THORNTON WILDER

Thornton Wilder

COLLECTED PLAYS &
WRITINGS ON THEATER

THE LIBRARY OF AMERICA

J. D. McClatchy
SELECTED THE TEXTS AND WROTE THE NOTES
FOR THIS VOLUME

Contents

THE ANGEL THAT
TROUBLED THE WATERS
AND OTHER PLAYS

CONTENTS

Nascuntur Poetæ . . .

We are gazing into some strange incomprehensible painting of Piero di Cosimo; a world of pale blues and greens; of abrupt peaks in agate and of walled cities; of flying red stags with hounds at their throats; and of lions in tears beside their crowns. On the roads are seen traveling companies, in no haste and often lost in contemplation of the sky. A boy sits on a rock in the foreground. He is listening to the words of a woman dressed in a chlamys that takes on the color of the objects about her.

THE WOMAN IN THE CHLAMYS: In a far valley, boy, sit those who in their lifetime have possessed some special gift of eye or ear or finger. There they sit apart, choosing their successors. And when on the winds toward birth the souls of those about to live are borne past them, they choose the brighter spirits that cry along that wind. And you were chosen.

THE BOY: For what gift, lady, did the choice fall? Am I to mould in clay, or paint? Shall I sing or mime, lady? What choice fell on me and from what master?

THE WOMAN IN THE CHLAMYS: It is enough to know that you were chosen.

THE BOY: What further remains to be done? You have poured on my eyes and ears and mouth the divine ointment; you have laid on my tongue the burning ember. Why do we delay?

THE WOMAN IN THE CHLAMYS: Be not so eager for life. Too soon you will be shaken by breath; too soon and too long you will be tossed in the tumult of the senses.

THE BOY: I am not afraid of life. I will astonish it. Why are we delaying?

THE WOMAN IN THE CHLAMYS: My sister is coming now. Listen to her.

> (THE WOMAN IN THE CHLAMYS *withdraws and gives place to her sister whose feet stir not the shells upon the path. She wears a robe of deep and noble red and bears in her hands a long golden chain hung about with pendants. Her face is*

fixed in concentration and compassion, like the face of one taking part in a sacrifice of great moment.)

THE BOY: All is ready. What do you come to do?

THE WOMAN IN DEEP RED: My sister has given you the gifts of pride and of joy. But those are not all.

THE BOY: What gifts remain? I have been chosen. I am ready.

THE WOMAN IN DEEP RED: Those gifts are vain without these. He who carries much gold stumbles. I bring the dark and necessary gifts. This golden chain. . . .

THE BOY: (*With mounting fear.*) Your face is shadowed. Draw back, take back all the gifts, if I must accept these also.

THE WOMAN IN DEEP RED: Too late. Too late. You had no choice in this. You must bow your head.

THE BOY: I am trembling. My knees are hot with my tears.

THE WOMAN IN DEEP RED: Since only tears can give sight to the eyes. (*She drops the chain about his neck.*)

THE BOY: Then am I permitted to know the meaning of these pendants?

THE WOMAN IN DEEP RED: This is a tongue of fire. It feeds upon the brain. It is a madness that in a better country has a better name.

THE BOY: These are mysteries. Give them no names.

THE WOMAN IN DEEP RED: This is a leaf of laurel from a tree not often plucked. You shall know pride and the shining of the eyes—of that I do not speak now.

THE BOY: And this, lady?

THE WOMAN IN DEEP RED: That is a staff and signifies the journey that awaits you your life long; for you are homeless.

THE BOY: And this . . . this is of crystal. . . .

THE WOMAN IN DEEP RED: That is yours alone, and you shall smart for it. It is wonderful and terrible. Others shall know a certain peace and shall live well enough in the limits of the life they know; but you shall be forever hindered. For you there shall be ever beyond the present a lost meaning and a more meaningful love.

THE BOY: Take back the chain. Take back your gifts. Take back life. For at its end what can there be that is worth such pain?

THE WOMAN IN DEEP RED: (*Slowly drawing back into the shadow of the wood.*) Farewell, child of the muses, playfellow in the bird-haunted groves. The life of man awaits you, the light laughter and the misery in the same day, in the selfsame hour the trivial and the divine. You are to give it a voice. Among the bewildered and the stammering thousands you are to give it a voice and to mark its meaning. Farewell, child of the muses, playfellow in the bird-haunted. . . .

(THE WOMAN IN THE CHLAMYS *returns.*)

THE WOMAN IN THE CHLAMYS: You must go now. Listen to that wind. It is the great fan of time that whirls on the soul for a season.

THE BOY: Stay a moment. I am not yet brave.

(*She leads him into a grotto and the young soul and his chain are lost in the profound shade.*)

Proserpina and the Devil

A Play for Marionettes

A puppet-show has been set up in Venice, 1640 A.D. The characters of this play are its manager and two manipulators; the puppets are DEMETER, PROSERPINA, HERMES *and* DÎS.

THE MANAGER: (*Winningly.*) Citizens and little citizens! We are going to give you a delicious foretaste of our great performance this afternoon, to which the whole world is coming. This is a pantomime about how a beautiful girl named Proserpina was snatched away by the Devil; and how her mother searched for her over all the hills of the world; and how at last she was able to bring her back to the earth for six months out of every year.

THE FIRST MANIPULATOR: (*Behind the scenes.*) Let go them strings.

THE MANAGER: At our great performance this afternoon this same play will be given *with words*; and besides it the story of the brave Melusina and her wanderings when she was driven out of Parma.

THE SECOND MANIPULATOR: (*His voice rising in anger.*) You don't have to show me!

THE MANAGER: On with the play!—but don't forget to bring your rich aunts this afternoon. (*To the Manipulators.*) Hurry through with it. I'm off for a cup of wine.

> (*The curtain rises with indecent haste and shows the underworld. The rivers Styx and Acheron have been replaced by a circular piece of cloth, sulphur-colored, with waves delicately embroidered about the margin. This is the Lake of Wrath and in it are seen floating arms and legs—all that are left, alas, of great puppets,* ABRAHAM, PENELOPE *and* JEPHTHA'S *daughter,* MIDAS *and* HARLEQUIN. *Beside the lake* PROSERPINA *is straying, robed in bluish black as one anticipating grief.* PLUTO—*now a medieval Satan—is stealthily approaching her. Suddenly* PROSERPINA *throws up her arms, runs to him and buries her face in his scarlet bosom.* NOAH'S ARK—*mutely protesting against*

the part it must play, with all its Christianized animals within it, of CHARON's *barge—is lowered from the proscenium and the curtain falls.*)

THE FIRST MANIPULATOR: (*Sotto voce.*) Beard of Medusa! You made her run in the wrong direction: the hussy courted death. Didn't I tell you he was to chase her three times around the lake?

THE SECOND MANIPULATOR: (*Sulkily.*) I don't care. A person can't tell which is his right hand and which is his left in this place.

THE FIRST MANIPULATOR: Here, you let me take her; you take the Devil.—Got the orange?

(*When the puppets are next seen* PROSERPINA *is exhibiting grief in pantomime. Her lord with affectionate gestures urges her to eat of a yellow pomegranate. Sadly she puts it to her mouth. With an odd recollection of the Garden of Eden, she tempts him into eating the remaining half. They go out cheerlessly.*)

THE FIRST MANIPULATOR: All right for that. Now I'll take the mother and the Devil. You take the other fellow and the daughter.

(DEMETER, *a handsome Italian matron in a wide gown of brocade, enters with her arms outstretched. At her elbow* HERMES, *the Archangel Gabriel, guides her through the Lake of Perdition.* PROSERPINA *and her husband return and throw up their hands in amazement. Again the frantic girl runs in the wrong direction and casts herself into the arms of Satan.* DEMETER *tries to draw her away, but a matter of pins and hooks-and-eyes prevents her rescue.*)

THE FIRST MANIPULATOR: Oh, you Gazoon! You lack-eyed Silenus! Your hands are nothing but feet.

THE SECOND MANIPULATOR: The Devil take your show and you with it.

(*The altercation behind the scenes grows out of bounds and one blow knocks down the stage. The Archangel falls upon the pavement and is cherished by gamins unto the third generation; the Devil rolls into the Lake;* PROSERPINA *is struck by a falling cloud, and lies motionless on her face;* DEMETER *by reason of the stiffness of her brocade stands upright, viewing with staring eyes the ills of her daughter.*)

Fanny Otcott

That great actress, MRS. OTCOTT, *an actress in the tradition of the Siddons, the Oldfield, Bracegirdle, O'Neill, is spending a quiet month in Wales. We do not see the cottage; we do not even see the mountains, but there is a stretch of lawn on whose gentle slope there stands an ancient round tower overgrown with ivy. In the shadow of this Arthurian monument* MRS. OTCOTT *has placed a table whereon she is sorting old engravings, playbills, letters, contracts, ribbons—in short, her past. She is still the handsome, humorous, Irish soul from whom every item out of the old trunks exacts its exclamation, its gesture, its renewed indignation or pleasure. She is attended by a blackamoor boy in livery, half asleep against a flower-pot.*

MRS. OTCOTT: Sampson! Tay!

SAMPSON: (*Springing up.*) Yes, mam. Wid or widout a streak o' cream?

MRS. OTCOTT: Widout. And Sampson, tell Pence I am not at home. Not even to the one in the yellow curls, or to the good black beard. And if they seem to know that I am at home, tell them . . . that I have gone up the tower, or that I have the vapors.

SAMPSON: You wants tea widout, and tell Mrs. Pence you don't want to see none of de gentlemen from de Village Inn,—dat you has de vapors.

MRS. OTCOTT: There! Do you see that, Sampson? I wore that the night the King dined with me on the stage.

SAMPSON: (*His eyes as big as soup-plates.*) King . . . James!

MRS. OTCOTT: (*Shuddering.*) No, stupid—Charles.—Go away! —This afternoon I shall devote to another woman, to another and a different woman and yet to myself, to myself, to myself.

SAMPSON: I'll tell Mrs. Pence.

> (*He goes out.* MRS. OTCOTT *picks up a packet of letters. One look, tosses them away, then rises muttering, goes and stamps on them and laughs. She returns to pick up a playbill and reads the heading with glistening eyes: "Fanny Otcott as*

Faizella in the 'Princess of Cathay.' First time." She strides about lost in thought. She almost walks into a gentleman who has entered through the hedge. He is wearing a black hat and cape, and has a serious worn face.)

ATCHESON: Your servant, Mrs. Otcott.

MRS. OTCOTT: (*Thunderstruck.*) Why, *no!* Yes! By the garter, it is George Atcheson. Oh! Oh! Oh!

ATCHESON: I do not disturb you, Mrs. Otcott? I . . . I came to discuss a thing that is very serious to me.

MRS. OTCOTT: (*Suddenly very pleased.*) Everything is—sit down, my friend. You always were very serious. That's why you made such a bad Hamlet. Delay your serious talk, George, and tell me about the women you have loved since you loved me, and confess that I finally made them all unendurable to you.

ATCHESON: You misunderstand me, Mrs. Otcott. . . .

MRS. OTCOTT: (*Loudly.*) Fanny.

ATCHESON: Ah . . . Fanny?

MRS. OTCOTT: All you need is a little coaxing. Well, George, a woman drove you on to the stage when you were preparing for the Church, and a woman drove you off, and it was my greatest service to the stage. Look, George, you remember me as Faizella in the *Princess of Cathay.* I never did better than that. Great Rufus, you played opposite me in it. Look!

ATCHESON: Perhaps you remember . . . I lost consciousness. . . .

MRS. OTCOTT: Ah yes! The pale divinity student fainted. Oh! George, you were the first of my lovers. No, it wasn't love, perhaps, but it was beautiful. It was like hawthorn-buds and meadow-larks and Mr. Handel's Water-music. And since, I have never ceased searching for love. Perhaps love strikes the first time or never at all. Then I was too much in love with my work. And oh, George, how young we were! But you were very dear to me in the old garret, and I'm sorry to see you're growing stout, for it's one more reminder that I shall probably live and die without having known the lightning of love.

(She sits down with a great flow of silken draperies and shakes her head at him ruefully.)

ATCHESON: I have come to discuss our . . . our association. . . .

MRS. OTCOTT: Thunder and Hell! don't you call that an association!

ATCHESON: . . . but my view of it is very different. (*Her shoe commences to mark time nervously on the turf.*) After my retirement from the Stage I resumed my theological studies, and I am now Bishop of Westholmstead. (*The shoe is now motionless.*) None of my friends know of that . . . that experience in my life, but it has always remained as a bitter . . . as a distressing spot in my conscience.

MRS. OTCOTT: (*After a pause, very rapidly.*) I see, you want to make a clean breast of the perilous stuff. You want to make a public confession, probably. You are married?

ATCHESON: Yes.

MRS. OTCOTT: You have several sons probably?

ATCHESON: Yes.

MRS. OTCOTT: And you lie awake nights, saying: Hypocrisy, hypocrisy. (*Pause.*) Well, make your confession. But why consult me?

ATCHESON: I have followed your course, madam, and seen the growing admiration your art commands in Court,—I might almost say in the Church.

MRS. OTCOTT: You do not suppose that that revelation would cast any deeper shadow on the good name of Fanny Otcott, such as it is. Remember, George, the months you call sinful. It wasn't love, perhaps, but it was grace and poetry. The heavens rained odors on us. It was as childlike and harmless as paintings on fans. I was a girl tragedienne reciting verses endlessly before a mirror and you were a young student who for the first time had seen a young girl braid her hair and sing at her work. Since then you have learned long names from books and heard a great many sneers from women as old as myself. You have borrowed your ideas from those who have never begun to live and who dare not.

ATCHESON: (*His head in his hands and his elbows on his knees.*) I do not know what to think. Your reasoning is full of perils.

MRS. OTCOTT: Go away and tell your congregations what you please. I feel as though you were communicating to my mind some of those pitiable remorses that have weakened you. I have sinned, but I have not that year on my conscience. It is that year and my playing of Faizella that will bring troops of angels to welcome me to Paradise. Go away and tell your congregations what you please.

ATCHESON: You give me no help in the matter, Mrs. Otcott.

MRS. OTCOTT: Go away. In the name of Heaven, go!

(*Crooked with doubt and hesitation, the Bishop of Westholmstead goes out through the hedge. For a few moments* MRS. OTCOTT *sits on the table, swinging one foot and muttering savagely in an imaginary conversation.*)

(*Reënter* SAMPSON *with a tray.*)

SAMPSON: Three gentlemen waited on you from de Village Inn, but Mrs. Pence sent dem away. She said you was up de tower, mam.

MRS. OTCOTT: (*Showily.*) Go call them back, Sampson. Tell them I have come down from de tower. Bring up the best box of wine, the one with my picture painted on it. I shall be young again.

Brother Fire

A hut in the mountains of Northern Italy. ANNUNZIATA, *a peasant woman, is preparing the evening meal over the fire. Her daughter,* ISOLA, *about eight years of age, is playing beside her.*

ANNUNZIATA: Now, now! Not so near. One of these days you'll be falling into the fire and there'll be nothing left to tell us about you but your shoes. Put them on and get out the bowls for supper.

ISOLA: I like to play with the fire.

ANNUNZIATA: What a thing to say!

ISOLA: I'd like to let my hair into it, gently, gently, gently, gently.

ANNUNZIATA: Don't you hear me tell you it's a wicked thing?

ISOLA: Brother Francis says it's our brother, and one of the best things in the world.

ANNUNZIATA: Tchk, Tchk! What makes the starling sing in his cage all of a sudden?

ISOLA: It's Brother Francis himself looking at us.

ANNUNZIATA: Tell him to come in and have some supper.

ISOLA: Come in, my mother says, and have some supper.

(FRANCIS *appears at the door. He blesses the house.*)

BROTHER FRANCIS: I can very well go on to my own supper and need not lighten your kettle.

ANNUNZIATA: Come in, Brother Francis. What you take will not even make a new ring around the kettle. Besides, I see you have been up to the top of the mountain again. You are cold and wet. Come and sit by the fire.

BROTHER FRANCIS: Yes, I have been up to the very top since yesterday, among the rocks and the birds in the rocks. Brother Wind was there and Sister Rain was there, but Brother Fire was not.

ANNUNZIATA: Now you sit by him, Isola, while I get some more wood; but don't ask him any questions. Now, Brother, put this fur skin across your knees.

(*She goes out.*)

15

ISOLA: What did you do, Brother Francis?

BROTHER FRANCIS: I watched and waited to see what they would let me see. For a long while there was nothing; then they nodded to one another, meaning that it was permitted to me. I watched seven stars closely. Suddenly they turned and fled inwards, and I saw the Queen of Heaven leading forth her company before all the shipwrecked seamen of this world.—However, do not tell thy mother, for she believes in no one's miracles but her own.

ISOLA: My mother says the fire is a wicked thing.

BROTHER FRANCIS: (*Turning.*) What, Sister Annunziata, how can you say that?—Why, what would cook your broth, what would keep you warm? And when you return from the mountain-tops, what else shines out from all the friendly windows of the world? Look at its flames, how they lean towards us!

ISOLA: It says: Give me something to eat. Give me something to eat.

BROTHER FRANCIS: (*Excitedly.*) Yes, yes. Its warmth is a kind of hunger. I have a love for all things in fur, feathers and scales, but I have not less a love for the fire that warms us. (*He edges the cloak into the fire.*) Look how it reaches for it. Wicked? Wicked? Never.

ISOLA: But, Brother Francis, it will . . . it will . . .

(*The flames suddenly seize the cloak.* FRANCIS *rises, wrapped in fire.*)

Brother Francis, you are on fire! Mother, mother!

(*She rushes from the hut and returns with her mother.* ANNUNZIATA *snatches the fur from* BROTHER FRANCIS *and throws it into the hearth.*)

BROTHER FRANCIS: (*Still standing ecstatically with lifted hands.*) Eat, Brother Fire. I knew you wanted this. I knew that you loved me too. (*He looks about him; then ruefully to* ANNUZIATA.) Sister, you have spoiled his supper.

ANNUNZIATA: (*With somber and averted face.*) I do not know what you mean. Here is your bowl of broth. Sit down and eat it.

BROTHER FRANCIS: Sister, do not be angry with me.

ANNUNZIATA: (*Breaking out.*) Come now, should we kill every-thing, the animals for their furs, yes, and one another, to feed them to the fire? Is it not enough that it takes our good pine tree by our road? There, that is logic, Brother Francis.

BROTHER FRANCIS: Bring me not logic, sister. She is the least of the handmaids of Love. I am often troubled when she speaks.

ANNUNZIATA: Must we give what makes us often warm, for that which makes us warm only for a moment?

BROTHER FRANCIS: (*Waving his wooden spoon about humor-ously.*) My mind is strangely light to-night, like the flames that play about the relics of Saint James. I could wander again through the whole night.

ANNUNZIATA: Where is your mother that she should watch over you? Had I not these other duties I should leave every-thing and watch over you myself.

BROTHER FRANCIS: She is in Paradise with a golden crook, leading the flames that died of hunger in this wicked world. She leads them to pasture on drifts of dried leaves. Look, Isola, I know that there is flame to burn all evil in the Lake of the Damned. I do not speak of that now,—but I know also that fire is at all times useful to the great Blessed. It sur-rounds them and they dwell in it. And even now . . .

(*And so on.*)

The Penny That Beauty Spent

The little heartbreak takes place in a rococo jeweler's shop in Paris. The shop is elegantly small and elegantly polished. The few jewels and the few pieces of brocade are tossed from surface to surface in a world of glass, from the chandelier to the mirrors and from the mirrors to the cases. It is Royalty's own place of purchase and the great egotistical head is present in bust and in miniature and on the backs of spoons. The old jeweler, enigmatic and smiling, is suddenly called to the door by a great clatter. A girl enters borne on the shoulders of a boy little older than herself. LA GRACILE *is thin and pinch-faced, but long penury has only made her the more elfin. Illness is already writing its progress in the eyes and on the brow of* QUINTE, *her husband. But they are deliciously happy and full of their secrets.* QUINTE *lifts her onto the counter and draws back.*

LA GRACILE: While you are with me I need never touch the ground. You can carry me from cushion to cushion.

QUINTE: And on your gravestone will be inscribed: Here lies an exquisite dancer, she who never touched the ground.

LA GRACILE: And beside mine yours will read: Here lies her husband, the soul of her life, the sole of her shoes.

THE JEWELER: Mademoiselle is in pain? The feet of Mademoiselle are in pain?

LA GRACILE: (*After she has recovered, with* QUINTE, *from the whirlwind of intimate amusement that this preposterous idea has caused them.*) No. I am the new dancer. I am La Gracile. Except when I dance I wear nothing on my feet but little velvet pockets. So when I am not wearing my practice slippers, my husband carries me about.

THE JEWELER: Oh, you are La Gracile. We have already heard of your great success last night. The King is delighted with you.

LA GRACILE: (*Shrilly, clapping her hands.*) Yes, yes, yes. I was a great success. Even the King's favorite, Madame d'Hautillon, was jealous. She tried to stand on my foot. They call me the moth of Versailles.

THE JEWELER: And now the King has sent you here to choose a present for yourself.

LA GRACILE: How did you know?

THE JEWELER: The King sends to me for a gift every young lady who pleases him. Madame d'Hautillon was here last.

LA GRACILE: (*Chattering on.*) I want nothing myself. It is to be for Quinte. A chronometer, please, that strikes every hour with a gavotte and midnight with a sarabande.

QUINTE: Nothing for me, Claire-Louise. When my cough returns it will shake every ornament off me, the buttons from my coat, the rings from my thin fingers. You must have something in pearls.

LA GRACILE: Silly Quinte, I want nothing.

QUINTE: But I suppose . . . You must wear something for the King.

LA GRACILE: (*Suddenly under a passing cloud of melancholy, resting her cheek on his hair, plaintively.*) I do not want a great showy pin on my breast. I want only a little white daisy from our beloved Brittany, from Grandmother's field that had too many stones.

QUINTE: Tell her what you have, Monsieur Jeweler.

THE JEWELER: Mademoiselle will look at this chain? Its art is secret. It is painted gold, the work of aged nuns in Hamburg.

QUINTE: Oh look, Claire-Louise, this flower for your hair. Many topazes were splintered to powder on the wheel before this perfect one.

THE JEWELER: Etiquette forbids, Mademoiselle, your buying that; it happens to be the very thing that Madame d'Hautillon bought for herself.

LA GRACILE: (*Arousing herself, imperiously.*) Have you a little fat chronometer with many jewels in it?

THE JEWELER: (*Proffering a tray.*) The best in Paris.

LA GRACILE: (*Giving one to* QUINTE.) That is for you, Quinte, from myself and from the dull King. Like my thoughts, it will rest on your heart, but long after it is sold as wire and rust my love will go on in the land where clocks do not mark off one sad moment from another.

QUINTE: (*With tears.*) Claire-Louise, it can be of no pleasure to me. In a while it will only please me because it is a little cool in my hot hand.

LA GRACILE: (*Softly, in pain.*) Courage, dearest Quinte, courage.

THE JEWELER: (*Interrupting formally.*) Remember, Mademoiselle, that etiquette demands that you will choose a present that His Majesty will admire on you.

LA GRACILE: (*Stormily.*) I shall choose what I please.

THE JEWELER: (*Insinuatingly.*) Your life is only to please the King. He has chosen you. By sending you here he is telling you that.

LA GRACILE: You are mistaken. . . . But I am only a poor thin dancer that . . . that has worked too hard. Besides, this is my husband.

THE JEWELER: (*Smiling.*) No, Mademoiselle, he is not your husband.

LA GRACILE: (*Jumps down and walks away, weeping bitterly, her little feet-sacks flopping against the polished floor. She suddenly turns with blazing eyes.*) I shall run away to Brittany . . . I shall scratch his eyes out.

THE JEWELER: (*Smiles at this foolish notion and leans across the counter, holding towards her a great jewel-encrusted buckle.*)

LA GRACILE: (*Wildly.*) Even though all Versailles kill me with steel pins, Quinte shall have the watch. (*But he has fallen among the gilt chairs.*)

The Angel on the Ship

The fore-deck of the Nancy Bray *lying disabled in mid-ocean. The figure-head of the ship has been torn from its place and nailed to the forepost, facing the stern,—back to back, as it were, with its former position. It is the half-length of an angel bearing wreaths; she is highly colored and buxom and has flowing yellow hair. On the deck lie three persons in the last stages of rags and exhaustion:* MINNA, *the captain's wife, the remnant of a stout, coarse woman;* VAN, *the under-cook, a little, sharp youth; and a fat, old, sleepy member of the crew,* JAMAICA SAM.

VAN: (*Driving the last nail into the figurehead.*) There she is. She's the new gawd of the Atlantic. It's only a she-gawd, but that's a good enough gawd for a sailor.

MINNA: (*Seated on the deck.*) Us'll call her Lily. That's a name like a god's.

SAM: Youm be quick. Youm say your prayers quick.

MINNA: (*Blubbering.*) Her can't hear us. Her's just the old figgerhead we had thirty years.

VAN: Her's an angel. Her knows everything. (*He throws himself on his knees and lays his forehead on the boards. In a hoarse whisper.*) That's the joss way. We all got t'do it.

(*The others do likewise.*)

SAM: Us'll pray in turns. Us must be quick. There ain't no more water to drink, and there ain't no more sails left to carry us on. Us'll have to be quick. Youm begin, Van. Youms a great lad with the words.

VAN: (*With real fanaticism.*) Great Gawd Lily, on the ship "Nancy Bray," all's lost with us if you don't bring us rain to drink. All the secret water I saved aside is drunk up, and we got to go over the side with the rest, if you don't bring us rain to-day,—or to-morrow. Youm allus been the angel on the front of this yere ship "Nancy Bray" and you ain't goin' to leave us rot now. I finished my prayer, great gawd Lily. Amen.

MINNA: Great God Lily, I'm the captain's wife that's sailed

behind you for twenty years. Many's the time, great God Lily, that I shined your face so you'd look spick and span and we sailing into London in the morning, or into heathen lands. You knows everything, and you knows what I did to my husband and that I didn't let him have none of the secret water that me and Van saved up, and that when he died he knew it and cursed me and Van to hell. But youms forgiven everything and send us some rain or bye-and-bye we'll die and there'll be no one here prayin' to you. This is the end of my prayin', great God Lily.

VAN: (*Whispers.*) Say Amen.

MINNA: Amen, great God Lily.

SAM: I ain't goin' to pray. I'm just a dog that's been on the sea since I was born. I don' know no land eddication.

MINNA: We all got to pray for some rain.

VAN: You got t'say your word, too.

SAM: God forgive me, great God Lily, I'm old Jamaica Sam that don't never go ashore. Amen. I'd be drowned, too, only for Van and the captain's wife who gave me some of the secret water, so that if they died I could roll 'em over the side and not leave 'em on the clean deck. Amen. Youms known my whole life, great God Lily, and how I stole the Portagee's red bag, only it was almost empty, and . . . and that other thing. Send a lot of rain and a ship to save us. Amen.

VAN: (*Crawling up beneath the figure and throwing himself full-length, hysterically.*) You've gone and forgiven me everything. Sure you have. I didn't kill the captain. The secret water was mine. Save us now, great gawd Lily, and bring me back to my uncle in Amsterdam and make him leave me his three coal barges.

MINNA: (*Rocking herself.*) We'm lost. She'll save Sam, but I've done what the gods don't like. They'm after me. They've got me now. (*Suddenly staring off the deck.*) Van! Van! Them's a ship coming to us. Van, look! (*She falls back crying.*)

VAN: Them's comin'!

SAM: (*Trying to jump up and down.*) It's the "Maria Theresa Third," comin' right at us.

VAN: (*His eye falls on the angel.*) What'll they say to the figger-head here?

SAM: (*Sententiously.*) But that's the great God Lily. Her's saved us. You ain't goin' to do anything to her?

VAN: (*Starting to beat the angel forward with his hammer.*) They'll call us heathen, bowin' down to wood and stone. Get the rope, Sam. We'll put her back.

MINNA: (*Frightened.*) But I can't never forget her and her great starey eyes. Her I've prayed to.

The Message and Jehanne

The interior of a goldsmith's shop in the Paris of the Renaissance. The tops of the windows are just above the level of the street, and through them we see the procession of shoes, any one of them a novel or a play or a poem. In the workshop one finds not only medals and salad forks for prelates, but unexpected things, a viola d'amore and folios ruled for music.

> (TULLIO, *the apprentice, enters from the street and confronts his master,* CHARLES OF BENICET. TULLIO *stands with his back to the door and lets his breath out slowly, as one who has just accomplished a great work.*)

CHARLES: (*Rubbing his hands.*) So you delivered the rings?

TULLIO: Yes, master.

CHARLES: And what did my little brown Jacquenetta say?

TULLIO: She twice read the verse you had written in the ring. Then she looked at me. Then she looked at the ring. "It is too cold," she said.

CHARLES: Too cold?

TULLIO: She said: "But . . . but I suppose it's what must go inside a ring!" Then she kissed the ring and bade me tell you she loved it.

CHARLES: (*Arrested and puzzled.*) Too cold, the verse!—But I'll make her another. We forget how they love us. And the other ring? Did you deliver the Graf's ring to the Lady Jehanne herself?

TULLIO: Yes, master. Into her very own hand. Her house is very old and in a bad part of the city. As I crossed the court and stood in the hall a great German, with fierce eyebrows, came in from the street with me.

CHARLES: Yes, that's the one she's to marry.

TULLIO: He asked me loudly what I had there. And I said, a box for the Lady Jehanne, and that it was for her hand alone, and I ran to the landing on the stairs. Then she came out herself. He cried out upon her: What gift was she receiving? And was it from a certain English student at Padua? And she said: "No, Baron, it is the wedding ring you have

24

sent me." And when I gave it to her she went in, very white, and without speaking to him. Then I went to Jacquenetta's with the other ring, and she gave me some supper.

CHARLES: Too cold, the verse! Start putting up the shutters; I must go and see her.

(*It has been growing darker. Suddenly a pair of shoes, a poem these, descends from the crowd, and* TULLIO *opens the door to a knock. A beautiful lady gives Christian greeting, and a seat is made for her among the littered chairs. She sits in silence until* TULLIO *has lighted the candles and retired.*)

JEHANNE: You are Charles of Benicet, master in precious metals?

CHARLES: *Carolus Benizentius auro argentoque magister*, and composer of music to God and to such men whose ears He chooses to open.

JEHANNE: You are a composer too?

CHARLES: They are callings like two sisters who have ever their arms about the other's neck. When I have made a wedding ring I compose a motet thereto. The boy who calls to see if the candlesticks are done takes back with him a Mass.

JEHANNE: (*Without a breath.*) Oh!

CHARLES: Can I serve you with music or with metals?

JEHANNE: You have served me to-day. I am the Lady Jehanne.

CHARLES: Ah, yes! The ring was unsatisfactory? I can make another to-night. I shall set about it at once.

JEHANNE: No, master. The ring is very beautiful.

CHARLES: (*After a pause, pretending to be embarrassed.*) I am overjoyed that it pleases you.

JEHANNE: (*Suddenly.*) The verses that you put in the rings—where do you find *them*?

CHARLES: Unless there is a special request, my lady, I put in nothing but the traditional legend: *fidelitas carior vita*.

JEHANNE: (*Without reproach.*) But there are liberties you allow yourself? Master, what meant you when you wrote within my ring?

CHARLES: My lady!

JEHANNE: (*Giving him the ring.*) Graf Klaus addresses me thus.

CHARLES: (*Reading around the inside of the ring.*) "As the

hermit his twilight, the countryman his holiday, the worshiper his peace, so do I love thee." It was the wrong ring that was delivered to you, my lady.

JEHANNE: It has broken my will. I am in flight for Padua. My family are truly become nothing but sparrows and God will feed them.

Childe Roland to the Dark Tower Came

The sun has set over the great marsh, leaving a yellow-brown Flemish light upon the scene. In the midst of the mire and among the tufts of iron-grass stands an old round-tower. Its lower narrow door is of green bronze, scarred with many assaults. Above the door are two small windows, behind which a gleam seems to come and go.

In the half-light that hangs over the plain a man in armor stumbles through the bog to the single step before the door. He is many times wounded; his blood flows freely to the ground. The knight blows his horn; the landscape collects itself to listen.

CHILDE ROLAND: I die . . . Open the door to me.

> (*The landscape laughs, then falls suddenly silent. Presently its subterranean waters are again heard sucking at buried tree-trunks.*)

I have seen your lights here from a long way off . . . You cannot hide from me now.

> (*The marsh becomes animated and fully interested in the stranger. One of the windows brightens slightly and a girl looks out. Her voice and manner are strangely detached and impersonal, as though she had been called away from some absorbing interest, and were eager to return to it.*)

Oh, you are here! Quick, descend to me. All my wounds are flowing. I am dying of thirst.

THE GIRL: Who are you to issue commands against this tower? Some emperor, surely.

CHILDE ROLAND: My name is written with many another upon the sword of Charlemagne: that is enough.

THE GIRL: You are some king, perhaps,—driven into the wilderness by your not too loving subjects?

CHILDE ROLAND: No king, but a friend and soldier of kings.

THE GIRL: Oh! This is some wise counselor. If you are so wise we will quickly open the door to you.

CHILDE ROLAND: Not wise, but often listened to in grave matters, having a voice equal with many others.

THE GIRL: (*Utterly untouched, lightly to some one within.*) I do believe this is some sweet singer. Let us bind on our slippers right quickly and put red wine to his lips, for poets are ever our delight.

CHILDE ROLAND: I am no singer, but one loving the string and the voice at all times. Open the door! For the wind is cold on the marsh, and the first terrible stars are stepping into their chains. Open the door, for my veins are emptied on your sill.

THE GIRL: (*Leaning far out, while her red hair falls almost to his shoulders.*) Beat upon the door, Sir Knight. Many things are gained by force.

CHILDE ROLAND: My hands are strengthless . . . I am fallen on my knees. . . . Pity me!

(THE GIRL *laughs pleasantly to her companion within.*)

Reach over the stars to me, Mary, Mother of God. To you I was committed in my first year, and have renewed yearly my promises. Send from thy golden mind and thy noiseless might the issue out of this difficulty.

(*A second girl, dark and thoughtful, appears at the other window.*)

THE FIRST GIRL: (*Intimately.*) He is praying now.

THE DARK GIRL: He is a little boy. His thoughts this last hour are returning to his earliest year.

THE FIRST GIRL: Is it not beautiful that a Knight should think of a little child?

THE DARK GIRL: What brought you here, Knight-at-arms?

CHILDE ROLAND: The battle passed suddenly into the west. This tower was all I could see. And here I brought my wounds.

THE FIRST GIRL: (*Softly.*) You see he is still able to reason; he reasons very well.

THE DARK GIRL: What led you to think that we could help you?

CHILDE ROLAND: I know your name! All my life I have heard of this tower. They say that on the outside you are dark and unlovely, but that within every hero stands with his fellows and the great queens step proudly on the stair.

THE DARK GIRL: And do you believe this?

CHILDE ROLAND: (*After a pause.*) Yes. (*With sudden fury.*) Open the door! There is a place for me within. Open the door, Death!

THE FIRST GIRL: (*Drawing up her hair languidly.*) He is irresistible, this great man.

CHILDE ROLAND: Oliver! Oliver! Charlemagne! I hear your voices. It is I, Roland, without, in the dark marsh. My body I cast away for you. My breath I returned to the sky in your defense. Open the door! . . .

> (*The marsh is a little put out by all this strong feeling. It lies quiet. The door slowly opens upon a hall full of drifting violet mists, some of which escape and fade over the marsh. The girl with the red hair is seen walking away in the hall, her mocking face looking back over her shoulder. The dark girl, robed in gray, leans across the threshold extending a chalice to the Knight's lips.*)

THE DARK GIRL: Take courage, high heart. How slow you have been to believe well of us. You gave us such little thought while living that we have made this little delay at your death.

Centaurs

The usual chattering audience of our theaters is waiting for the curtains to part on a performance of Ibsen's THE MASTER BUILDER. *Presently the lights are lowered to a colored darkness, and the warm glow of the footlights begins again the ancient magic. The orchestra draws its bows soothingly to a gradual close and files out gropingly into the rabbit-hutch prepared for it, leaving perhaps a sentimental viola-player staring upward into the darkness. Suddenly the curtains are parted by an earnest young man, who stares into the shadowy audience and starts, with some difficulty, to address it.*

SHELLEY: My name is Shelley. I . . . I am told that some of you may have heard of me, may even know my poems,—or some of my poems. I cannot imagine what they may seem like to you who live in this world that . . . that is, I have just seen your streets for the first time,—your machines, your buildings, and especially the machines with which you talk to one another. My poems must seem very strange in a world of such things. (*Awkward pause.*) Well, I wanted to say something about this play, but I don't know how to put it into words for you. You see, I feel that, in part, I wrote this play. (*With sudden relief calling back through the curtains.*) Hilda! Will you help me a moment?

HILDA WANGEL'S VOICE: Yes, I'm coming.

SHELLEY: (*Constrainedly, to the audience.*) A friend of mine.

HILDA: (*Appears in her mountaineering costume of the First Act, carrying an alpenstock. Vigorously, to the audience.*) He promised to do this by himself, but he has gotten into difficulties. Have you told them that you wrote it?

SHELLEY: I tried to. It didn't sound reasonable.

HILDA: Well, you were able to explain it to me. Help me to persuade Papa to come out here. (*She disappears.*)

SHELLEY: Hendrick, for my sake.

HILDA'S VOICE: There, did you hear that? For his sake, he said. Miss Fosli, will you kindly push forward the wicker settee from the last act? Thank you.

(*A wicker settee suddenly appears.*)

Now, Papa.

(*Hilda reappears leading the dramatist. Ibsen is smiling sternly through his spectacles and through his fringe of up-curling white whiskers.*)

Now sit down and Shelley will begin again.

IBSEN: Hurry, young man. My beautiful play is ready to begin. The kingdom is on the table, the nurseries are empty, and this house is full of unconverted people.

HILDA: (*Touching his shoe with the tip of her alpenstock.*) Hush, Papa. Let him go about it in his own way. Have you told them about the poem you were about to write when you died?

SHELLEY: No. (*To the audience.*) Ladies and Gentlemen, on the day I died,—drowned in the Mediterranean,—I was full of a poem to be called THE DEATH OF A CENTAUR, that I did not have time to put on paper.

HILDA: You forgot to say that it was a very good poem.

SHELLEY: I couldn't say that.

HILDA: You said it to me. (*Turning to the audience.*) You should know that this young man had come to a time when everything he wrote was valuable. He was as sure to write great poems as a good apple tree is to give good apples.

SHELLEY: Perhaps it would have been one of the better ones. At all events, it was never written. . . .

IBSEN: (*Rising excitedly and stamping his feet as though they had snow on them.*) And I claim that I wrote it. The poem hung for a while above the Mediterranean, and then drifted up toward the Tyrol and I caught it and wrote it down. And it is THE MASTER BUILDER.

HILDA: Now you must sit down, Papa, and keep calm. We must reason this out calmly. In the first place, both are certainly about centaurs. What do you say, Shelley?

SHELLEY: Well, it is not a strange idea, or a new one, that the stuff of which masterpieces are made drifts about the world waiting to be clothed with words. It is a truth that Plato would have understood that the mere language, the words of a masterpiece are the least of its offerings. Nay, in the world we have come into now, the languages of the planet have no value; but the impulse, the idea of "Comus" is a miracle, even in heaven. Let you remember this when you regret the work that has been lost through this war that has been laid upon your treasurable young men. The work they might have done is still with you, and will yet find its way into your lives and into your children's lives.

IBSEN: Enough, enough! You will be revealing all the mysteries soon. Enough has been said to prove that THE DEATH OF A CENTAUR and THE MASTER BUILDER are the same poem. Get in with you, children. The play is ready to start. Solness sits with his head in his hands and the harps are in the air.

(*He goes behind the curtains. Shelley lingers a moment; a shadow has fallen across his face.*)

HILDA: (*Laying her hand on his arm.*) What is the matter?

SHELLEY: That reminded me . . . of another poem . . . I did not write down.

Leviathan

Mid-Mediterranean. *Sunrise after a night of storm with the sea swaying prodigiously. A great Venetian argosy has been wrecked overnight; ships and men have disappeared, leaving only the cargo spread out upon the waters. Momently new treasures from the ship's holds float upward and, reaching the surface, are swept hither and thither for miles: Persian rugs, great lengths of brocade, boxes of spice, made from tropical leaves and bound with dried vine; and an apparently interminable swathe of gray silk unwinding from its ivory standard.*

In the foreground a mermaid is feeling her way among the stuffs with considerable distaste. To one used to the shadowed harmonies of deep-sea color these crimsons and oranges have no attraction. BRIGOMEÏDÉ *has the green wiry hair of her kind, entangled with the friendly snail; the iridescent shoulders of all sea-women, and the gray thin mouth.*

Suddenly she comes upon THE PRINCE. *The royal divan has been swept from the decks, and while the huge pillows are gradually soaking up the water and floating away, their Prince lies on them unconscious. For a moment the mermaid watches him open-mouthed. She steals nearer and holding on to the tassels of seed-pearls, leans cautiously over and scans his face long and wonderingly. She sighs faintly, splashes a little in discontent, and then gazes upon him again with a frown of concentration.*

BRIGOMEÏDÉ: It's breathing. He has not lost—what they call —the soul. I wonder where he keeps it. It is the great difference between us; we sea-people have no soul. I wonder where he keeps it! I have heard that it can be seen at times, in the eyes. Perhaps if I borrowed it from him while he slept he would never miss it. No,—I will ask him for it.

> (*She claps her hands suddenly to awake him, falling back, at the same time, into the water. The young man does not stir. She grows angry. She strikes the water sharply with the palms of her hands. By quick degrees a circling wind rises; great fantastic waves rear themselves, robed in silk; they break over the divan and the Prince stirs. Immediately* BRIGOMEÏDÉ

33

strokes the water to a stillness, and fixes her attention on the young man.)

THE PRINCE: My father, take not your hand away. My -
brothers, why have you ceased talking? Where am I?—All is
lost! *Ave Maris Stella!*

BRIGOMEÏDÉ: (*Watching him intently.*) How could you sleep
so—during the storm?

THE PRINCE: You—you are out of a dream. You are out of my
fever. Yes, yes—the storm—you—all this is but the painting
of my fever. I shall awake in Venice with the lute-player
fallen asleep by the window. I will call to him now and he
will wake me up: Amedeo!—Lute-player! Shake me out of
this dream!

(*The silence that follows is filled with the crackling noise as
the pith fillings of the heavier cushions become saturated.*)

BRIGOMEÏDÉ: (*Harshly.*) Who is it you are calling to? There is
no one here, but you and me only.

THE PRINCE: Amedeo!—he does not answer: this is real. But
you, you are dream; you are illusion. *Ave Maris Stella!*

BRIGOMEÏDÉ: (*Indignantly.*) I am not dream. I am not illusion. I am royal among all sea-women—I am of the Third
Order; on the three great tide days I am permitted to bind
my hair with Thetis-Agrandis and wear in my ears the higher
Muria.

THE PRINCE: You are out of an old ballad, taught me as a boy,
and you have come back to me in the last hour on the tide
of fever. In a moment my dream will have passed on from
you.

BRIGOMEÏDÉ: (*Vehemently.*) You think I am only dream because . . . you have heard it said . . . we sea-folk have no
souls.

THE PRINCE: Soul nor body.

BRIGOMEÏDÉ: (*More softly.*) Tell me where it is you keep your
soul. Have you it always with you?

THE PRINCE: (*As a great pillow floats away from under his
hand.*) *Flos undarum!* Save me! Deliver me! Hear my prayer!

BRIGOMEÏDÉ: Who are you speaking to? Did I not tell you
there was no one here but you and me only?

THE PRINCE: You! Tell me where is shore. You can swim for days. Draw me to some island. I will give you great riches . . . all you desire.

BRIGOMEÏDÉ: Give me your soul. All my days I have longed for two things, black hair and a soul. I have not lacked anything else. I will draw you to your home, if you will give me your soul.

THE PRINCE: (*Violently.*) It cannot be given away. No one has seen it; it cannot be felt with hands; seen or tasted.

BRIGOMEÏDÉ: And yet they say it is the greatest thing in the world; that without it life is a cold procession of hours; that it gives all sight to the eyes, and all hearing to the ears . . . you are mocking me! I see in your face that you have it now!

THE PRINCE: Yes, and am about to lose it.

BRIGOMEÏDÉ: Give it to me, and I will bring up from the bottom of the sea your father and your brothers. I will return to you all the pearls that have fallen here, and draw you softly into the narrows of Venice.

THE PRINCE: (*As the water closes over him.*) Amedeo! . . . Lute-player!

(BRIGOMEÏDÉ *turns away contemptuously.*)

BRIGOMEÏDÉ: It is something you cannot touch or see. What could I do with it so?

(THE PRINCE *rises, dead, entangled in scarves.* BRIGO-MEÏDÉ *stares into his face long and earnestly.*)

It is true! There is something gone . . . that lay about his eyes, that troubled his mouth. The soul, perhaps.

(*She claps her hands. From a great distance a sea-serpent swims hugely towards her. He is caught in the trailing lengths of gray brocade.*)

BRIGOMEÏDÉ: Gog–etar! There is no longer anything precious in this man. You may divide him among your young.

LEVIATHAN: It is terrible here, lady. These spices have made the streams unendurable. By to-morrow morning the waters will be tainted as far as Africa. Already my young are ill, lady. They lie motionless in the mud, dear lady. It is terrible to see them so. . . .

BRIGOMEÏDÉ: I do not want to hear your troubles. Take this man away.

LEVIATHAN: Thanks, gracious lady. Perhaps these hateful essences will have made him endurable . . .

BRIGOMEÏDÉ: Cease!

(*He drags* THE PRINCE *away. The frustrated* BRIGOMEÏDÉ *starts to comb the shell out of her hair, singing. Suddenly she breaks her song and adds musingly.*)

Perhaps it is better, although your body has passed to Leviathan, still to have another part of you somewhere about the world.

And the Sea Shall Give Up Its Dead

The clangor of Judgment Day's last trumpet dies away in the remotest pockets of space, and time comes to an end like a frayed ribbon. In the nave of creation the diaphanous amphitheater is already building for the trial of all flesh. Several miles below the surface of the North Atlantic, the spirits of the drowned rise through the water like bubbles in a neglected wineglass.

A WOMAN: (*To the gray weeds of whose soul still cling the vestiges of color, some stained purples and some wasted reds.*) At last I could struggle no longer. My head and lungs were under intense discomfort by reason of the water with which they were filled. I said to myself: "Only think, Gertruda, you have actually arrived at the moment of death!" Even then I was unwilling to believe it, though my lungs were on the point of bursting. One is never really able to believe that one will die. It is especially difficult for sovereigns who seldom, if ever, confront inevitable situations. Perhaps you know that I am Gertruda XXII, Empress of Newfoundland from 2638 to 2698?

A STOUT LITTLE MAN: Your Imperial Highness's experience is much like mine. I lived about five hundred years before Your Imperial Highness. I had always dreaded the moment of extinction, yet mine was less painful than a headache.

THE EMPRESS: We know now that the real pain comes to us in the ages that have passed since then. Have you too been swinging in mid-ocean, tangled in a cocoon of seaweed, slowly liberating your mind from the prides and prejudices and trivialities of a life-time? That is what is painful.

THE LITTLE MAN: I was a Jew and very proud of my race. Living under what I took to be the aspersions of my neighbors I had nourished the arrogant delusion that I was notable. It has taken me five hundred years of painful reflection to disembarrass myself of this notion. I was a theatrical producer and thought myself important to my time, wise, witty, and kindly. Each of these ideas I have shed with a hundred times the pain of losing a limb. Now I am reconciled to the fact that I am naked, a fool, a child.

THE EMPRESS: In my life I believed fiercely that everything of which I said MY had some peculiar excellence. It was impossible to imagine a citizen proud of any country save Newfoundland, or a woman vain of any hair save the golden. I had a passion for genealogies and antiquities and felt that such things merely looked forward to myself. Now these many years I have been wrapped in barnacles, divorcing my soul from all that it once loved. Even my love for my son and my son's love for me have vanished through sheer inconsequence. All this is the second death, and the one to be dreaded. I was afraid that when I had shed away my royalty and my beauty and my administrative talent and my pure descent and my astonishing memory for names, I was afraid that there would be nothing left. But fortunately, underneath all this litter I have found a tiny morsel of . . . but dare we say the Name?—But what was yours?

THE LITTLE MAN: Horatio Nissem.

THE EMPRESS: Speak to that man who is rising through the water beside you.

HORATIO NISSEM: Who are you, and what particular follies have you laid aside?

A TALL THIN DREAMY MAN: I was a priest of the gospel and a terrible time I have had taking leave of my sins. I tremble to think how but a few moments ago I still retained a longing for stupidities. Yes, sir, for the planets. I felt sure that they had personalities and I looked forward after my death to hearing their songs. Now I know that sun and moon and stars have fallen like dust into the lap of their maker. I told myself, also, that after death I should sit through eternity overhearing the conversation of Coleridge and Augustine and Our Lord; there I should embrace my loved ones and my enemies; there I should hear vindicated before the devils the great doctrines of Infant Baptism and Sacramental Confession. Only now have I been delivered from these follies. As I swayed in the meteoric slime I begged God to punish me for certain sins of my youth, moments I well remembered of rage and pride and shame. But these seemed of no importance to him: he seemed rather to be erasing from my mind the notion that my sins were of any consequence. I see now that even the idea that I was capable of sinning was a self-flattery and an impertinence. My name was Father Cosroe: now my name is Worm.

THE EMPRESS: We still cling obstinately to our identity, as though there were something valuable in it. This very moment I feel relics of pleasure in the fact that I am myself and no one else. Yet in a moment, if there is a moment, we shall all be reduced to our quintessential matter, and you, Mr. Nissem, will be exactly indistinguishable from me. God Himself will not be able to tell the Empress of Newfoundland from the Reverend Doctor Cosroe.

HORATIO NISSEM: (*In mounting terror.*) I am afraid. I refuse to give myself up.

THE EMPRESS: Do not cry out, fool. You have awakened all my rebellious nature. O God, do not take away my identity! I do not ask for my title or my features; do not take away my myself!

HORATIO NISSEM: Do you hear? I refuse to give myself up. O God, let me not be mistaken for a Gentile.

FATHER COSROE: Your screaming has aroused my madness. Let me keep my particular mind, O God, my own curious mind with all I have put into it!

> (*The three panic-stricken souls reach the surface of the sea. The extensive business of Domesday is over in a twinkling and the souls divested of all identification have tumbled, like falling stars, into the blaze of unicity. Soon nothing exists in space but the great unwinking eye, meditating a new creation.*)

Now the Servant's Name Was Malchus

In his father's house are many mansions, and it is from the windows of one of them that he stands looking out upon the clockwork of the skies. With the precision that is possible only to things dead in themselves, the stars weave incessantly their interlocking measures. At intervals the blackest pockets of space give birth to a nebula, whirling in new anguish, but for the most part the sky offers only its vast stars, eased in the first gradations of their cooling, and fulfilling happily and with a faint humming sound the long loops of their appointment.

(*To him comes* GABRIEL, *secretary and soldier.*)

GABRIEL: There are some unusually urgent petitions here. . . . There's this Colonel on a raft in the Bengal Sea—Here again is the widow and her two daughters in Moscow. A lady in Rome. (*He lays some papers on the table.*) Besides, there is someone outside who wishes to speak to you. He says he knew you on earth. I think he has something to complain of, even here.

OUR LORD: Let him wait a moment.

(*There is loud rapping at the door.*)

GABRIEL: There he is again.

OUR LORD: Then let him in.

(GABRIEL *admits* MALCHUS *and goes out.*)

MALCHUS: Please, sir, excuse me being so hasty, but I had to speak to you about something.

OUR LORD: You are displeased with Heaven?

MALCHUS: Oh no, sir—except for one thing.

OUR LORD: We will talk about it in a minute. Come by the window and look. Can you tell me which of those stars is mine?

MALCHUS: Lord, all are yours, surely.

OUR LORD: No, only one is mine, for only one bears living things upon it. And where there is no life I have no power. All the stars save one are lifeless; not even a blade of grass pushes through their powder or their flame. But one of them is so crowded with event that Heaven itself is scarcely able to attend to its needs. —But you are not interested?

MALCHUS: Oh, sir, it was so long ago that I was there that I cannot be expected to. . . . Even my children's children have long since left it. I cannot be very interested. Since I am so happy here,—except for one thing. But I should like to see it again. Which is it, sir?

OUR LORD: There, see! See where it floats for a moment out of a green mist. If your ears were accustomed to it as mine are, you would hear what I hear: the sigh as it turns. Now what is it you want of me?

MALCHUS: Well, as you know I was the High Priest's servant in the garden when you were taken. Sir, it's hardly worth mentioning.

OUR LORD: No, no. Speak out.

MALCHUS: And one of your fellows took out his sword and cut off my ear.

OUR LORD: Yes.

MALCHUS: It's . . . it's hardly worth mentioning. Most of the time, Lord, we're very happy up here and nothing disturbs us at our games. But whenever someone on earth thinks about us we are aware of it, pleasantly or unpleasantly. A sort of something crosses our mind. And because I'm in your book someone is always reading about me and thinking about me for a moment, and in the middle of my games I feel it. Especially at this season when your death is cele-brated, no moment goes by without this happening. And what they think is, that I'm ridiculous.

OUR LORD: I see. And you want your name to be erased from the book?

MALCHUS: (*Eagerly.*) Yes, sir. I thought you could just make the pages become blank at that place.

OUR LORD: Now that you have come here everything that you wish is granted to you. You know that.

MALCHUS: Yes, sir; thank you, sir.

OUR LORD: But stay a minute. At this season, Malchus, a num-ber of people are thinking of me, too.

MALCHUS: Yes, Lord, but as good, as great . . .

OUR LORD: But, Malchus, I am ridiculous too.

MALCHUS: Oh, no, no!

OUR LORD: Ridiculous because I suffered from the delusion that after my death I could be useful to men.

MALCHUS: They don't say that!

OUR LORD: And that my mind lay under a malady that many a doctor could cure. And that I have deceived and cheated millions and millions of souls who in their extremity called on me for the aid I had promised. They did not know that I died like any other man and their prayers mounted into vain air, for I no longer exist. My promises were so vast that I am either divine or ridiculous. (*Pause.*) Malchus, will you stay and be ridiculous with me?

MALCHUS: Yes, sir, I'll stay. I'm glad to stay. Though in a way I haven't any right to be there. I wasn't even the High Priest's servant; I only held his horse every now and then. And . . . and I used to steal a little,—only you've forgiven me that. Sure, I'm glad to stay.

OUR LORD: Thank you, Malchus.

MALCHUS: (*Smiling.*) It isn't even true in the book. It was my left ear and not my right.

OUR LORD: Yes, the book isn't always true about me, either.

MALCHUS: Excuse my troubling you, sir. Good day.

OUR LORD: Good day, Malchus.

> (MALCHUS *goes out.* GABRIEL *enters discreetly and lays down some more papers.*)

GABRIEL: (*In a low voice.*) The raft has capsized, sir, on the Bengal Sea, and the Colonel will be here at once. The woman in Moscow. . . .

Mozart and the Gray Steward

MOZART *is seated at a table in a mean room in Vienna orchestrating the "Magic Flute." Leaves of ruled paper are strewn about the floor. His wife enters in great excitement.*

CONSTANZE: There's someone come to see you, someone important. Pray God, it's a commission from Court.

MOZART: (*Unmoved.*) Not while Salieri's alive.

CONSTANZE: Put on your slippers, dear. It's some one dressed all in gray, with a gray mask over his eyes, and he's come in a great coach with its coat of arms all covered up with gray cloth. Pray God, it's a commission from Court for a *Te Deum* or something. (*She tidies up the room in six gestures.*)

MOZART: Not while Salieri's alive.

CONSTANZE: But, now, do be nice, 'Gangl, please. We must have some money, my treasure. Just listen to him and say "yes" and "thank you" and then you and I'll talk it over after he's gone. (*She holds his coat.*) Come, put this on. Step into your slippers.

MOZART: (Sighing.) I'm not well. I'm at home. I'm at work. There's not a single visitor in the whole world that could interest me. Bring him in.

CONSTANZE: (*Adjusting his stock.*) Now don't be proud. Just accept.

> (*She hurries out and presently reënters preceding the visitor. The visitor is dressed from head to foot in gray silk. His bright eyes look out through the holes in a narrow gray silk mask. He holds to his nose a gray perfumed handkerchief. One would say: an elegant undertaker.*)

THE GRAY STEWARD: Kappelmeister Mozart, *servus.* Gracious lady, *servus.*

MOZART: *Servus.*

THE GRAY STEWARD: Revered and noble master, wherever music reigns, wherever genius is valued, the name of Wolfgang Amadeus Mozart is . . .

MOZART: Sir, I have always been confused by compliments and

beg you to spare me that mortification by proceeding at once to the cause of your visit . . . the . . . the honor of your visit.

THE GRAY STEWARD: Revered master, before I lay my business before you, may I receive your promise that—whether you accept my commission or not—you both will . . .

MOZART: I promise you our secrecy, unless our silence would prove dishonorable to me or injurious to some one else. Pray continue.

THE GRAY STEWARD: Know then, gracious and revered genius, that I come from a prince who combines all the qualities of birth, station, generosity and wisdom.

MOZART: Ha! a European secret.

THE GRAY STEWARD: His Excellency moreover has just sustained a bitter misfortune. He has lately lost his wife and consort, a lady who was the admiration of her court and the sole light of her bereaved husband's life. Therefore, his Excellency, my master, commissions you to compose a Requiem Mass in honor of this lady. He asks you to pour into it the height of your invention and that wealth of melody and harmony that have made you the glory of our era. And for this music he asks leave to pay you the sum of four hundred crowns,—two hundred now, and the second two hundred crowns when you deliver the first four numbers.

MOZART: Well, Constanze, I must not be proud.

THE GRAY STEWARD: There is but one proviso.

MOZART: Yes, I heard it. The work must represent the height of my invention.

THE GRAY STEWARD: That was an easy assumption, master. The proviso is this: You shall let his Excellency have this music as an anonymous work, and you shall never by any sign, by so much as the nod of your head, acknowledge that the work is yours.

MOZART: And his Excellency is not aware that the pages I may compose at the height of my invention may be their own sufficient signature?

THE GRAY STEWARD: That may be. Naturally my master will see to it that no other composer will ever be able to claim the work as his.

MOZART: Quick, give me your paper and I will sign it. Leave your two hundred crowns with my wife at the foot of the stairs. Come back in August and you will have the first four numbers. *Servus. Servus.*

THE GRAY STEWARD: (*Backing out.*) *Servus*, master. *Servus*, madame.

> (CONSTANZE *returns in a moment and looks anxiously towards her husband.*)

CONSTANZE: A visit from Heaven, 'Gangl. Now you can go into the country. Now you can drink all the Bohemian water in the world.

MOZART: (*Bitterly.*) Good. And just at a time when I was contemplating a Requiem Mass. But for *myself.* However, I must not be proud.

CONSTANZE: (*Trying to divert him.*) Who can these people be? Try and think.

MOZART: Oh, there's no mystery about that. It's the Count von Walsegg. He composes himself. But for the most part he buys string quartets from us; he erases the signatures and has them played in his castle. The courtiers flatter him and pretend that they have guessed him to be the composer. He does not deny it. He tries to appear confused. And now he has succeeded in composing a Requiem. But that will reduce my pride.

CONSTANZE: You know he will only be laughed at. The music will speak for itself. Heaven wanted to give us four hundred crowns—

MOZART: And Heaven went about it humorously.

CONSTANZE: What was his wife like?

MOZART: Her impudences smelt to Heaven. She dressed like a page and called herself Cherubin. Her red cheeks and her black teeth and her sixty years are in my mind now.

CONSTANZE: (*After a pause.*) We'll give back the money. You can write the music, without writing it for them.

MOZART: No, I like this game. I like it for its very falseness. What does it matter who signs such music or to whom it is addressed? (*He flings himself upon the sofa and turns his face to the wall.*) For whom do we write music?—for musicians?

Salieri!—for patrons? Von Walsegg!—for the public? The Countess von Walsegg! I shall write this Requiem, but it shall be for myself, since I am dying.

CONSTANZE: My beloved, don't talk so! Go to sleep. (*She spreads a shawl over his body.*) How can you say such things? Imagine even thinking such a thing! You will live many years and write countless beautiful pages. We will return the money and refuse the commission. Then the matter will be closed. Now go to sleep, my treasure.

(*She goes out, quietly closing the door behind her.* MOZART, *at the mercy of his youth, his illness and his genius, is shaken by a violent fit of weeping. The sobs gradually subside and he falls asleep. In his dream* THE GRAY STEWARD *returns.*)

THE GRAY STEWARD: Mozart! Turn and look at me. You know who I am.

MOZART: (*Not turning.*) You are the steward of the Count von Walsegg. Go tell him to write his own music. I will not stain my pen to celebrate his lady, so let the foul bury the foul.

THE GRAY STEWARD: Lie then against the wall, and learn that it is Death itself that commissions. . . .

MOZART: Death is not so fastidious. Death carries no perfumed handkerchief.

THE GRAY STEWARD: Lie then against the wall. Know first that all the combinations of circumstance can suffer two interpretations, the apparent and the real.

MOZART: Then speak, sycophant, I know the apparent one. What other reading can this humiliation bear?

THE GRAY STEWARD: It is Death itself that commands you this Requiem. You are to give a voice to all those millions sleeping, who have no one but you to speak for them. There lie the captains and the thieves, the queens and the drudges, while the evening of their earthly remembrance shuts in, and from that great field rises an eternal *miserere nobis*. Only through the intercession of great love, and of great art which is love, can that despairing cry be eased. Was that not sufficient cause for this commission to be anonymous?

MOZART: (*Drops trembling on one knee beside the couch.*) Forgive me.

THE GRAY STEWARD: And it was for this that the pretext and

mover was chosen from among the weakest and vainest of humans. Death has her now, and all her folly has passed into the dignity and grandeur of her state. Where is your pride now? Here are her slippers and her trinkets. Press them against your lips. Again! Again! Know henceforth that only he who has kissed the leper can enter the kingdom of art.

MOZART: I have sinned, yet grant me one thing. Grant that I may live to finish the Requiem.

THE GRAY STEWARD: No! No!

(*And it remains unfinished.*)

Hast Thou Considered My Servant Job?

Now it came to pass on the day when the sons of God came to present themselves before SATAN *that* CHRIST *also came among them. And*

SATAN: (*Said unto* CHRIST.) *Whence comest Thou?*
CHRIST: (*Answered* SATAN *and said*) *From going to and fro in the earth, and from walking up and down in it.*

(*And*)

SATAN: (*Said unto* CHRIST) *Hast Thou considered my servant Judas? For there is none like him in the earth, an evil and a faithless man, one that feareth me and turneth away from God.*

(*Then*)

CHRIST: (*Answered* SATAN *and said*) *Doth Judas fear thee for naught? Hast thou not made a hedge about him, and about his house, and about all that he hath on every side? But draw back thy hand now and he will renounce thee to thy face.*

(*And*)

SATAN: (*Said unto* CHRIST) *Behold, all that he hath is in thy power.*

(*So* CHRIST *went forth from the presence of* SATAN.)

*   *   *   *   *

(*He descended to the earth. Thirty-three years are but a moment before* SATAN *and before* GOD, *and at the end of this moment* CHRIST *ascends again to His own place. He passes on this journey before the presence of the adversary.*)

SATAN: You are alone! Where is my son Judas whom I gave into your hands?
CHRIST: He follows me.
SATAN: I know what you have done. And the earth rejected you? The earth rejected you! All Hell murmurs in astonishment. But where is Judas, my son and my joy?

CHRIST: Even now he is coming.

SATAN: Even Heaven, when I reigned there, was not so tedious as this waiting. Know, Prince, that I am too proud to show all my astonishment at your defeat. But now that you are swallowing your last humiliation, now that your failure has shut the mouths of the angels, I may confess that for a while I feared you. There is a fretfulness in the hearts of men. Many are inconstant, even to me. Alas, every man is not a Judas. I knew even from the beginning that you would be able, for a season, to win their hearts with your mild eloquence. I feared that you would turn to your own uses this fretfulness that visits them. But my fears were useless. Even Judas, even when my power was withdrawn from him, even Judas betrayed you. Am I not right in this?

CHRIST: You are.

SATAN: You admitted him into your chosen company. Is it permitted to me to ask for how much he betrayed you?

CHRIST: For thirty pieces of silver.

SATAN: (*After a pause.*) Am I permitted to ask to what rôle he was assigned in your company?

CHRIST: He held its money-bags.

SATAN: (*Dazed.*) Does Heaven understand human nature as little as that? Surely the greater part of your closest companions stayed beside you to the end?

CHRIST: One stayed beside me.

SATAN: I have overestimated my enemy. Learn again, Prince, that if I were permitted to return to the earth in my own person, not for thirty years, but for thirty hours, I would seal all men to me and all the temptations in Heaven's gift could not persuade one to betray me. For I build not on intermittent dreams and timid aspirations, but on the unshakable passions of greed and lust and self-love. At last this is made clear: Judas, Judas, all the triumphs of Hell await you. Already above the eternal pavements of black marble the banquet is laid. Listen, how my nations are stirring in new hope and in new joy. Such music has not been lifted above my lakes and my mountains since the day I placed the apple of knowledge between the teeth of Adam.

(*Suddenly the thirty pieces of silver are cast upward from the revolted hand of* JUDAS. *They hurtle through the skies, flinging their enormous shadows across the stars and continue falling forever through the vast funnel of space.*

(*Presently* JUDAS *rises, the black stains about his throat and the rope of suicide.*)

SATAN: What have they done to you, my beloved son? What last poor revenge have they attempted upon you? Come to me. Here there is comfort. Here all this violence can be repaired. The futile spite of Heaven cannot reach you here. But why do you not speak to me? My son, my treasure!

(JUDAS *remains with lowered eyes.*)

CHRIST: Speak to him then, my beloved son.

JUDAS: (*Still with lowered eyes, softly, to* SATAN.) Accursed be thou, from eternity to eternity.

(*These two mount upward to their due place and* SATAN *remains to this day, uncomprehending, upon the pavement of Hell.*)

The Flight into Egypt

From time to time there are auctions of the fittings that made up the old Dime Museums, and at such an auction you should be able to pick up a revolving cyclorama of the Holy Land and Egypt, which is the scenery for this piece. Turn down the gas-lights, for it is night in Palestine, and introduce a lady and a child on a donkey. They are accompanied by an old man on foot. The Donkey's name is HEPZIBAH.

HEPZIBAH: (*For the tenth time.*) I'm tired.

OUR LADY: I know, I know.

HEPZIBAH: I'm willing to carry you as far and as fast as I can, but within reason.

ST. JOSEPH: If you didn't talk so much you'd have more strength for the journey.

HEPZIBAH: It's not my lungs that are tired, it's my legs. When I talk I don't notice how tired I am.

OUR LADY: Do as you think best, Hepzibah, but do keep moving. I can still hear Herod's soldiers behind us.

   (*Noise of ironmongery in the wings, right.*)

HEPZIBAH: Well, I'm doing my best.

   (*Silence. The Tigris passes on the cyclorama.*)

We must talk or I'll have to halt. We talked over the Romans and the whole political situation, and I must say again that I and every thinking person can only view such a situation with alarm, with real alarm. We talked over the village, and I don't think there's anything more to say about that. Did I remember to tell you that Issachbar's daughter's engagement had been broken?

OUR LADY: Yes.

HEPZIBAH: Well, there's always ideas. I hope I can say honestly that I am at home in ideas of all sorts. For instance, back in the yard I'm the leader of a group. Among the girls. Very interesting religious discussions, I can tell you. Very helpful.

ST. JOSEPH: (*As some more iron is heard failing in Judæa; the Euphrates passes.*) Can't you hurry a bit?

HEPZIBAH: I always say to the girls: Girls, even in faith we are supposed to use our reason. No one is intended to swallow hook, line and sinker, as the saying is. Now take these children that Herod is killing. Why were they born, since they must die so soon? Can any one answer that? Or put it another way: Why is the little boy in your arms being saved while the others must perish?

ST. JOSEPH: Is it necessary to stop?

HEPZIBAH: I was stopping for emphasis.—Mind you, it's not that I doubt. Honest discussion does not imply doubt necessarily.—What was that noise?

OUR LADY: I beg of you to make all the haste you can. The noise you hear is that of Herod's soldiers. My child will be slain while you argue about Faith. I beg of you, Hepzibah, to save him while you can.

HEPZIBAH: I assure you I'm doing the best I can, and I think I'm moving along smartly. I didn't mean that noise, anyway; it was a noise ahead. Of course, your child is dearer to you than others, but *theologically speaking*, there's no possible reason why you should escape safely into Egypt while the others should be put to the sword, as the Authorized Version has it. When the Messiah comes these things will be made clear, but until then I intend to exercise my reasoning faculty. My theory is this. . . .

OUR LADY: Hepzibah, we shall really have to beat you if you stop so often. Hepzibah, don't you remember me? Don't you remember how you fell on your knees in the stable? Don't you remember my child?

HEPZIBAH: What? What! Of course!

OUR LADY: Yes, Hepzibah.

HEPZIBAH: Let me stop just a moment and look around. No, I don't dare to stop. Why didn't I recognize you before! Really, my lady, you should have spoken more sharply to me. I didn't know I could run like this; it's a pleasure. Lord, what a donkey I was to be arguing about reason while my Lord was in danger.

(*A pyramid flies by.*)

Do you see the lights of the town yet? That's the Sphinx at the right, madam, yes, 3655 B.C. Well, well, it's a queer world where the survival of the Lord is dependent on donkeys, but so it is. Why didn't you tell me before, my lady?

ST. JOSEPH: We thought you could carry us forward on your own merit.

HEPZIBAH: Oh, forgive me, madam; forgive me, sir. You don't hear any more soldiers now, I warrant you. Please don't direct me so far—excuse me—to the right, madam. That's the Nile, and there are crocodiles. My lady, may I ask one question now that we're safe?

OUR LADY: Yes, Hepzibah.

HEPZIBAH: It's this matter of faith and reason, madam. I'd love to carry back to our group of girls whatever you might say about it. . . .

OUR LADY: Dear Hepzibah, perhaps some day. For the present just do as I do and bear your master on.

(*More pyramids fly by; Memnon sings; the Nile moves dreamily past, and the inn is reached.*)

The Angel That Troubled the Waters

The Pool.—*A vast gray hall with a hole in the ceiling open to the sky. Broad stone steps lead up from the water on its four sides. The water is continuously restless and throws blue reflections upon the walls. The sick, the blind and the malformed are lying on the steps. The long stretches of silence and despair are broken from time to time when one or another groans and turns in his rags, or raises a fretful wail or a sudden cry of exasperation at long-continued pain. A door leads out upon the porch where the attendants of the sick are playing at dice, waiting for the call to fling their masters into the water when the angel of healing stirs the pool. Beyond the porch there is a glimpse of the fierce sunlight and the empty streets of an oriental noonday.*

Suddenly the ANGEL *appears upon the top step. His face and robe shine with a color that is both silver and gold, and the wings of blue and green, tipped with rose, shimmer in the tremulous light. He walks slowly down among the shapeless sleepers and stands gazing into the water that already trembles in anticipation of its virtue.*

(*A new invalid enters.*)

THE NEWCOMER: Come, long-expected love. Come, long-expected love. Let the sacred finger and the sacred breath stir up the pool. Here on the lowest step I wait with festering limbs, with my heart in pain. Free me, long-expected love, from this old burden. Since I cannot stay, since I must return into the city, come now, renewal, come, release.

> (*Another invalid wakes suddenly out of a nightmare, calling: "The Angel! The Angel has come. I am cured." He flings himself into the pool, splashing his companions. They come to life and gaze eagerly at the water. They hang over the brink and several slide in. Then a great cry of derision rises: "The Fool! Fool! His nightmare again. Beat him! Drive him out into the Porch." The mistaken invalid and his dupes drag themselves out of the water and lie dripping disconsolately upon the steps.*)

THE MISTAKEN INVALID: I dreamt that an angel stood by me and that at last I should be free of this hateful place and its company. Better a mistake and this jeering than an opportunity lost. (*He sees the* NEWCOMER *beside him and turns on him plaintively.*) Aïe! You have no right to be here, at all events. You are able to walk about. You pass your days in the city. You come here only at great intervals, and it may be that by some unlucky chance you might be the first one to see the sign. You would rush into the water and a cure would be wasted. You are yourself a physician. You have restored my own children. Go back to your work and leave these miracles to us who need them.

THE NEWCOMER: (*Ignoring him; under his breath.*) My work grows faint. Heal me, long-expected Love; heal me that I may continue. Renewal, release; let me begin again without this fault that bears me down.

THE MISTAKEN INVALID: I shall sit here without ever lifting my eyes from the surface of the pool. I shall be the next. Many times, even since I have been here, many times the Angel has passed and has stirred the water, and hundreds have left the hall leaping and crying out with joy. I shall be the next.

THE ANGEL: (*Kneels down on the lowest step and meditatively holds his finger poised above the shuddering water.*) Joy and fulfilment, completion, content, rest and release have been promised.

THE NEWCOMER: Come, long-expected Love.

THE ANGEL: (*Without turning makes himself apparent to the* NEWCOMER *and addresses him.*) Draw back, physician, this moment is not for you.

THE NEWCOMER: Angelic visitor, I pray thee, listen to my prayer.

THE ANGEL: Healing is not for you.

THE NEWCOMER: Surely, surely, the angels are wise. Surely, O, Prince, you are not deceived by my apparent wholeness. Your eyes can see the nets in which my wings are caught; the sin into which all my endeavors sink half-performed cannot be concealed from you.

THE ANGEL: I know.

THE NEWCOMER: It is no shame to boast to an Angel of what I

might yet do in Love's service were I but freed from this bondage.

THE MISTAKEN INVALID: Surely the water is stirring strangely to-day! Surely I shall be whole!

THE ANGEL: I must make haste. Already the sky is afire with the gathering host, for it is the hour of the new song among us. The earth itself feels the preparation in the skies and attempts its hymn. Children born in this hour spend all their lives in a sharper longing for the perfection that awaits them.

THE NEWCOMER: Oh, in such an hour was I born, and doubly fearful to me is the flaw in my heart. Must I drag my shame, Prince and singer, all my days more bowed than my neighbor?

THE ANGEL: (*Stands a moment in silence.*) Without your wound where would your power be? It is your very remorse that makes your low voice tremble into the hearts of men. The very angels themselves cannot persuade the wretched and blundering children on earth as can one human being broken on the wheels of living. In Love's service only the wounded soldiers can serve. Draw back.

(*He swiftly kneels and draws his finger through the water. The pool is presently astir with running ripples. They increase and a divine wind strikes the gay surface. The waves are flung upon the steps.* The MISTAKEN MAN *casts himself into the Pool, and the whole company lurches, rolls, or hobbles in. The servants rush in from the porch. Turmoil. Finally the no longer* MISTAKEN INVALID *emerges and leaps joyfully up the steps. The rest, coughing and sighing, follow him. The* ANGEL *smiles for a moment and disappears.*)

THE HEALED MAN: Look, my hand is new as a child's. Glory be to God! I have begun again. (*To the* NEWCOMER.) May you be the next, my brother. But come with me first, an hour only, to my home. My son is lost in dark thoughts. I—I do not understand him, and only you have ever lifted his mood. Only an hour . . . my daughter since her child has died, sits in the shadow. She will not listen to us. . . .

THE LONG CHRISTMAS DINNER
AND OTHER PLAYS IN ONE ACT

CONTENTS

The Long Christmas Dinner

The dining-room of the Bayard home. Close to the footlights a long dining table is handsomely spread for Christmas dinner. The carver's place with a great turkey before it is at the spectator's right.

A door, left back, leads into the hall.

At the extreme left, by the proscenium pillar, is a strange portal trimmed with garlands of fruits and flowers. Directly opposite is another edged and hung with black velvet. The portals denote birth and death.

Ninety years are to be traversed in this play which represents in accelerated motion ninety Christmas dinners in the Bayard household. The actors are dressed in inconspicuous clothes and must indicate their gradual increase in years through their acting. Most of them carry wigs of white hair which they adjust upon their heads at the indicated moment, simply and without comment. The ladies may have shawls concealed beneath the table that they gradually draw up about their shoulders as they grow older.

Throughout the play the characters continue eating imaginary food with imaginary knives and forks.

There is no curtain. The audience arriving at the theatre sees the stage set and the table laid, though still in partial darkness. Gradually the lights in the auditorium become dim and the stage brightens until sparkling winter sunlight streams through the dining room windows.

Enter LUCIA. *She inspects the table, touching here a knife and there a fork. She talks to a servant girl who is invisible to us.*

LUCIA: I reckon we're ready now, Gertrude. We won't ring the chimes today. I'll just call them myself.

She goes into the hall and calls:

Roderick. Mother Bayard. We're all ready. Come to dinner.

Enter RODERICK *pushing* MOTHER BAYARD *in a wheel chair.*

MOTHER BAYARD: . . . and a new horse too, Roderick. I used

to think that only the wicked owned two horses. A new horse and a new house and a new wife!

RODERICK: Well, Mother, how do you like it? Our first Christmas dinner in the new house, hey?

MOTHER BAYARD: Tz-Tz-Tz! I don't know what your dear father would say!

LUCIA: Here, Mother Bayard, you sit between us.

RODERICK *says grace.*

MOTHER BAYARD: My dear Lucia, I can remember when there were still Indians on this very ground, and I wasn't a young girl either. I can remember when we had to cross the Mississippi on a new-made raft. I can remember when St. Louis and Kansas City were full of Indians.

LUCIA (*tying a napkin around* MOTHER BAYARD'S *neck*): Imagine that! There!—What a wonderful day for our first Christmas dinner: a beautiful sunny morning, snow, a splendid sermon. Dr. McCarthy preaches a splendid sermon. I cried and cried.

RODERICK (*extending an imaginary carving fork*): Come now, what'll you have, Mother? A little sliver of white?

LUCIA: Every least twig is wrapped around with ice. You almost never see that. Can I cut it up for you, dear? (*over her shoulder*) Gertrude, I forgot the jelly. You know,—on the top shelf.—Mother Bayard, I found your mother's gravy-boat while we were moving. What was her name, dear? What were all your names? You were . . . a . . . Genevieve Wainright. Now your mother—

MOTHER BAYARD: Yes, you must write it down somewhere. I was Genevieve Wainright. My mother was Faith Morrison. She was the daughter of a farmer in New Hampshire who was something of a blacksmith too. And she married young John Wainright—

LUCIA (*memorizing on her fingers*): Genevieve Wainright. Faith Morrison.

RODERICK: It's all down in a book somewhere upstairs. We have it all. All that kind of thing is very interesting. Come, Lucia, just a little wine. Mother, a little red wine for Christmas day. Full of iron. "Take a little wine for thy stomach's sake."

LUCIA: Really, I can't get used to wine! What would my father say? But I suppose it's all right.

Enter COUSIN BRANDON *from the hall. He takes his place by* LUCIA.

COUSIN BRANDON (*rubbing his hands*): Well, well, I smell turkey. My dear cousins, I can't tell you how pleasant it is to be having Christmas dinner with you all. I've lived out there in Alaska so long without relatives. Let me see, how long have you had this new house, Roderick?

RODERICK: Why, it must be . . .

MOTHER BAYARD: Five years. It's five years, children. You should keep a diary. This is your sixth Christmas dinner here.

LUCIA: Think of that, Roderick. We feel as though we had lived here twenty years.

COUSIN BRANDON: At all events it still looks as good as new.

RODERICK (*over his carving*): What'll you have, Brandon, light or dark?—Frieda, fill up Cousin Brandon's glass.

LUCIA: Oh, dear, I can't get used to these wines. I don't know what my father'd say, I'm sure. What'll you have, Mother Bayard?

During the following speeches MOTHER BAYARD'S *chair, without any visible propulsion, starts to draw away from the table, turns toward the right, and slowly goes toward the dark portal.*

MOTHER BAYARD: Yes, I can remember when there were Indians on this very land.

LUCIA (*softly*): Mother Bayard hasn't been very well lately, Roderick.

MOTHER BAYARD: My mother was a Faith Morrison. And in New Hampshire she married a young John Wainright, who was a Congregational minister. He saw her in his congregation one day . . .

LUCIA: Mother Bayard, hadn't you better lie down, dear?

MOTHER BAYARD: . . . and right in the middle of his sermon he said to himself: "I'll marry that girl." And he did, and I'm their daughter.

LUCIA (*half rising and looking after her with anxiety*): Just a little nap, dear?

MOTHER BAYARD: I'm all right. Just go on with your dinner. I was ten, and I said to my brother—

She goes out. A very slight pause.

COUSIN BRANDON: It's too bad it's such a cold dark day today. We almost need the lamps. I spoke to Major Lewis for a moment after church. His sciatica troubles him, but he does pretty well.

LUCIA (*dabbing her eyes*): I know Mother Bayard wouldn't want us to grieve for her on Christmas day, but I can't forget her sitting in her wheel chair right beside us, only a year ago. And she would be so glad to know our good news.

RODERICK (*patting her hand*): Now, now. It's Christmas. (*formally*) Cousin Brandon, a glass of wine with you, sir.

COUSIN BRANDON (*half rising, lifting his glass gallantly*): A glass of wine with you, sir.

LUCIA: Does the Major's sciatica cause him much pain?

COUSIN BRANDON: Some, perhaps. But you know his way. He says it'll be all the same in a hundred years.

LUCIA: Yes, he's a great philosopher.

RODERICK: His wife sends you a thousand thanks for her Christmas present.

LUCIA: I forget what I gave her.—Oh, yes, the workbasket!

Through the entrance of birth comes a nurse wheeling a perambulator trimmed with blue ribbons. LUCIA rushes toward it, the men following.

O my wonderful new baby, my darling baby! Who ever saw such a child! Quick, nurse, a boy or a girl? A boy! Roderick, what shall we call him? Really, nurse, you've never seen such a child!

RODERICK: We'll call him Charles after your father and grandfather.

LUCIA: But there are no Charleses in the Bible, Roderick.

RODERICK: Of course, there are. Surely there are.

LUCIA: Roderick!—Very well, but he will always be Samuel to me.—What miraculous hands he has! Really, they are the most beautiful hands in the world. All right, nurse. Have a good nap, my darling child.

RODERICK: Don't drop him, nurse. Brandon and I need him in our firm.

Exit nurse and perambulator into the hall. The others return to their chairs, LUCIA *taking the place left vacant by* MOTHER BAYARD *and* COUSIN BRANDON *moving up beside her.* COUSIN BRANDON *puts on his white hair.*

Lucia, a little white meat? Some stuffing? Cranberry sauce, anybody?

LUCIA *(over her shoulder)*: Margaret, the stuffing is very good today.—Just a little, thank you.

RODERICK: Now something to wash it down. *(half rising)* Cousin Brandon, a glass of wine with you, sir. To the ladies, God bless them.

LUCIA: Thank you, kind sirs.

COUSIN BRANDON: Pity it's such an overcast day today. And no snow.

LUCIA: But the sermon was lovely. I cried and cried. Dr. Spaulding does preach such a splendid sermon.

RODERICK: I saw Major Lewis for a moment after church. He says his rheumatism comes and goes. His wife says she has something for Charles and will bring it over this afternoon.

Enter nurse again with perambulator. Pink ribbons. Same rush toward the left.

LUCIA: O my lovely new baby! Really, it never occurred to me that it might be a girl. Why, nurse, she's perfect.

RODERICK: Now call her what you choose. It's your turn.

LUCIA: Loolooloolooloo. Aië. Aië. Yes, this time I shall have my way. She shall be called Genevieve after your mother. Have a good nap, my treasure.

She looks after it as the nurse wheels the perambulator into the hall.

Imagine! Sometime she'll be grown up and say "Good morning, Mother. Good morning, Father."—Really, Cousin Brandon, you don't find a baby like that every day.

COUSIN BRANDON: *And* the new factory.

LUCIA: A new factory? Really? Roderick, I shall be very

uncomfortable if we're going to turn out to be rich. I've been afraid of that for years.—However, we mustn't talk about such things on Christmas day. I'll just take a little piece of white meat, thank you. Roderick, Charles is destined for the ministry. I'm sure of it.

RODERICK: Woman, he's only twelve. Let him have a free mind. *We* want him in the firm, I don't mind saying. Anyway, no time passes as slowly as this when you're waiting for your urchins to grow up and settle down to business.

LUCIA: I don't want time to go any faster, thank you. I love the children just as they are.—Really, Roderick, you know what the doctor said: One glass a meal. (*putting her hand over his glass*) No, Margaret, that will be all.

> RODERICK *rises, glass in hand. With a look of dismay on his face he takes a few steps toward the dark portal.*

RODERICK: Now I wonder what's the matter with me.

LUCIA: Roderick, do be reasonable.

RODERICK (*tottering, but with gallant irony*): But, my dear, statistics show that we steady, moderate drinkers . . .

LUCIA (*rises, gazing at him in anguish*): Roderick! My dear! What . . . ?

RODERICK (*returns to his seat with a frightened look of relief*): Well, it's fine to be back at table with you again. How many good Christmas dinners have I had to miss upstairs? And to be back at a fine bright one, too.

LUCIA: O my dear, you gave us a very alarming time! Here's your glass of milk.—Josephine, bring Mr. Bayard his medicine from the cupboard in the library.

RODERICK: At all events, now that I'm better I'm going to start doing something about the house.

LUCIA: Roderick! You're not going to change the house?

RODERICK: Only touch it up here and there. It looks a hundred years old.

> CHARLES *enters casually from the hall. He kisses his mother's hair and sits down.*

LUCIA: Charles, you carve the turkey, dear. Your father's not well.—You always said you hated carving, though you *are* so clever at it.

Father and son exchange places.

CHARLES: It's a great blowy morning, Mother. The wind comes over the hill like a lot of cannon.

LUCIA: And such a good sermon. I cried and cried. Mother Bayard loved a good sermon so. And she used to sing the Christmas hymns all around the year. Oh, dear, oh, dear, I've been thinking of her all morning!

CHARLES: Sh, Mother. It's Christmas day. You mustn't think of such things.—You mustn't be depressed.

LUCIA: But sad things aren't the same as depressing things. I must be getting old: I like them.

CHARLES: Uncle Brandon, you haven't anything to eat. Pass his plate, Hilda . . . and some cranberry sauce . . .

Enter GENEVIEVE. *She kisses her father's temple and sits down.*

GENEVIEVE: It's glorious. Every least twig is wrapped around with ice. You almost never see that.

LUCIA: Did you have time to deliver those presents after church, Genevieve?

GENEVIEVE: Yes, Mama. Old Mrs. Lewis sends you a thousand thanks for hers. It was just what she wanted, she said. Give me lots, Charles, lots.

RODERICK (*rising and starting toward the dark portal*): Statistics, ladies and gentlemen, show that we steady, moderate . . .

CHARLES: How about a little skating this afternoon, Father?

RODERICK: I'll live till I'm ninety.

LUCIA: I really don't think he ought to go skating.

RODERICK (*at the very portal, suddenly astonished*): Yes, but . . . but . . . not yet!

He goes out.

LUCIA (*dabbing her eyes*): He was so young and so clever, Cousin Brandon. (*raising her voice for* COUSIN BRANDON'S *deafness*) I say he was so young and so clever.—Never forget your father, children. He was a good man.—Well, he wouldn't want us to grieve for him today.

CHARLES: White or dark, Genevieve? Just another sliver, Mother?

LUCIA (*putting on her white hair*): I can remember our first Christmas dinner in this house, Genevieve. Twenty-five years ago today. Mother Bayard was sitting here in her wheel chair. She could remember when Indians lived on this very spot and when she had to cross the river on a new-made raft.

CHARLES AND GENEVIEVE: She couldn't have, Mother. That can't be true.

LUCIA: It certainly was true—even I can remember when there was only one paved street. We were very happy to walk on boards. (*louder, to* COUSIN BRANDON) We can remember when there were no sidewalks, can't we, Cousin Brandon?

COUSIN BRANDON (*delighted*): Oh, yes! And those were the days.

CHARLES AND GENEVIEVE (*sotto voce. This is a family refrain*): Those were the days.

LUCIA: . . . and the ball last night, Genevieve? Did you have a nice time? I hope you didn't *waltz*, dear. I think a girl in our position ought to set an example. Did Charles keep an eye on you?

GENEVIEVE: He had none left. They were all on Leonora Banning. He can't conceal it any longer, Mother. I think he's engaged to marry Leonora Banning.

CHARLES: I'm not engaged to marry anyone.

LUCIA: Well, she's very pretty.

GENEVIEVE: I shall never marry, Mother—I shall sit in this house beside you forever, as though life were one long, happy Christmas dinner.

LUCIA: O my child, you mustn't say such things!

GENEVIEVE (*playfully*): You don't want me? You don't want me?

LUCIA *bursts into tears.*

Why, Mother, how silly you are! There's nothing sad about that—what could possibly be sad about that.

LUCIA (*drying her eyes*): Forgive me. I'm just unpredictable, that's all.

CHARLES *goes to the door and leads in* LEONORA BANNING.

LEONORA (*kissing* LUCIA'S *temple*): Good morning, Mother Bayard. Good morning, everybody. It's really a splendid Christmas day today.

CHARLES: Little white meat? Genevieve, Mother, Leonora?

LEONORA: Every least twig is encircled with ice.—You never see that.

CHARLES (*shouting*): Uncle Brandon, another?—Rogers, fill my uncle's glass.

LUCIA (*to Charles*): Do what your father used to do. It would please Cousin Brandon so. You know—(*pretending to raise a glass*)—"Uncle Brandon, a glass of wine—"

CHARLES (*rising*): Uncle Brandon, a glass of wine with you, sir.

BRANDON: A glass of wine with you, sir. To the ladies, God bless them every one.

THE LADIES: Thank you, kind sirs.

GENEVIEVE: And if I go to Germany for my music I promise to be back for Christmas. I wouldn't miss that.

LUCIA: I hate to think of you over there all alone in those strange pensions.

GENEVIEVE: But, darling, the time will pass so fast that you'll hardly know I'm gone. I'll be back in the twinkling of an eye.

Enter Left, the nurse and perambulator. Green ribbons.

LEONORA: Oh, what an angel! The darlingest baby in the world. Do let me hold it, nurse.

But the nurse resolutely wheels the perambulator across the stage and out the dark door.

Oh, I did love it so!

LUCIA goes to her, puts her arm around LEONORA'S shoulders, and they encircle the room whispering—LUCIA then hands her over to CHARLES who conducts her on the same circuit.

GENEVIEVE (*as her mother sits down,—softly*): Isn't there anything I can do?

LUCIA (*raises her eyebrows, ruefully*): No, dear. Only time, only the passing of time can help in these things.

CHARLES *and* LEONORA *return to the table.*

Don't you think we could ask Cousin Ermengarde to come and live with us here? There's plenty for everyone and there's no reason why she should go on teaching the First Grade for ever and ever. She wouldn't be in the way, would she, Charles?

CHARLES: No, I think it would be fine.—A little more potato and gravy, anybody? A little more turkey, Mother?

BRANDON *rises and starts slowly toward the dark portal.*
LUCIA *rises and stands for a moment with her face in her hands.*

COUSIN BRANDON (*muttering*): It was great to be in Alaska in those days . . .

GENEVIEVE (*half rising, and gazing at her mother in fear*): Mother, what is . . . ?

LUCIA (*hurriedly*): Hush, my dear. It will pass.—Hold fast to your music, you know. (*as* GENEVIEVE *starts toward her*) No, no. I want to be alone for a few minutes.

She turns and starts after COUSIN BRANDON *toward the Right.*

CHARLES: If the Republicans collected all their votes instead of going off into cliques among themselves, they might prevent his getting a second term.

GENEVIEVE: Charles, Mother doesn't tell us, but she hasn't been very well these days.

CHARLES: Come, Mother, we'll go to Florida for a few weeks.

Exit BRANDON.

LUCIA (*smiling at* GENEVIEVE *and waving her hand*): Don't be foolish. Don't grieve.

She clasps her hands under her chin; her lips move, whispering; she walks serenely into the portal.
GENEVIEVE *stares after her, frozen.*
At the same moment the nurse and perambulator enter from the Left. Pale yellow ribbons. LEONORA *rushes to it.*

LEONORA: O my darlings . . . twins . . . Charles, aren't they glorious! Look at them. Look at them.

GENEVIEVE (*sinks down on the table her face buried in her arms*): But what will I do? What's left for me to do?

CHARLES (*bending over the basket*): Which is which?

LEONORA: I feel as though I were the first mother who ever had twins.—Look at them now!—But why wasn't Mother Bayard allowed to stay and see them!

GENEVIEVE (*rising suddenly distraught, loudly*): I don't want to go on. I can't bear it.

CHARLES (*goes to her quickly. They sit down. He whispers to her earnestly taking both her hands*): But Genevieve, Genevieve! How frightfully Mother would feel to think that . . . Genevieve!

GENEVIEVE (*shaking her head wildly*): I never told her how wonderful she was. We all treated her as though she were just a friend in the house. I thought she'd be here forever.

LEONORA (*timidly*): Genevieve darling, do come one minute and hold my babies' hands. We shall call the girl Lucia after her grandmother,—will that please you? Do just see what adorable little hands they have.

GENEVIEVE *collects herself and goes over to the perambulator. She smiles brokenly into the basket.*

GENEVIEVE: They are wonderful, Leonora.

LEONORA: Give him your finger, darling. Just let him hold it.

CHARLES: And we'll call the boy Samuel.—Well, now everybody come and finish your dinners. Don't drop them, nurse; at least don't drop the boy. We need him in the firm.

LEONORA (*stands looking after them as the nurse wheels them into the hall*): Someday they'll be big. Imagine! They'll come in and say "Hello, Mother!" (*She makes clucking noises of rapturous consternation.*)

CHARLES: Come, a little wine, Leonora, Genevieve? Full of iron. Eduardo, fill the ladies' glasses. It certainly is a keen, cold morning. I used to go skating with Father on mornings like this and Mother would come back from church saying—

GENEVIEVE (*dreamily*): I know: saying "Such a splendid sermon. I cried and cried."

LEONORA: Why did she cry, dear?

GENEVIEVE: That generation all cried at sermons. It was their way.

LEONORA: Really, Genevieve?

GENEVIEVE: They had had to go since they were children and I suppose sermons reminded them of their fathers and mothers, just as Christmas dinners do us. Especially in an old house like this.

LEONORA: It really is pretty old, Charles. And so ugly, with all that ironwork filigree and that dreadful cupola.

GENEVIEVE: Charles! You aren't going to change the house!

CHARLES: No, no. I won't give up the house, but great heavens! it's fifty years old. This Spring we'll remove the cupola and build a new wing toward the tennis courts.

From now on GENEVIEVE *is seen to change. She sits up more straightly. The corners of her mouth become fixed. She becomes a forthright and slightly disillusioned spinster.* CHARLES *becomes the plain business man and a little pompous.*

LEONORA: And then couldn't we ask your dear old Cousin Ermengarde to come and live with us? She's really the self-effacing kind.

CHARLES: Ask her now. Take her out of the First Grade.

GENEVIEVE: We only seem to think of it on Christmas day with her Christmas card staring us in the face.

Enter Left, nurse and perambulator. Blue ribbons.

LEONORA: Another boy! Another boy! Here's a Roderick for you at last.

CHARLES: Roderick Brandon Bayard. A regular little fighter.

LEONORA: Goodbye, darling. Don't grow up too fast. Yes, yes. Aië, aië, aië—stay just as you are.—Thank you, nurse.

GENEVIEVE (*who has not left the table, repeats dryly*): Stay just as you are.

Exit nurse and perambulator. The others return to their places.

LEONORA: Now I have three children. One, two, three. Two boys and a girl. I'm collecting them. It's very exciting. (*over her shoulder*) What, Hilda? Oh, Cousin Ermengarde's come! Come in, Cousin.

She goes to the hall and welcomes COUSIN ERMENGARDE *who already wears her white hair.*

ERMENGARDE (*shyly*): It's such a pleasure to be with you all.

CHARLES (*pulling out her chair for her*): The twins have taken a great fancy to you already, Cousin.

LEONORA: The baby went to her at once.

CHARLES: Exactly how are we related, Cousin Ermengarde?— There, Genevieve, that's your specialty.—First a little more turkey and stuffing, Mother? Cranberry sauce, anybody?

GENEVIEVE: I can work it out: Grandmother Bayard was your . . .

ERMENGARDE: Your Grandmother Bayard was a second cousin of my Grandmother Haskins through the Wainrights.

CHARLES: Well, it's all in a book somewhere upstairs. All that kind of thing is awfully interesting.

GENEVIEVE: Nonsense. There are no such books. I collect my notes off gravestones, and you have to scrape a good deal of moss—let me tell you—to find one great-grandparent.

CHARLES: There's a story that my Grandmother Bayard crossed the Mississippi on a raft before there were any bridges or ferryboats. She died before Genevieve or I were born. Time certainly goes very fast in a great new country like this. Have some more cranberry sauce, Cousin Ermengarde.

ERMENGARDE (*timidly*): Well, time must be passing very slowly in Europe with this dreadful, dreadful war going on.

CHARLES: Perhaps an occasional war isn't so bad after all. It clears up a lot of poisons that collect in nations. It's like a boil.

ERMENGARDE: Oh, dear, oh, dear!

CHARLES (*with relish*): Yes, it's like a boil.—Ho! ho! Here are your twins.

> *The twins appear at the door into the hall.* SAM *is wearing the uniform of an ensign.* LUCIA *is fussing over some detail on it.*

LUCIA: Isn't he wonderful in it, Mother?

CHARLES: Let's get a look at you.

SAM: Mother, don't let Roderick fool with my stamp album while I'm gone.

LEONORA: Now, Sam, do write a letter once in a while. Do be a good boy about that, mind.

SAM: You might send some of those cakes of yours once in a while, Cousin Ermengarde.

ERMENGARDE (*in a flutter*): I certainly will, my dear boy.

CHARLES: If you need any money, we have agents in Paris and London, remember.

SAM: Well, goodbye . . .

> SAM *goes briskly out through the dark portal, tossing his un-needed white hair through the door before him.*
> LUCIA *sits down at the table with lowered eyes.*

ERMENGARDE (*after a slight pause, in a low, constrained voice, making conversation*): I spoke to Mrs. Fairchild for a moment coming out of church. Her rheumatism's a little better, she says. She sends you her warmest thanks for the Christmas present. The workbasket, wasn't it?—It was an admirable sermon. And our stained-glass window looked so beautiful, Leonora, so beautiful. Everybody spoke of it and so affectionately of Sammy. (LEONORA's *hand goes to her mouth.*) Forgive me, Leonora, but it's better to speak of him than not to speak of him when we're all thinking of him so hard.

LEONORA (*rising, in anguish*): He was a mere boy. He was a mere boy, Charles.

CHARLES: My dear, my dear.

LEONORA: I want to tell him how wonderful he was. We let him go so casually. I want to tell him how we all feel about him.—Forgive me, let me walk about a minute.—Yes, of course, Ermengarde—it's best to speak of him.

LUCIA (*in a low voice to Genevieve*): Isn't there anything I can do?

GENEVIEVE: No, no. Only time, only the passing of time can help in these things.

> LEONORA, *straying about the room finds herself near the door to the hall at the moment that her son* RODERICK *enters. He links his arm with hers and leads her back to the table.*

RODERICK: What's the matter, anyway? What are you all so glum about? The skating was fine today.

CHARLES: Sit down, young man. I have something to say to you.

RODERICK: Everybody was there. Lucia skated in the corners with Dan Creighton the whole time. When'll it be, Lucia, when'll it be?

LUCIA: I don't know what you mean.

RODERICK: Lucia's leaving us soon, Mother. Dan Creighton, of all people.

CHARLES (*ominously*): Roderick, I have something to say to you.

RODERICK: Yes, Father.

CHARLES: Is it true, Roderick, that you made yourself conspicuous last night at the Country Club—at a Christmas Eve dance, too?

LEONORA: Not now, Charles, I beg of you. This is Christmas dinner.

RODERICK (*loudly*): No, I didn't.

LUCIA: Really, Father, he didn't. It was that dreadful Johnny Lewis.

CHARLES: I don't want to hear about Johnny Lewis. I want to know whether a son of mine . . .

LEONORA: Charles, I beg of you . . .

CHARLES: The first family of this city!

RODERICK (*rising*): I hate this town and everything about it. I always did.

CHARLES: You behaved like a spoiled puppy, sir, an ill-bred spoiled puppy.

RODERICK: What did I do? What did I do that was wrong?

CHARLES: You were drunk and you were rude to the daughters of my best friends.

GENEVIEVE (*striking the table*): Nothing in the world deserves an ugly scene like this. Charles, I'm ashamed of you.

RODERICK: Great God, you gotta get drunk in this town to forget how dull it is. Time passes so slowly here that it stands still, that's what's the trouble.

CHARLES: Well, young man, we can employ your time. You will leave the university and you will come into the Bayard factory on January second.

RODERICK (*at the door into the hall*): I have better things to do than to go into your old factory. I'm going somewhere where time passes, my God!

He goes out into the hall.

LEONORA (*rising*): Roderick, Roderick, come here just a moment.—Charles where can he go?

LUCIA (*rising*): Sh, Mother. He'll come back. Now I have to go upstairs and pack my trunk.

LEONORA: I won't have any children left!

LUCIA: Sh, Mother. He'll come back. He's only gone to California or somewhere.—Cousin Ermengarde has done most of my packing—thanks a thousand times, Cousin Ermengarde. (*She kisses her mother.*) I won't be long.

She runs out into the hall.
GENEVIEVE *and* LEONORA *put on their white hair.*

ERMENGARDE: It's a very beautiful day. On the way home from church I stopped and saw Mrs. Foster a moment. Her arthritis comes and goes.

LEONORA: Is she actually in pain, dear?

ERMENGARDE: Oh, she says it'll all be the same in a hundred years!

LEONORA: Yes, she's a brave little stoic.

CHARLES: Come now, a little white meat, Mother?—Mary, pass my cousin's plate.

LEONORA: What is it, Mary?—Oh, here's a telegram from them in Paris! "Love and Christmas greetings to all." I told them we'd be eating some of their wedding cake and thinking about them today. It seems to be all decided that they will settle down in the East, Ermengarde. I can't even have my daughter for a neighbor. They hope to build before long somewhere on the shore north of New York.

GENEVIEVE: There is no shore north of New York.

LEONORA: Well, East or West or whatever it is.

Pause.

CHARLES: My, what a dark day.

He puts on his white hair. Pause.

How slowly time passes without any young people in the house.

LEONORA: I have three children somewhere.

CHARLES (*blunderingly offering comfort*): Well, one of them gave his life for his country.

LEONORA (*sadly*): And one of them is selling aluminum in China.

GENEVIEVE (*slowly working herself up to a hysterical crisis*): I can stand everything but this terrible soot everywhere. We should have moved long ago. We're surrounded by factories. We have to change the window curtains every week.

LEONORA: Why, Genevieve!

GENEVIEVE: I can't stand it. I can't stand it any more. I'm going abroad. It's not only the soot that comes through the very walls of this house; it's the *thoughts*, it's the thought of what has been and what might have been here. And the feeling about this house of the years *grinding away*. My mother died yesterday—not twenty-five years ago. Oh, I'm going to live and die abroad! Yes, I'm going to be the American old maid living and dying in a pension in Munich or Florence.

ERMENGARDE: Genevieve, you're tired.

CHARLES: Come, Genevieve, take a good drink of cold water. Mary, open the window a minute.

GENEVIEVE: I'm sorry. I'm sorry.

She hurries tearfully out into the hall.

ERMENGARDE: Dear Genevieve will come back to us, I think.

She rises and starts toward the dark portal.

You should have been out today, Leonora. It was one of those days when everything was encircled with ice. Very pretty, indeed.

CHARLES *rises and starts after her.*

CHARLES: Leonora, I used to go skating with Father on mornings like this—I wish I felt a little better.

LEONORA: What! Have I got two invalids on my hands at once? Now, Cousin Ermengarde, you must get better and help me nurse Charles.

ERMENGARDE: I'll do my best.

> ERMENGARDE *turns at the very portal and comes back to the table.*

CHARLES: Well, Leonora, I'll do what you ask. I'll write the puppy a letter of forgiveness and apology. It's Christmas day. I'll cable it. That's what I'll do.

He goes out the dark door.

LEONORA (*drying her eyes*): Ermengarde, it's such a comfort having you here with me. Mary, I really can't eat anything. Well, perhaps, a sliver of white meat.

ERMENGARDE (*very old*): I spoke to Mrs. Keene for a moment coming out of church. She asked after the young people.— At church I felt very proud sitting under our windows, Leonora, and our brass tablets. The Bayard aisle,—it's a regular Bayard aisle and I love it.

LEONORA: Ermengarde, would you be very angry with me if I went and stayed with the young people a little this Spring?

ERMENGARDE: Why, no. I know how badly they want you and need you. Especially now that they're about to build a new house.

LEONORA: You wouldn't be angry? This house is yours as long as you want it, remember.

ERMENGARDE: I don't see why the rest of you dislike it. I like it more than I can say.

LEONORA: I won't be long. I'll be back in no time and we can have some more of our readings-aloud in the evening.

> *She kisses her and goes into the hall.* ERMENGARDE *left alone, eats slowly and talks to* MARY.

ERMENGARDE: Really, Mary, I'll change my mind. If you'll ask Bertha to be good enough to make me a little eggnog. A dear little eggnog.—Such a nice letter this morning from Mrs. Bayard, Mary. Such a nice letter. They're having their first Christmas dinner in the new house. They must be very happy. They call her Mother Bayard, she says, as though she were an old lady. And she says she finds it more comfortable to come and go in a wheel chair.—Such a dear letter. . . . And Mary, I can tell you a secret. It's still a great secret,

mind! They're expecting a grandchild. Isn't that good news!
Now I'll read a little.

She props a book up before her, still dipping a spoon into a cus-
tard from time to time. She grows from very old to immensely
old. She sighs. The book falls down. She finds a cane beside her,
and soon totters into the dark portal, murmuring:

"Dear little Roderick and little Lucia."

THE END

Queens of France

A lawyer's office in New Orleans, 1869.
The door to the street is hung with a reed curtain, through which one obtains a glimpse of a public park in sunshine.
A small bell tinkles. After a pause it rings again.

MARIE-SIDONIE CRESSAUX *pushes the reeds apart and peers in. She is an attractive young woman equal to any situation in life except a summons to a lawyer's office.*

M'SU CAHUSAC, *a dry little man with sharp black eyes, enters from an inner room.*

MARIE-SIDONIE (*indicating a letter in her hand*): You . . . you have asked me to come and see you.

M. CAHUSAC (*severe and brief*): Your name, Madame?

MARIE-SIDONIE: Mamselle Marie-Sidonie Cressaux, M'su.

M. CAHUSAC (*after a pause*): Yes. Kindly be seated, Mamselle.

> *He goes to his desk and opens a great many drawers, collecting documents from each. Presently having assembled a large bundle he returns to the center of the room and says abruptly:*

Mamselle, this interview is to be regarded by you as strictly confidential.

MARIE-SIDONIE: Yes, M'su.

M. CAHUSAC (*after looking at her sternly a moment*): May I ask if Mamselle is able to bear the shock of surprise, of good or bad news?

MARIE-SIDONIE: Why . . . yes, M'su.

M. CAHUSAC: Then if you are Mamselle Marie-Sidonie Cressaux, the daughter of Baptiste-Anténor Cressaux, it is my duty to inform you that you are in danger.

MARIE-SIDONIE: I am in danger, M'su?

> *He returns to his desk, opens further drawers, and returns with more papers. She follows him with bewildered eyes.*

M. CAHUSAC: Mamselle, in addition to my duties as a lawyer in this city, I am the representative here of a Historical Society in Paris. Will you please try and follow me, Mamselle? This Historical Society has been engaged in tracing the descendants of the true heir to the French throne. As you know, at the time of the Revolution, in 1795, to be exact, Mamselle, the true, lawful, and legitimate heir to the French throne disappeared. It was rumored that this boy, who was then ten years old, came to America and lived for a time in New Orleans. We now know that the rumor was true. We now know that he here begot legitimate issue, that this legitimate issue in turn begot legitimate issue, and that—(MARIE-SIDONIE *suddenly starts searching for something in her shopping bag.*) Mamselle, may I have the honor of your attention a little longer?

MARIE-SIDONIE (*choking*): My fan—my, my fan, M'su. (*She finds it and at once begins to fan herself wildly. Suddenly she cries out*): M'su, what danger am I in?

M. CAHUSAC (*sternly*): If Mamselle will exercise a moment's—one moment's—patience, she will know all. . . . That legitimate issue here begot legitimate issue, and the royal line of France has been traced to a certain (*he consults his documents*) Baptiste-Anténor Cressaux.

MARIE-SIDONIE (*Her fan stops and she stares at him*): Ba't—ba'tiste . . . !

M. CAHUSAC (*leaning forward with menacing emphasis*): Mamselle, can you *prove* that you are the daughter of Baptiste-Anténor Cressaux?

MARIE-SIDONIE: Why . . . Why . . .

M. CAHUSAC: Mamselle, have you a certificate of your parents' marriage?

MARIE-SIDONIE: Yes, M'su.

M. CAHUSAC: If it turns out to be valid, and if it is true that you have no true lawful and legitimate brothers—

MARIE-SIDONIE: No, M'su.

M. CAHUSAC: Then, Mamselle, I have nothing further to do than to announce to you that you are the true and long-lost heir to the throne of France.

He draws himself up, approaches her with great dignity, and kisses her hand. MARIE-SIDONIE *begins to cry. He goes to the desk, pours out a glass of water and murmuring,* "Your Royal Highness," *offers it to her.*

MARIE-SIDONIE: M'su Cahusac, I am very sorry. . . . But there must be some mistake. My father was a poor sailor . . . a . . . a poor sailor.

M. CAHUSAC (*reading from his papers*): . . . A distinguished and esteemed navigator.

MARIE-SIDONIE: . . . A poor sailor . . .

M. CAHUSAC (*firmly*): . . . Navigator . . .

Pause. She looks about, stricken.

MARIE-SIDONIE (*as before, suddenly and loudly*): M'su, what danger am I in?

M. CAHUSAC (*approaching her and lowering his voice*): As Your Royal Highness knows there are several families in New Orleans that claim, without documents (*he rattles the vellum and seals in his hand*), without proof—that pretend to the blood royal. The danger from them, however, is not great. The real danger is from France. From the impassioned Republicans.

MARIE-SIDONIE: Impass . . .

M. CAHUSAC: But Your Royal Highness has only to put Herself into my hands.

MARIE-SIDONIE (*crying again*): Please do not call me "Your Royal Highness."

M. CAHUSAC: You . . . give me permission to call you Madame de Cressaux?

MARIE-SIDONIE: Yes, M'su. Mamselle Cressaux. I am Marie-Sidonie Cressaux.

M. CAHUSAC: Am I mistaken . . . hmm . . . in saying that you have children?

MARIE-SIDONIE (*faintly*): Yes, M'su. I have three children.

M. CAHUSAC *looks at her thoughtfully a moment and returns to his desk.*

M. CAHUSAC: Madame, from now on thousands of eyes will be fixed upon you, the eyes of the whole world, Madame. I cannot urge you too strongly to be very discreet, to be very circumspect.

MARIE-SIDONIE (*rising, abruptly, nervously*): M'su Cahusac, I do not wish to have anything to do with this. There is a mistake somewhere. I thank you very much, but there is a mistake somewhere. I do not know where. I must go now.

M. CAHUSAC (*darts forward*): But, Madame, you do not know what you are doing. Your rank cannot be dismissed as easily as that. Do you not know that in a month or two, all the newspapers in the world, including the New Orleans *Times-Picayune*, will publish your name? The first nobles of France will cross the ocean to call upon you. The Bishop of Louisiana will call upon you . . . Mayor . . .

MARIE-SIDONIE: No, no.

M. CAHUSAC: You will be given a great deal of money—and several palaces.

MARIE-SIDONIE: No, no.

M. CAHUSAC: And a guard of soldiers to protect you.

MARIE-SIDONIE: No, no.

M. CAHUSAC: You will be made president of Le Petit Salon and Queen of the Mardi Gras. . . . Another sip of water, Your Royal Highness.

MARIE-SIDONIE: Oh, M'su, what shall I do? . . . Oh, M'su, save me!—I do not want the Bishop or the Mayor.

M. CAHUSAC: You ask me what you shall do?

MARIE-SIDONIE: Oh, yes, oh, my God!

M. CAHUSAC: For the present, return to your home and lie down. A little rest and a little reflection will tell you what you have to do. Then come and see me Thursday morning.

MARIE-SIDONIE: I think there must be a mistake somewhere.

M. CAHUSAC: May I be permitted to ask Madame de Cressaux a question: Could I have the privilege of presenting Her—until the great announcement takes place—with a small gift of . . . money?

MARIE-SIDONIE: No, no.

M. CAHUSAC: The Historical Society is not rich. The Historical Society has difficulty in pursuing the search for the last documents that will confirm Madame's exalted rank, but they would be very happy to advance a certain sum to Madame, subscribed by her devoted subjects.

MARIE-SIDONIE: Please no. I do not wish any. I must go now.

M. CAHUSAC: Let me beg Madame not to be alarmed. For the present a little rest and reflection. . . .

The bell rings. He again bends over her hand, murmuring . . . "obedient servant and devoted subject."

MARIE-SIDONIE (*in confusion*): Goodbye, good morning, M. Cahusac. (*She lingers at the door a moment, then returns and says in great earnestness*): Oh, M. Cahusac, do not let the Bishop come and see me. The Mayor, yes—but not the Bishop.

Enter MADAME PUGEOT, *a plump little bourgeoise in black. Exit* MARIE-SIDONIE. M. CAHUSAC *kisses the graciously extended hand of* MADAME PUGEOT.

MME. PUGEOT: Good morning, M. Cahusac.

M. CAHUSAC: Your Royal Highness.

MME. PUGEOT: What business can you possibly be having with that dreadful Marie Cressaux! Do you not know that she is an abandoned woman?

M. CAHUSAC: Alas, we are in the world, Your Royal Highness. For the present I must earn a living as best I can. Mamselle Cressaux is arranging about the purchase of a house and garden.

MME. PUGEOT: Purchase, M. Cahusac, phi! You know very well that she has half a dozen houses and gardens already. She persuades every one of her lovers to give her a little house and garden. She is beginning to own the whole parish of Saint-Magloire.

M. CAHUSAC: Will Your Royal Highness condescend to sit down? (*She does.*) And how is the royal family this morning?

MME. PUGEOT: Only so-so, M'su Cahusac.

M. CAHUSAC: The Archduchess of Tuscany?

MME. PUGEOT (*fanning herself with a turkey's wing*): A cold. One of her colds. I sometimes think the dear child will never live to see her pearls.

M. CAHUSAC: And the Dauphin, Your Royal Highness?

MME. PUGEOT: Still, still amusing himself in the city, as young men will. Wine, gambling, bad company. At least it keeps him out of harm.

M. CAHUSAC: And the Duke of Burgundy?

MME. PUGEOT: Imagine! The poor child has a sty in his eye!

M. CAHUSAC: Tchk-tchk! (*with solicitude*) In which eye, Madame?

MME. PUGEOT: In the left!

M. CAHUSAC: Tchk-tchk! And the Prince of Lorraine and the Duke of Berry?

MME. PUGEOT: They are fairly well, but they seem to mope in their cradle. Their first teeth, my dear chamberlain.

M. CAHUSAC: And your husband, Madame?

MME. PUGEOT (*rises, walks back and forth a moment, then stands still*): From now on we are never to mention him again—while we are discussing these matters. It is to be understood that he is my husband in a manner of speaking only. He has no part in my true life. He has chosen to scoff at my birth and my rank, but he will see what he will see. . . . Naturally I have not told him about the proofs that you and I have collected. I have not the heart to let him see how unimportant he will become.

M. CAHUSAC: Unimportant, indeed!

MME. PUGEOT: So remember, we do not mention him in the same breath *with these matters!*

M. CAHUSAC: You must trust me, Madame. (*softly, with significance*) And *your* health, Your Royal Highness?

MME. PUGEOT: Oh, very well, thank you. Excellent. I used to do quite poorly, as you remember, but since this wonderful news I have been more than well, God be praised.

M. CAHUSAC (*as before, with lifted eyebrows*): I beg of you to do nothing unwise. I beg of you. . . . The little new life we are all anticipating . . .

MME. PUGEOT: Have no fear, my dear chamberlain. What is dear to France is dear to me.

M. CAHUSAC: When I think, Madame, of how soon we shall be able to announce your rank—when I think that this time next year you will be enjoying all the honors and privileges that are your due, I am filled with a pious joy.

MME. PUGEOT: God's will be done, God's will be done.

M. CAHUSAC: At all events, I am particularly happy to see that Your Royal Highness is in the best of health, for I have had a piece of disappointing news.

MME. PUGEOT: Chamberlain, you are not going to tell me that Germany has at last declared war upon my country?

M. CAHUSAC: No, Madame.

MME. PUGEOT: You greatly frightened me last week. I could scarcely sleep. Such burdens as I have! My husband tells me that I cried out in my sleep the words: *Paris, I come!*

M. CAHUSAC: Sublime, Madame!

MME. PUGEOT: *Paris, I come*, like that. I cried out twice in my sleep: *Paris, I come*. Oh, these are anxious times; I am on my way to the Cathedral now. This Bismarck does not understand me. We must avoid a war at all costs, M. Cahusac. . . . Then what is your news?

M. CAHUSAC: My anxiety at present is more personal. The Historical Society in Paris is now confirming the last proofs of your claim. They have secretaries at work in all the archives: Madrid, Vienna, Constantinople . . .

MME. PUGEOT: Constantinople!

M. CAHUSAC: All this requires a good deal of money and the Society is not rich. We have been driven to a painful decision. The Society must sell one of the royal jewels or one of the royal *fournitures* which I am guarding upstairs. The Historical Society has written me, Madame, ordering me to send them at once—the royal christening robe.

MME. PUGEOT: Never!

M. CAHUSAC: The very robe under which Charlemagne was christened, the Charles, the Henris, the Louis, to lie under a glass in the Louvre. (*softly*) And this is particularly painful to me because I had hoped—it was, in fact, the dream of my life—to see at least one of your children christened under all those fleurs-de-lis.

MME. PUGEOT: It shall not go to the Louvre. I forbid it.

M. CAHUSAC: But what can I do? I offered them the scepter. I offered them the orb. I even offered them the mug which Your Royal Highness has already purchased. But no! the christening robe it must be.

MME. PUGEOT: It shall not leave America! (*clutching her hand-bag*) How much are they asking for it?

M. CAHUSAC: Oh, Madame, since it is the Ministry of Museums and Monuments they are asking a great many thousands of francs.

MME. PUGEOT: And how much would they ask their Queen?

M. CAHUSAC (*sadly*): Madame, Madame, I cannot see you purchasing those things which are rightly yours.

MME. PUGEOT: I will purchase it. I shall sell the house on the Chausée Sainte Anne.

M. CAHUSAC (*softly*): If Your Majesty will give five hundred dollars of Her money I shall add five hundred of my own.

MME. PUGEOT (*shaken*): Five hundred. Five hundred. . . . Well, you will be repaid many times, my dear chamberlain, when I am restored to my position. (*She thinks a moment.*) To-morrow at three, I shall bring you the papers for the sale of the house. You will do everything quietly. My husband will be told about it in due time.

M. CAHUSAC: I understand. I shall be very discreet.

The bell rings. M. CAHUSAC *turns to the door as* MAMSELLE POINTEVIN *starts to enter.*

I shall be free to see you in a few moments, Mamselle. Madame Pugeot has still some details to discuss with me.

MLLE. POINTEVIN: I cannot wait long, M'su Cahusac.

M. CAHUSAC: A few minutes in the Park, thank you, Mamselle.

Exit MAMSELLE POINTEVIN.

MME. PUGEOT: Has that poor girl business with a lawyer, M. Cahusac? A poor school-teacher like that?

M. CAHUSAC (*softly*): Mamselle Pointevin has taken it into her head to make her will.

MME. PUGEOT (*laughs superiorly*): Three chairs and a broken plate. (*rising*) Well, to-morrow at three. . . . I am now going to the Cathedral. I do not forget the great responsibilities for which I must prepare myself—the army, the navy, the treasury, the appointment of bishops. When I am dead, my dear chamberlain—

M. CAHUSAC: Madame!

MME. PUGEOT: No, no!—even I must die some day. . . . When I am dead, when I am laid with my ancestors, let it never be said of me . . . By the way, where shall I be laid?

M. CAHUSAC: In the church of St. Denis, Your Royal Highness?

MME. PUGEOT: Not in Notre-Dame?

M. CAHUSAC: No, Madame.

MME. PUGEOT (*meditatively*): Not in Notre-Dame. Well (*brightening*) we will cross these bridges when we get to them. (*extending her hand*) Good morning and all my thanks, my dear chamberlain.

M. CAHUSAC: . . . Highness' most obedient servant and devoted subject.

MME. PUGEOT (*beautifully, filling the doorway*): Pray for us.

> *Exit* MADAME PUGEOT. M. CAHUSAC *goes to the door and bows to* MAMSELLE POINTEVIN *in the street.*

M. CAHUSAC: Now Mamselle, if you will have the goodness to enter.

> *Enter* MAMSELLE POINTEVIN, *a tall and indignant spinster.*

MLLE. POINTEVIN: M'su Cahusac, it is something new for you to keep me waiting in the public square while you carry on your wretched little business with a vulgar woman like Madame Pugeot. When I condescend to call upon you, my good man, you will have the goodness to receive me at once. Either I am, or I am not, Henriette, Queen of France, Queen of Navarre and Aquitania. It is not fitting that we cool our heels on a public bench among the nursemaids of remote New Orleans. It is hard enough for me to *hide myself* as a schoolmistress in this city, without having to suffer further humiliations at your hands. Is there no respect due to the blood of Charlemagne?

M. CAHUSAC: Madame . . .

MLLE. POINTEVIN: Or, Sir, are you bored and overfed on the company of queens?

M. CAHUSAC: Madame . . .

MLLE. POINTEVIN: You are busy with the law. Good! Know, then, *La loi-c'est moi.* (*sitting down and smoothing out her skirts*) Now what is it you have to say?

M. CAHUSAC (*pauses a moment, then approaches her with tightly pressed lips and narrowed eyes*): Your Royal Highness, I have received a letter from France. There is some discouraging news.

MLLE. POINTEVIN: No! I cannot afford to buy another thing. I possess the scepter and the orb. Sell the rest to the Louvre, if you must. I can buy them back when my rank is announced.

M. CAHUSAC: Alas!

MLLE. POINTEVIN: What do you mean—"alas"?

M. CAHUSAC: Will Your Royal Highness condescend to read the letter I have received from France?

MLLE. POINTEVIN (*unfurls the letter, but continues looking before her, splendidly*): Have they no bread? Give them cake. (*She starts to read, is shaken, suddenly returns it to him.*) It is too long. It is too long. . . . What does it say?

M. CAHUSAC: It is from the Secretary of the Historical Society. The Society remains convinced that you are the true and long-sought heir to the throne of France.

MLLE. POINTEVIN: Convinced? Convinced? I should hope so.

M. CAHUSAC: But to make this conviction public, Madame, to announce it throughout the newspapers of the world, including the New Orleans *Times-Picayune* . . .

MLLE. POINTEVIN: Yes go on!

M. CAHUSAC: To establish your claim among all your rivals. To establish your claim beyond any possible ridicule . . .

MLLE. POINTEVIN: Ridicule!

M. CAHUSAC: All they lack is one little document. One little but important document. They had hoped to find it in the archives of Madrid. Madame, it is not there.

MLLE. POINTEVIN: It is not there? Then where is it?

M. CAHUSAC: We do not know, Your Royal Highness. We are in despair.

MLLE. POINTEVIN: Ridicule, M. Cahusac!

She stares at him, her hand on her mouth.

M. CAHUSAC: It may be in Constantinople. It may be in Vienna. Naturally we shall continue to search for it. We shall continue to search for generations, for centuries, if need be. But I must confess this is a very discouraging blow.

MLLE. POINTEVIN: Generations! Centuries! But I am not a young girl, M'su Cahusac. Their letter says over and over again that I am the heir to the throne. (*She begins to cry.*)

M. CAHUSAC *discreetly proffers her a glass of water.*

MLLE. POINTEVIN: Thank you.

M. CAHUSAC (*suddenly changing his tone, with firmness*): Madame, you should know that the Society suspects the lost document to be in your possession. The Society feels sure that the document has been handed down from generation to generation in your family.

MLLE. POINTEVIN: In my possession!

M. CAHUSAC (*firmly*): Madame, are you concealing something from us?

MLLE. POINTEVIN: Why . . . no.

M. CAHUSAC: Are you playing with us, as a cat plays with a mouse?

MLLE. POINTEVIN: No, indeed I'm not.

M. CAHUSAC: Why is that paper not in Madrid, or in Constantinople or in Vienna? *Because it is in your house.* You live in what was once your father's house, do you not?

MLLE. POINTEVIN: Yes, I do.

M. CAHUSAC: Go back to it. Look through every old trunk . . .

MLLE. POINTEVIN: Every old trunk!

M. CAHUSAC: Examine especially the linings. Look through all the tables and desks. Pry into the joints. You will find perhaps a secret drawer, a secret panel.

MLLE. POINTEVIN: M'su Cahusac!

M. CAHUSAC: Examine the walls. Examine the boards of the floor. It may be hidden beneath them.

MLLE. POINTEVIN: I will. I'll go now.

M. CAHUSAC: Have you any old clothes of your father?

MLLE. POINTEVIN: Yes, I have.

M. CAHUSAC: It may be sewn into the lining.

MLLE. POINTEVIN: I'll look.

M. CAHUSAC: Madame, in what suit of clothes was your father buried?

MLLE. POINTEVIN: In his best, M'su.

She gives a sudden scream under her hand as this thought strikes home. They stare at one another significantly.

M. CAHUSAC: Take particular pains to look under all steps.

These kinds of document are frequently found under steps. You will find it. If it is not in Madrid, it is there.

MLLE. POINTEVIN: But if I can't find it! (*She sits down, suddenly spent.*) No one will ever know that I am the Queen of France. (*pause*) I am very much afraid, M'su Cahusac, that I shall never find that document in my four rooms. I know every inch of them. But I shall look. (*She draws her hand across her forehead, as though awaking from a dream.*) It is all very strange. You know, M'su Cahusac, I think there may have been a mistake somewhere. It was so beautiful while it lasted. It made even school-teaching a pleasure, M'su. . . . And my memoirs. I have just written my memoirs up to the moment when your wonderful announcement came to me —the account of my childhood *incognito*, the little girl in Louisiana who did not guess the great things before her. But before I go, may I ask something of you? Will you have the Historical Society write me a letter saying that they seriously think I may be . . . the person . . . the person they are looking for? I wish to keep the letter in the trunk with the orb and . . . with the scepter. You know . . . the more I think of it, the more I think there must have been a mistake somewhere.

M. CAHUSAC: The very letter you have in mind is here, Madame.

He gives it to her.

MLLE. POINTEVIN: Thank you. And M'su Cahusac, may I ask another favor of you?

M. CAHUSAC: Certainly, Madame.

MLLE. POINTEVIN: Please, never mention this . . . this whole affair to anyone in New Orleans.

M. CAHUSAC: Madame, not unless you wish it.

MLLE. POINTEVIN: Good morning—good morning, and thank you.

Her handkerchief to one eye she goes out.
M. CAHUSAC goes to his desk.
The bell rings.
The reed curtain is parted and a Negro boy pushes in a

wheel chair containing a woman of some hundred years of age. She is wrapped in shawls, like a mummy, and wears a scarf about her head, and green spectacles on her nose. The mummy extends a hand which M. CAHUSAC *kisses devotedly, murmuring,* "Your Royal Highness."

The curtain falls.

Pullman Car Hiawatha

At the back of the stage is a balcony or bridge or runway leading out of sight in both directions. Two flights of stairs descend from it to the stage. There is no further scenery.

At the rise of the curtain the STAGE MANAGER *is making lines with a piece of chalk on the floor of the stage by the footlights.*

THE STAGE MANAGER: This is the plan of a Pullman car. Its name is Hiawatha and on December twenty-first it is on its way from New York to Chicago. Here at your left are three compartments. Here is the aisle and five lowers. The berths are all full, uppers and lowers, but for the purposes of this play we are limiting our interest to the people in the lower berths on the further side only.

The berths are already made up. It is half-past nine. Most of the passengers are in bed behind the green curtains. They are dropping their shoes on the floor, or wrestling with their trousers, or wondering whether they dare hide their valuables in the pillow-slips during the night.

All right! Come on, everybody!

The actors enter carrying chairs. Each improvises his berth by placing two chairs "facing one another" in his chalk-marked space. They then sit in one chair, profile to the audience, and rest their feet on the other. This must do for lying in bed.

The passengers in the compartments do the same. Reading from left to right we have:

Compartment Three: *An insane woman with a male attendant and a trained nurse.*

Compartment Two: Philip *and*

Compartment One: Harriet, *his young wife.*

Lower One: *A maiden lady.*

Lower Three: *A middle-aged doctor.*

Lower Five: *A stout, amiable woman of fifty.*

Lower Seven: *An engineer going to California.*

Lower Nine: *Another engineer.*

LOWER ONE: Porter, be sure and wake me up at quarter of six.

PORTER: Yes, mam.

LOWER ONE: I know I shan't sleep a wink, but I want to be told when it's quarter of six.

PORTER: Yes, mam.

LOWER SEVEN (*putting his head through the curtains*): Hsst! Porter! Hsst! How the hell do you turn on this other light?

PORTER (*fussing with it*): I'm afraid it's outa order, suh. You'll have to use the other end.

THE STAGE MANAGER (*falsetto, substituting for some woman in an upper berth*): May I ask if some one in this car will be kind enough to lend me some aspirin?

PORTER (*rushing about*): Yes, mam.

LOWER NINE (*one of these engineers, descending the aisle and falling into Lower Five*): Sorry, lady, sorry. Made a mistake.

LOWER FIVE (*grumbling*): Never in all my born days!

LOWER ONE (*in a shrill whisper*): Porter! Porter!

PORTER: Yes, mam.

LOWER ONE: My hot water bag's leaking. I guess you'll have to take it away. I'll have to do without it tonight. How awful!

LOWER FIVE (*sharply to the passenger above her*): Young man, you mind your own business, or I'll report you to the conductor.

STAGE MANAGER (*substituting for* UPPER FIVE): Sorry, mam, I didn't mean to upset you. My suspenders fell down and I was trying to catch them.

LOWER FIVE: Well, here they are. Now go to sleep. Everybody seems to be rushing into my berth tonight.

She puts her head out.

Porter! Porter! Be a good soul and bring me a glass of water, will you? I'm parched.

LOWER NINE: Bill!

No answer.

Bill!

LOWER SEVEN: Ye'? Wha' d'y'a want?

LOWER NINE: Slip me one of those magazines, willya?

LOWER SEVEN: Which one d'y'a want?

LOWER NINE: Either one. "Detective Stories." Either one.

LOWER SEVEN: Aw, Fred. I'm just in the middle of one of'm in "Detective Stories."

LOWER NINE: That's all right. I'll take the "Western."—Thanks.

THE STAGE MANAGER (*to the actors*): All right!—Sh! Sh! Sh!—.

To the audience.

Now I want you to hear them thinking.

There is a pause and then they all begin a murmuring-swishing noise, very soft. In turn each one of them can be heard above the others.

LOWER FIVE (*the lady of fifty*): Let's see: I've got the doll for the baby. And the slip-on for Marietta. And the fountain pen for Herbert. And the subscription to *Time* for George. . . .

LOWER SEVEN (*Bill*): God! Lillian, if you don't turn out to be what I think you are, I don't know what I'll do.—I guess it's bad politics to let a woman know that you're going all the way to California to see her. I'll think up a song-and-dance about a business trip or something. Was I ever as hot and bothered about anyone like this before? Well, there was Martha. But that was different. I'd better try and read or I'll go cookoo. "How did you know it was ten o'clock when the visitor left the house?" asked the detective. "Because at ten o'clock," answered the girl, "I always turn out the lights in the conservatory and in the back hall. As I was coming down the stairs I heard the master talking to someone at the front door. I heard him say, 'Well, good night . . .'" —Gee, I don't feel like reading; I'll just think about Lillian. That yellow hair. Them eyes! . . .

LOWER THREE (*the doctor reads aloud to himself from a medical journal the most hair-raising material, every now and then punctuating his reading with an interrogative "So?"*).

LOWER ONE (*the maiden lady*): I know I'll be awake all night. I might just as well make up my mind to it now. I can't imagine what got hold of that hot water bag to leak on the train of all places. Well now, I'll lie on my right side and breathe deeply and think of beautiful things, and perhaps I can doze off a bit.

and lastly:

LOWER NINE (*Fred*): That was the craziest thing I ever did. It's set me back three whole years. I could have saved up thirty thousand dollars by now, if I'd only stayed over here. What business had I got to fool with contracts with the goddam Soviets. Hell, I thought it would be interesting. Interesting, what-the-hell! It's set me back three whole years. I don't even know if the company'll take me back. I'm green, that's all. I just don't grow up.

> *The* STAGE MANAGER *strides toward them with lifted hand crying "Hush," and their whispering ceases.*

THE STAGE MANAGER: That'll do!—Just one minute. Porter!
THE PORTER (*appearing at the left*): Yessuh.
THE STAGE MANAGER: It's your turn to think.
THE PORTER (*is very embarrassed*).
THE STAGE MANAGER: Don't you want to? You have a right to.
THE PORTER (*torn between the desire to release his thoughts and his shyness*): Ah . . . ah . . . I'm only thinkin' about my home in Chicago and . . . and my life insurance.
THE STAGE MANAGER: That's right.
THE PORTER: . . . well, thank you. . . . Thank you.

> *He slips away, blushing violently, in an agony of self-consciousness and pleasure.*

THE STAGE MANAGER (*to the audience*): He's a good fellow, Harrison is. Just shy.

> *To the actors again.*

Now the compartments, please.

> *The berths fall into shadow.*
> PHILIP *is standing at the door connecting his compartment with his wife's.*

PHILIP: Are you all right, angel?
HARRIET: Yes. I don't know what was the matter with me during dinner.
PHILIP: Shall I close the door?
HARRIET: Do see whether you can't put a chair against it that will hold it half open without banging.

PHILIP: There.—Good night, angel. If you can't sleep, call me and we'll sit up and play Russian Bank.

HARRIET: You're thinking of that awful time when we sat up every night for a week. . . . But at least I know I shall sleep tonight. The noise of the wheels has become sort of nice and homely. What state are we in?

PHILIP: We're tearing through Ohio. We'll be in Indiana soon.

HARRIET: I know those little towns full of horse-blocks.

PHILIP: Well, we'll reach Chicago very early. I'll call you. Sleep tight.

HARRIET: Sleep tight, darling.

> *He returns to his own compartment. In Compartment Three, the male attendant tips his chair back against the wall and smokes a cigar. The trained nurse knits a stocking. The insane woman leans her forehead against the window-pane, that is: stares into the audience.*

THE INSANE WOMAN (*her words have a dragging, complaining sound, but lack any conviction*): Don't take me there. Don't take me there.

THE FEMALE ATTENDANT: Wouldn't you like to lie down, dearie?

THE INSANE WOMAN: I want to get off the train. I want to go back to New York.

THE FEMALE ATTENDANT: Wouldn't you like me to brush your hair again? It's such a nice feeling.

THE INSANE WOMAN (*going to the door*): I want to get off the train. I want to open the door.

THE FEMALE ATTENDANT (*taking one of her hands*): Such a noise! You'll wake up all the nice people. Come and I'll tell you a story about the place we're going to.

THE INSANE WOMAN: I don't want to go to that place.

THE FEMALE ATTENDANT: Oh, it's lovely! There are lawns and gardens everywhere. I never saw such a lovely place. Just lovely.

THE INSANE WOMAN (*lies down on the bed*): Are there roses?

THE FEMALE ATTENDANT: Roses! Red, yellow, white . . . just everywhere.

THE MALE ATTENDANT (*after a pause*): That musta been Cleveland.

THE FEMALE ATTENDANT: I had a case in Cleveland once. Diabetes.

THE MALE ATTENDANT (*after another pause*): I wisht I had a radio here. Radios are good for *them*. I had a patient once that had to have the radio going every minute.

THE FEMALE ATTENDANT: Radios are lovely. My married niece has one. It's always going. It's wonderful.

THE INSANE WOMAN (*half rising*): I'm not beautiful. I'm not beautiful as she was.

THE FEMALE ATTENDANT: Oh, I think you're beautiful! Beautiful.—Mr. Morgan, don't you think Mrs. Churchill is beautiful?

THE MALE ATTENDANT: Oh, fine lookin'! Regular movie star, Mrs. Churchill.

> *She looks inquiringly at them and subsides.*
> HARRIET *groans slightly. Smothers a cough. She gropes about with her hand and finds the bell.*
> *The* PORTER *knocks at her door.*

HARRIET (*whispering*): Come in. First, please close the door into my husband's room. Softly. Softly.

PORTER (*a plaintive porter*): Yes, mam.

HARRIET: Porter, I'm not well. I'm sick. I must see a doctor.

PORTER: Why, mam, they ain't no doctor . . .

HARRIET: Yes, when I was coming out from dinner I saw a man in one of the seats on *that* side, reading medical papers. Go and wake him up.

PORTER (*flabbergasted*): Mam, I cain't wake anybody up.

HARRIET: Yes, you can. Porter. Porter. Now don't argue with me. I'm very sick. It's my heart. Wake him up. Tell him it's my heart.

PORTER: Yes, mam.

> *He goes into the aisle and starts pulling the shoulder of the man in Lower Three.*

LOWER THREE: Hello. Hello. What is it? Are we there?

> *The* PORTER *mumbles to him.*

I'll be right there.—Porter, is it a young woman or an old one?

PORTER: I dono, suh. I guess she's kinda old, suh, but not so very old.

LOWER THREE: Tell her I'll be there in a minute and to lie quietly.

The PORTER *enters* HARRIET'S *compartment. She has turned her head away.*

PORTER: He'll be here in a minute, mam. He says you lie quiet.

LOWER THREE *stumbles along the aisle muttering:* "Damn these shoes!"

SOMEONE'S VOICE: Can't we have a little quiet in this car, please?

LOWER NINE (*Fred*): Oh, shut up!

The DOCTOR *passes the* PORTER *and enters* HARRIET'S *compartment. He leans over her, concealing her by his stooping figure.*

LOWER THREE: She's dead, porter. Is there anyone on the train traveling with her?

PORTER: Yessuh. Dat's her husband in dere.

LOWER THREE: Idiot! Why didn't you call him? I'll go in and speak to him.

The STAGE MANAGER *comes forward.*

THE STAGE MANAGER: All right. So much for the inside of the car. That'll be enough of that for the present. Now for its position geographically, meteorologically, astronomically, theologically considered.

Pullman Car Hiawatha, ten minutes of ten. December twenty-first, 1930. All ready.

Some figures begin to appear on the balcony.

No, no. It's not time for the planets yet. Nor the hours.

They retire.
The STAGE MANAGER *claps his hands. A grinning boy in overalls enters from the left behind the berths.*

GROVER'S CORNERS, OHIO (*in a foolish voice as though he were reciting a piece at a Sunday School entertainment*): I represent

Grover's Corners, Ohio. 821 souls. "There's so much good in the worst of us and so much bad in the best of us, that it ill behooves any of us to criticize the rest of us." Robert Louis Stevenson. Thankya.

He grins and goes out right.
Enter from the same direction somebody in shirt sleeves. This is a field.

THE FIELD: I represent a field you are passing between Grover's Corners, Ohio, and Parkersburg, Ohio. In this field there are 51 gophers, 206 field mice, 6 snakes and millions of bugs, insects, ants, and spiders. All in their winter sleep. "What is so rare as a day in June? Then, if ever, come perfect days." *The Vision of Sir Launfal*, William Cullen—I mean James Russell Lowell. Thank you.

Exit.
Enter a tramp.

THE TRAMP: I just want to tell you that I'm a tramp that's been traveling under this car, Hiawatha, so I have a right to be in this play. I'm going from Rochester, New York, to Joliet, Illinois. It takes a lotta people to make a world. "On the road to Mandalay, where the flying fishes play and the sun comes up like thunder, over China cross the bay." Frank W. Service. It's bitter cold. Thank you.

Exit.
Enter a gentle old farmer's wife with three stringy young people.

PARKERSBURG, OHIO: I represent Parkersburg, Ohio. 2604 souls. I have seen all the dreadful havoc that alcohol has done and I hope no one here will ever touch a drop of the curse of this beautiful country.

She beats a measure and they all sing unsteadily:

"Throw out the lifeline! Throw out the lifeline! Someone is sinking today-ay . . ."

The STAGE MANAGER *waves them away tactfully.*
Enter a workman.

THE WORKMAN: Ich bin der Arbeiter der hier sein Leben ver-
lor. Bei der Sprengung für diese Brücke über die Sie in dem
Moment fahren—

The engine whistles for a trestle crossing—

erschlug mich ein Felsbock. Ich spiele jetzt als Geist in
diesem Stuck mit. "Vor sieben und achtzig Jahren haben
unsere Väter auf diesem Continent eine neue Nation her-
vorgebracht. . . ."
THE STAGE MANAGER (*helpfully, to the audience*): I'm sorry;
that's in German. He says that he's the ghost of a workman
who was killed while they were building the trestle over
which the car Hiawatha is now passing—

The engine whistles again—

and he wants to appear in this play. A chunk of rock hit him
while they were dynamiting.—His motto you know: "Three
score and seven years ago our fathers brought forth upon
this continent a new nation dedicated," and so on. Thank
you, Mr. Krüger.

Exit the ghost.
Enter another worker.

THIS WORKER: I'm a watchman in a tower near Parkersburg,
Ohio. I just want to tell you that I'm not asleep and that the
signals are all right for this train. I hope you all have a fine
trip. "If you can keep your head when all about you are
losing theirs and blaming it on you. . . ." Rudyard Kipling.
Thank you.

Exit.
The STAGE MANAGER *comes forward.*

THE STAGE MANAGER: All right. That'll be enough of that.
Now the weather.

Enter a mechanic.

A MECHANIC: It is eleven degrees above zero. The wind is
north-northwest, velocity, 57. There is a field of low baro-
metric pressure moving eastward from Saskatchewan to the

Eastern Coast. Tomorrow it will be cold with some snow in the Middle Western States and Northern New York.

Exit.

THE STAGE MANAGER: All right. Now for the hours.

Helpfully to the audience:

The minutes are gossips; the hours are philosophers; the years are theologians. The hours are philosophers with the exception of Twelve O'clock who is also a theologian.— Ready Ten O'clock!

The hours are beautiful girls dressed like Elihu Vedder's Pleiades. Each carries a great gold Roman numeral. They pass slowly across the balcony at the back moving from right to left.

What are you doing, Ten O'clock? Aristotle?

TEN O'CLOCK: No, Plato, Mr. Washburn.

THE STAGE MANAGER: Good.—"Are you not rather convinced that he who thus . . ."

TEN O'CLOCK: "Are you not rather convinced that he who sees Beauty as only it can be seen will be specially favored? And since he is in contact not with images but with realities. . . ."

She continues the passage in a murmur as ELEVEN O'CLOCK *appears.*

ELEVEN O'CLOCK: "What else can I, Epictetus, do, a lame old man, but sing hymns to God? If then I were a nightingale, I would do the nightingale's part. If I were a swan I would do a swan's. But now I am a rational creature. . . ."

Her voice too subsides to a murmur. TWELVE O'CLOCK *appears.*

THE STAGE MANAGER: Good.—Twelve O'clock, what have you?

TWELVE O'CLOCK: Saint Augustine and his mother.

THE STAGE MANAGER: So.—"And we began to say: If to any the tumult of the flesh were hushed. . . ."

TWELVE O'CLOCK: "And we began to say: If to any the tumult

of the flesh were hushed; hushed the images of earth; of waters and of air; . . .

THE STAGE MANAGER: Faster.—"Hushed also the poles of Heaven."

TWELVE O'CLOCK: "Yea, were the very soul to be hushed to herself."

STAGE MANAGER: A little louder, Miss Foster.

TWELVE O'CLOCK (*a little louder*): "Hushed all dreams and imaginary revelations. . . ."

THE STAGE MANAGER (*waving them back*): All right. All right. Now the planets. December twenty-first, 1930, please.

The hours unwind and return to their dressing rooms at the right. The planets appear on the balcony. Some of them take their place halfway on the steps. These have no words, but each has a sound. One has a pulsating, zinging sound. Another has a thrum. One whistles ascending and descending scales. Saturn does a slow, obstinate:

M—M—M—M—

Louder, Saturn.—Venus, higher. Good. Now, Jupiter.— Now the earth.

He turns to the beds on the train.

Come, everybody. This is the earth's sound.

The towns, workmen, etc. appear at the edge of the stage. The passengers begin their "thinking" murmur.

Come, Grover's Corners. Parkersburg. You're in this. Watchman. Tramp. This is the earth's sound.

He conducts it as the director of an orchestra would. Each of the towns and workmen does his motto.

THE INSANE WOMAN *breaks into passionate weeping. She rises and stretches out her arms to the* STAGE MANAGER.

THE INSANE WOMAN: Use me. Give me something to do.

He goes to her quickly, whispers something in her ear, and leads her back to her guardians. She is unconsoled.

THE STAGE MANAGER: Now sh—sh—sh! Enter the archangels.

To the audience:

THE STAGE MANAGER: We have now reached the theological position of Pullman Car Hiawatha.

The towns and workmen have disappeared. The planets, off stage, continue a faint music. Two young men in blue serge suits enter along the balcony and descend the stairs at the right. As they pass each bed the passenger talks in his sleep.
GABRIEL *points out* BILL *to* MICHAEL *who smiles with raised eyebrows. They pause before* LOWER FIVE *and* MICHAEL *makes the sound of assent that can only be rendered "Hn-Hn." The remarks that the characters make in their sleep are not all intelligible, being lost in the sound of sigh or groan or whisper by which they are conveyed. But we seem to hear:*

LOWER NINE (*loud*): Some people are slower than others, that's all.

LOWER SEVEN (*Bill*): It's no fun, y'know. I'll try.

LOWER FIVE (*the lady of the Christmas presents, rapidly*): You know best, of course. I'm ready whenever you are. One year's like another.

LOWER ONE: I can teach sewing. I can sew.

They approach HARRIET'S *compartment.*
THE INSANE WOMAN *sits up and speaks to them.*

THE INSANE WOMAN: Me?

THE ARCHANGELS (*shake their heads*).

THE INSANE WOMAN: What possible use can there be in my simply waiting?—Well, I'm grateful for anything. I'm grateful for being so much better than I was. The old story, the terrible story, doesn't haunt me as it used to. A great load seems to have been taken off my mind.—But no one understands me any more. At last I understand myself perfectly, but no one else understands a thing I say.—So I must wait?

THE ARCHANGELS (*nod, smiling*).

THE INSANE WOMAN (*resignedly, and with a smile that implies their complicity*): Well, you know best. I'll do whatever is best; but everyone is so childish, so absurd. They have no logic. These people are all so mad. . . . These people are like children; they have never suffered.

> *She returns to her bed and sleeps. The* ARCHANGELS *stand beside* HARRIET. *The* DOCTOR *has drawn* PHILIP *into the next compartment and is talking to him in earnest whispers.* HARRIET'S *face has been toward the wall; she turns it slightly and speaks toward the ceiling.*

HARRIET: I wouldn't be happy there. Let me stay dead down here. I belong here. I shall be perfectly happy to roam about my house and be near Philip.—You know I wouldn't be happy there.

> GABRIEL *leans over and whispers into her ear. After a short pause she bursts into fierce tears.*

I'm ashamed to come with you. I haven't done anything. I haven't done anything with my life. Worse than that: I was angry and sullen. I never realized anything. I don't dare go a step in such a place.

> *They whisper to her again.*

But it's not possible to forgive such things. I don't want to be forgiven so easily. I want to be punished for it all. I won't stir until I've been punished a long, long time. I want to be freed of all that—by punishment. I want to be all new.

> *They whisper to her. She puts her feet slowly on the ground.*

But no one else could be punished for me. I'm willing to face it all myself. I don't ask anyone to be punished for me.

> *They whisper to her again. She sits long and brokenly looking at her shoes and thinking it over.*

It wasn't fair. I'd have been willing to suffer for it myself, —if I could have endured such a mountain.

> *She smiles.*

Oh, I'm ashamed! I'm just a stupid and you know it. I'm just another American.—But then what wonderful things must be beginning now. You really want me? You really want me?

They start leading her down the aisle of the car.

Let's take the whole train. There are some lovely faces on this train. Can't we all come? You'll never find anyone better than Philip. Please, please, let's all go.

They reach the steps. The ARCHANGELS *interlock their arms as a support for her as she leans heavily on them, taking the steps slowly. Her words are half singing and half babbling.*

But look at how tremendously high and far it is. I've a weak heart. I'm not supposed to climb stairs. "I do not ask to see the distant scene: One step enough for me." It's like Switzerland. My tongue keeps saying things. I can't control it.—Do let me stop a minute: I want to say goodbye.

She turns in their arms.

Just a minute, I want to cry on your shoulder.

She leans her forehead against GABRIEL'S *shoulder and laughs long and softly.*

Goodbye, Philip.—I begged him not to marry me, but he would. He believed in me just as you do.—Goodbye, 1312 Ridgewood Avenue, Oaksbury, Illinois. I hope I remember all its steps and doors and wallpapers forever. Goodbye, Emerson Grammar School on the corner of Forbush Avenue and Wherry Street. Goodbye, Miss Walker and Miss Cramer who taught me English and Miss Matthewson who taught me Biology. Goodbye, First Congregational Church on the corner of Meyerson Avenue and 6th Street and Dr. McReady and Mrs. McReady and Julia. Goodbye, Papa and Mama. . . .

She turns.

Now I'm tired of saying goodbye.—I never used to talk like this. I was so homely I never used to have the courage to talk. Until Philip came. I see now. I see now. I understand everything now.

The STAGE MANAGER *comes forward.*

THE STAGE MANAGER (*to the actors*): All right. All right.—Now we'll have the whole world together, please. The whole solar system, please.

The complete cast begins to appear at the edges of the stage. He claps his hands.

The whole solar system, please. Where's the tramp?— Where's the moon?

He gives two raps on the floor, like the conductor of an orchestra attracting the attention of his forces, and slowly lifts his hand. The human beings murmur their thoughts; the hours discourse; the planets chant or hum. HARRIET'S *voice finally rises above them all saying:*

HARRIET:
    "I was not ever thus, nor asked that Thou
      Shouldst lead me on, and spite of fears,
      Pride ruled my will: Remember not past years."

The STAGE MANAGER *waves them away.*

THE STAGE MANAGER: Very good. Now clear the stage, please. Now we're at Englewood Station, South Chicago. See the University's towers over there! The best of them all.

LOWER ONE (*the spinster*): Porter, you promised to wake me up at quarter of six.

PORTER: Sorry, mam, but it's been an awful night on this car. A lady's been terrible sick.

LOWER ONE: Oh! Is she better?

PORTER: No'm. She ain't one jot better.

LOWER FIVE: Young man, take your foot out of my face.

THE STAGE MANAGER (*again substituting for* UPPER FIVE): Sorry, lady, I slipped—

LOWER FIVE (*grumbling not unamiably*): I declare, this trip's been one long series of insults.

THE STAGE MANAGER: Just one minute, mam, and I'll be down and out of your way.

LOWER FIVE: Haven't you got anybody to darn your socks for you? You ought to be ashamed to go about that way.

THE STAGE MANAGER: Sorry, lady.

LOWER FIVE: You're too stuck up to get married. That's the trouble with you.

LOWER NINE: Bill!—Bill!

LOWER SEVEN: Ye'? Wha' d'y'a want?

LOWER NINE: Bill, how much d'y'a give the porter on a train like this? I've been outa the country so long . . .

LOWER SEVEN: Hell, Fred, I don't know myself.

THE PORTER: CHICAGO, CHICAGO. All out. This train don't go no further.

The passengers jostle their way out and an army of old women with mops and pails enter and prepare to clean up the car.

The curtain falls.

Love and How To Cure It

The stage of the Tivoli Palace of Music, Soho, London, April, 1895.
The stage is dark save for a gas jet forward left and an oil lamp on the table at the back right.
Bare, dark, dusty and cold.

LINDA, *dressed in a white ballet dress, is practicing steps and bending exercises. She is a beautiful, impersonal, remote, almost sullen girl of barely sixteen.*

At the table in the distance sit JOEY, *a stout comedian, and* ROWENA, *a mature soubrette.* JOEY *is reading aloud from a pink theatrical and sporting weekly and* ROWENA *is darning a stocking. When they speak the touch of cockney in their diction is insufficiently compensated by touches of exaggerated elegance.*

There is silence for a time, broken only by the undertone of the reading and the whispered counting of LINDA *at her practice.* *Then:*

ROWENA (*calling to* LINDA): They've put off the rehearsal. Mark my words. It's after half-past eight now. They must have got word to the others somehow. Or else we understood the day wrong.—Go on, Joey.

He reads for a few minutes, then ROWENA *calls again:*

Linda, the paper says Marjorie FitzMaurice has an engagement. An Ali Baba and the Forty Thieves company that Moss has collected for Folkstone, Brighton, and the piers. She must have got better.—You'd better take a rest, dearie. You'll be all blowed.—Go on, Joey, that's a good boy.

LINDA (*gravely describing an arc waist-high with her toe*): It's nine o'clock. I can hear the chimes.

Apparently JOEY *has finished the paper. He stretches and yawns.* ROWENA *puts down her work, picks up her chair and brings it toward the footlights, and starts firmly supervising* LINDA's *movements.*

ROWENA: One, two, three; one, two, three. Whatever are you doing with your hands, child? Madame Angellelli didn't teach you anything like that. Bend them back like you was discovering a flower by surprise. That's right.—Upsidaisy! That's the way.—Now that's enough kicks for one night. If you must do any more, just stick to the knee-highs.

She yawns and pats her yawn.

There's no rehearsal. We might just as well go home. It was all a mistake somehow.

LINDA (*almost upside down*): No, no. I don't want to go home. Besides, I'm hungry. Ask Joey to go around the corner and buy some fish and chips.

ROWENA: Goodness, I never saw such an eater. Well, I have two kippers here I was going to set on for breakfast.

Calling.

Joey, there's a stove downstairs still, isn't there?

JOEY: Yes.

ROWENA (*to Linda*): There you are! We could have a little supper and ask Joey. I have a packet of tea in my bag. How would you like that, angel?

LINDA: Lovely.

ROWENA: Joey, how would you like a little supper on the stage with kipper and tea and everything nice?

JOEY: Like it! I'm that starved I could eat bones and all. Wot's more, I'll cook it for you. I'm the best little cooker of a kipper for a copper you could 'ope to see.

ROWENA (*meditatively*): You could use that in a song someday, Joey.—Shall I let him cook it, Linda?

LINDA: Yes, let him cook it.

JOEY: I'll just go next door and get a spoonful of butter.

ROWENA: There's sixpence. Get some milk for the tea, too. Put some water on as you go out and I'll be down in a minute to make the tea.

JOEY: Won't be a minute, my dears.

He hurries out.
There is a pause. LINDA *stops her exercise and examines attentively each of the soles of her slippers in turn.*

ROWENA: Joey must have cooked thousands of kippers in his day. All those last years when his wife was ill, he cooked everything for her. Good old Joey! He's all lost without her. And he wants me to talk about her all the time, only he doesn't want to bring her into the conversation first. You know, Henrietta du Vaux was wonderful, but I can't talk about her forever.

Another pause.

Linda, whatever are you thinking about all the time?

LINDA: Nothing.

ROWENA: Don't you say "Nothing." Come now, tell your Auntie. What is it you keep turning over in your mind all the time?

LINDA (*indifferently*): Well, almost nothing,—except that I'm going to be shot any minute.

ROWENA: Don't say such things, dearie. No one's going to shoot you. You ought to be ashamed to say such things.

LINDA (*pointing scornfully to the door*): He's out waiting in the street this very minute.

ROWENA: Why, he went back to his university didn't he? He's a student. They don't let them come to London whenever they want.

LINDA: Oh, I don't care! Let him shoot me. I wish I'd never seen him. What was he doing, anyway,—worming his way into Madame Angellelli's swarrays. He'd oughta stayed among his own people.

ROWENA: I'm going out into the street this minute to see if he's there. I can get the police after him for hounding a poor girl so. What's his name?

LINDA: Arthur Warburton. I tell you I don't care if he shoots me.

ROWENA (*sharply*): Now I won't have you saying things like that! Now mind! If he's out there Joey'll go and get him and we'll have a talk. When did you see him last?

LINDA: Sunday. We had tea at Richmond and went boating on the river.

ROWENA: Did you let him kiss you?

LINDA: I let him kiss me once when we floated under some willow trees. And then he kept talking so hot-headed that I didn't let him kiss me again, and I liked him less and less. All the way back on the bus, I didn't pay any attention to him;

just looked into the street and said yes and no; and then I told him I was too busy to see him this week. I don't want to see him again.—Aunt Rowena, he breathes so hard.

ROWENA: He didn't look like he was rough and nasty.

LINDA: He's not rough and nasty. He just—suffers.

ROWENA: I know 'em.

LINDA: Aunt Rowena, isn't there any way discovered to make a man get over loving you. Can it be cured?

> ROWENA *does not answer. She walks meditatively back to the table in the corner.*

ROWENA: Give me a hand, will you, with this table. We'll bring it nearer to the gas jet. I'd better go downstairs and see what Joey's doing to everything. (*They bring the table forward.*) Dearie, what makes you say such things? What makes you say he's thinking of shooting you?

LINDA: He looked all . . . all crazy and said I oughtn't to be alive. He said if I didn't marry him . . .

ROWENA: *Marry him!* He asked you to marry him? Linda, you are a funny girl not to tell me these things before. Why do you keep everything so secret, dearie?

LINDA: I didn't think that was a secret. I don't want to marry him.

ROWENA (*passing her thumb along her teeth and looking at Linda narrowly*): Well, now try and remember what he said about shooting.

LINDA: He was standing at the door saying goodbye. I was playing with the key in my hand to show him I was in a hurry to be done with him. He said he couldn't think of anything but me—that he couldn't live without me and so on. Then he asked me was there someone else I loved instead of him, and I said no. And he said how about the Italian fellow at Madame Angellelli's swarray, and I said no, not in a thousand years. He meant Mario. And then he started to cry and take on terrible.—Imagine being jealous of Mario.

ROWENA: I'll teach that young man a lesson. That's what I'll do.

LINDA: Then he was trembling all over, and he took up the edge of my coat and cried: People like me ought not to be alive. Nature ought not to allow such soulless beauties like I.

She has risen on her toes, holding out her arms and has started drifting away with little rapid steps. From the back of the stage she calls scornfully:

I ought not to be alive, he said. I ought not to be alive.

Pause.

ROWENA: Someone's pounding on the street door down there. Joey must have dropped the latch.
LINDA: It's Arthur.
ROWENA: Don't be foolish.
LINDA: I know in my bones it's him.

JOEY *appears at the back.*

JOEY: There's a gentleman to see you, Linda. Says his name is Warburton.
LINDA: Yes. Send him up.
JOEY: Kipper is almost ready. Water's boiling, Rowena. What are you going to do about this visitor?
ROWENA: Listen dearie, I want to look at this Arthur again. You ask him pretty to have supper with us.
LINDA: Oh, Aunt Rowena, I couldn't eat!
ROWENA: This is serious. This is serious, Linda. Now you ask him to supper and send him around the corner for some bitters. In the meantime I'll catch a minute to tell Joey how we must watch him.
LINDA: I don't care if he shoots me. It's nothing to me.

In the gloom at the back ARTHUR *appears. He is wearing an opera hat and cape.*

ARTHUR (*he is very miserable. He expects and dreads Linda's in-difference but hopes that some miraculous change of heart may occur any minute. Tentatively*): Good evening, Linda.
LINDA: Hello, Arthur. Arthur, I'd like you to meet my aunt, Mrs. Rowena Stoker.
ARTHUR: It's a great pleasure to meet you, Mrs. Stoker. I hope I'm not intruding. I was just passing by and I thought . . . (*his voice trails off*)
ROWENA: We thought there was going to be a rehearsal of the new panto we're engaged for, Mr. Warburton. But nobody's

showed up so like as not we mistook the day. Linda's just been practicing a few steps for practice, haven't you, dovie?

LINDA (*by rote*): Arthur, we were just going to have a little supper. We hope you'll have some with us. Just a kippered herring and some tea.

ARTHUR: That's awfully good of you. I've just come from dinner. But I hope you won't mind if I sit by you, Mrs. Stoker.

ROWENA: Suit yourself, I always say. It isn't very attractive in an empty theatre. But you must have something, oh yes.

LINDA: Perhaps you'd like to do us a favor, Arthur. Joey's downstairs doing the cooking and can't go. Perhaps you'd like to go down to the corner and bring us a jug of ale and bitters.

ROWENA: I have a shilling here somewhere.

LINDA: Aunt Rowena, perhaps Arthur is dressed too grand to go to a pub. . . .

ROWENA: The pubs in this street is used to us coming in in all kinds of costumes, Mr. Warburton. They'll think you're rehearsing for a society play.

ARTHUR (*who has refused the shilling, and is all feverish willingness*): I'll be right back. I'll only be a minute, Mrs. Stoker.

> *He hurries out.*

ROWENA: The poor boy is off his head for fair. Makes me feel all *old* just to see him. But I imagine he's quite a nice young man when he's got his senses. But never mind, Linda, nobody wants you to marry anybody you don't want to marry. —Has he been drinking, dearie, or does he just look that way?

LINDA: He just looks that way.

> *Enter* JOEY, *with cups, knives, forks, etc.*

JOEY: Where's the duke?

ROWENA: He's gone to the corner for some ale and bitters. Thank God, he's eaten already. Now Joey, listen. This young man is off his head about Linda, crazy for fair. Now this is serious. Linda says he talks wild and might even be thinking of shooting her. (JOEY *whistles.*) Well, the papers are full of such things, Joey. And plays are full of it. It might be. It might be.

JOEY: Well, I've heard about such things, but it never happened in my family.

ROWENA: Just the same we must take steps. Joey, I'll have him take his cape off. You take it downstairs and see if there's anything in the pocket.

JOEY: What in the pocket?

ROWENA: Why . . . one of those small guns.

LINDA: Yes, of course, there's one in his pocket. I know there is.

ROWENA: It would be in his cape so as not to bulge his other pockets. Listen, Joey, if there is a gun there, you take out the bullets, and then put the gun back into his pocket empty. See? Then bring the cape back again. If this boy is going to shoot Linda, he's going to shoot her tonight, so we can have a good heart-to-heart talk about it.

JOEY: Yes, and then call the police, that's what!

ROWENA: No, this is a thing police and prisons can't cure. Now, Joey, if you find a gun in his pocket and have done what I told you, you come back on the stage whistling one of your songs. Whistle your song about Bank holidays. You know: *My holiday girl on a holiday bus.*

JOEY: Right-o!

ROWENA: Now, Linda, you act just natural. Let him have his murder and get it out of his system. Yes, you know I like the boy and I don't hold it against him. When we're twenty-one years old we all have a few drops of crazy melodrama in us.

LINDA (*suddenly*): Oh, I hate him, I 'ate 'im! Why can't he let me be?

ROWENA: Yes, yes. That's love.

LINDA (*on the verge of hysterics*): Auntie, can't it be cured? Can't you make him just forget me?

ROWENA: Well, dovie, they say there are some ways. Some say you can make fun of him and mock him out of it. And some say you can show yourself up at your worst or pretend you're worse than you are. But I say there's only one way to cure that kind of love when it's feverish and all upset.

She pauses groping for her thought.

Only love can cure love. Only being interested . . . only being real interested and fond of him can . . . can . . .

She gives it up.

It's all right, dearie. Don't you get jumpy. It's a lucky chance to get the thing cleared up. Only remember this: I like him. I like him. He's just somebody's boy that's not well for a few weeks.

LINDA: He breathes too hard.

Enter ARTHUR, *followed by* JOEY. ARTHUR'S *hands are laden with bundles and bottles.*

ROWENA: Why, Mr. Warburton, I never see such a load. Whatever did you find to bring? Fries? Salami, and I don't know what all. This *is* a feast. Take off your coat, Mr. Warburton. Joey, help Mr. Warburton off with his coat. Take it and hang it on the peg downstairs.

ARTHUR (*with concern*): I think I'll keep the coat, thanks.

ROWENA (*as* JOEY *attacks it*): Oh, no, no! You won't need your coat. There's nothing worse than sitting about in a heavy coat.

ARTHUR *follows it with his eyes, as* JOEY *bears it off.*

But Linda, you've been exercising. You slip that scarf about you, dearie, and draw up your chair. Well, this is going to be nice. What's nicer than friends sitting down to a bite to eat? And extra nice for you, Mr. Warburton, because you ought to be in your university, or am I mistaken?

ARTHUR: Yes, I ought to be at Cambridge.

ROWENA: Fancy that! It must be exciting to break the rule so boldly. Ah, well, life is so dull that it does us good every now and then to *make* a little excitement. Now, Mr. Warburton, you'll change your mind and have a little snack with us. A slice of Salami?

ARTHUR: I don't think I could eat anything. I'll have a little ale.

ROWENA (*busying herself over the table*): That's right.

ARTHUR (*ventures a word to Linda*): Madame Angellelli is having a soirée Thursday, Linda. Don't you go any more?

LINDA: No, I don't like them.

ARTHUR: I wondered where you were last Thursday. Madame Angellelli expected you every minute.

LINDA: I don't like them.

Silence.

ROWENA: What can be keeping Joey over the kipper? Have you seen Joey on the stage, Mr. Warburton?—Joey Weston he is.

ARTHUR: No, I don't think I have.

ROWENA: Oh, very fine, he is! Quite the best comedian in the pantos. But surely you must have seen his wife. She was Henrietta du Vaux. She was the most popular soubrette in all England, and very famous, she was. He lost her two years ago, Henrietta du Vaux. Everybody loved her. It was a terrible loss. Sh—here he comes!

> *Enter* JOEY *with the kipper and the tea. He is jubilantly whistling a tune that presently breaks out into the words:* "A holiday girl on a holiday bus."

What a noise you do make, Joey, for fair. Anybody'd think you were happy about something. Well, now, Mr. Warburton, you'll excuse us if we sit down and fall right to.

> ARTHUR *sits at the left turned toward them.* JOEY *faces the audience, with* ROWENA *and* LINDA *facing one another,* ROWENA *at his right and* LINDA *at his left.*

JOEY: It's cold here, Rowena, after the kitchen.

ROWENA: Yes, it's colder than I thought for. Joey, go and get Mr. Warburton's coat for him. I think he'll want it after all.

ARTHUR: Yes, I'd better keep it by me.

> *He follows* JOEY *to the door and takes the coat from him.*

ROWENA (*while the men are at the door*): How do you feel, dearie?

LINDA: I hate it. I wish I were home.

ROWENA: Joey, this is good. You're a good cook.

> *They eat absorbedly for a few moments; then* ROWENA *gazes out into the vault of the dark theatre.*

Oh, this old theatre has seen some wonderful nights! I'll never forget you, Joey, in *Robinson Crusoe the Second.* I'll never forget you standing right there and pretending you saw a ghost. I hurt myself laughing.

JOEY: No, it wasn't me. It was Henrietta. She sang *The Sultan of Bagdad* three hundred times in this very house. On these very same boards. Three hundred times the house went crazy when she sang *The Houseboat Song.* They'd sit so quiet you'd think they were holding their breaths, and then they'd break out into shouts and cries. Henrietta du Vaux was my wife, Mr. Warburton. She was the best soubrette in England since Nell Gwynne, sir.

ROWENA: I can hear her now, Joey. She was as good a friend as she was a singer.

JOEY: After the show I would be waiting for her at the corner, Mr. Warburton. (*He points to the corner.*) Do you know the corner, sir?

ARTHUR (*fascinated*): Yes.

JOEY: I did not always have an engagement and the manager did not think it right to have a husband waiting in the theatre to take the soubrette home. So I waited for her at that corner. She slipped away from all that applause, sir, to go home with a husband that did not always have an engagement.

ROWENA: Joey, I won't have you saying that. You're one of the best comics in England.—Joey, you're tired. Rest yourself a bit.

JOEY: No, Rowena, I want to say this about her: She never felt her success. And she had a hundred ways of pretending that she was no success at all. "Joey," she'd say, "I got it all wrong tonight." And then she'd ask me how she should do it.

ROWENA: Do draw up a chair, Mr. Warburton, and have a bite for good feelings' sake. We're all friends here. Linda, put a piece of sausage on some bread for him, with your own hands.

ARTHUR: Well, thanks, thank you very much.

JOEY (*with increasing impressiveness*): And when she was ill, she knew that her coughing hurt me. And she'd suffer four times over trying to hold back her coughing. "Cough, Henrietta," I'd say, "if it makes you more comfortable." But no!—she'd act like I was the sick person that had to be taken care of.

Turning on ARTHUR *with gravity and force.*

I read in the papers about people who shoot the persons

they love. I don't know what to think. What is it but that they want to be *noticed*, noticed even if they must shoot to get noticed? It's themselves—it's themselves they love.

JOEY *stares at* ARTHUR *so fixedly that* ARTHUR *breathes an all but involuntary "Yes." Then he rises abruptly and says:*

ARTHUR: I must go now. You've been very kind.

ROWENA (*rising*): Joey, come downstairs with me a minute and help me open that old chest. I think we can find Henrietta's shield and spear from *The Palace of Ice* and other things. The lock's been broken for years.

JOEY: All right, Rowena. Let's look.

ROWENA: We won't be a minute. You go on eating.

They go out.

ARTHUR: I won't trouble you any more, Linda. I want you to be happy, that's all.

LINDA: You don't trouble me, Arthur.

ARTHUR: What he said is true. I want to be noticed. I wish you liked me, Linda. I mean I wish you liked me more. I wish I could prove to you that I'd do anything for you. That I could bring to you all . . . that that he was describing. . . . I won't be a trouble to you any more. (*He turns*) I can prove it to you, Linda. I've been waiting at that corner for hours, just walking up and down. And I'd planned, Linda, to prove that I couldn't live without you, . . . and if you were going to be cold and . . . didn't like me, Linda, I was going to shoot myself right here . . . to prove to you.

He puts the revolver on the table.

To prove to you.—But you've all been so kind to me. And that . . . and Mr. Weston told about his wife. I think just loving isn't wasted.

He weeps silently.

LINDA (*horrified*): Arthur! I wish you wouldn't!

ARTHUR: I imagine I'm . . . I'm young still.—Goodbye and thanks. Goodbye.

He hurries out.

LINDA *shudders with distaste; peers at the revolver; starts to walk about the room and presently is sketching steps again.* JOEY *and* ROWENA *return.*

ROWENA: Was that he that went out? What happened, Linda?

LINDA (*interrupting her drill, indifferently*): He said goodbye forever. He left the gun to prove to me something or other. Thank you for nothing.

ROWENA: Linda, I hope you said a nice word to him.

LINDA: Thank you for nothing, I said.

ROWENA: Well, young lady, you're only sixteen. Wait 'til your turn comes. We'll have to take care of you.

LINDA: Don't let's talk about it. It makes me tired. So hot and excited and breathing so hard. Mario would never act like that. Mario . . . Mario doesn't even seem to notice you when you're there. . . .

And the curtain falls.

Such Things Only Happen in Books

A young novelist and his wife have taken an old house in a New Hampshire village. This is John's library and study and living-room in one. It is a Spring evening. John is playing solitaire on a card table before the hearth and Gabrielle is sewing.

Silence.

JOHN *finishes a game, takes up his fountain pen, makes a no-tation on a piece of paper beside him, and starts shuffling the cards.*

JOHN: Five.

GABRIELLE: What, dear?

JOHN: Five.

GABRIELLE: Oh! . . . Even that's more than the average.

JOHN: The average is two. Listen to the scores this evening; zero, two, five, three, zero, one, four, zero, three, one, six, zero, zero, zero, three, zero, six, and now five. The full fifty-two come out every twenty-one times. So that from now on my chances for getting it out increase seven point three two every game.

GABRIELLE (*not understanding, but thinking that this is an un-fortunate announcement*): Tchk—Tchk!

Pause.

JOHN: The doctor's still upstairs, isn't he?

GABRIELLE: Yes.

JOHN: It does seem that he's taking an awfully long time.

GABRIELLE: Yes, every other day he changes the dressing on the wounds, or burns, or whatever you call it. It takes about half an hour. I offered to help him but he didn't seem to need me. He'll call down the stairs if he needs us.

JOHN: Well, he certainly is taking a long time. Does it hurt Katie when the dressing is changed?

GABRIELLE: Not any more. (*pause*) When's this man coming?

JOHN: About half-past eight, I imagine. He may not come at all. He had to work tonight on some sort of report. I just told him to drop around if he'd like and we'd have a game of chess.

GABRIELLE: On his first call like that, I really ought to have thought about getting together something special for him to eat.

JOHN: No, no. I told him you and I always had some cocoa about half-past ten,—cocoa and biscuits, I said.

GABRIELLE: Well, it's too bad Katie's laid up. I wonder he didn't hear about Katie. The whole town seems to know about her pouring all that boiling water over her legs.

JOHN: Here's another zero, I'm afraid,—though it promised very well.

GABRIELLE: How'd you meet this man?

JOHN: Where I meet everybody. At the post-office Sunday morning waiting for the mail. People stop in on the way home from church and everybody falls into conversation with everybody else.

GABRIELLE: That's the way you met Miss Buckingham. The unexplained Miss Buckingham. The Miss Buckingham whom I soundly disliked. Why on earth she wanted to poke into this house is still a mystery to me.

JOHN: Anyway she's left town for good now. She's gone back to Australia.—On the whole, though, dear, you don't mind my bringing home stray acquaintances from time to time, do you?

GABRIELLE: Oh, no indeed! Usually I like it.

JOHN: We authors should make it our business to multiply just such acquaintances.

GABRIELLE: By all means. I like it.

JOHN: Besides, this Mr. . . . Mr. . . .

GABRIELLE: Graham.

JOHN: Yes, this Mr. Graham asked to come. He said he'd often admired the house sitting up among its elms. I told him it was over two hundred years old and that it had a story. These westerners take a great fancy to our New Hampshire local color.—Really, Gabrielle, the doctor's taking an awfully long time upstairs.

GABRIELLE: Did you tell Mr. Graham the story about the house?

JOHN: No. Anyway I don't really know it. Two young people

frightened their father to death,—killed him or frightened him to death. I must ask one of the old citizens about it. Every old house in the state claims its murder. Thank God I have too much literary conscience to write another novel about an old New England house.

GABRIELLE: Just the same, let's ask the doctor to tell us all about it. He'll know.

JOHN (*examining his game*): Well, I guess this is stuck. It really looked as though it were coming out. I can see that if I moved just one card it would open up a lot of combinations.

GABRIELLE (*without malice*): But you have too much conscience.

JOHN: Yes.—You see it's like fiction. You have to adjust the cards to make a plot. In life most people live along without plots. A plot breaks through about once in every twenty-one times.

GABRIELLE: Well, then, I think, a plot is just about due.

JOHN: Not unless we push back the cards and look under.—At all events, this one's no good. I'll take my pipe out into the garden and walk about.

GABRIELLE: Well, keep one eye on the gate, will you? I don't want to open the door to this Mr. Graham without being introduced.

JOHN: All right. I'll walk up and down in front of the house so I won't miss him. I'll leave the front door open; you might whistle to me when the doctor comes downstairs. (*He leans over the tobacco jar filling his pipe.*) Plots. Plots. If I had no conscience I could choose any one of these plots that are in everybody's novels and in nobody's lives. These poor battered old plots. Enoch Arden returns and looks through the window and sees his wife married to another.

GABRIELLE: I've always loved that one.

JOHN: The plot that murderers always steal back to the scene of their crime and gloat over the place.

GABRIELLE: Oh, John! how wonderful. They'll come back to this house. Imagine!

JOHN: The plot that all married women of thirty-five have lovers.

GABRIELLE: Otherwise known as the Marseillaise.

JOHN: They're as pathetic and futile as the type-jokes—you

know: that mothers-in-law are unpleasant, that . . . that cooks feed chicken and turkey to policemen and other callers in the kitchen . . .

GABRIELLE: Katie! Katie!—Once every twenty-one times these plots really do happen in real life, you say?

JOHN: Once in a thousand. Books and plays are a quiet, harmless fraud about life. . . .

GABRIELLE: Well, now, don't get excited, dear, or you won't be able to work.

JOHN: All right. One pipeful.

He goes out into the garden. The debonaire young doctor comes in from the Right. Hat and coat and satchel. He looks inquiringly at GABRIELLE. *She makes a sign to him that* JOHN *is before the house. She looks out of the door, is reassured, and smiles. The doctor takes her in his arms. They kiss with conjugal tranquillity.*

GABRIELLE: Ouch!

DR. BUMPAS: Ouch! *Ouch!*

GABRIELLE: How's Katie?

DR. BUMPAS: Katie, ma'am, will get better. I've got to run along.

GABRIELLE: Oh, stay a minute!

DR. BUMPAS: Very busy. Patients dying like flies.

GABRIELLE: Tchk—Tchk!

DR. BUMPAS: You wouldn't detain me, would you, on my errands of mercy? Hundreds, ma'am, are waiting for my step on the stair.

He puts down his coat and hat and satchel and kisses her again.

Twins are popping all over the place—every now and then an appendix goes tttttt-bang. Where'd you get that dress? Very chic, very eye-filling.—Can I trust you with a secret, Gabrielle? Would you like to know a secret?

GABRIELLE: Yes, but hurry.—Don't coquette about it. I told John I'd whistle to him when you came downstairs.

DR. BUMPAS: It's about Katie.

GABRIELLE: Goodness. Katie has no secrets.

DR. BUMPAS: And promise me it won't make any difference

between you and Katie. Katie's a fine girl. If you were a stuffy old woman you'd probably fetch up a lot of indignation. And promise not to tell your husband.

GABRIELLE: Oh, I never tell John anything! It would prevent his working.

DR. BUMPAS: Katie just confessed to me how the accident happened. (*a short laugh*) Weren't you surprised that a strong careful girl like Katie could spill a kettle of boiling water over her legs?

GABRIELLE: I certainly was. I thought it very funny indeed.

DR. BUMPAS: Well, it was her brother that did it.

GABRIELLE: I didn't know she had a brother.

DR. BUMPAS: He's been in prison for eight years with four to go. Forgeries and embezzlements and things. But not a bad fellow, you know. Used to be an orderly in my hospital in Boston. Well, three months ago he escaped from prison. Sirens at midnight (*he whines the alarm*), bloodhounds (*he barks*), but he escaped. Gabrielle, did you ever used to hear noises in your kitchen at night?

GABRIELLE: I certainly did. I certainly did. But, then, this house is full of noises. I'd just turn over in bed and say: Not until that ghost comes into this room will I do anything about it.

DR. BUMPAS: Well, it wasn't a ghost. It was Katie's brother. Katie's brother has been hidden, living in your house for three months.

GABRIELLE: Without our knowing it! Why Katie's a monster.

DR. BUMPAS: Oh, Katie's in anguish about it. What Katie suffered from burns was nothing compared to what Katie suffered from conscience. Katie is as honest as the day. Every single time that Katie fed her brother a dinner out of your kitchen she went without a dinner herself. And the rest of his meals she paid for out of her own pocket money.

GABRIELLE: My, isn't life complicated!

DR. BUMPAS: That night she had boiled some water to wash the brother's shirts and socks. He lifted the kettle off the stove and, not being used to hot handles, he dropped it and the water fell all over Katie's knees. I can tell you all this now because he has safely crossed over into Canada to get some work. And now I too must go.

GABRIELLE: You must see John a minute. (*She whistles.*) It's a lovely evening. The rain has stopped. John's expecting a visitor tonight, to play chess. Do you know a westerner named Graham?

Enter JOHN.

JOHN: Hello, doctor, you've been a long time about it. How's Katie?

DR. BUMPAS: Katie'll get well. She'll be up and about in a few days.

He takes up his things.

JOHN: Can't you stay a while? Gabrielle'll make us some cocoa.

DR. BUMPAS: Cocoa! Are people still drinking cocoa?—No, I've got to hurry on. Patients dying like flies. Must look in at the Hospital again.

GABRIELLE: Oh, I know! Every time he enters the door of the Hospital, the building almost leaves the ground.

DR. BUMPAS: I galvanize'm. I galvanize'm.—How's your new book getting on?

JOHN: Nothing begun yet. Groping about for a plot.

DR. BUMPAS: Life's full of plots.

JOHN: We like to think so. But when you come down to it, the rank and file—rich and poor—live much as we do. Not much plot. Work and a nice wife and a nice house and a nice Katie.

DR. BUMPAS: No, no, no—life's full of plots. Swarming with'm.

JOHN: Here's Mr. Graham now.

He goes to the door and shakes hands with a reticent bearded man of about fifty. Presentations.

MR. GRAHAM: I just stopped by to meet your wife and to explain that I'll have to come another time, if you'll be so good as to ask me.

GABRIELLE: Oh, I'm sorry.

MR. GRAHAM: Tonight I must work. I've been ordered to send in a report and I shall probably work all night. (*looking about*) It's a very interesting, a very attractive, house.

JOHN: And it has a story. I was just going to ask Dr. Bumpas to tell it to us.

DR. BUMPAS: Let's see . . . what was their name?

GABRIELLE: They call it the Hamburton place.

DR. BUMPAS: That's it. It must have been some thirty years ago. There was an old father, rich, hateful, miserly, beard and everything. And he buried a lot of money under the floor or between the bricks. (*He points to the hearth.*) There was a son and daughter he kept in rags. Yes, sir, rags, and they lived on potato peelings. They wanted just enough money to get some education and something to wear. And one night they meant to frighten him—they tied him with rope or something to frighten him into releasing some money. Some say they meant to kill him; anyway he died in this very room.

GABRIELLE: What became of the children?

DR. BUMPAS: They disappeared. Tell the truth no one tried very hard to find them.

GABRIELLE: Did they get any money?

DR. BUMPAS: We hope so. Let's hope they found some. Most of it lies down there in the bank to this day.

JOHN: Well, there you have it.

MR. GRAHAM: Very interesting.

GABRIELLE: Come now, can't you both stay and have a cup of cocoa? It won't take a minute.

DR. BUMPAS: Patients dying like flies. Very glad to have met you, Mr. Graham.—Zzzzt. Off I go.

> *He goes out.*

JOHN: All these houses collect folklore like moss. (*to Gabrielle*) You see there's nothing one can make out of a story like that —it's too naïf.

GABRIELLE: Excuse me, one minute. I hear Katie's cowbell. We have a maid upstairs sick in bed, Mr. Graham. When she needs me she rings a cowbell.

> *She goes Right.*

MR. GRAHAM: But I must go too. You'll say goodnight for me. —One question before I go. Did you know a Miss Buckingham, by any chance?

JOHN: Yes, oh, yes. Miss Buckingham came and spent an evening with us here. Yes, she used to be a trained nurse in

South Africa, or Australia. She went back there. Did you know her?

MR. GRAHAM: Yes, I used to know her.

JOHN: She liked this house too. She asked to come and see it.

MR. GRAHAM: And she went back to Australia? That's what I wanted to know.

GABRIELLE'S *voice calls "John! John!"*

JOHN: There's my wife calling me upstairs.—You probably can get Miss Buckingham's address at Mrs. Thorpe's boarding house. She stayed there.—I'm coming!—You'll excuse me. Just come any time, Mr. Graham, and we'll have a game.

JOHN *hurries out.*

MR. GRAHAM, *who has been at the front door, reënters, crosses the room with grave caution to the front right corner. He slowly picks up one corner of the carpet, and stares at a mottled portion of the floor. He lowers the carpet and goes out into the street.*

JOHN *and* GABRIELLE *return.*

JOHN: I guess she'll be comfortable now.

GABRIELLE: Here you see: here's our evening free after all.

JOHN: Didn't even have the excitement of a game of chess. Well, I like it best this way.

He sits down to his cards again. GABRIELLE *takes up her sewing, then rises and stands behind him watching the game over his shoulder.*

GABRIELLE: There! That Jack on the ten releases the ace.

JOHN: But even then we're at a standstill.

GABRIELLE: I don't see why that game shouldn't come out oftener. (*pause*) I don't think you see all the moves.

JOHN: I certainly do see all the moves that are to be seen.— You don't expect me to look under the cards, do you?

He sweeps the cards toward him and starts to shuffle.

One more game and then we'll have some cocoa.

The curtain falls.

The Happy Journey to Trenton and Camden

No scenery is required for this play. Perhaps a few dusty flats may be seen leaning against the brick wall at the back of the stage.

The five members of the Kirby family and the STAGE MANAGER *compose the cast.*

The STAGE MANAGER *not only moves forward and withdraws the few properties that are required, but he reads from a typescript the lines of all the minor characters. He reads them clearly, but with little attempt at characterization, scarcely troubling himself to alter his voice, even when he responds in the person of a child or a woman.*

As the curtain rises the STAGE MANAGER *is leaning lazily against the proscenium pillar at the audience's left. He is smoking.*

ARTHUR *is playing marbles in the center of the stage.*

CAROLINE *is at the remote back right talking to some girls who are invisible to us.*

MA KIRBY *is anxiously putting on her hat before an imaginary mirror.*

MA: Where's your pa? Why isn't he here? I declare we'll never get started.

ARTHUR: Ma, where's my hat? I guess I don't go if I can't find my hat.

MA: Go out into the hall and see if it isn't there. Where's Caroline gone to now, the plagued child?

ARTHUR: She's out waitin' in the street talkin' to the Jones girls.—I just looked in the hall a thousand times, ma, and it isn't there. (*He spits for good luck before a difficult shot and mutters:*) Come on, baby.

MA: Go and look again, I say. Look carefully.

> ARTHUR *rises, runs to the right, turns around swiftly, returns to his game, flinging himself on the floor with a terrible impact and starts shooting an aggie.*

ARTHUR: No, ma, it's not there.

MA (*serenely*): Well, you don't leave Newark without that hat, make up your mind to that. I don't go no journeys with a hoodlum.

ARTHUR: Aw, ma!

> MA *comes down to the footlights and talks toward the audience as through a window.*

MA: Oh, Mrs. Schwartz!

THE STAGE MANAGER (*consulting his script*): Here I am, Mrs. Kirby. Are you going yet?

MA: I guess we're going in just a minute. How's the baby?

THE STAGE MANAGER: She's all right now. We slapped her on the back and she spat it up.

MA: Isn't that fine!—Well now, if you'll be good enough to give the cat a saucer of milk in the morning and the evening, Mrs. Schwartz, I'll be ever so grateful to you.—Oh, good afternoon, Mrs. Hobmeyer!

THE STAGE MANAGER: Good afternoon, Mrs. Kirby, I hear you're going away.

MA (*modest*): Oh, just for three days, Mrs. Hobmeyer, to see my married daughter, Beulah, in Camden. Elmer's got his vacation week from the laundry early this year, and he's just the best driver in the world.

> CAROLINE *comes "into the house" and stands by her mother.*

THE STAGE MANAGER: Is the whole family going?

MA: Yes, all four of us that's here. The change ought to be good for the children. My married daughter was downright sick a while ago—

THE STAGE MANAGER: Tchk—Tchk—Tchk! Yes. I remember you tellin' us.

MA: And I just want to go down and see the child. I ain't seen her since then. I just won't rest easy in my mind without I see her. (*To Caroline*) Can't you say good afternoon to Mrs. Hobmeyer?

CAROLINE (*blushes and lowers her eyes and says woodenly*): Good afternoon, Mrs. Hobmeyer.

THE STAGE MANAGER: Good afternoon, dear.—Well, I'll wait and beat these rugs until after you're gone, because I don't want to choke you. I hope you have a good time and find everything all right.

MA: Thank you, Mrs. Hobmeyer, I hope I will.—Well, I guess that milk for the cat is all, Mrs. Schwartz, if you're sure you don't mind. If anything should come up, the key to the back door is hanging by the ice box.

ARTHUR AND CAROLINE: Ma! Not so loud. Everybody can hear yuh.

MA: Stop pullin' my dress, children. (*In a loud whisper*) The key to the back door I'll leave hangin' by the ice box and I'll leave the screen door unhooked.

THE STAGE MANAGER: Now have a good trip, dear, and give my love to Loolie.

MA: I will, and thank you a thousand times.

She returns "into the room."

What can be keeping your pa?

ARTHUR: I can't find my hat, ma.

Enter ELMER holding a hat.

ELMER: Here's Arthur's hat. He musta left it in the car Sunday.

MA: That's a mercy. Now we can start.—Caroline Kirby, what you done to your cheeks?

CAROLINE: (*defiant-abashed*): Nothin'.

MA: If you've put anything on 'em, I'll slap you.

CAROLINE: No, ma, of course I haven't. (*hanging her head*) I just rubbed'm to make'm red. All the girls do that at High School when they're goin' places.

MA: Such silliness I never saw. Elmer, what kep' you?

ELMER (*always even-voiced and always looking out a little anxiously through his spectacles*): I just went to the garage and had Charlie give a last look at it, Kate.

MA: I'm glad you did. I wouldn't like to have no breakdown miles from anywhere. Now we can start. Arthur, put those marbles away. Anybody'd think you didn't want to go on a journey to look at yuh.

They go out through the "hall," take the short steps that denote going downstairs, and find themselves in the street.

ELMER: Here, you boys, you keep away from that car.

MA: Those Sullivan boys put their heads into everything.

> *The* STAGE MANAGER *has moved forward four chairs and a low platform. This is the automobile. It is in the center of the stage and faces the audience. The platform slightly raises the two chairs in the rear.* PA'S *hands hold an imaginary steering wheel and continually shift gears.* CAROLINE *sits beside him.* ARTHUR *is behind him and* MA *behind* CAROLINE.

CAROLINE (*self-consciously*): Goodbye, Mildred. Goodbye, Helen.

THE STAGE MANAGER: Goodbye, Caroline. Goodbye, Mrs. Kirby. I hope y'have a good time.

MA: Goodbye, girls.

THE STAGE MANAGER: Goodbye, Kate. The car looks fine.

MA (*looking upward toward a window*): Oh, goodbye, Emma! (*modestly*) We think it's the best little Chevrolet in the world.—Oh, goodbye, Mrs. Adler!

THE STAGE MANAGER: What, are you going away, Mrs. Kirby?

MA: Just for three days, Mrs. Adler, to see my married daughter in Camden.

THE STAGE MANAGER: Have a good time.

> *Now* MA, CAROLINE, *and the* STAGE MANAGER *break out into a tremendous chorus of goodbyes. The whole street is saying goodbye.* ARTHUR *takes out his pea shooter and lets fly happily into the air. There is a lurch or two and they are off.*

ARTHUR (*in sudden fright*): Pa! Pa! Don't go by the school. Mr. Biedenbach might see us!

MA: I don't care if he does see us. I guess I can take my children out of school for one day without having to hide down back streets about it.

> ELMER *nods to a passerby.*
> MA *asks without sharpness:*

Who was that you spoke to, Elmer?

ELMER: That was the fellow who arranges our banquets down to the Lodge, Kate.

MA: Is he the one who had to buy four hundred steaks? (PA *nods.*) I declare, I'm glad I'm not him.

ELMER: The air's getting better already. Take deep breaths, children.

They inhale noisily.

ARTHUR: Gee, it's almost open fields already. *"Weber and Heilbronner Suits for Well-dressed Men."* Ma, can I have one of them some day?

MA: If you graduate with good marks perhaps your father'll let you have one for graduation.

CAROLINE (*whining*): Oh, Pa! do we have to wait while that whole funeral goes by?

> PA *takes off his hat.*
> MA *cranes forward with absorbed curiosity.*

MA: Take off your hat, Arthur. Look at your father.—Why, Elmer, I do believe that's a lodge-brother of yours. See the banner? I suppose this is the Elizabeth branch.

> ELMER *nods.* MA *sighs: Tchk—tchk—tchk. They all lean forward and watch the funeral in silence, growing momentarily more solemnized. After a pause,* MA *continues almost dreamily:*

Well, we haven't forgotten the one that we went on, have we? We haven't forgotten our good Harold. He gave his life for his country, we mustn't forget that. (*She passes her finger from the corner of her eye across her cheek. There is another pause.*) Well, we'll all hold up the traffic for a few minutes some day.

THE CHILDREN (*very uncomfortable*): Ma!

MA (*without self-pity*): Well I'm "ready," children. I hope everybody in this car is "ready." (*She puts her hand on* PA's *shoulder.*) And I pray to go first, Elmer. Yes. (*PA touches her hand.*)

THE CHILDREN: Ma, everybody's looking at you. Everybody's laughing at you.

MA: Oh, hold your tongues! I don't care what a lot of silly people in Elizabeth, New Jersey, think of me.—Now we can go on. That's the last.

> *There is another lurch and the car goes on.*

CAROLINE: *"Fit-Rite Suspenders. The Working Man's Choice."* Pa, why do they spell Rite that way?

ELMER: So that it'll make you stop and ask about it, Missy.

CAROLINE: Papa, you're teasing me.—Ma, why do they say *"Three Hundred Rooms Three Hundred Baths?"*

ARTHUR: *"Miller's Spaghetti: The Family's Favorite Dish."* Ma, why don't you ever have spaghetti?

MA: Go along, you'd never eat it.

ARTHUR: Ma, I like it now.

CAROLINE (*with gesture*): Yum-yum. It looks wonderful up there. Ma, make some when we get home?

MA (*dryly*): "The management is always happy to receive suggestions. We aim to please."

The whole family finds this exquisitely funny. The children scream with laughter. Even ELMER smiles. MA remains modest.

ELMER: Well, I guess no one's complaining, Kate. Everybody knows you're a good cook.

MA: I don't know whether I'm a good cook or not, but I know I've had practice. At least I've cooked three meals a day for twenty-five years.

ARTHUR: Aw, ma, you went out to eat once in a while.

MA: Yes. That made it a leap year.

This joke is no less successful than its predecessor. When the laughter dies down, CAROLINE turns around in an ecstasy of well-being and kneeling on the cushions says:

CAROLINE: Ma, I love going out in the country like this. Let's do it often, ma.

MA: Goodness, smell that air will you! It's got the whole ocean in it.—Elmer, drive careful over that bridge. This must be New Brunswick we're coming to.

ARTHUR (*jealous of his mother's successes*): Ma, when is the next comfort station?

MA (*unruffled*): You don't want one. You just said that to be awful.

CAROLINE (*shrilly*): Yes, he did, ma. He's terrible. He says that kind of thing right out in school and I want to sink through the floor, ma. He's terrible.

MA: Oh, don't get so excited about nothing, Miss Proper! I guess we're all yewman-beings in this car, at least as far as I know. And, Arthur, you try and be a gentleman.—Elmer, don't run over that collie dog. (*She follows the dog with her eyes.*) Looked kinda peakèd to me. Needs a good honest bowl of leavings. Pretty dog, too. (*Her eyes fall on a billboard.*) That's a pretty advertisement for Chesterfield cigarettes, isn't it? Looks like Beulah, a little.

ARTHUR: Ma?

MA: Yes.

ARTHUR (*"route" rhymes with "out"*): Can't I take a paper route with the Newark *Daily Post*?

MA: No, you cannot. No, sir. I hear they make the paper boys get up at four-thirty in the morning. No son of mine is going to get up at four-thirty every morning, not if it's to make a million dollars. Your *Saturday Evening Post* route on Thursday mornings is enough.

ARTHUR: Aw, ma.

MA: No, sir. No son of mine is going to get up at four-thirty and miss the sleep God meant him to have.

ARTHUR (*sullenly*): Hhm! Ma's always talking about God. I guess she got a letter from him this morning.

MA *rises, outraged.*

MA: Elmer, stop that automobile this minute. I don't go another step with anybody that says things like that. Arthur, you get out of this car. Elmer, you give him another dollar bill. He can go back to Newark, by himself. I don't want him.

ARTHUR: What did I say? There wasn't anything terrible about that.

ELMER: I didn't hear what he said, Kate.

MA: God has done a lot of things for me and I won't have him made fun of by anybody. Go away. Go away from me.

CAROLINE: Aw, Ma,—don't spoil the ride.

MA: No.

ELMER: We might as well go on, Kate, since we've got started. I'll talk to the boy tonight.

MA (*slowly conceding*): All right, if you say so, Elmer. But I won't sit beside him. Caroline, you come, and sit by me.

ARTHUR (*frightened*): Aw, ma, that wasn't so terrible.

MA: I don't want to talk about it. I hope your father washes your mouth out with soap and water.—Where'd we all be if

I started talking about God like that, I'd like to know! We'd be in the speak-easies and night-clubs and places like that, that's where we'd be.—All right, Elmer, you can go on now.
CAROLINE: What did he say, ma? I didn't hear what he said.
MA: I don't want to talk about it.

They drive on in silence for a moment, the shocked silence after a scandal.

ELMER: I'm going to stop and give the car a little water, I guess.
MA: All right, Elmer. You know best.
ELMER (*to a garage hand*): Could I have a little water in the radiator—to make sure?
THE STAGE MANAGER (*in this scene alone he lays aside his script and enters into a rôle seriously*): You sure can. (*He punches the tires.*) Air, all right? Do you need any oil or gas?
ELMER: No, I think not. I just got fixed up in Newark.
MA: We're on the right road for Camden, are we?
THE STAGE MANAGER: Yes, keep straight ahead. You can't miss it. You'll be in Trenton in a few minutes.

He carefully pours some water into the hood.

Camden's a great town, lady, believe me.
MA: My daughter likes it fine,—my married daughter.
THE STAGE MANAGER: Ye'? It's a great burg all right. I guess I think so because I was born near there.
MA: Well, well. Your folks still live there?
THE STAGE MANAGER: No, my old man sold the farm and they built a factory on it. So the folks moved to Philadelphia.
MA: My married daughter Beulah lives there because her husband works in the telephone company.—Stop pokin' me, Caroline!—We're all going down to see her for a few days.
THE STAGE MANAGER: Ye'?
MA: She's been sick, you see, and I just felt I had to go and see her. My husband and my boy are going to stay at the Y.M.C.A. I hear they've got a dormitory on the top floor that's real clean and comfortable. Had you ever been there?
THE STAGE MANAGER: No. I'm Knights of Columbus myself.
MA: Oh.

THE STAGE MANAGER: I used to play basketball at the Y though. It looked all right to me.

He has been standing with one foot on the rung of MA'S *chair. They have taken a great fancy to one another. He reluctantly shakes himself out of it and pretends to examine the car again, whistling.*

Well, I guess you're all set now, lady. I hope you have a good trip; you can't miss it.
EVERYBODY: Thanks. Thanks a lot. Good luck to you.

Jolts and lurches.

MA (*with a sigh*): The world's full of nice people.—That's what I call a nice young man.
CAROLINE (*earnestly*): Ma, you oughtn't to tell'm all everything about yourself.
MA: Well, Caroline, you do your way and I'll do mine.—He looked kinda thin to me. I'd like to feed him up for a few days. His mother lives in Philadelphia and I expect he eats at those dreadful Greek places.
CAROLINE: I'm hungry. Pa, there's a hot dog stand. K'n I have one?
ELMER: We'll all have one, eh, Kate? We had such an early lunch.
MA: Just as you think best, Elmer.
ELMER: Arthur, here's half a dollar.—Run over and see what they have. Not too much mustard either.

ARTHUR *descends from the car and goes off stage right.*
MA *and* CAROLINE *get out and walk a bit.*

MA: What's that flower over there?—I'll take some of those to Beulah.
CAROLINE: It's just a weed, ma.
MA: I like it.—My, look at the sky, wouldya! I'm glad I was born in New Jersey. I've always said it was the best state in the Union. Every state has something no other state has got.

They stroll about humming.
Presently ARTHUR *returns with his hands full of imaginary hot dogs which he distributes. He is still very much cast down*

by the recent scandal. He finally approaches his mother and says falteringly:

ARTHUR: Ma, I'm sorry. I'm sorry for what I said.

He bursts into tears and puts his forehead against her elbow.

MA: There. There. We all say wicked things at times. I know you didn't mean it like it sounded.

He weeps still more violently than before.

Why, now, now! I forgive you, Arthur, and tonight before you go to bed you . . . (*she whispers.*) You're a good boy at heart, Arthur, and we all know it.

CAROLINE *starts to cry too.*
MA *is suddenly joyously alive and happy.*

Sakes alive, it's too nice a day for us all to be cryin'. Come now, get in. You go up in front with your father, Caroline. Ma wants to sit with her beau. I never saw such children. Your hot dogs are all getting wet. Now chew them fine, everybody.—All right, Elmer, forward march.—Caroline, whatever are you doing?

CAROLINE: I'm spitting out the leather, ma.

MA: Then say: Excuse me.

CAROLINE: Excuse me, please.

MA: What's this place? Arthur, did you see the post office?

ARTHUR: It said Lawrenceville.

MA: Hhn. School kinda. Nice. I wonder what that big yellow house set back was.—Now it's beginning to be Trenton.

CAROLINE: Papa, it was near here that George Washington crossed the Delaware. It was near Trenton, mama. He was first in war and first in peace, and first in the hearts of his countrymen.

MA (*surveying the passing world, serene and didactic*): Well, the thing I like about him best was that he never told a lie.

The children are duly cast down.
There is a pause.

There's a sunset for you. There's nothing like a good sunset.

ARTHUR: There's an Ohio license in front of us. Ma, have you ever been to Ohio?

MA: No.

> *A dreamy silence descends upon them.*
> CAROLINE *sits closer to her father.*
> MA *puts her arm around* ARTHUR.

ARTHUR: Ma, what a lotta people there are in the world, ma. There must be thousands and thousands in the United States. Ma, how many are there?

MA: I don't know. Ask your father.

ARTHUR: Pa, how many are there?

ELMER: There are a hundred and twenty-six million, Kate.

MA (*giving a pressure about* ARTHUR'S *shoulder*): And they all like to drive out in the evening with their children beside'm.

> *Another pause.*

Why doesn't somebody sing something? Arthur, you're always singing something; what's the matter with you?

ARTHUR: All right. What'll we sing? (*He sketches:*)
"In the Blue Ridge mountains of Virginia,
    On the trail of the lonesome pine . . ."
No, I don't like that any more. Let's do:
"I been workin on de railroad
    All de liblong day.
    I been workin' on de railroad
    Just to pass de time away."

> CAROLINE *joins in at once.*
> *Finally even* MA *is singing.*
> *Even* PA *is singing.*
> MA *suddenly jumps up with a wild cry:*

MA: Elmer, that signpost said Camden, I saw it.

ELMER: All right, Kate, if you're sure.

> *Much shifting of gears, backing, and jolting.*

MA: Yes, there it is. Camden—five miles. Dear old Beulah.— Now, children, you be good and quiet during dinner. She's just got out of bed after a big sorta operation, and we must all move around kinda quiet. First you drop me and Caroline at the door and just say hello, and then you men-folk go over to the Y.M.C.A. and come back for dinner in about an hour.

CAROLINE (*shutting her eyes and pressing her fists passionately against her nose*): I see the first star. Everybody make a wish.

> Star light, star bright,
> First star I seen tonight.
> I wish I may, I wish I might
> Have the wish I wish tonight.

(*then solemnly*) Pins. Mama, you say "needles."

She interlocks little fingers with her mother.

MA: Needles.

CAROLINE: Shakespeare. Ma, you say "Longfellow."

MA: Longfellow.

CAROLINE: Now it's a secret and I can't tell it to anybody. Ma, you make a wish.

MA (*with almost grim humor*): No, I can make wishes without waiting for no star. And I can tell my wishes right out loud too. Do you want to hear them?

CAROLINE (*resignedly*): No, ma, we know'm already. We've heard'm. (*She hangs her head affectedly on her left shoulder and says with unmalicious mimicry:*) You want me to be a good girl and you want Arthur to be honest-in-word-and-deed.

MA (*majestically*): Yes. So mind yourself.

ELMER: Caroline, take out that letter from Beulah in my coat pocket by you and read aloud the places I marked with red pencil.

CAROLINE (*working*): "*A few blocks after you pass the two big oil tanks on your left . . .*"

EVERYBODY (*pointing backward*): There they are!

CAROLINE: "*. . . you come to a corner where there's an A and P store on the left and a firehouse kitty-corner to it . . .*"

They all jubilantly identify these landmarks.

"*. . . turn right, go two blocks, and our house is Weyerhauser St. Number 471.*"

MA: It's an even nicer street than they used to live in. And right handy to an A and P.

CAROLINE (*whispering*): Ma, it's better than our street. It's richer than our street.—Ma, isn't Beulah richer than we are?

MA (*looking at her with a firm and glassy eye*): Mind yourself, missy. I don't want to hear anybody talking about rich or not rich when I'm around. If people aren't nice I don't care how rich they are. I live in the best street in the world because my husband and children live there.

> *She glares impressively at* CAROLINE *a moment to let this lesson sink in, then looks up, sees* BEULAH *and waves.*

There's Beulah standing on the steps lookin' for us.

> BEULAH *has appeared and is waving.*
> *They, all call out:* Hello, Beulah—Hello.
> *Presently they are all getting out of the car.*
> BEULAH *kisses her father long and affectionately.*

BEULAH: Hello, papa. Good old papa. You look tired, pa.— Hello, mama.—Lookit how Arthur and Caroline are growing!

MA: They're bursting all their clothes!—Yes, your pa needs a rest. Thank Heaven, his vacation has come just now. We'll feed him up and let him sleep late. Pa has a present for you, Loolie. He would go and buy it.

BEULAH: Why, pa, you're terrible to go and buy anything for me. Isn't he terrible?

MA: Well, it's a secret. You can open it at dinner.

ELMER: Where's Horace, Loolie?

BEULAH: He was kep' over a little at the office. He'll be here any minute. He's crazy to see you all.

MA: All right. You men go over to the Y and come back in about an hour.

BEULAH (*as her father returns to the wheel, stands out in the street beside him*): Go straight along, pa, you can't miss it. It just stares at yuh. (*She puts her arm around his neck and rubs her nose against his temple.*) Crazy old pa, goin' buyin' things! It's me that ought to be buyin' things for you, pa.

ELMER: Oh, no! There's only one Loolie in the world.

BEULAH (*whispering, as her eyes fill with tears*): Are you glad I'm still alive, pa?

She kisses him abruptly and goes back to the house steps.
The STAGE MANAGER *removes the automobile with the help*
of ELMER *and* ARTHUR *who go off waving their goodbyes.*

Well, come on upstairs, ma, and take off your things.
Caroline, there's a surprise for you in the back yard.

CAROLINE: Rabbits?

BEULAH: No.

CAROLINE: Chickins?

BEULAH: No. Go and see.

> CAROLINE *runs off stage.*
> BEULAH *and* MA *gradually go upstairs.*

There are two new puppies. You be thinking over whether
you can keep one in Newark.

MA: I guess we can. It's a nice house, Beulah. You just got a
lovely home.

BEULAH: When I got back from the hospital, Horace had
moved everything into it, and there wasn't anything for me
to do.

MA: It's lovely.

> *The* STAGE MANAGER *pushes out a bed from the left. Its foot*
> *is toward the right.* BEULAH *sits on it, testing the springs.*

BEULAH: I think you'll find the bed comfortable, ma.

MA (*taking off her hat*): Oh, I could sleep on a heapa shoes,
Loolie! I don't have no trouble sleepin'. (*She sits down beside
her.*) Now let me look at my girl. Well, well, when I last saw
you, you didn't know me. You kep' saying: *When's mama
comin'? When's mama comin'?* But the doctor sent me away.

BEULAH (*puts her head on her mother's shoulder and weeps*): It
was awful, mama. It was awful. She didn't even live a few
minutes, mama. It was awful.

MA (*looking far away*): God thought best, dear. God thought
best. We don't understand why. We just go on, honey, doin'
our business.

> *Then almost abruptly—passing the back of her hand across*
> *her cheek.*

Well, now, what are we giving the men to eat tonight?

BEULAH: There's a chicken in the oven.

MA: What time didya put it in?

BEULAH (*restraining her*): Aw, ma, don't go yet. I like to sit here with you this way. You always get the fidgets when we try and pet yuh, mama.

MA (*ruefully, laughing*): Yes, it's kinda foolish. I'm just an old Newark bag-a-bones. (*She glances at the backs of her hands.*)

BEULAH (*indignantly*): Why, ma, you're good-lookin'! We always said you were good-lookin'.—And besides, you're the best ma we could ever have.

MA (*uncomfortable*): Well, I hope you like me. There's nothin' like being liked by your family.—Now I'm going downstairs to look at the chicken. You stretch out here for a minute and shut your eyes.—Have you got everything laid in for breakfast before the shops close?

BEULAH: Oh, you know! Ham and eggs.

They both laugh.

MA: I declare I never could understand what men see in ham and eggs. I think they're horrible.—What time did you put the chicken in?

BEULAH: Five o'clock.

MA: Well, now, you shut your eyes for ten minutes.

> BEULAH *stretches out and shuts her eyes.*
> MA *descends the stairs absent-mindedly singing:*

> "There were ninety and nine that safely lay
>   In the shelter of the fold,
>   But one was out on the hills away,
>   Far off from the gates of gold . . . "

And the curtain falls.

OUR TOWN

A Play in Three Acts

To Alexander Woollcott
of Castleton Township, Rutland County, Vermont

CHARACTERS (in the order of their appearance)

STAGE MANAGER
DR. GIBBS
JOE CROWELL
HOWIE NEWSOME
MRS. GIBBS
MRS. WEBB
GEORGE GIBBS
REBECCA GIBBS
WALLY WEBB
EMILY WEBB
PROFESSOR WILLARD
MR. WEBB
WOMAN IN THE BALCONY
MAN IN THE AUDITORIUM
LADY IN THE BOX
SIMON STIMSON
MRS. SOAMES
CONSTABLE WARREN
SI CROWELL
THREE BASEBALL PLAYERS
SAM CRAIG
JOE STODDARD

The entire play takes place in Grover's Corners, New Hampshire.

Act I

No curtain.
No scenery.
The audience, arriving, sees an empty stage in half-light.
Presently the STAGE MANAGER, *hat on and pipe in mouth, enters and begins placing a table and three chairs downstage left, and a table and three chairs downstage right. He also places a low bench at the corner of what will be the Webb house, left.*
"Left" and "right" are from the point of view of the actor facing the audience. "Up" is toward the back wall.
As the house lights go down he has finished setting the stage and leaning against the right proscenium pillar watches the late arrivals in the audience.
When the auditorium is in complete darkness he speaks:

STAGE MANAGER: This play is called "Our Town." It was written by Thornton Wilder; produced and directed by A. . . . (or: produced by A. . . . ; directed by B. . . .). In it you will see Miss C. . . . ; Miss D. . . . ; Miss E. . . . ; and Mr. F. . . . ; Mr. G. . . . ; Mr. H. . . . ; and many others. The name of the town is Grover's Corners, New Hampshire—just across the Massachusetts line: latitude 42 degrees 40 minutes; longitude 70 degrees 37 minutes. The First Act shows a day in our town. The day is May 7, 1901. The time is just before dawn.

A rooster crows.

The sky is beginning to show some streaks of light over in the East there, behind our mount'in.
The morning star always gets wonderful bright the minute before it has to go,—doesn't it?

He stares at it for a moment, then goes upstage.

Well, I'd better show you how our town lies. Up here—

That is: parallel with the back wall.

is Main Street. Way back there is the railway station; tracks go that way. Polish Town's across the tracks, and some Canuck families.

Toward the left.

Over there is the Congregational Church; across the street's the Presbyterian.
Methodist and Unitarian are over there. Baptist is down in the holla' by the river.
Catholic Church is over beyond the tracks.
Here's the Town Hall and Post Office combined; jail's in the basement.
Bryan once made a speech from these very steps here.
Along here's a row of stores. Hitching posts and horse blocks in front of them. First automobile's going to come along in about five years—belonged to Banker Cartwright, our richest citizen . . . lives in the big white house up on the hill.
Here's the grocery store and here's Mr. Morgan's drugstore. Most everybody in town manages to look into those two stores once a day.
Public School's over yonder. High School's still farther over. Quarter of nine mornings, noontimes, and three o'clock afternoons, the hull town can hear the yelling and screaming from those schoolyards.

He approaches the table and chairs downstage right.

This is our doctor's house,—Doc Gibbs'. This is the back door.

Two arched trellises, covered with vines and flowers, are pushed out, one by each proscenium pillar.

There's some scenery for those who think they have to have scenery.
This is Mrs. Gibbs' garden. Corn . . . peas . . . beans . . . hollyhocks . . . heliotrope . . . and a lot of burdock.

Crosses the stage.

In those days our newspaper come out twice a week—the Grover's Corners *Sentinel*—and this is Editor Webb's house.

And this is Mrs. Webb's garden.
Just like Mrs. Gibbs', only it's got a lot of sunflowers, too.

He looks upward, center stage.

Right here . . .'s a big butternut tree.

He returns to his place by the right proscenium pillar and looks at the audience for a minute.

Nice town, y'know what I mean?
Nobody very remarkable ever come out of it, s'far as we know.
The earliest tombstones in the cemetery up there on the mountain say 1670–1680—they're Grovers and Cartwrights and Gibbses and Herseys—same names as are around here now.
Well, as I said: it's about dawn.
The only lights on in town are in a cottage over by the tracks where a Polish mother's just had twins. And in the Joe Crowell house, where Joe Junior's getting up so as to deliver the paper. And in the depot, where Shorty Hawkins is gettin' ready to flag the 5:45 for Boston.

A train whistle is heard. The STAGE MANAGER *takes out his watch and nods.*

Naturally, out in the country—all around—there've been lights on for some time, what with milkin's and so on. But town people sleep late.
So—another day's begun.
There's Doc Gibbs comin' down Main Street now, comin' back from that baby case. And here's his wife comin' downstairs to get breakfast.

MRS. GIBBS, *a plump, pleasant woman in the middle thirties, comes "downstairs" right. She pulls up an imaginary window shade in her kitchen and starts to make a fire in her stove.*

Doc Gibbs died in 1930. The new hospital's named after him. Mrs. Gibbs died first—long time ago, in fact. She went out to visit her daughter, Rebecca, who married an insurance man in Canton, Ohio, and died there—pneumonia—but her body was brought back here. She's up in the cemetery there now—in with a whole mess of Gibbses and Herseys—she was Julia Hersey 'fore she married Doc Gibbs in the Congregational Church over there.

In our town we like to know the facts about everybody.

There's Mrs. Webb, coming downstairs to get her breakfast, too.—That's Doc Gibbs. Got that call at half past one this morning.

And there comes Joe Crowell, Jr., delivering Mr. Webb's *Sentinel.*

> DR. GIBBS *has been coming along Main Street from the left. At the point where he would turn to approach his house, he stops, sets down his—imaginary—black bag, takes off his hat, and rubs his face with fatigue, using an enormous handkerchief.*
>
> MRS. WEBB, *a thin, serious, crisp woman, has entered her kitchen, left, tying on an apron. She goes through the motions of putting wood into a stove, lighting it, and preparing breakfast.*
>
> *Suddenly,* JOE CROWELL, JR., *eleven, starts down Main Street from the right, hurling imaginary newspapers into doorways.*

JOE CROWELL, JR.: Morning, Doc Gibbs.

DR. GIBBS: Morning, Joe.

JOE CROWELL, JR.: Somebody been sick, Doc?

DR. GIBBS: No. Just some twins born over in Polish Town.

JOE CROWELL, JR.: Do you want your paper now?

DR. GIBBS: Yes, I'll take it.—Anything serious goin' on in the world since Wednesday?

JOE CROWELL, JR.: Yessir. My schoolteacher, Miss Foster, 's getting married to a fella over in Concord.

DR. GIBBS: I declare.—How do you boys feel about that?

JOE CROWELL, JR.: Well, of course, it's none of my business— but I think if a person starts out to be a teacher, she ought to stay one.

DR. GIBBS: How's your knee, Joe?

JOE CROWELL, JR.: Fine, Doc, I never think about it at all. Only like you said, it always tells me when it's going to rain.

DR. GIBBS: What's it telling you today? Goin' to rain?

JOE CROWELL, JR.: No, sir.
DR. GIBBS: Sure?
JOE CROWELL, JR.: Yessir.
DR. GIBBS: Knee ever make a mistake?
JOE CROWELL, JR.: No, sir.

JOE *goes off.* DR. GIBBS *stands reading his paper.*

STAGE MANAGER: Want to tell you something about that boy
Joe Crowell there. Joe was awful bright—graduated from
high school here, head of his class. So he got a scholarship
to Massachusetts Tech. Graduated head of his class there,
too. It was all wrote up in the Boston paper at the time.
Goin' to be a great engineer, Joe was. But the war broke out
and he died in France.—All that education for nothing.
HOWIE NEWSOME: (*Off left.*) Giddap, Bessie! What's the
matter with you today?
STAGE MANAGER: Here comes Howie Newsome, deliverin' the
milk.

HOWIE NEWSOME, *about thirty, in overalls, comes along
Main Street from the left, walking beside an invisible horse
and wagon and carrying an imaginary rack with milk bottles. The sound of clinking milk bottles is heard. He leaves
some bottles at Mrs. Webb's trellis, then, crossing the stage to
Mrs. Gibbs', he stops center to talk to Dr. Gibbs.*

HOWIE NEWSOME: Morning, Doc.
DR. GIBBS: Morning, Howie.
HOWIE NEWSOME: Somebody sick?
DR. GIBBS: Pair of twins over to Mrs. Goruslawski's.
HOWIE NEWSOME: Twins, eh? This town's gettin' bigger every
year.
DR. GIBBS: Goin' to rain, Howie?
HOWIE NEWSOME: No, no. Fine day—that'll burn through.
Come on, Bessie.
DR. GIBBS: Hello Bessie.

He strokes the horse, which has remained up center.

How old is she, Howie?
HOWIE NEWSOME: Going on seventeen. Bessie's all mixed up
about the route ever since the Lockharts stopped takin' their

quart of milk every day. She wants to leave 'em a quart just the same—keeps scolding me the hull trip.

He reaches Mrs. Gibbs' back door. She is waiting for him.

MRS. GIBBS: Good morning, Howie.

HOWIE NEWSOME: Morning, Mrs. Gibbs. Doc's just comin' down the street.

MRS. GIBBS: Is he? Seems like you're late today.

HOWIE NEWSOME: Yes. Somep'n went wrong with the separator. Don't know what 'twas.

He passes Dr. Gibbs up center.

Doc!

DR. GIBBS: Howie!

MRS. GIBBS: (*Calling upstairs.*) Children! Children! Time to get up.

HOWIE NEWSOME: Come on, Bessie!

He goes off right.

MRS. GIBBS: George! Rebecca!

> DR. GIBBS *arrives at his back door and passes through the trellis into his house.*

MRS. GIBBS: Everything all right, Frank?

DR. GIBBS: Yes. I declare—easy as kittens.

MRS. GIBBS: Bacon'll be ready in a minute. Set down and drink your coffee. You can catch a couple hours' sleep this morning, can't you?

DR. GIBBS: Hm! . . . Mrs. Wentworth's coming at eleven. Guess I know what it's about, too. Her stummick ain't what it ought to be.

MRS. GIBBS: All told, you won't get more'n three hours' sleep. Frank Gibbs, I don't know what's goin' to become of you. I do wish I could get you to go away someplace and take a rest. I think it would do you good.

MRS. WEBB: Emileeee! Time to get up! Wally! Seven o'clock!

MRS. GIBBS: I declare, you got to speak to George. Seems like something's come over him lately. He's no help to me at all. I can't even get him to cut me some wood.

DR. GIBBS: (*Washing and drying his hands at the sink.* MRS. GIBBS *is busy at the stove.*) Is he sassy to you?

MRS. GIBBS: No. He just whines! All he thinks about is that baseball— George! Rebecca! You'll be late for school.

DR. GIBBS: M-m-m . . .

MRS. GIBBS: George!

DR. GIBBS: George, look sharp!

GEORGE'S VOICE: Yes, Pa!

DR. GIBBS: (*As he goes off the stage.*) Don't you hear your mother calling you? I guess I'll go upstairs and get forty winks.

MRS. WEBB: Walleee! Emileee! You'll be late for school! Walleee! You wash yourself good or I'll come up and do it myself.

REBECCA GIBBS' VOICE: Ma! What dress shall I wear?

MRS. GIBBS: Don't make a noise. Your father's been out all night and needs his sleep. I washed and ironed the blue gingham for you special.

REBECCA: Ma, I hate that dress.

MRS. GIBBS: Oh, hush-up-with-you.

REBECCA: Every day I go to school dressed like a sick turkey.

MRS. GIBBS: Now, Rebecca, you always look *very* nice.

REBECCA: Mama, George's throwing soap at me.

MRS. GIBBS: I'll come and slap the both of you,—that's what I'll do.

> *A factory whistle sounds.*
> The CHILDREN *dash in and take their places at the tables.* Right, GEORGE, *about sixteen, and* REBECCA, *eleven.* Left, EMILY *and* WALLY, *same ages. They carry strapped schoolbooks.*

STAGE MANAGER: We've got a factory in our town too—hear it? Makes blankets. Cartwrights own it and it brung 'em a fortune.

MRS. WEBB: Children! Now I won't have it. Breakfast is just as good as any other meal and I won't have you gobbling like wolves. It'll stunt your growth,—that's a fact. Put away your book, Wally.

WALLY: Aw, Ma! By ten o'clock I got to know all about Canada.

MRS. WEBB: You know the rule's well as I do—no books at

table. As for me, I'd rather have my children healthy than bright.

EMILY: I'm both, Mama: you know I am. I'm the brightest girl in school for my age. I have a wonderful memory.

MRS. WEBB: Eat your breakfast.

WALLY: I'm bright, too, when I'm looking at my stamp collection.

MRS. GIBBS: I'll speak to your father about it when he's rested. Seems to me twenty-five cents a week's enough for a boy your age. I declare I don't know how you spend it all.

GEORGE: Aw, Ma,—I gotta lotta things to buy.

MRS. GIBBS: Strawberry phosphates—that's what you spend it on.

GEORGE: I don't see how Rebecca comes to have so much money. She has more'n a dollar.

REBECCA: (*Spoon in mouth, dreamily.*) I've been saving it up gradual.

MRS. GIBBS: Well, dear, I think it's a good thing to spend some every now and then.

REBECCA: Mama, do you know what I love most in the world—do you?—Money.

MRS. GIBBS: Eat your breakfast.

THE CHILDREN: Mama, there's first bell.—I gotta hurry.—I don't want any more.—I gotta hurry.

> The CHILDREN *rise, seize their books and dash out through the trellises. They meet, down center, and chattering, walk to Main Street, then turn left.*
> The STAGE MANAGER *goes off, unobtrusively, right.*

MRS. WEBB: Walk fast, but you don't have to run. Wally, pull up your pants at the knee. Stand up straight, Emily.

MRS. GIBBS: Tell Miss Foster I send her my best congratulations —can you remember that?

REBECCA: Yes, Ma.

MRS. GIBBS: You look real nice, Rebecca. Pick up your feet.

ALL: Good-by.

> MRS. GIBBS *fills her apron with food for the chickens and comes down to the footlights.*

MRS. GIBBS: Here, chick, chick, chick.

No, go away, you. Go away.

Here, chick, chick, chick.

What's the matter with *you*? Fight, fight, fight,—that's all you do.

Hm . . . *you* don't belong to me. Where'd you come from?

She shakes her apron.

Oh, don't be so scared. Nobody's going to hurt you.

MRS. WEBB *is sitting on the bench by her trellis, stringing beans.*

Good morning, Myrtle. How's your cold?

MRS. WEBB: Well, I still get that tickling feeling in my throat. I told Charles I didn't know as I'd go to choir practice tonight. Wouldn't be any use.

MRS. GIBBS: Have you tried singing over your voice?

MRS. WEBB: Yes, but somehow I can't do that and stay on the key. While I'm resting myself I thought I'd string some of these beans.

MRS. GIBBS: (*Rolling up her sleeves as she crosses the stage for a chat.*) Let me help you. Beans have been good this year.

MRS. WEBB: I've decided to put up forty quarts if it kills me. The children say they hate 'em, but I notice they're able to get 'em down all winter.

Pause. Brief sound of chickens cackling.

MRS. GIBBS: Now, Myrtle. I've got to tell you something, because if I don't tell somebody I'll burst.

MRS. WEBB: Why, Julia Gibbs!

MRS. GIBBS: Here, give me some more of those beans. Myrtle, did one of those secondhand-furniture men from Boston come to see you last Friday?

MRS. WEBB: No-o.

MRS. GIBBS: Well, he called on me. First I thought he was a patient wantin' to see Dr. Gibbs. 'N he wormed his way into my parlor, and, Myrtle Webb, he offered me three hundred and fifty dollars for Grandmother Wentworth's highboy, as I'm sitting here!

MRS. WEBB: Why, Julia Gibbs!

MRS. GIBBS: He did! That old thing! Why, it was so big I

didn't know where to put it and I almost give it to Cousin Hester Wilcox.

MRS. WEBB: Well, you're going to take it, aren't you?

MRS. GIBBS: I don't know.

MRS. WEBB: You don't know—three hundred and fifty dollars! What's come over you?

MRS. GIBBS: Well, if I could get the Doctor to take the money and go away someplace on a real trip, I'd sell it like that.— Y'know, Myrtle, it's been the dream of my life to see Paris, France.—Oh, I don't know. It sounds crazy, I suppose, but for years I've been promising myself that if we ever had the chance—

MRS. WEBB: How does the Doctor feel about it?

MRS. GIBBS: Well, I did beat about the bush a little and said that if I got a legacy—that's the way I put it—I'd make him take me somewhere.

MRS. WEBB: M-m-m . . . What did he say?

MRS. GIBBS: You know how he is. I haven't heard a serious word out of him since I've known him. No, he said, it might make him discontented with Grover's Corners to go traipsin' about Europe; better let well enough alone, he says. Every two years he makes a trip to the battlefields of the Civil War and that's enough treat for anybody, he says.

MRS. WEBB: Well, Mr. Webb just *admires* the way Dr. Gibbs knows everything about the Civil War. Mr. Webb's a good mind to give up Napoleon and move over to the Civil War, only Dr. Gibbs being one of the greatest experts in the country just makes him despair.

MRS. GIBBS: It's a fact! Dr. Gibbs is never so happy as when he's at Antietam or Gettysburg. The times I've walked over those hills, Myrtle, stopping at every bush and pacing it all out, like we were going to buy it.

MRS. WEBB: Well, if that secondhand man's really serious about buyin' it, Julia, you sell it. And then you'll get to see Paris, all right. Just keep droppin' hints from time to time—that's how I got to see the Atlantic Ocean, y'know.

MRS. GIBBS: Oh, I'm sorry I mentioned it. Only it seems to me that once in your life before you die you ought to see a country where they don't talk in English and don't even want to.

The STAGE MANAGER *enters briskly from the right. He tips his hat to the ladies, who nod their heads.*

STAGE MANAGER: Thank you, ladies. Thank you very much.

MRS. GIBBS *and* MRS. WEBB *gather up their things, return into their homes and disappear.*

Now we're going to skip a few hours.
But first we want a little more information about the town, kind of a scientific account, you might say.
So I've asked Professor Willard of our State University to sketch in a few details of our past history here.
Is Professor Willard here?

PROFESSOR WILLARD, *a rural savant, pince-nez on a wide satin ribbon, enters from the right with some notes in his hand.*

May I introduce Professor Willard of our State University.
A few brief notes, thank you, Professor,—unfortunately our time is limited.

PROFESSOR WILLARD: Grover's Corners . . . let me see . . . Grover's Corners lies on the old Pleistocene granite of the Appalachian range. I may say it's some of the oldest land in the world. We're very proud of that. A shelf of Devonian basalt crosses it with vestiges of Mesozoic shale, and some sandstone outcroppings; but that's all more recent: two hundred, three hundred million years old.
Some highly interesting fossils have been found . . . I may say: unique fossils . . . two miles out of town, in Silas Peckham's cow pasture. They can be seen at the museum in our University at any time—that is, at any reasonable time. Shall I read some of Professor Gruber's notes on the meteorological situation—mean precipitation, et cetera?

STAGE MANAGER: Afraid we won't have time for that, Professor. We might have a few words on the history of man here.

PROFESSOR WILLARD: Yes . . . anthropological data: Early Amerindian stock. Cotahatchee tribes . . . no evidence before the tenth century of this era . . . hm . . . now entirely disappeared . . . possible traces in three families. Migration toward the end of the seventeenth century of

English brachiocephalic blue-eyed stock . . . for the most part. Since then some Slav and Mediterranean—

STAGE MANAGER: And the population, Professor Willard?

PROFESSOR WILLARD: Within the town limits: 2,640.

STAGE MANAGER: Just a moment, Professor.

He whispers into the professor's ear.

PROFESSOR WILLARD: Oh, yes, indeed?—The population, *at the moment*, is 2,642. The Postal District brings in 507 more, making a total of 3,149.—Mortality and birth rates: constant.—By MacPherson's gauge: 6.032.

STAGE MANAGER: Thank you very much, Professor. We're all very much obliged to you, I'm sure.

PROFESSOR WILLARD: Not at all, sir; not at all.

STAGE MANAGER: This way, Professor, and thank you again.

Exit PROFESSOR WILLARD.

Now the political and social report: Editor Webb.—Oh, Mr. Webb?

MRS. WEBB *appears at her back door.*

MRS. WEBB: He'll be here in a minute. . . . He just cut his hand while he was eatin' an apple.

STAGE MANAGER: Thank you, Mrs. Webb.

MRS. WEBB: Charles! Everybody's waitin'.

Exit MRS. WEBB.

STAGE MANAGER: Mr. Webb is Publisher and Editor of the Grover's Corners *Sentinel*. That's our local paper, y'know.

MR. WEBB *enters from his house, pulling on his coat. His finger is bound in a handkerchief.*

MR. WEBB: Well . . . I don't have to tell you that we're run here by a Board of Selectmen.—All males vote at the age of twenty-one. Women vote indirect. We're lower middle class: sprinkling of professional men . . . ten per cent illiterate laborers. Politically, we're eighty-six per cent Republicans; six per cent Democrats; four per cent Socialists; rest, indifferent. Religiously, we're eighty-five per cent Protestants; twelve per cent Catholics; rest, indifferent.

STAGE MANAGER: Have you any comments, Mr. Webb?

MR. WEBB: Very ordinary town, if you ask me. Little better behaved than most. Probably a lot duller.

But our young people here seem to like it well enough.
Ninety per cent of 'em graduating from high school settle
down right here to live—even when they've been away to
college.

STAGE MANAGER: Now, is there anyone in the audience who
would like to ask Editor Webb anything about the town?

WOMAN IN THE BALCONY: Is there much drinking in Grover's
Corners?

MR. WEBB: Well, ma'am, I wouldn't know what you'd call
much. Satiddy nights the farmhands meet down in Ellery
Greenough's stable and holler some. We've got one or two
town drunks, but they're always having remorses every time
an evangelist comes to town. No, ma'am, I'd say likker ain't
a regular thing in the home here, except in the medicine
chest. Right good for snake bite, y'know—always was.

BELLIGERENT MAN AT BACK OF AUDITORIUM: Is there no one
in town aware of—

STAGE MANAGER: Come forward, will you, where we can all
hear you— What were you saying?

BELLIGERENT MAN: Is there no one in town aware of social injustice and industrial inequality?

MR. WEBB: Oh, yes, everybody is—somethin' terrible. Seems
like they spend most of their time talking about who's rich
and who's poor.

BELLIGERENT MAN: Then why don't they do something
about it?

He withdraws without waiting for an answer.

MR. WEBB: Well, I dunno. . . . I guess we're all hunting like
everybody else for a way the diligent and sensible can rise to
the top and the lazy and quarrelsome can sink to the bottom.
But it ain't easy to find. Meanwhile, we do all we can to help
those that can't help themselves and those that can we leave
alone.—Are there any other questions?

LADY IN A BOX: Oh, Mr. Webb? Mr. Webb, is there any culture
or love of beauty in Grover's Corners?

MR. WEBB: Well, ma'am, there ain't much—not in the sense

you mean. Come to think of it, there's some girls that play
the piano at High School Commencement; but they ain't
happy about it. No, ma'am, there isn't much culture; but
maybe this is the place to tell you that we've got a lot of
pleasures of a kind here: we like the sun comin' up over the
mountain in the morning, and we all notice a good deal
about the birds. We pay a lot of attention to them. And we
watch the change of the seasons; yes, everybody knows
about them. But those other things—you're right, ma'am,
—there ain't much.—*Robinson Crusoe* and the Bible; and
Handel's "Largo," we all know that; and Whistler's
"Mother"—those are just about as far as we go.

LADY IN A BOX: So I thought. Thank you, Mr. Webb.

STAGE MANAGER: Thank you, Mr. Webb.

> MR. WEBB *retires.*

Now, we'll go back to the town. It's early afternoon. All
2,642 have had their dinners and all the dishes have been
washed.

> MR. WEBB, *having removed his coat, returns and starts
> pushing a lawn mower to and fro beside his house.*

There's an early-afternoon calm in our town: a buzzin' and
a hummin' from the school buildings; only a few buggies on
Main Street—the horses dozing at the hitching posts; you
all remember what it's like. Doc Gibbs is in his office, tapping people and making them say "ah." Mr. Webb's cuttin'
his lawn over there; one man in ten thinks it's a privilege to
push his own lawn mower.

No, sir. It's later than I thought. There are the children
coming home from school already.

> *Shrill girls' voices are heard, off left.* EMILY *comes along
> Main Street, carrying some books. There are some signs that
> she is imagining herself to be a lady of startling elegance.*

EMILY: I *can't*, Lois. I've got to go home and help my mother.
I *promised.*

MR. WEBB: Emily, walk simply. Who do you think you are today?

EMILY: Papa, you're terrible. One minute you tell me to stand up straight and the next minute you call me names. I just don't listen to you.

She gives him an abrupt kiss.

MR. WEBB: Golly, I never got a kiss from such a great lady before.

He goes out of sight. EMILY *leans over and picks some flowers by the gate of her house.*

GEORGE GIBBS *comes careening down Main Street. He is throwing a ball up to dizzying heights, and waiting to catch it again. This sometimes requires his taking six steps backward. He bumps into an* OLD LADY *invisible to us.*

GEORGE: Excuse me, Mrs. Forrest.

STAGE MANAGER: (*As Mrs. Forrest.*) Go out and play in the fields, young man. You got no business playing baseball on Main Street.

GEORGE: Awfully sorry, Mrs. Forrest.—Hello, Emily.

EMILY: H'lo.

GEORGE: You made a fine speech in class.

EMILY: Well . . . I was really ready to make a speech about the Monroe Doctrine, but at the last minute Miss Corcoran made me talk about the Louisiana Purchase instead. I worked an awful long time on both of them.

GEORGE: Gee, it's funny, Emily. From my window up there I can just see your head nights when you're doing your homework over in your room.

EMILY: Why, can you?

GEORGE: You certainly do stick to it, Emily. I don't see how you can sit still that long. I guess you like school.

EMILY: Well, I always feel it's something you have to go through.

GEORGE: Yeah.

EMILY: I don't mind it really. It passes the time.

GEORGE: Yeah.—Emily, what do you think? We might work out a kinda telegraph from your window to mine; and once in a while you could give me a kinda hint or two about one of those algebra problems. I don't mean the answers, Emily, of course not . . . just some little hint . . .

EMILY: Oh, I think *hints* are allowed.—So—ah—if you get

stuck, George, you whistle to me; and I'll give you some hints.

GEORGE: Emily, you're just naturally bright, I guess.

EMILY: I figure that it's just the way a person's born.

GEORGE: Yeah. But, you see, I want to be a farmer, and my Uncle Luke says whenever I'm ready I can come over and work on his farm and if I'm any good I can just gradually have it.

EMILY: You mean the house and everything?

Enter MRS. WEBB *with a large bowl and sits on the bench by her trellis.*

GEORGE: Yeah. Well, thanks . . . I better be getting out to the baseball field. Thanks for the talk, Emily.—Good afternoon, Mrs. Webb.

MRS. WEBB: Good afternoon, George.

GEORGE: So long, Emily.

EMILY: So long, George.

MRS. WEBB: Emily, come and help me string these beans for the winter. George Gibbs let himself have a real conversation, didn't he? Why, he's growing up. How old would George be?

EMILY: I don't know.

MRS. WEBB: Let's see. He must be almost sixteen.

EMILY: Mama, I made a speech in class today and I was very good.

MRS. WEBB: You must recite it to your father at supper. What was it about?

EMILY: The Louisiana Purchase. It was like silk off a spool. I'm going to make speeches all my life.—Mama, are these big enough?

MRS. WEBB: Try and get them a little bigger if you can.

EMILY: Mama, will you answer me a question, serious?

MRS. WEBB: Seriously, dear—not serious.

EMILY: Seriously,—will you?

MRS. WEBB: Of course, I will.

EMILY: Mama, am I good looking?

MRS. WEBB: Yes, of course you are. All my children have got good features; I'd be ashamed if they hadn't.

EMILY: Oh, Mama, that's not what I mean. What I mean is: am I *pretty?*

MRS. WEBB: I've already told you, yes. Now that's enough of that. You have a nice young pretty face. I never heard of such foolishness.

EMILY: Oh, Mama, you never tell us the truth about anything.

MRS. WEBB: I *am* telling you the truth.

EMILY: Mama, were you pretty?

MRS. WEBB: Yes, I was, if I do say it. I was the prettiest girl in town next to Mamie Cartwright.

EMILY: But, Mama, you've got to say *some*thing about me. Am I pretty enough . . . to get anybody . . . to get people interested in me?

MRS. WEBB: Emily, you make me tired. Now stop it. You're pretty enough for all normal purposes.—Come along now and bring that bowl with you.

EMILY: Oh, Mama, you're no help at all.

STAGE MANAGER: Thank you. Thank you! That'll do. We'll have to interrupt again here. Thank you, Mrs. Webb; thank you, Emily.

> MRS. WEBB *and* EMILY *withdraw.*

There are some more things we want to explore about this town.

> *He comes to the center of the stage. During the following speech the lights gradually dim to darkness, leaving only a spot on him.*

I think this is a good time to tell you that the Cartwright interests have just begun building a new bank in Grover's Corners—had to go to Vermont for the marble, sorry to say. And they've asked a friend of mine what they should put in the cornerstone for people to dig up . . . a thousand years from now. . . . Of course, they've put in a copy of the *New York Times* and a copy of Mr. Webb's *Sentinel.* . . . We're kind of interested in this because some scientific fellas have found a way of painting all that reading matter with a glue—a silicate glue—that'll make it keep a thousand—two thousand years.

We're putting in a Bible . . . and the Constitution of the United States—and a copy of William Shakespeare's plays. What do you say, folks? What do you think?

Y'know—Babylon once had two million people in it, and all we know about 'em is the names of the kings and some copies of wheat contracts . . . and contracts for the sale of slaves. Yet every night all those families sat down to supper, and the father came home from his work, and the smoke went up the chimney,—same as here. And even in Greece and Rome, all we know about the *real* life of the people is what we can piece together out of the joking poems and the comedies they wrote for the theatre back then.

So I'm going to have a copy of this play put in the cornerstone and the people a thousand years from now'll know a few simple facts about us—more than the Treaty of Versailles and the Lindbergh flight.

See what I mean?

So—people a thousand years from now—this is the way we were in the provinces north of New York at the beginning of the twentieth century.—This is the way we were: in our growing up and in our marrying and in our living and in our dying.

> *A choir partially concealed in the orchestra pit has begun singing "Blessed Be the Tie That Binds."*
>
> SIMON STIMSON *stands directing them.*
>
> *Two ladders have been pushed onto the stage; they serve as indication of the second story in the Gibbs and Webb houses.* GEORGE *and* EMILY *mount them, and apply themselves to their schoolwork.*
>
> DR. GIBBS *has entered and is seated in his kitchen reading.*

Well!—good deal of time's gone by. It's evening.

You can hear choir practice going on in the Congregational Church.

The children are at home doing their schoolwork.

The day's running down like a tired clock.

SIMON STIMSON: Now look here, everybody. Music come into the world to give pleasure.—Softer! Softer! Get it out of your heads that music's only good when it's loud. You leave loudness to the Methodists. You couldn't beat 'em, even if you wanted to. Now again. Tenors!

GEORGE: Hssst! Emily!

EMILY: Hello.

GEORGE: Hello!

EMILY: I can't work at all. The moonlight's so *terrible*.

GEORGE: Emily, did you get the third problem?

EMILY: Which?

GEORGE: The *third*?

EMILY: Why, yes, George—that's the easiest of them all.

GEORGE: I don't see it. Emily, can you give me a hint?

EMILY: I'll tell you one thing: the answer's in yards.

GEORGE: ! ! ! In yards? How do you mean?

EMILY: In *square* yards.

GEORGE: Oh . . . in square yards.

EMILY: Yes, George, don't you see?

GEORGE: Yeah.

EMILY: In square yards of *wallpaper*.

GEORGE: Wallpaper,—oh, I see. Thanks a lot, Emily.

EMILY: You're welcome. My, isn't the moonlight *terrible*? And choir practice going on.—I think if you hold your breath you can hear the train all the way to Contoocook. Hear it?

GEORGE: M-m-m— What do you know!

EMILY: Well, I guess I better go back and try to work.

GEORGE: Good night, Emily. And thanks.

EMILY: Good night, George.

SIMON STIMSON: Before I forget it: how many of you will be able to come in Tuesday afternoon and sing at Fred Hersey's wedding?—show your hands. That'll be fine; that'll be right nice. We'll do the same music we did for Jane Trowbridge's last month.
—Now we'll do: "Art Thou Weary; Art Thou Languid?" It's a question, ladies and gentlemen, make it talk. Ready.

DR. GIBBS: Oh, George, can you come down a minute?

GEORGE: Yes, Pa.

He descends the ladder.

DR. GIBBS: Make yourself comfortable, George; I'll only keep you a minute. George, how old are you?

GEORGE: I? I'm sixteen, almost seventeen.

DR. GIBBS: What do you want to do after school's over?

GEORGE: Why, you know, Pa. I want to be a farmer on Uncle Luke's farm.

DR. GIBBS: You'll be willing, will you, to get up early and milk and feed the stock . . . and you'll be able to hoe and hay all day?

GEORGE: Sure, I will. What are you . . . what do you mean, Pa?

DR. GIBBS: Well, George, while I was in my office today I heard a funny sound . . . and what do you think it was? It was your mother chopping wood. There you see your mother—getting up early; cooking meals all day long; washing and ironing;—and still she has to go out in the back yard and chop wood. I suppose she just got tired of asking you. She just gave up and decided it was easier to do it herself. And you eat her meals, and put on the clothes she keeps nice for you, and you run off and play baseball,—like she's some hired girl we keep around the house but that we don't like very much. Well, I knew all I had to do was call your attention to it. Here's a handkerchief, son. George, I've decided to raise your spending money twenty-five cents a week. Not, of course, for chopping wood for your mother, because that's a present you give her, but because you're getting older—and I imagine there are lots of things you must find to do with it.

GEORGE: Thanks, Pa.

DR. GIBBS: Let's see—tomorrow's your payday. You can count on it—Hmm. Probably Rebecca'll feel she ought to have some more too. Wonder what could have happened to your mother. Choir practice never was as late as this before.

GEORGE: It's only half past eight, Pa.

DR. GIBBS: I don't know why she's in that old choir. She hasn't any more voice than an old crow. . . . Traipsin' around the streets at this hour of the night . . . Just about time you retired, don't you think?

GEORGE: Yes, Pa.

   GEORGE *mounts to his place on the ladder.*
   Laughter and good nights can be heard on stage left and

presently MRS. GIBBS, MRS. SOAMES *and* MRS. WEBB *come down Main Street. When they arrive at the corner of the stage they stop.*

MRS. SOAMES: Good night, Martha. Good night, Mr. Foster.

MRS. WEBB: I'll tell Mr. Webb; I *know* he'll want to put it in the paper.

MRS. GIBBS: My, it's late!

MRS. SOAMES: Good night, Irma.

MRS. GIBBS: Real nice choir practice, wa'n't it? Myrtle Webb! Look at that moon, will you! Tsk-tsk-tsk. Potato weather, for sure.

They are silent a moment, gazing up at the moon.

MRS. SOAMES: Naturally I didn't want to say a word about it in front of those others, but now we're alone—really, it's the worst scandal that ever was in this town!

MRS. GIBBS: What?

MRS. SOAMES: Simon Stimson!

MRS. GIBBS: Now, Louella!

MRS. SOAMES: But, Julia! To have the organist of a church *drink* and *drunk* year after year. You know he was drunk tonight.

MRS. GIBBS: Now, Louella! We all know about Mr. Stimson, and we all know about the troubles he's been through, and Dr. Ferguson knows too, and if Dr. Ferguson keeps him on there in his job the only thing the rest of us can do is just not to notice it.

MRS. SOAMES: *Not to notice it!* But it's getting worse.

MRS. WEBB: No, it isn't, Louella. It's getting better. I've been in that choir twice as long as you have. It doesn't happen anywhere near so often. . . . My, I hate to go to bed on a night like this.—I better hurry. Those children'll be sitting up till all hours. Good night, Louella.

They all exchange good nights. She hurries downstage, enters her house and disappears.

MRS. GIBBS: Can you get home safe, Louella?

MRS. SOAMES: It's as bright as day. I can see Mr. Soames

scowling at the window now. You'd think we'd been to a
dance the way the menfolk carry on.

More good nights. MRS. GIBBS *arrives at her home and
passes through the trellis into the kitchen.*

MRS. GIBBS: Well, we had a real good time.

DR. GIBBS: You're late enough.

MRS. GIBBS: Why, Frank, it ain't any later 'n usual.

DR. GIBBS: And you stopping at the corner to gossip with a lot
of hens.

MRS. GIBBS: Now, Frank, don't be grouchy. Come out and
smell the heliotrope in the moonlight.

They stroll out arm in arm along the footlights.

Isn't that wonderful? What did you do all the time I was
away?

DR. GIBBS: Oh, I read—as usual. What were the girls gossiping
about tonight?

MRS. GIBBS: Well, believe me, Frank—there is something to
gossip about.

DR. GIBBS: Hmm! Simon Stimson far gone, was he?

MRS. GIBBS: Worst I've ever seen him. How'll that end, Frank?
Dr. Ferguson can't forgive him forever.

DR. GIBBS: I guess I know more about Simon Stimson's affairs
than anybody in this town. Some people ain't made for
small-town life. I don't know how that'll end; but there's
nothing we can do but just leave it alone. Come, get in.

MRS. GIBBS: No, not yet . . . Frank, I'm worried about
you.

DR. GIBBS: What are you worried about?

MRS. GIBBS: I think it's my duty to make plans for you to get a
real rest and change. And if I get that legacy, well, I'm going
to insist on it.

DR. GIBBS: Now, Julia, there's no sense in going over that
again.

MRS. GIBBS: Frank, you're just *unreasonable*!

DR. GIBBS: (*Starting into the house.*) Come on, Julia, it's getting
late. First thing you know you'll catch cold. I gave George a
piece of my mind tonight. I reckon you'll have your wood
chopped for a while anyway. No, no, start getting upstairs.

MRS. GIBBS: Oh, dear. There's always so many things to pick up, seems like. You know, Frank, Mrs. Fairchild always locks her front door every night. All those people up that part of town do.

DR. GIBBS: (*Blowing out the lamp.*) They're all getting citified, that's the trouble with them. They haven't got nothing fit to burgle and everybody knows it.

> *They disappear.*
> REBECCA *climbs up the ladder beside* GEORGE.

GEORGE: Get out, Rebecca. There's only room for one at this window. You're always spoiling everything.

REBECCA: Well, let me look just a minute.

GEORGE: Use your own window.

REBECCA: I did, but there's no moon there. . . . George, do you know what I think, do you? I think maybe the moon's getting nearer and nearer and there'll be a big 'splosion.

GEORGE: Rebecca, you don't know anything. If the moon were getting nearer, the guys that sit up all night with telescopes would see it first and they'd tell about it, and it'd be in all the newspapers.

REBECCA: George, is the moon shining on South America, Canada and half the whole world?

GEORGE: Well—prob'ly is.

> *The* STAGE MANAGER *strolls on.*
> *Pause. The sound of crickets is heard.*

STAGE MANAGER: Nine thirty. Most of the lights are out. No, there's Constable Warren trying a few doors on Main Street. And here comes Editor Webb, after putting his newspaper to bed.

> MR. WARREN, *an elderly policeman, comes along Main Street from the right,* MR. WEBB *from the left.*

MR. WEBB: Good evening, Bill.

CONSTABLE WARREN: Evenin', Mr. Webb.

MR. WEBB: Quite a moon!

CONSTABLE WARREN: Yepp.

MR. WEBB: All quiet tonight?

CONSTABLE WARREN: Simon Stimson is rollin' around a little.

Just saw his wife movin' out to hunt for him so I looked the other way—there he is now.

> SIMON STIMSON *comes down Main Street from the left, only a trace of unsteadiness in his walk.*

MR. WEBB: Good evening, Simon . . . Town seems to have settled down for the night pretty well. . . .

> SIMON STIMSON *comes up to him and pauses a moment and stares at him, swaying slightly.*

Good evening . . . Yes, most of the town's settled down for the night, Simon. . . . I guess we better do the same. Can I walk along a ways with you?

> SIMON STIMSON *continues on his way without a word and disappears at the right.*

Good night.

CONSTABLE WARREN: I don't know how that's goin' to end, Mr. Webb.

MR. WEBB: Well, he's seen a peck of trouble, one thing after another. . . . Oh, Bill . . . if you see my boy smoking cigarettes, just give him a word, will you? He thinks a lot of you, Bill.

CONSTABLE WARREN: I don't think he smokes no cigarettes, Mr. Webb. Leastways, not more'n two or three a year.

MR. WEBB: Hm . . . I hope not.—Well, good night, Bill.

CONSTABLE WARREN: Good night, Mr. Webb.

> *Exit.*

MR. WEBB: Who's that up there? Is that you, Myrtle?

EMILY: No, it's me, Papa.

MR. WEBB: Why aren't you in bed?

EMILY: I don't know. I just can't sleep yet, Papa. The moonlight's so *won*-derful. And the smell of Mrs. Gibbs' heliotrope. Can you smell it?

MR. WEBB: Hm . . . Yes. Haven't any troubles on your mind, have you, Emily?

EMILY: *Troubles*, Papa? *No.*

MR. WEBB: Well, enjoy yourself, but don't let your mother catch you. Good night, Emily.

EMILY: Good night, Papa.

> MR. WEBB *crosses into the house, whistling "Blessed Be the Tie That Binds" and disappears.*

REBECCA: I never told you about that letter Jane Crofut got from her minister when she was sick. He wrote Jane a letter and on the envelope the address was like this: It said: Jane Crofut; The Crofut Farm; Grover's Corners; Sutton County; New Hampshire; United States of America.

GEORGE: What's funny about that?

REBECCA: But listen, it's not finished: the United States of America; Continent of North America; Western Hemisphere; the Earth; the Solar System; the Universe; the Mind of God—that's what it said on the envelope.

GEORGE: What do you know!

REBECCA: And the postman brought it just the same.

GEORGE: What do you know!

STAGE MANAGER: That's the end of the First Act, friends. You can go and smoke now, those that smoke.

Act II

The tables and chairs of the two kitchens are still on the stage.
The ladders and the small bench have been withdrawn.

The STAGE MANAGER *has been at his accustomed place watching the audience return to its seats.*

STAGE MANAGER: Three years have gone by.

Yes, the sun's come up over a thousand times.

Summers and winters have cracked the mountains a little bit more and the rains have brought down some of the dirt.

Some babies that weren't even born before have begun talking regular sentences already; and a number of people who thought they were right young and spry have noticed that they can't bound up a flight of stairs like they used to, without their heart fluttering a little.

All that can happen in a thousand days.

Nature's been pushing and contriving in other ways, too: a number of young people fell in love and got married.

Yes, the mountain got bit away a few fractions of an inch; millions of gallons of water went by the mill; and here and there a new home was set up under a roof.

Almost everybody in the world gets married,—you know what I mean? In our town there aren't hardly any exceptions. Most everybody in the world climbs into their graves married.

The First Act was called the Daily Life. This act is called Love and Marriage. There's another act coming after this: I reckon you can guess what that's about.

So:

It's three years later. It's 1904.

It's July 7th, just after High School Commencement.

That's the time most of our young people jump up and get married.

Soon as they've passed their last examinations in solid geometry and Cicero's Orations, looks like they suddenly feel themselves fit to be married.

It's early morning. Only this time it's been raining. It's been pouring and thundering.

Mrs. Gibbs' garden, and Mrs. Webb's here: drenched.

All those bean poles and pea vines: drenched.

All yesterday over there on Main Street, the rain looked like curtains being blown along.

Hm . . . it may begin again any minute.

There! You can hear the 5:45 for Boston.

> MRS. GIBBS *and* MRS. WEBB *enter their kitchens and start the day as in the First Act.*

And there's Mrs. Gibbs and Mrs. Webb come down to make breakfast, just as though it were an ordinary day. I don't have to point out to the women in my audience that those ladies they see before them, both of those ladies cooked three meals a day—one of 'em for twenty years, the other for forty—and no summer vacation. They brought up two children apiece, washed, cleaned the house,—and *never a nervous breakdown.*

It's like what one of those Middle West poets said: You've got to love life to have life, and you've got to have life to love life. . . . It's what they call a vicious circle.

HOWIE NEWSOME: (*Off stage left.*) Giddap, Bessie!

STAGE MANAGER: Here comes Howie Newsome delivering the milk. And there's Si Crowell delivering the papers like his brother before him.

> SI CROWELL *has entered hurling imaginary newspapers into doorways;* HOWIE NEWSOME *has come along Main Street with Bessie.*

SI CROWELL: Morning, Howie.

HOWIE NEWSOME: Morning, Si.—Anything in the papers I ought to know?

SI CROWELL: Nothing much, except we're losing about the best baseball pitcher Grover's Corners ever had—George Gibbs.

HOWIE NEWSOME: Reckon he is.

SI CROWELL: He could hit and run bases, too.

HOWIE NEWSOME: Yep. Mighty fine ball player.—Whoa! Bessie! I guess I can stop and talk if I've a mind to!

SI CROWELL: I don't see how he could give up a thing like that just to get married. Would you, Howie?

HOWIE NEWSOME: Can't tell, Si. Never had no talent that way.

CONSTABLE WARREN enters. They exchange good mornings.

You're up early, Bill.

CONSTABLE WARREN: Seein' if there's anything I can do to prevent a flood. River's been risin' all night.

HOWIE NEWSOME: Si Crowell's all worked up here about George Gibbs' retiring from baseball.

CONSTABLE WARREN: Yes, sir; that's the way it goes. Back in '84 we had a player, Si—even George Gibbs couldn't touch him. Name of Hank Todd. Went down to Maine and become a parson. Wonderful ball player.—Howie, how does the weather look to you?

HOWIE NEWSOME: Oh, 'tain't bad. Think maybe it'll clear up for good.

CONSTABLE WARREN and SI CROWELL continue on their way.

HOWIE NEWSOME brings the milk first to Mrs. Gibbs' house. She meets him by the trellis.

MRS. GIBBS: Good morning, Howie. Do you think it's going to rain again?

HOWIE NEWSOME: Morning, Mrs. Gibbs. It rained so heavy, I think maybe it'll clear up.

MRS. GIBBS: Certainly hope it will.

HOWIE NEWSOME: How much did you want today?

MRS. GIBBS: I'm going to have a houseful of relations, Howie. Looks to me like I'll need three-a-milk and two-a-cream.

HOWIE NEWSOME: My wife says to tell you we both hope they'll be very happy, Mrs. Gibbs. Know they *will.*

MRS. GIBBS: Thanks a lot, Howie. Tell your wife I hope she gits there to the wedding.

HOWIE NEWSOME: Yes, she'll be there; she'll be there if she kin.

HOWIE NEWSOME crosses to Mrs. Webb's house.

Morning, Mrs. Webb.

MRS. WEBB: Oh, good morning, Mr. Newsome. I told you four quarts of milk, but I hope you can spare me another.

HOWIE NEWSOME: Yes'm . . . and the two of cream.

MRS. WEBB: Will it start raining again, Mr. Newsome?

HOWIE NEWSOME: Well. Just sayin' to Mrs. Gibbs as how it may lighten up. Mrs. Newsome told me to tell you as how we hope they'll both be very happy, Mrs. Webb. Know they *will.*

MRS. WEBB: Thank you, and thank Mrs. Newsome and we're counting on seeing you at the wedding.

HOWIE NEWSOME: Yes, Mrs. Webb. We hope to git there. Couldn't miss that. Come on, Bessie.

> *Exit* HOWIE NEWSOME.
>
> DR. GIBBS *descends in shirt sleeves, and sits down at his breakfast table.*

DR. GIBBS: Well, Ma, the day has come. You're losin' one of your chicks.

MRS. GIBBS: Frank Gibbs, don't you say another word. I feel like crying every minute. Sit down and drink your coffee.

DR. GIBBS: The groom's up shaving himself—only there ain't an awful lot to shave. Whistling and singing, like he's glad to leave us.—Every now and then he says "I do" to the mirror, but it don't sound convincing to me.

MRS. GIBBS: I declare, Frank, I don't know how he'll get along. I've arranged his clothes and seen to it he's put warm things on,—Frank! they're too *young.* Emily won't think of such things. He'll catch his death of cold within a week.

DR. GIBBS: I was remembering my wedding morning, Julia.

MRS. GIBBS: Now don't start that, Frank Gibbs.

DR. GIBBS: I was the scaredest young fella in the State of New Hampshire. I thought I'd make a mistake for sure. And when I saw you comin' down that aisle I thought you were the prettiest girl I'd ever seen, but the only trouble was that I'd never seen you before. There I was in the Congregational Church marryin' a total stranger.

MRS. GIBBS: And how do you think I felt!—Frank, weddings are perfectly awful things. Farces,—that's what they are! (*She puts a plate before him.*) Here, I've made something for you.

DR. GIBBS: Why, Julia Hersey—French toast!

MRS. GIBBS: 'Tain't hard to make and I had to do *some*thing.

Pause. DR. GIBBS *pours on the syrup.*

DR. GIBBS: How'd you sleep last night, Julia?

MRS. GIBBS: Well, I heard a lot of the hours struck off.

DR. GIBBS: Ye-e-s! I get a shock every time I think of George setting out to be a family man—that great gangling thing!—I tell you Julia, there's nothing so terrifying in the world as a *son*. The relation of father and son is the darndest, awkwardest—

MRS. GIBBS: Well, mother and daughter's no picnic, let me tell you.

DR. GIBBS: They'll have a lot of troubles, I suppose, but that's none of our business. Everybody has a right to their own troubles.

MRS. GIBBS: (*At the table, drinking her coffee, meditatively.*) Yes . . . people are meant to go through life two by two. 'Tain't natural to be lonesome.

Pause. DR. GIBBS *starts laughing.*

DR. GIBBS: Julia, do you know one of the things I was scared of when I married you?

MRS. GIBBS: Oh, go along with you!

DR. GIBBS: I was afraid we wouldn't have material for conversation more'n'd last us a few weeks.

Both laugh.

I was afraid we'd run out and eat our meals in silence, that's a fact.—Well, you and I been conversing for twenty years now without any noticeable barren spells.

MRS. GIBBS: Well,—good weather, bad weather—'tain't very choice, but I always find something to say. (*She goes to the foot of the stairs.*) Did you hear Rebecca stirring around upstairs?

DR. GIBBS: No. Only day of the year Rebecca hasn't been managing everybody's business up there. She's hiding in her room.—I got the impression she's crying.

MRS. GIBBS: Lord's sakes!—This has got to stop.—Rebecca! Rebecca! Come and get your breakfast.

GEORGE *comes rattling down the stairs, very brisk.*

GEORGE: Good morning, everybody. Only five more hours to live. (*Makes the gesture of cutting his throat, and a loud "k-k-k," and starts through the trellis.*)

MRS. GIBBS: George Gibbs, where are you going?

GEORGE: Just stepping across the grass to see my girl.

MRS. GIBBS: Now, George! You put on your overshoes. It's raining torrents. You don't go out of this house without you're prepared for it.

GEORGE: Aw, Ma. It's just a *step*!

MRS. GIBBS: George! You'll catch your death of cold and cough all through the service.

DR. GIBBS: George, do as your mother tells you!

> DR. GIBBS *goes upstairs.*
> GEORGE *returns reluctantly to the kitchen and pantomimes putting on overshoes.*

MRS. GIBBS: From tomorrow on you can kill yourself in all weathers, but while you're in my house you'll live wisely, thank you.—Maybe Mrs. Webb isn't used to callers at seven in the morning.—Here, take a cup of coffee first.

GEORGE: Be back in a minute. (*He crosses the stage, leaping over the puddles.*) Good morning, Mother Webb.

MRS. WEBB: Goodness! You frightened me!—Now, George, you can come in a minute out of the wet, but you know I can't ask you in.

GEORGE: Why not—?

MRS. WEBB: George, you know's well as I do: the groom can't see his bride on his wedding day, not until he sees her in church.

GEORGE: Aw!—that's just a superstition.—Good morning, Mr. Webb.

> *Enter* MR. WEBB.

MR. WEBB: Good morning, George.

GEORGE: Mr. Webb, you don't believe in that superstition, do you?

MR. WEBB: There's a lot of common sense in some superstitions, George. (*He sits at the table, facing right.*)

MRS. WEBB: Millions have folla'd it, George, and you don't want to be the first to fly in the face of custom.

GEORGE: How is Emily?

MRS. WEBB: She hasn't waked up yet. I haven't heard a sound out of her.

GEORGE: Emily's *asleep*!!!

MRS. WEBB: No wonder! We were up 'til all hours, sewing and packing. Now I'll tell you what I'll do; you set down here a minute with Mr. Webb and drink this cup of coffee; and I'll go upstairs and see she doesn't come down and surprise you. There's some bacon, too; but don't be long about it.

> *Exit* MRS. WEBB.
> *Embarrassed silence.*
> MR. WEBB *dunks doughnuts in his coffee.*
> *More silence.*

MR. WEBB: (*Suddenly and loudly.*) Well, George, how are you?

GEORGE: (*Startled, choking over his coffee.*) Oh, fine, I'm fine. (*Pause.*) Mr. Webb, what sense could there be in a superstition like that?

MR. WEBB: Well, you see,—on her wedding morning a girl's head's apt to be full of . . . clothes and one thing and another. Don't you think that's probably it?

GEORGE: Ye-e-s. I never thought of that.

MR. WEBB: A girl's apt to be a mite nervous on her wedding day.

> *Pause.*

GEORGE: I wish a fellow could get married without all that marching up and down.

MR. WEBB: Every man that's ever lived has felt that way about it, George; but it hasn't been any use. It's the womenfolk who've built up weddings, my boy. For a while now the women have it all their own. A man looks pretty small at a wedding, George. All those good women standing shoulder to shoulder making sure that the knot's tied in a mighty public way.

GEORGE: But . . . you *believe* in it, don't you, Mr. Webb?

MR. WEBB: (*With alacrity.*) Oh, yes; *oh, yes.* Don't you misunderstand me, my boy. Marriage is a wonderful thing,—wonderful thing. And don't you forget that, George.

GEORGE: No, sir.—Mr. Webb, how old were you when you got married?

MR. WEBB: Well, you see: I'd been to college and I'd taken a little time to get settled. But Mrs. Webb—she wasn't much older than what Emily is. Oh, age hasn't much to do with it, George,—not compared with . . . uh . . . other things.

GEORGE: What were you going to say, Mr. Webb?

MR. WEBB: Oh, I don't know.—Was I going to say something? (*Pause.*) George, I was thinking the other night of some advice my father gave me when I got married. Charles, he said, Charles, start out early showing who's boss, he said. Best thing to do is to give an order, even if it don't make sense; just so she'll learn to obey. And he said: if anything about your wife irritates you—her conversation, or anything—just get up and leave the house. That'll make it clear to her, he said. And, oh, yes! he said never, *never* let your wife know how much money you have, never.

GEORGE: Well, Mr. Webb . . . I don't think I could . . .

MR. WEBB: So I took the opposite of my father's advice and I've been happy ever since. And let that be a lesson to you, George, never to ask advice on personal matters.—George, are you going to raise chickens on your farm?

GEORGE: What?

MR. WEBB: Are you going to raise chickens on your farm?

GEORGE: Uncle Luke's never been much interested, but I thought—

MR. WEBB: A book came into my office the other day, George, on the Philo System of raising chickens. I want you to read it. I'm thinking of beginning in a small way in the back yard, and I'm going to put an incubator in the cellar—

Enter MRS. WEBB.

MRS. WEBB: Charles, are you talking about that old incubator again? I thought you two'd be talking about things worth while.

MR. WEBB: (*Bitingly.*) Well, Myrtle, if you want to give the boy some good advice, I'll go upstairs and leave you alone with him.

MRS. WEBB: (*Pulling* GEORGE *up.*) George, Emily's got to

come downstairs and eat her breakfast. She sends you her love but she doesn't want to lay eyes on you. Good-by.

GEORGE: Good-by.

> GEORGE *crosses the stage to his own home, bewildered and crestfallen. He slowly dodges a puddle and disappears into his house.*

MR. WEBB: Myrtle, I guess you don't know about that older superstition.

MRS. WEBB: What do you mean, Charles?

MR. WEBB: Since the cave men: no bridegroom should see his father-in-law on the day of the wedding, or near it. Now remember that.

> *Both leave the stage.*

STAGE MANAGER: Thank you very much, Mr. and Mrs. Webb. —Now I have to interrupt again here. You see, we want to know how all this began—this wedding, this plan to spend a lifetime together. I'm awfully interested in how big things like that begin.

You know how it is: you're twenty-one or twenty-two and you make some decisions; then whisssh! you're seventy: you've been a lawyer for fifty years, and that white-haired lady at your side has eaten over fifty thousand meals with you.

How do such things begin?

George and Emily are going to show you now the conversation they had when they first knew that . . . that . . . as the saying goes . . . they were meant for one another.

But before they do it I want you to try and remember what it was like to have been very young.

And particularly the days when you were first in love; when you were like a person sleepwalking, and you didn't quite see the street you were in, and didn't quite hear everything that was said to you.

You're just a little bit crazy. Will you remember that, please? Now they'll be coming out of high school at three o'clock. George has just been elected President of the Junior Class, and as it's June, that means he'll be President of the Senior

Class all next year. And Emily's just been elected Secretary and Treasurer.
I don't have to tell you how important that is.

He places a board across the backs of two chairs, which he takes from those at the Gibbs family's table. He brings two high stools from the wings and places them behind the board. Persons sitting on the stools will be facing the audience. This is the counter of Mr. Morgan's drugstore. The sounds of young people's voices are heard off left.

Yepp,—there they are coming down Main Street now.

EMILY, *carrying an armful of—imaginary—schoolbooks, comes along Main Street from the left.*

EMILY: I can't, Louise. I've got to go home. Good-by. Oh, Ernestine! Ernestine! Can you come over tonight and do Latin? Isn't that Cicero the worst thing—! Tell your mother you *have* to. G'by. G'by, Helen. G'by, Fred.

GEORGE, *also carrying books, catches up with her.*

GEORGE: Can I carry your books home for you, Emily?
EMILY: (*Coolly.*) Why . . . uh . . . Thank you. It isn't far. (*She gives them to him.*)
GEORGE: Excuse me a minute, Emily.—Say, Bob, if I'm a little late, start practice anyway. And give Herb some long high ones.
EMILY: Good-by, Lizzy.
GEORGE: Good-by, Lizzy.—I'm awfully glad you were elected, too, Emily.
EMILY: Thank you.

They have been standing on Main Street, almost against the back wall. They take the first steps toward the audience when GEORGE *stops and says:*

GEORGE: Emily, why are you mad at me?
EMILY: I'm not mad at you.
GEORGE: You've been treating me so funny lately.
EMILY: Well, since you ask me, I might as well say it right out, George,— (*She catches sight of a teacher passing.*) Good-by, Miss Corcoran.

GEORGE: Good-by, Miss Corcoran.—Wha—what is it?

EMILY: (*Not scoldingly; finding it difficult to say.*) I don't like the whole change that's come over you in the last year. I'm sorry if that hurts your feelings, but I've got to—tell the truth and shame the devil.

GEORGE: A *change*?—Wha—what do you mean?

EMILY: Well, up to a year ago I used to like you a lot. And I used to watch you as you did everything . . . because we'd been friends so long . . . and then you began spending all your time at *baseball* . . . and you never stopped to speak to anybody any more. Not even to your own family you didn't . . . and, George, it's a fact, you've got awful conceited and stuck-up, and all the girls say so. They may not say so to your face, but that's what they say about you behind your back, and it hurts me to hear them say it, but I've got to agree with them a little. I'm sorry if it hurts your feelings . . . but I can't be sorry I said it.

GEORGE: I . . . I'm glad you said it, Emily. I never thought that such a thing was happening to me. I guess it's hard for a fella not to have faults creep into his character.

They take a step or two in silence, then stand still in misery.

EMILY: I always expect a man to be perfect and I think he should be.

GEORGE: Oh . . . I don't think it's possible to be perfect, Emily.

EMILY: Well, my *father* is, and as far as I can see *your* father is. There's no reason on earth why you shouldn't be, too.

GEORGE: Well, I feel it's the other way round. That men aren't naturally good; but girls are.

EMILY: Well, you might as well know right now that I'm not perfect. It's not as easy for a girl to be perfect as a man, because we girls are more—more—nervous.—Now I'm sorry I said all that about you. I don't know what made me say it.

GEORGE: Emily,—

EMILY: Now I can see it's not the truth at all. And I suddenly feel that it isn't important, anyway.

GEORGE: Emily . . . would you like an ice-cream soda, or something, before you go home?

EMILY: Well, thank you. . . . I would.

They advance toward the audience and make an abrupt right turn, opening the door of Morgan's drugstore. Under strong emotion, EMILY *keeps her face down.* GEORGE *speaks to some passers-by.*

GEORGE: Hello, Stew,—how are you?—Good afternoon, Mrs. Slocum.

The STAGE MANAGER, *wearing spectacles and assuming the role of Mr. Morgan, enters abruptly from the right and stands between the audience and the counter of his soda fountain.*

STAGE MANAGER: Hello, George. Hello, Emily.—What'll you have?—Why, Emily Webb,—what you been crying about?

GEORGE: (*He gropes for an explanation.*) She . . . she just got an awful scare, Mr. Morgan. She almost got run over by that hardware-store wagon. Everybody says that Tom Huckins drives like a crazy man.

STAGE MANAGER: (*Drawing a drink of water.*) Well, now! You take a drink of water, Emily. You look all shook up. I tell you, you've got to look both ways before you cross Main Street these days. Gets worse every year.—What'll you have?

EMILY: I'll have a strawberry phosphate, thank you, Mr. Morgan.

GEORGE: No, no, Emily. Have an ice-cream soda with me. Two strawberry ice-cream sodas, Mr. Morgan.

STAGE MANAGER: (*Working the faucets.*) Two strawberry ice-cream sodas, yes sir. Yes, sir. There are a hundred and twenty-five horses in Grover's Corners this minute I'm talking to you. State Inspector was in here yesterday. And now they're bringing in these auto-mo-biles, the best thing to do is to just stay home. Why, I can remember when a dog could go to sleep all day in the middle of Main Street and nothing come along to disturb him. (*He sets the imaginary glasses before them.*) There they are. Enjoy 'em. (*He sees a customer, right.*) Yes, Mrs. Ellis. What can I do for you? (*He goes out right.*)

EMILY: They're so expensive.

GEORGE: No, no,—don't you think of that. We're celebrating our election. And then do you know what else I'm celebrating?

EMILY: N-no.

GEORGE: I'm celebrating because I've got a friend who tells me all the things that ought to be told me.

EMILY: George, *please* don't think of that. I don't know why I said it. It's not true. You're—

GEORGE: No, Emily, you stick to it. I'm glad you spoke to me like you did. But you'll *see*: I'm going to change so quick— you bet I'm going to change. And, Emily, I want to ask you a favor.

EMILY: What?

GEORGE: Emily, if I go away to State Agriculture College next year, will you write me a letter once in a while?

EMILY: I certainly will. I certainly will, George . . .

Pause. They start sipping the sodas through the straws.

It certainly seems like being away three years you'd get out of touch with things. Maybe letters from Grover's Corners wouldn't be so interesting after a while. Grover's Corners isn't a very important place when you think of all—New Hampshire; but I think it's a very nice town.

GEORGE: The day wouldn't come when I wouldn't want to know everything that's happening here. I know *that's* true, Emily.

EMILY: Well, I'll try to make my letters interesting.

Pause.

GEORGE: Y'know, Emily, whenever I meet a farmer I ask him if he thinks it's important to go to Agriculture School to be a good farmer.

EMILY: Why, George—

GEORGE: Yeah, and some of them say that it's even a waste of time. You can get all those things, anyway, out of the pamphlets the government sends out. And Uncle Luke's getting old,—he's about ready for me to start in taking over his farm tomorrow, if I could.

EMILY: My!

GEORGE: And, like you say, being gone all that time . . . in other places and meeting other people . . . Gosh, if anything like that can happen I don't want to go away. I guess new people aren't any better than old ones. I'll bet they almost never are. Emily . . . I feel that you're as good a friend as I've got. I don't need to go and meet the people in other towns.

EMILY: But, George, maybe it's very important for you to go and learn all that about—cattle judging and soils and those things. . . . Of course, I don't know.

GEORGE: (*After a pause, very seriously.*) Emily, I'm going to make up my mind right now. I won't go. I'll tell Pa about it tonight.

EMILY: Why, George, I don't see why you have to decide right now. It's a whole year away.

GEORGE: Emily, I'm glad you spoke to me about that . . . that fault in my character. What you said was right; but there was *one* thing wrong in it, and that was when you said that for a year I wasn't noticing people, and . . . you, for instance. Why, you say you were watching me when I did everything . . . I was doing the same about you all the time. Why, sure,—I always thought about you as one of the chief people I thought about. I always made sure where you were sitting on the bleachers, and who you were with, and for three days now I've been trying to walk home with you; but something's always got in the way. Yesterday I was standing over against the wall waiting for you, and you walked home with *Miss Corcoran*.

EMILY: George! . . . Life's awful funny! How could I have known that? Why, I thought—

GEORGE: Listen, Emily, I'm going to tell you why I'm not going to Agriculture School. I think that once you've found a person that you're very fond of . . . I mean a person who's fond of you, too, and likes you enough to be interested in your character . . . Well, I think that's just as important as college is, and even more so. That's what I think.

EMILY: I think it's awfully important, too.

GEORGE: Emily.

EMILY: Y-yes, George.

GEORGE: Emily, if I *do* improve and make a big change . . . would you be . . . I mean: *could* you be . . .

EMILY: I . . . I am now; I always have been.

GEORGE: (*Pause.*) So I guess this is an important talk we've been having.

EMILY: Yes . . . yes.

GEORGE: (*Takes a deep breath and straightens his back.*) Wait just a minute and I'll walk you home.

> *With mounting alarm he digs into his pockets for the money. The* STAGE MANAGER *enters, right.*
> GEORGE, *deeply embarrassed, but direct, says to him:*

Mr. Morgan, I'll have to go home and get the money to pay you for this. It'll only take me a minute.

STAGE MANAGER: (*Pretending to be affronted.*) What's that? George Gibbs, do you mean to tell me—!

GEORGE: Yes, but I had reasons, Mr. Morgan.—Look, here's my gold watch to keep until I come back with the money.

STAGE MANAGER: That's all right. Keep your watch. I'll trust you.

GEORGE: I'll be back in five minutes.

STAGE MANAGER: I'll trust you ten years, George,—not a day over.—Got all over your shock, Emily?

EMILY: Yes, thank you, Mr. Morgan. It was nothing.

GEORGE: (*Taking up the books from the counter.*) I'm ready.

> *They walk in grave silence across the stage and pass through the trellis at the Webbs' back door and disappear.*
> *The* STAGE MANAGER *watches them go out, then turns to the audience, removing his spectacles.*

STAGE MANAGER: Well,— (*He claps his hands as a signal.*) Now we're ready to get on with the wedding.

> *He stands waiting while the set is prepared for the next scene.*
> STAGEHANDS *remove the chairs, tables and trellises from the Gibbs and Webb houses.*
> *They arrange the pews for the church in the center of the stage. The congregation will sit facing the back wall. The aisle of the church starts at the center of the back wall and comes toward the audience.*
> *A small platform is placed against the back wall on which the* STAGE MANAGER *will stand later, playing the minister. The image of a stained-glass window is cast from a lantern slide upon the back wall.*
> *When all is ready the* STAGE MANAGER *strolls to the center*

*of the stage, down front, and, musingly, addresses the audi-
ence.*

There are a lot of things to be said about a wedding; there
are a lot of thoughts that go on during a wedding.

We can't get them all into one wedding, naturally, and especially not into a wedding at Grover's Corners, where they're
awfully plain and short.

In this wedding I play the minister. That gives me the right
to say a few more things about it.

For a while now, the play gets pretty serious.

Y'see, some churches say that marriage is a sacrament. I
don't quite know what that means, but I can guess. Like
Mrs. Gibbs said a few minutes ago: People were made to live
two-by-two.

This is a good wedding, but people are so put together that
even at a good wedding there's a lot of confusion way down
deep in people's minds and we thought that that ought to
be in our play, too.

The real hero of this scene isn't on the stage at all, and you
know who that is. It's like what one of those European fellas
said: every child born into the world is nature's attempt
to make a perfect human being. Well, we've seen nature
pushing and contriving for some time now. We all know that
nature's interested in quantity; but I think she's interested
in quality, too,—that's why I'm in the ministry.

And don't forget all the other witnesses at this wedding,—
the ancestors. Millions of them. Most of them set out to live
two-by-two, also. Millions of them.

Well, that's all my sermon. 'Twan't very long, anyway.

> *The organ starts playing Handel's "Largo."*
> *The congregation streams into the church and sits in silence.*
> *Church bells are heard.*
> MRS. GIBBS *sits in the front row, the first seat on the aisle,*
> *the right section; next to her are* REBECCA *and* DR. GIBBS.
> *Across the aisle* MRS. WEBB, WALLY *and* MR. WEBB. *A small*
> *choir takes its place, facing the audience under the stained-*
> *glass window.*
> MRS. WEBB, *on the way to her place, turns back and speaks*
> *to the audience.*

MRS. WEBB: I don't know why on earth I should be crying. I
suppose there's nothing to cry about. It came over me at
breakfast this morning; there was Emily eating her breakfast
as she's done for seventeen years and now she's going off to
eat it in someone else's house. I suppose that's it.

And Emily! She suddenly said: I can't eat another mouthful,
and she put her head down on the table and *she* cried. (*She
starts toward her seat in the church, but turns back and adds:*)
Oh, I've got to say it: you know, there's something downright cruel about sending our girls out into marriage this way.
I hope some of her girl friends have told her a thing or two.
It's cruel, I know, but I couldn't bring myself to say anything. I went into it blind as a bat myself. (*In half-amused
exasperation.*) The whole world's wrong, that's what's the
matter.

There they come.

> (*She hurries to her place in the pew.*)
> GEORGE *starts to come down the right aisle of the theatre,
> through the audience.*
> *Suddenly* THREE MEMBERS *of his baseball team appear by
> the right proscenium pillar and start whistling and cat-
> calling to him. They are dressed for the ball field.*

THE BASEBALL PLAYERS: Eh, George, George! Hast—yaow!
Look at him, fellas—he looks scared to death. Yaow! George,
don't look so innocent, you old geezer. We know what
you're thinking. Don't disgrace the team, big boy. Whoo-
oo-oo.

STAGE MANAGER: All right! All right! That'll do. That's
enough of that.

> *Smiling, he pushes them off the stage. They lean back to shout
> a few more catcalls.*

There used to be an awful lot of that kind of thing at weddings in the old days,—Rome, and later. We're more civilized now,—so they say.

> *The choir starts singing "Love Divine, All Love Excelling—."*
> GEORGE *has reached the stage. He stares at the congrega-
> tion a moment, then takes a few steps of withdrawal,*

toward the right proscenium pillar. His mother, from the
front row, seems to have felt his confusion. She leaves her seat
and comes down the aisle quickly to him.

MRS. GIBBS: George! George! What's the matter?

GEORGE: Ma, I don't want to grow old. Why's everybody
pushing me so?

MRS. GIBBS: Why, George . . . you wanted it.

GEORGE: No, Ma, listen to me—

MRS. GIBBS: No, no, George,—you're a man now.

GEORGE: Listen, Ma,—for the last time I ask you . . . All I
want to do is to be a fella—

MRS. GIBBS: George! If anyone should hear you! Now stop.
Why, I'm ashamed of you!

GEORGE: (*He comes to himself and looks over the scene.*) What?
Where's Emily?

MRS. GIBBS: (*Relieved.*) George! You gave me such a turn.

GEORGE: Cheer up, Ma. I'm getting married.

MRS. GIBBS: Let me catch my breath a minute.

GEORGE: (*Comforting her.*) Now, Ma, you save Thursday
nights. Emily and I are coming over to dinner every Thursday night . . . you'll see. Ma, what are you crying for?
Come on; we've got to get ready for this.

> MRS. GIBBS, *mastering her emotion, fixes his tie and whis-*
> *pers to him.*
> In the meantime, EMILY, *in white and wearing her wed-*
> *ding veil, has come through the audience and mounted onto*
> *the stage. She too draws back, frightened, when she sees the*
> *congregation in the church. The choir begins: "Blessed Be the*
> *Tie That Binds."*

EMILY: I never felt so alone in my whole life. And George over
there, looking so . . . ! *I hate* him. I wish I were dead.
Papa! Papa!

MR. WEBB: (*Leaves his seat in the pews and comes toward her*
anxiously.) Emily! Emily! Now don't get upset. . . .

EMILY: But, Papa,—I don't want to get married. . . .

MR. WEBB: Sh—sh—Emily. Everything's all right.

EMILY: Why can't I stay for a while just as I am? Let's go
away,—

MR. WEBB: No, no, Emily. Now stop and think a minute.

EMILY: Don't you remember that you used to say,—all the time you used to say—all the time: that I was *your* girl! There must be lots of places we can go to. I'll work for you. I could keep house.

MR. WEBB: Sh . . . You mustn't think of such things. You're just nervous, Emily. (*He turns and calls:*) George! George! Will you come here a minute? (*He leads her toward George.*) Why you're marrying the best young fellow in the world. George is a fine fellow.

EMILY: But Papa,—

> MRS. GIBBS *returns unobtrusively to her seat.*
> MR. WEBB *has one arm around his daughter. He places his hand on* GEORGE'S *shoulder.*

MR. WEBB: I'm giving away my daughter, George. Do you think you can take care of her?

GEORGE: Mr. Webb, I want to . . . I want to try. Emily, I'm going to do my best. I love you, Emily. I need you.

EMILY: Well, if you love me, help me. All I want is someone to love me.

GEORGE: I will, Emily. Emily, I'll try.

EMILY: And I mean for *ever.* Do you hear? For ever and ever.

> *They fall into each other's arms.*
> *The March from* Lohengrin *is heard.*
> *The* STAGE MANAGER, *as* CLERGYMAN, *stands on the box, up center.*

MR. WEBB: Come, they're waiting for us. Now you know it'll be all right. Come, quick.

> GEORGE *slips away and takes his place beside the* STAGE MANAGER-CLERGYMAN.
> EMILY *proceeds up the aisle on her father's arm.*

STAGE MANAGER: Do you, George, take this woman, Emily, to be your wedded wife, to have . . .

> MRS. SOAMES *has been sitting in the last row of the congregation.*

*She now turns to her neighbors and speaks in a shrill voice.
Her chatter drowns out the rest of the clergyman's words.*

MRS. SOAMES: Perfectly lovely wedding! Loveliest wedding I
  ever saw. Oh, I do love a good wedding, don't you? Doesn't
  she make a lovely bride?
GEORGE: I do.
STAGE MANAGER: Do you, Emily, take this man, George, to be
  your wedded husband,—

Again his further words are covered by those of MRS. SOAMES.

MRS. SOAMES: Don't know *when* I've seen such a lovely wedding. But I always cry. Don't know why it is, but I always
  cry. I just like to see young people happy, don't you? Oh, I
  think it's lovely.

  The ring.
  The kiss.
  The stage is suddenly arrested into silent tableau.
  The STAGE MANAGER, *his eyes on the distance, as though to
  himself:*

STAGE MANAGER: I've married over two hundred couples in
  my day.
  Do I believe in it?
  I don't know.
  M. . . . marries N. . . . millions of them.
  The cottage, the go-cart, the Sunday-afternoon drives in the
  Ford, the first rheumatism, the grandchildren, the second
  rheumatism, the deathbed, the reading of the will,— (*He
  now looks at the audience for the first time, with a warm smile
  that removes any sense of cynicism from the next line.*)
  Once in a thousand times it's interesting.
  —Well, let's have Mendelssohn's "Wedding March"!

  The organ picks up the March.
  The BRIDE *and* GROOM *come down the aisle, radiant, but
  trying to be very dignified.*

MRS. SOAMES: Aren't they a lovely couple? Oh, I've never been
  to such a nice wedding. I'm sure they'll be happy. I always

say: *happiness*, that's the great thing! The important thing is to be happy.

> *The* BRIDE *and* GROOM *reach the steps leading into the audience. A bright light is thrown upon them. They descend into the auditorium and run up the aisle joyously.*

STAGE MANAGER: That's all the Second Act, folks. Ten minutes' intermission.

CURTAIN

Act III

During the intermission the audience has seen the STAGE-HANDS *arranging the stage. On the right-hand side, a little right of the center, ten or twelve ordinary chairs have been placed in three openly spaced rows facing the audience.*

These are graves in the cemetery.

Toward the end of the intermission the ACTORS *enter and take their places. The front row contains: toward the center of the stage, an empty chair; then* MRS. GIBBS; SIMON STIMSON.

The second row contains, among others, MRS. SOAMES.

The third row has WALLY WEBB.

The dead do not turn their heads or their eyes to right or left, but they sit in a quiet without stiffness. When they speak their tone is matter-of-fact, without sentimentality and, above all, without lugubriousness.

The STAGE MANAGER *takes his accustomed place and waits for the house lights to go down.*

STAGE MANAGER: This time nine years have gone by, friends—summer, 1913.

Gradual changes in Grover's Corners. Horses are getting rarer. Farmers coming into town in Fords.

Everybody locks their house doors now at night. Ain't been any burglars in town yet, but everybody's heard about 'em. You'd be surprised, though—on the whole, things don't change much around here.

This is certainly an important part of Grover's Corners. It's on a hilltop—a windy hilltop—lots of sky, lots of clouds,—often lots of sun and moon and stars.

You come up here, on a fine afternoon and you can see range on range of hills—awful blue they are—up there by Lake Sunapee and Lake Winnipesaukee . . . and way up, if you've got a glass, you can see the White Mountains and Mt. Washington—where North Conway and Conway is. And, of course, our favorite mountain, Mt. Monadnock, 's right here—and all these towns that lie around it: Jaffrey, 'n East Jaffrey, 'n Peterborough, 'n Dublin; and (*Then pointing down in the audience.*) there, quite a ways down, is Grover's Corners.

Yes, beautiful spot up here. Mountain laurel and li-lacks. I often wonder why people like to be buried in Woodlawn and Brooklyn when they might pass the same time up here in New Hampshire.

Over there—(*Pointing to stage left.*) are the old stones,—1670, 1680. Strong-minded people that come a long way to be independent. Summer people walk around there laughing at the funny words on the tombstones . . . it don't do any harm. And genealogists come up from Boston—get paid by city people for looking up their ancestors. They want to make sure they're Daughters of the American Revolution and of the *Mayflower*. . . . Well, I guess that don't do any harm, either. Wherever you come near the human race, there's layers and layers of nonsense. . . .

Over there are some Civil War veterans. Iron flags on their graves . . . New Hampshire boys . . . had a notion that the Union ought to be kept together, though they'd never seen more than fifty miles of it themselves. All they knew was the name, friends—the United States of America. The United States of America. And they went and died about it. This here is the new part of the cemetery. Here's your friend Mrs. Gibbs. 'N let me see—Here's Mr. Stimson, organist at the Congregational Church. And Mrs. Soames who enjoyed the wedding so—you remember? Oh, and a lot of others. And Editor Webb's boy, Wallace, whose appendix burst while he was on a Boy Scout trip to Crawford Notch.

Yes, an awful lot of sorrow has sort of quieted down up here. People just wild with grief have brought their relatives up to this hill. We all know how it is . . . and then time . . . and sunny days . . . and rainy days . . . 'n snow . . . We're all glad they're in a beautiful place and we're coming up here ourselves when our fit's over.

Now there are some things we all know, but we don't take'm out and look at'm very often. We all know that *something* is eternal. And it ain't houses and it ain't names, and it ain't earth, and it ain't even the stars . . . everybody knows in their bones that *something* is eternal, and that something has to do with human beings. All the greatest people ever lived have been telling us that for five thousand years and yet you'd be surprised how people are always losing hold of it. There's something way down deep that's eternal about every human being. (*Pause.*) You know as well as I do that the dead don't stay interested in us living people for very long. Gradually, gradually, they lose hold of the earth . . . and the ambitions they had . . . and the pleasures they had . . . and the things they suffered . . . and the people they loved.

They get weaned away from earth—that's the way I put it,—weaned away.

And they stay here while the earth part of 'em burns away, burns out; and all that time they slowly get indifferent to what's goin' on in Grover's Corners.

They're waitin'. They're waitin' for something that they feel is comin'. Something important, and great. Aren't they waitin' for the eternal part in them to come out clear?

Some of the things they're going to say maybe'll hurt your feelings—but that's the way it is: mother 'n daughter . . . husband 'n wife . . . enemy 'n enemy . . . money 'n miser . . . all those terribly important things kind of grow pale around here. And what's left when memory's gone, and your identity, Mrs. Smith? (*He looks at the audience a minute, then turns to the stage.*)

Well! There are some *living* people. There's Joe Stoddard, our undertaker, supervising a new-made grave. And here comes a Grover's Corners boy, that left town to go out West.

> JOE STODDARD *has hovered about in the background.* SAM CRAIG *enters left, wiping his forehead from the exertion. He carries an umbrella and strolls front.*

SAM CRAIG: Good afternoon, Joe Stoddard.

JOE STODDARD: Good afternoon, good afternoon. Let me see now: do I know you?

SAM CRAIG: I'm Sam Craig.

JOE STODDARD: Gracious sakes' alive! Of all people! I should'a knowed you'd be back for the funeral. You've been away a long time, Sam.

SAM CRAIG: Yes, I've been away over twelve years. I'm in

business out in Buffalo now, Joe. But I was in the East when I got news of my cousin's death, so I thought I'd combine things a little and come and see the old home. You look well.

JOE STODDARD: Yes, yes, can't complain. Very sad, our journey today, Samuel.

SAM CRAIG: Yes.

JOE STODDARD: Yes, yes. I always say I hate to supervise when a young person is taken. They'll be here in a few minutes now. I had to come here early today—my son's supervisin' at the home.

SAM CRAIG: (*Reading stones.*) Old Farmer McCarty, I used to do chores for him—after school. He had the lumbago.

JOE STODDARD: Yes, we brought Farmer McCarty here a number of years ago now.

SAM CRAIG: (*Staring at Mrs. Gibbs' knees.*) Why, this is my Aunt Julia . . . I'd forgotten that she'd . . . of course, of course.

JOE STODDARD: Yes, Doc Gibbs lost his wife two-three years ago . . . about this time. And today's another pretty bad blow for him, too.

MRS. GIBBS: (*To Simon Stimson: in an even voice.*) That's my sister Carey's boy, Sam . . . Sam Craig.

SIMON STIMSON: I'm always uncomfortable when *they're* around.

MRS. GIBBS: Simon.

SAM CRAIG: Do they choose their own verses much, Joe?

JOE STODDARD: No . . . not usual. Mostly the bereaved pick a verse.

SAM CRAIG: Doesn't sound like Aunt Julia. There aren't many of those Hersey sisters left now. Let me see: where are . . . I wanted to look at my father's and mother's . . .

JOE STODDARD: Over there with the Craigs . . . Avenue F.

SAM CRAIG: (*Reading Simon Stimson's epitaph.*) He was organist at church, wasn't he?—Hm, drank a lot, we used to say.

JOE STODDARD: Nobody was supposed to know about it. He'd seen a peck of trouble. (*Behind his hand.*) Took his own life, y' know?

SAM CRAIG: Oh, did he?

JOE STODDARD: Hung himself in the attic. They tried to hush

it up, but of course it got around. He chose his own epy-
taph. You can see it there. It ain't a verse exactly.

SAM CRAIG: Why, it's just some notes of music—what is it?

JOE STODDARD: Oh, I wouldn't know. It was wrote up in the
Boston papers at the time.

SAM CRAIG: Joe, what did she die of?

JOE STODDARD: Who?

SAM CRAIG: My cousin.

JOE STODDARD: Oh, didn't you know? Had some trouble
bringing a baby into the world. 'Twas her second, though.
There's a little boy 'bout four years old.

SAM CRAIG: (*Opening his umbrella.*) The grave's going to be
over there?

JOE STODDARD: Yes, there ain't much more room over here
among the Gibbses, so they're opening up a whole new
Gibbs section over by Avenue B. You'll excuse me now. I see
they're comin'.

*From left to center, at the back of the stage, comes a proces-
sion.* FOUR MEN *carry a casket, invisible to us. All the rest
are under umbrellas. One can vaguely see:* DR. GIBBS,
GEORGE, *the* WEBBS, *etc. They gather about a grave in the
back center of the stage, a little to the left of center.*

MRS. SOAMES: Who is it, Julia?

MRS. GIBBS: (*Without raising her eyes.*) My daughter-in-law,
Emily Webb.

MRS. SOAMES: (*A little surprised, but no emotion.*) Well, I declare! The road up here must have been awful muddy. What
did she die of, Julia?

MRS. GIBBS: In childbirth.

MRS. SOAMES: Childbirth. (*Almost with a laugh.*) I'd forgotten
all about that. My, wasn't life awful— (*With a sigh.*) and
wonderful.

SIMON STIMSON: (*With a sideways glance.*) Wonderful, was it?

MRS. GIBBS: Simon! Now, remember!

MRS. SOAMES: I remember Emily's wedding. Wasn't it a lovely
wedding! And I remember her reading the class poem at
Graduation Exercises. Emily was one of the brightest girls
ever graduated from High School. I've heard Principal

Wilkins say so time after time. I called on them at their new farm, just before I died. Perfectly beautiful farm.

A WOMAN FROM AMONG THE DEAD: It's on the same road we lived on.

A MAN AMONG THE DEAD: Yepp, right smart farm.

> *They subside. The group by the grave starts singing "Blessed Be the Tie That Binds."*

A WOMAN AMONG THE DEAD: I always liked that hymn. I was hopin' they'd sing a hymn.

> *Pause. Suddenly* EMILY *appears from among the umbrellas. She is wearing a white dress. Her hair is down her back and tied by a white ribbon like a little girl. She comes slowly, gazing wonderingly at the dead, a little dazed.*
>
> *She stops halfway and smiles faintly. After looking at the mourners for a moment, she walks slowly to the vacant chair beside Mrs. Gibbs and sits down.*

EMILY: (*To them all, quietly, smiling.*) Hello.

MRS. SOAMES: Hello, Emily.

A MAN AMONG THE DEAD: Hello, M's Gibbs.

EMILY: (*Warmly.*) Hello, Mother Gibbs.

MRS. GIBBS: Emily.

EMILY: Hello. (*With surprise.*) It's raining. (*Her eyes drift back to the funeral company.*)

MRS. GIBBS: Yes . . . They'll be gone soon, dear. Just rest yourself.

EMILY: It seems thousands and thousands of years since I . . . Papa remembered that that was my favorite hymn.

Oh, I wish I'd been here a long time. I don't like being new here.—How do you do, Mr. Stimson?

SIMON STIMSON: How do you do, Emily.

> EMILY *continues to look about her with a wondering smile; as though to shut out from her mind the thought of the funeral company she starts speaking to Mrs. Gibbs with a touch of nervousness.*

EMILY: Mother Gibbs, George and I have made that farm into just the best place you ever saw. We thought of you all the time. We wanted to show you the new barn and a great long ce-ment drinking fountain for the stock. We bought that out of the money you left us.

MRS. GIBBS: I did?

EMILY: Don't you remember, Mother Gibbs—the legacy you left us? Why, it was over three hundred and fifty dollars.

MRS. GIBBS: Yes, yes, Emily.

EMILY: Well, there's a patent device on the drinking fountain so that it never overflows, Mother Gibbs, and it never sinks below a certain mark they have there. It's fine. (*Her voice trails off and her eyes return to the funeral group.*) It won't be the same to George without me, but it's a lovely farm. (*Suddenly she looks directly at Mrs. Gibbs.*) Live people don't understand, do they?

MRS. GIBBS: No, dear—not very much.

EMILY: They're sort of shut up in little boxes, aren't they? I feel as though I knew them last a thousand years ago . . . My boy is spending the day at Mrs. Carter's. (*She sees* MR. CARTER *among the dead.*) Oh, Mr. Carter, my little boy is spending the day at your house.

MR. CARTER: Is he?

EMILY: Yes, he loves it there.—Mother Gibbs, we have a Ford, too. Never gives any trouble. I don't drive, though. Mother Gibbs, when does this feeling go away?—Of being . . . one of *them*? How long does it . . . ?

MRS. GIBBS: Sh! dear. Just wait and be patient.

EMILY: (*With a sigh.*) I know.—Look, they're finished. They're going.

MRS. GIBBS: Sh—.

> *The umbrellas leave the stage.* DR. GIBBS *has come over to his wife's grave and stands before it a moment.* EMILY *looks up at his face.* MRS. GIBBS *does not raise her eyes.*

EMILY: Look! Father Gibbs is bringing some of my flowers to you. He looks just like George, doesn't he? Oh, Mother Gibbs, I never realized before how troubled and how . . . how in the dark live persons are. Look at him. I loved him so. From morning till night, that's all they are—troubled.

> DR. GIBBS *goes off.*

THE DEAD: Little cooler than it was.—Yes, that rain's cooled it off a little. Those northeast winds always do the same thing, don't they? If it isn't a rain, it's a three-day blow.—

A patient calm falls on the stage. The STAGE MANAGER *appears at his proscenium pillar, smoking.* EMILY *sits up abruptly with an idea.*

EMILY: But, Mother Gibbs, one can go back; one can go back there again . . . into living. I feel it. I know it. Why just then for a moment I was thinking about . . . about the farm . . . and for a minute I *was* there, and my baby was on my lap as plain as day.

MRS. GIBBS: Yes, of course you can.

EMILY: I can go back there and live all those days over again . . . why not?

MRS. GIBBS: All I can say is, Emily, don't.

EMILY: (*She appeals urgently to the stage manager.*) But it's true, isn't it? I can go and live . . . back there . . . again.

STAGE MANAGER: Yes, some have tried—but they soon come back here.

MRS. GIBBS: Don't do it, Emily.

MRS. SOAMES: Emily, don't. It's not what you think it'd be.

EMILY: But I won't live over a sad day. I'll choose a happy one—I'll choose the day I first knew that I loved George. Why should that be painful?

THEY *are silent. Her question turns to the stage manager.*

STAGE MANAGER: You not only live it; but you watch yourself living it.

EMILY: Yes?

STAGE MANAGER: And as you watch it, you see the thing that they—down there—never know. You see the future. You know what's going to happen afterwards.

EMILY: But is that—painful? Why?

MRS. GIBBS: That's not the only reason why you shouldn't do it, Emily. When you've been here longer you'll see that our life here is to forget all that, and think only of what's ahead, and be ready for what's ahead. When you've been here longer you'll understand.

EMILY: (*Softly.*) But, Mother Gibbs, how can I *ever* forget that life? It's all I know. It's all I had.

MRS. SOAMES: Oh, Emily. It isn't wise. Really, it isn't.

EMILY: But it's a thing I must know for myself. I'll choose a happy day, anyway.

MRS. GIBBS: *No!*—At least, choose an unimportant day. Choose the least important day in your life. It will be important enough.

EMILY: (*To herself.*) Then it can't be since I was married; or since the baby was born. (*To the stage manager, eagerly.*) I can choose a birthday at least, can't I?—I choose my twelfth birthday.

STAGE MANAGER: All right. February 11th, 1899. A Tuesday.— Do you want any special time of day?

EMILY: Oh, I want the whole day.

STAGE MANAGER: We'll begin at dawn. You remember it had been snowing for several days; but it had stopped the night before, and they had begun clearing the roads. The sun's coming up.

EMILY: (*With a cry; rising.*) There's Main Street . . . why, that's Mr. Morgan's drugstore before he changed it! . . . And there's the livery stable.

> *The stage at no time in this act has been very dark; but now the left half of the stage gradually becomes very bright—the brightness of a crisp winter morning.*
> EMILY *walks toward Main Street.*

STAGE MANAGER: Yes, it's 1899. This is fourteen years ago.

EMILY: Oh, that's the town I knew as a little girl. And, *look*, there's the old white fence that used to be around our house. Oh, I'd forgotten that! Oh, I love it so! Are they inside?

STAGE MANAGER: Yes, your mother'll be coming downstairs in a minute to make breakfast.

EMILY: (*Softly.*) Will she?

STAGE MANAGER: And you remember: your father had been away for several days; he came back on the early-morning train.

EMILY: No . . . ?

STAGE MANAGER: He'd been back to his college to make a speech—in western New York, at Clinton.

EMILY: Look! There's Howie Newsome. There's our policeman. But he's *dead*; he *died*.

The voices of HOWIE NEWSOME, CONSTABLE WARREN *and* JOE CROWELL, JR., *are heard at the left of the stage.* EMILY *listens in delight.*

HOWIE NEWSOME: Whoa, Bessie!—Bessie! 'Morning, Bill.

CONSTABLE WARREN: Morning, Howie.

HOWIE NEWSOME: You're up early.

CONSTABLE WARREN: Been rescuin' a party; darn near froze to death, down by Polish Town thar. Got drunk and lay out in the snowdrifts. Thought he was in bed when I shook'm.

EMILY: Why, there's Joe Crowell. . . .

JOE CROWELL: Good morning, Mr. Warren. 'Morning, Howie.

MRS. WEBB *has appeared in her kitchen, but* EMILY *does not see her until she calls.*

MRS. WEBB: Chil-*dren* Wally! Emily! . . . Time to get up.

EMILY: Mama, I'm here! Oh! how young Mama looks! I didn't know Mama was ever that young.

MRS. WEBB: You can come and dress by the kitchen fire, if you like; but hurry.

HOWIE NEWSOME *has entered along Main Street and brings the milk to Mrs. Webb's door.*

Good morning, Mr. Newsome. Whhhh—it's cold.

HOWIE NEWSOME: Ten below by my barn, Mrs. Webb.

MRS. WEBB: Think of it! Keep yourself wrapped up. (*She takes her bottles in, shuddering.*)

EMILY: (*With an effort.*) Mama, I can't find my blue hair ribbon anywhere.

MRS. WEBB: Just open your eyes, dear, that's all. I laid it out for you special—on the dresser, there. If it were a snake it would bite you.

EMILY: Yes, yes . . .

She puts her hand on her heart. MR. WEBB *comes along Main Street, where he meets* CONSTABLE WARREN. *Their movements and voices are increasingly lively in the sharp air.*

MR. WEBB: Good morning, Bill.

CONSTABLE WARREN: Good morning, Mr. Webb. You're up early.

MR. WEBB: Yes, just been back to my old college in New York State. Been any trouble here?

CONSTABLE WARREN: Well, I was called up this mornin' to rescue a Polish fella—darn near froze to death he was.

MR. WEBB: We must get it in the paper.

CONSTABLE WARREN: 'Twan't much.

EMILY: (*Whispers.*) Papa.

> MR. WEBB *shakes the snow off his feet and enters his house.* CONSTABLE WARREN *goes off, right.*

MR. WEBB: Good morning, Mother.

MRS. WEBB: How did it go, Charles?

MR. WEBB: Oh, fine, I guess. I told'm a few things.—Everything all right here?

MRS. WEBB: Yes—can't think of anything that's happened, special. Been right cold. Howie Newsome says it's ten below over to his barn.

MR. WEBB: Yes, well, it's colder than that at Hamilton College. Students' ears are falling off. It ain't Christian.—Paper have any mistakes in it?

MRS. WEBB: None that I noticed. Coffee's ready when you want it.

> *He starts upstairs.*

Charles! Don't forget; it's Emily's birthday. Did you remember to get her something?

MR. WEBB: (*Patting his pocket.*) Yes, I've got something here. (*Calling up the stairs.*) Where's my girl? Where's my birthday girl? (*He goes off left.*)

MRS. WEBB: Don't interrupt her now, Charles. You can see her at breakfast. She's slow enough as it is. Hurry up, children! It's seven o'clock. Now, I don't want to call you again.

EMILY: (*Softly, more in wonder than in grief.*) I can't bear it. They're so young and beautiful. Why did they ever have to get old? Mama, I'm here. I'm grown up. I love you all, everything.—I can't look at everything hard enough.

> *She looks questioningly at the* STAGE MANAGER, *saying or suggesting: "Can I go in?" He nods briefly. She crosses to the inner door to the kitchen, left of her mother, and as though*

entering the room, says, suggesting the voice of a girl of twelve:

Good morning, Mama.

MRS. WEBB: (*Crossing to embrace and kiss her, in her characteristic matter-of-fact manner.*) Well, now, dear, a very happy birthday to my girl and many happy returns. There are some surprises waiting for you on the kitchen table.

EMILY: Oh, Mama, you *shouldn't* have. (*She throws an anguished glance at the stage manager.*) I can't—I can't.

MRS. WEBB: (*Facing the audience, over her stove.*) But birthday or no birthday, I want you to eat your breakfast good and slow. I want you to grow up and be a good strong girl.
That in the blue paper is from your Aunt Carrie; and I reckon you can guess who brought the post-card album. I found it on the doorstep when I brought in the milk— George Gibbs . . . must have come over in the cold pretty early . . . right nice of him.

EMILY: (*To herself.*) Oh, George! I'd forgotten that. . . .

MRS. WEBB: Chew that bacon good and slow. It'll help keep you warm on a cold day.

EMILY: (*With mounting urgency.*) Oh, Mama, just look at me one minute as though you really saw me. Mama, fourteen years have gone by. I'm dead. You're a grandmother, Mama. I married George Gibbs, Mama. Wally's dead, too. Mama, his appendix burst on a camping trip to North Conway. We felt just terrible about it—don't you remember? But, just for a moment now we're all together. Mama, just for a moment we're happy. *Let's look at one another.*

MRS. WEBB: That in the yellow paper is something I found in the attic among your grandmother's things. You're old enough to wear it now, and I thought you'd like it.

EMILY: And this is from you. Why, Mama, it's just lovely and it's just what I wanted. It's beautiful!

> *She flings her arms around her mother's neck. Her* MOTHER *goes on with her cooking, but is pleased.*

MRS. WEBB: Well, I hoped you'd like it. Hunted all over. Your Aunt Norah couldn't find one in Concord, so I had to send all the way to Boston. (*Laughing.*) Wally has something for you, too. He made it at manual-training class and he's very proud of it. Be sure you make a big fuss about it.—Your father has a surprise for you, too; don't know what it is myself. Sh—here he comes.

MR. WEBB: (*Off stage.*) Where's my girl? Where's my birthday girl?

EMILY: (*In a loud voice to the stage manager.*) I can't. I can't go on. It goes so fast. We don't have time to look at one another. (*She breaks down sobbing.*)

> *The lights dim on the left half of the stage.* MRS. WEBB *disappears.*

I didn't realize. So all that was going on and we never noticed. Take me back—up the hill—to my grave. But first: Wait! One more look.

Good-by, Good-by, world. Good-by, Grover's Corners . . . Mama and Papa. Good-by to clocks ticking . . . and Mama's sunflowers. And food and coffee. And new-ironed dresses and hot baths . . . and sleeping and waking up. Oh, earth, you're too wonderful for anybody to realize you. (*She looks toward the stage manager and asks abruptly, through her tears:*) Do any human beings ever realize life while they live it?—every, every minute?

STAGE MANAGER: No. (*Pause.*) The saints and poets, maybe— they do some.

EMILY: I'm ready to go back. (*She returns to her chair beside Mrs. Gibbs.*)

> *Pause.*

MRS. GIBBS: Were you happy?

EMILY: No . . . I should have listened to you. That's all human beings are! Just blind people.

MRS. GIBBS: Look, it's clearing up. The stars are coming out.

EMILY: Oh, Mr. Stimson, I should have listened to them.

SIMON STIMSON: (*With mounting violence; bitingly.*) Yes, now you know. Now you know! That's what it was to be alive. To move about in a cloud of ignorance; to go up and down trampling on the feelings of those . . . of those about you. To spend and waste time as though you had a million years. To be always at the mercy of one self-centered passion, or another. Now you know—that's the happy existence you wanted to go back to. Ignorance and blindness.

MRS. GIBBS: (*Spiritedly.*) Simon Stimson, that ain't the whole truth and you know it. Emily, look at that star. I forget its name.

A MAN AMONG THE DEAD: My boy Joel was a sailor,—knew 'em all. He'd set on the porch evenings and tell 'em all by name. Yes, sir, wonderful!

ANOTHER MAN AMONG THE DEAD: A star's mighty good company.

A WOMAN AMONG THE DEAD: Yes. Yes, 'tis.

SIMON STIMSON: Here's one of *them* coming.

THE DEAD: That's funny. 'Tain't no time for one of them to be here.—Goodness sakes.

EMILY: Mother Gibbs, it's George.

MRS. GIBBS: Sh, dear. Just rest yourself.

EMILY: It's George.

> GEORGE *enters from the left, and slowly comes toward them.*

A MAN FROM AMONG THE DEAD: And my boy, Joel, who knew the stars—he used to say it took millions of years for that speck o' light to git to the earth. Don't seem like a body could believe it, but that's what he used to say—millions of years.

> GEORGE *sinks to his knees then falls full length at Emily's feet.*

A WOMAN AMONG THE DEAD: Goodness! That ain't no way to behave!

MRS. SOAMES: He ought to be home.

EMILY: Mother Gibbs?

MRS. GIBBS: Yes, Emily?

EMILY: They don't understand, do they?

MRS. GIBBS: No, dear. They don't understand.

> *The* STAGE MANAGER *appears at the right, one hand on a dark curtain which he slowly draws across the scene.*
> *In the distance a clock is heard striking the hour very faintly.*

STAGE MANAGER: Most everybody's asleep in Grover's Corners. There are a few lights on: Shorty Hawkins, down at the depot, has just watched the Albany train go by. And at the livery stable somebody's setting up late and talking.— Yes, it's clearing up. There are the stars—doing their old, old crisscross journeys in the sky. Scholars haven't settled the matter yet, but they seem to think there are no living beings up there. Just chalk . . . or fire. Only this one is straining away, straining away all the time to make something of itself. The strain's so bad that every sixteen hours everybody lies down and gets a rest. (*He winds his watch.*) Hm. . . . Eleven o'clock in Grover's Corners.—You get a good rest, too. Good night.

THE END

THE SKIN OF OUR TEETH

A Play in Three Acts

CHARACTERS (in the order of their appearance)

Act I. Home, Excelsior, New Jersey.

Act II. Atlantic City Boardwalk.

Act III. Home, Excelsior, New Jersey.

Act I

A projection screen in the middle of the curtain. The first lantern slide: the name of the theatre, and the words: NEWS EVENTS OF THE WORLD. An ANNOUNCER'S *voice is heard.*

ANNOUNCER: The management takes pleasure in bringing to you—The News Events of the World:

Slide of the sun appearing above the horizon.

Freeport, Long Island.
The sun rose this morning at 6:32 a.m. This gratifying event was first reported by Mrs. Dorothy Stetson of Freeport, Long Island, who promptly telephoned the Mayor.
The Society for Affirming the End of the World at once went into a special session and postponed the arrival of that event for TWENTY-FOUR HOURS.
All honor to Mrs. Stetson for her public spirit.

New York City:

Slide of the front doors of the theatre in which this play is playing; three cleaning WOMEN *with mops and pails.*

The X Theatre. During the daily cleaning of this theatre a number of lost objects were collected as usual by Mesdames Simpson, Pateslewski, and Moriarty.
Among these objects found today was a wedding ring, inscribed: To Eva from Adam. Genesis II:18.
The ring will be restored to the owner or owners, if their credentials are satisfactory.

Tippehatchee, Vermont:

Slide representing a glacier.

The unprecedented cold weather of this summer has produced a condition that has not yet been satisfactorily explained. There is a report that a wall of ice is moving

southward across these counties. The disruption of communications by the cold wave now crossing the country has
rendered exact information difficult, but little credence is
given to the rumor that the ice had pushed the Cathedral of
Montreal as far as St. Albans, Vermont.

For further information see your daily papers.

Excelsior, New Jersey:

Slide of a modest suburban home.

The home of Mr. George Antrobus, the inventor of the
wheel. The discovery of the wheel, following so closely on
the discovery of the lever, has centered the attention of the
country on Mr. Antrobus of this attractive suburban residence district. This is his home, a commodious seven-room
house, conveniently situated near a public school, a Methodist church, and a firehouse; it is right handy to an A. and P.

Slide of MR. ANTROBUS *on his front steps, smiling and lifting
his straw hat. He holds a wheel.*

Mr. Antrobus, himself. He comes of very old stock and has
made his way up from next to nothing.

It is reported that he was once a gardener, but left that situation under circumstances that have been variously reported.
Mr. Antrobus is a veteran of foreign wars, and bears a number of scars, front and back.

Slide of MRS. ANTROBUS, *holding some roses.*

This is Mrs. Antrobus, the charming and gracious president
of the Excelsior Mothers' Club.

Mrs. Antrobus is an excellent needlewoman; it is she who
invented the apron on which so many interesting changes
have been rung since.

Slide of the FAMILY *and* SABINA.

Here we see the Antrobuses with their two children, Henry
and Gladys, and friend. The friend in the rear, is Lily Sabina,
the maid.

I know we all want to congratulate this typical American
family on its enterprise. We all wish Mr. Antrobus a success-

ful future. Now the management takes you to the interior of this home for a brief visit.

> *Curtain rises. Living room of a commuter's home.* SABINA *—straw-blonde, over-rouged—is standing by the window back center, a feather duster under her elbow.*

SABINA: Oh, oh, oh! Six o'clock and the master not home yet. Pray God nothing serious has happened to him crossing the Hudson River. If anything happened to him, we would certainly be inconsolable and have to move into a less desirable residence district.

The fact is I don't know what'll become of us. Here it is the middle of August and the coldest day of the year. It's simply freezing; the dogs are sticking to the sidewalks; can anybody explain that? No.

But I'm not surprised. The whole world's at sixes and sevens, and why the house hasn't fallen down about our ears long ago is a miracle to me.

> *A fragment of the right wall leans precariously over the stage.* SABINA *looks at it nervously and it slowly rights itself.*

Every night this same anxiety as to whether the master will get home safely: whether he'll bring home anything to eat. In the midst of life we are in the midst of death, a truer word was never said.

> *The fragment of scenery flies up into the lofts.* SABINA *is struck dumb with surprise, shrugs her shoulders and starts dusting* MR. ANTROBUS' *chair, including the under side.*

Of course, Mr. Antrobus is a very fine man, an excellent husband and father, a pillar of the church, and has all the best interests of the community at heart. Of course, every muscle goes tight every time he passes a policeman; but what I think is that there are certain charges that ought not to be made, and I think I may add, ought not to be allowed to be made; we're all human; who isn't?

> *She dusts* MRS. ANTROBUS' *rocking chair.*

Mrs. Antrobus is as fine a woman as you could hope to see. She lives only for her children; and if it would be any benefit to her children she'd see the rest of us stretched out dead at her feet without turning a hair,—that's the truth. If you want to know anything more about Mrs. Antrobus, just go and look at a tigress, and look hard.

As to the children—

Well, Henry Antrobus is a real, clean-cut American boy. He'll graduate from High School one of these days, if they make the alphabet any easier.—Henry, when he has a stone in his hand, has a perfect aim; he can hit anything from a bird to an older brother—Oh! I didn't mean to say that!— but it certainly was an unfortunate accident, and it was very hard getting the police out of the house.

Mr. and Mrs. Antrobus' daughter is named Gladys. She'll make some good man a good wife some day, if he'll just come down off the movie screen and ask her.

So here we are!

We've managed to survive for some time now, catch as catch can, the fat and the lean, and if the dinosaurs don't trample us to death, and if the grasshoppers don't eat up our garden, we'll all live to see better days, knock on wood.

Each new child that's born to the Antrobuses seems to them to be sufficient reason for the whole universe's being set in motion; and each new child that dies seems to them to have been spared a whole world of sorrow, and what the end of it will be is still very much an open question.

We've rattled along, hot and cold, for some time now—

A portion of the wall above the door, right, flies up into the air and disappears.

—and my advice to you is not to inquire into why or whither, but just enjoy your ice cream while it's on your plate,—that's my philosophy.

Don't forget that a few years ago we came through the depression by the skin of our teeth! One more tight squeeze like that and where will we be?

This is a cue line. SABINA *looks angrily at the kitchen door and repeats:*

. . . we came through the depression by the skin of our teeth; one more tight squeeze like that and where will we be?

Flustered, she looks through the opening in the right wall; then goes to the window and reopens the Act.

Oh, oh, oh! Six o'clock and the master not home yet. Pray God nothing has happened to him crossing the Hudson. Here it is the middle of August and the coldest day of the year. It's simply freezing; the dogs are sticking. One more tight squeeze like that and where will we be?

VOICE:

Off stage.

Make up something! Invent something!

SABINA: Well . . . uh . . . this certainly is a fine American home . . . and—uh . . . everybody's very happy . . . and—uh . . .

Suddenly flings pretense to the winds and coming downstage says with indignation:

I can't invent any words for this play, and I'm glad I can't. I hate this play and every word in it.

As for me, I don't understand a single word of it, anyway,— all about the troubles the human race has gone through, there's a subject for you.

Besides, the author hasn't made up his silly mind as to whether we're all living back in caves or in New Jersey today, and that's the way it is all the way through.

Oh—why can't we have plays like we used to have—*Peg o' My Heart*, and *Smilin' Thru*, and *The Bat*—good entertainment with a message you can take home with you?

I took this hateful job because I had to. For two years I've sat up in my room living on a sandwich and a cup of tea a day, waiting for better times in the theatre. And look at me now: I—I who've played *Rain* and *The Barretts of Wimpole Street* and *First Lady*—God in Heaven!

The STAGE MANAGER puts his head out from the hole in the scenery.

MR. FITZPATRICK: Miss Somerset! ! Miss Somerset!

SABINA: Oh! Anyway!—nothing matters! It'll all be the same in a hundred years.

Loudly.

We came through the depression by the skin of our teeth,—
that's true!—one more tight squeeze like that and where
will we be?

Enter MRS. ANTROBUS, *a mother.*

MRS. ANTROBUS: Sabina, you've let the fire go out.

SABINA: (*In a lather.*) One-thing-and-another; don't-know-
whether-my-wits-are-upside-or-down; might-as-well-be-dead-
as-alive-in-a-house-all-sixes-and-sevens. . . .

MRS. ANTROBUS: You've let the fire go out. Here it is the coldest day of the year right in the middle of August, and you've
let the fire go out.

SABINA: Mrs. Antrobus, I'd like to give my two weeks' notice,
Mrs. Antrobus. A girl like I can get a situation in a home
where they're rich enough to have a fire in every room, Mrs.
Antrobus, and a girl don't have to carry the responsibility of
the whole house on her two shoulders. And a home without
children, Mrs. Antrobus, because children are a thing only a
parent can stand, and a truer word was never said; and a
home, Mrs. Antrobus, where the master of the house don't
pinch decent, self-respecting girls when he meets them in a
dark corridor. I mention no names and make no charges. So
you have my notice, Mrs. Antrobus. I hope that's perfectly
clear.

MRS. ANTROBUS: You've let the fire go out!—Have you milked
the mammoth?

SABINA: I don't understand a word of this play.—Yes, I've
milked the mammoth.

MRS. ANTROBUS: Until Mr. Antrobus comes home we have no
food and we have no fire. You'd better go over to the neighbors and borrow some fire.

SABINA: Mrs. Antrobus! I can't! I'd die on the way, you know
I would. It's worse than January. The dogs are sticking to
the sidewalks. I'd die.

MRS. ANTROBUS: Very well, I'll go.

SABINA: (*Even more distraught, coming forward and sinking on
her knees.*) You'd never come back alive; we'd all perish; if
you weren't here, we'd just perish. How do we know Mr.

Antrobus'll be back? We don't know. If you go out, I'll just kill myself.

MRS. ANTROBUS: Get up, Sabina.

SABINA: Every night it's the same thing. Will he come back safe, or won't he? Will we starve to death, or freeze to death, or boil to death or will we be killed by burglars? I don't know why we go on living. I don't know why we go on living at all. It's easier being dead.

She flings her arms on the table and buries her head in them. In each of the succeeding speeches she flings her head up— and sometimes her hands—then quickly buries her head again.

MRS. ANTROBUS: The same thing! Always throwing up the sponge, Sabina. Always announcing your own death. But give you a new hat—or a plate of ice cream—or a ticket to the movies, and you want to live forever.

SABINA: You don't care whether we live or die; all you care about is those children. If it would be any benefit to them you'd be glad to see us all stretched out dead.

MRS. ANTROBUS: Well, maybe I would.

SABINA: And what do they care about? Themselves—that's all they care about. (*Shrilly.*) They make fun of you behind your back. Don't tell me: they're ashamed of you. Half the time, they pretend they're someone else's children. Little thanks you get from them.

MRS. ANTROBUS: I'm not asking for any thanks.

SABINA: And Mr. Antrobus—you don't understand *him.* All that work he does—trying to discover the alphabet and the multiplication table. Whenever he tries to learn anything you fight against it.

MRS. ANTROBUS: Oh, Sabina, I know you.

When Mr. Antrobus raped you home from your Sabine hills, he did it to insult me.

He did it for your pretty face, and to insult me.

You were the new wife, weren't you?

For a year or two you lay on your bed all day and polished the nails on your hands and feet:

You made puff-balls of the combings of your hair and you blew them up to the ceiling.

And I washed your underclothes and I made you chicken broths.

I bore children and between my very groans I stirred the cream that you'd put on your face.

But I knew you wouldn't last.

You didn't last.

SABINA: But it was I who encouraged Mr. Antrobus to make the alphabet. I'm sorry to say it, Mrs. Antrobus, but you're not a beautiful woman, and you can never know what a man could do if he tried. It's girls like I who inspire the multiplication table.

I'm sorry to say it, but you're not a beautiful woman, Mrs. Antrobus, and that's the God's truth.

MRS. ANTROBUS: And you didn't last—you sank to the kitchen. And what do you do there? *You let the fire go out!* No wonder to you it seems easier being dead.

Reading and writing and counting on your fingers is all very well in their way,—but I keep the home going.

MRS. ANTROBUS: —There's that dinosaur on the front lawn again.—Shoo! Go away. Go away.

The baby DINOSAUR *puts his head in the window.*

DINOSAUR: It's cold.

MRS. ANTROBUS: You go around to the back of the house where you belong.

DINOSAUR: It's cold.

The DINOSAUR *disappears.* MRS. ANTROBUS *goes calmly out.* SABINA *slowly raises her head and speaks to the audience. The central portion of the center wall rises, pauses, and disappears into the loft.*

SABINA: Now that you audience are listening to this, too, I understand it a little better.

I wish eleven o'clock were here; I don't want to be dragged through this whole play again.

The TELEGRAPH BOY *is seen entering along the back wall of the stage from the right. She catches sight of him and calls:*

Mrs. Antrobus! Mrs. Antrobus! Help! There's a strange man coming to the house. He's coming up the walk, help!

Enter MRS. ANTROBUS *in alarm, but efficient.*

MRS. ANTROBUS: Help me quick!

They barricade the door by piling the furniture against it.

Who is it? What do you want?

TELEGRAPH BOY: A telegram for Mrs. Antrobus from Mr. Antrobus in the city.

SABINA: Are you sure, are you sure? Maybe it's just a trap!

MRS. ANTROBUS: I know his voice, Sabina. We can open the door.

Enter the TELEGRAPH BOY, *12 years old, in uniform.*
The DINOSAUR *and* MAMMOTH *slip by him into the room and settle down front right.*

I'm sorry we kept you waiting. We have to be careful, you know. (*To the* ANIMALS.) Hm! . . . Will you be quiet?

They nod.

Have you had your supper?

They nod.

Are you *ready* to come in?

They nod.

Young man, have you any fire with you? Then light the grate, will you?

He nods, produces something like a briquet; and kneels by the imagined fireplace, footlights center.
Pause.

What are people saying about this cold weather?

He makes a doubtful shrug with his shoulders.

Sabina, take this stick and go and light the stove.

SABINA: Like I told you, Mrs. Antrobus; two weeks. That's the law. I hope that's perfectly clear.

Exit.

MRS. ANTROBUS: What about this cold weather?

TELEGRAPH BOY: (*Lowered eyes.*) Of course, I don't know

anything . . . but they say there's a wall of ice moving down from the North, that's what they say. We can't get Boston by telegraph, and they're burning pianos in Hartford.

. . . It moves everything in front of it, churches and post offices and city halls.

I live in Brooklyn myself.

MRS. ANTROBUS: What are people doing about it?

TELEGRAPH BOY: Well . . . uh . . . Talking, mostly.

Or just what you'd do a day in February.

There are some that are trying to go South and the roads are crowded; but you can't take old people and children very far in a cold like this.

MRS. ANTROBUS: —What's this telegram you have for me?

TELEGRAPH BOY: (*Fingertips to his forehead.*) If you wait just a minute; I've got to remember it.

> *The* ANIMALS *have left their corner and are nosing him. Presently they take places on either side of him, leaning against his hips, like heraldic beasts.*

This telegram was flashed from Murray Hill to University Heights! And then by puffs of smoke from University Heights to Staten Island.

And then by lantern from Staten Island to Plainfield, New Jersey. What hath God wrought! (*He clears his throat.*)

"To Mrs. Antrobus, Excelsior, New Jersey:

My dear wife, will be an hour late. Busy day at the office. Don't worry the children about the cold just keep them warm burn everything except Shakespeare."

> *Pause.*

MRS. ANTROBUS: Men! —He knows I'd burn ten Shakespeares to prevent a child of mine from having one cold in the head. What does it say next?

> *Enter* SABINA.

TELEGRAPH BOY: "Have made great discoveries today have separated em from en."

SABINA: I know what that is, that's the alphabet, yes it is. Mr. Antrobus is just the cleverest man. Why, when the alphabet's finished, we'll be able to tell the future and everything.

TELEGRAPH BOY: Then listen to this: "Ten tens make a hundred semi-colon consequences far-reaching." (*Watches for effect.*)

MRS. ANTROBUS: The earth's turning to ice, and all he can do is to make up new numbers.

TELEGRAPH BOY: Well, Mrs. Antrobus, like the head man at our office said: a few more discoveries like that and we'll be worth freezing.

MRS. ANTROBUS: What does he say next?

TELEGRAPH BOY: I . . . I can't do this last part very well. (*He clears his throat and sings.*) "Happy w'dding ann'vers'ry to you, Happy ann'vers'ry to you—"

> The ANIMALS *begin to howl soulfully;* SABINA *screams with pleasure.*

MRS. ANTROBUS: Dolly! Frederick! Be quiet.

TELEGRAPH BOY: (*Above the din.*) "Happy w'dding ann'-vers'ry, dear Eva; happy w'dding ann'vers'ry to you."

MRS. ANTROBUS: Is that in the telegram? Are they singing telegrams now?

> *He nods.*

The earth's getting so silly no wonder the sun turns cold.

SABINA: Mrs. Antrobus, I want to take back the notice I gave you. Mrs. Antrobus, I don't want to leave a house that gets such interesting telegrams and I'm sorry for anything I said. I really am.

MRS. ANTROBUS: Young man, I'd like to give you something for all this trouble; Mr. Antrobus isn't home yet and I have no money and no food in the house—

TELEGRAPH BOY: Mrs. Antrobus . . . I don't like to . . . appear to . . . ask for anything, but . . .

MRS. ANTROBUS: What is it you'd like?

TELEGRAPH BOY: Do you happen to have an old needle you could spare? My wife just sits home all day thinking about needles.

SABINA: (*Shrilly.*) We only got two in the house. Mrs. Antrobus, you know we only got two in the house.

MRS. ANTROBUS: (*After a look at* SABINA *taking a needle from her collar.*) Why yes, I can spare this.

TELEGRAPH BOY: (*Lowered eyes.*) Thank you, Mrs. Antrobus. Mrs. Antrobus, can I ask you something else? I have two sons of my own; if the cold gets worse, what should I do?

SABINA: I think we'll all perish, that's what I think. Cold like this in August is just the end of the whole world.

Silence.

MRS. ANTROBUS: I don't know. After all, what does one do about anything? Just keep as warm as you can. And don't let your wife and children see that you're worried.

TELEGRAPH BOY: Yes. . . . Thank you, Mrs. Antrobus. Well, I'd better be going.—Oh, I forgot! There's one more sentence in the telegram. "Three cheers have invented the wheel."

MRS. ANTROBUS: A wheel? What's a wheel?

TELEGRAPH BOY: I don't know. That's what it said. The sign for it is like this. Well, goodbye.

The WOMEN *see him to the door, with goodbyes and injunctions to keep warm.*

SABINA: (*Apron to her eyes, wailing.*) Mrs. Antrobus, it looks to me like all the nice men in the world are already married; I don't know why that is.

Exit.

MRS. ANTROBUS: (*Thoughtful; to the* ANIMALS.) Do you ever remember hearing tell of any cold like this in August?

The ANIMALS *shake their heads.*

From your grandmothers or anyone?

They shake their heads.

Have you any suggestions?

They shake their heads.
She pulls her shawl around, goes to the front door and opening it an inch calls:

HENRY. GLADYS. CHILDREN. Come right in and get warm. No, no, when mama says a thing she means it.

Henry! HENRY. Put down that stone. You know what happened last time.

Shriek.

HENRY! Put down that stone!
Gladys! Put down your dress!! Try and be a lady.

The CHILDREN *bound in and dash to the fire. They take off
their winter things and leave them in heaps on the floor.*

GLADYS: Mama, I'm hungry. Mama, why is it so cold?
HENRY: (*At the same time.*) Mama, why doesn't it snow? Mama,
when's supper ready? Maybe, it'll snow and we can make
snowballs.
GLADYS: Mama, it's so cold that in one more minute I just
couldn't of stood it.
MRS. ANTROBUS: Settle down, both of you, I want to talk to
you.

*She draws up a hassock and sits front center over the orches-
tra pit before the imaginary fire. The* CHILDREN *stretch out
on the floor, leaning against her lap. Tableau by Raphael.
The* ANIMALS *edge up and complete the triangle.*

It's just a cold spell of some kind. Now listen to what I'm
saying:
When your father comes home I want you to be extra quiet.
He's had a hard day at the office and I don't know but what
he may have one of his moods.
I just got a telegram from him very happy and excited, and
you know what that means. Your father's temper's uneven; I
guess you know that.

Shriek.

Henry! Henry!
Why—why can't you remember to keep your hair down
over your forehead? You must keep that scar covered up.
Don't you know that when your father sees it he loses all
control over himself? He goes crazy. He wants to die.

*After a moment's despair she collects herself decisively, wets
the hem of her apron in her mouth and starts polishing his
forehead vigorously.*

Lift your head up. Stop squirming. Blessed me, sometimes I think that it's going away—and then there it is: just as red as ever.

HENRY: Mama, today at school two teachers forgot and called me by my old name. They forgot, Mama. You'd better write another letter to the principal, so that he'll tell them I've changed my name. Right out in class they called me: Cain.

MRS. ANTROBUS: (*Putting her hand on his mouth, too late; hoarsely.*) Don't say it. (*Polishing feverishly.*)

If you're good they'll forget it. Henry, you didn't hit anyone . . . today, did you?

HENRY: Oh . . . no-o-o!

MRS. ANTROBUS: (*Still working, not looking at Gladys.*) And, Gladys, I want you to be especially nice to your father tonight. You know what he calls you when you're good— his little angel, his little star. Keep your dress down like a little lady. And keep your voice nice and low. Gladys Antrobus!! What's that red stuff you have on your face? (*Slaps her.*)

You're a filthy detestable child! (*Rises in real, though temporary, repudiation and despair.*) Get away from me, both of you! I wish I'd never seen sight or sound of you. Let the cold come! I can't stand it. I don't want to go on. (*She walks away.*)

GLADYS: (*Weeping.*) All the girls at school do, Mama.

MRS. ANTROBUS: (*Shrieking.*) I'm through with you, that's all!—Sabina! Sabina!—Don't you know your father'd go crazy if he saw that paint on your face? Don't you know your father thinks you're perfect? Don't you know he couldn't live if he didn't think you were perfect?—Sabina!

Enter SABINA.

SABINA: Yes, Mrs. Antrobus!

MRS. ANTROBUS: Take this girl out into the kitchen and wash her face with the scrubbing brush.

MR. ANTROBUS: (*Outside, roaring.*) "I've been working on the railroad, all the livelong day . . . etc."

The ANIMALS *start running around in circles, bellowing.* SABINA *rushes to the window.*

MRS. ANTROBUS: Sabina, what's that noise outside?

SABINA: Oh, it's a drunken tramp. It's a giant, Mrs. Antrobus. We'll all be killed in our beds, I know it!

MRS. ANTROBUS: Help me quick. Quick. Everybody.

> *Again they stack all the furniture against the door.* MR. ANTROBUS *pounds and bellows.*

Who is it? What do you want?—Sabina, have you any boiling water ready?—Who is it?

MR. ANTROBUS: Broken-down camel of a pig's snout, open this door.

MRS. ANTROBUS: God be praised! It's your father.—Just a minute, George! —Sabina, clear the door, quick. Gladys, come here while I clean your nasty face!

MR. ANTROBUS: She-bitch of a goat's gizzard, I'll break every bone in your body. Let me in or I'll tear the whole house down.

MRS. ANTROBUS: Just a minute, George, something's the matter with the lock.

MR. ANTROBUS: Open the door or I'll tear your livers out. I'll smash your brains on the ceiling, and Devil take the hindmost.

MRS. ANTROBUS: Now, you can open the door, Sabina. I'm ready.

> *The door is flung open. Silence.* MR. ANTROBUS—*face of a Keystone Comedy Cop—stands there in fur cap and blanket. His arms are full of parcels, including a large stone wheel with a center in it. One hand carries a railroad man's lantern. Suddenly he bursts into joyous roar.*

MR. ANTROBUS: Well, how's the whole crooked family?

> *Relief. Laughter. Tears. Jumping up and down.* ANIMALS *cavorting.* ANTROBUS *throws the parcels on the ground. Hurls his cap and blanket after them. Heroic embraces. Melee of* HUMANS *and* ANIMALS, SABINA *included.*

I'll be scalded and tarred if a man can't get a little welcome when he comes home. Well, Maggie, you old gunny-sack, how's the broken down old weather hen? —Sabina, old fishbait, old skunkpot.—And the children,—how've the little smellers been?

GLADYS: Papa, Papa, Papa, Papa, Papa.

MR. ANTROBUS: How've they been, Maggie?

MRS. ANTROBUS: Well, I must say, they've been as good as gold. I haven't had to raise my voice once. I don't know what's the matter with them.

ANTROBUS: (*Kneeling before* GLADYS.) Papa's little weasel, eh?—Sabina, there's some food for you.—Papa's little gopher?

GLADYS: (*Her arm around his neck.*) Papa, you're always teasing me.

ANTROBUS: And Henry? Nothing rash today, I hope. Nothing rash?

HENRY: No, Papa.

ANTROBUS: (*Roaring.*) Well that's good, that's good—I'll bet Sabina let the fire go out.

SABINA: Mr. Antrobus, I've given my notice. I'm leaving two weeks from today. I'm sorry, but I'm leaving.

ANTROBUS: (*Roar.*) Well, if you leave now you'll freeze to death, so go and cook the dinner.

SABINA: Two weeks, that's the law.

  Exit.

ANTROBUS: Did you get my telegram?

MRS. ANTROBUS: Yes.—What's a wheel?

  He indicates the wheel with a glance. HENRY *is rolling it around the floor. Rapid, hoarse interchange:* MRS. ANTRO-BUS: *What does this cold weather mean? It's below freezing.* ANTROBUS: *Not before the children!* MRS. ANTROBUS: *Shouldn't we do something about it?—start off, move?* ANTROBUS: *Not before the children!!!* He gives HENRY a sharp slap.

HENRY: Papa, you hit me!

ANTROBUS: Well, remember it. That's to make you remember today. Today. The day the alphabet's finished; and the day that we *saw* the hundred—the hundred, the hundred, the hundred, the hundred, the hundred—there's no end to 'em. I've had a day at the office!

Take a look at that wheel, Maggie—when I've got that to rights: you'll see a sight.

There's a reward there for all the walking you've done.

MRS. ANTROBUS: How do you mean?

ANTROBUS: (*On the hassock looking into the fire; with awe.*) Maggie, we've reached the top of the wave. There's not much more to be done. We're there!

MRS. ANTROBUS: (*Cutting across his mood sharply.*) And the ice?

ANTROBUS: The ice!

HENRY: (*Playing with the wheel.*) Papa, you could put a chair on this.

ANTROBUS: (*Broodingly.*) Ye-e-s, any booby can fool with it now,—but I thought of it first.

MRS. ANTROBUS: Children, go out in the kitchen. I want to talk to your father alone.

> The CHILDREN *go out.*
>
> ANTROBUS *has moved to his chair up left. He takes the gold-fish bowl on his lap; pulls the canary cage down to the level of his face. Both the* ANIMALS *put their paws up on the arm of his chair.* MRS. ANTROBUS *faces him across the room, like a judge.*

MRS. ANTROBUS: Well?

ANTROBUS: (*Shortly.*) It's cold.—How things been, eh? Keck, keck, keck.— And you, Millicent?

MRS. ANTROBUS: I know it's cold.

ANTROBUS: (*To the canary.*) No spilling of sunflower seed, eh? No singing after lights-out, y'know what I mean?

MRS. ANTROBUS: You can try and prevent us freezing to death, can't you? You can do something? We can start moving. Or we can go on the animals' backs?

ANTROBUS: The best thing about animals is that they don't talk much.

MAMMOTH: It's cold.

ANTROBUS: Eh, eh, eh! Watch that!

—By midnight we'd turn to ice. The roads are full of people now who can scarcely lift a foot from the ground. The grass out in front is like iron,—which reminds me, I have another needle for you.—The people up north—where are they? Frozen . . . crushed. . . .

MRS. ANTROBUS: Is that what's going to happen to us?—Will you answer me?

ANTROBUS: I don't know. I don't know anything. Some say that the ice is going slower. Some say that it's stopped. The sun's growing cold. What can I do about that? Nothing we can do but burn everything in the house, and the fenceposts and the barn. Keep the fire going. When we have no more fire, we die.

MRS. ANTROBUS: Well, why didn't you say so in the first place?

> MRS. ANTROBUS *is about to march off when she catches sight of two* REFUGEES, *men, who have appeared against the back wall of the theatre and who are soon joined by others.*

REFUGEES: Mr. Antrobus! Mr. Antrobus! Mr. An-nn-tro-bus!

MRS. ANTROBUS: Who's that? Who's that calling you?

ANTROBUS: (*Clearing his throat guiltily.*) Hm—let me see.

> *Two* REFUGEES *come up to the window.*

REFUGEE: Could we warm our hands for a moment, Mr. Antrobus. It's very cold, Mr. Antrobus.

ANOTHER REFUGEE: Mr. Antrobus, I wonder if you have a piece of bread or something that you could spare.

> *Silence. They wait humbly.* MRS. ANTROBUS *stands rooted to the spot. Suddenly a knock at the door, then another hand knocking in short rapid blows.*

MRS. ANTROBUS: Who are these people? Why, they're all over the front yard. What have they come *here* for?

> *Enter* SABINA.

SABINA: Mrs. Antrobus! There are some tramps knocking at the back door.

MRS. ANTROBUS: George, tell these people to go away. Tell them to move right along. I'll go and send them away from the back door. Sabina, come with me. (*She goes out energetically.*)

ANTROBUS: Sabina! Stay here! I have something to say to you. (*He goes to the door and opens it a crack and talks through it.*) Ladies and gentlemen! I'll have to ask you to wait a few minutes longer. It'll be all right . . . while you're waiting you might each one pull up a stake of the fence. We'll need them all for the fireplace. There'll be coffee and sandwiches in a moment.

> SABINA *looks out door over his shoulder and suddenly extends her arm pointing, with a scream.*

SABINA: Mr. Antrobus, what's that??—that big white thing? Mr. Antrobus, it's ICE. It's ICE!!

ANTROBUS: Sabina, I want you to go in the kitchen and make a lot of coffee. Make a whole pail full.

SABINA: Pail full!!

ANTROBUS: (*With gesture.*) And sandwiches . . . piles of them . . . like this.

SABINA: Mr. An . . . !! (*Suddenly she drops the play, and says in her own person as* MISS SOMERSET, *with surprise.*) Oh, *I* see what this part of the play means now! This means refugees. (*She starts to cross to the proscenium.*) Oh, I don't like it. I don't like it. (*She leans against the proscenium and bursts into tears.*)

ANTROBUS: Miss Somerset!

> *Voice of the* STAGE MANAGER.

Miss Somerset!

SABINA: (*Energetically, to the audience.*) Ladies and gentlemen! Don't take this play serious. The world's not coming to an end. You know it's not. People exaggerate! Most people really have enough to eat and a roof over their heads. Nobody actually starves—you can always eat grass or something. That ice-business—why, it was a long, long time ago. Besides they were only savages. Savages don't love their families—not like we do.

ANTROBUS *and* STAGE MANAGER: Miss Somerset!!

> *There is renewed knocking at the door.*

SABINA: All right. I'll say the lines, but I won't think about the play.

> *Enter* MRS. ANTROBUS.

SABINA: (*Parting thrust at the audience.*) And I advise *you* not to think about the play, either.

Exit SABINA.

MRS. ANTROBUS: George, these tramps say that you asked them to come to the house. What does this mean?

Knocking at the door.

ANTROBUS: Just . . . uh . . . There are a few friends, Maggie, I met on the road. Real nice, real useful people. . . .

MRS. ANTROBUS: (*Back to the door.*) Now, don't you ask them in!
George Antrobus, not another soul comes in here over my dead body.

ANTROBUS: Maggie, there's a doctor there. Never hurts to have a good doctor in the house. We've lost a peck of children, one way and another. You can never tell when a child's throat will get stopped up. What you and I have seen—!!! (*He puts his fingers on his throat, and imitates diphtheria.*)

MRS. ANTROBUS: Well, just one person then, the Doctor. The others can go right along the road.

ANTROBUS: Maggie, there's an old man, particular friend of mine—

MRS. ANTROBUS: I won't listen to you—

ANTROBUS: It was he that really started off the A.B.C.'s.

MRS. ANTROBUS: I don't care if he perishes. We can do without reading or writing. We can't do without food.

ANTROBUS: Then let the ice come!! Drink your coffee!! I don't want any coffee if I can't drink it with some good people.

MRS. ANTROBUS: Stop shouting. Who else is there trying to push us off the cliff?

ANTROBUS: Well, there's the man . . . who makes all the laws. Judge Moses!

MRS. ANTROBUS: Judges can't help us now.

ANTROBUS: And if the ice melts? . . . and if we pull through? Have you and I been able to bring up Henry? What have we done?

MRS. ANTROBUS: Who are those old women?

ANTROBUS: (*Coughs.*) Up in town there are nine sisters. There are three or four of them here. They're sort of music teachers . . . and one of them recites and one of them—

MRS. ANTROBUS: That's the end. A singing troupe! Well, take

your choice, live or die. Starve your own children before your face.

ANTROBUS: (*Gently.*) These people don't take much. They're used to starving.

They'll sleep on the floor.

Besides, Maggie, listen: no, listen:

Who've we got in the house, but Sabina? Sabina's always afraid the worst will happen. Whose spirits can she keep up? Maggie, these people never give up. They think they'll live and work forever.

MRS. ANTROBUS: (*Walks slowly to the middle of the room.*) All right, let them in. Let them in. You're master here. (*Softly.*) —But these animals must go. Enough's enough. They'll soon be big enough to push the walls down, anyway. Take them away.

ANTROBUS: (*Sadly.*) All right. The dinosaur and mammoth—! Come on, baby, come on Frederick. Come for a walk. That's a good little fellow.

DINOSAUR: It's cold.

ANTROBUS: Yes, nice cold fresh air. Bracing.

He holds the door open and the ANIMALS *go out. He beckons to his friends. The* REFUGEES *are typical elderly out-of-works from the streets of New York today.* JUDGE MOSES *wears a skull cap.* HOMER *is a blind beggar with a guitar. The seedy crowd shuffles in and waits humbly and expectantly.* ANTROBUS *introduces them to his wife who bows to each with a stately bend of her head.*

Make yourself at home, Maggie, this the doctor . . . m . . . Coffee'll be here in a minute. . . . Professor, this is my wife. . . . And: . . . Judge . . . Maggie, you know the Judge.

An old blind man with a guitar.

Maggie, you know . . . you know Homer?—Come right in, Judge.—

Miss Muse—are some of your sisters here? Come right in. Miss E. Muse; Miss T. Muse, Miss M. Muse.

MRS. ANTROBUS: Pleased to meet you. Just . . . make yourself comfortable. Supper'll be ready in a minute. (*She goes out, abruptly.*)

ANTROBUS: Make yourself at home, friends. I'll be right back. (*He goes out.*)

The REFUGEES *stare about them in awe. Presently several voices start whispering "Homer! Homer!" All take it up.* HOMER *strikes a chord or two on his guitar, then starts to speak:*

HOMER: **Μῆνιν ἄειδε, θεὰ, Πηληϊάδεω 'Αχιλῆος, οὐλομένην, ἣ μυρί' 'Αχαιοῖς ἄλγε' ἔθηκεν, πολλὰs δ' ἰφθίμουs ψυχὰs—**

HOMER'S *face shows he is lost in thought and memory and the words die away on his lips. The* REFUGEES *likewise nod in dreamy recollection. Soon the whisper "Moses, Moses!" goes around. An aged Jew parts his beard and recites dramatically:*

MOSES:

בְּֽרֵאשִׁית בָּרָא אֱלֹהִים אֵת הַשָּׁמַיִם וְאֵת הָאָרֶץ: וְהָאָרֶץ הָיְתָה תֹהוֹ
וָבֹהוּ וְחשֶׁךְ עַל־פְּנֵי תְהוֹם וְרוּחַ אֱלֹהִים מְרַחֶפֶת עַל־פְּנֵי הַמָּיִם:

The same dying away of the words take place, and on the part of the REFUGEES *the same retreat into recollection. Some of them murmur, "Yes, yes."*

The mood is broken by the abrupt entrance of MR. *and* MRS. ANTROBUS *and* SABINA *bearing platters of sandwiches and a pail of coffee.* SABINA *stops and stares at the guests.*

MR. ANTROBUS: Sabina, pass the sandwiches.

SABINA: I thought I was working in a respectable house that had respectable guests. I'm giving my notice, Mr. Antrobus: two weeks, that's the law.

MR. ANTROBUS: Sabina! Pass the sandwiches.

SABINA: Two weeks, that's the law.

MR. ANTROBUS: There's the law. That's Moses.

SABINA: (*Stares.*) The Ten Commandments—FAUGH!!—(*To Audience*) That's the worst line I've ever had to say on any stage.

ANTROBUS: I think the best thing to do is just not to stand on ceremony, but pass the sandwiches around from left to right.—Judge, help yourself to one of these.

MRS. ANTROBUS: The roads are crowded, I hear?

THE GUESTS: (*All talking at once.*) Oh, ma'am, you can't imagine. . . . You can hardly put one foot before you . . . people are trampling one another.

Sudden silence.

MRS. ANTROBUS: Well, you know what I think it is,—I think it's sun-spots!

THE GUESTS: (*Discreet hubbub.*) Oh, you're right, Mrs. Antrobus . . . that's what it is. . . . That's what I was saying the other day.

Sudden silence.

ANTROBUS: Well, I don't believe the whole world's going to turn to ice.

All eyes are fixed on him, waiting.

I can't believe it. Judge! Have we worked for nothing? Professor! Have we just failed in the whole thing?

MRS. ANTROBUS: It is certainly very strange—well fortunately on both sides of the family we come of very hearty stock.— Doctor, I want you to meet my children. They're eating their supper now. And of course I want them to meet you.

MISS M. MUSE: How many children have you, Mrs. Antrobus?

MRS. ANTROBUS: I have two,—a boy and a girl.

MOSES: (*Softly.*) I understood you had two sons, Mrs. Antrobus.

> MRS. ANTROBUS *in blind suffering; she walks toward the footlights.*

MRS. ANTROBUS: (*In a low voice.*) Abel, Abel, my son, my son, Abel, my son, Abel, Abel, my son.

> *The* REFUGEES *move with few steps toward her as though in comfort murmuring words in Greek, Hebrew, German, et cetera.*
> *A piercing shriek from the kitchen,—*SABINA'S *voice. All heads turn.*

ANTROBUS: What's that?

SABINA *enters, bursting with indignation, pulling on her gloves.*

SABINA: Mr. Antrobus—that son of yours, that boy Henry Antrobus—I don't stay in this house another moment!— He's not fit to live among respectable folks and that's a fact.

MRS. ANTROBUS: Don't say another word, Sabina. I'll be right back. (*Without waiting for an answer she goes past her into the kitchen.*)

SABINA: Mr. Antrobus, Henry has thrown a stone again and if he hasn't killed the boy that lives next door, I'm very much mistaken. He finished his supper and went out to play; and I heard such a fight; and then I saw it. I saw it with my own eyes. And it looked to me like stark murder.

> MRS. ANTROBUS *appears at the kitchen door, shielding* HENRY *who follows her. When she steps aside, we see on* HENRY'S *forehead a large ochre and scarlet scar in the shape of a C.* MR. ANTROBUS *starts toward him. A pause.* HENRY *is heard saying under his breath:*

HENRY: He was going to take the wheel away from me. He started to throw a stone at me first.

MRS. ANTROBUS: George, it was just a boyish impulse. Remember how young he is. (*Louder, in an urgent wail.*) George, he's only four thousand years old.

SABINA: And everything was going along so nicely!

> *Silence.* ANTROBUS *goes back to the fireplace.*

ANTROBUS: Put out the fire! Put out all the fires. (*Violently.*) No wonder the sun grows cold. (*He starts stamping on the fireplace.*)

MRS. ANTROBUS: Doctor! Judge! Help me!—George, have you lost your mind?

ANTROBUS: There is no mind. We'll not try to live. (*To the guests.*) Give it up. Give up trying.

> MRS. ANTROBUS *seizes him.*

SABINA: Mr. Antrobus! I'm downright ashamed of you.

MRS. ANTROBUS: George, have some more coffee.—Gladys! Where's Gladys gone?

> GLADYS *steps in, frightened.*

GLADYS: Here I am, mama.

MRS. ANTROBUS: Go upstairs and bring your father's slippers. How could you forget a thing like that, when you know how tired he is?

> ANTROBUS *sits in his chair. He covers his face with his hands.*
> MRS. ANTROBUS *turns to the* REFUGEES:

Can't some of you sing? It's your business in life to sing, isn't it? Sabina!

> *Several of the women clear their throats tentatively, and with frightened faces gather around* HOMER'S *guitar. He establishes a few chords. Almost inaudibly they start singing, led by* SABINA: *"Jingle Bells."* MRS. ANTROBUS *continues to* ANTROBUS *in a low voice, while taking off his shoes:*

George, remember all the other times. When the volcanoes came right up in the front yard.
And the time the grasshoppers ate every single leaf and blade of grass, and all the grain and spinach you'd grown with your own hands. And the summer there were earthquakes every night.

ANTROBUS: Henry! Henry! (*Puts his hand on his forehead.*) Myself. All of us, we're covered with blood.

MRS. ANTROBUS: Then remember all the times you were pleased with him and when you were proud of yourself.— Henry! Henry! Come here and recite to your father the multiplication table that you do so nicely.

> HENRY *kneels on one knee beside his father and starts whispering the multiplication table.*

HENRY: (*Finally.*) Two times six is twelve; three times six is eighteen—I don't think I know the sixes.

> *Enter* GLADYS *with the slippers.* MRS. ANTROBUS *makes stern gestures to her: Go in there and do your best. The* GUESTS *are now singing "Tenting Tonight."*

GLADYS: (*Putting slippers on his feet.*) Papa . . . papa . . . I was very good in school today. Miss Conover said right out in class that if all the girls had as good manners as Gladys Antrobus, that the world would be a very different place to live in.

MRS. ANTROBUS: You recited a piece at assembly, didn't you? Recite it to your father.

GLADYS: Papa, do you want to hear what I recited in class?

Fierce directorial glance from her mother.

"THE STAR" by Henry Wadsworth LONGFELLOW.

MRS. ANTROBUS: Wait!!! The fire's going out. There isn't enough wood! Henry, go upstairs and bring down the chairs and start breaking up the beds.

Exit HENRY. *The singers return to "Jingle Bells," still very softly.*

GLADYS: Look, Papa, here's my report card. Lookit. Conduct A! Look, Papa. Papa, do you want to hear the Star, by Henry Wadsworth Longfellow? Papa, you're not mad at me, are you?—I know it'll get warmer. Soon it'll be just like spring, and we can go to a picnic at the Hibernian Picnic Grounds like you always like to do, don't you remember? Papa, just look at me once.

Enter HENRY *with some chairs.*

ANTROBUS: You recited in assembly, did you?

She nods eagerly.

You didn't forget it?

GLADYS: No!!! I was perfect.

Pause. Then ANTROBUS *rises, goes to the front door and opens it. The* REFUGEES *draw back timidly; the song stops; he peers out of the door, then closes it.*

ANTROBUS: (*With decision, suddenly.*) Build up the fire. It's cold. Build up the fire. We'll do what we can. Sabina, get some more wood. Come around the fire, everybody. At least the young ones may pull through. Henry, have you eaten something?

HENRY: Yes, papa.

ANTROBUS: Gladys, have you had some supper?

GLADYS: I ate in the kitchen, papa.

ANTROBUS: If you do come through this—what'll you be able to do? What do you know? Henry, did you take a good look at that wheel?

HENRY: Yes, papa.

ANTROBUS: (*Sitting down in his chair.*) Six times two are—

HENRY: —twelve; six times three are eighteen; six times four are—Papa, it's hot and cold. It makes my head all funny. It makes me sleepy.

ANTROBUS: (*Gives him a cuff.*) Wake up. I don't care if your head is sleepy. Six times four are twenty-four. Six times five are—

HENRY: Thirty. Papa!

ANTROBUS: Maggie, put something into Gladys' head on the chance she can use it.

MRS. ANTROBUS: What do you mean, George?

ANTROBUS: Six times six are thirty-six.

Teach her the beginning of the Bible.

GLADYS: But, Mama, it's so cold and close.

> HENRY *has all but drowsed off. His father slaps him sharply and the lesson goes on.*

MRS. ANTROBUS: "In the beginning God created the heavens and the earth; and the earth was waste and void; and the darkness was upon the face of the deep—"

> *The singing starts up again louder.* SABINA *has returned with wood.*

SABINA: (*After placing wood on the fireplace comes down to the footlights and addresses the audience:*) Will you please start handing up your chairs? We'll need everything for this fire. Save the human race.—Ushers, will you pass the chairs up here? Thank you.

HENRY: Six times nine are fifty-four; six times ten are sixty.

> *In the back of the auditorium the sound of chairs being ripped up can be heard.* USHERS *rush down the aisles with chairs and hand them over.*

GLADYS: "And God called the light Day and the darkness he called Night."

SABINA: Pass up your chairs, everybody. Save the human race.

CURTAIN

Act II

Toward the end of the intermission, though with the house-lights still up, lantern slide projections begin to appear on the curtain. Timetables for trains leaving Pennsylvania Station for Atlantic City. Advertisements of Atlantic City hotels, drugstores, churches, rug merchants; fortune tellers, Bingo parlors.

When the house-lights go down, the voice of an ANNOUNCER *is heard.*

ANNOUNCER: The Management now brings you the News Events of the World. Atlantic City, New Jersey:

Projection of a chrome postcard of the waterfront, trimmed in mica with the legend: FUN AT THE BEACH.

This great convention city is playing host this week to the anniversary convocation of that great fraternal order,—the Ancient and Honorable Order of Mammals, Subdivision Humans. This great fraternal, militant and burial society is celebrating on the Boardwalk, ladies and gentlemen, its six hundred thousandth Annual Convention.
It has just elected its president for the ensuing term,—

Projection of MR. *and* MRS. ANTROBUS *posed as they will be shown a few moments later.*

Mr. George Antrobus of Excelsior, New Jersey. We show you President Antrobus and his gracious and charming wife, every inch a mammal. Mr. Antrobus has had a long and che-quered career. Credit has been paid to him for many useful enterprises including the introduction of the lever, of the wheel and the brewing of beer. Credit has been also extended to President Antrobus's gracious and charming wife for many practical suggestions, including the hem, the gore, and the gusset; and the novelty of the year,—frying in oil. Before we show you Mr. Antrobus accepting the nomination, we have an important announcement to make. As many of you know, this great celebration of the Order of the Mammals has re-ceived delegations from the other rival Orders,—or shall we say: esteemed concurrent Orders: the WINGS, the FINS, the SHELLS, and so on. These Orders are holding their conventions also, in various parts of the world, and have sent representatives to our own, two of a kind.

Later in the day we will show you President Antrobus broadcasting his words of greeting and congratulation to the collected assemblies of the whole natural world.

Ladies and Gentlemen! We give you President Antrobus!

The screen becomes a Transparency. MR. ANTROBUS *stands beside a pedestal;* MRS. ANTROBUS *is seated wearing a corsage of orchids.* ANTROBUS *wears an untidy Prince Albert; spats; from a red rosette in his buttonhole hangs a fine long purple ribbon of honor. He wears a gay lodge hat,—something between a fez and a legionnaire's cap.*

ANTROBUS: Fellow-mammals,   fellow-vertebrates,   fellow-humans, I thank you. Little did my dear parents think,—when they told me to stand on my own two feet,—that I'd arrive at this place.

My friends, we have come a long way.

During this week of happy celebration it is perhaps not fitting that we dwell on some of the difficult times we have been through. The dinosaur is extinct—

Applause.

—the ice has retreated; and the common cold is being pursued by every means within our power.

MRS. ANTROBUS *sneezes, laughs prettily, and murmurs: "I beg your pardon."*

In our memorial service yesterday we did honor to all our friends and relatives who are no longer with us, by reason of cold, earthquakes, plagues and . . . and . . . (*Coughs.*) differences of opinion.

As our Bishop so ably said . . . uh . . . so ably said. . . .

MRS. ANTROBUS: (*Closed lips.*) Gone, but not forgotten.

ANTROBUS: 'They are gone, but not forgotten.'

I think I can say, I think I can prophesy with complete . . . uh . . . with complete. . . .

MRS. ANTROBUS: Confidence.

ANTROBUS: Thank you, my dear,—With complete lack of confidence, that a new day of security is about to dawn.

The watchword of the closing year was: Work. I give you the watchword for the future: Enjoy Yourselves.

MRS. ANTROBUS: George, sit down!

ANTROBUS: Before I close, however, I wish to answer one of those unjust and malicious accusations that were brought against me during this last electoral campaign.

Ladies and gentlemen, the charge was made that at various points in my career I leaned toward joining some of the rival orders,—that's a lie.

As I told reporters of the *Atlantic City Herald*, I do not deny that a few months before my birth I hesitated between . . . uh . . . between pinfeathers and gill-breathing,—and so did many of us here,—but for the last million years I have been viviparous, hairy and diaphragmatic.

> *Applause. Cries of 'Good old Antrobus,' 'The Prince chap!' 'Georgie,' etc.*

ANNOUNCER: Thank you. Thank you very much, Mr. Antrobus.

Now I know that our visitors will wish to hear a word from that gracious and charming mammal, Mrs. Antrobus, wife and mother,—Mrs. Antrobus!

> MRS. ANTROBUS *rises, lays her program on her chair, bows and says:*

MRS. ANTROBUS: Dear friends, I don't really think I should say anything. After all, it was my husband who was elected and not I.

Perhaps, as president of the Women's Auxiliary Bed and Board Society,—I had some notes here, oh, yes, here they are:—I should give a short report from some of our committees that have been meeting in this beautiful city.

Perhaps it may interest you to know that it has at last been decided that the tomato is edible. Can you all hear me? The tomato *is* edible.

A delegate from across the sea reports that the thread woven by the silkworm gives a cloth . . . I have a sample of it here . . . can you see it? smooth, elastic. I should say that it's rather attractive,—though personally I prefer less shiny surfaces. Should the windows of a sleeping apartment be open or shut? I know all mothers will follow our debates on this matter with close interest. I am sorry to say that the most expert authorities have not yet decided. It does seem to me that the night air would be bound to be unhealthy for our children, but there are many distinguished authorities on both sides. Well, I could go on talking forever,—as Shakespeare says: a woman's work is seldom done; but I think I'd better join my husband in saying thank you, and sit down. Thank you. (*She sits down.*)

ANNOUNCER: Oh, Mrs. Antrobus!

MRS. ANTROBUS: Yes?

ANNOUNCER: We understand that you are about to celebrate a wedding anniversary. I know our listeners would like to extend their felicitations and hear a few words from you on that subject.

MRS. ANTROBUS: I have been asked by this kind gentleman . . . yes, my friends, this Spring Mr. Antrobus and I will be celebrating our five thousandth wedding anniversary.

I don't know if I speak for my husband, but I can say that, as for me, I regret every moment of it.

Laughter of confusion.

I beg your pardon. What I *mean* to say is that I do not regret one moment of it. I hope none of you catch my cold. We have two children. We've always had two children, though it hasn't always been the same two. But as I say, we have two fine children, and we're very grateful for that. Yes, Mr. Antrobus and I have been married five thousand years. Each wedding anniversary reminds me of the times when there were no weddings. We had to crusade for marriage. Perhaps there are some women within the sound of my voice who remember that crusade and those struggles; we fought for it, didn't we? We chained ourselves to lampposts and we made disturbances in the Senate,—anyway, at last we women got the ring.

A few men helped us, but I must say that most men blocked our way at every step: they said we were unfeminine.

I only bring up these unpleasant memories, because I see some signs of backsliding from that great victory.

Oh, my fellow mammals, keep hold of that.

My husband says that the watchword for the year is Enjoy Yourselves. I think that's very open to misunderstanding. My watchword for the year is: Save the Family. It's held together for over five thousand years: Save it! Thank you.

ANNOUNCER: Thank you, Mrs. Antrobus.

The transparency disappears.

We had hoped to show you the Beauty Contest that took place here today.

President Antrobus, an experienced judge of pretty girls, gave the title of Miss Atlantic City 1942, to Miss Lily-Sabina Fairweather, charming hostess of our Boardwalk Bingo Parlor.

Unfortunately, however, our time is up, and I must take you to some views of the Convention City and conveeners,—enjoying themselves.

A burst of music; the curtain rises.

The Boardwalk. The audience is sitting in the ocean. A handrail of scarlet cord stretches across the front of the stage. A ramp—also with scarlet hand rail—descends to the right corner of the orchestra pit where a great scarlet beach umbrella or a cabana stands. Front and right stage left are benches facing the sea; attached to each bench is a street-lamp. The only scenery is two cardboard cut-outs six feet high, representing shops at the back of the stage. Reading from left to right they are: SALT WATER TAFFY: FORTUNE TELLER; then the blank space; BINGO PARLOR; TURKISH BATH. They have practical doors, that of the Fortune Teller's being hung with bright gypsy curtains.

By the left proscenium and rising from the orchestra pit is the weather signal; it is like the mast of a ship with cross bars. From time to time black discs are hung on it to indicate the storm and hurricane warnings. Three roller chairs, pushed by melancholy NEGROES, *file by empty. Throughout the act they traverse the stage in both directions.*

From time to time, CONVEENERS, *dressed like* MR. ANTRO-

BUS, *cross the stage. Some walk sedately by; others engage in inane horseplay. The old gypsy* FORTUNE TELLER *is seated at the door of her shop, smoking a corncob pipe.*
From the Bingo Parlor comes the voice of the CALLER.

BINGO CALLER: A-Nine; A-Nine. C-Twenty-six; C-Twenty-six. A-Four; A-Four. B-Twelve.
CHORUS: (*Back-stage.*) Bingo!!!

> *The front of the Bingo Parlor shudders, rises a few feet in the air and returns to the ground trembling.*

FORTUNE TELLER: (*Mechanically, to the unconscious back of a passerby, pointing with her pipe.*) Bright's disease! Your partner's deceiving you in that Kansas City deal. You'll have six grandchildren. Avoid high places. (*She rises and shouts after another:*) Cirrhosis of the liver!

> SABINA *appears at the door of the Bingo Parlor. She hugs about her a blue raincoat that almost conceals her red bathing suit. She tries to catch the* FORTUNE TELLER'S *attention.*

SABINA: Sssst! Esmeralda! Sssst!
FORTUNE TELLER: Keck!
SABINA: Has President Antrobus come along yet?
FORTUNE TELLER: No, no, no. Get back there. Hide yourself.
SABINA: I'm afraid I'll miss him. Oh, Esmeralda, if I fail in this, I'll die; I know I'll die. President Antrobus!!! And I'll be his wife! If it's the last thing I'll do, I'll be Mrs. George Antrobus.—Esmeralda, tell me my future.
FORTUNE TELLER: Keck!
SABINA: All right, I'll tell *you* my future. (*Laughing dreamily and tracing it out with one finger on the palm of her hand.*) I've won the Beauty Contest in Atlantic City,—well, I'll win the Beauty Contest of the whole world. I'll take President Antrobus away from that wife of his. Then I'll take every man away from his wife. I'll turn the whole earth upside down.
FORTUNE TELLER: Keck!
SABINA: When all those husbands just think about me they'll

get dizzy. They'll faint in the streets. They'll have to lean against lampposts.—Esmeralda, who was Helen of Troy?

FORTUNE TELLER: (*Furiously.*) Shut your foolish mouth. When Mr. Antrobus comes along you can see what you can do. Until then,—go away.

> SABINA *laughs. As she returns to the door of her Bingo Parlor a group of* CONVEENERS *rush over and smother her with attentions: "Oh, Miss Lily, you know me. You've known me for years."*

SABINA: Go away, boys, go away. I'm after bigger fry than you are.—Why, Mr. Simpson!! How *dare* you!! I expect that even you nobodies must have girls to amuse you; but where you find them and what you do with them, is of absolutely no interest to me.

> *Exit. The* CONVEENERS *squeal with pleasure and stumble in after her.*
> *The* FORTUNE TELLER *rises, puts her pipe down on the stool, unfurls her voluminous skirts, gives a sharp wrench to her bodice and strolls towards the audience, swinging her hips like a young woman.*

FORTUNE TELLER: I tell the future. Keck. Nothing easier. Everybody's future is in their face. Nothing easier.

But who can tell your past,—eh? Nobody!

Your youth,—where did it go? It slipped away while you weren't looking. While you were asleep. While you were drunk? Puh! You're like our friends, Mr. and Mrs. Antrobus; you lie awake nights trying to know your past. What did it mean? What was it trying to say to you?

Think! Think! Split your heads. I can't tell the past and neither can you. If anybody tries to tell you the past, take my word for it, they're charlatans! Charlatans! But I can tell the future. (*She suddenly barks at a passing chair-pusher.*)

Apoplexy! (*She returns to the audience.*)

Nobody listens.—Keck! I see a face among you now—I won't embarrass him by pointing him out, but, listen, it may be you: Next year the watchsprings inside you will crumple up. Death by regret,—Type Y. It's in the corners of your mouth. You'll decide that you should have lived for pleasure, but that you missed it. Death by regret,—Type Y. . . . Avoid mirrors. You'll try to be angry,—but no!—no anger. (*Far forward, confidentially.*)

And now what's the immediate future of our friends, the Antrobuses? Oh, you've seen it as well as I have, keck,—that dizziness of the head; that Great Man dizziness? The inventor of beer and gunpowder? The sudden fits of temper and then the long stretches of inertia? "I'm a sultan; let my slave-girls fan me?"

You know as well as I what's coming. Rain. Rain. Rain in floods. The deluge. But first you'll see shameful things— shameful things. Some of you will be saying: "Let him drown. He's not worth saving. Give the whole thing up." I can see it in your faces. But you're wrong. Keep your doubts and despairs to yourselves.

Again there'll be the narrow escape. The survival of a handful. From destruction,—total destruction. (*She points sweeping with her hand to the stage.*)

Even of the animals, a few will be saved: two of a kind, male and female, two of a kind.

> *The heads of* CONVEENERS *appear about the stage and in the orchestra pit, jeering at her.*

CONVEENERS: Charlatan! Madam Kill-joy! Mrs. Jeremiah! Charlatan!

FORTUNE TELLER: And *you!* Mark my words before it's too late. Where'll *you* be?

CONVEENERS: The croaking raven. Old dust and ashes. Rags, bottles, sacks.

FORTUNE TELLER: Yes, stick out your tongues. You can't stick your tongues out far enough to lick the death-sweat from your foreheads. It's too late to work now—bail out the flood with your soup spoons. You've had your chance and you've lost.

CONVEENERS: Enjoy yourselves!!!

> *They disappear. The* FORTUNE TELLER *looks off left and puts her finger on her lip.*

FORTUNE TELLER: They're coming—the Antrobuses. Keck. Your hope. Your despair. Your selves.

Enter from the left, MR. *and* MRS. ANTROBUS *and* GLADYS.

MRS. ANTROBUS: Gladys Antrobus, stick your stummick in.

GLADYS: But it's easier this way.

MRS. ANTROBUS: Well, it's too bad the new president has such a clumsy daughter, that's all I can say. Try and be a lady.

FORTUNE TELLER: Aijah! That's been said a hundred billion times.

MRS. ANTROBUS: Goodness! Where's Henry? He was here just a minute ago. Henry!

> *Sudden violent stir. A roller-chair appears from the left. About it are dancing in great excitement* HENRY *and a* NEGRO CHAIR-PUSHER.

HENRY: (*Slingshot in hand.*) I'll put your eye out. I'll make you yell, like you never yelled before.

NEGRO: (*At the same time.*) Now, I warns you. I warns you. If you make me mad, you'll get hurt.

ANTROBUS: Henry! What is this? Put down that slingshot.

MRS. ANTROBUS: (*At the same time.*) Henry! HENRY! Behave yourself.

FORTUNE TELLER: That's right, young man. There are too many people in the world as it is. Everybody's in the way, except one's self.

HENRY: All I wanted to do was—have some fun.

NEGRO: Nobody can't touch my chair, nobody, without I allow 'em to. You get clean away from me and you get away fast. (*He pushes his chair off, muttering.*)

ANTROBUS: What were you doing, Henry?

HENRY: Everybody's always getting mad. Everybody's always trying to push you around. I'll make him sorry for this; I'll make him sorry.

ANTROBUS: Give me that slingshot.

HENRY: I won't. I'm sorry I came to this place. I wish I weren't here. I wish I weren't anywhere.

MRS. ANTROBUS: Now, Henry, don't get so excited about nothing. I declare I don't know what we're going to do with you. Put your slingshot in your pocket, and don't try to take hold of things that don't belong to you.

ANTROBUS: After this you can stay home. I wash my hands of you.

MRS. ANTROBUS: Come now, let's forget all about it. Everybody take a good breath of that sea air and calm down.

A passing CONVEENER *bows to* ANTROBUS *who nods to him.*

Who was that you spoke to, George?

ANTROBUS: Nobody, Maggie. Just the candidate who ran against me in the election.

MRS. ANTROBUS: The man who ran against you in the election!! (*She turns and waves her umbrella after the disappearing* CONVEENER.) My husband didn't speak to you and he never will speak to you.

ANTROBUS: Now, Maggie.

MRS. ANTROBUS: After those lies you told about him in your speeches! Lies, that's what they were.

GLADYS AND HENRY: Mama, everybody's looking at you. Everybody's laughing at you.

MRS. ANTROBUS: If you must know, my husband's a SAINT, a downright SAINT, and you're not fit to speak to him on the street.

ANTROBUS: Now, Maggie, now, Maggie, that's enough of that.

MRS. ANTROBUS: George Antrobus, you're a perfect worm. If you won't stand up for yourself, I will.

GLADYS: Mama, you just act awful in public.

MRS. ANTROBUS: (*Laughing.*) Well, I must say I enjoyed it. I feel better. Wish his wife had been there to hear it. Children, what do you want to do?

GLADYS: Papa, can we ride in one of those chairs? Mama, I want to ride in one of those chairs.

MRS. ANTROBUS: No, Sir. If you're tired you just sit where you are. We have no money to spend on foolishness.

ANTROBUS: I guess we have money enough for a thing like that. It's one of the things you do at Atlantic City.

MRS. ANTROBUS: Oh, we have? I tell you it's a miracle my children have shoes to stand up in. I didn't think I'd ever live to see them pushed around in chairs.

ANTROBUS: We're on a vacation, aren't we? We have a right to some treats, I guess. Maggie, some day you're going to drive me crazy.

MRS. ANTROBUS: All right, go. I'll just sit here and laugh at you. And you can give me my dollar right in my hand. Mark my words, a rainy day is coming. There's a rainy day ahead of us. I feel it in my bones. Go on, throw your money around. I can starve. I've starved before. I know how.

A CONVEENER *puts his head through Turkish Bath window, and says with raised eyebrows:*

CONVEENER: Hello, George. How are ya? I see where you brought the WHOLE family along.
MRS. ANTROBUS: And what do you mean by that?

CONVEENER *withdraws head and closes window.*

ANTROBUS: Maggie, I tell you there's a limit to what I can stand. God's Heaven, haven't I worked *enough*? Don't I get *any* vacation? Can't I even give my children so much as a ride in a roller-chair?
MRS. ANTROBUS: (*Putting out her hand for raindrops.*) Anyway, it's going to rain very soon and you have your broadcast to make.
ANTROBUS: Now, Maggie, I warn you. A man can stand a family only just so long. I'm warning you.

Enter SABINA *from the Bingo-Parlor. She wears a flounced red silk bathing suit, 1905. Red stockings, shoes, parasol. She bows demurely to* ANTROBUS *and starts down the ramp.* ANTROBUS *and the* CHILDREN *stare at her.* ANTROBUS *bows gallantly.*

MRS. ANTROBUS: Why, George Antrobus, how can you say such a thing! You have the best family in the world.
ANTROBUS: Good morning, Miss Fairweather.

SABINA *finally disappears behind the beach umbrella or in a cabana in the orchestra pit.*

MRS. ANTROBUS: Who on earth was that you spoke to, George?
ANTROBUS: (*Complacent; mock-modest.*) Hm . . . m . . . just a . . . solambaka keray.
MRS. ANTROBUS: What? I can't understand you.
GLADYS: Mama, wasn't she beautiful?
HENRY: Papa, introduce her to me.
MRS. ANTROBUS: Children, will you be quiet while I ask your father a simple question?—Who did you say it was, George?

ANTROBUS: Why-uh . . . a friend of mine. Very nice refined girl.

MRS. ANTROBUS: I'm waiting.

ANTROBUS: Maggie, that's the girl I gave the prize to in the beauty contest,—that's Miss Atlantic City 1942.

MRS. ANTROBUS: Hm! She looked like Sabina to me.

HENRY: (*At the railing.*) Mama, the life-guard knows her, too. Mama, he knows her well.

ANTROBUS: Henry, come here.—She's a very nice girl in every way and the sole support of her aged mother.

MRS. ANTROBUS: So was Sabina, so was Sabina; and it took a wall of ice to open your eyes about Sabina.—Henry, come over and sit down on this bench.

ANTROBUS: She's a very different matter from Sabina. Miss Fairweather is a college graduate, Phi Beta Kappa.

MRS. ANTROBUS: Henry, you sit here by mama. Gladys—

ANTROBUS: (*Sitting.*) Reduced circumstances have required her taking a position as hostess in a Bingo Parlor; but there isn't a girl with higher principles in the country.

MRS. ANTROBUS: Well, let's not talk about it.—Henry, I haven't seen a whale yet.

ANTROBUS: She speaks seven languages and has more culture in her little finger than you've acquired in a lifetime.

MRS. ANTROBUS: (*Assumed amiability.*) All right, all right, George. I'm glad to know there are such superior girls in the Bingo Parlors.—Henry, what's that?

Pointing at the storm signal, which has one black disk.

HENRY: What is it, Papa?

ANTROBUS: What? Oh, that's the storm signal. One of those black disks means bad weather; two means storm; three means hurricane; and four means the end of the world.

As they watch it a second black disk rolls into place.

MRS. ANTROBUS: Goodness! I'm going this very minute to buy you all some raincoats.

GLADYS: (*Putting her cheek against her father's shoulder.*) Mama, don't go yet. I like sitting this way. And the ocean coming in and coming in. Papa, don't you like it?

MRS. ANTROBUS: Well, there's only one thing I lack to make me a perfectly happy woman: I'd like to see a whale.

HENRY: Mama, we saw two. Right out there. They're delegates to the convention. I'll find you one.

GLADYS: Papa, ask me something. Ask me a question.

ANTROBUS: Well . . . how big's the ocean?

GLADYS: Papa, you're teasing me. It's—three-hundred and sixty million square-miles—and—it—covers—three-fourths —of—the—earth's—surface—and—its—deepest-place— is—five—and—a—half—miles—deep—and—its—average —depth—is—twelve-thousand—feet. No, Papa, ask me something hard, real hard.

MRS. ANTROBUS: (*Rising.*) Now I'm going off to buy those raincoats. I think that bad weather's going to get worse and worse. I hope it doesn't come before your broadcast. I should think we have about an hour or so.

HENRY: I hope it comes and zzzzzz everything before it. I hope it—

MRS. ANTROBUS: Henry!—George, I think . . . maybe, it's one of those storms that are just as bad on land as on the sea. When you're just as safe and safer in a good stout boat.

HENRY: There's a boat out at the end of the pier.

MRS. ANTROBUS: Well, keep your eye on it. George, you shut your eyes and get a good rest before the broadcast.

ANTROBUS: Thundering Judas, do I have to be told when to open and shut my eyes? Go and buy your raincoats.

MRS. ANTROBUS: Now, children, you have ten minutes to walk around. Ten minutes. And, Henry: control yourself. Gladys, stick by your brother and don't get lost.

They run off.

MRS. ANTROBUS: Will you be all right, George?

CONVEENERS *suddenly stick their heads out of the Bingo Parlor and Salt Water Taffy store, and voices rise from the orchestra pit.*

CONVEENERS: George. Geo-r-r-rge! George! Leave the old hen-coop at home, George. Do-mes-ticated Georgie!

MRS. ANTROBUS: (*Shaking her umbrella.*) Low common oafs! That's what they are. Guess a man has a right to bring his wife to a convention, if he wants to. (*She starts off.*) What's the matter with a family, I'd like to know. What else have they got to offer?

Exit. ANTROBUS *has closed his eyes. The* FORTUNE TELLER *comes out of her shop and goes over to the left proscenium. She leans against it watching* SABINA *quizzically.*

FORTUNE TELLER: Heh! Here she comes!

SABINA: (*Loud whisper.*) What's he doing?

FORTUNE TELLER: Oh, he's ready for you. Bite your lips, dear, take a long breath and come on up.

SABINA: I'm nervous. My whole future depends on this. I'm nervous.

FORTUNE TELLER: Don't be a fool. What more could you want? He's forty-five. His head's a little dizzy. He's just been elected president. He's never known any other woman than his wife. Whenever he looks at her he realizes that she knows every foolish thing he's ever done.

SABINA: (*Still whispering.*) I don't know why it is, but every time I start one of these I'm nervous.

The FORTUNE TELLER *stands in the center of the stage watching the following:*

FORTUNE TELLER: You make me tired.

SABINA: First tell me my fortune.

The FORTUNE TELLER *laughs drily and makes the gesture of brushing away a nonsensical question.* SABINA *coughs and says:*

Oh, Mr. Antrobus,—dare I speak to you for a moment?

ANTROBUS: What?—Oh, certainly, certainly, Miss Fairweather.

SABINA: Mr. Antrobus . . . I've been so unhappy. I've wanted . . . I've wanted to make sure that you don't think that I'm the kind of girl who goes out for beauty contests.

FORTUNE TELLER: That's the way!

ANTROBUS: Oh, I understand. I understand perfectly.

FORTUNE TELLER: Give it a little more. Lean on it.

SABINA: I knew you would. My mother said to me this morning: Lily, she said, that fine Mr. Antrobus gave you the prize because he saw at once that you weren't the kind of girl who'd go in for a thing like that. But, honestly, Mr. Antrobus, in this world, honestly, a good girl doesn't know where to turn.

FORTUNE TELLER: Now you've gone too far.

ANTROBUS: My dear Miss Fairweather!

SABINA: You wouldn't know how hard it is. With that lovely wife and daughter you have. Oh, I think Mrs. Antrobus is the finest woman I ever saw. I wish I were like her.

ANTROBUS: There, there. There's . . . uh . . . room for all kinds of people in the world, Miss Fairweather.

SABINA: How wonderful of you to say that. How generous!— Mr. Antrobus, have you a moment free? . . . I'm afraid I may be a little conspicuous here . . . could you come down, for just a moment, to my beach cabana . . . ?

ANTROBUS: Why-uh . . . yes, certainly . . . for a moment . . . just for a moment.

SABINA: There's a deck chair there. Because: you know you *do* look tired. Just this morning my mother said to me: Lily, she said, I hope Mr. Antrobus is getting a good rest. His fine strong face has deep deep lines in it. Now isn't it true, Mr. Antrobus: you work too hard?

FORTUNE TELLER: Bingo! (*She goes into her shop.*)

SABINA: Now you will just stretch out. No, I shan't say a word, not a word. I shall just sit there,—privileged. That's what I am.

ANTROBUS: (*Taking her hand.*) Miss Fairweather . . . you'll . . . spoil me.

SABINA: Just a moment. I have something I wish to say to the audience.—Ladies and gentlemen. I'm not going to play this particular scene tonight. It's just a short scene and we're going to skip it. But I'll tell you what takes place and then we can continue the play from there on. Now in this scene—

ANTROBUS: (*Between his teeth.*) But, Miss Somerset!

SABINA: I'm sorry. I'm sorry. But I have to skip it. In this scene, I talk to Mr. Antrobus, and at the end of it he decides to leave his wife, get a divorce at Reno and marry me. That's all.

ANTROBUS: Fitz!—Fitz!

SABINA: So that now I've told you we can jump to the end of it,—where you say:

Enter in fury MR. FITZPATRICK, *the stage manager.*

MR. FITZPATRICK: Miss Somerset, we insist on your playing
  this scene.
SABINA: I'm sorry, Mr. Fitzpatrick, but I can't and I won't.
  I've told the audience all they need to know and now we can
  go on.

Other ACTORS *begin to appear on the stage, listening.*

MR. FITZPATRICK: And *why* can't you play it?
SABINA: Because there are some lines in that scene that would
  hurt some people's feelings and I don't think the theatre is a
  place where people's feelings ought to be hurt.
MR. FITZPATRICK: Miss Somerset, you can pack up your things
  and go home. I shall call the understudy and I shall report
  you to Equity.
SABINA: I sent the understudy up to the corner for a cup of
  coffee and if Equity tries to penalize me I'll drag the case
  right up to the Supreme Court. Now listen, everybody,
  there's no need to get excited.
MR. FITZPATRICK *and* ANTROBUS: Why can't you play it . . .
  what's the matter with the scene?
SABINA: Well, if you must know, I have a personal guest in the
  audience tonight. Her life hasn't been exactly a happy one. I
  wouldn't have my friend hear some of these lines for the
  whole world. I don't suppose it occurred to the author that
  some other women might have gone through the experience of losing their husbands like this. Wild horses wouldn't
  drag from me the details of my friend's life, but . . . well,
  they'd been married twenty years, and before he got rich,
  why, she'd done the washing and everything.
MR. FITZPATRICK: Miss Somerset, your friend will forgive you.
  We must play this scene.
SABINA: Nothing, nothing will make me say some of those
  lines . . . about "a man outgrows a wife every seven years"
  and . . . and that one about "the Mohammedans being
  the only people who looked the subject square in the face."
  Nothing.
MR. FITZPATRICK: Miss Somerset! Go to your dressing room.
  I'll *read* your lines.

SABINA: Now everybody's nerves are on edge.

MR. ANTROBUS: Skip the scene.

> MR. FITZPATRICK *and the other* ACTORS *go off.*

SABINA: Thank you. I knew you'd understand. We'll do just what I said. So Mr. Antrobus is going to divorce his wife and marry me. Mr. Antrobus, you say: "It won't be easy to lay all this before my wife."

> *The* ACTORS *withdraw.* ANTROBUS *walks about, his hand to his forehead muttering:*

ANTROBUS: Wait a minute. I can't get back into it as easily as all that. "My wife is a very obstinate woman." Hm . . . then you say . . . hm . . . Miss Fairweather, I mean Lily, it won't be easy to lay all this before my wife. It'll hurt her feelings a little.

SABINA: Listen, George: *other* people haven't got feelings. Not in the same way that we have,—we who are presidents like you and prize-winners like me. Listen, other people haven't got feelings; they just imagine they have. Within two weeks they go back to playing bridge and going to the movies.

Listen, dear: everybody in the world except a few people like you and me are just people of straw. Most people have no insides at all. Now that you're president you'll see that. Listen, darling, there's a kind of secret society at the top of the world,—like you and me,—that know this. The world was made for us. What's life anyway? Except for two things, pleasure and power, what is life? Boredom! Foolishness. You know it is. Except for those two things, life's nau-se-at-ing. So,—come here!

> *She moves close. They kiss.*

So.

Now when your wife comes, it's really very simple; just tell her.

ANTROBUS: Lily, Lily: you're a wonderful woman.

SABINA: Of course I am.

> *They enter the cabana and it hides them from view. Distant roll of thunder. A third black disk appears on the weather*

signal. Distant thunder is heard. MRS. ANTROBUS *appears carrying parcels. She looks about, seats herself on the bench left, and fans herself with her handkerchief. Enter* GLADYS *right, followed by two* CONVEENERS. *She is wearing red stockings.*

MRS. ANTROBUS: Gladys!

GLADYS: Mama, here I am.

MRS. ANTROBUS: Gladys Antrobus!!! Where did you get those dreadful things?

GLADYS: Wha-a-t? Papa liked the color.

MRS. ANTROBUS: You go back to the hotel this minute!

GLADYS: I won't. I won't. Papa liked the color.

MRS. ANTROBUS: All right. All right. You stay here. I've a good mind to let your father see you that way. You stay right here.

GLADYS: I . . . I don't want to stay if . . . if you don't think he'd like it.

MRS. ANTROBUS: Oh . . . it's all one to me. I don't care what happens. I don't care if the biggest storm in the whole world comes. Let it come. (*She folds her hands.*) Where's your brother?

GLADYS: (*In a small voice.*) He'll be here.

MRS. ANTROBUS: Will he? Well, let him get into trouble. I don't care. I don't know where your father is, I'm sure.

Laughter from the cabana.

GLADYS: (*Leaning over the rail.*) I think he's . . . Mama, he's talking to the lady in the red dress.

MRS. ANTROBUS: Is that so? (*Pause.*) We'll wait till he's through. Sit down here beside me and stop fidgeting . . . what are you crying about?

Distant thunder. She covers GLADYS'S *stockings with a raincoat.*

GLADYS: You don't like my stockings.

Two CONVEENERS *rush in with a microphone on a standard and various paraphernalia. The* FORTUNE TELLER *appears at the door of her shop. Other characters gradually gather.*

BROADCAST OFFICIAL: Mrs. Antrobus! Thank God we've found you at last. Where's Mr. Antrobus? We've been hunting everywhere for him. It's about time for the broadcast to the conventions of the world.

MRS. ANTROBUS: (*Calm.*) I expect he'll be here in a minute.

BROADCAST OFFICIAL: Mrs. Antrobus, if he doesn't show up in time, I hope you will consent to broadcast in his place. It's the most important broadcast of the year.

SABINA *enters from cabana followed by* ANTROBUS.

MRS. ANTROBUS: No, I shan't. I haven't one single thing to say.

BROADCAST OFFICIAL: Then won't you help us find him, Mrs. Antrobus? A storm's coming up. A hurricane. A deluge!

SECOND CONVEENER: (*Who has sighted* ANTROBUS *over the rail.*) Joe! Joe! Here he is.

BROADCAST OFFICIAL: In the name of God, Mr. Antrobus, you're on the air in five minutes. Will you kindly please come and test the instrument? That's all we ask. If you just please begin the alphabet slowly.

ANTROBUS, *with set face, comes ponderously up the ramp. He stops at the point where his waist is level with the stage and speaks authoritatively to the* OFFICIALS.

ANTROBUS: I'll be ready when the time comes. Until then, move away. Go away. I have something I wish to say to my wife.

BROADCAST OFFICIAL: (*Whimpering.*) Mr. Antrobus! This is the most important broadcast of the year.

The OFFICIALS *withdraw to the edge of the stage.* SABINA *glides up the ramp behind* ANTROBUS.

SABINA: (*Whispering.*) Don't let her argue. Remember arguments have nothing to do with it.

ANTROBUS: Maggie, I'm moving out of the hotel. In fact, I'm moving out of everything. For good. I'm going to marry Miss Fairweather. I shall provide generously for you and the children. In a few years you'll be able to see that it's all for the best. That's all I have to say.

BROADCAST OFFICIAL: Mr. Antrobus! I hope you'll be ready. This is the most important broadcast of the year.

GLADYS: What did Papa say, Mama? I didn't hear what papa said.

BROADCAST OFFICIAL: Mr. Antrobus. All we want to do is test your voice with the alphabet.

ANTROBUS: Go away. Clear out.

BINGO ANNOUNCER: A—nine; A—nine. D—forty-two; D—forty-two. C—thirty; C—thirty. B—seventeen; B—seventeen. C—forty; C—forty.

CHORUS: Bingo!!

MRS. ANTROBUS: (*Composedly with lowered eyes.*) George, I can't talk to you until you wipe those silly red marks off your face.

ANTROBUS: I think there's nothing to talk about. I've said what I have to say.

SABINA: Splendid!!

ANTROBUS: You're a fine woman, Maggie, but . . . but a man has his own life to lead in the world.

MRS. ANTROBUS: Well, after living with you for five thousand years I guess I have a right to a word or two, haven't I?

ANTROBUS: (*To* SABINA.) What can I answer to that?

SABINA: Tell her that conversation would only hurt her feelings. It's-kinder-in-the-long-run-to-do-it-short-and-quick.

ANTROBUS: I want to spare your feelings in every way I can, Maggie.

BROADCAST OFFICIAL: Mr. Antrobus, the hurricane signal's gone up. We could begin right now.

MRS. ANTROBUS: (*Calmly, almost dreamily.*) I didn't marry you because you were perfect. I didn't even marry you because I loved you. I married you because you gave me a promise. (*She takes off her ring and looks at it.*) That promise made up for your faults. And the promise I gave you made up for mine. Two imperfect people got married and it was the promise that made the marriage.

ANTROBUS: Maggie, . . . I was only nineteen.

MRS. ANTROBUS: (*She puts her ring back on her finger.*) And when our children were growing up, it wasn't a house that protected them; and it wasn't our love, that protected them—it was that promise.

And when that promise is broken—this can happen! (*With a sweep of the hand she removes the raincoat from* GLADYS' *stockings.*)

ANTROBUS: (*Stretches out his arm, apoplectic.*) Gladys!! Have you gone crazy? Has everyone gone crazy? (*Turning on* SABINA.) You did this. You gave them to her.

SABINA: I never said a word to her.

ANTROBUS: (*To* GLADYS.) You go back to the hotel and take those horrible things off.

GLADYS: (*Pert.*) Before I go, I've got something to tell you,— it's about Henry.

MRS. ANTROBUS: (*Claps her hands peremptorily.*) Stop your noise,—I'm taking her back to the hotel, George. Before I go I have a letter. . . . I have a message to throw into the ocean. (*Fumbling in her handbag.*)

Where is the plagued thing? Here it is. (*She flings something —invisible to us—far over the heads of the audience to the back of the auditorium.*) It's a bottle. And in the bottle's a letter. And in the letter is written all the things that a woman knows.

It's never been told to any man and it's never been told to any woman, and if it finds its destination, a new time will come. We're not what books and plays say we are. We're not what advertisements say we are. We're not in the movies and we're not on the radio.

We're not what you're all told and what you think we are: We're ourselves. And if any man can find one of us he'll learn why the whole universe was set in motion. And if any man harm any one of us, his soul—the only soul he's got— had better be at the bottom of that ocean,—and that's the only way to put it. Gladys, come here. We're going back to the hotel.

> She drags GLADYS *firmly off by the hand, but* GLADYS *breaks away and comes down to speak to her father.*

SABINA: Such goings-on. Don't give it a minute's thought.

GLADYS: Anyway, I think you ought to know that Henry hit a man with a stone. He hit one of those colored men that push the chairs and the man's very sick. Henry ran away and hid and some policemen are looking for him very hard. And I don't care a bit if you don't want to have anything to do with mama and me, because I'll never like you again and I hope nobody ever likes you again,—so there!

She runs off. ANTROBUS *starts after her.*

ANTROBUS: I . . . I have to go and see what I can do about this.

SABINA: You stay right here. Don't you go now while you're excited. Gracious sakes, all these things will be forgotten in a hundred years. Come, now, you're on the air. Just say anything,—it doesn't matter what. Just a lot of birds and fishes and things.

BROADCAST OFFICIAL: Thank you, Miss Fairweather. Thank you very much. Ready, Mr. Antrobus.

ANTROBUS: (*Touching the microphone.*) What is it, what is it? Who am I talking to?

BROADCAST OFFICIAL: Why, Mr. Antrobus! To our order and to all the other orders.

ANTROBUS: (*Raising his head.*) What are all those birds doing?

BROADCAST OFFICIAL: Those are just a few of the birds. Those are the delegates to our convention,—two of a kind.

ANTROBUS: (*Pointing into the audience.*) Look at the water. Look at them all. Those fishes jumping. The children should see this! —There's Maggie's whales!! Here are your whales, Maggie!!

BROADCAST OFFICIAL: I hope you're ready, Mr. Antrobus.

ANTROBUS: And look on the beach! You didn't tell me these would be here!

SABINA: Yes, George. Those are the animals.

BROADCAST OFFICIAL: (*Busy with the apparatus.*) Yes, Mr. Antrobus, those are the vertebrates. We hope the lion will have a word to say when you're through. Step right up, Mr. Antrobus, we're ready. We'll just have time before the storm. (*Pause. In a hoarse whisper:*) They're wait-ing.

It has grown dark. Soon after he speaks a high whistling noise begins. Strange veering lights start whirling about the stage. The other characters disappear from the stage.

ANTROBUS: Friends. Cousins. Four score and ten billion years ago our forefather brought forth upon this planet the spark of life,—

> *He is drowned out by thunder. When the thunder stops the* FORTUNE TELLER *is seen standing beside him.*

FORTUNE TELLER: Antrobus, there's not a minute to be lost. Don't you see the four disks on the weather signal? Take your family into that boat at the end of the pier.

ANTROBUS: My family? I have no family. Maggie! Maggie! They won't come.

FORTUNE TELLER: They'll come.—Antrobus! Take these animals into that boat with you. All of them,—two of each kind.

SABINA: George, what's the matter with you? This is just a storm like any other storm.

ANTROBUS: Maggie!

SABINA: Stay with me, we'll go . . . (*Losing conviction.*) This is just another thunderstorm,—isn't it? Isn't it?

ANTROBUS: Maggie!!!

> MRS. ANTROBUS *appears beside him with* GLADYS.

MRS. ANTROBUS: (*Matter-of-fact.*) Here I am and here's Gladys.

ANTROBUS: Where've you been? Where have you been? Quick, we're going into that boat out there.

MRS. ANTROBUS: I know we are. But I haven't found Henry. (*She wanders off into the darkness calling "Henry!"*)

SABINA: (*Low urgent babbling, only occasionally raising her voice.*) I don't believe it. I don't believe it's anything at all. I've seen hundreds of storms like this.

FORTUNE TELLER: There's no time to lose. Go. Push the animals along before you. Start a new world. Begin again.

SABINA: Esmeralda! George! Tell me,—is it really serious?

ANTROBUS: (*Suddenly very busy.*) Elephants first. Gently, gently.—Look where you're going.

GLADYS: (*Leaning over the ramp and striking an animal on the back.*) Stop it or you'll be left behind!

ANTROBUS: Is the Kangaroo there? *There* you are! Take those turtles in your pouch, will you? (*To some other animals,*

pointing to his shoulder.) Here! You jump up here. You'll be
trampled on.

GLADYS: (*To her father, pointing below.*) Papa, look,—the
snakes!

MRS. ANTROBUS: I can't find Henry. Hen-ry!

ANTROBUS: Go along. Go along. Climb on their backs.—
Wolves! Jackals,—whatever you are,—tend to your own
business!

GLADYS: (*Pointing, tenderly.*) Papa,—look.

SABINA: Mr. Antrobus—take me with you. Don't leave me
here. I'll work. I'll help. I'll do anything.

> THREE CONVEENERS *cross the stage, marching with a
> banner.*

CONVEENERS: George! What are you scared of?—George!
Fellas, it looks like rain.—"Maggie, where's my umbrella?"
—George, setting up for Barnum and Bailey.

ANTROBUS: (*Again catching his wife's hand.*) Come on now,
Maggie,—the pier's going to break any minute.

MRS. ANTROBUS: I'm not going a step without Henry. Henry!

GLADYS: (*On the ramp.*) Mama! Papa! Hurry. The pier's crack-
ing, Mama. It's going to break.

MRS. ANTROBUS: Henry! Cain! CAIN!

> HENRY *dashes onto the stage and joins his mother.*

HENRY: Here I am, Mama.

MRS. ANTROBUS: Thank God!—now come quick.

HENRY: I didn't think you wanted me.

MRS. ANTROBUS: Quick! (*She pushes him down before her into
the aisle.*)

SABINA: (*All the* ANTROBUSES *are now in the theatre aisle.*
SABINA *stands at the top of the ramp.*) Mrs. Antrobus, take
me. Don't you remember me? I'll work. I'll help. Don't leave
me here!

MRS. ANTROBUS: (*Impatiently, but as though it were of no importance.*) Yes, yes. There's a lot of work to be done. Only
hurry.

FORTUNE TELLER: (*Now dominating the stage. To* SABINA *with
a grim smile.*) Yes, go—back to the kitchen with you.

SABINA: (*Half-down the ramp. To* FORTUNE TELLER.) I don't

know why my life's always being interrupted—just when everything's going fine!! (*She dashes up the aisle.*)

> Now the CONVEENERS *emerge doing a serpentine dance on the stage. They jeer at the* FORTUNE TELLER.

CONVEENERS: Get a canoe—there's not a minute to be lost! Tell me my future, Mrs. Croaker.

FORTUNE TELLER: Paddle in the water, boys—enjoy yourselves.

VOICE FROM THE BINGO PARLOR: A-nine; A-nine. C-Twenty-four. C-Twenty-four.

CONVEENERS: Rags, bottles, and sacks.

FORTUNE TELLER: Go back and climb on your roofs. Put rags in the cracks under your doors.—Nothing will keep out the flood. You've had your chance. You've had your day. You've failed. You've lost.

VOICE FROM THE BINGO PARLOR: B-fifteen. B-Fifteen.

FORTUNE TELLER: (*Shading her eyes and looking out to sea.*) They're safe. George Antrobus! Think it over! A new world to make.—think it over!

CURTAIN

Act III

Just before the curtain rises, two sounds are heard from the stage: a cracked bugle call.

The curtain rises on almost total darkness. Almost all the flats composing the walls of MR. ANTROBUS'S *house, as of Act I, are up, but they lean helter-skelter against one another, leaving irregular gaps. Among the flats missing are two in the back wall, leaving the frames of the window and door crazily out of line. Off stage, back right, some red Roman fire is burning. The bugle call is repeated. Enter* SABINA *through the tilted door. She is dressed as a Napoleonic camp follower, "la fille du regiment," in begrimed reds and blues.*

SABINA: Mrs. Antrobus! Gladys! Where are you?

The war's over. The war's over. You can come out. The peace treaty's been signed.

Where are they?—Hmpf! Are they dead, too? Mrs. Annnntrobus! Glaaaadus! Mr. Antrobus'll be here this afternoon. I just saw him downtown. Huuuurry and put things in order. He says that now that the war's over we'll all have to settle down and be perfect.

> *Enter* MR. FITZPATRICK, *the stage manager, followed by the whole company, who stand waiting at the edges of the stage.* MR. FITZPATRICK *tries to interrupt* SABINA.

MR. FITZPATRICK: Miss Somerset, we have to stop a moment.

SABINA: They may be hiding out in the back—

MR. FITZPATRICK: Miss Somerset! We have to stop a moment.

SABINA: What's the matter?

MR. FITZPATRICK: There's an explanation we have to make to the audience.—Lights, please. (*To the actor who plays* MR. ANTROBUS.) Will you explain the matter to the audience?

> *The lights go up. We now see that a balcony or elevated runway has been erected at the back of the stage, back of the wall of the Antrobus house. From its extreme right and left ends ladder-like steps descend to the floor of the stage.*

ANTROBUS: Ladies and gentlemen, an unfortunate accident has taken place back stage. Perhaps I should say *another* unfortunate accident.

SABINA: I'm sorry. I'm sorry.

ANTROBUS: The management feels, in fact, we all feel that you are due an apology. And now we have to ask your indulgence for the most serious mishap of all. Seven of our actors have . . . have been taken ill. Apparently, it was something they ate. I'm not exactly clear what happened.

All the actors start to talk at once. ANTROBUS *raises his hand.*

Now, now—not all at once. Fitz, do you know what it was?

MR. FITZPATRICK: Why, it's perfectly clear. These seven actors had dinner together, and they ate something that disagreed with them.

SABINA: Disagreed with them!!! They have ptomaine poisoning. They're in Bellevue Hospital this very minute in agony. They're having their stomachs pumped out this very minute, in perfect agony.

ANTROBUS: Fortunately, we've just heard they'll all recover.

SABINA: It'll be a miracle if they do, a downright miracle. It was the lemon meringue pie.

ACTORS: It was the fish . . . it was the canned tomatoes . . . it was the fish.

SABINA: It was the lemon meringue pie. I saw it with my own eyes; it had blue mould all over the bottom of it.

ANTROBUS: Whatever it was, they're in no condition to take part in this performance. Naturally, we haven't enough understudies to fill all those roles; but we do have a number of splendid volunteers who have kindly consented to help us out. These friends have watched our rehearsals, and they assure me that they know the lines and the business very well. Let me introduce them to you—my dresser, Mr. Tremayne, —himself a distinguished Shakespearean actor for many years; our wardrobe mistress, Hester; Miss Somerset's maid, Ivy; and Fred Bailey, captain of the ushers in this theatre.

These persons bow modestly. IVY *and* HESTER *are colored girls.*

Now this scene takes place near the end of the act. And I'm
sorry to say we'll need a short rehearsal, just a short run-
through. And as some of it takes place in the auditorium,
we'll have to keep the curtain up. Those of you who wish
can go out in the lobby and smoke some more. The rest of
you can listen to us, or . . . or just talk quietly among
yourselves, as you choose. Thank you. Now will you take it
over, Mr. Fitzpatrick?

MR. FITZPATRICK: Thank you.—Now for those of you who are
listening perhaps I should explain that at the end of this act,
the men have come back from the War and the family's
settled down in the house. And the author wants to show
the hours of the night passing by over their heads, and the
planets crossing the sky . . . uh . . . over their heads. And
he says—this is hard to explain—that each of the hours of
the night is a philosopher, or a great thinker. Eleven o'clock,
for instance, is Aristotle. And nine o'clock is Spinoza. Like
that. I don't suppose it means anything. It's just a kind of
poetic effect.

SABINA: Not mean anything! Why, it certainly does. Twelve
o'clock goes by saying those wonderful things. I think it
means that when people are asleep they have all those lovely
thoughts, much better than when they're awake.

IVY: Excuse me, I think it means,—excuse me, Mr. Fitzpatrick—

SABINA: What were you going to say, Ivy?

IVY: Mr. Fitzpatrick, you let my father come to a rehearsal; and
my father's a Baptist minister, and he said that the author
meant that—just like the hours and stars go by over our
heads at night, in the same way the ideas and thoughts of
the great men are in the air around us all the time and
they're working on us, even when we don't know it.

MR. FITZPATRICK: Well, well, maybe that's it. Thank you, Ivy.
Anyway,—the hours of the night are philosophers. My
friends, are you ready? Ivy, can you be eleven o'clock? "This
good estate of the mind possessing its object in energy we
call divine." Aristotle.

IVY: Yes, sir. I know that and I know twelve o'clock and I
know nine o'clock.

MR. FITZPATRICK: Twelve o'clock? Mr. Tremayne, the Bible.

TREMAYNE: Yes.

MR. FITZPATRICK: Ten o'clock? Hester,—Plato? (*She nods eagerly.*) Nine o'clock, Spinoza,—Fred?

BAILEY: Yes, *sir*.

> FRED BAILEY *picks up a great gilded cardboard numeral IX and starts up the steps to the platform.* MR. FITZPATRICK *strikes his forehead.*

MR. FITZPATRICK: The planets!! We forgot all about the planets.

SABINA: O my God! The planets! Are they sick too?

> ACTORS *nod.*

MR. FITZPATRICK: Ladies and gentlemen, the planets are singers. Of course, we can't replace them, so you'll have to imagine them singing in this scene. Saturn sings from the orchestra pit down here. The Moon is way up there. And Mars with a red lantern in his hand, stands in the aisle over there—Tz-tz-tz. It's too bad; it all makes a very fine effect. However! Ready—nine o'clock: Spinoza.

BAILEY: (*Walking slowly across the balcony, left to right.*) "After experience had taught me that the common occurrences of daily life are vain and futile—"

FITZPATRICK: Louder, Fred. "And I saw that all the objects of my desire and fear—"

BAILEY: "And I saw that all the objects of my desire and fear were in themselves nothing good nor bad save insofar as the mind was affected by them—"

FITZPATRICK: Do you know the rest? All right. Ten o'clock. Hester. Plato.

HESTER: "Then tell me, O Critias, how will a man choose the ruler that shall rule over him? Will he not—"

FITZPATRICK: Thank you. Skip to the end, Hester.

HESTER: ". . . can be multiplied a thousand fold in its effects among the citizens."

FITZPATRICK: Thank you.—Aristotle, Ivy?

IVY: "This good estate of the mind possessing its object in energy we call divine. This we mortals have occasionally and it is this energy which is pleasantest and best. But God has it always. It is wonderful in us; but in Him how much more wonderful."

FITZPATRICK: Midnight. Midnight, Mr. Tremayne. That's right,—you've done it before.—All right, everybody. You know what you have to do.—Lower the curtain. House lights up. Act Three of THE SKIN OF OUR TEETH. (*As the curtain descends he is heard saying:*) You volunteers, just wear what you have on. Don't try to put on the costumes today.

> *House lights go down. The Act begins again. The Bugle call. Curtain rises. Enter* SABINA.

SABINA: Mrs. Antrobus! Gladys! Where are you?
   The war's over.—You've heard all this— (*She gabbles the main points.*)
   Where—are—they? Are—they—dead, too, et cetera.
   I—just—saw—Mr.—Antrobus—down town, et cetera. (*Slowing up:*)
   He says that now that the war's over we'll all have to settle down and be perfect. They may be hiding out in the back somewhere. Mrs. An-tro-bus.

> *She wanders off. It has grown lighter.*
> *A trapdoor is cautiously raised and* MRS. ANTROBUS *emerges waist-high and listens. She is disheveled and worn; she wears a tattered dress and a shawl half covers her head. She talks down through the trapdoor.*

MRS. ANTROBUS: It's getting light. There's still something burning over there—Newark, or Jersey City. What? Yes, I could swear I heard someone moving about up here. But I can't see anybody. I say: I can't see anybody.

> *She starts to move about the stage.* GLADYS' *head appears at the trapdoor. She is holding a* BABY.

GLADYS: Oh, Mama. Be careful.
MRS. ANTROBUS: Now, Gladys, you stay out of sight.
GLADYS: Well, let me stay here just a minute. I want the baby to get some of this fresh air.
MRS. ANTROBUS: All right, but keep your eyes open. I'll see what I can find. I'll have a good hot plate of soup for you before you can say Jack Robinson. Gladys Antrobus! Do you know what I think I see? There's old Mr. Hawkins

sweeping the sidewalk in front of his A. and P. store. Sweeping it with a broom. Why, he must have gone crazy, like the others! I see some other people moving about, too.

GLADYS: Mama, come back, come back.

MRS. ANTROBUS *returns to the trapdoor and listens.*

MRS. ANTROBUS: Gladys, there's something in the air. Everybody's movement's sort of different. I see some women walking right out in the middle of the street.

SABINA'S VOICE: Mrs. An-tro-bus!

MRS. ANTROBUS AND GLADYS: What's that?!!

SABINA'S VOICE: Glaaaadys! Mrs. An-tro-bus!

Enter SABINA.

MRS. ANTROBUS: Gladys, that's Sabina's voice as sure as I live.—Sabina! Sabina!—Are you *alive?!!*

SABINA: Of course, I'm alive. How've you girls been?—*Don't* try and kiss me. I never want to kiss another human being as long as I live. Sh-sh, there's nothing to get emotional about. Pull yourself together, the war's over. Take a deep breath,— the war's over.

MRS. ANTROBUS: The war's over!! I don't believe you. I don't believe you. I can't believe you.

GLADYS: Mama!

SABINA: Who's that?

MRS. ANTROBUS: That's Gladys and her baby. I don't believe you. Gladys, Sabina says the war's over. Oh, Sabina.

SABINA: (*Leaning over the* BABY.) Goodness! Are there any babies left in the world! Can it *see?* And can it cry and everything?

GLADYS: Yes, he can. He notices everything very well.

SABINA: Where on earth did you get it? Oh, I won't ask.— Lord, I've lived all these seven years around camp and I've forgotten how to behave.—Now we've got to think about the men coming home.—Mrs. Antrobus, go and wash your face, I'm ashamed of you. Put your best clothes on. Mr. Antrobus'll be here this afternoon. I just saw him downtown.

MRS. ANTROBUS AND GLADYS: He's alive!! He'll be here!! Sabina, you're not joking?

MRS. ANTROBUS: And Henry?

SABINA: (*Dryly.*) Yes, Henry's alive, too, that's what they say.
Now don't stop to talk. Get yourselves fixed up. Gladys, you
look terrible. Have you any decent clothes?

SABINA *has pushed them toward the trapdoor.*

MRS. ANTROBUS: (*Half down.*) Yes, I've something to wear just
for this very day. But, Sabina,—who won the war?

SABINA: Don't stop now,—just wash your face.

A whistle sounds in the distance.

Oh, my God, what's that silly little noise?

MRS. ANTROBUS: Why, it sounds like . . . it sounds like what
used to be the noon whistle at the shoe-polish factory. (*Exit.*)

SABINA: That's what it is. Seems to me like peacetime's coming
along pretty fast—shoe polish!

GLADYS: (*Half down.*) Sabina, how soon after peacetime begins does the milkman start coming to the door?

SABINA: As soon as he catches a cow. Give him time to catch a
cow, dear.

Exit GLADYS. SABINA *walks about a moment, thinking.*

Shoe polish! My, I'd forgotten what peacetime was like. (*She
shakes her head, then sits down by the trapdoor and starts
talking down the hole.*) Mrs. Antrobus, guess what I saw Mr.
Antrobus doing this morning at dawn. He was tacking up a
piece of paper on the door of the Town Hall. You'll die
when you hear: it was a recipe for grass soup, for a grass
soup that doesn't give you the diarrhea. Mr. Antrobus is still
thinking up new things.—He told me to give you his love.
He's got all sorts of ideas for peacetime, he says. No more
laziness and idiocy, he says. And oh, yes! Where are his
books? What? Well, pass them up. The first thing he wants
to see are his books. He says if you've burnt those books, or
if the rats have eaten them, he says it isn't worthwhile starting
over again. Everybody's going to be beautiful, he says, and
diligent, and very intelligent.

A hand reaches up with two volumes.

What language is that? Pu-u-gh,—mold! And he's got such

plans for you, Mrs. Antrobus. You're going to study history and algebra—and so are Gladys and I—and philosophy. You should hear him talk:

Taking two more volumes.

Well, these are in English, anyway.—To hear him talk, seems like he expects you to be a combination, Mrs. Antrobus, of a saint and a college professor, and a dancehall hostess, if you know what I mean.

Two more volumes.

Ugh. German!

She is lying on the floor; one elbow bent, her cheek on her hand, meditatively.

Yes, peace will be here before we know it. In a week or two we'll be asking the Perkinses in for a quiet evening of bridge. We'll turn on the radio and hear how to be big successes with a new toothpaste. We'll trot down to the movies and see how girls with wax faces live—all *that* will begin again. Oh, Mrs. Antrobus, God forgive me but I enjoyed the war. Everybody's at their best in wartime. I'm sorry it's over. And, oh, I forgot! Mr. Antrobus sent you another message—can you hear me?—

Enter HENRY, *blackened and sullen. He is wearing torn overalls, but has one gaudy admiral's epaulette hanging by a thread from his right shoulder, and there are vestiges of gold and scarlet braid running down his left trouser leg. He stands listening.*

Listen! Henry's never to put foot in this house again, he says. He'll kill Henry on sight, if he sees him.
You don't know about Henry??? Well, where have you been? What? Well, Henry rose right to the top. Top of *what?* Listen, I'm telling you. Henry rose from corporal to captain, to major, to general.—I don't know how to say it, but the enemy is *Henry;* Henry *is* the enemy. Everybody knows that.
HENRY: He'll kill me, will he?
SABINA: Who are *you?* I'm not afraid of you. The war's over.

HENRY: I'll kill him so fast. I've spent seven years trying to find him; the others I killed were just substitutes.

SABINA: Goodness! It's Henry!—

He makes an angry gesture.

Oh, I'm not afraid of you. The war's over, Henry Antrobus, and you're not any more important than any other unemployed. You go away and hide yourself, until we calm your father down.

HENRY: The first thing to do is to burn up those old books; it's the ideas he gets out of those old books that . . . that makes the whole world so you can't live in it. (*He reels forward and starts kicking the books about, but suddenly falls down in a sitting position.*)

SABINA: You leave those books alone!! Mr. Antrobus is looking forward to them a-special.—Gracious sakes, Henry, you're so tired you can't stand up. Your mother and sister'll be here in a minute and we'll think what to do about you.

HENRY: What did they ever care about me?

SABINA: There's that old whine again. All you people think you're not loved enough, nobody loves you. Well, you start being lovable and we'll love you.

HENRY: (*Outraged.*) I don't want anybody to love me.

SABINA: Then stop talking about it all the time.

HENRY: I *never* talk about it. The last thing I want is anybody to pay any attention to me.

SABINA: I can hear it behind every word you say.

HENRY: I want everybody to hate me.

SABINA: Yes, you've decided that's second best, but it's still the same thing.—Mrs. Antrobus! Henry's here. He's so tired he can't stand up.

MRS. ANTROBUS *and* GLADYS, *with her* BABY, *emerge. They are dressed as in Act I.* MRS. ANTROBUS *carries some objects in her apron, and* GLADYS *has a blanket over her shoulder.*

MRS. ANTROBUS AND GLADYS: Henry! Henry! Henry!

HENRY: (*Glaring at them.*) Have you anything to eat?

MRS. ANTROBUS: Yes, I have, Henry. I've been saving it for this very day,—two good baked potatoes. No! Henry! one of them's for your father. Henry!! Give me that other potato back this minute.

> SABINA *sidles up behind him and snatches the other potato away.*

SABINA: He's so dog-tired he doesn't know what he's doing.

MRS. ANTROBUS: Now you just rest there, Henry, until I can get your room ready. Eat that potato good and slow, so you can get all the nourishment out of it.

HENRY: You all might as well know right now that I haven't come back here to live.

MRS. ANTROBUS: Sh. . . . I'll put this coat over you. Your room's hardly damaged at all. Your football trophies are a little tarnished, but Sabina and I will polish them up to-morrow.

HENRY: Did you hear me? I don't live here. I don't belong to anybody.

MRS. ANTROBUS: Why, how can you say a thing like that! You certainly do belong right here. Where else would you want to go? Your forehead's feverish, Henry, seems to me. You'd better give me that gun, Henry. You won't need that any more.

GLADYS: (*Whispering.*) Look, he's fallen asleep already, with his potato half-chewed.

SABINA: Puh! The terror of the world.

MRS. ANTROBUS: Sabina, you mind your own business, and start putting the room to rights.

> HENRY *has turned his face to the back of the sofa.* MRS. ANTROBUS *gingerly puts the revolver in her apron pocket, then helps* SABINA. SABINA *has found a rope hanging from the ceiling. Grunting, she hangs all her weight on it, and as she pulls the walls begin to move into their right places.* MRS. ANTROBUS *brings the overturned tables, chairs and hassock into the positions of Act I.*

SABINA: That's all we do—always beginning again! Over and over again. Always beginning again. (*She pulls on the rope and a part of the wall moves into place. She stops. Meditatively:*) How do we know that it'll be any better than before? Why do we go on pretending? Some day the whole earth's going to have to turn cold anyway, and until that time all these other things'll be happening again: it will be more wars and more walls of ice and floods and earthquakes.

MRS. ANTROBUS: Sabina!! Stop arguing and go on with your work.

SABINA: All right. I'll go on just out of *habit*, but I won't believe in it.

MRS. ANTROBUS: (*Aroused.*) Now, Sabina. I've let you talk long enough. I don't want to hear any more of it. Do I have to explain to you what everybody knows,—everybody who keeps a home going? Do I have to say to you what nobody should ever *have* to say, because they can read it in each other's eyes?

Now listen to me: (MRS. ANTROBUS *takes hold of the rope.*) I could live for seventy years in a cellar and make soup out of grass and bark, without ever doubting that this world has a work to do and will do it.

Do you hear me?

SABINA: (*Frightened.*) Yes, Mrs. Antrobus.

MRS. ANTROBUS: Sabina, do you see this house,—216 Cedar Street,—do you see it?

SABINA: Yes, Mrs. Antrobus.

MRS. ANTROBUS: Well, just to have known this house is to have seen the idea of what we can do someday if we keep our wits about us. Too many people have suffered and died for my children for us to start reneging now. So we'll start putting this house to rights. Now, Sabina, go and see what you can do in the kitchen.

SABINA: Kitchen! Why is it that however far I go away, I always find myself back in the kitchen? (*Exit.*)

MRS. ANTROBUS: (*Still thinking over her last speech, relaxes and says with a reminiscent smile:*) Goodness gracious, wouldn't you know that my father was a parson? It was just like I heard his own voice speaking and he's been dead five thousand years. There! I've gone and almost waked Henry up.

HENRY: (*Talking in his sleep, indistinctly.*) Fellows . . . what have they done for us? . . . Blocked our way at every step. Kept everything in their own hands. And you've stood it. When are you going to wake up?

MRS. ANTROBUS: Sh, Henry. Go to sleep. Go to sleep. Go to sleep.—Well, that looks better. Now let's go and help Sabina.

GLADYS: Mama, I'm going out into the backyard and hold the baby right up in the air. And show him that we don't have to be afraid any more.

> *Exit* GLADYS *to the kitchen.*
>
> MRS. ANTROBUS *glances at* HENRY, *exits into kitchen.* HENRY *thrashes about in his sleep. Enter* ANTROBUS, *his arms full of bundles, chewing the end of a carrot. He has a slight limp. Over the suit of Act I he is wearing an overcoat too long for him, its skirts trailing on the ground. He lets his bundles fall and stands looking about. Presently his attention is fixed on* HENRY, *whose words grow clearer.*

HENRY: All right! What have you got to lose? What have they done for us? That's right—nothing. Tear everything down. I don't care what you smash. We'll begin again and we'll show 'em.

> ANTROBUS *takes out his revolver and holds it pointing downwards. With his back towards the audience he moves toward the footlights.*
>
> HENRY'S *voice grows louder and he wakes with a start. They stare at one another. Then* HENRY *sits up quickly. Throughout the following scene* HENRY *is played, not as a misunderstood or misguided young man, but as a representation of strong unreconciled evil.*

All right! Do something.

> *Pause.*

Don't think I'm afraid of you, either. All right, do what you were going to do. Do it. (*Furiously.*) Shoot me, I tell you. You don't have to think I'm any relation of yours. I haven't got any father or any mother, or brothers or sisters. And I don't want any. And what's more I haven't got anybody over me; and I never will have. I'm alone, and that's all I want to be: alone. So you can shoot me.

ANTROBUS: You're the last person I wanted to see. The sight of you dries up all my plans and hopes. I wish I were back at war still, because it's easier to fight you than to live with you. War's a pleasure—do you hear me?—War's a pleasure compared to what faces us now: trying to build up a peace-time with you in the middle of it. (ANTROBUS *walks up to the window.*)

HENRY: I'm not going to be a part of any peacetime of yours. I'm going a long way from here and make my own world that's fit for a man to live in. Where a man can be free, and have a chance, and do what he wants to do in his own way.

ANTROBUS: (*His attention arrested; thoughtfully. He throws the gun out of the window and turns with hope.*) . . . Henry, let's try again.

HENRY: Try what? Living *here*?— Speaking polite downtown to all the old men like you? Standing like a sheep at the street corner until the red light turns to green? Being a good boy and a good sheep, like all the stinking ideas you get out of your books? Oh, no. I'll make a world, and I'll show you.

ANTROBUS: (*Hard.*) How can you make a world for people to live in, unless you've first put order in yourself? Mark my words: I shall continue fighting you until my last breath as long as you mix up your idea of liberty with your idea of hogging everything for yourself. I shall have no pity on you. I shall pursue you to the far corners of the earth. You and I want the same thing; but until you think of it as something that everyone has a right to, you are my deadly enemy and I will destroy you.—I hear your mother's voice in the kitchen. Have you seen her?

HENRY: I have no mother. Get it into your head. I don't be-long here. I have nothing to do here. I have no home.

ANTROBUS: Then why did you come here? With the whole world to choose from, why did you come to this one place: 216 Cedar Street, Excelsior, New Jersey. . . . Well?

HENRY: What if I did? What if I wanted to look at it once more, to see if—

ANTROBUS: Oh, you're related, all right—When your mother comes in you must behave yourself. Do you hear me?

HENRY: (*Wildly.*) What is this?—*must behave* yourself. Don't you say *must* to me.

ANTROBUS: Quiet!

Enter MRS. ANTROBUS *and* SABINA.

HENRY: Nobody can say *must* to me. All my life everybody's been crossing me,—everybody, everything, all of you. I'm going to be free, even if I have to kill half the world for it. Right now, too. Let me get my hands on his throat. I'll show him.

He advances toward ANTROBUS. *Suddenly,* SABINA *jumps between them and calls out in her own person:*

SABINA: Stop! Stop! Don't play this scene. You know what happened last night. Stop the play.

The men fall back, panting. HENRY *covers his face with his hands.*

Last night you almost strangled him. You became a regular savage. Stop it!

HENRY: It's true. I'm sorry. I don't know what comes over me. I have nothing against him personally. I respect him very much . . . I . . . I admire him. But something comes over me. It's like I become fifteen years old again. I . . . I . . . listen: my own father used to whip me and lock me up every Saturday night. I never had enough to eat. He never let me have enough money to buy decent clothes. I was ashamed to go downtown. I never could go to the dances. My father and my uncle put rules in the way of everything I wanted to do. They tried to prevent my living at all.—I'm sorry. I'm sorry.

MRS. ANTROBUS: (*Quickly.*) No, go on. Finish what you were saying. Say it all.

HENRY: In this scene it's as though I were back in High School again. It's like I had some big emptiness inside me,—the emptiness of being hated and blocked at every turn. And the emptiness fills up with the one thought that you have to strike and fight and kill. Listen, it's as though you have to kill somebody else so as not to end up killing yourself.

SABINA: That's not true. I knew your father and your uncle and your mother. You imagined all that. Why, they did everything they could for you. How can you say things like that? They didn't lock you up.

HENRY: They did. They did. They wished I hadn't been born.

SABINA: That's not true.

ANTROBUS: (*In his his own person, with self-condemnation, but cold and proud.*) Wait a minute. I have something to say, too. It's not wholly his fault that he wants to strangle me in this scene. It's my fault, too. He wouldn't feel that way unless there were something in me that reminded him of all that. He talks about an emptiness. Well, there's an emptiness in me, too. Yes,—work, work, work,—that's all I do. I've ceased to *live.* No wonder he feels that anger coming over him.

MRS. ANTROBUS: There! At least you've said it.

SABINA: We're all just as wicked as we can be, and that's the God's truth.

MRS. ANTROBUS: (*Nods a moment, then comes forward; quietly:*) Come. Come and put your head under some cold water.

SABINA: (*In a whisper.*) I'll go with him. I've known him a long while. You have to go on with the play. Come with me.

> HENRY *starts out with* SABINA, *but turns at the exit and says to* ANTROBUS:

HENRY: Thanks. Thanks for what you said. I'll be all right to-morrow. I won't lose control in that place. I promise.

> *Exeunt* HENRY *and* SABINA.
> ANTROBUS *starts toward the front door, fastens it.*
> MRS. ANTROBUS *goes up stage and places the chair close to table.*

MRS. ANTROBUS: George, do I see you limping?

ANTROBUS: Yes, a little. My old wound from the other war started smarting again. I can manage.

MRS. ANTROBUS: (*Looking out of the window.*) Some lights are coming on,—the first in seven years. People are walking up and down looking at them. Over in Hawkins' open lot they've built a bonfire to celebrate the peace. They're dancing around it like scarecrows.

ANTROBUS: A bonfire! As though they hadn't seen enough things burning.—Maggie,—the dog died?

MRS. ANTROBUS: Oh, yes. Long ago. There are no dogs left in Excelsior.—You're back again! All these years. I gave up counting on letters. The few that arrived were anywhere from six months to a year late.

ANTROBUS: Yes, the ocean's full of letters, along with the other things.

MRS. ANTROBUS: George, sit down, you're tired.

ANTROBUS: No, you sit down. I'm tired but I'm restless. (*Suddenly, as she comes forward:*) Maggie! I've lost it. I've lost it.

MRS. ANTROBUS: What, George? What have you lost?

ANTROBUS: The most important thing of all: The desire to begin again, to start building.

MRS. ANTROBUS: (*Sitting in the chair right of the table.*) Well, it will come back.

ANTROBUS: (*At the window.*) I've lost it. This minute I feel like all those people dancing around the bonfire—just relief. Just the desire to settle down; to slip into the old grooves and keep the neighbors from walking over my lawn.—Hm. But during the war,—in the middle of all that blood and dirt and hot and cold—every day and night, I'd have moments, Maggie, when I *saw* the things that we could do when it was over. When you're at war you think about a better life; when you're at peace you think about a more comfortable one. I've lost it. I feel sick and tired.

MRS. ANTROBUS: Listen! The baby's crying.

I hear Gladys talking. Probably she's quieting Henry again. George, while Gladys and I were living here—like moles, like rats, and when we were at our wits' end to save the baby's life—the only thought we clung to was that you were going to bring something good out of this suffering. In the night, in the dark, we'd whisper about it, starving and sick. —Oh, George, you'll have to get it back again. Think! What else kept us alive all these years? Even now, it's not comfort we want. We can suffer whatever's necessary; only give us back that promise.

Enter SABINA *with a lighted lamp. She is dressed as in Act I.*

SABINA: Mrs. Antrobus . . .

MRS. ANTROBUS: Yes, Sabina?

SABINA: Will you need me?

MRS. ANTROBUS: No, Sabina, you can go to bed.

SABINA: Mrs. Antrobus, if it's all right with you, I'd like to go to the bonfire and celebrate seeing the war's over. And, Mrs. Antrobus, they've opened the Gem Movie Theatre and they're giving away a hand-painted soup tureen to every lady, and I thought one of us ought to go.

ANTROBUS: Well, Sabina, I haven't any money. I haven't seen any money for quite a while.

SABINA: Oh, you don't need money. They're taking anything you can give them. And I have some . . . some . . . Mrs. Antrobus, promise you won't tell anyone. It's a little against the law. But I'll give you some, too.

ANTROBUS: What is it?

SABINA: I'll give you some, too. Yesterday I picked up a lot of . . . of beef-cubes!

> MRS. ANTROBUS *turns and says calmly:*

MRS. ANTROBUS: But, Sabina, you know you ought to give that in to the Center downtown. They know who needs them most.

SABINA: (*Outburst.*) Mrs. Antrobus, I didn't make this war. I didn't ask for it. And, in my opinion, after anybody's gone through what we've gone through, they have a right to grab what they can find. You're a very nice man, Mr. Antrobus, but you'd have got on better in the world if you'd realized that dog-eat-dog was the rule in the beginning and always will be. And most of all now. (*In tears.*) Oh, the world's an awful place, and you know it is. I used to think something could be done about it; but I know better now. I hate it. I hate it. (*She comes forward slowly and brings six cubes from the bag.*) All right. All right. You can have them.

ANTROBUS: Thank you, Sabina.

SABINA: Can I have . . . can I have one to go to the movies?

> ANTROBUS *in silence gives her one.*

Thank you.

ANTROBUS: Good night, Sabina.

SABINA: Mr. Antrobus, don't mind what I say. I'm just an ordinary girl, you know what I mean, I'm just an ordinary girl. But you're a bright man, you're a very bright man, and of course you invented the alphabet and the wheel, and, my God, a lot of things . . . and if you've got any other plans, my God, don't let me upset them. Only every now and then I've got to go to the movies. I mean my nerves can't stand it. But if you have any ideas about improving the crazy old world, I'm really with you. I really am. Because it's . . . it's . . . Good night.

She goes out. ANTROBUS *starts laughing softly with exhilaration.*

ANTROBUS: Now I remember what three things always went together when I was able to see things most clearly: three things. Three things: (*He points to where* SABINA *has gone out.*) The voice of the people in their confusion and their need. And the thought of you and the children and this house . . . And . . . Maggie! I didn't dare ask you: my books! They haven't been lost, have they?

MRS. ANTROBUS: No. There are some of them right here. Kind of tattered.

ANTROBUS: Yes.—Remember, Maggie, we almost lost them once before? And when we finally did collect a few torn copies out of old cellars they ran in everyone's head like a fever. They as good as rebuilt the world. (*Pauses, book in hand, and looks up.*) Oh, I've never forgotten for long at a time that living is struggle. I know that every good and excellent thing in the world stands moment by moment on the razor-edge of danger and must be fought for—whether it's a field, or a home, or a country. All I ask is the chance to build new worlds and God has always given us that. And has given us (*Opening the book*) voices to guide us; and the memory of our mistakes to warn us. Maggie, you and I will remember in peacetime all the resolves that were so clear to us in the days of war. We've come a long ways. We've learned. We're learning. And the steps of our journey are marked for us here. (*He stands by the table turning the leaves of a book.*) Sometimes out there in the war,—standing all night on a hill —I'd try and remember some of the words in these books. Parts of them and phrases would come back to me. And after a while I used to give names to the hours of the night. (*He sits, hunting for a passage in the book.*) Nine o'clock I used to call Spinoza. Where is it: "After experience had taught me—"

The back wall has disappeared, revealing the platform.
FRED BAILEY *carrying his numeral has started from left to*
right. MRS. ANTROBUS *sits by the table sewing.*

BAILEY: "After experience had taught me that the common
occurrences of daily life are vain and futile; and I saw that all
the objects of my desire and fear were in themselves nothing
good nor bad save insofar as the mind was affected by them;
I at length determined to search out whether there was
something truly good and communicable to man."

Almost without break HESTER, *carrying a large Roman*
numeral ten, starts crossing the platform. GLADYS *appears*
at the kitchen door and moves towards her mother's chair.

HESTER: "Then tell me, O Critias, how will a man choose the
ruler that shall rule over him? Will he not choose a man who
has first established order in himself, knowing that any decision that has its spring from anger or pride or vanity can be
multiplied a thousand fold in its effects upon the citizens?"

HESTER disappears and IVY, *as eleven o'clock starts speaking.*

IVY: "This good estate of the mind possessing its object in energy we call divine. This we mortals have occasionally and it
is this energy which is pleasantest and best. But God has it
always. It is wonderful in us; but in Him how much more
wonderful."

As MR. TREMAYNE *starts to speak,* HENRY *appears at the*
edge of the scene, brooding and unreconciled, but present.

TREMAYNE: "In the beginning, God created the Heavens and
the earth; And the Earth was waste and void; And the darkness was upon the face of the deep. And the Lord said let
there be light and there was light."

Sudden black-out and silence, except for the last strokes of
the midnight bell. Then just as suddenly the lights go up,
and SABINA *is standing at the window, as at the opening of*
the play.

SABINA: Oh, oh, oh. Six o'clock and the master not home yet.

Pray God nothing serious has happened to him crossing the Hudson River. But I wouldn't be surprised. The whole world's at sixes and sevens, and why the house hasn't fallen down about our ears long ago is a miracle to me. (*She comes down to the footlights.*) This is where you came in. We have to go on for ages and ages yet.

You go home.

The end of this play isn't written yet.

Mr. and Mrs. Antrobus! Their heads are full of plans and they're as confident as the first day they began,—and they told me to tell you: good night.

THE MATCHMAKER

A Farce in Four Acts

CHARACTERS

HORACE VANDERGELDER   *A merchant of Yonkers, New York*
CORNELIUS HACKL ⎫
BARNABY TUCKER ⎬ *Clerks in his store*
MALACHI STACK ⎭
AMBROSE KEMPER   *An artist*
JOE SCANLON   *A barber*
RUDOLPH ⎫
AUGUST ⎭ *Waiters*
A CABMAN
MRS. DOLLY LEVI ⎫ *Friends of Vandergelder's*
MISS FLORA VAN HUYSEN ⎭ *late wife*
MRS. IRENE MOLLOY   *A milliner*
MINNIE FAY   *Her assistant*
ERMENGARDE   *Vandergelder's niece*
GERTRUDE   *Vandergelder's housekeeper*
MISS VAN HUYSEN'S COOK

TIME: The early 80's.

> Act I.   Vandergelder's house in Yonkers, New York.
>
> Act II.   Mrs. Molloy's hat shop, New York.
>
> Act III.   The Harmonia Gardens Restaurant on the Battery, New York.
>
> Act IV.   Miss Van Huysen's house, New York.

This play is based upon a comedy by Johann Nestroy, *Einen Jux will es sich Machen* (Vienna, 1842), which was in turn based upon an English original, *A Day Well Spent* (London, 1835) by John Oxenford.

Act I

Living room of Mr. Vandergelder's house, over his hay, feed and provision store in Yonkers, fifteen miles north of New York City. Articles from the store have overflowed into this room; it has not been cleaned for a long time and is in some disorder, but it is not sordid or gloomy.

There are three entrances. One at the center back leads into the principal rooms of the house. One on the back right (all the directions are from the point of view of the actors) opens on steps which descend to the street door. One on the left leads to Ermengarde's room.

In the center of the room is a trap door; below it is a ladder descending to the store below.

Behind the trap door and to the left of it is a tall accountant's desk; to the left of it is an old-fashioned stove with a stovepipe going up into the ceiling. Before the desk is a tall stool. On the right of the stage is a table with some chairs about it.

Mr. Vandergelder's Gladstone bag, packed for a journey, is beside the desk.

It is early morning.

VANDERGELDER, *sixty, choleric, vain and sly, wears a soiled dressing gown. He is seated with a towel about his neck, in a chair beside the desk, being shaved by* JOE SCANLON. VANDERGELDER *is smoking a cigar and holding a hand mirror.* AMBROSE KEMPER *is angrily striding about the room.*

VANDERGELDER: (*Loudly.*) I tell you for the hundredth time you will never marry my niece.

AMBROSE: (*Thirty; dressed as an "artist."*) And I tell you for the thousandth time that I will marry your niece; and right soon, too.

VANDERGELDER: Never!

AMBROSE: Your niece is of age, Mr. Vandergelder. Your niece has consented to marry me. This is a free country, Mr. Vandergelder—not a private kingdom of your own.

VANDERGELDER: There are no free countries for fools, Mr.

Kemper. Thank you for the honor of your visit—good morning.

JOE: (*Fifty; lanky, mass of gray hair falling into his eyes.*) Mr. Vandergelder, will you please sit still one minute? If I cut your throat it'll be practically unintentional.

VANDERGELDER: Ermengarde is not for you, nor for anybody else who can't support her.

AMBROSE: I tell you I can support her. I make a very good living.

VANDERGELDER: No, sir! A living is made, Mr. Kemper, by selling something that everybody needs at least once a year. Yes, sir! And a million is made by producing something that everybody needs every day. You artists produce something that nobody needs at any time. You may sell a picture once in a while, but you'll make no living. Joe, go over there and stamp three times. I want to talk to Cornelius.

> JOE *crosses to trap door and stamps three times.*

AMBROSE: Not only can I support her now, but I have considerable expectations.

VANDERGELDER: *Expectations!* We merchants don't do business with them. I don't keep accounts with people who promise somehow to pay something someday, and I don't allow my niece to marry such people.

AMBROSE: Very well, from now on you might as well know that I regard any way we can find to get married is right and fair. Ermengarde is of age, and there's no law . . .

> VANDERGELDER *rises and crosses toward Ambrose.* JOE SCANLON *follows him complainingly and tries to find a chance to cut his hair even while he is standing.*

VANDERGELDER: Law? Let me tell you something, Mr. Kemper: most of the people in the world are fools. The law is there to prevent crime; we men of sense are there to prevent foolishness. It's I, and not the law, that will prevent Ermengarde from marrying you, and I've taken some steps already. I've sent her away to get this nonsense out of her head.

AMBROSE: Ermengarde's . . . not here?

VANDERGELDER: She's gone—east, west, north, south. I thank you for the honor of your visit.

Enter GERTRUDE—*eighty; deaf; half blind; and very pleased with herself.*

GERTRUDE: Everything's ready, Mr. Vandergelder. Ermengarde and I have just finished packing the trunk.

VANDERGELDER: Hold your tongue!

JOE *is shaving Vandergelder's throat, so he can only wave his hands vainly.*

GERTRUDE: Yes, Mr. Vandergelder, Ermengarde's ready to leave. Her trunk's all marked. Care Miss Van Huysen, 8 Jackson Street, New York.

VANDERGELDER: (*Breaking away from Joe.*) Hell and damnation! Didn't I tell you it was a secret?

AMBROSE: (*Picks up hat and coat—kisses Gertrude.*) Care Miss Van Huysen, 8 Jackson Street, New York. Thank you very much. Good morning, Mr. Vandergelder.

Exit AMBROSE, *to the street.*

VANDERGELDER: It won't help you, Mr. Kemper— (*To Gertrude.*) Deaf! And blind! At least you can do me the favor of being dumb!

GERTRUDE: Chk—chk! Such a temper! Lord save us!

CORNELIUS *puts his head up through the trap door. He is thirty-three; mock-deferential—he wears a green apron and is in his shirt-sleeves.*

CORNELIUS: Yes, Mr. Vandergelder?

VANDERGELDER: Go in and get my niece's trunk and carry it over to the station. Wait! Gertrude, has Mrs. Levi arrived yet?

CORNELIUS *comes up the trap door, steps into the room and closes the trap door behind him.*

GERTRUDE: Don't shout. I can hear perfectly well. Everything's clearly marked.

Exit left.

VANDERGELDER: Have the buggy brought round to the front of the store in half an hour.

CORNELIUS: Yes, Mr. Vandergelder.

VANDERGELDER: This morning I'm joining my lodge parade and this afternoon I'm going to New York. Before I go, I have something important to say to you and Barnaby. Good news. Fact is—I'm going to promote you. How old are you?

CORNELIUS: Thirty-three, Mr. Vandergelder.

VANDERGELDER: What?

CORNELIUS: Thirty-three.

VANDERGELDER: That all? That's a foolish age to be at. I thought you were forty.

CORNELIUS: Thirty-three.

VANDERGELDER: A man's not worth a cent until he's forty. We just pay 'em wages to make mistakes—don't we, Joe?

JOE: You almost lost an ear on it, Mr. Vandergelder.

VANDERGELDER: I was thinking of promoting you to chief clerk.

CORNELIUS: What am I now, Mr. Vandergelder?

VANDERGELDER: You're an impertinent fool, that's what you are. Now, if you behave yourself, I'll promote you from impertinent fool to chief clerk, with a raise in your wages. And Barnaby may be promoted from idiot apprentice to incompetent clerk.

CORNELIUS: Thank you, Mr. Vandergelder.

VANDERGELDER: However, I want to see you again before I go. Go in and get my niece's trunk.

CORNELIUS: Yes, Mr. Vandergelder.

Exit CORNELIUS, *left.*

VANDERGELDER: Joe—the world's getting crazier every minute. Like my father used to say: the horses'll be taking over the world soon.

JOE: (*Presenting mirror.*) I did what I could, Mr. Vandergelder, what with you flying in and out of the chair. (*He wipes last of the soap from Vandergelder's face.*)

VANDERGELDER: Fine, fine. Joe, you do a fine job, the same fine job you've done me for twenty years. Joe . . . I've got special reasons for looking my best today . . . isn't there something a little extry you could do, something a little special? I'll pay you right up to fifty cents—see what I mean? Do some of those things you do to the young fellas. Touch me up; smarten me up a bit.

JOE: All I know is fifteen cents' worth, like usual, Mr. Vander-gelder; and that includes everything that's decent to do to a man.

VANDERGELDER: Now hold your horses, Joe—all I meant was . . .

JOE: I've shaved you for twenty years and you never asked me no such question before.

VANDERGELDER: Hold your horses, I say, Joe! I'm going to tell you a secret. But I don't want you telling it to that riffraff down to the barbershop what I'm going to tell you now. All I ask of you is a little extry because I'm thinking of getting married again; and this very afternoon I'm going to New York to call on my intended, a very refined lady.

JOE: Your gettin' married is none of my business, Mr. Van-dergelder. I done everything to you I know, and the charge is fifteen cents like it always was, and . . .

> CORNELIUS *crosses, left to right, and exit, carrying a trunk on his shoulder.* ERMENGARDE *and* GERTRUDE *enter from left.*

I don't dye no hair, not even for fifty cents I don't!

VANDERGELDER: Joe Scanlon, get out!

JOE: And lastly, it looks to me like you're pretty rash to judge which is fools and which isn't fools, Mr. Vandergelder. People that's et onions is bad judges of who's et onions and who ain't. Good morning, ladies; good morning, Mr. Vander-gelder.

> *Exit* JOE.

VANDERGELDER: Well, what do you want?

ERMENGARDE: (*Twenty-four; pretty, sentimental.*) Uncle! You said you wanted to talk to us.

VANDERGELDER: Oh yes. Gertrude, go and get my parade regalia—the uniform for my lodge parade.

GERTRUDE: What? Oh yes. Lord have mercy!

> *Exit* GERTRUDE, *back center.*

VANDERGELDER: I had a talk with that artist of yours. He's a fool.

ERMENGARDE *starts to cry.*

Weeping! Weeping! You can go down and weep for a while in New York where it won't be noticed. (*He sits on desk chair, puts tie round neck and calls her over to tie it for him.*) Ermengarde! I told him that when you were old enough to marry you'd marry someone who could support you. I've done you a good turn. You'll come and thank me when you're fifty.

ERMENGARDE: But Uncle, I love him!

VANDERGELDER: I tell you you don't.

ERMENGARDE: But I *do*!

VANDERGELDER: And I tell you you don't. Leave those things to me.

ERMENGARDE: If I don't marry Ambrose I know I'll die.

VANDERGELDER: What of?

ERMENGARDE: A broken heart.

VANDERGELDER: Never heard of it. Mrs. Levi is coming in a moment to take you to New York. You are going to stay two or three weeks with Miss Van Huysen, an old friend of your mother's.

GERTRUDE *re-enters with coat, sash and sword. Enter from the street, right,* MALACHI STACK.

You're not to receive any letters except from me. I'm coming to New York myself today and I'll call on you tomorrow. (*To Malachi.*) Who are you?

MALACHI: (*Fifty. Sardonic. Apparently innocent smile; pretense of humility.*) Malachi Stack, your honor. I heard you wanted an apprentice in the hay, feed, provision and hardware business.

VANDERGELDER: An apprentice at your age?

MALACHI: Yes, your honor; I bring a lot of experience to it.

VANDERGELDER: Have you any letters of recommendation?

MALACHI: (*Extending a sheaf of soiled papers.*) Yes, indeed, your honor! First-class recommendation.

VANDERGELDER: Ermengarde! Are you ready to start?

ERMENGARDE: Yes.

VANDERGELDER: Well, go and get ready some more. Ermengarde! Let me know the minute Mrs. Levi gets here.

ERMENGARDE: Yes, Uncle Horace.

> ERMENGARDE *and* GERTRUDE *exit.*
> VANDERGELDER *examines the letters, putting them down one by one.*

VANDERGELDER: I don't want an able seaman. Nor a type-setter. And I don't want a hospital cook.

MALACHI: No, your honor, but it's all experience. Excuse me! (*Selects a letter.*) This one is from your former partner, Joshua Van Tuyl, in Albany. (*He puts letters from table back into pocket.*)

VANDERGELDER: ". . . for the most part honest and reliable . . . occasionally willing and diligent." There seems to be a certain amount of hesitation about these recommendations.

MALACHI: Businessmen aren't writers, your honor. There's only one businessman in a thousand that can write a good letter of recommendation, your honor. Mr. Van Tuyl sends his best wishes and wants to know if you can use me in the provision and hardware business.

VANDERGELDER: Not so fast, not so fast! What's this "your honor" you use so much?

MALACHI: Mr. Van Tuyl says you're President of the Hudson River Provision Dealers' Recreational, Musical and Burial Society.

VANDERGELDER: I am; but there's no "your honor" that goes with it. Why did you come to Yonkers?

MALACHI: I heard that you'd had an apprentice that was a good-for-nothing, and that you were at your wit's end for another.

VANDERGELDER: Wit's end, wit's end! There's no dearth of good-for-nothing apprentices.

MALACHI: That's right, Mr. Vandergelder. It's employers there's a dearth of. Seems like you hear of a new one dying every day.

VANDERGELDER: What's that? Hold your tongue. I see you've been a barber, and a valet too. Why have you changed your place so often?

MALACHI: Changed my place, Mr. Vandergelder? When a man's interested in experience . . .

VANDERGELDER: Do you drink?

MALACHI: No, thanks. I've just had breakfast.

VANDERGELDER: I didn't ask you whether—Idiot! I asked you if you were a drunkard.

MALACHI: No, sir! No! Why, looking at it from all sides I don't even like liquor.

VANDERGELDER: Well, if you keep on looking at it from all sides, out you go. Remember that. Here. (*Gives him remaining letters.*) With all your faults, I'm going to give you a try.

MALACHI: You'll never regret it, Mr. Vandergelder. You'll never regret it.

VANDERGELDER: Now today I want to use you in New York. I judge you know your way around New York?

MALACHI: Do I know New York? Mr. Vandergelder, I know every hole and corner in New York.

VANDERGELDER: Here's a dollar. A train leaves in a minute. Take that bag to the Central Hotel on Water Street, have them save me a room. Wait for me. I'll be there about four o'clock.

MALACHI: Yes, Mr. Vandergelder. (*Picks up the bag, starts out, then comes back.*) Oh, but first, I'd like to meet the other clerks I'm to work with.

VANDERGELDER: You haven't time. Hurry now. The station's across the street.

MALACHI: Yes, sir. (*Away—then back once more.*) You'll see, sir, you'll never regret it. . . .

VANDERGELDER: I regret it already. Go on. Off with you.

> *Exit* MALACHI, *right.*
> *The following speech is addressed to the audience. During it* MR. VANDERGELDER *takes off his dressing gown, puts on his scarlet sash, his sword and his bright-colored coat. He is already wearing light blue trousers with a red stripe down the sides.*

VANDERGELDER: Ninety-nine per cent of the people in the world are fools and the rest of us are in great danger of contagion. But I wasn't always free of foolishness as I am now. I was once young, which was foolish; I fell in love, which was foolish; and I got married, which was foolish; and for a while I was poor, which was more foolish than all the other things put together. Then my wife died, which was foolish of her; I grew older, which was sensible of me; then I became a rich man, which is as sensible as it is rare. Since you see I'm a man of sense, I guess you were surprised to hear that I'm planning to get married again. Well, I've two reasons for it. In the first place, I like my house run with order, comfort and economy. That's a woman's work; but even a woman can't do it well if she's merely being paid for it. In order to run a house well, a woman must have the feeling that she owns it. Marriage is a bribe to make a housekeeper think she's a householder. Did you ever watch an ant carry a burden twice its size? What excitement! What patience! What will! Well, that's what I think of when I see a woman running a house. What giant passions in those little bodies—what quarrels with the butcher for the best cut—what fury at discovering a moth in a cupboard! Believe me!—if women could harness their natures to something bigger than a house and a baby carriage—tck! tck!—they'd change the world. And the second reason, ladies and gentlemen? Well, I see by your faces you've guessed it already. There's nothing like mixing with women to bring out all the foolishness in a man of sense. And that's a risk I'm willing to take. I've just turned sixty, and I've just laid side by side the last dollar of my first half million. So if I should lose my head a little, I still have enough money to buy it back. After many years' caution and hard work, I have a right to a little risk and adventure, and I'm thinking of getting married. Yes, like all you other fools, I'm willing to risk a little security for a certain amount of adventure. Think it over.

Exit back center.

AMBROSE *enters from the street, crosses left, and whistles softly.* ERMENGARDE *enters from left.*

ERMENGARDE: Ambrose! If my uncle saw you!

AMBROSE: Sh! Get your hat.

ERMENGARDE: My hat!

AMBROSE: Quick! Your trunk's at the station. Now quick! We're running away.

ERMENGARDE: Running away!

AMBROSE: Sh!

ERMENGARDE: Where?

AMBROSE: To New York. To get married.

ERMENGARDE: Oh, Ambrose, I can't do that. Ambrose dear—
it wouldn't be proper!

AMBROSE: Listen. I'm taking you to my friend's house. His
wife will take care of you.

ERMENGARDE: But, Ambrose, a girl can't go on a train with a
man. I can see you don't know anything about girls.

AMBROSE: But I'm telling you we're going to get married!

ERMENGARDE: Married! But what would *Uncle* say?

AMBROSE: We don't care what Uncle'd say—we're eloping.

ERMENGARDE: Ambrose Kemper! How can you use such an
awful word!

AMBROSE: Ermengarde, you have the soul of a field mouse.

ERMENGARDE: (*Crying.*) Ambrose, why do you say such cruel
things to me?

Enter MRS. LEVI, *from the street, right. She stands listening.*

AMBROSE: For the last time I beg you—get your hat and coat.
The train leaves in a few minutes. Ermengarde, we'll get
married tomorrow. . . .

ERMENGARDE: Oh, Ambrose! I see you don't understand anything about weddings. Ambrose, don't you *respect* me? . . .

MRS. LEVI: (*Uncertain age; mass of sandy hair; impoverished
elegance; large, shrewd but generous nature, an assumption of
worldly cynicism conceals a tireless amused enjoyment of life.
She carries a handbag and a small brown paper bag.*) Good
morning, darling girl—how are you?

They kiss.

ERMENGARDE: Oh, good morning, Mrs. Levi.

MRS. LEVI: And who is this gentleman who is so devoted to
you?

ERMENGARDE: This is Mr. Kemper, Mrs. Levi. Ambrose, this is
. . . Mrs. Levi . . . she's an old friend. . . .

MRS. LEVI: Mrs. Levi, born Gallagher. Very happy to meet you,
Mr. Kemper.

AMBROSE: Good morning, Mrs. Levi.

MRS. LEVI: Mr. Kemper, *the artist!* Delighted! Mr. Kemper,
may I say something very frankly?

AMBROSE: Yes, Mrs. Levi.

MRS. LEVI: This thing you were planning to do is a very great mistake.

ERMENGARDE: Oh, Mrs. Levi, please explain to Ambrose—of *course*! I want to marry him, but to *elope*! . . . How . . .

MRS. LEVI: Now, my dear girl, you go in and keep one eye on your uncle. I wish to talk to Mr. Kemper for a moment. You give us a warning when you hear your Uncle Horace coming. . . .

ERMENGARDE: Ye-es, Mrs. Levi.

   Exit ERMENGARDE, *back center.*

MRS. LEVI: Mr. Kemper, I was this dear girl's mother's oldest friend. Believe me, I am on your side. I hope you two will be married very soon, and I think I can be of real service to you. Mr. Kemper, I always go right to the point.

AMBROSE: What is the point, Mrs. Levi?

MRS. LEVI: Mr. Vandergelder is a very rich man, Mr. Kemper, and Ermengarde is his only relative.

AMBROSE: But I am not interested in Mr. Vandergelder's money. I have enough to support a wife and family.

MRS. LEVI: Enough? How much is enough when one is thinking about children and the future? The future is the most expensive luxury in the world, Mr. Kemper.

AMBROSE: Mrs. Levi, what is the point.

MRS. LEVI: Believe me, Mr. Vandergelder wishes to get rid of Ermengarde, and if you follow my suggestions he will even permit her to marry you. You see, Mr. Vandergelder is planning to get married himself.

AMBROSE: What? That monster!

MRS. LEVI: Mr. Kemper!

AMBROSE: Married! To you, Mrs. Levi?

MRS. LEVI: (*Taken aback.*) Oh, no, no . . . NO! I am merely arranging it. I am helping him find a suitable bride.

AMBROSE: For Mr. Vandergelder there are no suitable brides.

MRS. LEVI: I think we can safely say that Mr. Vandergelder will be married to someone by the end of next week.

AMBROSE: What are you suggesting, Mrs. Levi?

MRS. LEVI: I am taking Ermengarde to New York on the next train. I shall not take her to Miss Van Huysen's, as is planned;

I shall take her to my house. I wish you to call for her at my house at five thirty, Here is my card.

AMBROSE: "Mrs. Dolly Gallagher Levi. Varicose veins reduced."

MRS. LEVI: (*Trying to take back card.*) I beg your pardon . . .

AMBROSE: (*Holding card.*) I beg *your* pardon. "Consultations free."

MRS. LEVI: I meant to give you my other card. Here.

AMBROSE: "Mrs. Dolly Gallagher Levi. Aurora Hosiery. Instruction in the guitar and mandolin." You do all these things, Mrs. Levi?

MRS. LEVI: Two and two make four, Mr. Kemper—always did. So you will come to my house at five thirty. At about six I shall take you both with me to the Harmonia Gardens Restaurant on the Battery; Mr. Vandergelder will be there and everything will be arranged.

AMBROSE: How?

MRS. LEVI: Oh, I don't know. One thing will lead to another.

AMBROSE: How do I know that I can trust you, Mrs. Levi? You could easily make our situation worse.

MRS. LEVI: Mr. Kemper, your situation could not possibly be worse.

AMBROSE: I wish I knew what you get out of this, Mrs. Levi.

MRS. LEVI: That is a very proper question. I get two things: profit and pleasure.

AMBROSE: How?

MRS. LEVI: Mr. Kemper, I am a woman who arranges things. At present I am arranging Mr. Vandergelder's domestic affairs. Out of it I get—shall we call it: little pickings? I need little pickings, Mr. Kemper, and especially just now, when I haven't got my train fare back to New York. You see: I am frank with you.

AMBROSE: That's your profit, Mrs. Levi; but where do you get your pleasure?

MRS. LEVI: My pleasure? Mr. Kemper, when you artists paint a hillside or a river you change everything a little, you make thousands of little changes, don't you? Nature is never completely satisfactory and must be corrected. Well, I'm like you artists. Life as it is is never quite interesting enough for me—I'm bored, Mr. Kemper, with life as it is—and so I do things. I put my hand in here, and I put my hand in there, and I watch and I listen—and often I'm very much amused.

AMBROSE: (*Rises.*) Not in my affairs, Mrs. Levi.

MRS. LEVI: Wait, I haven't finished. There's another thing. I'm very interested in this household here—in Mr. Vandergelder and all that idle, frozen money of his. I don't like the thought of it lying in great piles, useless, motionless, in the bank, Mr. Kemper. Money should circulate like rain water. It should be flowing down among the people, through dressmakers and restaurants and cabmen, setting up a little business here, and furnishing a good time there. Do you see what I mean?

AMBROSE: Yes, I do.

MRS. LEVI: New York should be a very happy city, Mr. Kemper, but it isn't. My late husband came from Vienna; now there's a city that understands this. I want New York to be more like Vienna and less like a collection of nervous and tired ants. And if you and Ermengarde get a good deal of Mr. Vandergelder's money, I want you to see that it starts flowing in and around a lot of people's lives. And for that reason I want you to come with me to the Harmonia Gardens Restaurant tonight.

Enter ERMENGARDE.

ERMENGARDE: Mrs. Levi, Uncle Horace is coming.

MRS. LEVI: Mr. Kemper, I think you'd better be going. . . .

AMBROSE *crosses to trap door and disappears down the ladder, closing trap as he goes.*

Darling girl, Mr. Kemper and I have had a very good talk. You'll see: Mr. Vandergelder and I will be dancing at your wedding very soon—

Enter VANDERGELDER *at back. He has now added a splendid plumed hat to his costume and is carrying a standard or small flag bearing the initials of his lodge.*

Oh, Mr. Vandergelder, how handsome you look! You take my breath away. Yes, my dear girl, I'll see you soon.

Exit ERMENGARDE *back center.*

Oh, Mr. Vandergelder, I wish Irene Molloy could see you

now. But then! I don't know what's come over you lately. You seem to be growing younger every day.

VANDERGELDER: Allowing for exaggeration, Mrs. Levi. If a man eats careful there's no reason why he should look old.

MRS. LEVI: You never said a truer word.

VANDERGELDER: I'll never see fifty-five again.

MRS. LEVI: Fifty-five! Why, I can see at a glance that you're the sort that will be stamping about at a hundred—and eating five meals a day, like my Uncle Harry. At fifty-five my Uncle Harry was a mere boy. I'm a judge of hands, Mr. Vandergelder—show me your hand. (*Looks at it.*) Lord in heaven! What a life line!

VANDERGELDER: Where?

MRS. LEVI: From *here* to *here*. It runs right off your hand. I don't know where it goes. They'll have to hit you on the head with a mallet. They'll have to stifle you with a sofa pillow. You'll bury us all! However, to return to our business—Mr. Vandergelder, I suppose you've changed your mind again. I suppose you've given up all idea of getting married.

VANDERGELDER: (*Complacently.*) Not at all, Mrs. Levi. I have news for you.

MRS. LEVI: News?

VANDERGELDER: Mrs. Levi, I've practically decided to ask Mrs. Molloy to be my wife.

MRS. LEVI: (*Taken aback.*) You have?

VANDERGELDER: Yes, I have.

MRS. LEVI: Oh, you have! Well, I guess that's just about the best news I ever heard. So there's nothing more for me to do but wish you every happiness under the sun and say good-by. (*Crosses as if to leave.*)

VANDERGELDER: (*Stopping her.*) Well—Mrs. Levi—Surely I thought—

MRS. LEVI: Well, I did have a little suggestion to make—but I won't. You're going to marry Irene Molloy, and that closes the matter.

VANDERGELDER: What suggestion was that, Mrs. Levi?

MRS. LEVI: Well—I *had* found *another* girl for you.

VANDERGELDER: Another?

MRS. LEVI: The most wonderful girl, the ideal wife.

VANDERGELDER: Another, eh? What's her name?

MRS. LEVI: Her name?

VANDERGELDER: Yes!

MRS. LEVI: (*Groping for it.*) Err . . . er . . . her *name?*—
Ernestina—Simple. *Miss* Ernestina Simple. But now of
course all that's too late. After all, you're engaged—you're
practically engaged to marry Irene Molloy.

VANDERGELDER: Oh, I ain't engaged to Mrs. Molloy!

MRS. LEVI: Nonsense! You can't break poor Irene's heart now
and change to another girl. . . . When a man at your time
of life calls four times on an attractive widow like that—and
sends her a pot of geraniums—that's practically an engagement!

VANDERGELDER: That ain't an engagement!

MRS. LEVI: And yet—! If only you were free! I've found this
treasure of a girl. Every moment I felt like a traitor to Irene
Molloy—but let me tell you: I couldn't help it. I told this
girl all about you, just as though you were a free man. Isn't
that dreadful? The fact is: she has fallen in love with you
already.

VANDERGELDER: Ernestina?

MRS. LEVI: Ernestina Simple.

VANDERGELDER: Ernestina Simple.

MRS. LEVI: Of course she's a very different idea from Mrs.
Molloy, Ernestina is. Like her name—simple, domestic,
practical.

VANDERGELDER: Can she cook?

MRS. LEVI: Cook, Mr. Vandergelder? I've had two meals from
her hands, and—as I live—I don't know what I've done that
God should reward me with such meals.

MRS. LEVI: (*Continues.*) Her duck! Her steak!

VANDERGELDER: Eh! Eh! In this house we don't eat duck and
steak every day, Mrs. Levi.

MRS. LEVI: But didn't I tell you?—that's the wonderful part
about it. Her duck—what was it? Pigeon! I'm alive to tell
you. I don't know how she does it. It's a secret that's come
down in her family. The greatest chefs would give their right
hands to know it. And the steaks? Shoulder of beef—four
cents a pound. Dogs wouldn't eat. But when Ernestina
passes her hands over it—!!

VANDERGELDER: Allowing for exaggeration, Mrs. Levi.

MRS. LEVI: No exaggeration.

I'm the best cook in the world myself, and I *know* what's good.

VANDERGELDER: Hm. How old is she, Mrs. Levi?

MRS. LEVI: Nineteen, well—say twenty.

VANDERGELDER: Twenty, Mrs. Levi? Girls of twenty are apt to favor young fellows of their own age.

MRS. LEVI: But you don't listen to me. And you don't know the girl. Mr. Vandergelder, she has a positive horror of flighty, brainless young men. A fine head of gray hair, she says, is worth twenty shined up with goose grease. No, sir. "I like a man that's *settled*"—in so many words she said it.

VANDERGELDER: That's . . . that's not usual, Mrs. Levi.

MRS. LEVI: Usual? I'm not wearing myself to the bone hunting up *usual* girls to interest you, Mr. Vandergelder. Usual, indeed. Listen to me. Do you know the sort of pictures she has on her wall? Is it any of these young Romeos and Lochinvars? No!—it's Moses on the Mountain—that's what she's got. If you want to make her happy, you give her a picture of Methuselah surrounded by his grandchildren. That's my advice to you.

VANDERGELDER: I hope . . . hm . . . that she has some means, Mrs. Levi. I have a large household to run.

MRS. LEVI: Ernestina? She'll bring you five thousand dollars a year.

VANDERGELDER: Eh! Eh!

MRS. LEVI: Listen to me, Mr. Vandergelder. You're a man of sense, I hope. A man that can reckon. In the first place, she's an orphan. She's been brought up with a great saving of food. What does she eat herself? Apples and lettuce. It's what she's been used to eat and what she likes best. She saves you two thousand a year right there. Secondly, she makes her own clothes—out of old tablecloths and window curtains. And she's the best-dressed woman in Brooklyn this minute. She saves you a thousand dollars right there. Thirdly, her health is of iron—

VANDERGELDER: But, Mrs. Levi, that's not money in the pocket.

MRS. LEVI: We're talking about marriage, aren't we, Mr. Vandergelder? The money she saves while she's in Brooklyn is none of your affair—but if she were your wife that would be *money.* Yes, sir, that's money.

VANDERGELDER: What's her family?

MRS. LEVI: Her father?—God be good to him! He was the best —what am I trying to say?—the best undertaker in Brooklyn, respected, esteemed. He knew all the best people— knew them well, even before they died. So—well, that's the way it is. (*Lowering her voice, intimately.*) Now let me tell you a little more of her appearance. Can you hear me: as I say, a beautiful girl, beautiful, I've seen her go down the street—you know what I mean?—the young men get dizzy. They have to lean against lampposts. And she? Modest, eyes on the ground—I'm not going to tell you any more. . . . Couldn't you come to New York today?

VANDERGELDER: I was thinking of coming to New York this afternoon. . . .

MRS. LEVI: You were? Well now, I wonder if something could be arranged—oh, she's so eager to see you! Let me see . . .

VANDERGELDER: Could I . . . Mrs. Levi, could I give you a little dinner, maybe?

MRS. LEVI: Really, come to think of it, I don't see where I could get the time. I'm so busy over that wretched lawsuit of mine. Yes. If I win it, I don't mind telling you, I'll be what's called a very rich woman. I'll own half of Long Island, that's a fact. But just now I'm at my wit's end for a little help, just enough money to finish it off. My wit's end! (*She looks in her handbag.*)

> In order not to hear this, VANDERGELDER *has a series of coughs, sneezes and minor convulsions.*

But perhaps I could arrange a little dinner; I'll see. Yes, for that lawsuit all I need is fifty dollars, and Staten Island's as good as mine. I've been trotting all over New York for you, trying to find you a suitable wife.

VANDERGELDER: Fifty dollars!!

MRS. LEVI: Two whole months I've been . . .

VANDERGELDER: Fifty dollars, Mrs. Levi . . . is no joke. (*Producing purse.*) I don't know where money's gone to these days. It's in hiding. . . . There's twenty . . . well, there's twenty-five. I can't spare no more, not now I can't.

MRS. LEVI: Well, this will help—will help somewhat. Now let me tell you what we'll do. I'll bring Ernestina to that restaurant on the Battery. You know it: the Harmonia Gardens. It's good, but it's not flashy. Now, Mr. Vandergelder, I think it'd be nice if just this once you'd order a real nice dinner. I guess you can afford it.

VANDERGELDER: Well, just this once.

MRS. LEVI: A chicken wouldn't hurt.

VANDERGELDER: Chicken!!—Well, just this once.

MRS. LEVI: And a little wine.

VANDERGELDER: Wine? Well, just this once.

MRS. LEVI: Now about Mrs. Molloy—what do you think? Shall we call that subject closed?

VANDERGELDER: No, not at all, Mrs. Levi, I want to have dinner with Miss . . . with Miss . . .

MRS. LEVI: Simple.

VANDERGELDER: With Miss Simple; but first I want to make another call on Mrs. Molloy.

MRS. LEVI: Dear, dear, dear! And Miss Simple? What races you make me run! Very well; I'll meet you on one of those benches in front of Mrs. Molloy's hat store at four thirty, as usual.

Trap door rises, and CORNELIUS' *head appears.*

CORNELIUS: The buggy's here, ready for the parade, Mr. Vandergelder.

VANDERGELDER: Call Barnaby. I want to talk to both of you.

CORNELIUS: Yes, Mr. Vandergelder.

Exit CORNELIUS *down trap door. Leaves trap open.*

MRS. LEVI: Now do put your thoughts in order, Mr. Vandergelder. I can't keep upsetting and disturbing the finest women in New York City unless you mean business.

VANDERGELDER: Oh, I mean business all right!

MRS. LEVI: I hope so. Because, you know, you're playing a very dangerous game.

VANDERGELDER: Dangerous?—Dangerous, Mrs. Levi?

MRS. LEVI: Of course, it's dangerous—and there's a name for it! You're tampering with these women's affections, aren't you? And the only way you can save yourself now is to be married to *someone* by the end of next week. So think that over!

Exit center back.
Enter CORNELIUS *and* BARNABY, *by the trap door.*

VANDERGELDER: This morning I'm joining my lodge parade, and this afternoon I'm going to New York. When I come back, there are going to be some changes in the house here. I'll tell you what the change is, but I don't want you discussing it amongst yourselves: you're going to have a mistress.

BARNABY: (*Seventeen; round-faced, wide-eyed innocence; wearing a green apron.*) I'm too young, Mr. Vandergelder!

VANDERGELDER: Not yours! Death and damnation! Not yours, idiot—*mine!* (*Then, realizing:*) Hey! Hold your tongue until you're spoken to! I'm thinking of getting married.

CORNELIUS: (*Crosses, hand outstretched.*) Many congratulations, Mr. Vandergelder, and my compliments to the lady.

VANDERGELDER: That's none of your business. Now go back to the store.

The BOYS *start down the ladder,* BARNABY *first.*

Have you got any questions you want to ask before I go?

CORNELIUS: Mr. Vandergelder—er—Mr. Vandergelder, does the chief clerk get one evening off every week?

VANDERGELDER: So that's the way you begin being chief clerk, is it? When I was your age I got up at five; I didn't close the shop until ten at night, and then I put in a good hour at the account books. The world's going to pieces. You elegant ladies lie in bed until six and at nine o'clock at night you rush to close the door so fast the line of customers bark their noses. No, sir—you'll attend to the store as usual, and on Friday and Saturday nights you'll remain open until ten—now hear what I say! This is the first time I've been away from the store overnight. When I come back I want to hear that you've run the place perfectly in my absence. If I hear of any foolishness, I'll discharge you. An evening free! Do you suppose that *I* had evenings free? (*At the top of his complacency.*) If I'd had evenings free I wouldn't be what I am now! (*He marches out, right.*)

BARNABY: (*Watching him go.*) The horses nearly ran away when they saw him. What's the matter, Cornelius?

CORNELIUS: (*Sits in dejected thought.*) Chief clerk! Promoted from chief clerk to chief clerk.

BARNABY: Don't you like it?

CORNELIUS: Chief clerk!—and if I'm good, in ten years I'll be promoted to chief clerk again. Thirty-three years old and I still don't get an evening free? When am I going to begin to live?

BARNABY: Well—ah . . . you can begin to live on Sundays, Cornelius.

CORNELIUS: That's not living. Twice to church, and old Wolf-trap's eyes on the back of my head the whole time. And as for holidays! What did we do last Christmas? All those canned tomatoes went bad and exploded. We had to clean up the mess all afternoon. Was that living?

BARNABY: (*Holding his nose at the memory of the bad smell.*) No!!!

CORNELIUS: (*Rising with sudden resolution.*) Barnaby, how much money have you got—where you can get at it?

BARNABY: Oh—three dollars. Why, Cornelius?

CORNELIUS: You and I are going to New York.

BARNABY: Cornelius!!! We can't! Close the store?

CORNELIUS: Some more rotten-tomato cans are going to explode.

BARNABY: Holy cabooses! How do you know?

CORNELIUS: I know they're rotten. All you have to do is to light a match under them. They'll make such a smell that customers can't come into the place for twenty-four hours. That'll get us an evening free. We're going to New York too, Barnaby, we're going to live! I'm going to have enough adventures to last me until I'm *partner*. So go and get your Sunday clothes on.

BARNABY: Wha-a-a-t?

CORNELIUS: Yes, I mean it. We're going to have a good meal; and we're going to be in danger; and we're going to get almost arrested; and we're going to spend all our money.

BARNABY: Holy cabooses!!

CORNELIUS: And one more thing: we're not coming back to Yonkers until we've kissed a girl.

BARNABY: Kissed a girl! Cornelius, you can't do that. You don't know any girls.

CORNELIUS: I'm thirty-three. I've got to begin sometime.

BARNABY: I'm only seventeen, Cornelius. It isn't so urgent for me.

CORNELIUS: Don't start backing down now—if the worst comes to the worst and we get discharged from here we can always join the Army.

BARNABY: Uh—did I hear you say that you'd be old Wolf-trap's partner?

CORNELIUS: How can I help it? He's growing old. If you go to bed at nine and open the store at six, you get promoted upward whether you like it or not.

BARNABY: My! Partner.

CORNELIUS: Oh, there's no way of getting away from it. You and I will be Vandergelders.

BARNABY: I? Oh, no—I may rise a little, but I'll never be a Vandergelder.

CORNELIUS: Listen—everybody thinks when he gets rich he'll be a different kind of rich person from the rich people he sees around him; later on he finds out there's only one kind of rich person, and he's it.

BARNABY: Oh, but I'll—

CORNELIUS: No. The best of all would be a person who has all the good things a poor person has, and all the good meals a rich person has, but that's never been known. No, you and I are going to be Vandergelders; all the more reason, then, for us to try and get some living and some adventure into us now—will you come, Barnaby?

BARNABY: (*In a struggle with his fears, a whirlwind of words.*) But Wolf-trap—KRR-pt, Gertrude-KRR-pt— (*With a sudden cry of agreement.*) Yes, Cornelius!

Enter MRS. LEVI, ERMENGARDE *and* GERTRUDE *from back center. The* BOYS *start down the ladder,* CORNELIUS *last.*

MRS. LEVI: Mr. Hackl, is the trunk waiting at the station?

CORNELIUS: Yes, Mrs. Levi. (*Closes the trap door.*)

MRS. LEVI: Take a last look, Ermengarde.

ERMENGARDE: What?

MRS. LEVI: Take a last look at your girlhood home, dear. I

remember when I left my home. I gave a whinny like a young colt, and off I went.

ERMENGARDE *and* GERTRUDE *exit.*

ERMENGARDE: (*As they go.*) Oh, Gertrude, do you think I ought to get married this way? A young girl has to be so careful!

MRS. LEVI *is alone. She addresses the audience.*

MRS. LEVI: You know, I think I'm going to have this room with *blue* wallpaper,—yes, in blue! (*Hurries out after the others.*)

BARNABY *comes up trap door, looks off right, then lies on floor, gazing down through the trap door.*

BARNABY: All clear up here, Cornelius! Cornelius—hold the candle steady a minute—the bottom row's all right—but try the top now . . . they're swelled up like they are ready to bust!

BANG.

Holy CABOOSES!

BANG, BANG.

Cornelius! I can smell it up here! (*Rises and dances about, holding his nose.*)

CORNELIUS: (*Rushing up the trap door.*) Get into your Sunday clothes, Barnaby. We're going to New York!

As they run out . . . there is a big explosion. A shower of tomato cans comes up from below, as—
THE
CURTAIN
FALLS

Act II

Mrs. Molloy's hat shop, New York City.

There are two entrances. One door at the extreme right of the back wall, to Mrs. Molloy's workroom; one at the back left corner, to the street. The whole left wall is taken up with the show windows, filled with hats. It is separated from the shop by a low brass rail, hung with net; during the act both MRS. MOLLOY *and* BARNABY *stoop under the rail and go into the shop window. By the street door stands a large cheval glass. In the middle of the back wall is a large wardrobe or clothes cupboard, filled with ladies' coats, large enough for* CORNELIUS *to hide in. At the left, beginning at the back wall, between the wardrobe and the workroom door, a long counter extends toward the audience, almost to the footlights. In the center of the room is a large round table with a low-hanging red cloth. There are a small gilt chair by the wardrobe and two chairs in front of the counter. Over the street door and the workroom door are bells which ring when the doors are opened.*

As the curtain rises, MRS. MOLLOY *is in the window, standing on a box, reaching up to put hats on the stand.* MINNIE FAY *is sewing by the counter.* MRS. MOLLOY *has a pair of felt overshoes, to be removed later.*

MRS. MOLLOY: Minnie, you're a fool. Of course I shall marry Horace Vandergelder.

MINNIE: Oh, Mrs. Molloy! I didn't ask you. I wouldn't dream of asking you such a personal question.

MRS. MOLLOY: Well, it's what you meant, isn't it? And there's your answer. I shall certainly marry Horace Vandergelder if he asks me. (*Crawls under window rail, into the room, singing loudly.*)

MINNIE: I know it's none of my business . . .

MRS. MOLLOY: Speak up, Minnie, I can't hear you.

MINNIE: . . . but do you . . . do you . . . ?

MRS. MOLLOY: (*Having crossed the room, is busy at the counter.*) Minnie, you're a fool. Say it: Do I love him? Of course, I don't love him. But I have two good reasons for marrying him just the same. Minnie, put something on that hat. It's not ugly enough. (*Throws hat over counter.*)

MINNIE: (*Catching and taking hat to table.*) Not ugly enough!

MRS. MOLLOY: I couldn't sell it. Put a . . . put a sponge on it.

MINNIE: Why, Mrs. Molloy, you're in such a *mood* today.

MRS. MOLLOY: In the first place I shall marry Mr. Vandergelder to get away from the millinery business. I've hated it from the first day I had anything to do with it. Minnie, I hate hats. (*Sings loudly again.*)

MINNIE: Why, what's the matter with the millinery business?

MRS. MOLLOY: (*Crossing to window with two hats.*) I can no longer stand being suspected of being a wicked woman, while I have nothing to show for it. I can't stand it. (*She crawls under rail into window.*)

MINNIE: Why, no one would dream of suspecting you—

MRS. MOLLOY: (*On her knees, she looks over the rail.*) Minnie, you're a fool. All millineresses are suspected of being wicked women. Why, half the time all those women come into the shop merely to look at me.

MINNIE: Oh!

MRS. MOLLOY: They enjoy the suspicion. But they aren't certain. If they were *certain* I was a wicked woman, they wouldn't put foot in this place again. Do I go to restaurants? No, it would be bad for business. Do I go to balls, or theatres, or operas? No, it would be bad for business. The only men I ever meet are feather merchants. (*Crawls out of window, but gazes intently into the street.*) What are those two young men doing out there on that park bench? Take my word for it, Minnie, either I marry Horace Vandergelder, or I break out of this place like a fire engine. I'll go to every theatre and ball and opera in New York City. (*Returns to counter, singing again.*)

MINNIE: But Mr. Vandergelder's not . . .

MRS. MOLLOY: Speak up, Minnie, I can't hear you.

MINNIE: . . . I don't think he's attractive.

MRS. MOLLOY: But what I think he is—and it's very important —I think he'd make a good fighter.

MINNIE: Mrs. Molloy!

MRS. MOLLOY: Take my word for it, Minnie: the best part of married life is the fights. The rest is merely so-so.

MINNIE: (*Fingers in ears.*) I won't listen.

MRS. MOLLOY: Peter Molloy—God rest him!—was a fine arguing man. I pity the woman whose husband slams the door and walks out of the house at the beginning of an argument. Peter Molloy would stand up and fight for hours on end. He'd even throw things, Minnie, and there's no pleasure to equal that. When I felt tired I'd start a good bloodwarming fight and it'd take ten years off my age; now Horace Vandergelder would put up a good fight; I know it. I've a mind to marry him.

MINNIE: I think they're just awful, the things you're saying today.

MRS. MOLLOY: Well, I'm enjoying them myself, too.

MINNIE: (*At the window.*) Mrs. Molloy, those two men out in the street—

MRS. MOLLOY: What?

MINNIE: Those men. It looks as if they meant to come in here.

MRS. MOLLOY: Well now, it's time some men came into this place. I give you the younger one, Minnie.

MINNIE: Aren't you terrible!

> MRS. MOLLOY *sits on center table, while* MINNIE *takes off her felt overshoes.*

MRS. MOLLOY: Wait till I get my hands on that older one! Mark my words, Minnie, we'll get an adventure out of this yet. Adventure, adventure! Why does everybody have adventures except me, Minnie? Because I have no spirit, I have no gumption. Minnie, they're coming in here. Let's go into the workroom and make them wait for us for a minute.

MINNIE: Oh, but Mrs. Molloy . . . my work! . . .

MRS. MOLLOY: (*Running to workroom.*) Hurry up, be quick now, Minnie!

> *They go out to workroom.*
> BARNABY *and* CORNELIUS *run in from street, leaving front door open. They are dressed in the stiff discomfort of their Sunday clothes.* CORNELIUS *wears a bowler hat,* BARNABY *a straw hat too large for him.*

BARNABY: No one's here.

CORNELIUS: Some women were here a minute ago. I saw them.

They jump back to the street door and peer down the street.

That's Wolf-trap all right!

Coming back.

Well, we've got to hide here until he passes by.

BARNABY: He's sitting down on that bench. It may be quite a while.

CORNELIUS: When these women come in, we'll have to make conversation until he's gone away. We'll pretend we're buying a hat. How much money have you got now?

BARNABY: (*Counting his money.*) Forty cents for the train—seventy cents for dinner—twenty cents to see the whale—and a dollar I lost—I have seventy cents.

CORNELIUS: And I have a dollar seventy-five. I wish I knew how much hats cost!

BARNABY: Is this an adventure, Cornelius?

CORNELIUS: No, but it may be.

BARNABY: I think it is. There we wander around New York all day and nothing happens; and then we come to the quietest street in the whole city and suddenly Mr. Vandergelder turns the corner. (*Going to door.*) I think that's an adventure. I think . . . Cornelius! That Mrs. Levi is there now. She's sitting down on the bench with him.

CORNELIUS: What do you know about that! We know only one person in all New York City, and there she is!

BARNABY: Even if our adventure came along now I'd be too tired to enjoy it. Cornelius, why isn't this an adventure?

CORNELIUS: Don't be asking that. When you're in an adventure, you'll know it all right.

BARNABY: Maybe I wouldn't. Cornelius, let's arrange a signal for you to give me when an adventure's really going on. For instance, Cornelius, you say . . . uh . . . uh . . . *pudding;* you say *pudding* to me if it's an adventure we're in.

CORNELIUS: I wonder where the lady who runs this store is? What's her name again?

BARNABY: "Mrs. Molloy, hats for ladies."

CORNELIUS: Oh yes. I must think over what I'm going to say when she comes in. (*To counter.*) "Good afternoon, Mrs.

Molloy, wonderful weather we're having. We've been looking everywhere for some beautiful hats."

BARNABY: That's fine, Cornelius!

CORNELIUS: "Good afternoon, Mrs. Molloy; wonderful weather . . ." We'll make her think we're very rich. (*One hand in trouser pocket, the other on back of chair.*) "Good afternoon, Mrs. Molloy . . ." You keep one eye on the door the whole time. "We've been looking everywhere for . . ."

Enter MRS. MOLLOY *from the workroom.*

MRS. MOLLOY: (*Behind the counter.*) Oh, I'm sorry. Have I kept you waiting? Good afternoon, gentlemen.

CORNELIUS: (*Hat off.*) Here, Cornelius Hackl.

BARNABY: (*Hat off.*) Here, Barnaby Tucker.

MRS. MOLLOY: I'm very happy to meet you. Perhaps I can help you. Won't you sit down?

CORNELIUS: Thank you, we will.

The BOYS *place their hats on the table, then sit down at the counter facing Mrs. Molloy.*

You see, Mrs. Molloy, we're looking for hats. We've looked everywhere. Do you know what we heard? Go to Mrs. Molloy's, they said. So we came here. Only place we *could* go . . .

MRS. MOLLOY: Well now, that's *very* complimentary.

CORNELIUS: . . . and we were right. Everybody was right.

MRS. MOLLOY: You wish to choose some hats for a friend?

CORNELIUS: Yes, exactly. (*Kicks Barnaby.*)

BARNABY: Yes, exactly.

CORNELIUS: We were thinking of five or six, weren't we, Barnaby?

BARNABY: Er—five.

CORNELIUS: You see, Mrs. Molloy, money's no object with us. None at all.

MRS. MOLLOY: Why, Mr. Hackl . . .

CORNELIUS: (*Rises and goes toward street door.*) . . . I beg your pardon, what an interesting street! Something happening every minute. Passers-by, and . . .

BARNABY runs to join him.

MRS. MOLLOY: You're from out of town, Mr. Hackl?

CORNELIUS: (*Coming back.*) Yes, ma'am—Barnaby, just keep your eye on the street, will you? You won't see that in Yonkers every day.

BARNABY *remains kneeling at street door.*

BARNABY: Oh yes, I will.

CORNELIUS: Not all of it.

MRS. MOLLOY: Now this friend of yours—couldn't she come in with you someday and choose her hats herself?

CORNELIUS: (*Sits at counter.*) No. Oh, no. It's a surprise for her.

MRS. MOLLOY: Indeed? That may be a little difficult, Mr. Hackl. It's not entirely customary.—Your friend's very interested in the street, Mr. Hackl.

CORNELIUS: Oh yes. Yes. He has reason to be.

MRS. MOLLOY: You said you were from out of town?

CORNELIUS: Yes, we're from Yonkers.

MRS. MOLLOY: Yonkers?

CORNELIUS: Yonkers . . . yes, Yonkers. (*He gazes rapt into her eyes.*) You should know Yonkers, Mrs. Molloy. Hudson River; Palisades; drives; some say it's the most beautiful town in the world; that's what they say.

MRS. MOLLOY: Is that so!

CORNELIUS: (*Rises.*) Mrs. Molloy, if you ever had a Sunday free, I'd . . . we'd like to show you Yonkers. Y'know, it's very historic, too.

MRS. MOLLOY: That's very kind of you. Well, perhaps . . . now about those hats. (*Takes two hats from under counter, and crosses to back center of the room.*)

CORNELIUS: (*Following.*) Is there . . . Have you a . . . Maybe Mr. Molloy would like to see Yonkers too?

MRS. MOLLOY: Oh, I'm a widow, Mr. Hackl.

CORNELIUS: (*Joyfully.*) You are! (*With sudden gravity.*) Oh, that's too bad. Mr. Molloy would have enjoyed Yonkers.

MRS. MOLLOY: Very likely. Now about these hats. Is your friend dark or light?

CORNELIUS: Don't think about that for a minute. Any hat you'd like would be perfectly all right with her.

MRS. MOLLOY: Really! (*She puts one on.*) Do you like this one?

CORNELIUS: (*In awe-struck admiration.*) Barnaby! (*In sudden anger.*) Barnaby! Look!

> BARNABY *turns; unimpressed, he laughs vaguely, and turns to door again.*

Mrs. Molloy, that's the most beautiful hat I ever saw.

> BARNABY *now crawls under the rail into the window.*

MRS. MOLLOY: Your friend is acting very strangely, Mr. Hackl.

CORNELIUS: Barnaby, stop acting strangely. When the street's quiet and empty, come back and talk to us. What was I saying? Oh yes: Mrs. Molloy, you should know Yonkers.

MRS. MOLLOY: (*Hat off.*) The fact is, I have a friend in Yonkers. Perhaps you know him. It's always so foolish to ask in cases like that, isn't it?

> *They both laugh over this with increasing congeniality.* MRS. MOLLOY *goes to counter with hats from table.* CORNELIUS *follows.*

It's a Mr. Vandergelder.

CORNELIUS: (*Stops abruptly.*) What was that you said?

MRS. MOLLOY: Then you do know him?

CORNELIUS: Horace Vandergelder?

MRS. MOLLOY: Yes, that's right.

CORNELIUS: Know him! (*Look to Barnaby.*) Why, no. No!

BARNABY: No! No!

CORNELIUS: (*Starting to glide about the room, in search of a hiding place.*) I beg your pardon, Mrs. Molloy—what an attractive shop you have! (*Smiling fixedly at her he moves to the workshop door.*) And where does this door lead to? (*Opens it, and is alarmed by the bell which rings above it.*)

MRS. MOLLOY: Why, Mr. Hackl, that's my workroom.

CORNELIUS: Everything here is so interesting. (*Looks under counter.*) Every corner. Every door, Mrs. Molloy. Barnaby, notice the interesting doors and cupboards. (*He opens the cupboard door.*) Deeply interesting. Coats for ladies. (*Laughs.*) Barnaby, make a note of the table. Precious piece of furniture, with a low-hanging cloth, I see. (*Stretches his leg under table.*)

MRS. MOLLOY: (*Taking a hat from box left of wardrobe.*) Perhaps your friend might like some of this new Italian straw. Mr. Vandergelder's a substantial man and very well liked, they tell me.

CORNELIUS: A lovely man, Mrs. Molloy.

MRS. MOLLOY: Oh yes—charming, charming!

CORNELIUS: (*Smiling sweetly.*) Has only one fault, as far as I know; he's hard as nails; but apart from that, as you say, a charming nature, ma'am.

MRS. MOLLOY: And a large circle of friends—?

CORNELIUS: Yes, indeed, yes indeed—five or six.

BARNABY: Five!

CORNELIUS: He comes and calls on you here from time to time, I suppose.

MRS. MOLLOY: (*Turns from mirror where she has been putting a hat on.*) This summer we'll be wearing ribbons down our back. Yes, as a matter of fact I am expecting a call from him this afternoon. (*Hat off.*)

BARNABY: I think . . . Cornelius! I think . . . !!

MRS. MOLLOY: Now to show you some more hats—

BARNABY: Look out! (*He takes a flying leap over the rail and flings himself under the table.*)

CORNELIUS: Begging your pardon, Mrs. Molloy. (*He jumps into the cupboard.*)

MRS. MOLLOY: Gentlemen! Mr. Hackl! Come right out of there this minute!

CORNELIUS: (*Sticking his head out of the wardrobe door.*) Help us just this once, Mrs. Molloy! We'll explain later!

MRS. MOLLOY: Mr. Hackl!

BARNABY: We're as innocent as can be, Mrs. Molloy.

MRS. MOLLOY: But really! Gentlemen! I can't have this! *What are you doing?*

BARNABY: Cornelius! Cornelius! Pudding?

CORNELIUS: (*A shout.*) Pudding!

> *They disappear. Enter from the street* MRS. LEVI, *followed by* MR. VANDERGELDER. VANDERGELDER *is dressed in a too-bright checked suit, and wears a green derby—or bowler—hat. He is carrying a large ornate box of chocolates in one hand, and a cane in the other.*

MRS. LEVI: Irene, my darling child, how *are* you? Heaven be good to us, how well you look!

They kiss.

MRS. MOLLOY: But what a surprise! And Mr. Vandergelder in New York—what a pleasure!

VANDERGELDER: (*Swaying back and forth on his heels complacently.*) Good afternoon, Mrs. Molloy.

They shake hands. MRS. MOLLOY *brings chair from counter for him. He sits at left of table.*

MRS. LEVI: Yes, Mr. Vandergelder's in New York. Yonkers lies up there—*decimated* today. Irene, we thought we'd pay you a very short call. Now you'll tell us if it's inconvenient, won't you?

MRS. MOLLOY: (*Placing a chair for Mrs. Levi at right of table.*) Inconvenient, Dolly! The idea! Why, it's sweet of you to come. (*She notices the boys' hats on the table—sticks a spray of flowers into crown of Cornelius' bowler and winds a piece of chiffon round Barnaby's panama.*)

VANDERGELDER: We waited outside a moment.

MRS. LEVI: Mr. Vandergelder thought he saw two customers coming in—two men.

MRS. MOLLOY: Men! Men, Mr. Vandergelder? Why, what will you be saying next?

MRS. LEVI: Then we'll sit down for a minute or two. . . .

MRS. MOLLOY: (*Wishing to get them out of the shop into the workroom.*) Before you sit down— (*She pushes them both.*) Before you sit down, there's something I want to show you. I want to show Mr. Vandergelder my workroom, too.

MRS. LEVI: I've seen the workroom a hundred times. I'll stay right here and try on some of these hats.

MRS. MOLLOY: No, Dolly, you come too. I have something for you. Come along, everybody.

Exit MRS. LEVI *to workroom.*

Mr. Vandergelder, I want your advice. You don't know how helpless a woman in business is. Oh, I feel I need advice every minute from a fine business head like yours.

Exit VANDERGELDER *to workroom.* MRS. MOLLOY *shouts this line and then slams the workroom door.*

Now I shut the door!!

Exit MRS. MOLLOY.
CORNELIUS *puts his head out of the wardrobe door and gradually comes out into the room, leaving door open.*

CORNELIUS: Hsst!

BARNABY: (*Pokes his head out from under the table.*) Maybe she wants us to go, Cornelius?

CORNELIUS: Certainly I won't go. Mrs. Molloy would think we were just thoughtless fellows. No, all I want is to stretch a minute.

BARNABY: What are you going to do when he's gone, Cornelius? Are we just going to run away?

CORNELIUS: Well . . . I don't know yet. I like Mrs. Molloy a lot. I wouldn't like her to think badly of me. I think I'll buy a hat. We can walk home to Yonkers, even if it takes us all night. I wonder how much hats cost. Barnaby, give me all the money you've got.

As he leans over to take the money, he sneezes. Both return to their hiding places in alarm; then emerge again.

My, all those perfumes in that cupboard tickle my nose! But I like it in there . . . it's a woman's world, and very different.

BARNABY: I like it where I am, too; only I'd like it better if I had a pillow.

CORNELIUS: (*Taking coat from wardrobe.*) Here, take one of these coats. I'll roll it up for you so it won't get mussed. Ladies don't like to have their coats mussed.

BARNABY: That's fine. Now I can just lie here and hear Mr. Vandergelder talk.

CORNELIUS *goes slowly above table towards cheval mirror, repeating Mrs. Molloy's line dreamily:*

CORNELIUS: This summer we'll be wearing ribbons down our back. . . .

BARNABY: Can I take off my shoes, Cornelius?

CORNELIUS *does not reply. He comes to the footlights and addresses the audience, in completely simple naïve sincerity:*

CORNELIUS: Isn't the world full of wonderful things. There we sit cooped up in Yonkers for years and years and all the time wonderful people like Mrs. Molloy are walking around in New York and we don't know them at all. I don't know whether—from where you're sitting—you can see—well, for instance, the way (*He points to the edge of his right eye.*) her eye and forehead and cheek come together, up here. Can you? And the kind of fireworks that shoot out of her eyes all the time. I tell you right now: a fine woman is the greatest work of God. You can talk all you like about Niagara Falls and the Pyramids; they aren't in it at all. Of course, up there at Yonkers they came into the store all the time, and bought this and that, and I said, "Yes, ma'am," and "That'll be seventy-five cents, ma'am"; and I *watched* them. But today I've talked to one, equal to equal, equal to equal, and to the finest one that ever existed, in my opinion. They're so different from men! Everything that they say and do is so different that you feel like laughing all the time. (*He laughs.*) Golly, they're different from men. And they're awfully mysterious, too. You never can be really sure what's going on in their heads. They have a kind of wall around them all the time—of pride and a sort of play-acting: I bet you could know a woman a hundred years without ever being really sure whether she liked you or not. This minute I'm in danger. I'm in danger of losing my job and my future and everything that people think is important; but I don't care. Even if I have to dig ditches for the rest of my life, I'll be a ditch digger who once had a wonderful day. Barnaby!

BARNABY: Oh, you woke me up!

CORNELIUS: (*Kneels.*) Barnaby, we can't go back to Yonkers yet and you know why.

BARNABY: Why not?

CORNELIUS: We've had a good meal. We've had an adventure. We've been in danger of getting arrested. There's only one more thing we've got to do before we go back to be successes in Yonkers.

BARNABY: Cornelius! You're never going to kiss Mrs. Molloy!

CORNELIUS: Maybe.

BARNABY: But she'll scream.

CORNELIUS: Barnaby, you don't know anything at all. You might as well know right now that everybody except us goes through life kissing right and left all the time.

BARNABY: (*Pauses for reflection: humbly:*) Well, thanks for telling me, Cornelius. I often wondered.

Enter MRS. LEVI *from workroom.*

MRS. LEVI: Just a minute, Irene. I must find my handkerchief.

> CORNELIUS, *caught by the arrival of Mrs. Levi, drops to his hands and knees, and starts very slowly to crawl back to the wardrobe, as though the slowness rendered him invisible.* MRS. LEVI, *leaning over the counter, watches him. From the cupboard he puts his head out of it and looks pleadingly at her.*

Why, Mr. Hackl, I thought you were up in Yonkers.

CORNELIUS: I almost always am, Mrs. Levi. Oh, Mrs. Levi, don't tell Mr. Vandergelder! I'll explain everything later.

BARNABY: (*Puts head out.*) We're terribly innocent, Mrs. Levi.

MRS. LEVI: Why, who's that?

BARNABY: Barnaby Tucker—just paying a call.

MRS. LEVI: (*Looking under counter and even shaking out her skirts.*) Well, who else is here?

CORNELIUS: Just the two of us, Mrs. Levi, that's all.

MRS. LEVI: Old friends of Mrs. Molloy's, is that it?

CORNELIUS: We never knew her before a few minutes ago, but we like her a lot—don't we, Barnaby? In fact, I think she's . . . I think she's the finest person in the world. I'm ready to tell that to anybody.

MRS. LEVI: And does she think *you're* the finest person in the world?

CORNELIUS: Oh, no. I don't suppose she even notices that I'm alive.

MRS. LEVI: Well, I think she must notice that you're alive in that cupboard, Mr. Hackl. Well, if I were you, I'd get back into it right away. Somebody could be coming in any minute.

> CORNELIUS *disappears. She sits unconcernedly in chair right. Enter* MRS. MOLLOY.

MRS. MOLLOY: (*Leaving door open and looking about in concealed alarm.*) Can I help you, Dolly?

MRS. LEVI: No, no, no. I was just blowing my nose.

Enter VANDERGELDER *from workroom.*

VANDERGELDER: Mrs. Molloy, I've got some advice to give you about your business.

MRS. MOLLOY *comes to the center of the room and puts Barnaby's hat on floor in window, then Cornelius' hat on the counter.*

MRS. LEVI: Oh, advice from Mr. Vandergelder! The whole city should hear this.

VANDERGELDER: (*Standing in the workroom door, pompously.*) In the first place, the aim of business is to make profit.

MRS. MOLLOY: Is that so?

MRS. LEVI: I never heard it put so clearly before. Did you hear it?

VANDERGELDER: (*Crossing the room to the left.*) You pay those girls of yours too much. You pay them as much as men. Girls like that enjoy their work. Wages, Mrs. Molloy, are paid to make people do work they don't want to do.

MRS. LEVI: Mr. Vandergelder thinks so ably. And that's exactly the way his business is run up in Yonkers.

VANDERGELDER: (*Patting her hand.*) Mrs. Molloy, I'd like for you to come up to Yonkers.

MRS. MOLLOY: That would be very nice.

He hands her the box of chocolates.

Oh, thank you. As a matter of fact, I know someone from Yonkers, someone else.

VANDERGELDER: (*Hangs hat on the cheval mirror.*) Oh? Who's that?

MRS. MOLLOY *puts chocolates on table and brings gilt chair forward and sits center at table facing the audience.*

MRS. MOLLOY: Someone quite well-to-do, I believe, though a little free and easy in his behavior. Mr. Vandergelder, do you know Mr. Cornelius Hackl in Yonkers?

VANDERGELDER: I know him like I know my own boot. He's my head clerk.

MRS. MOLLOY: Is that so?

VANDERGELDER: He's been in my store for ten years.

MRS. MOLLOY: Well, I never!

VANDERGELDER: Where would you have known him?

> MRS. MOLLOY *is in silent confusion. She looks for help to Mrs. Levi, seated at right end of table.*

MRS. LEVI: (*Groping for means to help Mrs. Molloy.*) Err . . . blah . . . err . . . bl . . . er . . . Oh, just one of those chance meetings, I suppose.

MRS. MOLLOY: Yes, oh yes! One of those chance meetings.

VANDERGELDER: What? Chance meetings? Cornelius Hackl has no right to chance meetings. Where was it?

MRS. MOLLOY: Really, Mr. Vandergelder, it's very unlike you to question me in such a way. I think Mr. Hackl is better known than you think he is.

VANDERGELDER: Nonsense.

MRS. MOLLOY: He's in New York often, and he's very well liked.

MRS. LEVI: (*Having found her idea, with decision.*) Well, the truth might as well come out now as later. Mr. Vandergelder, Irene is quite right. Your head clerk is often in New York. Goes everywhere; has an army of friends. Everybody knows Cornelius Hackl.

VANDERGELDER: (*Laughs blandly and sits in chair at left of table.*) He never comes to New York. He works all day in my store and at nine o'clock at night he goes to sleep in the bran room.

MRS. LEVI: So you think. But it's not true.

VANDERGELDER: Dolly Gallagher, you're crazy.

MRS. LEVI: Listen to me. You keep your nose so deep in your account books you don't know what goes on. Yes, by day, Cornelius Hackl is your faithful trusted clerk—that's true; but by night! Well, he leads a double life, that's all! He's here at the opera; at the great restaurants; in all the fashionable homes . . . why, he's at the Harmonia Gardens Restaurant three nights a week. The fact is, he's the wittiest, gayest, naughtiest, most delightful man in New York. Well, he's just *the* famous Cornelius Hackl!

VANDERGELDER: (*Sure of himself.*) It ain't the same man. If I

ever thought Cornelius Hackl came to New York, I'd discharge him.

MRS. LEVI: Who took the horses out of Jenny Lind's carriage
and pulled her through the streets?

MRS. MOLLOY: Who?

MRS. LEVI: Cornelius Hackl! Who dressed up as a waiter at the
Fifth Avenue Hotel the other night and took an oyster and
dropped it right down Mrs . . . (*Rises.*) No, it's too wicked
to tell you!

MRS. MOLLOY: Oh yes, Dolly, tell it! Go on!

MRS. LEVI: No. But it *was* Cornelius Hackl.

VANDERGELDER: (*Loud.*) It ain't the same man. Where'd he
get the money?

MRS. LEVI: But he's very rich.

VANDERGELDER: (*Rises.*) Rich! I keep his money in my own
safe. He has a hundred and forty-six dollars and thirty-five
cents.

MRS. LEVI: Oh, Mr. Vandergelder, you're killing me! Do come
to your senses. He's one of *the* Hackls.

> MRS. MOLLOY *sits at chair right of table where Mrs. Levi has
> been sitting.*

VANDERGELDER: *The* Hackls?

MRS. LEVI: They built the Raritan Canal.

VANDERGELDER: Then why should he work in my store?

MRS. LEVI: Well, I'll tell you. (*Sits at the center of the table, facing
the audience.*)

VANDERGELDER: (*Striding about.*) I don't want to hear! I've
got a headache! I'm going home. *It ain't the same man!!* He
sleeps in my bran room. You can't get away from facts. I just
made him my chief clerk.

MRS. LEVI: If you had any sense you'd make him partner.
(*Rises, crosses to Mrs. Molloy.*)
Now Irene, I can see you were as taken with him as every-
body else is.

MRS. MOLLOY: Why, I only met him once, very hastily.

MRS. LEVI: Yes, but I can see that you were taken with him.
Now don't you be thinking of marrying him!

MRS. MOLLOY: (*Her hands on her cheeks.*) Dolly! What are you
saying! Oh!

MRS. LEVI: Maybe it'd be fine. But think it over carefully. He breaks hearts like hickory nuts.

VANDERGELDER: Who?

MRS. LEVI: Cornelius Hackl!

VANDERGELDER: Mrs. Molloy, how often has he called on you?

MRS. MOLLOY: Oh, I'm telling the truth. I've only seen him once in my life. Dolly Levi's been exaggerating so. I don't know where to look!

Enter MINNIE *from workroom and crosses to window.*

MINNIE: Excuse me, Mrs. Molloy. I must get together that order for Mrs. Parkinson.

MRS. MOLLOY: Yes, we must get that off before closing.

MINNIE: I want to send it off by the errand girl. (*Having taken a hat from the window.*) Oh, I almost forgot the coat. (*She starts for the wardrobe.*)

MRS. MOLLOY: (*Running to the wardrobe to prevent her.*) Oh, oh! I'll do that, Minnie!

But she is too late. MINNIE *opens the right-hand cupboard door and falls back in terror, and screams:*

MINNIE: Oh, Mrs. Molloy! Help! There's a man!

MRS. MOLLOY *with the following speech pushes her back to the workroom door.* MINNIE *walks with one arm pointing at the cupboard. At the end of each of Mrs. Molloy's sentences she repeats—at the same pitch and degree—the words: "There's a man!"*

MRS. MOLLOY: (*Slamming cupboard door.*) Minnie, you imagined it. You're tired, dear. You go back in the workroom and lie down. Minnie, you're a fool; hold your tongue!

MINNIE: There's a man!

Exit MINNIE *to workroom.*
MRS. MOLLOY *returns to the front of the stage.*
VANDERGELDER *raises his stick threateningly.*

VANDERGELDER: If there's a man there, we'll get him out. Whoever you are, come out of there! (*Strikes table with his stick.*)

MRS. LEVI: (*Goes masterfully to the cupboard—sweeps her um-*

brella around among the coats and closes each door as she does so.) Nonsense! There's no man there. See! Miss Fay's nerves have been playing tricks on her. Come now, let's sit down again. What were you saying, Mr. Vandergelder?

They sit, MRS. MOLLOY *right,* MRS. LEVI *center,* VANDER-GELDER *left.*
A sneeze is heard from the cupboard. They all rise, look towards cupboard, then sit again.

Well now . . .

Another tremendous sneeze.
With a gesture that says, "I can do no more":

God bless you!

They all rise. MRS. MOLLOY *stands with her back to the cupboard.*

MRS. MOLLOY: (*To* VANDERGELDER) Yes, there is a man in there. I'll explain it all to you another time. Thank you very much for coming to see me. Good afternoon, Dolly. Good afternoon, Mr. Vandergelder.
VANDERGELDER: You're protecting a man in there!
MRS. MOLLOY: (*With back to cupboard.*) There's a very simple explanation, but for the present, good afternoon.

BARNABY *now sneezes twice, lifting the table each time.*
VANDERGELDER, *right of table, jerks off the tablecloth.*
BARNABY *pulls cloth under table and rolls himself up in it.*
MRS. MOLLOY *picks up the box of chocolates, which has rolled on to the floor.*

MRS. LEVI: Lord, the whole room's *crawling* with men! I'll never get over it.
VANDERGELDER: The world is going to pieces! I can't believe my own eyes!
MRS. LEVI: Come, Mr. Vandergelder. Ernestina Simple is waiting for us.
VANDERGELDER: (*Finds his hat and puts it on.*) Mrs. Molloy, I shan't trouble you again, and *vice versa.*

MRS. MOLLOY *is standing transfixed in front of cupboard,*

clasping the box of chocolates. VANDERGELDER *snatches the box from her and goes out.*

MRS. LEVI: (*Crosses to her.*) Irene, when I think of all the interesting things you have in this room! (*Kisses her.*) Make the most of it, dear. (*Raps cupboard.*) Good-by! (*Raps on table with umbrella.*) Good-by!

Exit MRS. LEVI.
MRS. MOLLOY *opens door of cupboard.* CORNELIUS *steps out.*

MRS. MOLLOY: So that was one of your practical jokes, Mr. Hackl?

CORNELIUS: No, no, Mrs. Molloy!

MRS. MOLLOY: Come out from under that, Barnaby Tucker, you troublemaker! (*She snatches the cloth and spreads it back on table.*)

MINNIE *enters.*

There's nothing to be afraid of, Minnie, I know all about these gentlemen.

CORNELIUS: Mrs. Molloy, we realize that what happened here—

MRS. MOLLOY: You think because you're rich you can make up for all the harm you do, is that it?

CORNELIUS: No, no!

BARNABY: (*On the floor putting shoes on.*) No, no!

MRS. MOLLOY: Minnie, this is the famous Cornelius Hackl who goes round New York tying people into knots; and that's Barnaby Tucker, another troublemaker.

BARNABY: How d'you do?

MRS. MOLLOY: Minnie, choose yourself any hat and coat in the store. We're going out to dinner. If this Mr. Hackl is so rich and gay and charming, he's going to be rich and gay and charming to us. He dines three nights a week at the Harmonia Gardens Restaurant, does he? Well, he's taking us there now.

MINNIE: Mrs. Molloy, are you sure it's safe?

MRS. MOLLOY: Minnie, hold your tongue. We're in a position to put these men into jail if they so much as squeak.

CORNELIUS: Jail, Mrs. Molloy?

MRS. MOLLOY: Jail, Mr. Hackl. Officer Cogarty does everything I tell him to do. Minnie, you and I have been respectable for years; now we're in disgrace, we might as well
make the most of it. Come into the workroom with me; I
know some ways we can perk up our appearances. Gentlemen, we'll be back in a minute.

CORNELIUS: Uh—Mrs. Molloy, I hear there's an awfully good
restaurant at the railway station.

MRS. MOLLOY: (*High indignation.*) Railway station? Railway
station? Certainly not! No, sir! You're going to give us a
good dinner in the heart of the fashionable world. Go on in,
Minnie! Don't you boys forget that you've made us lose our
reputations, and now the fashionable world's the only place
we *can* eat.

   MRS. MOLLOY *exits to workroom.*

BARNABY: She's angry at us, Cornelius. Maybe we'd better run
away now.

CORNELIUS: No, I'm going to go through with this if it kills
me. Barnaby, for a woman like that a man could consent to
go back to Yonkers and be a success.

BARNABY: All I know is no woman's going to make a success
out of me.

CORNELIUS: Jail or no jail, we're going to take those ladies out
to dinner. So grit your teeth.

   Enter MRS. MOLLOY *and* MINNIE *from workroom dressed
   for the street.*

MRS. MOLLOY: Gentlemen, the cabs are at the corner, so forward march! (*She takes a hat—which will be Barnaby's at the
end of Act III—and gives it to* MINNIE.)

CORNELIUS: Yes, ma'am.

   BARNABY *stands shaking his empty pockets warningly.*

Oh, Mrs. Molloy . . . is it far to the restaurant? Couldn't
we walk?

MRS. MOLLOY: (*Pauses a moment, then*) Minnie, take off your
things. We're not going.

OTHERS: Mrs. Molloy!

MRS. MOLLOY: Mr. Hackl, I don't go anywhere I'm not wanted. Good night. I'm not very happy to have met you. (*She crosses the stage as though going to the workroom door.*)

OTHERS: Mrs. Molloy!

MRS. MOLLOY: I suppose you think we're not fashionable enough for you? Well, I won't be a burden to you. Good night, Mr. Tucker.

> *The others follow her behind counter:* CORNELIUS, BARN-ABY, *then* MINNIE.

CORNELIUS: We want you to come with us more than anything in the world, Mrs. Molloy.

> MRS. MOLLOY *turns and pushes the three back. They are now near the center of the stage, to the right of the table,* MRS. MOLLOY *facing the audience.*

MRS. MOLLOY: No, you don't! Look at you! Look at the pair of them, Minnie! Scowling, both of them!

CORNELIUS: Please, Mrs. Molloy!

MRS. MOLLOY: Then smile. (*To Barnaby.*) Go on, smile! No, that's not enough. Minnie, you come with me and we'll get our own supper.

CORNELIUS: Smile, Barnaby, you lout!

BARNABY: My face can't smile any stronger than that.

MRS. MOLLOY: Then do something! Show some interest. Do something lively: sing!

CORNELIUS: I can't sing, really I can't.

MRS. MOLLOY: We're wasting our time, Minnie. They don't want us.

CORNELIUS: Barnaby, what can you sing? Mrs. Molloy, all we know are sad songs.

MRS. MOLLOY: That doesn't matter. If you want us to go out with you, you've got to sing something.

> *All this has been very rapid; the boys turn up to counter, put their heads together, confer and abruptly turn, stand stiffly and sing "Tenting tonight; tenting tonight; tenting on the old camp ground." The four of them now repeat the refrain, softly harmonizing.*

At the end of the song, after a pause, MRS. MOLLOY, *moved, says:*

MRS. MOLLOY: We'll come!

The boys shout joyfully.

You boys go ahead.

CORNELIUS *gets his hat from counter; as he puts it on he discovers the flowers on it.* BARNABY *gets his hat from window. They go out whistling.*
MINNIE *turns and puts her hat on at the mirror.*

Minnie, get the front door key—I'll lock the workroom.

MRS. MOLLOY *goes to workroom.*
MINNIE *takes key from hook left of wardrobe and goes to Mrs. Molloy, at the workroom door. She turns her around.*

MINNIE: Why, Mrs. Molloy, you're crying!

MRS. MOLLOY *flings her arms round Minnie.*

MRS. MOLLOY: Oh, Minnie, the world is full of wonderful things. Watch me, dear, and tell me if my petticoat's showing.

She crosses to door, followed by MINNIE, *as—*
THE
CURTAIN
FALLS

Act III

Veranda at the Harmonia Gardens Restaurant on the Battery, New York.

This room is informal and rustic. The main restaurant is indicated to be off stage back right.

There are three entrances: swinging double doors at the center of the back wall leading to the kitchen; one on the right wall (perhaps up a few steps and flanked by potted palms) to the street; one on the left wall to the staircase leading to the rooms above.

On the stage are two tables, left and right, each with four chairs. It is now afternoon and they are not yet set for dinner.

Against the back wall is a large folding screen. Also against the back wall are hat and coat racks.

As the curtain rises, VANDERGELDER *is standing, giving orders to* RUDOLPH, *a waiter.* MALACHI STACK *sits at table left.*

VANDERGELDER: Now, hear what I say. I don't want you to make any mistakes. I want a table for three.

RUDOLPH: (*Tall "snob" waiter, alternating between cold superiority and rage. German accent.*) For three.

VANDERGELDER: There'll be two ladies and myself.

MALACHI: It's a bad combination, Mr. Vandergelder. You'll regret it.

VANDERGELDER: And I want a chicken.

MALACHI: A chicken! You'll regret it.

VANDERGELDER: Hold your tongue. Write it down: chicken.

RUDOLPH: Yes, sir. Chicken Esterhazy? Chicken cacciatore? Chicken à la crème—?

VANDERGELDER: (*Exploding.*) A chicken! A chicken like everybody else has. And with the chicken I want a bottle of wine.

RUDOLPH: Moselle? Chablis? Vouvray?

MALACHI: He doesn't understand you, Mr. Vandergelder. You'd better speak louder.

VANDERGELDER: (*Spelling.*) W-I-N-E.

RUDOLPH: Wine.

VANDERGELDER: Wine! And I want this table removed. We'll eat at that table alone.

Exit RUDOLPH *through service door at back.*

MALACHI: There are some people coming in here now, Mr. Vandergelder.

VANDERGELDER *goes to back right to look at the newcomers.*

VANDERGELDER: What! Thunder and damnation! It's my niece Ermengarde! What's she doing here?!—Wait till I get my hands on her.

MALACHI: (*Running up to him.*) Mr. Vandergelder! You must keep your temper!

VANDERGELDER: And there's that rascal artist with her. Why, it's a plot. I'll throw them in jail.

MALACHI: Mr. Vandergelder! They're old enough to come to New York. You can't throw people into jail for coming to New York.

VANDERGELDER: And there's Mrs. Levi! What's she doing with them? It's a plot. It's a conspiracy! What's she saying to the cabman? Go up and hear what she's saying.

MALACHI: (*Listening at entrance, right.*) She's telling the cabman to wait, Mr. Vandergelder. She's telling the young people to come in and have a good dinner, Mr. Vandergelder.

VANDERGELDER: I'll put an end to this.

MALACHI: Now, Mr. Vandergelder, if you lose your temper, you'll make matters worse. Mr. Vandergelder, come here and take my advice.

VANDERGELDER: Stop pulling my coat. What's your advice?

MALACHI: Hide, Mr. Vandergelder. Hide behind this screen, and listen to what they're saying.

VANDERGELDER: (*Being pulled behind the screen.*) Stop pulling at me.

They hide behind the screen as MRS. LEVI, ERMENGARDE *and* AMBROSE *enter from the right.* AMBROSE *is carrying Ermengarde's luggage.*

ERMENGARDE: But I don't want to eat in a restaurant. It's not proper.

MRS. LEVI: Now, Ermengarde, dear, there's nothing wicked about eating in a restaurant. There's nothing wicked, even, about being in New York. Clergymen just make those things up to fill out their sermons.

ERMENGARDE: Oh, I wish I were in Yonkers, where *nothing* ever happens!

MRS. LEVI: Ermengarde, you're hungry. That's what's troubling you.

ERMENGARDE: Anyway, after dinner you must promise to take me to Aunt Flora's. She's been waiting for me all day and she must be half dead of fright.

MRS. LEVI: All right but of course, you know at Miss Van Huysen's you'll be back in your uncle's hands.

AMBROSE: (*Hands raised to heaven.*) I can't stand it.

MRS. LEVI: (*To Ambrose.*) Just keep telling yourself how pretty she is. Pretty girls have very little opportunity to improve their other advantages.

AMBROSE: Listen, Ermengarde! You don't want to go back to your uncle. Stop and think! That old man with one foot in the grave!

MRS. LEVI: And the other three in the cashbox.

AMBROSE: Smelling of oats—

MRS. LEVI: And axle grease.

MALACHI: That's not true. It's only partly true.

VANDERGELDER: (*Loudly.*) Hold your tongue! I'm going to teach them a lesson.

MALACHI: (*Whisper.*) Keep your temper, Mr. Vandergelder. Listen to what they say.

MRS. LEVI: (*Hears this; throws a quick glance toward the screen; her whole manner changes.*) Oh dear, what was I saying? The Lord be praised, how glad I am that I found you two dreadful children just as you were about to break poor dear Mr. Vandergelder's heart.

AMBROSE: He's got no heart to break!

MRS. LEVI: (*Vainly signaling.*) Mr. Vandergelder's a much kinder man than you think.

AMBROSE: Kinder? He's a wolf.

MRS. LEVI: Remember that he leads a very lonely life. Now you're going to have dinner upstairs. There are some private rooms up there,—just meant for shy timid girls like Ermengarde. Come with me.

> She pushes the young people out left, AMBROSE *carrying the luggage.*

VANDERGELDER: (*Coming forward.*) I'll show them! (*He sits at table right.*)

MALACHI: Everybody should eavesdrop once in a while, I always say. There's nothing like eavesdropping to show you that the world outside your head is different from the world inside your head.

VANDERGELDER: (*Producing a pencil and paper.*) I want to write a note. Go and call that cabman in here. I want to talk to him.

MALACHI: No one asks advice of a cabman, Mr. Vandergelder. They see so much of life that they have no ideas left.

VANDERGELDER: Do as I tell you.

MALACHI: Yes, sir. Advice of a cabman!

> *Exit right.*
> VANDERGELDER *writes his letter.*

VANDERGELDER: "My dear Miss Van Huysen"—(*To audience:*) Everybody's dear in a letter. It's enough to make you give up writing 'em. "My dear Miss Van Huysen. This is Ermengarde and that rascal Ambrose Kemper. They are trying to run away. Keep them in your house until I come."

> MALACHI *returns with an enormous* CABMAN *in a high hat and a long coat. He carries a whip.*

CABMAN: (*Entering.*) What's he want?

VANDERGELDER: I want to talk to you.

CABMAN: I'm engaged. I'm waiting for my parties.

VANDERGELDER: (*Folding letter and writing address.*) I know you are. Do you want to earn five dollars?

CABMAN: Eh?

VANDERGELDER: I asked you, do you want to earn five dollars?

CABMAN: I don't know. I never tried.

VANDERGELDER: When those parties of yours come downstairs, I want you to drive them to this address. Never mind what they say, drive them to this address. Ring the bell: give this letter to the lady of the house: see that they get in the door and keep them there.

CABMAN: I can't make people go into a house if they don't want to.

VANDERGELDER: (*Producing purse.*) Can you for ten dollars?

CABMAN: Even for ten dollars, I can't do it alone.

VANDERGELDER: This fellow here will help you.

MALACHI: (*Sitting at table left.*) Now I'm pushing people into houses.

VANDERGELDER: There's the address: Miss Flora Van Huysen, 8 Jackson Street.

CABMAN: Even if I get them in the door I can't be sure they'll stay there.

VANDERGELDER: For fifteen dollars you can.

MALACHI: Murder begins at twenty-five.

VANDERGELDER: Hold your tongue! (*To cabman.*) The lady of the house will help you. All you have to do is to sit in the front hall and see that the man doesn't run off with the girl. I'll be at Miss Van Huysen's in an hour or two and I'll pay you then.

CABMAN: If they call the police, I can't do anything.

VANDERGELDER: It's perfectly honest business. Perfectly honest.

MALACHI: Every man's the best judge of his own honesty.

VANDERGELDER: The young lady is my niece.

> *The* CABMAN *laughs, skeptically.*

The young lady is my niece!!

> *The* CABMAN *looks at Malachi and shrugs.*

She's trying to run away with a good-for-nothing and we're preventing it.

CABMAN: Oh, I know them, sir. They'll win in the end. Rivers don't run uphill.

MALACHI: What did I tell you, Mr. Vandergelder? Advice of a cabman.

VANDERGELDER: (*Hits table with his stick.*) Stack! I'll be back in half an hour. See that the table's set for three. See that nobody else eats here. Then go and join the cabman on the box.

MALACHI: Yes, sir.

> *Exit* VANDERGELDER *right.*

CABMAN: Who's your friend?

MALACHI: Friend!! That's not a friend; that's an employer I'm trying out for a few days.

CABMAN: You won't like him.

MALACHI: I can see you're in business for yourself because you talk about liking employers. No one's ever liked an employer since business began.

CABMAN: AW—!

MALACHI: No, sir. I suppose you think *your horse* likes you?

CABMAN: My old Clementine? She'd give her right feet for me.

MALACHI: That's what all employers think. You imagine it. The streets of New York are full of cab horses winking at one another. Let's go in the kitchen and get some whiskey. I can't push people into houses when I'm sober. No, I've had about fifty employers in my life, but this is the most employer of them all. He talks to everybody as though he were paying them.

CABMAN: I had an employer once. He watched me from eight in the morning until six at night—just sat there and watched me. Oh, dear! Even my mother didn't think I was as interesting as that.

CABMAN *exits through service door.*

MALACHI: (*Following him off.*) Yes, being employed is like being loved: you know that somebody's thinking about you the whole time.

Exits.
Enter right, MRS. MOLLOY, MINNIE, BARNABY *and* CORNELIUS.

MRS. MOLLOY: See! Here's the place I meant! Isn't it fine? Minnie, take off your things; we'll be here for hours.

CORNELIUS: (*Stopping at door.*) Mrs. Molloy, are you sure you'll like it here? I think I feel a draught.

MRS. MOLLOY: Indeed, I do like it. We're going to have a fine dinner right in this room; it's private, and it's elegant. Now we're all going to forget our troubles and call each other by our first names. Cornelius! Call the waiter.

CORNELIUS: Wait—wait—I can't make a sound. I must have caught a cold on that ride. Wai—No! It won't come.

MRS. MOLLOY: I don't believe you. Barnaby, you call him.

BARNABY: (*Boldly.*) Waiter! Waiter!

CORNELIUS *threatens him.* BARNABY *runs left.*

MINNIE: I never thought I'd be in such a place in my whole life. Mrs. Molloy, is this what they call a "café"?

MRS. MOLLOY: (*Sits at table left, facing audience.*) Yes, this is a café. Sit down, Minnie. Cornelius, Mrs. Levi gave us to understand that every waiter in New York knew you.

CORNELIUS: They will.

> BARNABY *sits at chair left;* MINNIE *in chair back to audience. Enter* RUDOLPH *from service door.*

RUDOLPH: Good evening, ladies and gentlemen.

CORNELIUS: (*Shaking his hand.*) How are you, Fritz? How are you, my friend?

RUDOLPH: I am Rudolph.

CORNELIUS: Of course. Rudolph, of course. Well, Rudolph, these ladies want a little something to eat—you know what I mean? Just if you can find the time—we know how busy you are.

MRS. MOLLOY: Cornelius, there's no need to be so familiar with the waiter. (*Takes menu from* RUDOLPH.)

CORNELIUS: Oh, yes, there is.

MRS. MOLLOY: (*Passing menu across.*) Minnie, what do you want to eat?

MINNIE: Just anything, Irene.

MRS. MOLLOY: No, speak up, Minnie. What do you want?

MINNIE: No, really, I have no appetite at all. (*Swings round in her chair and studies the menu, horrified at the prices.*) Oh . . . Oh . . . I'd like some sardines on toast and a glass of milk.

CORNELIUS: (*Takes menu from her.*) Great grindstones! What a sensible girl. Barnaby, shake Minnie's hand. She's the most sensible girl in the world. Rudolph, bring us gentlemen two glasses of beer, a loaf of bread and some cheese.

MRS. MOLLOY: (*Takes menu.*) I never heard such nonsense. Cornelius, we've come here for a good dinner and a good time. Minnie, have you ever eaten pheasant?

MINNIE: Pheasant? No-o-o-o!

MRS. MOLLOY: Rudolph, have you any pheasant?

RUDOLPH: Yes, ma'am. Just in from New Jersey today.

MRS. MOLLOY: Even the pheasants are leaving New Jersey. (*She laughs loudly, pushing* CORNELIUS, *then* RUDOLPH; *not from menu*.) Now, Rudolph, write this down: mock turtle soup; pheasant; mashed chestnuts; green salad; and some nice red wine.

RUDOLPH *repeats each item after her.*

CORNELIUS: (*Losing all his fears, boldly*.) All right, Barnaby, you watch me. (*He reads from the bill of fare.*) Rudolph, write this down: Neapolitan ice cream; hothouse peaches; champagne . . .
ALL: Champagne!

BARNABY *spins round in his chair.*

CORNELIUS: (*Holds up a finger.*) . . . and a German band. Have you got a German band?
MRS. MOLLOY: No, Cornelius, I won't let you be extravagant. Champagne, but no band. Now, Rudolph, be quick about this. We're hungry.

Exit RUDOLPH *to kitchen.* MRS. MOLLOY *crosses to right.*

Minnie, come upstairs. I have an idea about your hair. I think it'd be nice in two wee horns—
MINNIE: (*Hurrying after her, turns and looks at the boys.*) Oh! Horns!

They go out right.
There is a long pause. CORNELIUS *sits staring after them.*

BARNABY: Cornelius, in the Army, you have to peel potatoes all the time.
CORNELIUS: (*Not turning.*) Oh, that doesn't matter. By the time we get out of jail we can move right over to the Old Men's Home.

Another waiter, AUGUST, *enters from service door bearing a bottle of champagne in cooler, and five glasses.* MRS. MOL- LOY *re-enters right, followed by* MINNIE, *and stops* AUGUST.

MRS. MOLLOY: Waiter! What's that? What's that you have?
AUGUST: (*Young waiter; baby face; is continually bursting into tears.*) It's some champagne, ma'am.
MRS. MOLLOY: Cornelius; it's our champagne.

ALL *gather round August.*

AUGUST: No, no. It's for His Honor the Mayor of New York and he's very impatient.

MRS. MOLLOY: Shame on him! The Mayor of New York has more important things to be impatient about. Cornelius, open it.

CORNELIUS takes the bottle, opens it and fills the glasses.

AUGUST: Ma'am, he'll kill me.

MRS. MOLLOY: Well, have a glass first and die happy.

AUGUST: (*Sits at table right, weeping.*) He'll kill me.

RUDOLPH lays the cloth on the table, left.

MRS. MOLLOY: I go to a public restaurant for the first time in ten years and all the waiters burst into tears. There, take that and stop crying, love. (*She takes a glass to August and pats his head, then comes back.*)

Barnaby, make a toast!

BARNABY: (*Center of the group, with naïve sincerity.*) I? . . . uh . . . To all the ladies in the world . . . may I get to know more of them . . . and . . . may I get to know them better.

There is a hushed pause.

CORNELIUS: (*Softly.*) To the ladies!

MRS. MOLLOY: That's *very* sweet and *very* refined. Minnie, for that I'm going to give Barnaby a kiss.

MINNIE: Oh!

MRS. MOLLOY: Hold your tongue, Minnie. I'm old enough to be his mother, and—(*Indicating a height three feet from the floor.*) a dear wee mother I would have been too. Barnaby, this is for you from all the ladies in the world.

She kisses him. BARNABY is at first silent and dazed, then:

BARNABY: Now I can go back to Yonkers, Cornelius. Pudding. Pudding. Pudding! (*He spins round and falls on his knees.*)

MRS. MOLLOY: Look at Barnaby. He's not strong enough for a kiss. His head can't stand it.

Exit AUGUST, right service door, with tray and cooler.
The sound of "Les Patineurs" waltz comes from off left.

*CORNELIUS sits in chair facing audience, top of table.
MINNIE at left. BARNABY at right and MRS. MOLLOY back
to audience.*

Minnie, I'm enjoying myself. To think that this goes on in
hundreds of places every night, while I sit at home darning
my stockings.

*MRS. MOLLOY rises and dances, alone, slowly about the
stage.*

Cornelius, dance with me.

CORNELIUS: (*Rises.*) Irene, the Hackls don't dance. We're
Presbyterian.

MRS. MOLLOY: Minnie, you dance with me.

MINNIE joins her. CORNELIUS sits again.

MINNIE: Lovely music.

MRS. MOLLOY: Why, Minnie, you dance beautifully.

MINNIE: We girls dance in the workroom when you're not
looking, Irene.

MRS. MOLLOY: You thought I'd be angry! Oh dear, no one in
the world understands anyone else in the world.

*The girls separate. MINNIE dances off to her place at the
table. MRS. MOLLOY sits thoughtfully at table right. The
music fades away.*

Cornelius! Jenny Lind and all those other ladies—do you
see them all the time?

CORNELIUS: (*Rises and joins her at table right.*) Irene, I've put
them right out of my head. I'm interested in . . .

*RUDOLPH has entered by the service door. He now flings a
tablecloth between them on table.*

MRS. MOLLOY: Rudolph, what are you doing?

RUDOLPH: A table's been reserved here. Special orders.

MRS. MOLLOY: Stop right where you are. That party can eat inside. This veranda's ours.

RUDOLPH: I'm very sorry. This veranda is open to anybody who
wants it. Ah, there comes the man who brought the order.

Enter MALACHI *from the kitchen, drunk.*

MRS. MOLLOY: (*To Malachi.*) Take your table away from here. We got here first, Cornelius, throw him out.

MALACHI: Ma'am, my employer reserved this room at four o'clock this afternoon. You can go and eat in the restaurant. My employer said it was very important that he have a table alone.

MRS. MOLLOY: No, sir. We got here first and we're going to stay here—alone, too.

MINNIE *and* BARNABY *come forward.*

RUDOLPH: Ladies and gentlemen!

MRS. MOLLOY: Shut up, you. (*To Malachi.*) You're an impertinent, idiotic kill-joy.

MALACHI: (*Very pleased.*) That's an insult!

MRS. MOLLOY: All the facts about you are insults. (*To Cornelius.*) Cornelius, do something. Knock it over! The table.

CORNELIUS: Knock it over.

After a shocked struggle with himself CORNELIUS *calmly overturns the table.* AUGUST *rights the table and picks up cutlery, weeping copiously.*

RUDOLPH: (*In cold fury.*) I'm sorry, but this room can't be reserved for anyone. If you want to eat alone, you must go upstairs. I'm sorry, but that's the rule.

MRS. MOLLOY: We're having a nice dinner alone and we're going to stay here. Cornelius, knock it over.

CORNELIUS *overturns the table again. The girls squeal with pleasure. The waiter* AUGUST *again scrambles for the silver.*

MALACHI: Wait till you see my employer!

RUDOLPH: (*Bringing screen down.*) Ladies and gentlemen! I tell you what we'll do. There's a big screen here. We'll put the screen up between the tables. August, come and help me.

MRS. MOLLOY: I won't eat behind a screen. I won't. Minnie, make a noise. We're not animals in a menagerie. Cornelius, no screen. Minnie, there's a fight. I feel ten years younger. No screen! No screen!

During the struggle with the screen all talk at once.

MALACHI: (*Loud and clear and pointing to entrance right.*) Now you'll learn something. There comes my employer now, getting out of that cab.

CORNELIUS: (*Coming to him, taking off his coat.*) Where? I'll knock him down too.

> BARNABY *has gone up to right entrance. He turns and shouts clearly:*

BARNABY: Cornelius, it's Wolf-trap. Yes, it is!

CORNELIUS: Wolf-trap! Listen, everybody. I think the screen's a good idea. Have you got any more screens, Rudolph? We could use three or four. (*He pulls the screen forward again.*)

MRS. MOLLOY: Quiet down, Cornelius, and stop changing your mind. Hurry up, Rudolph, we're ready for the soup.

> *During the following scene* RUDOLPH *serves the meal at the table left, as unobtrusively as possible.*
> *The stage is now divided in half. The quartet's table is at the left. Enter* VANDERGELDER *from the right. Now wears overcoat and carries the box of chocolates.*

VANDERGELDER: Stack! What's the meaning of this? I told you I wanted a table alone. What's that?

> VANDERGELDER *hits the screen twice with his stick.* MRS. MOLLOY *hits back twice with a spoon. The four young people sit:* BARNABY *facing audience;* MRS. MOLLOY *right,* MINNIE *left, and* CORNELIUS *back to audience.*

MALACHI: Mr. Vandergelder, I did what I could. Mr. Vandergelder, you wouldn't believe what wild savages the people of New York are. There's a woman over there, Mr. Vandergelder—civilization hasn't touched her.

VANDERGELDER: Everything's wrong. You can't even manage a thing like that. Help me off with my coat. Don't kill me. Don't kill me.

> *During the struggle with the overcoat* MR. VANDERGELDER'S *purse flies out of his pocket and falls by the screen.* VANDERGELDER *goes to the coat tree and hangs his coat up.*

MRS. MOLLOY: Speak up! I can't hear you.

CORNELIUS: My voice again. Barnaby, how's your throat? Can you speak?

BARNABY: Can't make a sound.

MRS. MOLLOY: Oh, all right. Bring your heads together, and we'll whisper.

VANDERGELDER: Who are those people over there?

MALACHI: Some city sparks and their girls, Mr. Vandergelder. What goes on in big cities, Mr. Vandergelder—best not think of it.

VANDERGELDER: Has that couple come down from upstairs yet? I hope they haven't gone off without your seeing them.

MALACHI: No, sir. Myself and the cabman have kept our eyes on everything.

VANDERGELDER: (*Sits at right of table right, profile to the audience.*) I'll sit here and wait for my guests. You go out to the cab.

MALACHI: Yes, sir.

> VANDERGELDER *unfurls newspaper and starts to read.* MALACHI *sees the purse on the floor and picks it up.*

Eh? What's that? A purse. Did you drop something, Mr. Vandergelder?

VANDERGELDER: No. Don't bother me any more. Do as I tell you.

MALACHI: (*Stopping over. Coming center.*) A purse. That fellow over there must have let it fall during the misunderstanding about the screen. No, I won't look inside. Twenty-dollar bills, dozens of them. I'll go over and give it to him. (*Starts towards Cornelius, then turns and says to audience:*) You're surprised? You're surprised to see me getting rid of this money so quickly, eh? I'll explain it to you. There was a time in my life when my chief interest was picking up money that didn't belong to me. The law is there to protect property, but—sure, the law doesn't care whether a property owner deserves his property or not, and the law has to be corrected. There are several thousands of people in this country engaged in correcting the law. For a while, I too was engaged in the redistribution of superfluities. A man works all his life and leaves a million to his widow. She sits in hotels and eats great meals and plays cards all afternoon and evening,

with ten diamonds on her fingers. Call in the robbers! Call in
the robbers! Or a man leaves it to his son who stands leaning
against bars all night boring a bartender. Call in the robbers!
Stealing's a weakness. There are some people who say you
shouldn't have any weaknesses at all—no vices. But if a man
has no vices, he's in great danger of making vices out of his
virtues, and there's a spectacle. We've all seen them: men
who were monsters of philanthropy and women who were
dragons of purity. We've seen people who told the truth,
though the Heavens fall,— and the Heavens fell. No, no—
nurse one vice in your bosom. Give it the attention it deserves and let your virtues spring up modestly around it.
Then you'll have the miser who's no liar; and the drunkard
who's the benefactor of a whole city. Well, after I'd had that
weakness of stealing for a while, I found another: I took to
whisky—whisky took to me. And then I discovered an important rule that I'm going to pass on to you: Never support
two weaknesses at the same time. It's your combination
sinners—your lecherous liars and your miserly drunkards—
who dishonor the vices and bring them into bad repute. So
now you see why I want to get rid of this money: I want to
keep my mind free to do the credit to whisky that it deserves. And my last word to you, ladies and gentlemen, is
this: one vice at a time. (*Goes over to Cornelius.*) Can I speak
to you for a minute?

CORNELIUS: (*Rises.*) You certainly can. We all want to apologize to you about that screen—that little misunderstanding.

They all rise, with exclamations of apology.

What's your name, sir?

MALACHI: Stack, sir. Malachi Stack. If the ladies will excuse
you, I'd like to speak to you for a minute.

Draws CORNELIUS *down to front of stage.*

Listen, boy, have you lost . . . ? Come here . . .

Leads him further down, out of Vandergelder's hearing.

Have you lost something?

CORNELIUS: Mr. Stack, in this one day I've lost everything I
own.

MALACHI: There it is. (*Gives him purse.*) Don't mention it.

CORNELIUS: Why, Mr. Stack . . . you know what it is? It's a miracle. (*Looks toward the ceiling.*)

MALACHI: Don't mention it.

CORNELIUS: Barnaby, come here a minute. I want you to shake hands with Mr. Stack.

BARNABY, *napkin tucked into his collar, joins them.*

Mr. Stack's just found the purse I lost, Barnaby. You know—the purse full of money.

BARNABY: (*Shaking his hand vigorously.*) You're a wonderful man, Mr. Stack.

MALACHI: Oh, it's nothing—nothing.

CORNELIUS: I'm certainly glad I went to church all these years. You're a good person to know, Mr. Stack. In a way. Mr. Stack, where do you work?

MALACHI: Well, I've just begun. I work for a Mr. Vandergelder in Yonkers.

CORNELIUS *is thunderstruck. He glances at Barnaby and turns to Malachi with awe. All three are swaying slightly, back and forth.*

CORNELIUS: You do? It's a miracle. (*He points to the ceiling.*) Mr. Stack, I know you don't need it—but can I give you something for . . . for the good work?

MALACHI: (*Putting out his hand.*) Don't mention it. It's nothing. (*Starts to go left.*)

CORNELIUS: Take that. (*Hands him a note.*)

MALACHI: (*Taking note.*) Don't mention it.

CORNELIUS: And that. (*Another note.*)

MALACHI: (*Takes it and moves away.*) I'd better be going.

CORNELIUS: Oh, here. And that.

MALACHI: (*Hands third note back.*) No . . . I might get to like them.

Exit left.

CORNELIUS *bounds exultantly back to table.*

CORNELIUS: Irene, I feel a lot better about everything. Irene, I feel so well that I'm going to tell the truth.

MRS. MOLLOY: I'd forgotten that, Minnie. Men get drunk so differently from women. All right, what is the truth?

CORNELIUS: If I tell the truth, will you let me . . . will you let me put my arm around your waist?

MINNIE *screams and flings her napkin over her face.*

MRS. MOLLOY: Hold your tongue, Minnie. All right, you can put your arm around my waist just to show it can be done in a gentlemanly way; but I might as well warn you: a corset is a corset.

CORNELIUS: (*His arm around her; softly.*) You're a wonderful person, Mrs. Molloy.

MRS. MOLLOY: Thank you. (*She removes his hand from around her waist.*) All right, now that's enough. What is the truth?

CORNELIUS: Irene, I'm not rich as Mrs. Levi said I was.

MRS. MOLLOY: Not rich!

CORNELIUS: I almost never came to New York. And I'm not like she said I was,—bad. And I think you ought to know that at this very minute Mr. Vandergelder's sitting on the other side of that screen.

MRS. MOLLOY: What!! Well, he's not going to spoil any party of mine. So *that's* why we've been whispering? Let's forget all about Mr. Vandergelder and have some more wine.

They start to sing softly: "The Sidewalks of New York."
Enter MRS. LEVI, *from the street, in an elaborate dress.*
VANDERGELDER *rises.*

MRS. LEVI: Good evening, Mr. Vandergelder.

VANDERGELDER: Where's—where's Miss Simple?

MRS. LEVI: Mr. Vandergelder, I'll never trust a woman again as long as I live.

VANDERGELDER: Well? What is it?

MRS. LEVI: She ran away this afternoon and got married!

VANDERGELDER: She did?

MRS. LEVI: Married, Mr. Vandergelder, to a young boy of fifty.

VANDERGELDER: She did?

MRS. LEVI: Oh, I'm as disappointed as you are. I-can't-eat-a-thing-what-have-you-ordered?

VANDERGELDER: I ordered what you told me to, a chicken.

Enter AUGUST. *He goes to Vandergelder's table.*

MRS. LEVI: I don't think I could face a chicken. Oh, waiter. How do you do? What's your name?

AUGUST: August, ma'am.

MRS. LEVI: August, this is Mr. Vandergelder of Yonkers—Yonkers' most influential citizen, in fact. I want you to see that he's served with the best you have and served promptly. And there'll only be the two of us.

> MRS. LEVI *gives one set of cutlery to* AUGUST.
> VANDERGELDER *puts chocolate box under table.*

Mr. Vandergelder's been through some trying experiences today—what with men hidden all over Mrs. Molloy's store—like Indians in ambush.

VANDERGELDER: (*Between his teeth.*) Mrs. Levi, you don't have to tell him everything about me.

The quartet commences singing again very softly.

MRS. LEVI: Mr. Vandergelder, if you're thinking about getting married, you might as well learn right now you have to let women be women. Now, August, we want excellent service.

AUGUST: Yes, ma'am.

> *Exits to kitchen.*

VANDERGELDER: You've managed things very badly. When I plan a thing it takes place.

> MRS. LEVI *rises.*

Where are you going?

MRS. LEVI: Oh, I'd just like to see who's on the other side of that screen.

> MRS. LEVI *crosses to the other side of the stage and sees the quartet. They are frightened and fall silent.*

CORNELIUS: (*Rising.*) Good evening, Mrs. Levi.

> MRS. LEVI *takes no notice, but, taking up the refrain where they left off, returns to her place at the table right.*

VANDERGELDER: Well, who was it?

MRS. LEVI: Oh, just some city sparks entertaining their girls, I guess.

VANDERGELDER: Always wanting to know everything; always curious about everything; always putting your nose into other people's affairs. Anybody who lived with you would get as nervous as a cat.

MRS. LEVI: What? What's that you're saying?

VANDERGELDER: I said anybody who lived with you would—

MRS. LEVI: Horace Vandergelder, get that idea right out of your head this minute. I'm surprised that you even mentioned such a thing. Understand once and for all that I have no intention of marrying you.

VANDERGELDER: I didn't mean that.

MRS. LEVI: You've been hinting around at such a thing for some time, but from now on put such ideas right out of your head.

VANDERGELDER: Stop talking that way. That's not what I meant at all.

MRS. LEVI: I hope not. I should hope not. Horace Vandergelder, you go your way (*Points a finger.*) and I'll go mine. (*Points again in same direction.*) I'm not some Irene Molloy, whose head can be turned by a pot of geraniums. Why, the idea of your even suggesting such a thing.

VANDERGELDER: Mrs. Levi, you misunderstood me.

MRS. LEVI: I certainly hope I did. If I had any intention of marrying again it would be to a far more pleasure-loving man than you. Why I'd marry Cornelius Hackl before I'd marry you.

> CORNELIUS *raises his head in alarm. The others stop eating and listen.*

However, we won't discuss it any more.

> *Enter* AUGUST *with a tray.*

Here's August with our food. I'll serve it, August.

AUGUST: Yes, ma'am.

> *Exit* AUGUST.

MRS. LEVI: Here's some white meat for you, and some giblets, very tender and very good for you. No, as I said before, you go your way and I'll go mine.—Start right in on the wine. I think you'll feel better at once. However, since you brought the matter up, there's one more thing I think I ought to say.

VANDERGELDER: (*Rising in rage.*) I didn't bring the matter up
    at all.

MRS. LEVI: We'll have forgotten all about it in a moment, but
    —sit down, sit down, we'll close the matter forever in just a
    moment, but there's one more thing I ought to say:

> VANDERGELDER *sits down.*

It's true, I'm a woman who likes to know everything that's
going on; who likes to manage things, you're perfectly right
about that. But I wouldn't like to manage anything as dis-
orderly as your household, as out of control, as untidy.
You'll have to do that yourself, God helping you.

VANDERGELDER: It's not out of control.

MRS. LEVI: Very well, let's not say another word about it. Take
    some more of that squash, it's good. No, Horace, a com-
    plaining, quarrelsome, friendless soul like you is no sort of
    companion for me. You go your way (*Peppers her own plate.*)
    and I'll go mine. (*Peppers his plate.*)

VANDERGELDER: Stop saying that.

MRS. LEVI: I won't say another word.

VANDERGELDER: Besides . . . I'm not those things you said
    I am.

MRS. LEVI: What?—Well, I guess you're friendless, aren't you?
    Ermengarde told me this morning you'd even quarreled
    with your barber—a man who's held a razor to your throat
    for twenty years! Seems to me that that's sinking pretty low.

VANDERGELDER: Well, . . . but . . . my clerks, they . . .

MRS. LEVI: They like you? Cornelius Hackl and that Barnaby?
    Behind your back they call you Wolf-trap.

> *Quietly the quartet at the other table have moved up to the
> screens—bringing chairs for Mrs. Molloy and Minnie. Wine
> glasses in hand, they overhear this conversation.*

VANDERGELDER: (*Blanching.*) They don't.

MRS. LEVI: No, Horace. It looks to me as though I were the last
    person in the world that liked you, and even I'm just so-so.
    No, for the rest of my life I intend to have a good time.
    You'll be able to find some housekeeper who can prepare
    you three meals for a dollar a day—it can be done, you

know, if you like cold baked beans. You'll spend your last days listening at keyholes, for fear someone's cheating you. Take some more of that.

VANDERGELDER: Dolly, you're a damned exasperating woman.

MRS. LEVI: There! You see? That's the difference between us. I'd be nagging you all day to get some spirit into you. You could be a perfectly charming, witty, amiable man, if you wanted to.

VANDERGELDER: (*Rising, bellowing.*) I don't want to be charming.

MRS. LEVI: But you are. Look at you now. You can't hide it.

VANDERGELDER: (*Sits.*) Listening at keyholes! Dolly, you have no right to say such things to me.

MRS. LEVI: At your age you ought to enjoy hearing the honest truth.

VANDERGELDER: My age! My age! You're always talking about my age.

MRS. LEVI: I don't know what your age is, but I do know that up at Yonkers with bad food and bad temper you'll double it in six months. Let's talk of something else; but before we leave the subject there's one more thing I *am* going to say.

VANDERGELDER: Don't!

MRS. LEVI: Sometimes, just sometimes, I think I'd be tempted to marry you out of sheer pity; and if the confusion in your house gets any worse I may *have* to.

VANDERGELDER: I haven't asked you to marry me.

MRS. LEVI: Well, *please don't.*

VANDERGELDER: And my house is not in confusion.

MRS. LEVI: What? With your niece upstairs in the restaurant right now?

VANDERGELDER: I've fixed that better than you know.

MRS. LEVI: And your clerks skipping around New York behind your back?

VANDERGELDER: They're in Yonkers where they always are.

MRS. LEVI: Nonsense!

VANDERGELDER: What do you mean, nonsense?

MRS. LEVI: Cornelius Hackl's the other side of that screen this very minute.

VANDERGELDER: It ain't the same man!

MRS. LEVI: All right. Go on. Push it, knock it down. Go and see.

VANDERGELDER: (*Goes to screen, pauses in doubt, then returns to his chair again.*) I don't believe it.

MRS. LEVI: All right. All right. Eat your chicken. Of course, Horace, if your affairs went from bad to worse and you became actually miserable, I might feel that it was my duty to come up to Yonkers and be of some assistance to you. After all, I was your wife's oldest friend.

VANDERGELDER: I don't know how you ever got any such notion. Now understand once and for all, I have *no intention of marrying anybody*. Now, I'm tired and I don't want to talk.

> CORNELIUS *crosses to extreme left,* MRS. MOLLOY *following him.*

MRS. LEVI: I won't say another word, either.

CORNELIUS: Irene, I think we'd better go. You take this money and pay the bill. Oh, don't worry, it's not mine.

MRS. MOLLOY: No, no, I'll tell you what we'll do. You boys put on our coats and veils, and if he comes stamping over here, he'll think you're girls.

CORNELIUS: What! Those things!

MRS. MOLLOY: Yes. Come on.

> *She and* MINNIE *take the clothes from the stand.*

VANDERGELDER: (*Rises.*) I've got a headache. I've had a bad day. I'm going to Flora Van Huysen's, and then I'm going back to my hotel. (*Reaches for his purse.*) So, here's the money to pay for the dinner. (*Searching another pocket.*) Here's the money to pay for the . . . (*Going through all his pockets.*) Here's the money . . . I've lost my purse!!

MRS. LEVI: Impossible! I can't imagine you without your purse.

VANDERGELDER: It's been stolen. (*Searching overcoat.*) Or I left it in the cab. What am I going to do? I'm new at the hotel; they don't know me. I've never been here before. . . . Stop eating the chicken, I can't pay for it!

MRS. LEVI: (*Laughing gaily.*) Horace, I'll be able to find some money. Sit down and calm yourself.

VANDERGELDER: Dolly Gallagher, I gave you twenty-five dollars this morning.

MRS. LEVI: I haven't a cent. I gave it to my lawyer. We can borrow it from Ambrose Kemper, upstairs.

VANDERGELDER: I wouldn't take it.
MRS. LEVI: Cornelius Hackl will lend it to us.
VANDERGELDER: He's in Yonkers.—Waiter!

> CORNELIUS *comes forward dressed in Mrs. Molloy's coat, thrown over his shoulder like a cape.*
> MRS. LEVI *is enjoying herself immensely.* VANDERGELDER *again goes to back wall to examine the pockets of his overcoat.*

MRS. MOLLOY: Cornelius, is that Mr. Vandergelder's purse?
CORNELIUS: I didn't know it myself. I thought it was money just wandering around loose that didn't belong to anybody.
MRS. MOLLOY: Goodness! That's what politicians think!
VANDERGELDER: Waiter!

> *A band off left starts playing a polka.* BARNABY *comes forward dressed in Minnie's hat, coat and veil.*

MINNIE: Irene, doesn't Barnaby make a lovely girl? He just ought to stay that way.

> MRS. LEVI *and* VANDERGELDER *move their table upstage while searching for the purse.*

MRS. MOLLOY: Why should we have our evening spoiled? Cornelius, I can teach you to dance in a few minutes. Oh, he won't recognize you.
MINNIE: Barnaby, it's the easiest thing in the world.

> *They move their table up against the back wall.*

MRS. LEVI: Horace, you danced with me at your wedding and you danced with me at mine. Do you remember?
VANDERGELDER: No. Yes.
MRS. LEVI: Horace, you were a good dancer then. Don't confess to me that you're too old to dance.
VANDERGELDER: I'm not too old. I just don't want to dance.
MRS. LEVI: Listen to that music. Horace, do you remember the dances in the firehouse at Yonkers on Saturday nights? You gave me a fan. Come, come on!

> VANDERGELDER *and* MRS. LEVI *start to dance.* CORNELIUS, *dancing with* MRS. MOLLOY, *bumps into Vandergelder, back*

to back. VANDERGELDER, *turning, fails at first to recognize him, then does and roars:*

VANDERGELDER: You're discharged! Not a word! You're fired! Where's that idiot, Barnaby Tucker? He's fired, too.

The four young people, laughing, start rushing out the door to the street. VANDERGELDER, *pointing at Mrs. Molloy, shouts:*

You're discharged!

MRS. MOLLOY: (*Pointing at him.*) *You're* discharged!

Exit.

VANDERGELDER: You're discharged!

Enter from left, AMBROSE *and* ERMENGARDE. *To Ermengarde.*

I'll lock you up for the rest of your life, young lady.

ERMENGARDE: Uncle! (*She faints in* AMBROSE'S *arms.*)

VANDERGELDER: (*To Ambrose.*) I'll have you arrested. Get out of my sight. I never want to see you again.

AMBROSE: (*Carrying* ERMENGARDE *across to exit right.*) You can't do anything to me, Mr. Vandergelder.

Exit AMBROSE *and* ERMENGARDE.

MRS. LEVI: (*Who has been laughing heartily, follows the distraught* VANDERGELDER *about the stage as he continues to hunt for his purse.*) Well, there's your life, Mr. Vandergelder! Without niece—without clerks—without bride—and without your purse. *Will you marry me now?*

VANDERGELDER: No!

To get away from her, he dashes into the kitchen. MRS. LEVI, *still laughing, exclaims to the audience:*

MRS. LEVI: Damn!! (*And rushes off right.*)

THE
CURTAIN
FALLS

Act IV

Miss Flora Van Huysen's house.

This is a prosperous spinster's living room and is filled with knickknacks, all in bright colors, and hung with family portraits, bird cages, shawls, etc.

There is only one entrance—a large double door in the center of the back wall. Beyond it one sees the hall which leads left to the street door and right to the kitchen and the rest of the house. On the left are big windows hung with lace curtains on heavy draperies. Front left is Miss Van Huysen's sofa, covered with bright-colored cushions, and behind it a table. On the right is another smaller sofa. MISS VAN HUYSEN *is lying on the sofa. The* COOK *is at the window, left.* MISS VAN HUYSEN, *fifty, florid, stout and sentimental, is sniffing at smelling salts.* COOK *(enormous) holds a china mixing bowl.*

COOK: No, ma'am. I could swear I heard a cab drawing up to the door.

MISS VAN H.: You imagined it. Imagination. Everything in life . . . like that . . . disappointment . . . illusion. Our plans . . . our hopes . . . what becomes of them? Nothing. The story of my life.

She sings for a moment.

COOK: Pray God nothing's happened to the dear girl. Is it a long journey from Yonkers?

MISS VAN H.: No; but long enough for a thousand things to happen.

COOK: Well, we've been waiting all day. Don't you think we ought to call the police about it?

MISS VAN H.: The police! If it's God's will, the police can't prevent it. Oh, in three days, in a week, in a year, we'll know what's happened. . . . And if anything *has* happened to Ermengarde, it'll be a lesson to *him*—that's what it'll be.

COOK: To who?

MISS VAN H.: To that cruel uncle of hers, of course,—to Horace Vandergelder, and to everyone else who tries to separate

young lovers. Young lovers have enough to contend with as
it is. Who should know that better than I? No one. The story
of my life. (*Sings for a moment, then:*) There! Now I hear a
cab. Quick!

COOK: No. No, ma'am. I don't see anything.

MISS VAN H.: There! What did I tell you? Everything's
imagination—illusion.

COOK: But surely, if they'd changed their plans Mr. Vandergelder would have sent you a message.

MISS VAN H.: Oh, I know what's the matter. That poor child
probably thought she was coming to another prison—to another tyrant. If she'd known that I was her friend, and a
friend of all young lovers, she'd be here by now. Oh, yes, she
would. Her life shall not be crossed with obstacles and disappointments as . . . Cook, a minute ago my smelling salts
were on this table. Now they've completely disappeared.

COOK: Why, there they are, ma'am, right there in your hand.

MISS VAN H.: Goodness! How did they get there? I won't inquire. Stranger things have happened!

COOK: I suppose Mr. Vandergelder was sending her down with
someone?

MISS VAN H.: Two can go astray as easily as . . . (*She sneezes.*)

COOK: God bless you! (*Runs to window.*) Now, here's a carriage
stopping.

The doorbell rings.

MISS VAN H.: Well, open the door, Cook.

COOK *exits.*

It's probably some mistake . . . (*Sneezes again.*)
God bless you!

Sounds of altercation off in hall.

It almost sounds as though I heard voices.

CORNELIUS: (*Off.*) I don't want to come in. This is a free
country, I tell you.

CABMAN: (*Off.*) Forward march!

MALACHI: (*Off.*) In you go. We have orders.

CORNELIUS: (*Off.*) You can't make a person go where he
doesn't want to go.

Enter MALACHI, *followed by* COOK. *The* CABMAN *bundles* BARNABY *and* CORNELIUS *into the room, but they fight their way back into the hall.* CORNELIUS *has lost Mrs. Molloy's coat, but* BARNABY *is wearing Minnie's clothes.*

MALACHI: Begging your pardon, ma'am, are you Miss Van Huysen?

MISS VAN H.: Yes, I am, unfortunately. What's all this noise about?

MALACHI: There are two people here that Mr. Vandergelder said must be brought to this house and kept here until he comes. And here's his letter to you.

MISS VAN H.: No one has any right to tell me whom I'm to keep in my house if they don't want to stay.

MALACHI: You're right, ma'am. Everybody's always talking about people breaking into houses, ma'am; but there are more people in the world who want to break out of houses, that's what I always say.—Bring them in, Joe.

Enter CORNELIUS *and* BARNABY *being pushed by the* CABMAN.

CORNELIUS: This young lady and I have no business here. We jumped into a cab and asked to be driven to the station and these men brought us to the house and forced us to come inside. There's been a mistake.

CABMAN: Is your name Miss Van Huysen?

MISS VAN H.: Everybody's asking me if my name's Miss Van Huysen. I think that's a matter I can decide for myself. Now will you all be quiet while I read this letter? . . . "This is Ermengarde and that rascal Ambrose Kemper . . ." Now I know who you two are, anyway. "They are trying to run away . . ." Story of my life. "Keep them in your house until I come." Mr. Kemper, you have nothing to fear. (*To Cabman.*) Who are you?

CABMAN: I'm Joe. I stay here until the old man comes. He owes me fifteen dollars.

MALACHI: That's right, Miss Van Huysen, we must stay here to see they don't escape.

MISS VAN H.: (*To Barnaby*) My dear child, take off your things. We'll all have some coffee. (*To Malachi and cabman.*) You

two go out and wait in the hall. I'll send coffee out to you.
Cook, take them.

 COOK *pushes* MALACHI *and* CABMAN *into the hall.*

CORNELIUS: Ma'am, we're not the people you're expecting,
 and there's no reason . . .

MISS VAN H.: Mr. Kemper, I'm not the tyrant you think I am.
 . . . You don't have to be afraid of me. . . . I know you're
 trying to run away with this innocent girl. . . . All my life I
 have suffered from the interference of others. You shall not
 suffer as I did. So put yourself entirely in my hands. (*She lifts
 Barnaby's veil.*) Ermengarde! (*Kisses him on both cheeks.*)
 Where's your luggage?

BARNABY: It's—uh—uh—it's . . .

CORNELIUS: Oh, I'll find it in the morning. It's been mislaid.

MISS VAN H.: Mislaid! How like life! Well, Ermengarde; you
 shall put on some of my clothes.

BARNABY: Oh, I know I wouldn't be happy, really.

MISS VAN H.: She's a shy little thing, isn't she? Timid little darling! . . . Cook! Put some gingerbread in the oven and get
 the coffee ready . . .

COOK: Yes, ma'am.

 Exits to kitchen.

MISS VAN H.: . . . while I go and draw a good hot bath for
 Ermengarde.

CORNELIUS: Oh, oh—Miss Van Huysen . . .

MISS VAN H.: Believe me, Ermengarde, your troubles are at an
 end. You two will be married tomorrow. (*To Barnaby.*) My
 dear, you look just like I did at your age, and your sufferings
 have been as mine. While you're bathing, I'll come and tell
 you the story of my life.

BARNABY: Oh, I don't want to take a bath. I always catch cold.

MISS VAN H.: No, dear, you won't catch cold. I'll slap you all
 over. I'll be back in a minute.

 Exit.

CORNELIUS: (*Looking out of window.*) Barnaby, do you think
 we could jump down from this window?

BARNABY: Yes—we'd kill ourselves.

CORNELIUS: We'll just have to stay here and watch for something to happen. Barnaby, the situation's desperate.

BARNABY: It began getting desperate about half-past four and it's been getting worse ever since. Now I have to take a bath and get slapped all over.

Enter MISS VAN HUYSEN *from kitchen.*

MISS VAN H.: Ermengarde, you've still got those wet things on. Your bath's nearly ready. Mr. Kemper, you come into the kitchen and put your feet in the oven.

The doorbell rings. Enter COOK.

What's that? It's the doorbell. I expect it's your uncle.

COOK: There's the doorbell. (*At window.*) It's *another* man and a girl in a cab!

MISS VAN H.: Well, go and let them in, Cook. Now, come with me, you two. Come, Ermengarde.

Exit COOK. MISS VAN HUYSEN *drags* CORNELIUS *and the protesting* BARNABY *off into the kitchen.*

COOK: (*Off.*) No, that's impossible. Come in, anyway.

Enter ERMENGARDE, *followed by* AMBROSE, *carrying the two pieces of luggage.*

There's some mistake. I'll tell Miss Van Huysen, but there's some mistake.

ERMENGARDE: But, I tell you, I *am* Mr. Vandergelder's niece; I'm Ermengarde.

COOK: Beg your pardon, Miss, but you *can't* be Miss Ermengarde.

ERMENGARDE: But—but—here I *am.* And that's my baggage.

COOK: Well, I'll tell Miss Van Huysen who you *think* you are, but she won't like it.

Exits.

AMBROSE: You'll be all right now, Ermengarde. I'd better go before she sees me.

ERMENGARDE: Oh, no. You must stay. I feel so strange here.

AMBROSE: I know, but Mr. Vandergelder will be here in a minute. . . .

ERMENGARDE: Ambrose, you can't go. You can't leave me in this crazy house with those drunken men in the hall. Ambrose . . . Ambrose, let's say you're someone else that my uncle sent down to take care of me. Let's say you're—you're Cornelius Hackl!

AMBROSE: Who's Cornelius Hackl?

ERMENGARDE: You know. He's chief clerk in Uncle's store.

AMBROSE: I don't want to be Cornelius Hackl. No, no, Ermengarde, come away with me now. I'll take you to my friend's house. Or I'll take you to Mrs. Levi's house.

ERMENGARDE: Why, it was Mrs. Levi who threw us right at Uncle Horace's face. Oh, I wish I were back in Yonkers where nothing ever happens.

Enter MISS VAN HUYSEN.

MISS VAN H.: What's all this I hear? Who do you say you are?

ERMENGARDE: Aunt Flora . . . don't you remember me? I'm Ermengarde.

MISS VAN H.: And you're Mr. Vandergelder's niece?

ERMENGARDE: Yes, I am.

MISS VAN H.: Well, that's very strange indeed, because he has just sent me another niece named Ermengarde. She came with a letter from him, explaining everything. Have you got a letter from him?

ERMENGARDE: No . . .

MISS VAN H.: Really!—And who is this?

ERMENGARDE: This is Cornelius Hackl, Aunt Flora.

MISS VAN H.: Never heard of him.

ERMENGARDE: He's chief clerk in Uncle's store.

MISS VAN H.: Never heard of him. The other Ermengarde came with the man she's in love with, and that *proves* it. She came with Mr. Ambrose Kemper.

AMBROSE: (*Shouts.*) Ambrose Kemper!

MISS VAN H.: Yes, Mr. Hackl, and Mr. Ambrose Kemper is in the kitchen there now *with his feet in the oven.*

ERMENGARDE *starts to cry.* MISS VAN HUYSEN *takes her to the sofa. They both sit.*

Dear child, what is your trouble?

ERMENGARDE: Oh, dear. I don't know what to do.

MISS VAN H.: (*In a low voice.*) Are you in love with this man?

ERMENGARDE: Yes, I am.

MISS VAN H.: I could see it—and are people trying to separate you?

ERMENGARDE: Yes, they are.

MISS VAN H.: I could see it—who? Horace Vandergelder?

ERMENGARDE: Yes.

MISS VAN H.: That's enough for me. I'll put a stop to Horace Vandergelder's goings on.

> MISS VAN HUYSEN *draws* AMBROSE *down to sit on her other side.*

Mr. Hackl, think of me as your friend. Come in the kitchen and get warm. . . . (*She rises and starts to go out.*) We can decide later who everybody is. My dear, would you like a good hot bath?

ERMENGARDE: Yes, I would.

MISS VAN H.: Well, when Ermengarde comes out you can go in.

> *Enter* CORNELIUS *from the kitchen.*

CORNELIUS: Oh, Miss Van Huysen . . .

ERMENGARDE: Why, Mr. Hack—!!

CORNELIUS: (*Sliding up to her, urgently.*) Not yet! I'll explain. I'll explain everything.

MISS VAN H.: Mr. Kemper!—Mr. Kemper! This is Mr. Cornelius Hackl. (*To Ambrose.*) Mr. Hackl, this is Mr. Ambrose Kemper.

> *Pause, while the men glare at one another.*

Perhaps you two know one another?

AMBROSE: No!

CORNELIUS: No, we don't.

AMBROSE: (*Hotly.*) Miss Van Huysen, I know that man is not Ambrose Kemper.

CORNELIUS: (*Ditto.*) And he's not Cornelius Hackl.

MISS VAN H.: My dear young men, what does it matter what your names are? The important thing is that you are you. (*To Ambrose.*) You are alive and breathing, aren't you, Mr. Hackl? (*Pinches Ambrose's left arm.*)

AMBROSE: Ouch, Miss Van Huysen.

MISS VAN H.: This dear child imagines she is Horace Vandergelder's niece Ermengarde.

ERMENGARDE: But I am.

MISS VAN H.: The important thing is that you're all in love.
Everything else is illusion. (*She pinches Cornelius' arm.*)

CORNELIUS: Ouch! Miss Van Huysen!

MISS VAN H.: (*Comes down and addresses the audience.*) Everybody keeps asking me if I'm Miss Van Huys . . .

*She seems suddenly to be stricken with doubt as to who she is;
her face shows bewildered alarm. She pinches herself on the
upper arm and is abruptly and happily relieved.*

Now, you two gentlemen sit down and have a nice chat
while this dear child has a good hot bath.

The doorbell rings. ERMENGARDE *exits,* MISS VAN HUYSEN
about to follow her, but stops. Enter COOK.

COOK: There's the doorbell again.

MISS VAN H.: Well, answer it.

She and ERMENGARDE *exit to kitchen.*

COOK: (*At window, very happy about all these guests.*) It's a cab
and three ladies. I never saw such a night.

Exit to front door.

MISS VAN H.: Gentlemen, you can rest easy. I'll see that Mr.
Vandergelder lets his nieces marry you both.

Enter MRS. LEVI.

MRS. LEVI: Flora, how are you?

MISS VAN H.: Dolly Gallagher! What brings you here?

MRS. LEVI: Great Heavens, Flora, what are those two drunken
men doing in your hall?

MISS VAN H.: I don't know. Horace Vandergelder sent them
to me.

MRS. LEVI: Well, I've brought you two girls in much the same
condition. Otherwise they're the finest girls in the world.

She goes up to the door and leads in MRS. MOLLOY. MINNIE
follows.

I want you to meet Irene Molloy and Minnie Fay.

MISS VAN H.: Delighted to know you.

MRS. LEVI: Oh, I see you two gentlemen are here, too. Mr. Hackl, I was about to look for you (*Pointing about the room.*) *somewhere* here.

CORNELIUS: No, Mrs. Levi. I'm ready to face anything now.

MRS. LEVI: Mr. Vandergelder will be here in a minute. He's downstairs trying to pay for a cab without any money.

MRS. MOLLOY: (*Holding Vandergelder's purse.*) Oh, I'll help him.

MRS. LEVI: Yes, will you, dear? You had to pay the restaurant bills. You must have hundreds of dollars there it seems.

MRS. MOLLOY: This is his own purse he lost. I can't give it back to him without seeming . . .

MRS. LEVI: I'll give it back to him.—There, you help him with this now. (*She gives Mrs. Molloy a bill and puts the purse airily under her arm.*)

VANDERGELDER: (*Off.*) Will somebody please pay for this cab?

> MRS. MOLLOY *exits to front door.*

MRS. MOLLOY: (*Off stage.*) I'll take care of that, Mr. Vandergelder.

> *As* MR. VANDERGELDER *enters,* MALACHI *and the* CABMAN *follow him in.* VANDERGELDER *carries overcoat, stick and box of chocolates.*

CABMAN: Fifteen dollars, Mr. Vandergelder.

MALACHI: Hello, Mr. Vandergelder.

VANDERGELDER: (*To Malachi.*) You're discharged! (*To Cabman.*) You too!

> MALACHI *and* CABMAN *go out and wait in the hall.*

So I've caught up with you at last! (*To Ambrose.*) I never want to see you again! (*To Cornelius.*) You're discharged! Get out of the house, both of you.

> *He strikes sofa with his stick; a second after,* MISS VAN HUYSEN *strikes him on the shoulder with a folded newspaper or magazine.*

MISS VAN H.: (*Forcefully.*) Now then you. Stop ordering people

out of my house. You can shout and carry on in Yonkers,
but when you're in my house you'll behave yourself.

VANDERGELDER: They're both dishonest scoundrels.

MISS VAN H.: Take your hat off. Gentlemen, you stay right
where you are.

CORNELIUS: Mr. Vandergelder, I can explain—

MISS VAN H.: There aren't going to be any explanations. Horace, stop scowling at Mr. Kemper and forgive him.

VANDERGELDER: That's not Kemper, that's a dishonest rogue
named Cornelius Hackl.

MISS VAN H.: You're crazy. (*Points to Ambrose.*) That's Cornelius Hackl.

VANDERGELDER: I guess I know my own chief clerk.

MISS VAN H.: I don't care what their names are. You shake
hands with them both, or out you go.

VANDERGELDER: Shake hands with those dogs and scoundrels!

MRS. LEVI: Mr. Vandergelder, you've had a hard day. You don't
want to go out in the rain now. Just for form's sake, you
shake hands with them. You can start quarreling with them
tomorrow.

VANDERGELDER: (*Gives* CORNELIUS *one finger to shake.*) There!
Don't regard that as a handshake.

He turns to AMBROSE, *who mockingly offers him one finger.*

Hey! I never want to see you again.

MRS. MOLLOY enters from front door.

MRS. MOLLOY: Miss Van Huysen.

MISS VAN H.: Yes, dear?

MRS. MOLLOY: Do I smell coffee?

MISS VAN H.: Yes, dear.

MRS. MOLLOY: Can I have some, good and black?

MISS VAN H.: Come along, everybody. We'll all go into the
kitchen and have some coffee.

As they all go:

Horace, you'll be interested to know there are two Ermengardes in there. . . .

VANDERGELDER: Two!!

Last to go is MINNIE, *who revolves about the room dreamily waltzing, a finger on her forehead.* MRS. LEVI *has been standing at one side. She now comes forward, in thoughtful mood.* MINNIE *continues her waltz round the left sofa and out to the kitchen.*

MRS. LEVI, *left alone, comes to front, addressing an imaginary Ephraim.*

MRS. LEVI: Ephraim Levi, I'm going to get married again. Ephraim, I'm marrying Horace Vandergelder for his money. I'm going to send his money out doing all the things you taught me. Oh, it won't be a marriage in the sense that we had one—but I shall certainly make him happy, and Ephraim —I'm tired. I'm tired of living from hand to mouth, and I'm asking your permission, Ephraim—will you give me away? (*Now addressing the audience, she holds up the purse.*) Money! Money!—it's like the sun we walk under; it can kill or cure.—Mr. Vandergelder's money! Vandergelder's never tired of saying most of the people in the world are fools, and in a way he's right, isn't he? Himself, Irene, Cornelius, myself! But there comes a moment in everybody's life when he must decide whether he'll live among human beings or not—a fool among fools or a fool alone.
As for me, I've decided to live among them.
I wasn't always so. After my husband's death I retired into myself. Yes, in the evenings, I'd put out the cat, and I'd lock the door, and I'd make myself a little rum toddy; and before I went to bed I'd say a little prayer, thanking God that I was independent—that no one else's life was mixed up with mine. And when ten o'clock sounded from Trinity Church tower, I fell off to sleep and I was a perfectly contented woman. And one night, after two years of this, an oak leaf fell out of my Bible. I had placed it there on the day my husband asked me to marry him; a perfectly good oak leaf— but without color and without life. And suddenly I realized that for a long time I had not shed one tear; nor had I been filled with the wonderful hope that something or other would turn out well. I saw that I was like that oak leaf, and on that night I decided to rejoin the human race.
Yes, we're all fools and we're all in danger of destroying the

world with our folly. But the surest way to keep us out of harm is to give us the four or five human pleasures that are our right in the world,—and that takes a little *money*!

The difference between a little money and no money at all is enormous—and can shatter the world. And the difference between a little money and an enormous amount of money is very slight—and that, also, can shatter the world.

Money, I've always felt, money—pardon my expression—is like manure; it's not worth a thing unless it's spread about encouraging young things to grow.

Anyway,—that's the opinion of the second Mrs. Vandergelder.

> VANDERGELDER *enters with two cups of coffee. With his back, he closes both doors.*

VANDERGELDER: Miss Van Huysen asked me to bring you this.

MRS. LEVI: Thank you both. Sit down and rest yourself. What's been going on in the kitchen?

VANDERGELDER: A lot of foolishness. Everybody falling in love with everybody. I forgave 'em; Ermengarde and that artist.

MRS. LEVI: I knew you would.

VANDERGELDER: I made Cornelius Hackl my partner.

MRS. LEVI: You won't regret it.

VANDERGELDER: Dolly, you said some mighty unpleasant things to me in the restaurant tonight . . . all that about my house . . . and everything.

MRS. LEVI: Let's not say another word about it.

VANDERGELDER: Dolly, you have a lot of faults—

MRS. LEVI: Oh, I know what you mean.

VANDERGELDER: You're bossy, scheming, inquisitive . . .

MRS. LEVI: Go on.

VANDERGELDER: But you're a wonderful woman. Dolly, marry me.

MRS. LEVI: Horace! (*Rises.*) Stop right there.

VANDERGELDER: I know I've been a fool about Mrs. Molloy, and that other woman. But, Dolly, forgive me and marry me. (*He goes on his knees.*)

MRS. LEVI: Horace, I don't dare. No. I don't dare.

VANDERGELDER: What do you mean?

MRS. LEVI: You know as well as I do that you're the first citizen of Yonkers. Naturally, you'd expect your wife to keep open house, to have scores of friends in and out all the time. Any wife of yours should be used to that kind of thing.

VANDERGELDER: (*After a brief struggle with himself.*) Dolly, you can live any way you like.

MRS. LEVI: Horace, you can't deny it, your wife would have to be a *somebody*. Answer me: am I a somebody?

VANDERGELDER: You are . . . you are. Wonderful woman.

MRS. LEVI: Oh, you're partial. (*She crosses, giving a big wink at the audience, and sits on sofa right.*)

> VANDERGELDER *follows her on his knees.*

Horace, it won't be enough for you to load your wife with money and jewels; to insist that she be a benefactress to half the town.

> *He rises and, still struggling with himself, coughs so as not to hear this.*

No, she must be a somebody. Do you really think I have it in me to be a credit to you?

VANDERGELDER: Dolly, everybody knows that you could do anything you wanted to do.

MRS. LEVI: I'll try. With your help, I'll try—and by the way, I found your purse. (*Holds it up.*)

VANDERGELDER: Where did you—! Wonderful woman!

MRS. LEVI: It just walked into my hand. I don't know how I do it. Sometimes I frighten myself. Horace, take it. Money walks out of my hands, too.

VANDERGELDER: Keep it. Keep it.

MRS. LEVI: Horace! (*Half laughing, half weeping, and with an air of real affection for him.*) I never thought . . . I'd ever . . . hear you say a thing like that!

> BARNABY *dashes in from the kitchen in great excitement. He has discarded Minnie's clothes.*

BARNABY: Oh! Excuse me. I didn't know anybody was here.

VANDERGELDER: (*Bellowing.*) Didn't know anybody was here. Idiot!

MRS. LEVI: (*Putting her hand on Vandergelder's arm; amiably:*) Come in, Barnaby. Come in.

> VANDERGELDER *looks at her a minute; then says, imitating her tone:*

VANDERGELDER: Come in, Barnaby. Come in.
BARNABY: Cornelius is going to marry Mrs. Molloy!!
MRS. LEVI: Isn't that fine! Horace! . . .

> MRS. LEVI *rises, and indicates that he has an announcement to make.*

VANDERGELDER: Barnaby, go in and tell the rest of them that Mrs. Levi has consented—
MRS. LEVI: *Finally* consented!
VANDERGELDER: Finally consented to become my wife.
BARNABY: Holy cabooses. (*Dashes back to the doorway.*) Hey! Listen, everybody! Wolf-trap—I mean—Mr. Vandergelder is going to marry Mrs. Levi.

> MISS VAN HUYSEN *enters followed by all the people in this act. She is now carrying the box of chocolates.*

MISS VAN H.: Dolly, that's the best news I ever heard. (*She addresses the audience.*) There isn't any more coffee; there isn't any more gingerbread; but there are three couples in my house and they're all going to get married. And do you know, one of those Ermengardes wasn't a dear little girl at all—she was a boy! Well, that's what life is: disappointment, illusion.
MRS. LEVI: (*To audience.*) There isn't any more coffee; there isn't any more gingerbread, and there isn't any more play— but there is one more thing we have to do. . . . Barnaby, come here. (*She whispers to him, pointing to the audience. Then she says to the audience:*) I think the youngest person here ought to tell us what the moral of the play is.

> BARNABY *is reluctantly pushed forward to the footlights.*

BARNABY: Oh, I think it's about . . . I think it's about adventure. The test of an adventure is that when you're in the middle of it, you say to yourself, "Oh, now I've got myself into an awful mess; I wish I were sitting quietly at home."

And the sign that something's wrong with you is when you sit quietly at home wishing you were out having lots of adventure. What we would like for you is that you have just the right amount of sitting quietly at home, and just the right amount of—adventure! So that now we all want to thank you for coming tonight, and we all hope that in your lives you have just the right amount of—adventure!

THE
    CURTAIN
        FALLS

THE ALCESTIAD

Characters in Order of Appearance

THE ALCESTIAD

APOLLO
DEATH
FIRST WATCHMAN
ALCESTIS
AGLAIA
TEIRESIAS
BOY
ADMETUS
FIRST HERDSMAN
SECOND HERDSMAN
THIRD HERDSMAN
FOURTH HERDSMAN
RHODOPE
HERCULES
SECOND WATCHMAN
EPIMENES
CHERIANDER
AGIS
FIRST GUARD
SECOND GUARD
THIRD GUARD
FOURTH GUARD
SERVANTS
PEOPLE OF THESSALY

THE DRUNKEN SISTERS

APOLLO
CLOTHO ⎫
LACHESIS ⎬ THE THREE FATES
ATROPOS ⎭

Act I

No curtain, except at the end of Act III and after *The Drunken Sisters.* All three acts of *The Alcestiad* take place in the rear court of the palace of ADMETUS, King of Thessaly, many centuries before the Great Age of Greece. Each act begins at dawn and ends at sunset of the same day.

The palace is a low, squat house of roughly dressed stone, with a flat roof. There is a suggestion of a portico, however, supported by sections of the trunks of great trees. The palace doors are of wood and a gilded ox skull is affixed to each of them. Before these doors is a platform with low steps leading down to the soil floor of the courtyard.

The front of the palace fills the left three-quarters of the back of the stage. The rest of the stage is enclosed by clay-brick walls. In the wall to the right is a large wooden gate leading to the road outside and to the city of Pherai. The wall on the left is less high; a small door in it leads to the servants' quarters.

From the front center of the stage a path leads down (descending to the right) to what in a conventional theater would be the orchestra pit. At the bottom of this path is a "grotto"— a spring with practical flowing water; a bronze door to the Underworld, overhung by vines, but large enough for actors to pass through. Here is also (not seen, only assumed) the snake PYTHO.

———

First streaks of dawn.
Gradually a light rises to brilliancy, revealing APOLLO *standing on the roof of the palace. He wears a costume of gold with a long dark-blue mantle over his right shoulder. A blue light begins to glow from the entrance to Hell, down by the spring.* DEATH—*in a garment of large black patches, in which he looks like a bat or a beetle—comes waddling up the path and sniffs at the gate left and at the palace gate.*
Throughout the scene APOLLO *gazes off toward the rising sun— cool, measured, and with a faint smile on His lips.*

APOLLO: (*Like a "Good morning."*) Death!

DEATH: Aaah! You are here! The palace of Admetus has an honored guest! We are to have a wedding here today. What a guest! Or have you come to steal the bride away, illustrious Apollo?

APOLLO: Death, you live in the dark.

DEATH: I do, I do. Have you come, Lord Apollo, to show us some great sign, some wonder today?

> The NIGHT WATCHMAN, *sounding his rattle and carrying a waxed parchment lantern, comes around the palace, up center.*

WATCHMAN: (*Singsong.*) The watch before dawn, and all is well in the palace of Admetus the Hospitable, King of Thessaly, rich in horses. (*Starting to go off left.*) Dawn. The day of the wedding—of the greatest of all weddings.

> *Exit left into the servants' quarters.*

DEATH: I was asking, Lord Apollo, if you had come to show us some great wonder. (*Pause.*) Yes? No? "Yes," I hope. When the gods come near to men, sooner or later someone is killed. Am I to welcome some admired guest in my kingdom to-day? Am I to have King Admetus or the Princess Alcestis?

APOLLO: No.

DEATH: I shall watch and hope. (*He waddles to the center.*) In which of your powers and capacities are you here today, may I ask? As healer? (*Pause.*) As bringer of light and life? (*Pause.*) As singer?

APOLLO: (*Still gazing off, casually.*) They are all one and the same. I have come to set a song in motion—a story—

DEATH: A story!

APOLLO: A story that will be told many times . . .

DEATH: Ah! A lesson! Will there be a lesson in it for me?

APOLLO: Yes.

DEATH: (*Beating with his flippers on the ground.*) No!

APOLLO: Yes. You are to learn something.

DEATH: (*Scuttling about in rage.*) No! There is no lesson you can teach me. I am here forever, and I do not change. It's you Gods of the Upper Air that need lessons. And I'll read you a lesson right now. (*Shrilly.*) Leave these human beings alone. Stay up on Mount Olympus, where you belong, and enjoy yourselves. I've watched this foolishness coming over you for a long time. You made these creatures and then you became infatuated with them. You've thrown the whole world into confusion and it's getting worse every day. All you do is to torment them—who knows better than I? (*He waddles back to the top of the path, shaking himself furiously.*) They will never understand your language. The more you try to say something, the more you drive them distraught.

APOLLO: They have begun to understand me. At first they were like the beasts—more savage, more fearful. Like beasts in a cage, themselves the cage to themselves. Then two things broke on their minds and they lifted their heads: my father's thunder, which raised their fears to awe; and my sunlight, for which they gave thanks. In thanks they discovered speech, and I gave them song. These were signs and they knew them. First one, then another, knew that I prompted their hearts and was speaking.

DEATH: Yes, they're not like they used to be: "Apollo *loves* Thessaly. Apollo *loves* the house of Pherai." Go back to Olympus, where you belong. All this loving . . . It's hard to tell which is the unhappier—you or these wretched creatures. When you try to come into their lives you're like a giant in a small room: with every movement you break something. And whom are you tormenting today? The King? Or his bride?

APOLLO: You.

DEATH: Me? Me? So you've decided to love me, too? No, thank you! (*He flaps all his flippers, scrambles down the path, then scrambles up again; shrilly.*) You can't trouble me, and you can't give me any lessons. I and my Kingdom were made to last forever. How could you possibly trouble me?

APOLLO: You live in the dark and you cannot see that all things change.

DEATH: (*Screaming.*) Change! There'll be no change. (*He looks around in apprehension.*) It's getting light. And this story you're starting today is about a change? A change for *me*?

APOLLO: For you and for me.

DEATH: (*Disappearing into his cave, with one last sneering scream.*) For *you*!

The light on APOLLO *fades and he disappears.*
The WATCHMAN *returns on his rounds. He shakes his rattle,*
then blows out the lamp.

WATCHMAN: Dawn. Dawn. And all is well in the palace of Admetus the Hospitable, King of Thessaly, rich in horses. (*Descends toward audience.*) It is the day of the wedding, the
greatest of all weddings, and all is *not* well. Why can't she
sleep—the princess, the bride, our future queen? Eight, ten
times during the night, I've found her here—wandering
about, looking at the sky. Sometimes she goes out into the
road, as though she were waiting for a messenger. She stands
here and raises her arms—whispers: "Apollo! A sign! One
sign!" Sign of what? That she is right to marry King Admetus? Eh! Where will she find clearer signs than those written
on his face? Oh, I have lived a long time. I know that a bride
can be filled with fears on the night before her wedding. But
to be afraid of our Admetus who has won her hand in such a
wonderful way that all Greece is amazed. Oh, my friends,
take an old watchman's advice. Don't meditate upon the
issues of life at three in the morning. At that hour no warmth
reaches your heart and mind. At that hour—huuu—you see
your house in flames and your children stretched out dead at
your feet. Wait until the sun rises. The facts are the same—
the facts of a human life are the same—but the sunlight gives
them a meaning. Take the advice of a night watchman. Now
I want a drink of water. (*He descends to the spring and greets
the snake* PYTHO.) Good day to you, Pytho, old friend. It
will be a great day for you, too. You shall have a part in the
marriage banquet—a great sheep, or half an ox. Now come!
Leave my hands free to make the offering. (*He lets the water
slip through his cupped hands. And mumbles the ritual: "You
sources of life—earth, air, fire, and water . . ." Then he scoops
once more and drinks. He addresses the audience.*) Look,
friends. Do you see this cave under the vines? This is one of
the five entrances into Hell, and our good Pytho is here to
guard it. No man has ever entered it, and no man has ever
come out of it. That's what it is—merely one of the ten
thousand things we do not understand. (*He drinks again.
Shriek of a slain animal.*) Well, the great day has begun.

They are slaughtering the animals for the feast. The cooks are building great fires. The meadows are filled with the tents of kings and of chiefs who have come to celebrate the wedding of King Admetus, and of the Princess Alcestis, daughter of Pelias, King of Iolcos.

> *He starts up the path.* ALCESTIS, *in white, glides out of the palace doors. Animal cries.*

Hsst! There she is again!

> *He hides on the path below the level of the stage.* ALCESTIS *comes to the center of the stage, raises her arms, and whispers:*

ALCESTIS: Apollo! A sign! One sign! (*She goes out the gate, right, leading to the road.*)

WATCHMAN: (*Softly to the audience, mimicking her.*) Apollo! One sign!

> *Animal cries.* AGLAIA, *the old nurse, comes out quickly from the palace. She looks about, sees the* WATCHMAN.

AGLAIA: (*Whispers:*) Where is the princess? (*He points.*) All night —this restlessness, this unhappiness! "Apollo! One sign!"

WATCHMAN: "Apollo! One sign!"

> ALCESTIS *comes in from the gate, in nervous decisiveness.*

ALCESTIS: Watchman!

WATCHMAN: Yes, Princess?

ALCESTIS: Find my drivers. Tell them to harness the horses for a journey. Aglaia, call together my maids; tell them to get everything ready.

AGLAIA: A journey, Princess—on your wedding day, a journey?

ALCESTIS: (*Who has swept by her, from the palace steps.*) Aglaia, I have no choice in this. I must go. Forgive me. No, hate me; despise me—but finally forget me.

AGLAIA: Princess, the shame—and the insult to King Admetus.

ALCESTIS: I know all that, Aglaia. Aglaia, when I have gone, tell the King—tell Admetus—that I take all the shame; that I do not ask him to forgive me, but to despise me and forget me.

AGLAIA: Princess, I am an old woman. I am no ordinary slave in this house. I nursed the child Admetus and his father before him. (*To the* WATCHMAN.) Watchman, leave us alone.

Exit WATCHMAN.

You do not know King Admetus. In all Greece and the Islands you would not find a better husband.

ALCESTIS: I know this.

AGLAIA: You will find men who are more warlike, more adventurous, stronger perhaps—but not one more just, more . . . more beloved.

ALCESTIS: All this I know, Aglaia. I, too, love Admetus. Because of that I am doubly unhappy. But there is One I love more.

AGLAIA: Another? Another man? Above Admetus? Then go, Princess, and go quickly. We have been mistaken in you. You have no business here. If you have no eyes; if you have no mind; if you cannot see— (*Harshly.*) Watchman! Watchman! Everything will be ready for your journey, Princess. But go quickly.

ALCESTIS: No, Aglaia, not another man. The thing that I love more than Admetus is . . . is a God. Is Apollo.

AGLAIA: Apollo?

ALCESTIS: Yes. Since a young girl I have had only one wish—to be His priestess at Delphi. (*She despairs of expressing herself. Then suddenly cries, with passion:*) I wish to live in the real. With one life to live, one life to give—not these lives we see about us: fever and pride and . . . and possessionship—but in the real; at Delphi, where the truth is.

AGLAIA: But the God has not called you? (*Pause.*) The God has not sent for you?

ALCESTIS: (*Low; in shame.*) No.

AGLAIA: And this real—it is not real enough to be the wife of Admetus, the mother of his children, and the Queen of Thessaly?

ALCESTIS: Any woman can be wife and mother; and hundreds have been queens. My husband. My children. To center your life upon these five or six, to be bound and shut in with everything that concerns them . . . each day filled—so filled—with the thousand occupations that help or comfort them, that finally one sinks into the grave loved and honored, but as ignorant as the day one was born—

AGLAIA: Ignorant?

ALCESTIS: Knowing as little of why we live and why we die—of why the hundred thousand live and die—as the day we were born.

AGLAIA: (*Dryly.*) And that you think you can learn at Delphi? But the God has not called you.

ALCESTIS: (*In shame.*) I sent offerings . . . messages . . . offerings . . . (*Pause.*) I was my father's favorite daughter. He wished me never to marry, but to remain with him until his death. But suitors came to seek my hand from all Greece. He imposed upon them an impossible task. He required of them that they yoke together a lion and a boar and drive them thrice about the walls of our city of Iolcos. They came from all Greece: Jason came, and Nestor; Hercules, son of Zeus, came; and Atreus. And all failed. Month after month the new suitors failed and barely escaped with their lives. My father and I sat at the city gates and my father laughed. And I smiled—not because I wished to live with my father, but because I wished for only this one thing: to live and die as a priestess of Apollo at Delphi.

AGLAIA: And then Admetus came. And he drove the lion and the boar—like mild oxen he drove them about the city; and won your hand, Princess.

ALCESTIS: But I loved Apollo more.

AGLAIA: Yes. But it was Apollo who made this marriage.

ALCESTIS: We cannot know that.

AGLAIA: The sign you are asking for, Princess, is before you—the clearest of signs. (*Drastically.*) You have not been called to Delphi: you cannot read the simplest words of the God.

ALCESTIS *shields her face.*

Now listen to what I am telling you: were you not amazed that Admetus was able to yoke together the lion and the boar? Where Atreus failed, and Hercules, son of Zeus? I will tell you how he did it: in a dream, the God Apollo taught him how to yoke together a lion and a boar.

ALCESTIS *takes two steps backward.*

First, he saw and loved you. Before he returned to Iolcos that second time—after his first failure—he fell ill. Love and despair brought him to the point of death—and I nursed him. Three nights he lay at the point of death. And the third night, I was sitting beside him—his agony and his delirium —and I heard, I *saw*, that in a dream Apollo was teaching him to yoke together a lion and a boar.

> ALCESTIS *gazes at her.*

This is true. I swear it is true.

ALCESTIS: True, yes—but we have heard enough of these deliriums and dreams, fevers and visions. Aglaia, it is time we asked for certainties. The clear open presence of the God— that is at Delphi.

AGLAIA: Clear? Open? Even at Delphi the sibyl is delirious; she raves; she is beside herself. Who ever heard of them speaking clearly?

ALCESTIS: (*Turning with irresolute step toward the palace, in despair.*) I am alone, alone. . . .

AGLAIA: (*Firmly but affectionately.*) Now listen to me, Princess. Go to your room and sleep. (*Looking upward.*) It is two hours to noon. If, after a little rest, you are still of the same mind, you can go on any journey you want, and no one will try to stop you. (*Holding* ALCESTIS'S *elbow, she guides her to the palace doors, prattling in maternal fashion.*) You want the gods to speak to us clearly and openly, Princess? What can you be thinking they are, Princess? I hope you don't think of them as men!

> *Both exit into the palace. For a moment the stage is empty. A sound of voices at the gate rises almost to clamor. Pounding and knocking at right. The* WATCHMAN *comes around the palace up center.*

WATCHMAN: Well, now, what's that? What's all this noise? (*Opens the gate and talks through it, ajar.*) The wedding guests enter at the gate in front of the palace. This is the rear gate. What? Don't everybody talk at once! What? Very well, very well. Let the old man in.

> *Enter* TEIRESIAS, *blind, unbelievably old, irascible, truculent, domineering, and very near to senile incoherence. One hand is on the shoulder of a* BOY *who guides him; the other ceaselessly brandishes a great stick.* TOWNSPEOPLE *follow*

him into the court; and some SERVANTS *come into the court both from the palace doors and from around the palace.*

TEIRESIAS: (*Surprisingly loud and strong.*) Is this the palace of Minos, King of Crete?

Laughter; the BOY *starts pulling his sleeve and whispering into his ear.*

I mean, is this the palace of Oedipus, King of Thebes? (*Striking the* BOY *with his stick.*) Stop pulling at me! I know what I'm saying. (*Warding off those pressing about him.*) Bees, wasps, and hornets!

WATCHMAN: No, old man. This is the palace of Admetus, King of Thessaly.

TEIRESIAS: (*Repeating his words.*) King of Thessaly. Well, that's what I said. That's what I meant. Call Admetus, King of Thessaly. I have a message for him.

WATCHMAN: Old man, the King is to be married today. He is busy with his guests. You sit here in the sun now; we shall wash your feet. The King will come and hear you later.

TEIRESIAS: (*Threatening with his stick.*) Marrying . . . washing. What have I got to do with marrying and washing? I'll not wait a minute. (*Stamping.*) Call King What's-his-name.

Enter AGLAIA *from the palace.*

AGLAIA: Who are you, old man? I shall tell the King—

TEIRESIAS: Tell the King that I am Delphi, priest of Teiresias— Apollo, priest of Delphi. . . . Boy, what is this I'm saying?

BOY *whispers.*

Tell the King I am Teiresias, priest of Apollo. That I come from Delphi with a message and that I am in a hurry to go back there.

AGLAIA: You are Teiresias? Teiresias!

WATCHMAN and BYSTANDERS: Teiresias!

TEIRESIAS: (*Beating with his stick on the ground.*) Call the King! Plague and pestilence! Call King What's-his-name.

AGLAIA: Coming, great Teiresias.

She is hurrying to the palace door as it opens and ADMETUS *comes out. More* SERVANTS *gather.*

ADMETUS: What is it? Who is this, Aglaia?

AGLAIA: (*Confidentially.*) It is Teiresias, come from Delphi.

ADMETUS: Teiresias!

AGLAIA: (*Points to her forehead.*) As old as the mountains, King Admetus.

ADMETUS: Welcome, welcome, noble Teiresias, my father's old friend. Welcome to Pherai. I am Admetus, King of Thessaly.

TEIRESIAS: (*Waving his stick.*) Back. Stand back. All this crowding and pushing . . . Have you ears, fellow?

ADMETUS: Yes, Teiresias.

TEIRESIAS: Then pull the wax out of them and listen to what the God says.

ADMETUS: They are open, Teiresias.

TEIRESIAS: Atreus, King of Mycenae, hear what the God says—

ADMETUS: Atreus? Noble Teiresias, I am Admetus, King of—

TEIRESIAS: Admetus? All right—Admetus, then. Hold your tongue and let me get my message out. I bring a message to you from Apollo's temple at Delphi. An honor, a great honor has come to Thessaly. Boy, is this Thessaly? (*He puts hands on the* BOY'S *head; the* BOY *nods.*) A great honor and a great peril has come to Thessaly.

ADMETUS: A peril, Teiresias?

TEIRESIAS: An honor and a peril. A peril is an honor, fool. No—an honor is a peril. Don't you know the first things up here in Thessaly?

ADMETUS: One moment, Teiresias. A message to me is also a message to my future queen. Aglaia, call the princess.

AGLAIA *hurries into the palace.*

Today I am to be married to Alcestis, daughter of King Pelias of Iolcos. No guest is more to be honored than Teiresias. Rest first, Teiresias. . . .

TEIRESIAS: There are ten thousand weddings. Let this queen make haste. Hear me, Minos, King of Crete. . . . Boy, what is his name?

BOY *whispers.*

Well, what does it matter? Is this queen here?

Enter from the palace ALCESTIS, *breathless with wonder.*

ADMETUS: She is here.

ALCESTIS: Noble Teiresias . . . great Teiresias! My father's old friend. I am Alcestis, daughter of King Pelias of Iolcos.

TEIRESIAS: (*Waving his stick testily at those pressing around him.*) Back! Keep back! Geese and ducks and quacklings. Silence and hold your tongues. Zeus, father of gods and men, has commanded . . . has commanded . . . Boy, what has he commanded?

> BOY *whispers.* TEIRESIAS *strikes him.*

Well, you don't have to run on. . . . Has commanded that Apollo, my master—that Apollo come down from Olympus; and that he live on earth for one year, solstice to solstice . . . live as a man among men. I have given my message. Boy, lead me to the road. (*He turns to go.*)

ALCESTIS: (*While the* BOY *whispers into* TEIRESIAS'S *ear.*) Apollo is to live on the earth?

TEIRESIAS: (*To the* BOY.) Yes, yes. Don't deafen me. And Apollo, my master, has chosen to live here— (*He strikes the ground with his stick.*) here as a servant of Admetus, King of Thessaly.

ADMETUS: Here? Here, noble Teiresias? (*Goes quickly to him.*) One moment more, Teiresias. How do I understand this? You do not mean, divine Teiresias, that Apollo will be here, with us, as a servant, every day? With us, each day?

> *As all watch him breathlessly,* TEIRESIAS, *hand to brow, seems to fall into a deep sleep. Suddenly he awakes and says:*

TEIRESIAS: Outside the gate are four herdsmen. They are to be your servants for a year. Assign them their duties. One of them is Apollo.

ADMETUS: (*Repeating.*) One of them is Apollo?

TEIRESIAS: Four herdsmen. One of them is Apollo. Do not try to know which one is the God. I do not know. You will never know. And ask me no more questions, for I have no more answers. Boy, call the herdsmen.

> *The* BOY *goes out. Silence.*

ADMETUS: Teiresias, should we not . . . fall on our knees, on our faces?

TEIRESIAS: You do not listen to what's said to you. Apollo is here, *as a man.* As a man. As a common herdsman or shepherd. . . . Do as I do!

> *The* BOY *returns and presses close to* TEIRESIAS. *Enter the* FOUR HERDSMEN. *They are dusty, dirty, unshaven common oafs. They are deeply abashed by the great folk before them, touch their forelocks obsequiously, shuffle into a line against the wall, and don't know what to do with their eyes. Two have great wineskins; all have big sticks.* TEIRESIAS *speaks gruffly to them.*

TEIRESIAS: Come, don't be slow about it. Make your bow to your new master. Anyone can see you've been drinking. A nice way to begin your service. (*Waving his stick.*) If I had eyes to see, I'd beat you. Forward; pick up your feet. Boy, are they all four here? Well, has the King lost his voice?

ADMETUS: (*Pulling himself together.*) You are welcome to Thessaly. You are welcome to the wedding feast, for I am to be married today. Tomorrow I shall assign you your herds and flocks. You have made a long journey. You are welcome to Thessaly. . . . Teiresias, you, too, have made a long journey. Will you not bathe and rest?

TEIRESIAS: I have a longer journey to go. My message has been delivered. Boy, lead me out the gate.

ALCESTIS: (*Coming to a few steps before him; in a low voice.*) Divine Teiresias? Have you no message for Alcestis?

TEIRESIAS: Who's this woman?

ALCESTIS: I am Alcestis, daughter of King Pelias of Iolcos. I sent many messages and offerings to Delphi and—

TEIRESIAS: Messages and offerings. There are mountains of them. Boy, lead me to the road.

> *But the* BOY *keeps pulling at his sleeve and shoulder and trying to whisper to him.*

Oh, yes, I had a message for some girl or woman—for Jocasta, or Alcestis, or Dejaneira, or I care not whom, but I have forgotten it. Boy, stop dragging at me! (*He strikes the* BOY *with his stick.*) Worthless! Impudent!

The BOY *falls.* TEIRESIAS *continues to beat him.*

BOY: (*Screaming.*) Teiresias! Help! Help! King Admetus!

ADMETUS: Surely, great Teiresias, the boy has not—

ALCESTIS: It was a small fault, Teiresias. I beg you spare the boy. He will learn.

TEIRESIAS: (*Suddenly stopping and peering at* ALCESTIS.) Whatever your name is: Jocasta, Leda, Hermione—

ALCESTIS: Alcestis.

TEIRESIAS: I had a message for some girl, but I have forgotten it. Or else I've delivered it already. That's it: I've delivered it. By thunder and lightning, by the holy tripod—what use is Delphi if men and women cannot learn to listen?

> TEIRESIAS *is following the* BOY *out of the gate, when* ADMETUS *takes some steps forward.*

ADMETUS: You said . . . you said there was peril, Teiresias?

TEIRESIAS: (*Half out of the gate.*) Of course there's peril, imbecile. When they (*Brusque gesture upward.*) draw near it is always peril.

ADMETUS: But my father said that Apollo has always loved Thessaly. . . .

TEIRESIAS: Yes—love, love, love. Let them keep their love to themselves. Look at me: five—six hundred years old and pretty well loved by the gods and I am not allowed to die. If the gods didn't love men, we'd all be happy; and the other way round is true, too: if we men didn't love the gods, we'd all be happy.

> *Exit, with the* BOY.
> *A bewildered pause.*
> ADMETUS *collects himself and says in a more matter-of-fact, authoritative tone to the* FOUR HERDSMEN:

ADMETUS: Again, you are welcome to Thessaly and to Pherai. (*To the* WATCHMAN.) See that they are well provided for. (*Again to the* HERDSMEN.) I am happy that you are to be guests at my wedding today.

> ADMETUS *and all on the stage watch in confused awe as the* WATCHMAN *guides them down the path to the spring. They pass* ADMETUS *with servile timidity; by the spring they*

stretch out, pass the wineskin from one to another; one promptly falls asleep. ADMETUS *has not looked at* ALCESTIS. *Partly to her and partly to himself, he says reflectively:*

I do not know what to think of these things. . . . I am a mere herdsman myself. Alcestis, there is great need of you in Pherai.

He stretches his hand out behind him. She, frozen in thought, does not take it.

I must return to my guests. (*With a last echo of his awe.*) I do not know what to think of these things. (*Then with a smile.*) Alcestis, there is an old custom here in Thessaly that a bridegroom should not see the face of his bride until the evening of his wedding day. This has been said for many hundreds of years. Is there also such a custom at Iolcos?

ALCESTIS: (*Low.*) Yes, Admetus.

ADMETUS: (*Passing her with youthful vigor, his hand shielding his face.*) Hereafter—by the God's gift—I may look upon your face until I die.

At the door of the palace, he is arrested by a thought. Still shielding his face, he comes in slow deliberation to the point of the stage, overhanging the HERDSMEN *by the spring. After taking a deep breath of resolution, he says with unemphatic directness:*

Apollo, friend of my father and my ancestors and my land, I am a simple man, devout. I am not learned in piety. If, in ignorance, I blunder and fall short, may He who has been the friend of my house and my people forgive me. You have come on a day when I am the happiest of all men. Continue your favor to me and to my descendants. . . . (*Slight pause.*) I am not skilled in speech. You can read all minds. Read what is in mine, or rather . . . yourself plant in my mind those wishes which only you can fulfill. (*He turns and goes quickly into the palace.*)

ALCESTIS: (*Who has not ceased to keep her eyes on the* HERDSMEN, *half in longing and half in doubt and repulsion— though they are now hidden from where she is standing, murmuring.*) Is Apollo there?

AGLAIA: Princess!

ALCESTIS: One of those? And could that old man have been Teiresias of Delphi—that broken, crazy old man?

AGLAIA: (*Really shocked; firmly.*) Do not doubt these things, Princess.

ALCESTIS: (*After taking a few steps toward them; in sudden resolve.*) Leave me alone with them.

> AGLAIA *makes a gesture to the* WATCHMAN *and both go out. During the following speech, though one* HERDSMAN *is asleep and snoring, the others are embarrassed by her presence. The wineskin is being passed around; they scarcely dare to raise their eyes to her.*

Are you here? I have spoken to you a thousand times—to the sky and the stars and the sun. And I have sent messages to Delphi. Are you now, truly, within the hearing of my voice?

> *Silence, broken by a snore and a grunt.*

Some say that you do not exist. Some say that the gods are far away; they are feasting on Olympus, or are asleep, or drunk. I have offered you my life. You know that I have wished to live only for you: to learn—to be taught by you— the meaning of our life.

> *No answer.*

Are we human beings to be left without any sign, any word? Are we abandoned?

> *She waits another second above the embarrassed silence of the* HERDSMEN, *then turns toward the palace, and says to herself, bitterly:*

Then we must find our way by ourselves . . . and life is a meaningless grasping at this and that; it is a passionate nonsense. . . .

> *The* FIRST HERDSMAN—*the dirtiest, most insignificant of the four—rises. He touches his cap in humble embarrassment and says:*

HERDSMAN: Princess, did that old man say that there was a

god among us? Did I hear him say that? The God Apollo? Then, lady, I am as surprised as you are. Lady, for thirty days we four have walked all across Greece. We have drunk from the same wineskin; we have put our hands in the same dish; we have slept by the same fire. If there had been a god among us, would I not have known it?

ALCESTIS, *in hope and revulsion, has taken several steps toward him.*

By all I value, lady, I swear we are just ordinary herdsmen. Ignorant herdsmen. But . . . but one thing I will say, lady: we are not quite ordinary herdsmen. Why, that fellow there—the one that's snoring: there's no illness he cannot cure. Snakebite or a broken back. Yet I know that he is not a god, Princess. And that fellow beside him, that one! (*He goes forward and kicks the* HERDSMAN.) Can't you stop drinking while the princess is looking at you? He never loses his way. In the darkest night he knows his north from his south and his east from his west. Oh, it's wonderful. Yet I know well that he's not the god of the sun. (*Adding under his breath:*) Besides, his habits are filthy, are filthy.

ALCESTIS: (*Barely breathing it.*) And that one?

HERDSMAN: That man? He's our singer.

ALCESTIS: Ah!

HERDSMAN: Believe me, when he plays the lyre and sings—oh, Princess! It is true that at times I have said to myself, "Surely this is a god." He can fill us to the brim with joy or sadness when we have no reason at all to be joyful or sad. He can make the memory of love more sweet than love itself. But, Princess, he is no god. (*As though she had contradicted him; with sudden argumentative energy.*) How can he be a god when he's in misery all the time and drinking himself to death? Killing himself, you might say, before our own eyes. The gods don't hate themselves, Princess.

ALCESTIS: And you?

HERDSMAN: I? *I*, Apollo? Not only am I not Apollo, but I'm not ready to believe that Apollo is here.

ALCESTIS: Teiresias . . . Teiresias said . . .

HERDSMAN: Was that Teiresias—that half-witted, crumbling

old man? Can they find no better messenger than that? Can't they say what they have to say in any clearer way than this?

Again ALCESTIS *turns toward the palace; then turns toward the* HERDSMAN *and says, as though talking to herself:*

ALCESTIS: Then we are indeed miserable. Not only because we have no aid, but because we are cheated with the hope that we might have aid. . . .

HERDSMAN: (*Taking more steps onto the stage.*) But if they did exist, these gods, how would they speak to us? In what language would they talk to us? Compared to them, we are diseased and dying and deaf and blind and as busy as clowns. Why, there are some who even say that they love us. Could you understand that? What kind of love is that, Princess, when there is so great a gulf between the lovers? (*He starts to return to his place in the path.*) That would be an unhappy love, no doubt about that.

ALCESTIS: (*Earnestly and sharply.*) No, not unhappy!

HERDSMAN: (*With equal spirit.*) Yes. For if they showed themselves to us in their glory, it would kill us. (*Pause.*) I did have an idea this morning: maybe there is another way—a way to bridge that gulf, I mean. Maybe they can find a way to bring those they love up—up nearer to them. If Teiresias is right, Apollo is here in Thessaly. Now, maybe that foolish old man got his message wrong. Maybe he was supposed to say that Apollo is here divided up among many people—us four herdsmen and others! Take Admetus, for example. I've only seen him for a few hours. I must confess, Princess, at first I was very disappointed in Admetus. There's nothing very extraordinary about him. Did you ever see Hercules, Princess?

ALCESTIS: (*Nods her head slightly.*) Yes.

HERDSMAN: (*Suddenly recollecting.*) Ah, yes. He sought your hand. There's a man! Hercules, son of Zeus and Alcmene. And you can see it at once. I've seen a dozen better men than Admetus. But . . . slowly I began to see that King Admetus has something that all those other heroes haven't got. . . . The world changes; it changes slowly. What good would this world be, Princess, unless new kinds of men came into it—and new kinds of women?

Enter ADMETUS, *wearing on his right shoulder a light-blue cloak like Apollo's. He stands watching from the top step.*

And wouldn't that be, maybe, the way those unhappy lovers (*He points upward.*) would try to throw a bridge across the gulf I was talking about? (*He becomes aware of* ADMETUS. *Obsequiously bowing his head, and pulling his forelock, murmuring.*) We wish you all happiness . . . many years. (*He goes back to his place.*)

The sun is setting. The sky behind the palace roof is filled with color.

ADMETUS: (*With set face.*) Aglaia has told me of your wish to leave, Princess Alcestis. You are, of course, free to go. There are no constraints here. There are no slaves in Thessaly, Princess—not even its queen. I have just given orders that your drivers and your maids be prepared for the journey. (*He takes one step down.*) Before you leave, I wish to say one thing. I do not say this in order to win your pity, nor to dissuade you from what you have planned to do. I say this because you and I are not children; and we should not conceal from one another what is in our hearts. (*Slight pause.*) It is still a great wonder to me that I was able to yoke the lion and the boar. But I am in no doubt as to *why* I was able to do it: I loved you. I shall never see you again. I shall never marry. And I shall never be the same. From now on I shall know that there is something wrong and false in this world into which we have been born. I am an ordinary man, but the love that filled me is not an ordinary love. When such love is not met by a love in return, then life is itself a deception. And it is best that men live at random, as best they may. For justice . . . and honor . . . and love are just things we invent for a short time, as suits the moment. May you have a good journey, Princess Alcestis.

ALCESTIS *has been standing with raised head but lowered eyes. She now puts out her hand.*

ALCESTIS: Admetus. (*Slight pause.*) Admetus, ask me again to marry you. (*He takes one quick step toward her; she again puts out her hand quickly to stop him.*) Ask me to love all the things that you love . . . and to be the queen of your Thessaly. Ask me in pain to bear you children. To walk beside you at the great festivals. To comfort you when you are despairing. To make sure that when you return from a journey the water for your bath will be hot, and that your house, Admetus, will be as well ordered as your mind. To live for you and for your children and for your people—to live for you as though every moment I were ready to die for you. . . .

ADMETUS: (*Joyously and loudly.*) No—no Alcestis! It is I . . .

He takes her outstretched hand. They do not embrace.

Alcestis, will you be the wife of Admetus, King of Thessaly?
ALCESTIS: With my whole self, Admetus . . .

They go into the palace.

Act II

The same scene, twelve years later.
Again first dawn. The same WATCHMAN *comes around the palace.*
He does not shake his rattle. He speaks softly, slowly, and dejectedly.

WATCHMAN: The watch before dawn . . . the palace of Admetus the Hospitable, King of Thessaly, rich in horses. (*He stands a moment, his eyes on the ground; then to the audience.*) And all is as bad as it possibly could be . . . as it possibly could be. (*He goes to the gate, which is ajar, and talks to a whispering crowd outside.*) No, my friends. There is no news. The King is still alive; he has lived through another night. The Queen is sitting by his bed. She is holding his hand. . . . No news. No change. . . . Take that dog away; we must have no barking. Yes, the King drank some ox blood mixed with wine. (*He returns to the center of the stage and addresses the audience.*) Our King is at the point of death, there is no doubt about it. You remember those herdsmen, twelve years ago, that Teiresias brought here, saying that one of them was Apollo—and that Apollo would live here as a servant for a year? You remember all that?

Well, at the end of the year did they go away? No; all four of them are still here. Was Apollo in one of them? Nobody knows. Don't try to think about it; you'll lose your senses if you try to understand things like that. But, friends, that first year was a wonderful year. I cannot explain this to you: it was no more or less prosperous than other years. To a visitor, to a passer-by, everything would have appeared the same. But to us who were living it, everything was different. The facts of our human life never change; it is our way of seeing them that changes. Apollo was certainly here. (*Pause.*) What? How did King Admetus come by his illness? Well, as I say, those four herdsmen stayed on. They were good fellows and good workers—though they talked south-country Greek. But two of them—eh!—drank their wine without water. And one evening at sunset time those two were sitting drinking—there, right there!—and a quarrel arose between them. There was shouting and chasing about, and King Admetus came out to put a stop to it. Then—oh, my friends—one of the herdsmen whipped out his knife and stabbed King Admetus by mistake, stabbed him from here (*Points to his throat.*) right down his side to the waist. You could put your hand in it. That was weeks ago. The wound didn't heal. It got angry and boiled and watered and boiled and watered, and now the King must surely die. No one's wanted to punish the herdsman whose body held Apollo— you see? And the crime may have been Apollo's will—try to think that through! And that herdsman's outside the gate now—is always there—flat on the ground, flat on his face, wishing he were dead.

There is a rising murmur of excited voices at the gate.

Now what's all that noise about?

AGLAIA comes hurriedly out of the palace.

AGLAIA: What's all that noise? Watchman, how can you allow that noise?

WATCHMAN: (*Hobbling to the gate.*) They've only just begun it.

AGLAIA: (*At the gate.*) What's all this cackling about? Don't you know you must be quiet?

WATCHMAN: Have you no sense? Have you no hearts? What? What?

AGLAIA: What? What messenger? Tell him to go around to the front of the palace and to go quietly. What messenger? Where's he from?

Enter ALCESTIS, from the palace.

ALCESTIS: There must be no noise. There must be no noise. Aglaia, how can you allow this noise?

AGLAIA: Queen Alcestis, they say that a messenger has come.

ALCESTIS: What messenger?

WATCHMAN: (*Has received through the gate a small rectangular leaf of gold, which he gives to ALCESTIS.*) They are saying that a messenger came during the night and left this.

ALCESTIS stands looking at it in her hand. The WATCHMAN leans over and examines it in her hand and continues talking officiously.

It is of gold, lady. See, those are the signs—that is the writing—of the Southland. There is the sun . . . and the tripod . . . and the laurel. . . . Queen Alcestis, it is from Delphi. It is a message from Delphi!

ALCESTIS suddenly performs the ritual: she places the leaf first to her forehead, then on her heart, then on her lips.

ALCESTIS: Where is the messenger?

The WATCHMAN goes to the gate—now slightly open—and holds a whispered colloquy.

WATCHMAN: (*Turning back toward ALCESTIS.*) He went away —hours ago, they say.

ALCESTIS: Who can read this writing? Watchman, go call those four herdsmen!

WATCHMAN: They are here, lady—all four of them.

Again a busy colloquy at the gate. It opens further to admit the four HERDSMEN. The HERDSMAN who held the long conversation with ALCESTIS in Act I flings himself on the ground, face downward, holding his head in his hands.

ALCESTIS: Can one of you read the writing of the Southland?

HERDSMAN: (*Raising his head.*) I can . . . a little, Queen Alcestis.

ALCESTIS: Then stand. Stand up.

He rises. She puts the leaf in his hand. He looks at it a moment, then puts it to his forehead, heart, and lips; and says in awe:

HERDSMAN: It is from the temple of Apollo at Delphi.

Some TOWNSPEOPLE have pressed through the gate. The HERDSMAN starts reading with great difficulty.

"Peace . . . and long life . . . to Admetus the Hospitable, King of Thessaly, rich in horses."

ALCESTIS: Long life?

HERDSMAN: "Peace and long life to Admetus the Hospitable—"
ALCESTIS: Stop. (*To the* WATCHMAN.) Close the gate.

The WATCHMAN *pushes the* TOWNSPEOPLE *off the stage, and after a glance at* ALCESTIS, *also drives off the three other* HERDSMEN. *He closes the gate.* ALCESTIS *returns to the reader, who has been trying to decipher the text.*

HERDSMAN: "King Admetus . . . *not* . . . will not . . . die."
AGLAIA: Great is Apollo! Great is Apollo!
HERDSMAN: "Will not die . . . if . . . if . . . because . . . no, if . . . another . . . if someone else . . . if a second person . . . desires . . . (*He points to his heart.*) wishes . . . longs . . . desires to die . . ." Lady, I do not know this last word.
ALCESTIS: I know it.
HERDSMAN: (*Struggling, finds it.*) "In his place . . . in his stead." Great is Apollo!
AGLAIA: What does it say? What does it say?
WATCHMAN: I. I shall die. (*Starting left.*) My sword, where is my sword?
AGLAIA: (*Getting the idea.*) No. (*Strongly, to the* WATCHMAN.) No. This message is for me. I was there when he was born: I shall die for him. I shall throw myself in the river.
WATCHMAN: (*Returning; to* AGLAIA.) This is not for a woman to do.
HERDSMAN: (*Kneeling, his fists pressed against his eyes in concentration.*) I have begun to die already.
AGLAIA: Queen Alcestis, tell me . . . I must do it properly: how does one die for King Admetus?
WATCHMAN: (*Self-importantly, placing himself between* AGLAIA *and* ALCESTIS.) Give your orders to me, Queen Alcestis. It is very clear that this message was meant for me.
HERDSMAN: (*Again throwing himself full length on the ground.*) I struck him. I am to blame for all!
ALCESTIS: (*Who has waited, motionless, for silence.*) How would you die in his stead? (*Pause.*) Do you think it is enough to fling yourself into the river—or to run a sword through your heart? (*Pause.*) No—the gods do not ask what is easy of us, but what is difficult.

AGLAIA: (*Sobbing.*) Queen Alcestis, how does one die for King Admetus?

HERDSMAN: I know. I know. (*He turns and starts to go to the gate.*) Peace and long life to King Admetus!

ALCESTIS: (*To the* HERDSMAN.) Wait!

They all watch her. She says quietly:

Aglaia, go and lay out the dress in which I was married.

AGLAIA: (*Stares at her in sudden realization; horrified whisper.*) No. No . . . you must not . . .

ALCESTIS: Tell the children I am coming to see them. Tell the King the sun is warm here. He must come out and sit in it.

Sudden clamor from the others.

AGLAIA: No. No, Queen Alcestis. We are old. Our lives are over.

WATCHMAN: Lady, look at me—I am an old man.

AGLAIA: You cannot do this. He would not wish it. You are queen; you are mother.

ALCESTIS: (*Restraining their noise by voice and gesture.*) First! First I order you to say nothing of this to anyone. Aglaia, do you hear me?

AGLAIA: Yes, Queen Alcestis.

ALCESTIS: Watchman!

WATCHMAN: Yes, Queen Alcestis.

ALCESTIS: To no one—until tomorrow. No matter what takes place here, you will show no surprise, no grief. Now leave me alone with this man. (*Pointing to the* HERDSMAN.)

> AGLAIA *goes into the palace; the* WATCHMAN *out left.*
> *The* HERDSMAN *stands with one fist on his forehead in concentration, and suddenly cries:*

HERDSMAN: King Admetus—rise up! Rise up!

ALCESTIS: You cannot save him.

HERDSMAN: I have begun to die already.

ALCESTIS: Yes, maybe you could do it. But you would do it imperfectly. You wish to die, yes . . . not for love of Admetus, but to lift the burden of that crime from off your heart. This is work of love, Herdsman; not work of expiation, but of love.

HERDSMAN: (*Almost angrily.*) I, too, love Admetus.

ALCESTIS: Who does not love Admetus? But your death would be a small death. You long to die: I dread, fear, hate to die. I must die for Admetus— (*She looks upward.*) from this sunlight. Only so will he be restored. Can you give him that?

He is silent. She continues, as though talking to herself.

I know now what I have to do and how to do it. But I do not know why . . . why this has been asked of me. You . . . you can help me to understand why I must die.

HERDSMAN: I?

ALCESTIS: Yes, you—who came from Delphi; in whom Apollo—

HERDSMAN: (*In sincere repudiation.*) Lady . . . Princess, I told you—again and again. If Apollo was in us herdsmen, he was not in me!

ALCESTIS: (*Softly and lightly.*) You made clear to me that Apollo willed my marriage.

HERDSMAN: (*Still almost angrily.*) No. No. You asked me questions. I answered as any man would answer. You know well that I am an ordinary man.

ALCESTIS *turns in suffering frustration toward the palace door; then turns back again to the* HERDSMAN.

ALCESTIS: Then speak again as an ordinary man, and tell me why Apollo asks me to die.

HERDSMAN: (*Still with a touch of anger.*) Then as an ordinary man I answer you—as many an ordinary man would: Delphi has said that one of us must die. I am ready to die. Why should I try to understand it?

ALCESTIS: But if we do not understand, our lives are little better than those of the animals.

HERDSMAN: No! Princess, to understand means to see the whole of a thing. Do we men ever see the whole of a story, the end of a story? If you let me die now for Admetus, I would not know what followed after my death, but I would die willingly. For I have always seen that there are two kinds of death: one which is an end; and one which is a going forward, which is big with what follows after it. And I would know that a death which had been laid on me by Delphi would be a death which led on to something. For if the gods exist, that is their sign: that whatever they do is an unfolding —a part of something larger than we can see. Let me die this death, Princess—for it would save me from that other death which I dread and which all men dread: the mere ceasing to be; the dust in the grave.

> ALCESTIS *has received his words as full answer and solution. Her mood changes; she says lightly and quickly:*

ALCESTIS: No, Herdsman, live—live for Admetus, for me, and for my children. Are you not the friend of Epimenes—he who hates you now because you struck his father? You have almost broken his heart. He thought you were his friend— you who taught him to swim and to fish. Before I go I shall tell Epimenes that you have done me a great kindness.

> *In silence the* HERDSMAN *goes out the gate.*
> ALCESTIS *again makes the ritual gesture with the gold leaf—forehead, heart, lips. Enter* AGLAIA *from the palace.*

AGLAIA: (*With lowered head.*) The dress is ready, Queen Alcestis.

ALCESTIS: Aglaia, for what I have to do now I cannot—I must not—see the children. Their heads smell so sweet. Do you understand?

AGLAIA: Yes, Queen Alcestis.

ALCESTIS: You are to tell Epimenes—from me—that he is to go to the herdsman who struck his father . . . that he is to forgive him, and to thank him for a great kindness which he has done me.

AGLAIA: I shall tell him.

ALCESTIS: You are to cut a lock of my hair. Say nothing to anyone, and place it on the altar (*Pointing to the gate.*) in the grove of Apollo, across the road. Aglaia, after I am gone, you are to tell King Admetus that I have said that I wish him to marry again.

AGLAIA: Queen Alcestis!

ALCESTIS: A man must have that comfort. But oh, Aglaia! They say that stepmothers often bear ill will toward the children of the former wife. Stay by them! Stay near them! And oh, Aglaia—from time to time recall me to him. (*Her voice breaking.*) Recall me to him! (*She rushes into the palace.*)

> AGLAIA *is about to follow when she is stopped by excited whispering and talking at the gate. Some* TOWNSPEOPLE *take a few steps into the court.* RHODOPE, *a young girl of the palace servants, smothering her happy giggling, runs from the gate to the palace door.*

AGLAIA: What is this? What is this noise? Rhodope!

RHODOPE: He's coming along the road!

AGLAIA: Who?

RHODOPE and TOWNSPEOPLE: Hercules is coming! He's down the valley! Hercules, son of Zeus!

AGLAIA: Hush, all of you. Go out of the court. Have you forgotten that there is sickness in this house! Rhodope, go in the house and hold your tongue!

> TOWNSPEOPLE *disappear.* RHODOPE *slips through the palace door as it is opened by the* WATCHMAN, *who enters, preceding two* SERVANTS, *who are not yet seen with the day bed. Then to* AGLAIA, *whose head is lowered in anxiety.*

WATCHMAN: Hercules! Today of all days!

AGLAIA: (*In a bad humor.*) Yes. Yes. And every year. Why does he come every year? Do we know?

WATCHMAN: But . . . so great a friend!

AGLAIA: Yes, but great friends can sometimes make us a present of their absence.

WATCHMAN: Aglaia, I don't understand you!

AGLAIA: (*Irritably.*) I know what I know.

> From the palace come two SERVANTS. They are bearing a day bed and a low stool.

WATCHMAN: (*To the* SERVANTS.) Come on . . . put them down here. You know where.

AGLAIA: (*Taking over the ordering, while the* WATCHMAN *turns back to help* ADMETUS.) Here, right here! (*Getting her bearings by the sun.*) Turn it so. (*She takes the cushions from them.*) So. There. And the Queen likes to sit here.

Enter ADMETUS, *supported, his arms around the shoulders of the* WATCHMAN *and a* GUARD.

ADMETUS: The sun is already halfway up the sky. (*To the* WATCHMAN.) You have watched all night. You should be asleep.

WATCHMAN: Oh, we old men, King Admetus, we sleep very little. Gently. Gently now.

ADMETUS: I don't know where the Queen is, Aglaia.

AGLAIA: (*Busies herself with the cushions.*) She'll be here in a minute, King Admetus. You can be sure of that. (*She goes quickly into the palace.*)

WATCHMAN: Now, sire, when you're comfortably settled on that couch, I have some news for you. You'll scarcely believe it. (*He squints up at the sun.*) Yes, sire, it will be a very hot day. We are in the solstice. The sailors say that the sun swings low, that He is very near us these days. That's what they say.

ADMETUS: What is your news?

WATCHMAN: A great friend, sire, is coming to see you—a very good friend.

ADMETUS: Hercules!

WATCHMAN: Yes, Hercules, son of Zeus!

ADMETUS: Today! Today of all days!

WATCHMAN: The whole town knows it. Oh, he comes slowly enough. At every village, every farm, they bring him wine; they put garlands on his head. He is very drunk. . . . Oh, King Admetus, we must prevent his embracing you. You remember his embraces. He would surely kill you today.

ADMETUS: Does the Queen know?

WATCHMAN: Oh, the maids will have told her all about it.

ADMETUS: I wish he could have come at another time.

WATCHMAN: Every time is a good time for Hercules. Your sons, sire, are beside themselves. Epimenes will ask him all over again how he killed the Nemean lion and how he cleaned the stables of King Augeas.

ADMETUS: Call Aglaia.

Enter AGLAIA *from the palace door.*

WATCHMAN: Here she is now.

AGLAIA: Yes, King Admetus?

Behind the KING'S *back, with her hand she directs the* WATCHMAN *to leave. He exits left.*

ADMETUS: Aglaia—come near to me. You have heard the news?

The WATCHMAN *as he leaves gives* AGLAIA *an anxious look and is relieved by her answer.*

AGLAIA: Yes, I have: the son of Zeus is coming to visit us.
ADMETUS: (*Without pathos.*) Aglaia, this is my last day. I know it. I feel it.
AGLAIA: Sire, how would any of us know that? You must not talk now. You must save your strength.
ADMETUS: I shall die before sundown. Now, if it is possible— and you must make it possible—my death must be hidden from Hercules, for at least a day or two. You must say that one of the servants has died. And you must go about your life as though nothing had happened. The Queen will show you the way of it. You know what Hercules's life is like— those great labors, one after another. When he comes to us as a happy visitor, we would not wish to show him a house of mourning. Especially Hercules, who is so often on the point of losing his life, and who has such an aversion to all that has to do with burial and mourning.
AGLAIA: (*Again arranging his cushions.*) King Admetus, I am not a fool. All these things I understand very well. Now lie back and shut your eyes. This sunlight is going to give you strength.
ADMETUS: If it could only give me strength for one more day—to welcome Hercules! Go and see where the Queen is.
AGLAIA: Here she is.

Exit AGLAIA *left.*
Enter ALCESTIS *from the palace door. She stands on the top step. She is wearing the dress of Act I.* ADMETUS *turns and gazes at her in silence.*

ADMETUS: Our wedding dress!
ALCESTIS: (*Smiling, puts her finger on her lips to silence him; she goes to him and says lightly:*) Most wives save it for their burial. I wear it for life.
ADMETUS: Sit here, dearest. I was just saying to Aglaia—

ALCESTIS *sits on the stool beside* ADMETUS *and rests her hand beside his.*

ALCESTIS: Yes, yes, I know—when Hercules comes . . .

ADMETUS: He will soon be here.

ALCESTIS: Oh, he is being detained on the road. Hercules goes quickly only to danger. Perhaps he will be here tonight . . . perhaps not till tomorrow. We have time. (*She rises and goes to the center of the stage and stands there listening.*) I hear shouts of joy in the valley. (*She walks slowly back to her stool and repeats:*) We have time. (*In the center of the stage, gazing at the sun as if for help.*) This is the healing sun—the sun of the summer solstice. Do you feel it?

ADMETUS: It is the healing sun, but for others. I have put all that behind me: I do not need hope. My life was short, but a single hour can hold the whole fullness of time. The fullness of time was given to me. A man who has been happy is no longer the subject of time. . . . Come, we'll say to each other what is still to be said on this last day.

ALCESTIS: (*Returning to her place beside him; with a gentle smile.*) This last day? You must rest and save your strength and breath. I shall talk. I shall talk for two—for you and for me. I do not know who gave me that second name: Alcestis the Silent. I think it was you, but also it was Hercules who carried it over Greece.

ADMETUS: Were you always silent?

ALCESTIS: I? No. As a girl—oh, I was a contentious and argumentative girl, as you know well. But there are times when I am impatient with my silence—this tiresome, silent Alcestis! There are times when I wish to be like other women, who can freely say what is in their hearts. What do other wives say? I think they must say something like this: Admetus . . . have I ever told you—let me look into your eyes again—have I ever told you that I have loved you more than life itself?

> *Leaning over him, she is suddenly stricken with great pain. She rises, whirls about, one hand to her head, the other to her left side, where his wound is.* ADMETUS *has not noticed it. He has closed his eyes again, and starts to laugh in a low, long murmur.*

ADMETUS: That does not sound . . . no, that does not sound like my silent Alcestis. And if you were to speak for me, what would you say?

ALCESTIS: (*The pain has slackened and she replies almost serenely.*) I would say that I—I, Admetus—have chosen neither the day of my birth nor the day of my death. That having been born is a gift that fell to our lot—a wonderful gift—and that Alcestis's death—or my own—comes from the same hand.

ADMETUS: (*Almost amused.*) *Your* death, Alcestis?

ALCESTIS: Were it to come from the same hand that gives life . . . Are you in pain, Admetus?

ADMETUS: (*Puts his hand to his side wonderingly.*) No. I do not know why it is, but the pain seems to have . . .

ALCESTIS: Lift your hand!

> As he slowly raises his paralyzed left hand, the pain passes into her body; she clutches her side, bending in agony.

ADMETUS: This lightness! (*He stares before him with hope.*) No, I must not think of such things. I have put that behind me. We who have known what we have known . . . are not the subjects of time.

ALCESTIS: (*The great pain has passed, but she moves guardedly; she has sat down again and speaks with her cheek pressed close to his.*) Yes, we, who were happy . . .

ADMETUS: (*Suddenly grasping her hand, ardently.*) And you hated me once!

ALCESTIS: (*Withdrawing her hand.*) No, never.

ADMETUS: That young man who kept coming back to that trial of the lion and the boar . . . There he is again—that young idiot from Thessaly.

> They are both laughing.

ALCESTIS: Oh, what a road I have come!

ADMETUS: You didn't hate me, as I came around the corner straining over those damned beasts?

ALCESTIS: No. I suffered the more for it. I had begun to love that stern-faced young man from Thessaly. You were the only suitor who attempted that trial twice. . . . Even Hercules gave up. . . . To think that I could not see where life was carrying me!

ADMETUS: (*Proudly, ardently.*) I, I saw.

ALCESTIS: Beloved Admetus . . . you saw. You married this self-willed, obstinate girl.

ADMETUS: (*More ardently.*) Our love! Our love! . . . Our whisperings in the night! . . . The birth of Epimenes, when I almost lost you . . . (*She makes gestures of trying to silence him.*) Alcestis! What we have known, what we have lived . . . Oh, to live forever—with you—beside you.

ALCESTIS: Ssh! There are things that we human beings are not permitted to say aloud.

ADMETUS: (*Tentatively putting his foot on the ground.*) I do not understand. . . . My knee does not tremble. (*With joyous hope.*) Alcestis! It may be . . . it may be I shall live.

ALCESTIS: (*Equally ecstatic, to the sky.*) Living or dead, we are watched; we are guided; we are understood. Oh, Admetus, lie quiet, lie still!

ADMETUS: I dare not . . . believe . . . hope . . .

ALCESTIS: (*The pain returns; she is starting toward the palace door.*) Admetus, I would find it a natural thing, if a message came from Delphi to me, saying that I should give my life for my children or for Thessaly or . . . for my husband—

ADMETUS: No. No. No man would wish another to die for him. Every man is ready to die his own death.

ALCESTIS: (*Mastering her suffering.*) What are you saying, Admetus? Think of all the soldiers—thousands and thousands of them—who have died for others. And we women, poor cowardly soldiers, have died—a great many of us—for our husbands and children. (*She starts stumbling toward the palace door.*)

ADMETUS: I would think less of the gods who could lay such a decision between husband and wife. . . . (*Rising; in loud amazement.*) Look! This lightness!

ALCESTIS: Aglaia! Aglaia!

ADMETUS: (*Springs up and rushes to her.*) Alcestis, you are in trouble! Aglaia! Aglaia!

AGLAIA *hurries to her from the palace door.*

ALCESTIS: Take me to my bed.

ADMETUS: You are ill. Are you ill, Alcestis?

ALCESTIS: (*Turning.*) Take my life. Be happy. Be happy.

> *She collapses in their arms and is carried into the palace.*
> *From beyond the gate come sounds of an excited crowd, frag-*
> *ments of singing, etc., and the roar of* HERCULES'S *voice.*

HERCULES: Where is my old friend Ad-meeee-tus?

TOWNSPEOPLE: Hercules is here! Hercules is here!

HERCULES: Al-cess-stis! Where is the divine Al-cess-stis? Alcestis the Silent! Admetus the Hoss-s-spitable!

> *The* WATCHMAN *enters.*

TOWNSPEOPLE: Hercules is here! Hercules!

WATCHMAN: The gods preserve us! What can be done?

> *More* TOWNSPEOPLE *pour in the gate, shouting, "Long live*
> *Hercules, son of Zeus!" Enter* HERCULES—*drunk, happy,*
> *garlanded—a jug in his hand. Two* VILLAGERS *laughingly*
> *carry* HERCULES'S *club as a great burden.*

HERCULES: Alcestis, fairest of the daughters of Iolcos! Admetus, crown of friends! Where are they?

TOWNSPEOPLE: Hercules, the destroyer of beasts! Hercules,
the friend of man! Long live Hercules!

WATCHMAN: Welcome a thousand times to Pherai, great
Hercules!

HERCULES: Where is my friend Epimenes—the mighty hunter,
the mighty fisherman? Epimenes, I shall wrestle with you.
By the God's thunder, you shall not throw me again!

WATCHMAN: All of them will be here in a minute, Hercules.
They are beside themselves with joy.

> *A wailing, a keening, is heard in the palace.*

HERCULES: That's weeping I hear. What is that wailing, old
man?

WATCHMAN: Wailing, Hercules! The women and girls are re-
joicing that Hercules has come.

> *Enter* AGLAIA *in haste from the palace.*

AGLAIA: A thousand times welcome, divine Hercules. The
King and Queen will be here in a moment. Happy, happy

they are—you can be sure of that. Oh, son of Zeus, what a joy to see you!

HERCULES: (*Loudly.*) I'm not the son of Zeus!

AGLAIA: (*Covering her ears.*) Hercules, what are you saying?

HERCULES: I'm the son of Amphytrion and Alcmene. I'm a common man, Aglaia; and the work I do is as hard for me as for any other.

AGLAIA: Oh, may the gods prevent misfortune from coming to this house! You're very drunk, Hercules, to say such a wicked thing as that.

HERCULES: I'm a man, just an ordinary man, I tell you.

AGLAIA: God or man, Hercules, what do I see? Hercules, you are filthy! Is this the handsomest man in all Greece? By the immortal gods, I would never have known you! Now listen: you remember the baths that Aglaia prepares? They'd take the skin off an ordinary man. And the oil I have ready for you—you remember the oil, don't you?

HERCULES: (*Confidentially.*) First, Aglaia—first! (*He makes a gesture of drinking.*)

AGLAIA: You haven't forgotten our wine, is that it? You shall have some immediately!

HERCULES: (*Suddenly roaring.*) On the road they told me that Admetus had been stabbed and wounded. Who struck him, Aglaia?

AGLAIA: Oh, that's all forgotten, Hercules. He's as well now as you or I!

> RHODOPE *and another* GIRL *come from the palace bearing a wine jar and some cups.*

Come, sit here and refresh yourself.

> HERCULES *tries to catch one of the girls, who eludes him. He then starts in pursuit of the other. He catches her.*

HERCULES: What's your name, little pigeon?

AGLAIA: (*Angrily.*) Hercules!

> *The* GIRL *escapes.* HERCULES *runs after her, stumbles, and falls flat on the ground.*

HERCULES: Oh! I've hurt myself! Hell and confusion! My knee! My knee!

AGLAIA: Hercules! I haven't one bit of pity for you. Can you have forgotten where you are? Immortal heavens, what would Queen Alcestis think—you behaving like that!

HERCULES: (*Who has slowly got up and sat down.*) Twenty days I've walked. Where are they? Where are my friends, Admetus and Alcestis?

AGLAIA: (*Confidentially.*) Now, Hercules, you're an old friend of the house, aren't you?

HERCULES: I am!

AGLAIA: We can talk quite plainly to you, can't we? You're not one of those guests we have to conceal things from, thank the gods!

HERCULES: I'm their brother! Their brother!

AGLAIA: Now listen: one of the women in the house, an orphan . . . one of the women in the house . . .

HERCULES: What? Dead?

AGLAIA: (*Finger on lips.*) And you know how loyal and kind King Admetus and Queen Alcestis are to all of us who serve here. . . .

HERCULES: Dead? An orphan?

AGLAIA: Yes, she'd lost both her father and mother. Now, they'll be here in just a minute—after you've had your bath. But now, just now—you know: they are by that poor girl, in friendship and piety. You understand everything, Hercules?

HERCULES: No. No, Aglaia, there are too many things I do not understand. But do you know who understands them all? (*Pause.*) Alcestis. Am I not right, Aglaia?

AGLAIA: Yes. Yes, Hercules.

HERCULES: Now I am going to talk frankly to you, Aglaia: I have come here—I have walked twenty days—to ask Alcestis one question.

AGLAIA: A question, Hercules?

For answer, HERCULES *twice points quickly and emphatically toward the zenith.*

About the gods?

He nods. AGLAIA *recovers herself and says briskly:*

Well, first you must have that bath. You will come out of it looking like a boy of seventeen. And I have such a garland for you. And such perfumes!

He rises and starts to follow her to the palace steps.

HERCULES: And while I'm taking the bath you will sit beside me and tell me again how Apollo came to Thessaly?

AGLAIA: Yes, I will. I'll tell you once more.

HERCULES: (*Stopping her; with urgency.*) And no one knew which was Apollo?

She shakes her head.

A whole year, and no one knew which was Apollo—not even Alcestis?

Again she shakes her head. HERCULES *clutches his forehead.*

Aglaia, who can understand them? We shall never understand them. When I try to think of them, I start trembling; I get dizzy.

AGLAIA: Hercules! You are tired. Come. . . .

Enter ADMETUS. *He stands at the top of the stairs as* HERCULES *and* AGLAIA *reach the bottom step.*

ADMETUS: (*Loudly.*) Welcome, Hercules, friend of all men; Hercules, benefactor of all men!

HERCULES: Admetus! Old friend!

ADMETUS *puts his hands on* HERCULES'S *shoulders. They gaze into one another's eyes.*

ADMETUS: From where have you come, Hercules?

HERCULES: From labors, Admetus . . . from labors.

AGLAIA: King Admetus, Hercules's bath is ready. You can begin talking when he comes out. (*Looking up.*) It will be evening soon.

ADMETUS: No, first we will drink a bowl of wine together! Come, sit down, Hercules. For a short time I was ill, and this foolish womanish couch is where I used to sit in the sun. Now tell me—what has been your latest great labor?

AGLAIA *and the* GIRLS *have gone into the palace.*

HERCULES: (*Hushed, wide-eyed.*) Admetus, Admetus—I killed the Hydra.

ADMETUS: (*Rising, in awed astonishment.*) Great-hearted Hercules! You slew the Hydra! By the immortal gods, Hercules, you are the friend of man. Slew the Hydra! The Hydra!

HERCULES: (*Beckoning to* ADMETUS *to draw his face nearer for a confidence.*) Admetus— (*Again beckoning.*) It wasn't easy!

ADMETUS: I can well believe it!

HERCULES: (*Almost bitterly; gazing into his face.*) It was not easy. (*Abrupt change to urgent earnestness.*) Admetus, am I the son of Zeus?

ADMETUS: Hercules! Everyone knows that you are the son of Zeus and Alcmene.

HERCULES: One person can tell me. That is what I have come to ask Alcestis. Where is Alcestis, queen of women?

ADMETUS: But Aglaia told you!

HERCULES: Oh, yes. Who is this orphan girl that has died? Was she one of the first in the house?

ADMETUS: She called herself the servant of the servants.

HERCULES: But you were all fond of her?

ADMETUS: Yes. We all loved her.

HERCULES: You see, Admetus, everyone says I am the son of Zeus and therefore my labors must be easier for me than for another man. If I have the blood and the heart and the lungs of Him (*Pointing upward.*) in me, shouldn't they be easy? But, Admetus, they are not easy. The Hydra! (*He wraps his arms around Admetus in imitation of a snake and sets his face in extreme horror.*) I was about to burst. The blood sprang out of my ears like fountains. If I am only a man—the son of Amphytrion and Alcmene—then, Admetus, (*Peering into* ADMETUS'S *face with strained urgency.*) then I'm a very good man!

ADMETUS: God or man, Hercules—god or man, all men honor and are grateful to you.

HERCULES: But I want to know. Some days I feel that I am the son of Zeus. Other days I am . . . I am a beast, Admetus, a beast and a brute. Every month messengers arrive from all over Greece, asking me to come and do this and do that. I'll do no more; I won't do a single thing until I've settled this matter. One of these days—yes, I foresee it—someone will come to me and ask me to . . . descend into the under-world . . . into Hell, Admetus, and bring back someone who has died. (*Rising, in terrified repudiation.*) No! No! *That* I will not do. God or man, *no one* may ask that of me!

ADMETUS: (*Sincerely shocked.*) No, Hercules—that has never been done, nor even thought of.

HERCULES: Every time I come here I look at that—that entrance to Hell—with great fear, Admetus.

ADMETUS: You must not think such thoughts!

HERCULES: Even a son of Zeus couldn't do that, could he? So—so do you see the question? Isn't that an important question? And who can answer it? Who is wisest in just these matters where you and I are most ignorant? You know who: she who never speaks, or speaks so little. The Silent. She is silent, isn't she?

ADMETUS: Yes, she is silent.

HERCULES: But she'll speak to me . . . to her old friend Hercules? She'll speak for me, won't she? (*He pours himself more wine.*) Do you know, Admetus—do you know what your Alcestis is?

> ADMETUS, *in pain, rises, and sits down.*

No, you don't know. I journey from place to place—from court to court. I've seen them all—the queens and princesses of Greece. The daughters of the men we knew and the girls we courted are growing up. Oedipus of Thebes has a daughter, Antigone; and there is Penelope, who's just married the son of Laertes of Ithaca. Leda of Sparta has two daughters, Helen and Clytemnestra. I've seen 'em all, talked to 'em all. What are they beside Alcestis? Dirt. Trash.

> AGLAIA *comes from the palace bearing a garland of vine leaves. The* WATCHMAN *follows with a jar of oil. They stand listening.*
> HERCULES *rises and, in drunken energy close to violence, turns* ADMETUS *about, shouting.*

Do you know? Do you know to the full?

ADMETUS: (*In agony, raising his arms.*) I know, Hercules.

HERCULES: Do you know all—her power to forgive, to pardon? No, you don't know a thing. Alcestis is the crown of Greece. The crown of women.

ADMETUS: (*Taking three steps backward.*) Hercules! Alcestis is dead. (*Pause.*) The servant of servants. Forgive us, Hercules!

HERCULES: (*Silence. A great rage rises in him. Then with savage bitterness.*) Admetus . . . you are no friend. By the immortal gods, you are my worst enemy!

> *He grasps him by the throat and, walking backward, drags the unresisting* ADMETUS *with him.*

If you were not Admetus, I would kill you now!

AGLAIA and WATCHMAN: Hercules! Hercules, Queen Alcestis wished it! She wanted us not to tell you until later.

HERCULES: You have treated me as no friend. I thought I was your brother.

AGLAIA: (*Pounding with her fists on his back.*) Hercules! Hercules!

HERCULES: Alcestis dead—and I was not worthy to be told! You let me boast and drink and revel . . .

AGLAIA: It was her wish, Hercules. Alcestis commanded it.

HERCULES: (*Broodingly, holding* ADMETUS *bent far backward before him.*) You think I have no mind or heart or soul. What do I care for the thanks and praise of the world if I am not fit to share the grief of my friends?

> *Pause.*

AGLAIA: It was for hospitality, Hercules. She wished it!

HERCULES: Hospitality is for guests, not brothers.

ADMETUS: (*Quietly.*) Forgive us, Hercules.

HERCULES: (*Releasing* ADMETUS.) Alcestis is dead. Alcestis is in the underworld. (*Suddenly struck by an idea; loudly.*) In Hell! Where is my club? My club! I shall go and get her!

AGLAIA: Hercules!

ADMETUS: No, Hercules. Live! She died in my place. She died for me. It is not right that still another die.

HERCULES: My club! My club! Admetus, now I shall tell you something—something that no man knows. Now all the world may know it. (*He has advanced to the top of the path.*) I once came near to Alcestis in violence, in brutish violence. Yes, I, Hercules, son of Zeus, did that! A god—some god—intervened in time, to save her and to save me. Alcestis forgave me. How can that be? How can any man understand that? She spoke of it to no one in the world. And when I came to Pherai there was no sign in her face, in her eyes, that I had been the criminal. Only a god can understand that—only that loving smile. Forgiveness is not within our power—we commoner men. Only the strong and pure can forgive. I never wanted that she should forget that evil moment—no!—for in her remembering it lay my happiness; for her remembering and her forgiving were one.

ADMETUS: Hercules, I shall come with you.

HERCULES: Stay and rule, Admetus. Your labors I cannot do; you cannot do mine. What god shall I call on? Not my father—father and no father. Who is the god you mainly worship here?

AGLAIA: Have you forgotten, Hercules? This is Apollo's land.

HERCULES: Yes, now I remember. I have had little to do with Him, but . . . (*Looking to heaven.*) Apollo, I am Hercules, called the son of Zeus and Alcmene. All Greece says that you have loved these two—Admetus and Alcestis. You know what I'm about to do. You know I can't do it by myself. Put into my arm a strength that's never been there before. You do this—or let's say, you and I do this together. And if we can do it, let everybody see that a new knowledge has been given to us of what gods and men can do together.

ADMETUS: One moment, Hercules. (*He goes down the path.*) Pytho! Pytho! This is Hercules, the loved friend of Alcestis and of me and of Epimenes. Let him pass, Pytho—going and coming.

HERCULES: Go into the palace, Admetus—all of you. I must work as I must live—alone.

> It is dark. The characters on the stage withdraw, except for ADMETUS, who stands by the palace door, covering his face with his cloak. A low beating on tympani, like distant thunder, grows louder, strikes a sharp blow, and jumps up a fourth. HERCULES has disappeared into the door of the cave. Presently he returns, leading ALCESTIS. Over her white dress and head she wears a dark veil, which trails many yards behind her. As they reach the stage, HERCULES releases her

hand. She sways, with groping steps, as though drugged with sleep. HERCULES *shoulders his club and goes off in his solitary way.* ADMETUS, *holding his cloak before him, as before a strong light, approaches, enfolds her. She rests her head on his breast. He leads her into the palace.*

Act III

Twelve years later. Again, first streaks of dawn.
Enter left, ALCESTIS—*old, broken, in rags. She is carrying a water jar. She descends to the spring to fill it.*
Noise of a crowd on the road.

TOWNSPEOPLE: (*Outside the palace gates.*) King Agis, help us! Save us! . . . King Agis must help us. . . . We want to talk to King Agis!

> *Enter hurriedly, in horrified protest, a new and younger* NIGHT WATCHMAN. *He also carries a lighted lantern and a rattle. His face is smeared with ashes. He opens the gate a crack and speaks through it.*

WATCHMAN: You know the order: anyone who puts foot in these gates will be killed.

TOWNSPEOPLE: (*Pressing in and overrunning the* WATCHMAN.) Let him kill us! We're dying already! . . . The King must do something.

WATCHMAN: (*Looking over his shoulder toward the palace, in terror.*) The King's doing everything he can. Pestilences and plagues come from the gods, he says, and only the gods can stop them. Bury your dead, he says, bury them the moment they fall. And smear your faces with ashes; rub your whole body with ashes and cinders. That way the plague can't see you, he says, and it will pass you by.

TOWNSPEOPLE: We've heard all that before. We want to see Queen Alcestis. Queen Alcestis! She can help us. Queen Alcestis!

WATCHMAN: (*Indignantly.*) What do you mean—Queen Alcestis? There's no Queen Alcestis here. She's a slave, and the lowest of the slaves!

> ALCESTIS *has come up the path, her jar on her shoulder. She stands and listens. The* WATCHMAN *sees her.*

There she is! (*Violently.*) Look at her! *She* brought the plague.

She *is* the plague. It's she that's brought the curse on Thessaly!

TOWNSPEOPLE: (*After a shocked silence, an outburst of contradictory cries.*) No, never! Not Queen Alcestis! What did he say? How did she bring it?

ALCESTIS: (*Her head turning slowly as she looks into their faces; barely a question.*) I—brought the plague? I brought the plague?

WATCHMAN: She was dead, wasn't she? And Hercules brought her back from death, didn't he? She brought back death with her. Everybody belonging to her is dead. Her husband killed. Two of her children killed. One of her sons got away —but who's heard of him for a dozen years? The King will have her killed or driven from the country.

ALCESTIS: No, I did not bring this disease to Thessaly. Take me to these judges. If it is I who have brought misfortune to Thessaly, let them take my life and remove the disease from you and your children.

> ALCESTIS *moves off to the left, into the servants' quarters. Light slowly comes up on* APOLLO, *standing on the roof.*

TOWNSPEOPLE: No! She could not have brought evil to Thessaly! That is Alcestis the Wise!

WATCHMAN: (*Amid contradictory cries from the* CROWD.) Go to your homes! You'll all be killed here. (*To those in front.*) What do you know about it? Ignorant boors! Away, all of you! I've warned you. You know what kind of man King Agis is.

> TOWNSPEOPLE *disappear, murmuring and grumbling, through the palace gate. The* WATCHMAN *goes off left, shaking his rattle. As he goes:*

Dawn . . . dawn . . . and all is well in the palace of Agis, King of Thessaly, rich in horses. . . .

> DEATH *comes out of the cave, ascends the path, and sniffs at the doors.*

APOLLO: Death!

DEATH: (*Who hasn't noticed Him; taken unawares.*) Ah, you're here again!

APOLLO: It is getting light. You are shuddering.

DEATH: Yes. Yes, but I have some questions to ask you. Lord Apollo, I can't understand what you mean by this. So many dead! Down where I live there's such a crowding and trampling and waiting in line! And never have I seen so many children! But I confess to you, Lord Apollo, I don't know what you mean by it: you are the God of healing—of life and of healing—and here you are, the sender of plagues and pestilence. You loved Admetus, and his family, and his people; and all you do is kill them.

APOLLO: (*A smile.*) I loved Alcestis, and I killed her—once.

DEATH: Contemptible, what you did!

APOLLO: Have you mended the wall—that wall through which Hercules broke?

DEATH: Broke? Hercules? *You* broke it. You broke the ancient law and order of the world: that the living are the living and the dead are the dead.

APOLLO: Yes—one small ray of light fell where light had never fallen before.

DEATH: You broke that law, and now you're caught up in its consequences. You're losing your happiness and your very wits because you can't make yourself known to them. And you're behaving like the rejected lover who dashes into the beloved's house and kills everyone there.

APOLLO: I *have* made myself known to them. I have set my story in motion.

DEATH: Your lesson.

APOLLO: Yes, my lesson—that I can bring back from the dead only those who have offered their lives for others.

DEATH: You brought back *one*, and now you are hurling thousands and thousands into my kingdom.

APOLLO: Yes, I must bring ruin and havoc, for only so will they remember the story. In the stories that are longest remembered, death plays a large role.

DEATH: (*Shuddering.*) This light! This light! All these plague-stricken do not interest me. There is one mortal here that I am waiting for . . . she who escaped me once.

APOLLO: Alcestis? You will never have her.

DEATH: She is mortal!

APOLLO: Yes.

DEATH: She is *mortal*!

APOLLO: All mortal. Nothing but mortal.

DEATH: What are you going to do? You cannot steal her a second time?

APOLLO: Death, the sun is risen. You are shaking.

DEATH: Yes, but give me an answer. I am in a hurry.

APOLLO: Start accustoming yourself to a change.

DEATH: I?

APOLLO: One ray of light has already reached your kingdom.

DEATH: (*In headlong flight to his cave, shrieking.*) There'll be no more. No second one. No more light. No more. No change!

> *Exit. The light fades from* APOLLO, *who disappears. Enter from the road—through the palace gate, left open—* EPIMENES, *21, and* CHERIANDER, *also 21. They are holding their cloaks about their noses. Under their cloaks they wear short swords.* CHERIANDER *comes forward eagerly and looks about him with awe.* EPIMENES *follows him, morose and bitter.*

CHERIANDER: The palace of Admetus and Alcestis! . . . And was Apollo here? Where did He place His feet—here, or here?

> EPIMENES *nods, scarcely raising his eyes from the ground.*

And Hercules brought your mother back from the dead . . . where?

> EPIMENES *indicates the cave.* CHERIANDER *goes quickly down to it.*

That I have lived to see this place! Look, Epimenes! There is your old friend Pytho guarding the door. Speak to him so that we can drink at the spring. This water, at least, is not poisoned.

EPIMENES: You remember me, Pytho? He scarcely stirs.

CHERIANDER: Make the offering, and let us drink.

EPIMENES: "Sources of life—earth, air . . ." No, Cheriander, I cannot. How can I say the prayer we said here so many hundred times? In the morning my father and mother would bring us here. How could all this have happened? The God turned his face away. My father killed. My brother and sister killed. Myself sent away by night to live among strangers. My mother a slave—or dead. And the land under pestilence and the dead bodies lying unburied under the sun. To whom do I make a prayer?

CHERIANDER: (*With quiet resolution.*) We are leaving Pherai. We are going out of that gate now. You are not ready to do what we came to do, and I will not help you.

EPIMENES: I can do what I have to do without prayer or offering. Justice and revenge speak for themselves. To strike! To strike into his throat. Yes, and to strike his daughter, Laodamia, too.

CHERIANDER: Epimenes, I will not help you. This is not the way we planned it. Kill or be killed, as you wish. I have not crossed Greece with you to take part in a mere butchery.

EPIMENES: You want me to make a prayer? To whom? To Apollo, who has blasted this house with His hatred?

CHERIANDER: (*He descends, and putting his hands on* EPIMENES'S *shoulders, shakes him in solemn anger.*) Are you the first man to have suffered? Cruelty, injustice, murder, and humiliation—is it only here that those things can be found? Have you forgotten that we came here to establish justice? That you yourself said that men of themselves could never have arrived at justice—that it was planted in their minds by the gods?

They gaze sternly at one another.

EPIMENES: (*Quietly, looking down.*) I do not deserve to have such a friend.

Enter ALCESTIS, *left, carrying the water jar on her shoulder.*

CHERIANDER: Are you ready to make the offering?

EPIMENES recites the ritual, solemnly, but all but inaudibly. They both drink. CHERIANDER *starts up the path, vigorously.*

I am ready to knock at the palace doors.

He sees ALCESTIS. *He hurries back to the spring, and says to* EPIMENES:

There is an old woman here. We will see what we can learn from her.

ALCESTIS has taken a few steps down the path, but seeing the men, draws back. CHERIANDER comes up the path to her.

Old woman, is this the palace of Agis, King of Thessaly?

Her eyes go at once to the gate. CHERIANDER returns to EPIMENES.

She seems to be a slave. Perhaps it is your mother.

EPIMENES: (*Goes quickly up the path, looks closely at ALCESTIS, then says brusquely:*) No.

CHERIANDER: You are sure?

EPIMENES: (*Shortly.*) Sure. Certain.

CHERIANDER: Tell me, old woman, has this pestilence taken lives in the palace?

She shakes her head.

King Agis lives here with his family—with a young daughter, Laodamia?

She nods.

Tell me: the guards he has about him—did he bring them from Thrace, or are they of this country?

No answer.

EPIMENES: Perhaps she is deaf, or dumb. (*Louder.*) Does he often make journeys back to his own country—to Thrace?

ALCESTIS: You are in danger here. You must go—you must go at once.

EPIMENES: Oh, she can speak. Tell me, old mother, were you here in the days of King Admetus and Queen Alcestis?

ALCESTIS: Who are you? From where have you come?

EPIMENES: Did you know them? Had you talked with them?

She nods.

King Admetus is dead?

She nods.

Is Queen Alcestis alive?

No sign.

Here in the palace?

Her eyes return again to the gate. He adds impatiently:

By the immortal gods, since you can speak, speak!

ALCESTIS: You must go at once. But tell me . . . tell me: who are you?

CHERIANDER: (*Staring at* ALCESTIS, *but urgently striking* EPIMENES'S *forearm.*) Look again. Look closely. Are you sure?

EPIMENES: Sure! These mountain women are all the same. They all have this silence, this slyness.

ALCESTIS: How did you come in at that gate? King Agis will certainly have you killed.

CHERIANDER: No. We bring a message to King Agis that he will be glad to hear.

ALCESTIS: (*Repeatedly shaking her head.*) There is no message now that will save your lives, young man. Go. Take the road to the north and go quickly.

EPIMENES: The message we bring will make us very welcome. We have come to tell him of the death of an enemy—of his greatest enemy.

CHERIANDER: There is no need to tell it now.

EPIMENES: Whom he lives in dread of.

Shaking her head, ALCESTIS *passes him and starts down the path.*

We come to tell him of the death of Epimenes, the son of King Admetus and Queen Alcestis. He will be glad enough to hear of that.

ALCESTIS *is near the spring. She stops, lifts her head, and puts her hand to her heart, letting her jar slip.*

CHERIANDER: (*Going to her and taking her jar.*) Let me carry your jar, old woman.

ALCESTIS: (*Suddenly.*) You are Epimenes!

CHERIANDER: (*Short laugh.*) No, old woman. Epimenes is dead.

ALCESTIS: You have proof of this?

CHERIANDER: Yes, proof. (*He has filled the jar and is starting up the path.*)

ALCESTIS: We have always thought that he would return . . . in secret, or disguise. My eyes are failing. (*Eagerly.*) You are Epimenes!

CHERIANDER: No, mother, no.

ALCESTIS: You knew him—you talked with him?

CHERIANDER: Yes, many times. Where can I carry this for you?

ALCESTIS: (*At the top of the path, peers into* EPIMENES'S *face.*) Let me look at you. (*Then gazing into* CHERIANDER'S *face.*) Do not tell lies to an old woman. He sent no message?

EPIMENES: None.

ALCESTIS: None?

EPIMENES: None but this. Can you see this belt? Queen Alcestis wove this for King Admetus before Epimenes was born.

ALCESTIS: (*Peers at it, and gives a cry.*) What manner of young man was he who gave you this belt?

EPIMENES: (*Mastering his impatience; as to a deaf person.*) Old woman, is Queen Alcestis near? Make some answer: yes or no. This is unendurable. Can you call Queen Alcestis, or can't you?

ALCESTIS: I am Alcestis.

CHERIANDER: (*After amazed silence, falls on one knee; gazing into her face.*) You . . . you are Alcestis?

EPIMENES: (*Standing rigid, one fist on his forehead.*) I am ashamed to say my name. (*He also sinks to one knee.*) I am Epimenes.

ALCESTIS: Yes—yes. (*Her eyes turning from palace to road.*) But in this danger . . . this danger . . .

EPIMENES: Forgive . . . me.

ALCESTIS: (*Touching his head.*) You are an impatient self-willed young man, as I was an impatient, self-willed girl. It is time you were more like your father.

EPIMENES: You unhappy—

ALCESTIS: (*Almost sharply.*) No. No, Epimenes. Do not call me unhappy.

EPIMENES: This misery . . .

ALCESTIS: No! Learn to know unhappiness when you see it. There is only one misery, and that is ignorance—ignorance of what our lives are. That is misery and despair.

CHERIANDER: (*Rising, intent.*) Ignorance?

ALCESTIS: Great happiness was given to me once, yes . . . but shall I forget that now? And forget the one who gave it to me? All that has happened since came from the same hands that gave me the happiness. I shall not doubt that it is good and has a part in something I cannot see. . . . You must go now.

EPIMENES: (*Rising.*) We have come to kill King Agis and to regain the throne.

> ALCESTIS *starts turning her face from side to side and murmuring, "No. No."*

Our plans have been made in detail. This very night—

ALCESTIS: No. No, Epimenes. The plague, the pestilence, has taken the place of all that. King Agis has only one thought, and one fear—not for himself, but for his child, Laodamia. The God is bringing things to pass in His own way.

CHERIANDER: We will do what she says, Epimenes, and go now.

ALCESTIS: Come back . . . in ten days. Go north. Hold your cloaks before your faces and go north.

CHERIANDER: Get your cloak, Epimenes.

> EPIMENES *descends to the spring.*

ALCESTIS: Where is your home, young man?

CHERIANDER: In Euboea—under Mount Dirphys.

ALCESTIS: Is your mother living?

CHERIANDER: Yes, Queen Alcestis.

ALCESTIS: Does she know my name?

CHERIANDER: Every child in Greece knows your name!

ALCESTIS: Tell her . . . Alcestis thanks her.

> EPIMENES *is beside her; she touches him lightly.*

Remember—I have not been unhappy. I was once miserable and in despair: I was saved from that. (*Pointing.*) Go through that grove . . . and follow the river.

> *Sounds of* TOWNSPEOPLE *approaching. More breaking of gates. They come on to the edge of the stage, shouting. The* WATCHMAN *and* GUARDS *come out of the palace in alarm.*

ALCESTIS *beckons to the young men to descend and hide themselves by the spring. The* GUARDS *keep the people back by holding their spears horizontally before them.*

TOWNSPEOPLE: Water! We want water from the palace spring! The water's been poisoned. King Agis, help us!

GUARDS: Back! Back and out—all of you!

Enter from the palace KING AGIS. *He is dressed in a barbaric, ornate costume. He is 40; a thick cap of black hair over a low forehead. His face is also streaked with ashes.*

AGIS: How did these people get into the court?

TOWNSPEOPLE: King Agis, help us!

AGIS: This eternal "Help us!" I'm doing what I can. Which one of you let these people in?

GUARDS: (*In confusion.*) Sire—they've broken the gates. We can't hold them.

AGIS: Cowards! Do your duty. You're afraid to go near them, that's the trouble. (*To the* TOWNSPEOPLE.) Stand back! (*To a* GUARD.) What is that they were saying about water?

FIRST GUARD: They say, Your Greatness, they think that the springs in the town have been poisoned, and they want some water from the springs in the palace.

AGIS: Very well, you shall have water from these springs. (*Holding a corner of his robe before his nose, he points to a man who has crawled far forward on his knees.*) Get back, you! People of Pherai, I have news for you. I thought I had done all a king could do; and now I find there is one more thing to be done. Where's this Alcestis?

WATCHMAN: She is here, Your Greatness.

AGIS: (*Turns and looks at her in long, slow contempt, and says slowly:*) So . . . you . . . are . . . the bringer of all this evil! This is a great day, people of Pherai, for at last we have come to the heart of this matter. If it can be shown that this woman has brought this disease upon us, she will be stoned to death or driven from the country. (*To* ALCESTIS.) Woman, is it true that you were dead—dead and buried—and that you were brought back to life?

ALCESTIS: It is true.

AGIS: And that you and your husband believed that this was

done by Hercules, with the aid of Apollo, and as a sign of Apollo's favor?

ALCESTIS: We believed it, and it is true.

AGIS: And is it true that you and your husband believed that Apollo was here for a year's time, out of love and favor for you and Thessaly?

ALCESTIS: We believed it, and it is true.

AGIS: And where is that love now? People of Pherai, this is Apollo's land. If Apollo formerly extended favor to this woman and to her family, is it not clear to you now that His favor has turned to hatred?

The crowd is silent.

Yes or no?

Contradictory murmurs.

What? You are of mixed mind? You dolts! Have you forgotten that this plague is raging among you? Watchman!

WATCHMAN: Yes, sire?

AGIS: Before the gates of the palace were closed, did you see the effects of the disease, and how it struck?

WATCHMAN: Yes, sire, I saw it.

AGIS: Describe it!

WATCHMAN: Your Greatness, it is not just one—there are three diseases. The first comes suddenly, like—

A GUARD *has come from the palace, and presents himself before* KING AGIS.

AGIS: (*Irritably.*) Well, what is it? What is it?

SECOND GUARD: Sire, your daughter is beating on her door. She says she wishes to be let out. She says she wishes to be where you are. Without stopping she is beating on her door.

AGIS: (*With a reflection of his tenderness for her; urgently.*) Tell her that I shall be with her soon; that I have work to do here. Tell her to be patient; tell her that I shall come to her soon.

SECOND GUARD: Yes, sire. (*He starts toward the palace door.*)

AGIS: Wait! (*Torn.*) Tell her to be patient. I shall take her from her room for a walk in the garden later.

SECOND GUARD: Yes, sire.

Exit.

AGIS: (*To the* WATCHMAN.) Three? Three diseases, you say?

WATCHMAN: The first one strikes suddenly, Your Greatness, like lightning.

AGIS: (*With a shudder; turning to* ALCESTIS.) *Your* work, old woman!

ALCESTIS: No! No!

WATCHMAN: (*His hands on his stomach.*) Like fire. That's the one that strikes young people and children.

AGIS: (*Beside himself.*) Children! Idiot! Don't you know better than to say words of ill omen here? I'll have your tongue torn out. Avert, you immortal gods, avert the omen! Hear not the omen! (*To the* WATCHMAN.) I want no more of this. (*Turning to the palace in despairing frustration.*) Oh, go away—all of you! Who shall save us from this night . . . this swamp . . . this evil cloud? (*He turns his head from side to side in helplessness and revulsion; then suddenly pulls himself together; resolutely, pointing at* ALCESTIS.) Speak then! Apollo the God hates you, and through you has brought this curse upon Thessaly.

    ALCESTIS *in silence, looks at him with a level gaze.*

Is that not so? Speak!

ALCESTIS: (*Taking her time.*) When Apollo came to this city, King Agis, his priest Teiresias said that that great honor brought with it a great peril.

AGIS: Peril?

ALCESTIS: You stand in that peril now. This floor is still warm—is hot—from the footprints of the God. . . . (*As though to herself, almost dreamily.*) For a long time I did not understand this. It is solitude—and slavery—that have made it clear to me. Beware what you do here, King Agis.

AGIS: (*Throws up his chin, curtly dismissing this warning.*) Answer my question.

ALCESTIS: The gods are not like you and me, King Agis—but at times we are like them. They do not love us for a day or a year and then hate what they have loved. Nor do you love your child Laodamia today and tomorrow drive her out upon the road.

AGIS: (*Outraged.*) Do not name her, you . . . you bringer of death and destruction! (*He starts toward the palace door.*)

ALCESTIS: We ask of them health . . . and riches . . . and our happiness. But they are trying to give us something else, and better: understanding. And we are so quick to refuse their gift. . . . No! No! Apollo has not turned His face away from me. . . . People of Pherai, had you ever been told that King Admetus was unjust to you?

TOWNSPEOPLE: No, Queen Alcestis.

ALCESTIS: Or I?

TOWNSPEOPLE: No-o-o-o, Queen Alcestis!

ALCESTIS: Do you believe that this disease has been sent to punish you for any wickedness of ours?

TOWNSPEOPLE: No! No!

ALCESTIS: If Hercules brought someone back from the dead, do you think he could have done it without the full approval of the gods?

TOWNSPEOPLE: No! No!

AGIS: Then what is the cause of this pestilence?

ALCESTIS: It has been sent . . . to call our attention to . . . to make us stop, to open our eyes . . .

AGIS: To call our attention to what, Alcestis?

ALCESTIS: (*Lifted head, as though listening.*) I don't know. To some sign.

> *There is a moment of suspended waiting. Then suddenly the* FIRST GUARD, *at the head of the path, sees the two* YOUNG MEN *and cries:*

FIRST GUARD: Sire, there are two strangers here.

AGIS: (*Coming forward as near as he dares.*) How did they come here? Guards! Close in on them!

> GUARDS *gather above and in front of them.*

Throw down your swords!

EPIMENES: Never, King Agis!

AGIS: What can you do—caught in that hole there? Throw down your swords!

> ALCESTIS *has been shaking her head from side to side, and murmuring, "King Agis, King Agis . . ."*

To ALCESTIS.

You brought them in. Neither you nor they have put ashes on your faces. (*To the* GUARDS.) Kill them! Kill them!

Two GUARDS *start gingerly down the path.*

Cowards! Traitors! Do what I command!

Suddenly a THIRD GUARD *on the stage is stricken with the plague. He throws down his spear and cries:*

THIRD GUARD: King Agis! Water! The plague! I'm on fire. Save me! Help me! I'm on fire! (*Intermittently he yawns.*)

AGIS: (*Recoiling, as all recoil.*) Drive him out! Strike his back with your spears.

THIRD GUARD: (*Alternately lurching from side to side, and yawning, and crying out.*) Water! Water! Sleeeeep!

AGIS: (*Holding his hands before his face.*) Push him out into the road.

General tumult. The THIRD GUARD *tries to drag himself to the gate. Other* GUARDS *and* TOWNSPEOPLE, *averting their faces, try, with spears, with kicks, to hurry his departure. In these horrors, the* GUARDS *have removed their attention from* EPIMENES *and* CHERIANDER. *For a second all that can be heard is exhausted panting.*

AGIS: (*Screaming.*) My wagons! My horses! . . . To Thrace! To Thrace! (*To* ALCESTIS.) Take back your Thessaly the Hospitable, Queen Alcestis! Rule over your dead and dying. . . .

EPIMENES: Now, Cheriander!

They rush upon the stage.

CHERIANDER: Strike, Epimenes!

EPIMENES: Agis—I am Epimenes, son of King Admetus!

AGIS: Who? What is this? Guards!

ALCESTIS, *shaking her head, stands in front of* KING AGIS, *and with raised hands opposes* EPIMENES.

ALCESTIS: No, Epimenes! No!

EPIMENES: (*Outraged by* ALCESTIS'S *attitude.*) Mother! The moment has come. He killed my father!

ALCESTIS: Don't do it!

AGIS: Guards! (*Taking distraught steps, right and left.*) Coward! Guards!

CHERIANDER: Listen to your mother, Epimenes.

ALCESTIS: (*Her back to* AGIS, *but talking to him.*) Yes, King Agis, go back to your own kingdom.

AGIS: Is that your son? Alcestis, answer me: is this your son?

> *In rage and frustration at seeing his revenge frustrated,* EPIMENES *is on one knee, beating the floor with the hilt of his own sword.*

EPIMENES: Revenge! Revenge!

ALCESTIS: Epimenes, remember your father's words: that the murderer cuts the sinews of his own heart.

EPIMENES: (*Sobbing, his forehead near the ground.*) He killed my father . . . my brother . . . my sister . . .

> *The* SECOND GUARD *rushes from the palace.*

SECOND GUARD: King Agis! Your daughter, the Princess Laodamia! She is beating on her door and calling for you—in pain, King Agis, in pain!

AGIS: (*Arms upraised.*) The gods avert! Laodamia! Laodamia! Avert, you immortal gods!

> AGIS *rushes into the palace.*

ALCESTIS: (*Standing over* EPIMENES *and placing her hand on his shoulder.*) A man who has known the joys of revenge may never know any other joy. That is the voice of your father. (*She turns to the* TOWNSPEOPLE *and says calmly and impartially:*) Friends, go to your homes and get baskets and jars. Go to the quarries beyond the South Gate, where sulfur is. Epimenes, you remember the quarries where you played as a child? That yellow sulfur that the workers in iron used . . . Burn it in the streets. Spread it on the dead. (*To the* GUARDS.) Help them in this work; there is nothing more for you to do here. Epimenes, stand—stand up. Direct them in this.

EPIMENES: (*Getting up.*) Yes, Mother. (*With quiet authority; to* GUARDS *and* TOWNSPEOPLE.) Come with me.

They start off, but CHERIANDER *returns and adds softly, in awe:*

CHERIANDER: Queen Alcestis . . . the sign you spoke of— from Apollo the God. Was this decision of King Agis—was that the sign?

ALCESTIS: (*With lifted listening head.*) No . . . the sign has not come yet.

CHERIANDER: (*With youthful ardor.*) You are the sign! You are message and sign, Queen Alcestis!

ALCESTIS: (*Almost insensible, shaking her head; softly.*) No . . . no . . .

CHERIANDER *dashes out after* EPIMENES. *Enter from the palace* KING AGIS, *howling with grief.*

AGIS: She is dead! Laodamia is dead! Twelve years old. She is dead. . . . (*He beats his fists against columns and walls. He stamps down the stairs, then up them again.*) Twelve years old. Her arms around my neck. In excruciating pain. "Father, help me . . . Father, help me!" . . . Her hair. Her mother's face. Her eyes, her eyes. (*He sees* ALCESTIS.) You— you brought this! You did this!

ALCESTIS: (*Murmuring through his words, as if entreating.*) Agis . . . Agis . . . Agis . . .

AGIS: (*Seizing her hand and touching it to his forehead and chest.*) Give me this plague. Let it destroy us all. "Father, help me!" She was everything to me. And she is dead—dead —dead!

ALCESTIS: Agis . . . Agis . . .

AGIS: You—whom Hercules brought back from the dead— you could do this. (*An idea strikes him.*) Hercules brought you back. Where was it? Was it here? (*He stumbles down the path.*) There? (*He ascends the path quickly.*) Tell me, Alces- tis—how did Hercules do it? What happened below there?

ALCESTIS *shakes her head silently.*

Show me what he did and I shall do it. Laodamia, I shall come for you. Answer me, Alcestis!

ALCESTIS: Agis, I saw nothing. I heard nothing.

AGIS: You are lying.

ALCESTIS: Agis, listen to me—I have something to say to you.

AGIS: Speak! Speak!

ALCESTIS: "Father, help me!"

AGIS: Do not mock me.

ALCESTIS: I am not mocking you. What was Laodamia saying, King Agis?

AGIS: She was in pain, pain, excruciating pain!

ALCESTIS: Yes, but that was not all. What more did she mean?

AGIS: What more?

ALCESTIS: The bitterness of death, King Agis, is part pain—but that is not all. The last bitterness of death is not parting— though that is great grief. I died . . . once. What is the last bitterness of death, King Agis?

AGIS: Tell me!

ALCESTIS: It is the despair that one has not lived. It is the despair that one's life has been without meaning. That it has been nonsense; happy or unhappy, that it has been senseless. "Father, help me."

AGIS: She loved me, Alcestis.

ALCESTIS: Yes.

AGIS: She *loved* me.

ALCESTIS: Yes, but love is not enough.

AGIS: It *was*. It was for her and it was for me. I will not listen to you.

ALCESTIS: Love is not the meaning. It is one of the signs that there is a meaning—it is only one of the signs that there is a meaning. Laodamia is in despair and asks that you help her. That is what death is—it is despair. Her life is vain and empty, until you give it a meaning.

AGIS: What meaning could I give it?

ALCESTIS: (*Quietly.*) You are a brutal, cruel, and ignorant man.

Brief silence.

You killed *my* Laodamia. Three times. Senselessly. Even you do not know how many times you have killed Laodamia.

AGIS: No!

ALCESTIS: You don't know. Go back to your kingdom. There, and only there, can you help Laodamia.

AGIS *comes up the path and, passing her, goes toward the palace door.*

All the dead, King Agis . . . (*She points to the entrance to the underworld.*) all those millions lie imploring us to show them that their lives were not empty and foolish.

AGIS: And what is this meaning that I can give to Laodamia's life?

ALCESTIS: Today you have begun to understand that.

AGIS: (*His head against the post of the palace door.*) No.

ALCESTIS: I was taught these things. Even I. You will learn them, King Agis. . . . Through Laodamia's suffering you will learn them.

> *Broken, he goes through the palace door.*
> *During his slow exit, the light begins to fall on* APOLLO, *entering from the palace doors. In this descent, He wears His cloak, but the hood has fallen back on His shoulders, showing a garland around His head. He first addresses* ALCESTIS *from the doors; then moves behind her.*
> *Left alone,* ALCESTIS *closes her eyes and takes a few steps left. Her head seems to bend with great weariness; she seems to shrink to a great age. She turns right and starts to move toward the gate to the road, her eyes half open.*

APOLLO: A few more steps, Alcestis. Through the gate . . . and across the road . . . and into my grove.

ALCESTIS: So far . . . and so high . . .

APOLLO: Now another step. It is not a hill. You do not have to raise your foot.

ALCESTIS: It is too far. Let me find my grave here.

APOLLO: You will not have that grave, Alcestis.

ALCESTIS: Oh, yes. I want my grave. . . .

APOLLO: The grave means an end. You will not have that ending. You are the first of a great number that will not have that ending. Still another step, Alcestis.

ALCESTIS: And will there be grandchildren, and the grandchildren of grandchildren . . . ?

APOLLO: Beyond all counting.

ALCESTIS: Yes . . . What was his name?

APOLLO: Admetus.

ALCESTIS: Yes. And the shining one I wanted to serve?

APOLLO: Apollo.

ALCESTIS: Yes . . . (*Near the gate.*) All the thousands of days . . . and the world of cares . . . (*Raising her head, with closed eyes.*) And whom do I thank for all the happiness?

APOLLO: Friends do not ask one another that question. (*She goes out.*)

> APOLLO *raises His voice, as though to ensure that she will hear Him beyond the wall.*

Those who have loved one another do not ask one another that question . . . Alcestis.

CURTAIN

Transition from

THE ALCESTIAD

to

THE DRUNKEN SISTERS

At the close of the three acts of The Alcestiad a curtain falls. APOLLO *comes before the curtain.*

APOLLO: (*To the audience.*) Wait! Wait! We have still one more thing to do. We are in Greece, and here we do not believe that audiences should return to their homes immediately after watching stories that present what is difficult and painful in human life. Here we have this custom: we require that the poet write a short satyr play in the spirit of diversion —even of the comical. (*Confidentially.*) We claim that the tragic insight cannot stand alone. It tends to its own excess. As one of you (*Pointing into the audience.*) has said: Neither Death nor the Sun permits itself to be gazed at fixedly. And further, we require that this satyr play deal with some element —some secondary aspect—of the preceding play. So—what shall we show you? Teiresias—the six-hundred-year-old, the too-much-loved? How from time to time the gods made him young again; how from time to time they even changed him into a woman? And the quarrel between Zeus and Hera about that? (*He starts laughing but tries to control himself.*) No, no—that's not suitable here. That play is too coarse. The Greeks have stomachs strong enough to endure such unseemly matters, but (*He is again overcome with laughter.*) it is . . . No, no—not here. Or shall we show you the story about the sisters of Queen Alcestis? Her father, King Pelias, was an old fool and her two sisters were not very clever. That often happens in families—there is just one intelligent person. We could show you how the archcook Medea whispered into the sisters' ears, pretending to show them how they could make their dear father young again. . . . (*Suddenly changing his tone.*) No! It is true that there are people

431

who laugh only when they hear about something cruel. That play is a heap of cruelties, and when you went home you would be ashamed of yourselves for having been amused by it. We have another: it is not very funny. Tonight did you ask yourselves how it was possible that the life of King Admetus was extended? Those great ladies the weird sisters, the Fates—can they be bribed? We shall show you how it happened. (*He starts taking off his outer robes, under which he is dressed as a kitchen boy, and calls into the wings: "My hat! My hat!"*) In this little play I am again Apollo, in the disguise of a kitchen boy.

> *From the wings are reached out to him a large cone-shaped straw hat and a belt, from which the effects of a kitchen boy —onions, etc.—hang. He calls into the wings: "My bottles!," sets his hat on his head, and puts on the belt.*

I hate disguises, I hate drunkenness—

> *From the wings he receives a rope, from which three bottles hang.*

but see these bottles I have hanging around my neck? I hate lies and stratagems—but I've come to do crookedly what even All-Father Zeus could not do without guile: extend a human life. (*Calling through the curtain to the rear or into the wings: "All ready?" and then turning again to the audience.*) Yes, all is ready for the satyr play, to conclude the solemn trilogy of *The Alcestiad*.

> *He remains standing at the proscenium pillar as the curtain rises.*

THE DRUNKEN SISTERS

The three FATES *are seated on a bench largely hidden by their vo-luminous draperies. They wear the masks of old women, touched by the grotesque but with vestiges of nobility. Seated are* CLOTHO *with her spindle,* LACHESIS *with the bulk of the thread of life on her lap, and* ATROPOS *with her scissors. They rock back and forth as they work, passing the threads from right to left. The audience watches them for a time in silence, broken only by a faint humming from* CLOTHO.

CLOTHO: What is it that goes first on four legs, then on two legs? Don't tell me! Don't tell me!

LACHESIS: (*Bored.*) You know it!

CLOTHO: Let me pretend that I don't know it.

ATROPOS: There are no new riddles. We know them all.

LACHESIS: How boring our life is without riddles! Clotho, make up a riddle.

CLOTHO: Be quiet, then, and give me a moment to think. . . . What is it that . . . What is it that . . . ?

Enter APOLLO, *disguised.*

APOLLO: (*To the audience.*) These are the great sisters—the Fates. Clotho weaves the threads of life; Lachesis measures the length of each; Atropos cuts them short. In their monotonous work of deciding our lives they are terribly bored, and like so many people who are bored, they find great pleasure in games—in enigmas and riddles. Naturally they can't play cards, because their hands are always busy with the threads of life.

ATROPOS: Sister! Your elbow! Do your work without striking me.

LACHESIS: I can't help it—this thread is s-o-o l-o-o-ong! Never have I had to reach so far.

CLOTHO: Long and gray and dirty! All those years a slave!

LACHESIS: So it is! (*To* ATROPOS.) Cut it, dear sister.

ATROPOS *cuts it—click!*

And now this one; cut this. It's a blue one—blue for bravery: blue and short.

ATROPOS: So easy to see!

Click.

LACHESIS: You almost cut that purple one, Atropos.

ATROPOS: This one? Purple for a king?

LACHESIS: Yes; watch what you're doing, dear. It's the life of Admetus, King of Thessaly.

APOLLO: (*Aside.*) Aie!

LACHESIS: I've marked it clearly. He's to die at sunset.

APOLLO: (*To the audience.*) No! No!

LACHESIS: He's the favorite of Apollo, as was his father before him, and all that tiresome house of Thessaly. The queen Alcestis will be a widow tonight.

APOLLO: (*To the audience.*) Alcestis! Alcestis! No!

LACHESIS: There'll be howling in Thessaly. There'll be rolling on the ground and tearing of garments. . . . Not now, dear; there's an hour yet.

APOLLO: (*Aside.*) To work! To work, Apollo the Crooked! (*He starts the motions of running furiously while remaining in one place, but stops suddenly and addresses the audience.*) Is there anyone here who does not know that old story—the reason why King Admetus and his queen Alcestis are dear to me? (*He sits on the ground and continues talking with raised forefinger.*) Was it ten years ago? I am little concerned with time. I am the god of the sun; it is always light where I am. Perhaps ten years ago. My father and the father of us all was filled up with anger against me. What had I done? (*He moves his finger back and forth.*) Do not ask that now; let it be forgotten. . . . He laid upon me a punishment. He ordered that I should descend to earth and live for a year among men—I, as a man among men, as a servant. Half hidden, known and not known, I chose to be a herdsman of King Admetus of Thessaly. I lived the life of a man, as close to them as I am to you now, as close to the just and to the unjust. Each day the King gave orders to the other herdsmen and myself; each day the Queen gave thought to what went well or ill with us and our families. I came to love King Admetus and Queen Alcestis and through them I came to love all men. And now Admetus must die. (*Rising.*) No! I have laid my plans. I shall prevent it. To work. To work, Apollo the Crooked.

> *He again starts the motions of running furiously while remaining in one place. He complains noisily:*

Oh, my back! Aie, aie. They beat me, but worst of all they've made me late. I'll be beaten again.

LACHESIS: Who's the sniveler?

APOLLO: Don't stop me now. I haven't a moment to talk. I'm late already. Besides, my errand's a terrible secret. I can't say a word.

ATROPOS: Throw your yarn around him, Lachesis. What's the fool doing with a secret? It's we who have all the secrets.

> *The threads in the laps of the* SISTERS *are invisible to the audience.* LACHESIS *now rises and swings her hands three times in wide circles above her head as though she were about to fling a lasso, then hurls the noose across the stage.* APOLLO *makes the gesture of being caught. With each strong pull by* LACHESIS, APOLLO *is dragged nearer to her. During the following speeches* LACHESIS *lifts her end of the strands high in the air, alternately pulling* APOLLO *up, almost strangling him, and flinging him again to the ground.*

APOLLO: Ladies, beautiful ladies, let me go. If I'm late all Olympus will be in an uproar. Aphrodite will be mad with fear—but oh, already I've said too much. My orders were to come immediately, and to say nothing—especially not to women. The thing's of no interest to men. Dear ladies, let me go.

ATROPOS: Pull on your yarn, sister.

APOLLO: You're choking me. You're squeezing me to death.

LACHESIS: (*Forcefully.*) Stop your whining and tell your secret at once.

APOLLO: I can't. I dare not.

ATROPOS: Pull harder, sister. Boy, speak or strangle. (*She makes the gesture of choking him.*)

APOLLO: Ow! Ow!—Wait! I'll tell the half of it, if you let me go.

ATROPOS: Tell the whole or we'll hang you up in the air in that noose.

APOLLO: I'll tell, I'll tell. But— (*He looks about him fearfully.*) promise me! Swear by the Styx that you'll not tell anyone, and swear by Lethe that you'll forget it.

LACHESIS: We have only one oath—by Acheron. And we never swear it—least of all to a sniveling slave. Tell us what you know, or you'll be by all three rivers in a minute.

APOLLO: I tremble at what I am about to say. I . . . ssh . . . I carry . . . here . . . in these bottles . . . Oh, ladies, let me go. Let me go.

CLOTHO and ATROPOS: Pull, sister.

APOLLO: No! No! I'll tell you. I am carrying the wine for . . . for Aphrodite. Once every ten days she renews her beauty . . . by . . . drinking this.

ATROPOS: Liar! Fool! She has nectar and ambrosia, as they all have.

APOLLO: (*Confidentially.*) But is she not the fairest? . . . It is the love gift of Hephaistos; from the vineyards of Dionysos; from grapes ripened under the eye of Apollo—of Apollo who tells no lies.

> *The* SISTERS *confidentially to one another in blissful anticipation.*

LACHESIS and ATROPOS and CLOTHO: Sisters!

ATROPOS: (*Like sugar.*) Pass the bottles up, dear boy.

APOLLO: (*In terror.*) Not that! Ladies! It is enough that I have told you the secret! Not that!

ATROPOS: Surely, Lachesis, you can find on your lap the thread of this worthless slave—a yellow one destined for a long life?

APOLLO: (*Falling on his knees.*) Spare me!

ATROPOS: (*To* LACHESIS.) Look, that's it—the sallow one, with the tangle in it of dishonesty, and the stiffness of obstinacy, and the ravel-ravel of stupidity. Pass it over to me, dear.

APOLLO: (*His forehead touching the floor.*) Oh, that I had never been born!

LACHESIS: (*To* ATROPOS.) This is it. (*With a sigh.*) I'd planned to give him five score.

APOLLO: (*Rising and extending the bottles, sobbing.*) Here, take them! Take them! I'll be killed anyway. Aphrodite will kill me. My life's over.

ATROPOS: (*Strongly, as the* SISTERS *take the bottles.*) Not one more word out of you. Put your hand on your mouth. We're tired of listening to you.

> APOLLO, *released of the noose, flings himself face down upon the ground, his shoulders heaving. The* SISTERS *put the flagons to their lips. They drink and moan with pleasure.*

LACHESIS and ATROPOS and CLOTHO: Sisters!

LACHESIS: Sister, how do I look?

ATROPOS: Oh, I could eat you. And I?

CLOTHO: Sister, how do I look?

LACHESIS: Beautiful! Beautiful! And I?

ATROPOS: And not a mirror on all the mountain, or a bit of still water, to tell us which of us is the fairest.

LACHESIS: (*Dreamily, passing her hand over her face.*) I feel like . . . I feel as I did when Kronos followed me about, trying to catch me in a dark corner.

ATROPOS: Poseidon was beside himself—dashing across the plains trying to engulf me.

CLOTHO: My own father—who can blame him?—began to forget himself.

ATROPOS: (*Whispering.*) This is not such a worthless fellow, after all. And he's not bad-looking. (*To* CLOTHO.) Ask him what he sees.

LACHESIS: Ask him which of us is the fairest.

CLOTHO: Boy! Boy! You bay meek. I mean, you . . . you may thpeak. Thpeak to him, Lakethith; I've lotht my tongue.

LACHESIS: Boy, look at us well! You may tell us which is the fairest.

> APOLLO *has remained face downward on the ground. He now rises and gazes at the* SISTERS. *He acts as if blinded: he cowers and uncovers his eyes, gazing first at one and then at another.*

APOLLO: What have I done? This splendor! What have I done? You—and you—and you! Kill me if you will, but I cannot say which one is the fairest. (*Falling on his knees.*) Oh, ladies —if so much beauty has not made you cruel, let me now go and hide myself. Aphrodite will hear of this. Let me escape to Crete and take up my old work.

ATROPOS: What was your former work, dear boy?

APOLLO: I helped my father in the marketplace; I was a teller of stories and riddles.

The SISTERS *are transfixed. Then almost with a scream.*

SISTERS: What's that? What's that you said?

APOLLO: A teller of stories and riddles. Do the beautiful ladies enjoy riddles?

SISTERS: (*Rocking from side to side and slapping one another.*) Sisters, do we enjoy riddles?

ATROPOS: Oh, he would only know the old ones. Puh! The blind horse . . . the big toe . . .

LACHESIS: The cloud—the eyelashes of Hera . . .

CLOTHO: (*Harping on one string.*) What is it that first goes on four legs . . . ?

ATROPOS: The porpoise . . . Etna . . .

APOLLO: Everyone knows those! I have some new ones—

SISTERS: (*Again, a scream.*) New ones!

APOLLO: (*Slowly.*) What is it that is necessary to—

He pauses. The SISTERS *are riveted.*

LACHESIS: Go on, boy, go on. What is it that is necessary to—

APOLLO: But—I only play for forfeits. See! If I lose . . .

CLOTHO: If you looth, you mutht tell uth which one ith the faireth.

APOLLO: No! No! I dare not!

LACHESIS: (*Sharply.*) Yes!

APOLLO: And if I win?

ATROPOS: Win? Idiot! Stupid! Slave! No one has ever won from us.

APOLLO: But if I win?

LACHESIS: He doesn't know who we are!

APOLLO: But if I win?

CLOTHO: The fool talkth of winning!

APOLLO: If I win, you must grant me one wish. One wish, any wish.

LACHESIS: Yes, yes. Oh, what a tedious fellow! Go on with your riddle. What is it that is necessary to—

APOLLO: Swear by Acheron!

CLOTHO and LACHESIS: We swear! By Acheron! By Acheron!

APOLLO: (*To* ATROPOS.) You, too.

ATROPOS: (*After a moment's brooding resistance, loudly.*) By Acheron!

APOLLO: Then: ready?

LACHESIS: Wait! One moment. (*Leaning toward* ATROPOS, *confidentially.*) The sun is near setting. Do not forget the thread of Ad—You know, the thread of Ad—

ATROPOS: What? What Ad? What are you whispering about, silly?

LACHESIS: (*Somewhat louder.*) Not to forget the thread of Admetus, King of Thessaly. At sundown. Have you lost your shears, Atropos?

ATROPOS: Oh, stop your buzzing and fussing and tend to your own business. Of course I haven't lost my shears. Go on with your riddle, boy!

APOLLO: So! I'll give you as much time as it takes to recite the names of the Muses and their mother.

LACHESIS: Hm! Nine and one. Well, begin!

APOLLO: What is it that is necessary to every life—and that can save only one?

> The SISTERS *rock back and forth with closed eyes, mumbling the words of the riddle. Suddenly* APOLLO *starts singing his invocation to the Muses.*

> Mnemosyne, mother of the nine;
> Polyhymnia, incense of the gods—

LACHESIS: (*Shrieks.*) Don't sing! Unfair! How can we think?

CLOTHO: Stop your ears, sister.

ATROPOS: Unfair! (*Murmuring.*) What is it that can save every life—

> *They put their fingers in their ears.*

APOLLO: Erato, voice of love;
> Euterpe, help me now.

> Calliope, thief of our souls;
> Urania, clothed of the stars;

Clio of the backward glances;
Euterpe, help me now.

Terpsichore of the beautiful ankles;
Thalia of long laughter;
Melpomene, dreaded and welcome;
Euterpe, help me now.

Then, in a loud voice.

Forfeit! Forfeit!

CLOTHO *and* ATROPOS *bury their faces in* LACHESIS'S *neck, moaning.*

LACHESIS: (*In a dying voice.*) What is the answer?
APOLLO: (*Flinging away his hat, triumphantly.*) Myself! Apollo the sun.
SISTERS: Apollo! You?
LACHESIS: (*Savagely.*) Pah! What life can you save?
APOLLO: My forfeit! One wish! One life! The life of Admetus, King of Thessaly.

A horrified clamor arises from the SISTERS.

SISTERS: Fraud! Impossible! Not to be thought of!
APOLLO: By Acheron.
SISTERS: Against all law. Zeus will judge. Fraud.
APOLLO: (*Warning.*) By Acheron.
SISTERS: Zeus! We will go to Zeus about it. He will decide.
APOLLO: Zeus swears by Acheron and keeps his oath.

Sudden silence.

ATROPOS: (*Decisive but ominous.*) You will have your wish—the life of King Admetus. But—
APOLLO: (*Triumphantly.*) I shall have the life of Admetus!
SISTERS: But—
APOLLO: I shall have the life of Admetus! What is your *but?*
ATROPOS: Someone else must die in his stead.
APOLLO: (*Lightly.*) Oh—choose some slave. Some gray and greasy thread on your lap, divine Lachesis.
LACHESIS: (*Outraged.*) What? You ask me to take a life?
ATROPOS: You ask us to murder?

CLOTHO: Apollo thinks that we are criminals?

APOLLO: (*Beginning to be fearful.*) Then, great sisters, how is this to be done?

LACHESIS: Me—an assassin? (*She spreads her arms wide and says solemnly:*) Over my left hand is Chance; over my right hand is Necessity.

APOLLO: Then, gracious sisters, how will this be done?

LACHESIS: Someone must *give* his life for Admetus—of free choice and will. Over such deaths we have no control. Neither Chance nor Necessity rules the free offering of the will. Someone must choose to die in the place of Admetus, King of Thessaly.

APOLLO: (*Covering his face with his hands.*) No! No! I see it all! (*With a loud cry.*) Alcestis! Alcestis!

    And he runs stumbling from the scene.

CURTAIN

UNCOLLECTED PLAYS

The Marriage We Deplore

CHARACTERS

EVA, an aristocrat, fifty
CHARLES, her second husband
JULIA, Eva's daughter, twenty-five
GEORGE, Eva's son, Julia's brother
PHYLLIS, George's wife

SETTING

Living room of Mrs. Eva Hibbert-Havens, Boston.

At the rise of the curtain Eva Hibbert-Havens is seated, dressed for dinner, in a beautiful chair from which she does not rise until the close of the play. She is a stout aristocratic lady, assertive but illogical. In short, a Boston grande dame. She calls to her second husband who passes in the hall:

EVA: Charles! Come in, please.
CHARLES (*Offstage, reluctantly*): I could wait in the den, dear, until they come.
EVA (*Firmly*): Well, please sit down just for a minute.

> *Charles Havens comes in. He is an absentminded, slightly apologetic man in a tuxedo.*

I haven't told Daughter yet just who the guests are. I told her to dress for dinner quietly and she'd find out later who they were.
CHARLES (*indifferently*): Surely it wouldn't hurt her to say that her brother is coming to dinner.
EVA (*Severely*): Her brother, and her brother's wife.
CHARLES (*Mildly*): Yes, her brother's wife. Her sister, so to speak.
EVA: Well, if I had told Daughter that!—And I want her to look especially well tonight. (*Forcefully*) To contrast with the rouge and tinsel of her "sister."

447

CHARLES (*In surprised protest*): But George's wife won't wear rouge and tinsel.

EVA: How do we know what George's wife won't wear? Where did he find her, I'd like to know? In a station lunchroom, very likely. In a prize shooting gallery.

CHARLES (*Amusedly*): In a circus, perhaps.

EVA (*With indignation*): I mean that my son, George Hibbert *Junior*, of the Boston Hibberts, married miles beneath him.

CHARLES (*Absentmindedly*): Was that her name?

EVA: As you say, he may have married a trapeze artiste.

CHARLES (*Prosaically*): My dear, you're always reminding me that you married beneath you when you married me. Why blame George for doing what you have found fairly satisfactory?

EVA: I blame George because he is a young man with still some prestige to make. When I married you I had been for eight years the widow of the most distinguished citizen of Boston. I could have married someone much lower than my husband's assistant manager, and still faced the world.

CHARLES (*Gently*): My dear, I was not your husband's assistant manager. I was his foreman.

EVA: Foreman, never. I used to see you sign his checks for him. I married my husband's sub-manager; George has married his landlady's furnace-shaker.

CHARLES (*Shaking his head*): He has dragged the name of Hibbert in the coal bin.

> *Enter Daughter in evening dress. A beautiful girl of twenty-five is Julia Hibbert-Havens. She is strong-minded and so has naturally found with such a mother that concealment is the best policy. We know her to be excitingly tricky, so we are able to appreciate that her demureness in the presence of her mother is a trifle exaggerated.*

JULIA: Well, Mother, who are these secret guests we're having tonight?

EVA: Who, indeed!

CHARLES: It's your brother George.

JULIA: And his bride?

EVA: Yes, his acquirement. He holds an indignation meeting against me for two years because I married your present father, and then he marries a Nobody and breaks the silence by inviting himself to dinner.

JULIA: Who was she?

EVA: No one seems to know; a boardinghouse girl; someone says, a waitress in a station lunchroom—

CHARLES: —You said so yourself.

EVA: Perhaps the proprietress of a shooting gallery—

CHARLES: —That was your guess.

EVA: Don't interrupt! And Charles heard that she was from a circus.

CHARLES: I didn't hear, I guessed.

EVA: Well, take your choice. Those are the rumors. George has married beneath him. It's a wonder the church allows it. Every debutante marries her chauffeur; her brother marries her lady's maid. It is a national danger. If everybody married beneath them where should we be, I'd like to know. It is the peril that lurks for democratic nations. It shows a nationwide admiration for the lower classes that is deplorable. That's what George said in his terrible letter after I had married a second time. Such names he called me! It was like Forbes-Robertson talking to his mother in *Hamlet*.

CHARLES (*Vaguely*): Ah . . . is there a situation like that in *Hamlet*? (*He wanders to the bookcase*)

EVA (*With alarm*): No, there is not . . . not the slightest.

JULIA: What does it matter?

EVA (*Anxiously*): Do let us be frank with one another. You don't realize how difficult this is for me. What are you doing, Charles? You're not listening to me.

CHARLES: Oh, yes I was. I was seeing if I could find *Hamlet*.

EVA: Julia, I want you to burn every copy of *Hamlet* there is in the house.

JULIA: It'll spoil the sets, Mother.

EVA: There are more important things than preserving sets.

JULIA: Not in Boston.

EVA: What was I saying, Charles?

CHARLES: You wanted us to be frank with one another. My dear, I've been frank. I understand perfectly that your son was angry with you when you married me. I wrote him that I did not pretend to be more than a plain ordinary man.

JULIA: Mother, it's you that are not being frank.

EVA (*Crying*): Haven't I told you that she was a station restaurant waitress?

CHARLES (*Pained*): Dear me! What an affliction!

JULIA: All the better. Then he's in a glass house; and won't dare to throw stones at you anymore.

EVA: It's not *that* I mind. I'd like to give him a good talking to, myself. It's because I'm in a glass house.

CHARLES (*Gently*): My dear, seeing that this doesn't concern me, may I retire to my den until your son arrives? (*He is unnoticed*)

JULIA: Now there'll be peace in the family. No more mutual recriminations; everybody wears muzzles—in fact, they've married muzzles.

CHARLES: I daresay he's timorous about coming to see you now.

EVA (*Sharply*): Not at all! There's always you as a precedent.

CHARLES (*Cowed*): Dear me! So there is, so there is. There's the doorbell now.

EVA: Now don't anyone be tactless.

JULIA: Don't anyone mention boardinghouses or glass houses, or anything that might cause self-consciousness.

CHARLES: Am I to stay in the room all the time?

EVA: Yes; they are not to think I have any regrets.—I shall soon find out which rumor was correct.

> *Enter George and his wife. George is an obstinate young man; Phyllis is an extraordinarily pretty young girl with large blue eyes. Her hair is arranged to resemble Billie Burke's; she is exquisitely dressed and has charming manners. It is the most difficult moment in her life.*

GEORGE (*Kissing his mother*): How are you, Mother? Mother, this is my wife.

EVA (*Offering her cheek*): You may, my dear. (*After Phyllis has kissed her*) We meet at last, so to speak.

PHYLLIS (*Blushing*): Better late than never, as they say.

GEORGE (*To Charles, shaking hands stiffly*): How do you do, Mr. Havens. Phyllis, this is my father.

PHYLLIS (*Faintly*): I'm very happy to know you.

EVA: George, why don't you introduce your wife to Daughter?

JULIA: Oh, we have met, Mother.

EVA (*In astonishment*): When was that?

JULIA: I have called on them several times.

EVA (*With evident displeasure*): So *that's* how you spend your time in Atlantic City. And never say a word about it to me!

JULIA: I was saving it as a pleasant surprise.

EVA: You misjudged!—Were you ever in Boston before, Phyllis?

PHYLLIS: Unfortunately not. I have been kept pretty regularly to Atlantic City.

EVA (*Marveling*): And yet Boston so close!

PHYLLIS: I have occasionally run up to New York for shopping.

EVA (*Urgently*): Charles! My smelling salts—in the hall. (*He gets them*) But naturally from your position in the station you were able to see the trains depart for Boston.

PHYLLIS (*Agreeably*): Oh, yes. There are trains.

EVA (*Nodding her head enigmatically*): Hmm—yes . . . yes. Did you find it monotonous?—Standing over the counter, long hours . . . ?

PHYLLIS (*At sea*): You mean, did we come by boat?

JULIA: No, dear, Mother means: Did you find the trip longer than you expected?

PHYLLIS (*To her*): I like traveling.

EVA: I see! Naturally. How fortunate. There must be long waits while the tents are being nailed down.—Then there's the long, hot parade.

PHYLLIS (*To George*): I'm afraid—I do not understand . . .

GEORGE: You mean, Mother—?

JULIA (*To the rescue*): By parade, Mother means the boardwalk at Atlantic City we all hear so much about.

PHYLLIS (*To Eva, brightly*): Oh, no. It's a pleasure, I assure you. And on the hottest days there are the awnings—that's what you meant by "tents."

EVA: Yes, yes. But no doubt there are tents, too. Fortune tellers, and—

PHYLLIS: —A very few.—

EVA: —And among them, the shooting gallery.

PHYLLIS (*Seeking light*): *The* shooting gallery?

EVA (*Boldly*): The one you were interested in.

At last Phyllis is completely perplexed.

PHYLLIS (*In a pretty confusion*): I'm afraid I'm very dull. But

I've heard of the subtlety—the wit—of Boston conversation. I have always lived quietly with my mother in our little home on the North Shore. I've had little experience—

JULIA: —Don't apologize, Phyllis. Mother has a playful way you'll understand when you get to know her better.

EVA: I was not aware of it.

CHARLES (*Soothingly*): Now Eva! You know you're famous for your wit.

GEORGE: It has developed then in the last year—amazingly.

EVA (*Retorting*): Think of what I've had to bear.

GEORGE: I warned you in good time.

Fortunately dinner is announced at this point.

EVA (*Rising and repeating a formula used by all Boston hostesses at informal dinners to relatives*): We live very simply, but of such as it is we try to obtain the best, and to that you are always welcome. (*She leads the way out with Charles*)

PHYLLIS (*Turning, at the front of the stage; plaintively*): I don't understand your mother at all, George— (*She sees Julia and runs to her*) When are you to be married, Julia?

JULIA (*Smiling down at her happily*): On Saturday afternoon at four o' the clock.

PHYLLIS: Why at four?

JULIA: Because they don't let the dear boy out of the factory until three; and he says he *must* brush his hair.

They go on in to dinner.

END OF PLAY

The Unerring Instinct

A PLAY IN ONE ACT

CHARACTERS

LEONORA THORPE, a pleasant woman of middle age
BELINDA WATSON, a younger woman, Leonora's sister-in-law
ARTHUR ROGERS

SETTING

Leonora's home.

No curtain and scenery are required. Three comfortable chairs and a small table. At the players' right is a table or board on which there are three colored lights: red, blue and green. They are worked on dimmers.

Leonora enters and coming to the front of the stage addresses the audience.

LEONORA: My name is Leonora Thorpe. I've been asked to come here to tell you about a practical joke I played on a friend of mine—on my sister-in-law, in fact. Some of you may think I was a little cruel. Perhaps I was. My sister-in-law, Belinda Watson, has always been full of fears about people and full of sweeping judgments about those she wants to meet and those she doesn't want to meet. On this occasion I lost my patience with her. I decided to plant a brand-new prejudice in her mind—just to show her how susceptible she was to nonsense.

While we act this out I've asked some electricians to operate these three colored lights. They will show you the various emotions that were going on inside Belinda Watson during this session.

During the following explanation the lights are turned up as they are described.

This light is red. It's for fear and it needs no explanation.

This blue light indicates despair—bewilderment, confusion and despair. It denotes that state which we all get into when it seems that thinking is too difficult; that thinking never gets us anywhere; that reason and justice are simply too complicated; that it's easier to give up and just attack.

So this last light is green—that's the last resort of fear and despair: that's malice and snarl and bite and attack.

This thing took place in a friend's house in the town where we all live. There'd been an auction for some benefit—Visiting Nurses or Boys' Clubs. Hundreds of people had been there. In fact, it was the first time that I'd felt that our whole community had gotten together in a friendly way and had really met one another. At the end of the afternoon I went out to the veranda to sit down and rest. I'd been one of the auctioneers.

She sits down. Enter Belinda, fanning kerself with an auction program.

BELINDA: Well, dear, it's been a great success, a really great success. And I've shaken a great many hands that I hope I never shake again. I know they're very nice, I hope they're happy, I hope they eat three meals a day, but let them lead their lives and let me lead mine.

LEONORA: Now, Belinda, I'm too tired to listen to you protesting about how broad-minded you are.

BELINDA: Well, I am. You're always scolding me about what you call my prejudices. You're wrong. I'm the most broadminded woman in this town. As far as I'm concerned: color, religion, rich or poor—makes no difference to me.

LEONORA: Good heavens, here we go again.

BELINDA: It's only when it comes to my children that I draw the line. I want every association that they make to be of the *very best*. I don't want them to get into any situation that might be embarrassing—*ever*.

LEONORA: I know. And for that you have that infallible instinct of yours to guide you as to who is or is not suitable for them. Let's not talk about it.

BELINDA: Well, after all, you're their aunt. You must see what I mean.

LEONORA (*Sitting up*): Yes, I'm their aunt, aren't I?

BELINDA: And you've said a thousand times that they're perfectly beautiful children. And, of course, you have a certain responsibility to them, too. After all, little Leonora's named after you—she looks like you, she dotes on you.

Leonora has risen. She walks about and is seen to be forming a decision. Standing behind Belinda's chair, she says:

LEONORA: Belinda, I noticed something odd this afternoon. I wonder if you did.

BELINDA: Why . . . what?

LEONORA: Oh, George Smith and his brother and sister.

BELINDA: . . . Which ones? . . .

LEONORA: Belinda, do you happen to know many people named Smith?

BELINDA: No.—Yes, I know a few. Why do you ask?

LEONORA (*Sitting down*): Well, dear, have you ever noticed anything *funny* about them?

BELINDA: Funny? How do you mean? (*The red light begins to glow*)

LEONORA: Oh, well, if you haven't, I'm sorry I mentioned it. After all, you have enough to worry you as it is—to bring up the children and everything.

BELINDA: What were you going to say, dear?

LEONORA: Forget it.—My, what an attractive dress that is. Have I ever seen that before?

BELINDA: Yes, it's new.— No, I mean it's an old thing I've had for years. But what were you going to say about the Smiths? —Now, Leonora, if there's anything I ought to know, I insist on your telling me.

LEONORA: Well, it's nothing really. Yet I feel that it's something everybody should at least know *about*. Have you ever really stopped to think about the name Smith?

BELINDA: No-o-o-o. What do you mean? (*A brief flare-up of the red light*)

LEONORA: Before the War, I read a paper by a famous German scholar—oh, a *very* great scholar—about the Schmidts in Germany. And of course, they're the same thing as our Smiths.

BELINDA: Yes?

LEONORA: Don't you see? They're all descended finally from blacksmiths and ironworkers, aren't they?

BELINDA: I suppose so.

LEONORA: Swinging great hammers all day.

BELINDA: You mean . . . ? Leonora, hundreds of years have gone by since . . .

LEONORA: So you *do* see? This professor studies thousands of them. You must have read it; it was in all the magazines. Naturally, they'd be very *strong willed* and ruthless, wouldn't they? Heartless, really.

BELINDA: Leonora! I never thought of that.

LEONORA: Pounding. Hammering. Driving nails into poor horses' feet all day. Twisting white-hot iron into the strangest shapes. Well—that's all I meant.

BELINDA: Goodness! But, Leonora . . . what should we do about it?

LEONORA: The only thing for us to do is to *know* it and to keep our wits about us.

BELINDA: To think that I never, never thought of that before!

LEONORA: Of course, there are *some* nice Smiths—

BELINDA (*Sudden strong burst of red light; sudden cry*): But the principal of my boy's school is named Smith!! He *seemed* perfectly nice.

LEONORA: Oh, I don't deny it. But listen: a nice Smith is still a *Smith*. You keep your eyes open, dear—you'll see. Take another example—come nearer, dear, we mustn't talk so loud. Take that woman who sings on the radio—Rose Smith or Bessie Smith—what's her name?

BELINDA: Why, I always thought she was so nice and wholesome, so to speak. (*The blue light begins to glow. The red light off*)

LEONORA: Yes, but look at how *famous* she is! To arrive at a position like that, my dear, one must be . . . *strong willed*, believe me. Why, do you realize that Al Smith almost became president of the United States?

BELINDA: But, Leonora, the principal of my William's school is named Smith. (*A brief return of the red glow*)

LEONORA: Now you're beginning to misunderstand me. There are lots of perfectly nice Smiths.

BELINDA: Oh, dear, I'm almost sorry that you told me all this.

It's so upsetting. (*Brief intensity of blue; then back to blue glow*) Really, one doesn't know what to do or to think these days.

LEONORA: The answer to that is this: Don't try to think, just know what you know, trust to that instinct of yours, and keep your eyes open. You'll see the Smiths behaving in very Smithy ways wherever you look.

BELINDA: Oh, I just thought of . . . Who could have been kinder and better than Dr. Buckingham Smith?

LEONORA: Oh, yes. The one who was so kind to your mother all through her illness?

BELINDA: He was an angel, a perfect angel. (*Strong blue light*) Oh, Leonora, it's so hard to . . . I mean, it's really hard . . .

LEONORA: Of course, it's *easiest* just to distrust them *all*.

BELINDA (*No lights on; pause; then thoughtfully*): Do you know something? (*Green light begins full*) I never did really like that school.

LEONORA: Oh, Belinda, you've always been very enthusiastic about it.

BELINDA: No. From the first day I saw it I knew it wasn't right. Fortunately I have an instinct for such things . . . Of course, William admires this Mr. . . . this Mr. Blacksmith.

LEONORA: Smith, dear, Smith.

BELINDA (*Green reduced to red glow*): Whatever you call him. William admires him, but, of course, William's a mere child. Children don't sense these things. I'll speak to Wallace about it tonight.

LEONORA: About what, Belinda?

BELINDA (*Green light full for a moment; harshly*): Why, about taking William out of that dreadful place, of course. I'll speak to him about it this very night.

Enter Arthur, carrying a teacup.

ARTHUR (*Remaining at back of stage*): Oh, there you are, Leonora. Can I bring you ladies some tea?

All colored lights off.

LEONORA: No, Arthur, we've had some. Arthur, I want you to meet my sister-in-law, Belinda Watson.

ARTHUR: Happy to meet you, Mrs. Watson.—I'll be back in one minute.

Exit Arthur.

BELINDA (*Pleased*): Why, who's that? He seems . . . very nice man . . .

LEONORA: That's . . . old friend of my husband's. That's Arthur . . . uh . . . I'm surprised you don't know him. That's Arthur Smythe.

BELINDA (*Quickly*): What? Smythe?! How do you spell it?

LEONORA: S.M.Y.T.H.E.—Why?

BELINDA: Leonora!! (*Flare-up of red beside the green glow*) That's the same as Smith, isn't it?

LEONORA: Oh, that's all right. Everybody likes Arthur. I'm glad you're going to meet him.

BELINDA: Do you think it wise, dear? (*Red glow; green strong*) Really, I'd rather not.

LEONORA: Now, Belinda, you're getting hysterical. Arthur's an exceptional person. Wonderful war record. And besides, he's the best citizen in this town; your own husband says so. He should get all the credit for the new hospital wing.

BELINDA (*Add brief full strength of blue light*): But, dear, he's one of those Smiths!

Arthur reappears; he promptly drops his cup and saucer.

ARTHUR: Confound it! Holy blazes! If I'm not the awkwardest pigheadedest—

BELINDA (*Brief red flare; pointing dramatically*):—Look at that! Look at that!

Arthur kneels down and dabs at the floor with his handkerchief. All lights off except a faint green glow.

ARTHUR: Have I ruined this rug, Leonora?

LEONORA: Was there any cream in it?

ARTHUR: No.

LEONORA: Then it's all right. Come over and talk to us.

ARTHUR (*Crossing*): Well, at last, I'm very glad to meet you, Mrs. Watson. I've been seeing your husband almost every day. In fact, I had lunch with him yesterday.

BELINDA (*Flare-up of red light, then out; very gracious*): Did you? How nice!

ARTHUR: Yes, I was complaining to him that Amelia and I had never had the opportunity to meet you. I asked him: What's the matter with us?

Red and green lights begin to flicker on and off at medium strength. Belinda laughs nervously.

Anyway, I think you're coming to dinner with us next Thursday.

BELINDA (*Flickering continues; charming*): Oh, I *wish* we could. Now, isn't that too bad! I'm so sorry, but we're engaged on Thursday.

ARTHUR: Sorry. However, we'll hound you until you do come.

Belinda laughs prettily.

I believe my daughter Helen has been doing her algebra with your daughter Leonora.

BELINDA (*Red and green up*): Has she? Has she? Well, I've always believed—of course, I may be wrong!—that children should do their homework *alone*. I certainly hope that I shall have the pleasure of meeting Mrs. Black . . . I mean Mrs. . . . I mean Mrs. Smythe some day; but my husband's been overworking lately—in fact, he's a perfect wreck—and we almost never go out in the evening.

ARTHUR: Oh . . . uh . . . what Mrs. Smythe is that?

LEONORA (*Quickly*): Oh, I know you'll like each other enormously when you do meet. There's no doubt about it.

Red and green flicker at half strength.

ARTHUR: Mrs. Watson, your husband was telling me that your son William has been having a succession of colds all autumn. I suggested that just after Christmas he could go with my son Jim down to my mother's house in Florida.

BELINDA (*The blue light starts flickering with the other two*): Oh . . . uh . . . uh . . . uh . . .

LEONORA: Oh, Belinda, it would do him a world of good. I've been there; it's a perfectly beautiful place. They could be out in the sun all day.

ARTHUR: Of course, I have purely selfish reasons for urging it,

since my boy would have so much better a time with another boy along.

BELINDA (*All lights off, but a strong green; rises*): Mr. Smythe, I
thank you very much, really very much. But our family has
made the rule never to be separated. We may be unusual in
that; I don't know. But I couldn't let William . . . it's such
a distance . . . Thank you very much.

ARTHUR: That's as you think best, of course—I must be going
now. Leonora, I shall probably be telephoning your house
tonight . . . to ask about the weather. I'm glad to have
met you, Mrs. Watson. Perhaps Mrs. Rogers and I may hope
to meet you—*some day.*

Exit Arthur. All lights off.

BELINDA: Why did he say "Mrs. Rogers and I"?

LEONORA: What, dear?

BELINDA: Who's Mrs. Rogers? Why did he say "Mrs. Rogers
and I"?

LEONORA: Why not? That's Arthur Rogers.

BELINDA: But you said his name was SMYTHE! Leonora! —
Arthur Rogers! Why, my husband thinks the world of him.
How could you say that he was one of those *Smiths*?

LEONORA: Belinda, sit down. I have something to tell you.

BELINDA: What an awful mistake! Leonora, I might have hurt
his feelings.

LEONORA: You didn't hurt his feelings; he merely thought you
peculiar.

BELINDA: Leonora!

LEONORA: Now listen to what I'm saying, Belinda. Everything
I've told you about the Smiths today is nonsense. Do you
hear me?—perfect nonsense.

BELINDA (*Weeping*): I shouldn't have listened to you.

LEONORA: Exactly! You shouldn't have believed me. You have
no infallible instinct at all. What you call your instinct about
people is merely made of listening to nonsense like this.

BELINDA: Leonora, I don't know when I'll forgive you. You've
made a fool of me in front of a perfectly nice man.

Exit Belinda quickly. Leonora turns to the audience.

LEONORA: Well, that's the story. I realize that what you all want to know is whether Belinda profited by this lesson. Maybe not. Only one Belinda in ten ever learns anything. It's my nieces and nephews that I'm interested in.

Before bidding you good-bye I wish to ask the forgiveness of all Smiths who were for a moment disparaged in this play—of Kate Smith; of Mary Pickford, born Smith; of Smith College; and of the Smithsonian Institution.

But I have no apologies to make to those who were—even for a moment—shaken in their good opinion of the Smiths.

Good night.

END OF PLAY

SCENES FROM

The Emporium

CHARACTERS

STAGE HANDS
MEMBER OF THE AUDIENCE
MR. FOSTER, superintendent of the orphanage
MRS. FOSTER, his wife
MR. CONOVER, a janitor
MRS. GRAHAM, a farmer's wife, played by the same actress as
    Mrs. Foster
JOHN, the Grahams' adopted son
MR. GRAHAM, a farmer, played by the same actor as Mr. Foster
MR. HOBMEYER, guard and head floor-walker of the Empo-
    rium, played by the same actor as Mr. Foster
MISS LAURENCIA OBSTPFLUECKER
MR. DOBBS, played by same actor as Mr. Foster and Mr.
    Hobmeyer
MR. CORRIGAN
THREE OLD PEOPLE: MRS. FRISBEE, MISS COLEY, AND
    MR. BENJAMIN
MR. WILLISTON
MR. ALVAREZ
MISS WILHELMINA

The curtain of the stage is not used in this play.
Members of the audience arriving early will see the stage in half
light. The six screens and the furniture and properties will be seen
stacked about it at random.
Two Stage Hands dressed in light blue jumpers, like garage me-
chanics, will enter ten minutes before the beginning and will re-
move these properties and set the stage for Scene One.
The six screens are about six-and-a-half by twelve. They are like
the moveable walls of a Japanese house and are on rollers. They
are all slightly off white,—one faintly bluish, another toward
buff, or green, and so on.

There is a light chair on the left front of the stage (from the point of view of the actors), by the proscenium pillar.
A few minutes before the play begins the Member of the Audience enters from the wings at the left, looks about a little nervously and seats himself in this chair, turning it toward the center of the stage. He affects to be at ease, glances occasionally at the arriving audience, and studies his program. He is a modest but very earnest man of about fifty. He will be on the stage throughout the play and, except at the moments indicated, he will remain motionless, fixing an absorbed attention on the action before him.
A screen has been placed far front in the center of the stage, parallel with the footlights. The other screens are placed as though casually at the back of the stage though masking the entrances at the right and left. In front of the central screen is an old-fashioned "deacon's" chair. Beside it is a stand on which lies a vast Bible.
A bell starts ringing at the back of the auditorium.

SCENE ONE

The Amanda Gregory Foster Orphanage

Enter Mr. Foster, superintendent of the Orphanage. He is an excitable man of late middle age dressed in an old, faded and unpressed cutaway. He looks like a deacon or a small town undertaker.
He dashes out a few steps from the right and shakes his hand imperiously at the back of the auditorium, calling out loudly:

MR. FOSTER: Ring the bell, Mr. Conover. Ring it again. Ring it louder. I want every child in this orphanage to be in this auditorium in four minutes.

He disappears as rapidly as he came.
Enter from the same entrance Mrs. Foster, a worn woman of her husband's age, dressed in faded blue gingham. She also calls to the back of the auditorium:

MRS. FOSTER: Come in, children. Come in quietly. Take your places quietly, girls.—
Boys, behave yourselves!—Girls here on my left, as usual. Mr. Conover, are they ringing the bell out in the vegetable

garden, too? Thank you.—I wonder if the girls in the laundry can hear it, with all that machinery going.

Henry Smith Foster, is that you? Will you run over to the laundry and tell all the children that Mr. Foster wants them—all of them—here in the Assembly Hall.

Boys! Boys!—Don't play now. Just take your places quietly.

> *Exit Mrs. Foster.*
> *A second alarm bell starts ringing in dissonance.*
> *Enter Mr. Foster.*

MR. FOSTER: That's right, Mr. Conover. Ring all the bells. George Washington Foster, are *you* there? Form them into lines, two by two. They're all pushing and crowding.

Girls on this side (*left*); boys over here (*right*).

All children over eleven down here in front.

Very young children in the back. The blind children and the lame children in the last rows.

Children eight to eleven up in the balconies.

> *He shades his eyes and seems to be peering up to fourth, fifth and sixth balconies. Then again to the back of the auditorium:*

Now what's all that group late for? Oh, you've been working in the dairy. Very well, take your places.

> *Enter Mrs. Foster. She goes up to her husband and says in his ear:*

MRS. FOSTER: Now you mustn't get excited! You remember what the doctor said.

MR. FOSTER: Stragglers! Stragglers!

Yes.—Edgar Allan Poe Foster! Late as usual. Always trying to be different.

MRS. FOSTER: Remember your asthma! Remember your ulcers! You only hurt yourself when you get so excited. Remember, this has happened before and it will very certainly happen again.

(*Suddenly in irritation to a girl apparently coming down the aisle*) Sarah Bernhardt Foster! Stop making a show of yourself; sit down and take your place quietly among the other girls!

MR. FOSTER: I want you all to come to attention.
James Jones Foster!—you may assist George Washington Foster in closing the doors.

Impressive pause.

Wards of the Amanda Gregory Foster Orphanage! Of William County, Western Pennsylvania! Another of our children has attempted to run away!
That makes the twelfth since Christmas!

He has a moment's convulsion of asthmatic coughing and sneezing into an enormous red-checked handkerchief. During this his eyes fall on the Member of the Audience seated on the stage at his left. He stares at him a moment, then dropping his characterization, he says:

Who are you?
MEMBER OF THE AUDIENCE: I?
MR. FOSTER: Yes, you—who are you? What are you doing up here on the stage?
(*To the audience:*) Excuse me a moment. There's—there's something wrong here.
What are you doing—sitting up here on stage?
MEMBER OF THE AUDIENCE: Euh . . . the management sold me this seat . . . I told them I was a little hard of hearing.
MR. FOSTER: What? What's that? I can't hear you.
MEMBER OF THE AUDIENCE: The management sold me this seat. I . . . won't be in the way. I told them I was a little hard of hearing and they sold me this seat here.
MR. FOSTER: You certainly will be in the way. I never heard of such a thing.

He turns to Mrs. Foster.

We can't go on with this man here.
MRS. FOSTER: Perhaps. Anyway, we'd better not stop now. We'll try to do something about it at the intermission.
MR. FOSTER: At the intermission.—I must say I never heard of such a thing.—Anyway, while you're here,—draw your chair back against the wall. You're preventing those people from seeing the stage.

The Member of the Audience draws his chair back.

I hope you know enough not to distract the audience's attention in any way. It's important to us that you be as quiet as possible.

MEMBER OF THE AUDIENCE: Yes, oh, yes.

Mr. Foster glares at him and resumes his rôle.

MR. FOSTER: Wards of the Amanda Gregory Foster Orphanage! Of William County, Western Pennsylvania! Another of our children has attempted to run away. That makes the twelfth since Christmas.

He will be found. He will be brought back to us any moment now.

I have brought you together this morning to talk this over. You run away: To what? To whom?

Last fall *you* ran away (*fixing an orphan in the audience*), George Gordon Byron Foster! You were brought back after a week, but what kind of week was it? You slept in railroad stations; you fed yourself out of refuse cans, or from what you could beg at the back doors of restaurants.

We asked you why you ran away and you said you wanted to live—to live, to live, impatience to *live.*

—Joan Dark Foster, will you stop throwing yourself about in your seat! I shall not keep you long.—

And you said you wanted to be free.

Every lost dog and cat is free. The horse that has run away from the stable and wanders in the woods is free.

—Do I hear talking up there!—in the fourth and fifth balconies? Surely, you nine-year-olds can understand what I'm saying! The five-year-olds down here are quiet enough!

Gustav Froebel Foster!—Can't you keep order among the children up there?

He waits a moment in stern silence.

This orphanage was founded by a noble Christian woman, Amanda Gregory Foster, and here—for a time—you are taken care of.

You have all been given the name of Foster, in memory of our foundress, and some of you have been given the names of eminent—of great and useful—men and women. But you are all foundlings and orphans.

These are facts. Do not exhaust your minds and hearts by trying to resist these things *which are*.

Prometheus Foster! Ludwig van Beethoven Foster! Sit down, both of you! Glaring and shaking your fists at me cannot change these matters one iota.

What has to be, has to be. But that is not the only thing which you must patiently accept in life.

There is also much about each one of you which cannot be changed: your *self*.

Your eyes and nose and mouth. Your colour. Your height—when you have finally gained your growth.

And your disposition:

Some of you are timid. Some of you are proud. We know which ones of you are lazy and which of you are ambitious.

In addition, each of you has a different store of health. Your sum of health,—*yours!*

> *Mrs. Foster rises quickly and points to audience, left.*

MRS. FOSTER: What's that? John Keats Foster has fainted.

MR. FOSTER: Lower his head between his knees, boys; he will come to himself.

MRS. FOSTER: Who's sitting beside him? Joseph Severn Foster and Percy Shelley Foster,—carry him out into the open air, boys. You'd better take him to the Infirmary.

MR. FOSTER: And what's that noise I hear in the back row?

MRS. FOSTER: It's . . . it's the blind children.

Where's Helen Keller Foster?—Oh, there you are!—Will you comfort the . . . yes.

> *She returns to her seat.*

MR. FOSTER: There is no greater waste of time—and no greater enemy of character—than to wish that you were differently endowed and differently constituted.

From these things you cannot run away.

Now one of our number, John Vere Foster, has again tried to change all this.

For the third time he has tried to run away.

Ah, there he is!

Mr. Conover, will you bring John Vere Foster right down here, please. To the front row so that we can all see him.

Mr. Conover,—a shuffling old janitor—leads a boy, invisible to us, holding him by the ear, to a seat in the front row of the theatre aisle. Mr. Foster rises, steps forward, and fixes his eyes on the boy.

Now, young man, will you tell us—tell all of us—why is it that you tried to run away?

Pause.

What! You're going to be stubborn and silent?

Pause.

You all have enough to eat. You have suitable clothing. The work is not difficult. Many of you enjoy your classes and we hear all of you playing very happily among yourselves in your recreation hours. Mrs. Foster and I make every effort to be just. There is very little punishment here and what there is is light. Many visitors tell us that this is the best orphanage in the country.

Again he has an asthmatic convulsion.

MRS. FOSTER: Take a glass of water. Sit down a moment and take a glass of water.

He sits down, his shoulders heaving.
Mrs. Foster comes to the front of the stage and addresses John—more gently but unsentimentally:

John, tell us . . . tell us why you have tried to run away. I can't hear you. Oh—you want to *belong.*

MR. FOSTER: What did he say? What did he say?

MEMBER OF THE AUDIENCE (*helpfully*): He said he wanted to belong.

MR. FOSTER: Oh—to belong.

Children!—I am going to give John Vere Foster his wishes. He wishes—as you all say you do—to live and to belong.

A farmer and his wife called on me this morning. They wish to adopt a boy. Mr. Graham seems to me to be a just man. We do not usually place you—you, children—in homes until you are sixteen. John is only fourteen, but he is strong for his age—and, as you see, he is *impatient.*

John—go to Mrs. Hoskins: she will give you a new pair of shoes and a new overcoat; and she will pack your box.

You are leaving with your father and mother—Mr. and Mrs. Graham—on the railway train this afternoon.

You all *belong*.

Thousands of children have passed through this school—thousands of schools. The names of many of them you will find on tablets in the corridor. The names of many of them are forgotten. The very ink has faded on our school records. The generations of men are like the generations of leaves on the trees. They fall into the earth and new leaves are grown the following spring.

The world into which you have been born is one of eternal repetitions—already you can see that.

But there is something to which you *can* belong—you *do* belong. I am not yet empowered to tell you its name.

It is something which is constantly striving to bring something new into these repetitions, to lift them, to color them, to—

Belong!—to belong!

All of you have one thing in common: you do not belong to parents; you do not belong to homes; you do not belong to yourselves.

It's not by running away—from place to place—that you will find something to belong to—or that you will make yourself free—

Convulsions.

You are looking in the wrong place,
—You will find it when you least expect it.

He is shaken with coughing. His wife speaks to the children.

MRS. FOSTER: That will be all!

Go back to your rooms *quietly*, children.

Benvenuto Cellini Foster—put away your slingshot. This is no time for play.

SCENE TWO
The Graham Farm

The screens have been arranged to suggest a large room—the
kitchen of the Graham farmhouse. A gap between the two screens
at the back indicates the door into the parlor.
Stage left: a kitchen table. The chair at its left faces right.
Enter Mrs. Graham—played by the actress who has just played
Mrs. Foster.
She now seems gaunt and stony-faced. She has thrown a worn
blue shawl over her shoulders.
She carries a farm-lantern.
She comes to the front of the stage, opens an imaginary back-door.
She peers toward the back of the auditorium.

MRS. GRAHAM: John Graham, I want you should come in and
    eat your supper before Mr. Graham comes back from
    prayer-meeting.
    I've just heated it up for the second time and I want you
    should eat it.
    It's eight o'clock. It's cold and it's black as pitch. But I've
    seen you down by the corncrib there. You finished chores a
    long time ago and there's nothing for you to be doing down
    at the barn, and a growing boy should eat his food hot!
    It's real good. It's hominy cooked in bacon, and greens, and
    it's real good. And I put some molasses in it.

    She puts her lantern down and hugs her shawl tighter
    around her.

    All right, I won't call you by your whole name; I'll just call
    you John.
    Now, John, I want you to come and eat your supper.
    I know you think Mr. Graham's unjust—I know that—but
    you ought to see that he *thinks* he's doing the right thing.
    In his mind he's just. When he does that,—when he whips
    you, John, when he whips you on Wednesday nights,—he
    thinks he's doing it for your own good.
    And I've stewed up some of them crabapples that you
    picked yourself.
    I know what your argument is,—and I can understand it,—

that, what with all the work you've done, you've got a right
to take the horse and go into town nights, once in a while.
It's not *that* that Mr. Graham minds so much, I think,—
maybe it's that when you're in town you talk with those men
down in Kramer's livery stable . . . and learn swear words
. . . and . . . he prays to God that you don't touch liquor
and learn other things. That's the truth of the matter.
Now, John, I'm catching my death of cold here, and twice
I've heated up that good supper for you.

   She takes a step forward.

What's more, if you'll come in now, I'll tell you something—*something about yourself* that I never told you before.
Something real interesting that I learned when we called for
you at that orphanage.
It's about where you come from, where you were found.
I see now that I should've told you this a long time ago, because you're a grown-up man now, almost, and it's right
you should know everything important about yourself.

   *John seems suddenly to rise up in the middle aisle of the au-
   ditorium, about six rows from the stage. He is about eighteen
   and wears faded blue overalls.*

JOHN (*darkly*): You got something really to say? You're not
   just fooling me?
MRS. GRAHAM: I'm not fooling you. You come in and eat your
   supper and I'll tell you.
JOHN: You can tell it to me here.
MRS. GRAHAM: No, I can't. I'm perishing of cold. I can
   scarcely talk the way my teeth are chattering.
JOHN: Is it *long*—what you got to tell me?
MRS. GRAHAM: Oh, yes, it's long. I guess it'll take a whole
   quarter-hour to tell it right. So you come inside.
JOHN: I swore I wasn't ever going into that house again. I
   ain't going into any house where they call me a thief. I
   haven't ever stolen anything from anybody. It's him that's
   stolen from me: he steals from me every hour of the day,
   that's what he does. Maybe fathers can make their sons work
   for them for four years without one cent of pay,—but he's
   not my father and I'm not his son. He owes me a lot. I'll bet

you he owes me a whole hunnert dollars. I'll bet that by now I own that whole horse and I can take it wherever I want to.

MRS. GRAHAM: I know that's your argument, John.

JOHN: You go fetch a coat or something and tell me right here what you've got to tell me,—because I'm not going into that house another night to be whipped by him.

MRS. GRAHAM: Now, John, you know he's not coming back for a while yet. And you can tell when he's come by the bells on the horses, can't you?—Until he comes back, you come inside. Whatever you do then, I can't stop you.

JOHN: Well, I'll only just come inside the door. I won't go any farther than that.

MRS. GRAHAM: You don't have to come any farther than you want to,—but scrape the snow off your shoes when you come in.

> *She opens the imagined door and returns into the kitchen. After scraping his shoes, John follows her. She busies herself at the stove. He takes his stand down left center, his back to the audience, feet apart, proud and resentful.*

JOHN: Don't you worry about where I'll go.—Mr. Stahl-schneider's hired man gets five dollars a week. I guess I'm worth two dollars a week—leastways, these last two years I've been. I bet I've even been worth three dollars. And Mr. Graham hasn't given me anything except that blue suit,— and even that he locks up between Sundays.

MRS. GRAHAM: Now, John Graham,—if you're thinking of running away, I can't stop you, but I've got fourteen dollars I saved making buttermilk. It's right there behind the clock in a tobacco bag. If you must go, I'm glad you should have it.

JOHN (*loud*): I don't want no presents. I want what's *mine*. And my name's not John *Graham*. I haven't got any name, —only John.

MRS. GRAHAM: We tried to be a father and mother to you, best we could.

JOHN: I don't want no father or mother. I'm glad I didn't have any.

MRS. GRAHAM (*handing him an imagined plate*): Here's your supper.

JOHN: Put it on the table. I don't think I'm going to eat it.—
You can say what you were going to say.

MRS. GRAHAM (*putting the plate on the corner of the table, but speaking with spirit*): And I'm not going to say one living word until you take a mouthful of that good supper while it's hot.

Silence. War of wills. Suddenly John goes to the table, digs an unseen spoon into the dish and puts it in his mouth. He then resumes his former vindictive position.

JOHN: Well, say it!

MRS. GRAHAM: When we went to that Amanda Gregory Foster Orphanage to adopt you we had a talk with that Mr. and Mrs. Foster that run it. We asked them if they knew anything about you and where you come from.

Pause.

I must say I can't tell this very good with you standing there and showing hate in every muscle.

JOHN: Well, what do you want me to say? I run away three times and I'd run away again.

Their eyes meet. She points at the plate. He abruptly takes one more mouthful and replaces the plate on the table.

MRS. GRAHAM: You were found in a baskit, John—about three months old. Now maybe you'll think what I'm going to tell you isn't important, but you'll be mistaken there.
That baskit, and every stitch of clothes that baby had on— and the blankits and the rattle and milk bottle and the nipple —all of it, all of it come from the Gillespie and Schwinge- meister Emporium.

Pause.

Now I hope you see what that means.
There wasn't a thing there that was second-rate or skimped. Somebody thought a lot of you, John—thought enough of you to get you A-number-one fittings.

JOHN (*after a short pause*): Now I've et and I'm going back to the barn.

MRS. GRAHAM: I got something more to tell you. You eat

every mouthful on that plate. I guess you've heard of the G. and S. Emporium in Philadelphia, P.A.

There is a sound of sleigh bells at the rear of the auditorium. Both listen in suspense.

That's Deacon Riebenschneider's bells.

They relax.

JOHN: Course, I have.

MRS. GRAHAM: Well, it'd be a funny thing if you hadn't, because I've noticed that you're awful interested in stores. Goodness, when we take you into town, that's all you want to see—asking me a thousand questions. I never saw anybody so interested in anything like you're interested in stores.

—Well, I should think you'd be real proud,—that all your baby-fittings come from the G. and S.

JOHN: Well, I ain't proud of it.

MRS. GRAHAM: That just goes to show how ignorant you are. I guess you think that's a store like any other store. A store that buys a lot of things and then sells 'em; a store that don't do any more than that: just does the same thing over and over, buy-sell, buy-sell. I guess you think it's that kind of store.

JOHN: Have you ever . . . have you ever been in it?

MRS. GRAHAM: Have I ever been in it?

(*Without looking at him. Brooding, with muted exaltation*) There's a kind of well that goes up the middle of it—and balconies and balconies with little white colyums.

And red carpets with roses on them. And at the corners of the aisles, there's big brass cuspidors.

And over the sales-ladies' heads there's wires and when they sell something little iron boxes run along the wires with the change. And at one side there are these elevators that go up and down taking people where they want to go.

JOHN: It's . . . it's only one of these stores for rich people.

MRS. GRAHAM: That shows you know nothing about it, simply nothing at all.

(*Again brooding*) It'll never burn up—that's what they say. Never even been a little fire in it. Of course, they keep a whole fire-fighting outfit in it—but that's just for show.

Of course, if you buy goods there and bring them home—
then they'll burn. But not in the store they won't.

Why, if Philadelphia, P.A., had a fire like Chicago, Illinois,
had—you go in the G. and S. and you'll be perfectly safe.

That's what they say and I believe them.

JOHN: That's not reasonable.

MRS. GRAHAM: Reasonable? Ain't nothing reasonable about it.
Why, there are millions of people in the world who think
that the G. and S. is crazy. Why, my sister went in to buy a
wedding-dress and there was one there—all fine sewed. The
most beautiful dress in the world. And it looked like it cost a
hundred dollars and, of course, she couldn't pay that.

But the lady sold it to her for eighteen dollars, that's a fact.
Not a thing wrong with it.

My sister's husband—well, one terrible thing after another
happened; but it was a beautiful dress; and her daughter
wore it at *her* wedding.

Then on other days, little things, little everyday things cost a
world of money.

Nobody's ever been able to understand it—nobody.

Some days the G. and S. insults the customers—there's no
other way of putting it—and other days it loads you down.

It's not reasonable . . . but it's the greatest store in the
world.

JOHN: What's this other thing you were going to tell me?

MRS. GRAHAM: Before I tell you, I want you to promise me . . .
that you won't raise your hand against Mr. Graham when he
. . . when he thinks it's his duty to punish you. Mr.
Graham don't seem to notice that you're getting bigger and
stronger every month.

Will you promise me that?

*John, silent a moment; then goes to back wall and takes the
same pose facing the audience.*

JOHN: Say what you were going to say without making any
bargains. (*Relents*) Depends on what he does. (*Pause.*) Have
you been in it often?

MRS. GRAHAM: Have I been in it often?! . . .

Gravely she brings out a locket from the neck of her dress.

See that lockit? I got that lockit for three years' faithful service at the G. and S.

JOHN (*fascinated, peers at it*): That says Gertrude Foster. Your
name ain't Foster.

MRS. GRAHAM: 'Fore I married Mr. Graham it was.

JOHN (*backing; outraged*): I thought you was like that Mrs.
Foster that run the orphanage. Are you kin of hers? Are you
. . . *kin* of hers?

MRS. GRAHAM: Course not. Lots of people named Foster in
West Pennsylvania. Lots of 'em.—Now you eat these crab-
apples while I tell you what comes next.

You eat 'em slow . . . get the nourishment out of them.

> *She gives him the plate and goes back to the stove. She is
> again lost in thought.*

You can scarcely see to the top of it where there's painting—
hand-painting on the dome. And always, way up, very faint
—there's music. Music wrote special for the Emporium.

You never saw such a place.

JOHN (*now spell-bound*): And the superinten'ants and managers? Are they walking around? I mean Mr. Gillespie and
Mr. Schwingemeister?

MRS. GRAHAM (*sudden scorn*): Well, if you aren't the most ignorant boy in the world I don't know who is! Mr. Gillespie!
Mr. Schwingemeister, indeed!

Why nobody's ever seen even Mr. Sordini—and he's on the
fifth floor.

Looks like you think the Emporium's like other stores.

Huh! I wouldn't have called you in from the barn if your
baby-fittings come from an ordinary store.

If you want to work in any ordinary store you can go to
Craigie's—yes, sir, you can go to Craigie's Deepartmental
Store, that's next door to the G. and S.

In Craigie's you know where you are.

You're paid regular—

> *Sleighbells at back of auditorium. Same business.*

That's Widow Ochshofer's.

JOHN: Don't they *pay* you at the Emporium?

MRS. GRAHAM: And you can see Mr. Craigie, every day, ten times a day.

You're paid good and you're paid regular—and everything's perfectly clear.

At six o'clock you can go home.

Yes, sir, you can work there fifty years and any night you like you can go home and hang yourself.

At Craigie's Departmental Store, the color's green. Everything green. What color is the Emporium color?

JOHN (*weak*): I don't know.

MRS. GRAHAM (*whispers*): What color do I always wear?

JOHN: . . . Blue. . . .

MRS. GRAHAM: Of *course* I do . . . and what color you got on?

JOHN: Blue!

MRS. GRAHAM: And what color was all over that baskit you was found in?

Blue.

Now, I'll tell you something about yourself.

Where was your baskit found?

On the steps of the City Hall?

Or the hospital, like most babies?

Or at the Public Liberry?

No.

You were found on the steps of the G. and S. itself.

You kind of belong there—that's what I think.

You're an Emporium man.

But that ain't all:

You know what I think? I think that Amanda Gregory Foster Orphanage—I think that orphanage is run by the G. and S. —that's what I think. I think I've seen that Mr. and Mrs. Foster before—and I know *where* I saw 'em too.

JOHN (*excitedly*): You look like her. That's what I always thought—that you look like her.

MRS. GRAHAM (*contemptuously*): I don't look like her at all. But I've often said to myself: if anything happened to Mr. Graham—that's where I'd like to be. I'd like to be working at that orphanage, helping some way, working with all those children. Something like that.

You're an Emporium man.

Sleigh bells. This is it.

There he is. That's him.

JOHN (*frozen*): I'm going to stay right here.

MRS. GRAHAM: Now remember, John. You promised.

JOHN: I never made no promise in my life.

MRS. GRAHAM: I ironed your blue suit today. It's just inside that door. And if you think you've got to go—here it is. The buttermilk money.

> *She goes quickly to the mantel and pushes an (imaginary) bag toward him.*

JOHN: I don't need no money.

MRS. GRAHAM: Take it.

Hasn't anybody ever told you that this world is a terrible place—hasn't nobody ever told you that? *Take it!*

> *She returns to her chair and sits down.*
> *Enter Mr. Graham—fur cap; short green coat of blanket material.*
> *Strides down the auditorium aisle; on to the stage; without glancing right or left goes out stage-center.*
> *They stare motionless while he passes through the room.*

JOHN (*whispering*): What do you mean: the Emporium don't *pay* you?—It's no good, if it don't pay you when you work for it.

MR. GRAHAM'S VOICE (*from the parlor*): John Graham—you will come into the parlor.

MRS. GRAHAM: Listen, now—I haven't told you the whole truth about it: how *hard* it is.

And some days you just despair.

Yes, some weeks it forgets to pay you.

And some weeks it pays you too much—like there's been a mistake in the books.

And that it takes every bit of you and don't hardly leave you any life to yourself.

And that it doesn't thank you—and it almost never gives you a compliment for what you've done.

Just the same—it's something you can feel you can *belong* to. You go there! You'll see.

MR. GRAHAM'S VOICE: John!

Mr. Graham appears at the parlor door. He is holding a large stick.

John Graham, did you hear me?
You will go into the parlor and lower your overalls.
Mrs. Graham, you will go upstairs.

MRS. GRAHAM: Mr. Graham, I will stay right here.

MR. GRAHAM: Mrs. Graham, you will go upstairs.

MRS. GRAHAM: You and I, before God, adopted this boy for our own—together. (*She flinches.*) I'm going out on the porch, but I'm not going upstairs.

Hugging her shawl about her, she goes out on the porch, and stands with pursed mouth.

MR. GRAHAM: Did you hear me, John?

JOHN (*rapidly*): I'm coming in. But I tell you right now that you owe me a hunnert dollars and maybe more; and that any man that's hit by another man has a right to defend himself; and that that time the hook fell on you from the top of the barn and you were sick a week—you thought it was me but it wasn't; and the only lie I ever told you was about when the old heifer got in the lower pasture (and that was in the second week I was here): so I guess everything's square between us now.

He goes out back, center. Mr. Graham is astonished by this speech.

MR. GRAHAM: I don't know what you're talking about. Anybody'd think you'd gone crazy. Your smoking and your drinking have made you crazy,—that's what happened.

He follows John off. His voice can be heard.

We'll first kneel down and ask God's blessing.

Mrs. Graham slowly re-enters the kitchen; sits at the table. Sudden sounds of violence from the parlor. Stumbling. Breaking furniture.

MR. GRAHAM'S VOICE: How *dare* you—you young . . . *devil!*

Silence. Mrs. Graham does not move.

Gertrude! Gertrude!

John appears at the door. Sombre, and a little dazed. He is holding the stick. Mrs. Graham does not look at him.

JOHN: I'll take my blue suit.

MR. GRAHAM (*off*): Gertrude!

John becomes aware that he is holding the stick. He throws it back into the parlor. He returns to the parlor and reappears with his suit wrapped in a brown paper parcel. He starts to leave via the audience; then pauses, drops the parcel and going to Mrs. Graham leans over her with his hands approaching her throat.

JOHN: Give me that!

MRS. GRAHAM (*in terror, defending her throat*): John! What you doin'? What you doin'?

JOHN: I'm taking that lockit. (*He breaks it and holds it before him.*) That's the only thing I ever stole.

MRS. GRAHAM: All right. You didn't steal it. I give it to you.

JOHN (*looking about him*): Of all the hundreds and thousands of farms I could'a been sent to,—I was sent to this one!

MRS. GRAHAM (*proudly*): Anyway, in this one you got one thing: you heard about the Emporium firsthand.

JOHN: I'll bet it ain't much.

He dashes down into the audience and leaves the auditorium by the aisle.

MR. GRAHAM'S VOICE: Gertrude . . . get Dr. Krueger . . . Go, get him. . . .

Mr. Graham goes slowly out back.
Sound of galloping horse at the back of the auditorium.

MEMBER OF THE AUDIENCE (*looks at the audience; smiles, rubs his hands*): I guess that's the end of the scene.

SCENE THREE
First Floor of the Emporium

Again there is a bell,—this time, back stage.
Mr. Hobmeyer, guard and head floor-walker—played by the
same actor who played Mr. Foster—enters. He now wears a
splendid commissionaire's blue coat, trimmed with red and
gold frogs, braid, etc. and a magnificent commissionaire's
cap.

MR. HOBMEYER: That is the closing bell, madam. Yes, madam,
it is six o'clock. Very well, madam, complaints should be put
into writing and placed in one of the complaint boxes. You
will find a complaint box at each of the entrances.
(*Loudly*) The Emporium appreciates your patronage, ladies
and gentlemen, but must insist that all patrons now leave
the store.

Enter from right Miss Laurencia Obstpfluecker, walking
backward.

LAURENCIA: Yes, madam, that is the closing bell. We open at
eight o'clock every weekday morning, madam.
MR. HOBMEYER: There are exits in every direction, sir. *That*
corridor leads to the Market Street entrance. You're welcome, sir.
LAURENCIA: You have been separated from . . . Lost children, madam, are assembled at the Market Street entrance.
You're welcome, madam.

She sings to herself under her breath.

I'll be a little late tonight, Mr. Hobmeyer. I've got to get
some boxes from the stock room.
MR. HOBMEYER: That'll be all right, Miss Laurencia, as long as
you're out by seven. (*loud*) Ladies and gentlemen, the Gillespie and Schwingemeister Emporium appreciates your patronage, but must insist that all patrons now leave the store.
LAURENCIA: Yes, madam, the material will be waiting for you
here on Monday morning. You can make up your mind in
the meantime. You're welcome, madam.

She sings to herself, as she busily shifts boxes about.

Mr. Hobmeyer opens his coat, loosens his collar, stretches, and yawns.

MR. HOBMEYER: Well, that's another week.

LAURENCIA (*confidentially*): I'm afraid it was an awfully bad week for sales, Mr. Hobmeyer.—(*sharply*) Lost children, madam, are assembled at the Market Street entrance. I think you'd better hurry, madam—after ten minutes, the lost children are *disposed* of. (*She is convulsed with laughter and covers her face with her handkerchief.*) I love to tell them that; I learned it from Julia. (*She heads right, apparently arranging boxes:*) Six, navy blue; six and a quarter, navy blue; six and a half, navy blue—I only sold half what I usually sell. We'll go into bankr'acy, for sure. (*This also amuses her very much.*) Seven three-quarters, navy blue. Eight, navy blue.

MR. HOBMEYER (*has come to the front of the stage and is listening toward the dome*): Bee-thoven!

LAURENCIA: What?

MR. HOBMEYER: That music up there. Wrote special for the Emporium. Man name of Bee-thoven. Deef as a post, he was.

LAURENCIA (*stands beside him*): Wrote music when he was deef?!—oh, you're joking.—When I first came here I couldn't hear it at all,—not a note. Now I can a little.

John, wearing his blue suit, appears for a second at the back, trying to hear their conversation. He then disappears.

Mostly I like waltzes.

They listen in silence—dreamily.

This is the time I love best,—when *they've* gone. Mr. Hobmeyer, isn't the music often better at night,—after the crowds have gone, I mean?

MR. HOBMEYER: Why, Miss Laurencia, some nights it gets tremendous up there, tremendous.

LAURENCIA: Really?—And Mr. Hobmeyer, there's another question I've always wanted to ask you: after closing hours —after we've gone home—do *they* come down? The Higher-Ups, I mean, from the offices on the seventh and eighth floors? Do they come down and look around and see what we've been doing? I've wanted to ask you that for a long time.

MR. HOBMEYER: Miss Laurencia, I've been here forty years, and my father and grandfather before me,—we never seen any of those Higher-Ups. Emporium isn't like other stores. Here you never see 'em.

LAURENCIA (*with a sigh, going back to her work*): That's one of the things that makes it so hard. You never know if you're giving satisfaction. Six, black. Six and a quarter, black. Six and—

Suddenly she stops and says:

Mr. Hobmeyer, some days I want to just stay and work in the Emporium all my life. And other days I want to resign and go away tomorrow. I love it, I love it, I love it,—but it's so hard. Sometimes I think all I do is make mistakes. Really, it's as though each one of us has to carry the whole G. and S. on our shoulders every minute of the day. And with nobody to help us.

MR. HOBMEYER: That's my favorite.

LAURENCIA: What, Mr. Hobmeyer?

MR. HOBMEYER: Those pictures up around the dome. Hand-painted special for the Emporium. See that one?

She joins him. John appears, peeking around a wall.

LAURENCIA: Which one?

MR. HOBMEYER: God making the first man, Adam. Fellow lay on his back for years on a scaffold to paint it. Eyetalian. Just about lost his eyesight.

LAURENCIA: Lost his eyesight?!

MR. HOBMEYER: Michael-something. Michael, some such name. Eyetalian.

LAURENCIA: I hope they paid him,—you know what I mean. —Did the G. and S. *make* him lie on his back all those years to paint it?

MR. HOBMEYER: Didn't *make* him. You know what the Emporium's like: it just tells you to do what you do best and then it leaves you alone. As to paying him,—well, there isn't enough money in the world to pay for eyesight like that, is there? (*without transition*) You said that here in the G. and S. you work with no one to help you.

LAURENCIA (*with sudden force*): Yes, *that*'s what's so bad.

MR. HOBMEYER: Ah, but Miss Laurencia,—

Another bell rings backstage. John disappears.

Well, there's the second bell. I'd better go and start rounding up some of those stragglers.—Don't look now, Miss Laurencia, but there's one of those young fellas trying to get himself shut up in here after closing time. He's hiding in the raincoats.

LAURENCIA: They do that all the time.

MR. HOBMEYER: I think maybe he's trying to get to know you, Miss Laurencia.

LAURENCIA: Well, he's just wasting his time, Mr. Hobmeyer. You can tell him that.

Mr. Hobmeyer, leaving, suddenly cocks his ear to the dome, and says:

MR. HOBMEYER: Schubert?

LAURENCIA: What, Mr. Hobmeyer?

MR. HOBMEYER: That music. Wrote by Schubert. Young fella died at thirty-six. My grandfather remembered him bringing in his stuff every day, regular.

Exit.
Laurencia, humming, carries some boxes to left, and kneels, arranging them.
Suddenly John plunges forward from the back.

JOHN (*without turning*): Excuse me, can I ask you a question?

LAURENCIA: It's after closing time. Mr. Hobmeyer will let you out at the Market Street entrance.

JOHN: Before I go there's a question I want to ask you. What I want to know is why you work in a place like this?

She turns and glares at him.

I know some people think this is a wonderful store,—and maybe you do. But I mean, just look at it.

LAURENCIA (*balefully*): I have looked at it!

JOHN (*intimidated, hence doubly nervous*): It's . . . it's a broken-down fifth rate old store. It's old and it's so crowded you can't turn around in it . . . and, well, look at it. And besides, the air is so bad you can't breathe it. What I mean is, you could get a job at Craigie,—a girl like you—

LAURENCIA (*rising slowly, furious*): The air's bad!!

JOHN: And this store. Why, it doesn't even advertise, and . . . it hasn't even got a front door. Why, you have to look a dozen times even before you can find an entrance. What I think is that it's got you all hyp-notized because . . . (*finishing lamely, under her glare*) . . . There's just nothing here.

LAURENCIA: The air's bad! The air's bad!

JOHN: I just wanted to ask you that question.

LAURENCIA: Now listen to me: this store, with that big wall and that dome, has the best air in the world. Something's the matter with your *nose*—that's the trouble! Can't find the front door?! Why this store has ten doors, and every one is more beautiful than the other. Air! If you want some bad air, you go over to Craigie's store, next door. Over there, *all* the air is bad.

JOHN: Fact is, I work there.

LAURENCIA: Then what are you doing in here.—If you think so much of Craigie's, you can go back there. We don't want you here!—Mr. Hobmeyer! Mr. Hobmeyer!—Now I want you to apologize to me. You put your nose right under that dome and *smell*.

He glares at her.

Go on!

He comes forward and sniffs.

Again!—Now what do you say?

JOHN: Well, . . . it isn't so bad as I thought.

LAURENCIA: Can you hear the music up there?

She points. He listens. Then shakes his head, no.

Can you see all those pictures?

JOHN (*squinting*): Hardly.

LAURENCIA: You haven't any nose or ears or eyes,—that's the trouble with you. Now go away and leave me to work.

She kneels down and continues working, absorbedly. He watches her.

Seven—black; seven and a quarter, black; seven and a half, black.

JOHN: I came to Philadelphia about a year ago. And the first thing I did was to try to get a job here. And they wouldn't take me, but I could see they were taking other fellows my age. I tried every way. I guess I must have been throwed out of here a dozen times. . . . What I want to know is how do you get a job here? What kind of person have you got to be?

LAURENCIA: That's none of my business. I don't know anything about that.

JOHN: Would you be so kind as to . . . could you tell me how you got in here?

LAURENCIA (*sharply*): No!— (*She stands and faces him*)
If you *hate* the Emporium so, why are you so crazy to get a job here?

He stares back at her, reluctant to answer.

JOHN: Well, I'm interested in stores. I want to be the biggest department store man in the world. So I ought to know how every store is run.

She continues to stare at him. He adds haltingly:

I'm young. I have only one life to lead and I don't want to make any mistakes.

Still she does not answer. Out of his pocket he takes Mrs. Graham's medal.

You see that? That's a G. and S. medal. Someone gave me that once and said that . . . that I was an Emporium man.

LAURENCIA (*turning abruptly back to her tasks, curtly*): I don't know how you get a job here.

JOHN: I thought maybe in a few minutes you'd come to dinner with me. I've got money.

She doesn't answer.

I thought maybe if you knew me better, you could tell me

what was wrong with me,—why they won't give me a job here. I thought maybe you could improve me.

LAURENCIA (*turning suddenly, almost fiercely*): No! No! Go away.—Mr Hobmeyer! Mr. Hobmeyer!—You have no business here at all. Coming in here night after night and hiding in the raincoats. You're Craigie. Craigie's written all over you.

Enter Mr. Hobmeyer.

MR. HOBMEYER: What's this? What's this?—Young man, what are you doing here? Haven't I put you out of this store enough times? Now you get out of that door right now. You've got no business here.

JOHN: All right. I'm going.

Laurencia, head high, walks quickly out left.

MR. HOBMEYER: I don't know what I'm going to do with fellows like you.

John is moving sullenly to the right, when suddenly he stops. In great excitement he points to the dome.

JOHN: I can hear it . . . I *can* hear it!—Mr. Hobmeyer,—you know all about it. Help get me in!

MR. HOBMEYER: That's the point, boy, about the G. and S.—Nobody can help you. You must do it all yourself!

SCENE FOUR

Four chairs on the left. Audience member in one; four on the right.
Table right. Chairs behind it facing the audience.
Enter Mr. Dobbs, played by actor who played Mr. Foster. He carries many papers. Stops en route to table and gazes piercingly at the office.

MR. DOBBS: You may shut the doors, Mr. Corrigan.

Starts toward his table, then says abruptly:

I don't want anyone here who has come into this auditorium

by mistake. This is not the post office. And this is not the branch public library. I want it understood clearly that this is the Personnel Employment Office Number Seven of the Gillespie and Schwingemeister Emporium and nothing else. I assume that you are *all* applicants for employment at the G. and S. Is that clear?

Let the lady out, Mr. Corrigan. What did she think this was? . . .

He goes to his table, sits and with a very grave face shuffles his papers.
Then rises and comes to the center of the stage.

Ladies and gentlemen. I have good news for you this morning. I have received word—from very high quarters— that there will be a number of vacancies at the end of the month.

His eye is distracted by the entrance, from the back of the stage right, of three old people—Mrs. Frisbee, Miss Coley, and a few minutes after them of Mr. Benjamin. Just as in the case of the interruption in Scene One, he speaks to them in his voice as an actor.

I beg your pardon?—What are you doing here?

MRS. FRISBEE: This play is about department stores, isn't it?

MR. DOBBS: What? What did you say?

MRS. FRISBEE: Since this play is about department stores we want to hear every word of it—

MR. DOBBS (*at the end of his patience*): The place for members of the audience is *down there*, in the auditorium,—not here on the stage. We have one too many up here, as it is.

MRS. FRISBEE (*firmly and agreeably and very loquaciously taking over*): We are from the RRDSW. Retreat for Retired Department Store Workers. We've worked in department stores all our lives, and one of our board of directors thought that we'd like to see this play.

What's more, I worked in the store you're talking about.

MR. DOBBS: What's that?

MRS. FRISBEE: I know all about your Gillespie and Schwinge-meister.

MR. DOBBS: Why there is no such store. The author just made that up.

MRS. FRISBEE: Oh, we all know what lies behind that name.

MR. DOBBS: This is quite impossible!

MRS. FRISBEE: And since we're all over sixty-five—you have to be sixty-five to get into the Retreat for Retired Department Store Workers—we'd like to *see* and hear every word of it. So we're going to sit up here, like that nice man.

MR. DOBBS: We can't *act*! We can't *act* with all you people—

MRS. FRISBEE: Why, you're acting *splendidly*. Now, young man, you go right on with the play. We won't disturb you at all.

MR. DOBBS (*beaten, helpless, and in resigned despair to the audience*): You can see that I'm not responsible for what's been going on here today.

MRS. FRISBEE (*to her friends*): Are you comfortable, Julia?—Mr. Benjamin?—(*To Mr. Dobbs:*) We all have awards for long and faithful service in department store work. Miss Coley was thirty-five years in jewelry at John Wanamakers; Mr. Benjamin was thirty-three at Marshall Fields in men's hosiery. And I—now, I won't say another word. This is the Employment office of *your* store—we heard that. Now you go right on from where you were.

MR. DOBBS (*pauses in despair, then says icily*): Are you comfortable?

MRS. FRISBEE: Yes, yes, yes.—Very.

MR. DOBBS (*to himself*): Where was I?—Ladies and gentlemen, I have good news for you this morning. I have received word—from very high quarters—that there will be a number of vacancies at the end of the month. Several of these vacancies will be for the *young*; at least two will be for those of more advanced years.

> *Enter John in his blue suit, right, back. He stands truculently listening to Mr. Dobbs.*

I have the waiting list here,—but I will repeat what I have said before: your employment does not *primarily* depend upon your position on the waiting-list. It depends on your personal qualifications,—you know that.

Mrs. Herkiner and Mr. Bennhurst head the waiting-list. I believe Mrs. Herkiner has been waiting here . . . for . . .

sixty-three years, and Mr. Bennhurst . . . sixty, almost sixty-one. We can assure them that their turn will come— they will—pretty certainly—obtain employment at the G. and S. Though it may not be next month.

How often have I told you . . . when you think of the thousands—hundreds of thousands—who have waited here—here and in the twelve other agencies—for their call to the G. and S.—what reason is there for sobbing and fainting or—for self-pity and sentimentality.

Last week, Mr. Wentworth killed himself right there in the back row. Self-pity and sentimentality.

Mrs. Herkiner! Mrs. Herkiner! Control yourself. Tears and sobbing never got anybody anywhere.

As for the younger people—there is Wilfred Cusack: he has been waiting here since the age of five. He is an artist. He feels that he can be useful to the G. and S. perhaps in painting the dome, or in dressing the windows. Hm.

Mr. Kerry—yawning, yawning, here of all places. You will slip back four places in the waiting list. And I don't want to have to speak to you again. You are not at the theatre, or at a concert, or in church. You can go and yawn *there*. But you are here,—where your whole life and soul depends on what I tell you.

    His eye falls on John.

What are you doing here?

JOHN (*without moving from his place*): I want a job at the G. and S. (*He stretches out his hand.*) I want one of those blue cards.

MR. DOBBS: Then take your place with the others down here, and wait your turn with the others.

    John does not move and continues gazing at him somberly.

Now: I have to talk to you very seriously about something else.

Word has reached me that a number of you . . . have been making inquiries about obtaining employment in another department store. I will name it: In Craigie's dee-partmental store.

He goes over to his table and strikes it forcefully with his fist.

I could scarcely believe it. I could scarcely believe my ears. *You*—Craigie's!! When you had the chance, the possibility (*slapping the table*) of entering the service of the G. and S. Is Mr. Williston here? Mr. Williston, come forward.

Mr. Williston, 60, trembling, starts down the auditorium's aisle and starts mounting the steps to the stage.

Come up here where we can all see you.

Mr. Williston, halfway up the stairs. His knees give way. Sobbing, he falls, sprawled on the steps.

MR. WILLISTON: I can't. . . . I can't.
MR. DOBBS: You have waited here for thirty-two years looking forward to employment at the G. and S. You have appeared at this office three times a week, like everybody else. I believed you to be loyal. But you wavered. You backslid.

He goes back to his desk and shuffles papers.

Mr. Williston, you will lose twenty places in the waiting-list. You will fall back between Mr. Alvarez and Miss Wilhelmina Caffrey.

He turns to John.

I told you to join the other applicants in the auditorium.
JOHN (*without moving; cool impudence*): I'm watchin' this. I'm listening to what you have to say.
MR. DOBBS: Mr. Williston, you may return to your seat.
MR. WILLISTON: —I . . . there was . . . (*inarticulate mumbling*)
MR. DOBBS: What's that you're trying to say?
MR. WILLISTON: Mr. Dobbs . . . Mr. Dobbs . . . I tried only once to get a job at Craigie's . . . I'm no longer a young man. . . . My daughter-in-law humiliates me.
MR. DOBBS: Your daughter-in-law humiliates you? How often have I told you that the Gillespie and Schwingemeister Emporium is not interested in your private life?—You may go back to your seat.

Mr. Williston creeps back to his seat. John comes forward with a baleful step.

JOHN: What a lot of crazy fools you all are. This man here can't get anybody a job at the G. and S. He's just a fraud. I've been to all twelve G. and S. Employment Offices in this town. They're all frauds. Thousands of you, thousands, come into those places three times a week—for fifty-sixty years,—and nobody's ever got a job.

Mr. Dobbs stands at his table, glaring at John.

MR. DOBBS: Say what you have to say. I've heard it all before.
JOHN: Show me your papers. Show me even *one* letter from the G. and S.

To the audience:

Here you are, eating your hearts out to get work there. You've wasted your whole life.

Calling to the back of the auditorium:

Mr. Williston, you go and get a job at Craigie's. They're honest and they pay regular and they give you a pension when you're old. I work there. I came to Philadelphia about two years ago. I'd heard a lot about the G. and S. and I tried to get a job there. I tried every way. I was throwed out a dozen times, but I could see they were taking on other fellows my age every day. And then I went to Craigie's and I got a job right off. And I got paid better than people who've worked at the G. and S. for years. And I've got promoted, and I'm head of men's shirts and collars.
MR. DOBBS: Then why do you come here?
JOHN: I come in here because I . . . almost hate the Emporium. I don't understand it. But I'd even give up my job at Craigie's to work there . . . for a while. Because the thing I'm most interested in is stores. I'm not ashamed to say that I intend to be the biggest department store man in the world,—and . . . I got to get to know every kind of store.
MR. WILLISTON: You *hate* the Emporium!!
JOHN (*a little wildly*): I know there are people that think it's the best. But I went in it when I first came to Philadelphia

and . . . why, all I could see was an old fifth rate run-down store—so full of junk that you couldn't turn around in it . . . and . . . the air was so bad . . . and the doors into it were so little you could scarcely see them. . . .

MR. WILLISTON: Oh! Oh!

MR. DOBBS: Let the fool talk!

JOHN: And I heard all those stories about it. How it don't pay regular . . . and how it takes your whole life and don't give you anything in return. What I want to know is why some people think it's so wonderful. That's why I came here.—Because I'm a young man and I've only got one life to live and . . . I don't want to make any mistakes.

MRS. FRISBEE (*very much agitated, waving her hands*): I never saw such a play. I declare, I never saw such a play. Julia, do you want to go home?

MISS COLEY: Let's see what they have to say next, Emma. We can go home if it gets worse.

They hold each other's hands for a moment.

John goes to Mr. Dobbs, takes the lapels of his coat and presses them together under his—Mr. Dobbs's—neck.

JOHN: Can you get anybody a job at the G. and S.? Are you a fraud?

MR. DOBBS (*terrified*): Don't touch me. Help!

John goes close to Mr. Dobbs—and directs his wild emphatic words to both him and the audience.

JOHN: What we all want to know is: how does a person get a job at the G. and S.?—Can you find us a job or can't you. YES OR NO??

He grasps Mr. Dobbs by his coat lapels and starts backing him to stage right.

YES or NO.

MR. DOBBS: You take your hands off me. How dare you touch me.

JOHN: We're in earnest. We're not fooling.

MR. DOBBS: Help. Help me. Get this crazy one off me.

JOHN: Answer. Answer.

Mrs. Frisbee and Miss Coley rise shrieking and waving their hands in the air.

MRS. FRISBEE: Why, this is terrible. He's hurting him. (*To the Member of the Audience:*) *Do* something. You must stop this.

The three old people scatter like a flock of sparrows from their seats to the center of the stage.

JOHN (*as Mr. Dobbs falls exhausted into the chair vacated by Mrs. Frisbee*): Are you employed by the G. and S.? Do you get paid by them?

Mr. Dobbs, much shaken, tries to speak, at last pulls himself together and says with dignity:

MR. DOBBS: Many people have passed from this office to service in the G. and S. They all know that.

JOHN: *What* gets them in? How are they chosen?

MR. DOBBS: Nobody knows that.

JOHN: Well, you must'a been watching it for years. You must have *some* idea? (*Mr. Dobbs, his eyes on the distance, shakes his head faintly*) —And all these people come to you just for that and you haven't any suggestions?—Well, I'll tell you what you are: you're a real big fraud.

(*To the audience:*) Somebody—somewhere—must know a better way to get in.

He turns back to Mr. Dobbs.

Anyway, you must know something. What *is* the Emporium? What makes it different from other stores? Why do so many people give up everything else in their life for it?— WHAT IS IT?

Mr. Dobbs continues silent, exhausted, deaf. John, in heightened impatience, puts out his hands and is about to shake him.

MRS. FRISBEE: Now, stop it, young man. Don't be so impatient. Give him *time* to answer!

MR. DOBBS: Other stores just buy and sell. And thousands of goods come in and go out.

JOHN: Yes, of course.

MR. DOBBS: They just change hands, year after year. Like the leaves that grow and fall off. Like children born who grow up and then have children and they grow up and have children. . . . That's what stores are like—just the same coming and going, year after year. But not the Emporium.

He's not talking very loud. The Member on the Stage, cupping his left ear in his hand, crosses the stage to hear better.

Don't you think that maybe the G. and S.—maybe it isn't a store at all; it only pretends to be a store: that there's something else behind it?

JOHN: Behind it?—Of course, it's a store!

MR. DOBBS: It's not interested in buying and selling. It's . . . it's . . .

He dries up.

I must lie down. . . . (*His hand goes to his heart.*) I'm not well. (*Rises.*)

MR. WILLISTON (*also his hand to his heart, rising*): I'm not well, either. I'm dizzy.

JOHN: Everybody's kinda collapsin' around here.—There's a sofa in the next room.— (*To both of them*) Can you make it?

John takes for a moment the elbow each of them, then turns back in thought toward the Audience. The old men, bent over, go out. The retired old people sit down by the Member of the Audience on stage left.

I'm going to hide in the store after closing time. I don't care if they kick me out a hundred times. I'm going to get to know some of the people that work there.

PLAYS FOR BLEECKER STREET

The Seven Deadly Sins

Bernice

(*Pride*)

CHARACTERS

MR. MALLISON, Mr. Walbeck's lawyer, fifty-nine
BERNICE MAYHEW, Mr. Walbeck's maid, fifty
THE DRIVER
MR. WALBECK, forty-seven

SETTING

Drawing room of a house in Chicago, 1911.

Door into the hall at the back. All we need see are an elaborate, but not weighty, table in the center and two chairs. At the front of the stage are some andirons and a poker, indicating a fireplace.

Mallison, fifty-nine, all a lawyer, now very nervous, is standing before the table holding an open watch in his hand. By the door is Bernice, colored, fifty, in a maid's uniform.

MALLISON: Remind me . . . remind me, please . . . your name?

BERNICE (*Unimpressed*): Bernice.

MALLISON: Thank you.—Now Mr. Burgess, your employer, may be a little bit . . . moody. You do whatever he wants. Have you enough help to run the house?

BERNICE: I did what you told me. There's Jason for the heavy work and the furnace. This Mr. Burgess—will he be alone in this house?

MALLISON: Alone? Oh! Most probably. At all events, you are in charge. Get whatever help you need. I am Mr. Burgess's lawyer, but he will be getting another lawyer soon. All your bills will be paid, I'm sure . . . You have some dinner waiting for him now?

BERNICE (*Slowly*): Why do you talk so funny about this Mr. Burgess? Is he coming from the crazy house or something?

MALLISON (*Outraged*): No, indeed!! I don't know where you got such an idea. All that's expected of you is . . . uh . . . good meals and a well-run house.

BERNICE: You talk very funny, Mr. Mallison.

MALLISON (*After swallowing with dignity and glaring at her*): Mrs. Willard recommended you as an experienced cook and housekeeper, Bernice. My duty ends there.

BERNICE: I don't have to take any jobs unless I likes them, Mr. Mallison. I never agrees to work any place more than three days. Mrs. Willard don't like it, but that's my terms—if I likes it, I stays.

MALLISON: Well, I hope you like it here. You're getting very well paid and you can ask for any further help you need—within reason. There's an automobile stopping before the door now. I think you'd better go to the door.

Bernice doesn't move. Arms akimbo she looks musingly at Mallison.

BERNICE: I seen people like you before . . . You're up to something.

The front door bell rings.

MALLISON: I don't like your tone. You've been engaged to work here—for three days, anyway. You can begin by answering that door bell.

Bernice goes out. Mallison straightens his clothes, goes to the table and picks up his briefcase, then stands waiting with pursed lips. Sounds of altercation from the hall.

DRIVER'S VOICE: All right! The price is twenty dollars. But if I'd know'd it was a night like this—

Enter the Driver, a livery stable chauffeur, Irish, slightly drunk. He is carrying a small rattan suitcase, which he puts down by the door. He is followed by Walbeck, forty-seven, prematurely gray; he speaks softly, but gives an impression of controlled power. Bernice enters behind them.

WALBECK (*To Mallison, in a low voice*): I understood that the fare was paid in advance?

MALLISON: The twenty dollars was paid in advance.

DRIVER: Anybody'd charge twice to drive on a night like this. First it was rain and snow—

MALLISON: The livery stable was given twenty dollars— (*To Bernice*) You can prepare the dinner!

Exit Bernice.

DRIVER: Then it turned to ice. The worst night I've ever seen, to go to Joliet and pick up a I-don't-know-what. The car falling off the road every minute. To go to Joliet and pick up a criminal of some sort—

WALBECK (*Gesture of empty pockets*): I have no money.

MALLISON (*To the driver*): I will give you five dollars, but I shall report you to the livery stable.

DRIVER (*Taking the bill*): What do I care? Thirty-five miles each way and half the time you couldn't see the road five yards in front of you; and the other half sliding into the ditch. All right, tell 'em and see what I tell 'em.

MALLISON: You have your five dollars. If you go now, I'll say nothing to your superiors— But go!

DRIVER (*Starting for the door, then turning on Walbeck*): And who do you think you are, Mr. Bur-gessss! Keeping your mouth so shut! You a murderer or I-don't-know-what; and too big and mighty to talk to anybody.—Oh, you had to *think*, did you? So you had to think? Well, you've got enough to think about for the rest of your goddamned life.

He goes out.

MALLISON (*Stiffly*): Good evening, Mr. Walbeck.

The front door is heard closing with a slam.

WALBECK (*Always softly, but impersonally*): What is this name of . . . Burgess?

MALLISON: We assumed, Mr. Walbeck, that you would prefer

us to engage the household staff and . . . make certain other arrangements under . . . another name. Since you did not reply to our letters on this matter, we selected the name of Burgess.

WALBECK: I see.—Is . . . my wife here?

MALLISON (*Astonished*): You did not get Mrs. Walbeck's letters?

WALBECK: I did not open any letters.

MALLISON: And *our* letters, Mr. Walbeck?

WALBECK: I haven't opened any letters for six months.

MALLISON (*Controlling his outrage, primly*): Mrs. Walbeck left a week ago—with the children—for California. She has filed a petition for divorce. In her letters she probably explained it to you at length. She did not wish to make this move earlier . . . She wished it to be known that she stood by you through . . . your ordeal. When she heard that your sentence had been reduced and that you would be returning this week, she—

WALBECK (*Coolly*): There's no need to say anything more, Mr. Mallison.

MALLISON: A woman has been engaged to attend to your needs. Her name is Bernice. A wardrobe—that is, a wardrobe of clothes—you will find upstairs. Your measurements were obtained by your former tailor from the authorities at the . . . institution from which you have come. —Here are the keys of the house. Here are the statements from your bank. A checkbook. Here (*He places a long envelope on the table*) are five hundred dollars which I have drawn for your immediate needs.

WALBECK: Thank you. Good night.

MALLISON: Mr. Walbeck, hitherto the firm of Bremerton, Bremerton, Mallison and Mallison has been happy to serve as your legal representatives. From now on we trust that you will find other counsel. We relinquish—here (*He lays down another document*) our power of attorney. And in this envelope you will find all the documents and information that our successors will require. I wish you good night.

WALBECK (*Stonily*): Good night.

Mallison turns at the door.

MALLISON: You read no letters?

WALBECK (*His eyes on the ground*): No.

MALLISON: That reminds me. Your daughter Lavinia wished to leave a letter for you. Her mother forbade her to do so. However, I . . . I was prepared to take the responsibility. Your daughter gave me this letter to give to you.

He gives an envelope to Walbeck, who puts it in his breast pocket. His silence and level glance complete Mallison's discomfiture.

Good night, sir.

Exit Mallison. Walbeck stands motionless gazing fixedly before him. Suddenly, in a rage, he overturns the table before him; but immediately recovers his self-control. Enter Bernice.

BERNICE: Dinner's served, sir.

WALBECK: I won't have any dinner.

BERNICE: Yes, Mr. Burgess.

WALBECK: What?

BERNICE: I said, "Yes, Mr. Burgess." I'll just set that table to rights.

WALBECK (*Quickly*): I'll do it.

He does.

BERNICE (*Watchfully but unsentimentally*): I've got a real good steak in there. I'm the best cook in Chicago, Mr. Burgess. There's lots of people that knows that.

WALBECK: Is there any liquor in the house?

BERNICE: Oh, yes. There's everything.

WALBECK: Rye. Rye straight.—You eat the steak.

BERNICE: Thank you, Mr. Burgess.

She starts out, then turns.

Now, you don't want to eat that steak, Mr. Burgess, but I've got some tomato soup there that's the best tomato soup you ever ate. You aren't going to waste my time by refusing to eat that soup.

WALBECK (*Looking at her; impersonally*): What is your name?

BERNICE: My name's Bernice Mayhew. People calls me Bernice.

WALBECK: Bernice, I don't want to eat in that dining room. You can bring me the rye and some of that soup in here.

BERNICE: Yes, Mr. Burgess.

WALBECK: My name is Walbeck.

BERNICE: What's that?

WALBECK: My name: Wal-beck, Walbeck.

BERNICE: Yes, Mr. Walbeck.

WALBECK: And pour yourself some rye.

BERNICE: I don't touch it, Mr. Walbeck. Ten years ago I made my life over. I changed my name and I changed everything about myself. I thank you, but I don't touch liquor.

> *She goes out. Walbeck, standing straight, his eyes on the ground, puts his hand in his pocket and draws out his daughter's letter. After a moment's hesitation, he opens it. He holds it suspended in his hand a moment. Then he tears the letter and envelope, each two ways, and throws the fragments into the fire (invisible to us), between the andirons.*
>
> *Bernice returns, pushing a small service table. She gives him the rye, then unfurls a tablecloth and starts laying the table. Walbeck drinks half the rye in one swallow.*

WALBECK: Were you here when my wife was here?

BERNICE: No, sir. Nobody's been here today but that lawyer-man. I came here this morning and all day Jason and I have been cleaning the house.

WALBECK: Do you know where I come from?

BERNICE (*Quietly, lowered eyes*): Yes, I do.

WALBECK: Did that lawyer tell you?

BERNICE: No . . . I knew . . . I been there myself . . . So I knew. I'll get your soup.

> *She goes out. Suddenly Walbeck goes to the fireplace. Falling on his knees, he tries without burning his fingers to rake out the fragments of the letter. Apparently it is too late.*
>
> *Bernice enters with a covered soup tureen. Watchfully, but with no show of surprise, she tries to take in what he is doing. Walbeck rises, dusting off his knees.*

You want me to build up that fire, Mr. Walbeck?

WALBECK: No, it's all right as it is.

He seats himself at the table.

BERNICE (*Eyeing the fireplace speculatively*): There's some toast there, too.

WALBECK: You say you changed your name?

BERNICE: Yes. My born name was Sarah Temple. When I came out of prison I was Bernice Mayhew. Of course, I had some other names too. I was married twice. But Bernice Mayhew was the name I gave myself. (*Without emphasis; her eyes on the distance*) I was in because I killed somebody.

WALBECK (*The soup spoon at his mouth, speaks in her tone*): I was in because I cheated two or three hundred people out of money.

BERNICE (*Musingly*): Well, everybody's done something.

Pause. Walbeck eats.

WALBECK: You say you changed everything about yourself?

BERNICE: Yes. Everything was changed, anyway. I was in a disgrace—nobody can be in a bigger disgrace than I was. And some people were avoiding me and some people were laughing at me and some people were being kind to me, like I was a dog that came to the back door. And some people were saying: cheer up, Sarah, you've paid your price. There's lots of things to live for. You're young yet.—You're sure you wouldn't like a piece of that steak, Mr. Walbeck, rare or any way you'd like it?

WALBECK: No. I'm going downtown soon. If I get hungry, later, I'll pick up something to eat down there.

BERNICE (*After a short pause, while she continues to gaze into the distance*): Did anybody come to meet you when you came out of the door of the place you was at?

WALBECK: No.

BERNICE: That's what I mean. I don't blame them. I wouldn't want to go 'round with a person who's very much in a disgrace—like with a person who's killed somebody. I wouldn't choose 'em.

WALBECK: Or with a person who's stolen a lot of people's life savings.

BERNICE: I only mentioned that to show a big part of the change: you're alone.

WALBECK: Did that lawyer who was here, or the agency, know that you'd been in prison?

BERNICE: Oh, no. It was Sarah Temple who did that. She's dead. When I changed my name she became dead. You see the first part of my life I lived in Kansas City. Then I came to Chicago. Bernice Mayhew has never been to Kansas City. She don't even know what it looks like.

WALBECK (*Impersonally, without looking at her*): If you've been on your feet all day cleaning the house, I think you'd better sit down, Bernice.

BERNICE: Well, thank you, I will sit down.

WALBECK: Would you advise me to kill off George Walbeck?

BERNICE (*Seeming more and more remote, in her musings*): Not so much for your sake as for other people's sake. It's not good for other people to have to do with persons who are in a disgrace; it brings out the worst in them. I don't like to see that.

WALBECK (*Slowly, his eyes on the distance*): I guess you're right. I'd better do that.

BERNICE: It's like what happens about poor people. You're a thousand times richer than I am, but I'm richer than millions of people. What good does it do to think about them? I only need one real meal a day; the rest is just stuffing. But I don't notice as how I give up my other two meals. I'm always right there at mealtimes. When I went hungry, most times I didn't let people know about it; and when I'm in a disgrace, why should I make them uncomfortable?

WALBECK: Before you became Bernice Mayhew, did you have any children?

BERNICE: Yes, I did . . . Their mother's dead, of course. But I guess somebody's reminding them every day that their mother was a murderer.—That's bad enough, but it's not as bad as knowing their mother's alive.—Have you noticed that we gradually forgive them that's dead? If I was alive they'd be thinking about me, in one way or another: hating me or maybe trying to stand up for me. There are a lot of ideas young people could go through about a thing like that.

WALBECK (*As though to himself*): Yes.

The telephone rings in the hall. Walbeck rises uneasily.

Who could that be? Answer it, will you, Bernice? Don't say that I'm here.

Bernice goes into the hall. Her voice can be heard shouting as though she were unaccustomed to the telephone.

BERNICE: It's me talking—Bernice.
Yes. Who are you, talking?
Who? Oh.
I can't understand much.
A letter? I hear you, a letter.
Yes, miss. What? I can't hear good. The machine don't work good.
All right, you come. I'm here.
Bernice. Yes, you come. I'm here.

Bernice returns to the stage.

She says she's your daughter.

WALBECK: So-o-o! She didn't go to California with her mother.

BERNICE: She says she sent you a letter. In the letter she asked you to telephone her . . . that she could come and see you. She was asking over and over again if you was here, but I made out that the machine didn't work good. She says she'll be here soon.

Bernice has been clearing the table, putting the objects on the wheeled service table, which she starts pushing to the door.

WALBECK: I can't see her tonight.—What do you suppose she wants?

BERNICE (*At the door with lowered eyes*): I think I can figger that out: about what half the daughters in the world would want. She wants to make a home for you. And to give up her life for you.

She goes out with the service table.

WALBECK (*Softly*): Good God—

Bernice returns and stands at the door.

She's seventeen! How could she get such an idea! Her

mother must have told her what she thought of me—told her every day for eight years what she thought of me—

BERNICE (*Always without looking at him, broodingly*): Yes.

Slight pause.

Mr. Walbeck, you ought to know that women don't believe what women say. Least of all their mothers. They'll believe any old fool thing a man says.

WALBECK: She's seventeen! How did she do it? How did she get away from her mother? She must have run away at the railway station. She probably has very little money.

BERNICE (*"Seeing" it; staring before her*): She's got some rings, hasn't she? She'll be selling them. She'll be going to the stores hunting for a job.

WALBECK (*Staring at her*): Yes.—But her mother will have come back to look for her. Or will have telephoned the police to look for her.

BERNICE: Maybe not. Maybe not at all . . . It's terrible when young girls are brave.

WALBECK (*In a sort of terror. For the first time loudly*): Bernice!—What shall I do?

BERNICE (*A quick glance of somber anger*): It ain't right to ask advices. It ain't right, Mr. Walbeck.

WALBECK: See here, Bernice! Do this for me.

BERNICE: Do what, for you?

WALBECK: Do what you'd do, if it were your own daughter.

BERNICE (*Sudden flood of tormented emotion*): How do I know if I did right?—What I did about my own daughter? Maybe my daughter'd be having a good big life living with me. Maybe she's just having one of them silly lives, living with silly people and saying jabber-jabber silly things all day. (*Gazing before her*) I hate people who don't know that lots of people is hungry and that lots of people has done bad things. If my daughter was with me, we'd talk . . . I got so many things I've *learned* that I could tell to a girl like that . . . And we'd go downtown and we'd shop for her clothes together . . . and talk . . . I've got a weak heart; I shouldn't get excited. (*She looks at the floor a minute*) No, Mr. Walbeck, don't ask me to throw your daughter back into the trashy lives that most people live.

WALBECK: Bernice: when she comes, give her her choice. I'll go upstairs.

BERNICE: Young people can't make choices. They don't know what they're choosing.

WALBECK (*With increasing almost choked urgency*): Then tell her . . . she and I'll go away together. Somewhere. We'll start a new life.

Bernice is silent a moment. Then her mood changes. For the first time she brings a long deep gaze toward him.

BERNICE: No!—These are just fancies. We're a stone around their necks now! If we were with them we'd be a bigger stone. Sometimes I think death come into the world so we wouldn't *be* a stone around young people's necks. Besides you and I—we're alone. We did what we did because we were that kind of person—the kind that chooses to think they're smarter and better than other people . . . And people that think that way end up alone. We're not *company* for anybody.

Pause. Walbeck's mood also changes.

WALBECK (*His mind made up*): Then tell her that the doctors told me that I had only a few months to live . . . that I've gone off so as not to be a weight on anybody . . . on her, for instance. (*He pulls the envelope from his pocket*) If she's not followed her mother to California, she'll be needing some money. Give her this envelope. (*His tormented urgency returns*) And tell her . . . Tell her . . .

BERNICE (*Somberly but largely*): I knows what else to tell her, Mr. Walbeck. You go upstairs and hide youself. You's almost dead. You's dyin'.

Walbeck goes out. Bernice sits in a chair facing the audience, waitng, her eyes on the distance.

END OF PLAY

The Wreck on the Five-Twenty-Five

(*Sloth*)

CHARACTERS

MRS. HAWKINS, forty
MINNIE, her daughter, almost sixteen
MR. FORBES, a neighbor
MR. HERBERT HAWKINS, Mrs. Hawkins's husband

SETTING

Today. The Hawkins home.

Six o'clock in the evening. Mrs. Hawkins, forty, and her daughter Minnie, almost sixteen, are sewing and knitting. At the back is a door into the hall and beside it a table on which is a telephone.

MRS. HAWKINS: Irish stew doesn't seem right for Sunday dinner, somehow. (*Pause*) And your father doesn't really like roast or veal. (*Pause*) Thank Heaven, he's not crazy about steak.

Another pause while she takes some pins from her mouth.

I must say it's downright strange—his not being here. He hasn't telephoned for years, like that—that he'd take a later train.
MINNIE: Did he say what was keeping him?
MRS. HAWKINS: No . . . something at the office, I suppose. (*She changes pins again*) He never really did like chicken, either.
MINNIE: He ate pork last week without saying anything. You might try pork chops, Mama; I don't really mind them.
MRS. HAWKINS: He doesn't ever say anything. He eats what's there.—Oh, Minnie, men never realize that there's only a limited number of things to eat.
MINNIE: What did he say on the telephone exactly?

MRS. HAWKINS: "I'll try to catch the six-thirty."

Both look at their wristwatches.

MINNIE: But, Mama, Papa's not cranky about what he eats. He's always saying what a good cook you are.

MRS. HAWKINS: Men!

She has put down her sewing and is gazing before her.

They think they want a lot of change—variety and change, variety and change. But they don't really. Deep down, they don't.

MINNIE: Don't *what?*

MRS. HAWKINS: You know for a while he read all those Wild Western magazines: cowboys and horses and silly Indians . . . two or three a week. Then, suddenly, he stopped all that. It's as though he thought he were in a kind of jail or prison.—Keep an eye on that window, Minnie. He may be coming down the street any minute.

Minnie rises and, turning, peers through a window, back right.

MINNIE: No.—There's Mr. Wilkerson, though. He came back on the five-twenty-five, anyway. Sometimes Papa stops at the tobacco shop and comes down Spruce Street.

She moves to the left and looks through another window.

MRS. HAWKINS: Do you feel as though you were in a jail, Minnie?

MINNIE: *What?!*

MRS. HAWKINS: As though life were a jail?

MINNIE (*Returning to her chair*): No, of course not.—Mama, you're talking awfully funny tonight.

MRS. HAWKINS: I'm not myself. (*Laughs lightly*) I guess I'm not myself because of your father's phone call—his taking a later train, like that, for the first time in so many years.

MINNIE (*With a little giggle*): I don't know what the five-twenty-five will have done without him.

MRS. HAWKINS (*Not sharply*): And all those hoodlums he plays cards with every afternoon.

MINNIE: And all the jokes they make.

Mrs. Hawkins has been looking straight before her—through a window—over the audience's heads, intently.

MRS. HAWKINS: There's Mrs. Cochran cooking her dinner.

They both gaze absorbedly at Mrs. Cochran a moment.

Well, I'm not going to start dinner until your father puts foot in this house.

MINNIE (*Still gazing through the window; slowly*): There's Mr. Cochran at the door . . . They're arguing about something.

MRS. HAWKINS: Well, that shows that he got in on the five-twenty-five, all right.

MINNIE: Don't people look foolish when you see them, like that—and you can't hear what they're saying? Like ants or something. Somehow, you feel it's not right to look at them when they don't know it.

They return to their work.

MRS. HAWKINS: Yes, those men on the train will have missed those awful jokes your father makes. (*Minnie giggles*) I declare, Minnie, every year your father makes worse jokes. It's growing on him.

MINNIE: I don't think they're awful, but, I don't understand *all* of them. Do you? Like what he said to the minister Sunday. I was so embarrassed I didn't want to tell you.

MRS. HAWKINS: I don't want to hear it—not tonight.

(*Her gaze returns to the window*) I can't understand why Mrs. Cochran is acting so strangely. And Mr. Cochran has been coming in and out of the kitchen.

MINNIE: And they seem to keep looking at us all the time.

After a moment's gazing, they return to their work.

MRS. HAWKINS: Well, you might as well tell me what your father said to the minister.

MINNIE: I . . . I don't want to tell you, if it makes you nervous.

MRS. HAWKINS: I've lived with his jokes for twenty years. I guess I can stand one more.

MINNIE: Mr. Brown had preached a sermon about the atom

bomb . . . and about how terrible it would be . . . and at the church door Papa said to him: "Fine sermon, Joe. I enjoyed it. But have you ever thought of this, Joe"—he said—"suppose the atom bomb didn't fall, what would we do then? Have you ever thought of that?" Mr. Brown looked terribly put out.

MRS. HAWKINS (*Puts down her sewing*): He said that!! I declare, he's getting worse. I don't know where he gets such ideas. People will be beginning to think he's *bitter*. Your father isn't bitter. I know he's not bitter.

MINNIE: No, Mama. People like it. People stop me on the street and tell me what a wonderful sense of humor he has. Like . . . like . . . (*She gives up the attempt and says merely*) Oh, nothing.

MRS. HAWKINS: Go on. Say what you were going to say.

MINNIE: What did he mean by saying: "There we sit for twenty years playing cards on the five-twenty-five, hoping that something big and terrible and wonderful will happen —like a wreck, for instance"?

MRS. HAWKINS (*More distress than indignation*): I say to you seriously, Minnie, it's just *self-indulgence*. We do everything we know how to make him happy. He loves his home, you know he does. He likes his work—he's proud of what he does at the office.

(*She rises and looks down the street through the window at the back. Moved*) Oh, it's not *us* he's impatient at: it's the whole world. He simply wishes the whole world were different— that's the trouble with him.

MINNIE: Why, Mama, Papa doesn't complain about anything.

MRS. HAWKINS: Well, I wish he would complain once in a while.

(*She returns to her chair*) For Sunday I'll see if I can't get an extra good bit of veal.

They sit in silence a moment. The telephone rings.

Answer that, will you, dear?—No, I'll answer it.

Minnie returns to her work. Mrs. Hawkins has a special voice for answering the telephone, slow and measured.

This is Mrs. Hawkins speaking. Oh, yes, Mr. Cochran. What's that? I don't hear you.

(*A shade of anxiety*) Are you *sure*? You must be mistaken.

MINNIE: Mama, what is it? (*Mrs. Hawkins listens in silence*) Mama! Mama!!—What's he saying? Is it about Papa?

MRS. HAWKINS: Will you hold the line one minute, Mr. Cochran? I wish to speak to my daughter. (*She puts her hand over the mouthpiece*) No, Minnie. It's not about your father at all.

MINNIE (*Rising*): Then what *is* it?

MRS. HAWKINS (*In a low, distinct and firm voice*): Now you do what I tell you. Sit down and go on knitting. Don't look up at me and don't show any surprise.

MINNIE (*A groan of protest*): Mama!

MRS. HAWKINS: There's nothing to be alarmed about—but I want you to *obey* me.

(*She speaks into the telephone*) Yes, Mr. Cochran . . . No . . . Mr. Hawkins telephoned that he was taking a later train tonight. I'm expecting him on the six-thirty.

You do what you think best.

I'm not sure that's necessary but . . . you do what you think best.

We'll be right here.

She hangs up and stands thinking a moment.

MINNIE: Mama, I'm almost sixteen. *Tell* me what it's about.

MRS. HAWKINS (*Returns to her chair; bending over her work, she speaks as guardedly as possible*): Minnie, there's probably nothing to be alarmed about. Don't show any surprise at what I'm about to say to you. Mr. Cochran says that there's been somebody out on the lawn watching us—for ten minutes or more. A man. He's been standing in the shadow of the garage, just looking at us.

MINNIE (*Lowered head*): Is *that* all!

MRS. HAWKINS: Well, Mr. Cochran doesn't like it. He's . . . he says he's going to telephone the police.

MINNIE: The police!!

MRS. HAWKINS: Your father'll be home any minute, anyway. (*Slight pause*) I guess it's just some . . . some *moody* person on an evening walk. Maybe Mr. Cochran's done right to call the police, though. He says that we shouldn't pull the curtains or anything like that—but just act as though nothing has happened.—Now, I don't want you to get frightened.

MINNIE: I'm not, Mama. I'm just . . . interested. Most nights *nothing* happens.

MRS. HAWKINS (*Sharply*): I should hope not!

Slight pause.

MINNIE: Mama, all evening I *did* have the feeling that I was being watched . . . and *that* man was being watched by Mrs. Cochran; and (*Slight giggle*) Mrs. Cochran was being watched by us.

MRS. HAWKINS: We'll know what it's all about in a few minutes.

Silence.

MINNIE: But Mama, what would the man be looking at?—Just us two sewing.

MRS. HAWKINS: I think you'd better go in the kitchen. Go slowly—and don't look out the window.

MINNIE (*Without raising her head*): No! I'm going to stay right here. But I'd like to know *why* a man would do that— would just stand and look. Is he . . . a crazy man?

MRS. HAWKINS: No, I don't think so.

MINNIE: Well, say *something* about him.

MRS. HAWKINS: Minnie, the world is full of people who think that everybody's happy except themselves. They think their lives should be more exciting.

MINNIE: Does that man think that our lives are exciting, Mama?

MRS. HAWKINS: Our lives are just as exciting as they ought to be, Minnie.

MINNIE (*With a little giggle*): Well, they are tonight.

MRS. HAWKINS: They are all the time; and don't you forget it.

The front door bell rings.

Now, who can that be at the front door? I'll go, Minnie. (*Weighing the dangers*) No, *you* go.—No, I'll go.

She goes into the hall. The jovial voice of Mr. Forbes is heard.

MR. FORBES'S VOICE: Good evening, Mrs. Hawkins. Is Herb home?

MRS. HAWKINS'S VOICE: No, he hasn't come home yet, Mr. Forbes. He telephoned that he'd take a later train.

Enter Mr. Forbes, followed by Mrs. Hawkins.

MR. FORBES: Yes, I know. The old five-twenty-five wasn't the same without him. Darn near went off the rails.
(*To Minnie*) Good evening, young lady.

MINNIE (*Head bent; tiny voice*): Good evening, Mr. Forbes.

MR. FORBES: Well, I thought I'd drop in and see Herb for a minute. About how maybe he'd be wanting a new car—now that he's come into all that money.

MRS. HAWKINS: Come into *what* money, Mr. Forbes?

MR. FORBES: Why, sure, he telephoned you about it?

MRS. HAWKINS: He didn't say anything about any money.

MR. FORBES (*Laughing loudly*): Well, maybe I've gone and put my foot in it again. So he didn't tell you anything about it yet? Haw-haw-haw. (*Confidentially*) If he's got to pay taxes on it we figgered out he'd get about eighteen thousand dollars.—Well, you tell him I called, and tell him that I'll give him nine hundred dollars on that Chevrolet of his— maybe a little more after I've had a look at it.

MRS. HAWKINS: I'll tell him.—Mr. Forbes, I'm sorry I can't ask you to sit down, but my daughter's had a cold for days now and I wouldn't want you to take it home to your girls.

MR. FORBES: I'm sorry to hear that.—Well, as you say, I'd better not carry it with me.
(*He goes to the door, then turns and says confidentially*) Do you know what Herb said when he heard that he'd got that money? Haw-haw-haw. I've always said Herb Hawkins has more sense of humor than anybody I know. Why, he said, "All window glass is the same." Haw-haw. "All window glass is the same." Herb! You can't beat him.

MRS. HAWKINS: "All window glass is the same." What did he mean by that?

MR. FORBES: You know: that thing he's always saying. About life. He said it at Rotary in his speech. You know how crazy people look when you see them through a window— arguing and carrying on—and you can't hear a word they say? He says that's the way things look to him. Wars and politics . . . and everything in life.

Mrs. Hawkins is silent and unamused.

Well, I'd better be going. Tell Herb there's real good glass
—*unbreakable*—on the car I'm going to sell him. Good
night, miss; good night, Mrs. Hawkins.

*He goes out. Mrs. Hawkins does not accompany him to the
front door. She stands a moment looking before her. Then she
says, from deep thought:*

MRS. HAWKINS: That's your father who's been standing out by
the garage.
MINNIE: Why would he do that?
MRS. HAWKINS: Looking in.—I should have known it.
MINNIE (*Amazed but not alarmed*): Look! All over the lawn!
MRS. HAWKINS: The police have come. Those are their flash-
lights.
MINNIE: All over the place! I can hear them talking . . .
(*Pause*) . . . Papa's angry . . . Papa's *very* angry.

They listen.

Now they're driving away.
MRS. HAWKINS: I should have known it.

*She returns to her seat. Sound of the front door opening and
closing noisily.*

That's your father. Don't mention anything unless he men-
tions it first.

*They bend over their work. From the hall sounds of Hawkins
singing the first phrase of "Valencia." Enter Hawkins, a
commuter. His manner is of loud, forced geniality.*

HAWKINS: Well—HOW are the ladies?

He kisses each lightly on the cheek.

MRS. HAWKINS: I didn't start getting dinner until I knew when
you'd get here.
HAWKINS (*Largely*): Well, *don't* start it. I'm taking you two
ladies out to dinner.—There's no hurry, though. We'll go to
Michaelson's after the crowd's thinned out.

(*Starting for the hall on his way to the kitchen*) Want a drink, anybody?

MRS. HAWKINS: No. The ice is ready for you on the shelf.

He goes out. From the kitchen he can be heard singing "Valencia." He returns, glass in hand.

What kept you, Herbert?

HAWKINS: Nothing. Nothing. I decided to take another train.

He walks back and forth, holding his glass at the level of his face.

I decided to take another train. (*He leans teasingly a moment over his wife's shoulder, conspiratorially*) I thought maybe things might look different through the windows of another train. You know: all those towns I've never been in? Kenniston—Laidlaw—East Laidlaw—Bennsville. Let's go to Bennsville some day. Damn it, I don't know why people should go to Paris and Rome and Cairo when they could go to Bennsville. Bennsville! Oh, Bennsville—

MRS. HAWKINS: Have you been drinking, Herbert?

HAWKINS: This is the first swallow I've had since last night. Oh, Bennsville . . . breathes there a man with soul so dead—

Minnie's eyes have followed her father as he walks about with smiling appreciation.

MINNIE: I know a girl who lives in Bennsville.

HAWKINS: They're happy there, aren't they? No, not exactly happy, but they live it up to the full. In Bennsville they kick the hell out of life.

MINNIE: Her name's Eloise Brinton.

HAWKINS: Well, Bennsville and East Laidlaw don't look different through the windows of another train. It's not by looking through a train window that you can get at the *heart* of Bennsville.

Pause.

There all we fellows sit every night on the five-twenty-five playing cards and hoping against hope that there'll be that wonderful, beautiful—

MINNIE (*Laughing delightedly*): Wreck!!

MRS. HAWKINS: Herbert! I won't have you talking that way!

HAWKINS: A wreck, so that we can crawl out of the smoking, burning cars . . . and get into one of those houses. Do you know what you see from the windows of the train? Those people—those cars—that you see on the streets of Bennsville—they're just dummies. *Cardboard*. They've been put up there to deceive you. What really goes on in Bennsville—inside those houses—*that's* what's interesting. People with six arms and legs. People that can talk like Shakespeare. Children, Minnie, that can beat Einstein. Fabulous things.

MINNIE: Papa, *I* don't mind, but you make Mama nervous when you talk like that.

HAWKINS: Behind those walls. But it isn't only behind those walls that strange things go on. Right on that train, right in those cars. The damndest things. Fred Cochran and Phil Forbes—

MRS. HAWKINS: Mr. Forbes was here to see you.

HAWKINS: Fred Cochran and Phil Forbes—we've played cards together for twenty years. We're so expert at hiding things from one another—we're so cram-filled with things we can't say to one another that only a wreck could crack us open.

MINNIE (*Indicating her mother, reproachfully*): Papa!

MRS. HAWKINS: Herbert Hawkins, why did you stand out in the dark there, looking at us through the window?

HAWKINS: Well, I'll tell you . . . I got a lot of money today. But more than that I got a message. A message from beyond the grave. From the dead. There was this old lady—I used to do her income tax for her—old lady. She'd keep me on a while—God, how she wanted someone to talk to . . . I'd say anything that came into my head . . . I want another drink.

> *He goes into the kitchen. Again we hear him singing "Valencia."*

MINNIE (*Whispering*): Eighteen thousand dollars!

MRS. HAWKINS: We've just got to let him talk himself out.

MINNIE: But Mama, why did he go and stand out on the lawn?

MRS. HAWKINS: Shh!

Hawkins returns.

HAWKINS: I told her a lot of things. I told her—

MINNIE: I know! You told her that everything looked as though it were seen through glass.

HAWKINS: Yes, I did. (*Pause*) You don't hear the words, or if you hear the words, they don't fit what you see. And one day she said to me: "Mr. Hawkins, you say that all the time: why don't you do it?" "Do what?" I said. "Really stand outside and look through some windows."

Pause.

I knew she meant my own . . . Well, to tell the truth, I was afraid to. I preferred to talk about it.

He paces back and forth.

She died. Today some lawyer called me up and said she's left me twenty thousand dollars.

MRS. HAWKINS: Herbert!

HAWKINS (*His eyes on the distance*): "To Herbert Hawkins, in gratitude for many thoughtfulnesses and in appreciation of his sense of humor." From beyond the grave . . . It was an order. I took the four o'clock home . . . It took me a whole hour to get up the courage to go and stand (*He points*) out there.

MINNIE: But Papa, you didn't *see* anything! Just us sewing!

Hawkins stares before him, then, changing his mood, says briskly:

HAWKINS: What are we going to have for Sunday dinner?

MINNIE: I know!

HAWKINS (*Pinching her ear*): Buffalo steak?

MINNIE: No.

HAWKINS: I had to live for a week once on rattlesnake stew.

MINNIE: Papa, you're awful.

MRS. HAWKINS (*Putting down her sewing; in an even voice*): Were you planning to go away, Herbert?

HAWKINS: What?

MRS. HAWKINS (*For the first time, looking at him*): You were thinking of going away.

HAWKINS (*Looks into his glass a moment*): Far away.
(*Then again putting his face over her shoulder teasingly, but in a serious voice*) There is no "away." . . . There's only "here."—Get your hats; we're going out to dinner.—I've decided to move to "here." To take up residence, as they say. I'll move in tonight. I don't bring much baggage.—Get your hats.

MRS. HAWKINS (*Rising*): Herbert, we don't wear hats any more. That was in your mother's time.—Minnie, run upstairs and get my blue shawl.

HAWKINS: I'll go and get one more drop out in the kitchen.

MRS. HAWKINS: Herbert, I don't like your old lady.

HAWKINS (*Turning at the door in surprise*): Why, what's the matter with her?

MRS. HAWKINS: I can understand that she was in need of someone to talk to.—What business had she trying to make you look at Minnie and me *through windows*? As though we were strangers.

She crosses and puts her sewing on the telephone table.

People who've known one another as long as you and I have are not supposed to *see* one another. The pictures we have of one another are inside.—Herbert, last year one day I went to the city to have lunch with your sister. And as I was walking along the street, who do you think I saw coming toward me? From quite a ways off? *You!* My heart stopped beating and I *prayed*—I prayed that you wouldn't see me. And you passed by without seeing me. I didn't want you to see me in those silly clothes we wear when we go to the city—and in that silly hat—with that silly look we put on our face when we're in public places. The person that other people see.

HAWKINS (*With lowered eyes*): You saw *me*—with that silly look.

MRS. HAWKINS: Oh, no. I didn't look long enough for that. I was too busy hiding myself.—I don't know why Minnie's so long trying to find my shawl.

She goes out. The telephone rings.

HAWKINS: Yes, this is Herbert Hawkins.—Nat Fischer? Oh, hello, Nat . . . Oh! . . . All right. Sure, I see your point of view . . . Eleven o'clock. Yes, I'll be there. Eleven o'clock.

He hangs up. Mrs. Hawkins returns wearing a shawl.

MRS. HAWKINS: Was that call for me?

HAWKINS: No. It was for me all right.—I might as well tell you now what it was about.

He stares at the floor.

MRS. HAWKINS: Well?

HAWKINS: A few minutes ago the police tried to arrest me for standing on my own lawn. Well, I got them over that. But they found a revolver on me—without a license. So I've got to show up at court tomorrow, eleven o'clock.

MRS. HAWKINS (*Short pause; thoughtfully*): Oh . . . a revolver.

HAWKINS (*Looking at the floor*): Yes . . . I thought that maybe it was best . . . that I go away . . . a long way.

MRS. HAWKINS (*Looking up with the beginning of a smile*): To Bennsville?

HAWKINS: Yes.

MRS. HAWKINS: Where life's so exciting.

(*Suddenly briskly*) Well, you get the license for that revolver, Herbert, so that you can prevent people looking in at us through the window, when they have no business to.— Turn out the lights when you come.

END OF PLAY

A Ringing of Doorbells

(*Envy*)

CHARACTERS

MRS. BEATTIE, sixty-five, crippled with arthritis
MRS. McCULLUM, her housekeeper
MRS. KINKAID, a caller, forty-five
DAPHNE, Mrs. Kinkaid's daughter, eighteen

SETTING

The front room of Mrs. Beattie's small house in Mount Hope, Florida, circa 1939.

Mrs. Beattie, sixty-five, crippled with arthritis, ill, of a bad color, but proud, stoical and every inch the "General's Widow," wheels herself carefully into the room in her invalid's chair. She comes to a halt beside her worktable and starts to spread out the material for her knitting. A ball of yarn falls to the ground. She eyes it resentfully. Presently, and with great precautions, she gets out of her chair, stoops over and retrieves the wool. She has just regained her seat in the chair when Mrs. McCullum, her housekeeper, can be heard offstage.

MRS. McCULLUM: Mrs. Beattie, Mrs. Beattie! (*She puts her head in the door*) I have the most extraordinary thing to tell you. I mean it's perfectly terrible. I'll put the groceries in the kitchen. (*She enters from the back, her hands full of parcels and herself breathless with excitement*) —And they'll be here any minute! (*She comes to the front of the stage and peers through a window toward the right*) They'll be coming down that street in a minute.

MRS. BEATTIE: Now, do catch your breath, Mrs. McCullum, and tell me calmly what you have to say.

MRS. McCULLUM: I recognized them at once—both the mother and daughter. You won't *believe* what I have to tell you.

MRS. BEATTIE (*Calmly*): I think you'd better sit down.

MRS. McCULLUM: But they'll be here any minute.

MRS. BEATTIE: Who'll be here?

MRS. McCULLUM: These dreadful people . . . I know you won't want to see them. I'll just send them away.

MRS. BEATTIE: Did you get my medicine?

MRS. McCULLUM: Yes, I did.—Here's the bottle. And here's the change.—There I was sitting in Mr. Goheny's drugstore—and *they* came in.—The medicine was two-forty; you gave me a ten-dollar bill. Here's . . . seven . . . sixty . . . The mother asked Mr. Goheny where Willow Street was . . . and asked him if Mrs. Beattie was in town!! And she asked him if Mrs. Brigham lived in Mount Hope, too.—You see, *that's* what she does; she goes to people's houses. —People that have been in the army. *High up* in the army.

MRS. BEATTIE: Did you cash my check?

MRS. McCULLUM (*Fumbles in her handbag; brings out an envelope, which she gives to Mrs. Beattie*): Yes, I did. Here it is. Mr. Spottswood sends his regards and hopes that you are feeling better.—Oh, Mrs. Beattie, they're just common adventuresses. *Don't* see them.

MRS. BEATTIE (*She verifies the contents of the envelope; then says with decision*): Mrs. McCullum, I don't like fluster. Now, you go over there and sit by the piano; and you don't say a word until I've counted to five.—Then you tell me what this is all about—starting from the beginning.

> *Mrs. McCullum goes to the front of the stage and sits by an —invisible—piano, containing herself. Mrs. Beattie, calmly adjusting her knitting and starting a row, slowly counts to five.*

One . . . two . . . breathe tranquilly, Mrs. McCullum . . . three . . . four . . . Where did you *first* see or know about this mother and daughter?

MRS. McCULLUM: I do want to apologize, Mrs. Beattie, for being so excited, *but* (*Again peering through the window*) I wanted you—

MRS. BEATTIE: Yes, Mrs. McCullum. You first met them—?

MRS. McCULLUM: When I was working for Mrs. Ferguson in Winter Park two years ago, they came to the door. She said that her husband had been in the army under General Ferguson . . . in Panama . . . no, in Hawaii . . . and what good friends they'd been. They don't beg. I mean they don't *seem* to beg. She says that the daughter has a beautiful voice and that she hasn't the money to train this girl's beautiful voice. And the girl gets up to sing and she faints.

MRS. BEATTIE: What?

MRS. McCULLUM: Mrs. Beattie, the girl gets up as though she's about to sing, but she doesn't sing. She crumples up and falls on the floor. And the mother tells a whole story about how they're starving, and Mrs. Ferguson gave her two hundred dollars. But that's not all. The next day Mrs. Ogilvie called Mrs. Ferguson on the telephone and said that these two adventuresses had called at her house and the girl had fainted and she gave them one hundred dollars.

MRS. BEATTIE (*Knitting impassively*): Thank you. Did Mrs. Ferguson and Mrs. Ogilvie remember the names of these people?

MRS. McCULLUM: No . . . but this mother seemed to know *all about* General Ferguson and General Ogilvie . . . They go everywhere and get money.

MRS. BEATTIE: Now be quiet and let me think a minute!

Pause.

Do you remember their name?

MRS. McCULLUM (*Peering out the window*): No, I'm sorry I don't. But Mrs. Ferguson looked it up in the army register and it was there.

MRS. BEATTIE: How old is the girl?

MRS. McCULLUM: Well, that's the funny part about it. I think she must be all of eighteen, *now*, but her mother dresses her up as though she were much younger—so that she'll be more pathetic when she faints.

MRS. BEATTIE: Does the mother look like a lady?

MRS. McCULLUM: Yes . . . pretty much.

MRS. BEATTIE (*Her eyes on Mrs. McCullum with a sort of sardonic brooding*): Think of how full their lives must be!—Full . . . occupied!

MRS. McCULLUM (*With a start*): What? What's that you said, Mrs. Beattie? *Occupied!*—But what they're doing is immoral.

MRS. BEATTIE: I'd exchange places with them *like that*!

MRS. McCULLUM: You're in one of those moods when I don't begin to understand a word you *say*! Anyway, you're not going to see them, are you?

MRS. BEATTIE (*Calmly*): Of course, I'm going to see them.— Mrs. McCullum, will you kindly get the hot water bottle for my knees?

MRS. McCULLUM: I'll do that right now. But they'll be *here* in a minute. Won't you let me wheel you into your bedroom and bring you the bottle there?

MRS. BEATTIE: In the first place, I don't like to be wheeled anywhere. And whether they come at once or later, I'd like the hot water bottle now.

MRS. McCULLUM (*Starting*): Yes, Mrs. Beattie.

MRS. BEATTIE: One minute: tell me about the girl. She has lots of spirit.—Is this daughter pretty?

MRS. McCULLUM: Yes.—Yes, she is . . . and that reminds me: will you excuse, Mrs. Beattie, if I make a suggestion?

MRS. BEATTIE: Yes, indeed, what is it?

MRS. McCULLUM: Excuse me . . . but I think I should prepare you. The daughter—it struck me at once—resembles, very much resembles, that . . . dear photograph on the piano. I mean I couldn't help noticing it. Will you let me take the photograph into your bedroom?

MRS. BEATTIE (*Impassive, only her eyes concentrated*): I see no need to change anything in this room, Mrs. McCullum.

MRS. McCULLUM: I'll get the hot water bottle.

She goes out. Again Mrs. Beattie painfully descends from the chair. She moves to the piano and gazes long at the photograph. Then she moves farther forward on the stage and turns her head down the street. She sees the couple. She stares at them fixedly and somberly. Mrs. McCullum enters with a hot water bottle.

MRS. McCULLUM: Mrs. Beattie! You're up!

Mrs. Beattie indicates with a gesture the couple up the street. Mrs. McCullum rushes to her side.

Yes! That's they. She has that sort of list in her hand she

studies all the time.—Oh, let me send them away. They're just swindlers—common swindlers.

MRS. BEATTIE: Look!—She's studying her notes.—Yes, the girl—there is a resemblance . . . Isn't it strange . . . (*Broodingly, with a touch of bitterness*) Young . . . and beautiful . . . occupied . . .

MRS. McCULLUM: And wicked!

MRS. BEATTIE (*Dismissing this*): Oh! . . . Alive . . . (*Starting to hobble off*) Alive and together . . . Bring them in here. Be very polite to them. Tell them I'm lying down. We'll make them wait a bit . . . If they don't have calling cards, get their names very carefully and bring them in to me . . . I'm going to receive them without my wheelchair.

MRS. McCULLUM: Mrs. Beattie!

MRS. BEATTIE: And while they're waiting for me I'm going to ask you to bring some tea in to them.

MRS. McCULLUM (*Looking out the window*): Oh! They're almost here!

MRS. BEATTIE: Alive and together—that's the point.

She goes out.

MRS. McCULLUM (*Picking up her parcels and pushing the empty chair*): Why, Mrs. Beattie, you're better every day. You know you are. [(*She is out*)]

The doorbell rings.

(*Offstage*) Mrs. Beattie? Yes. Will you come in, please? Who shall I say is calling?

Enter Mrs. Kinkaid and Daphne. Mrs. Kinkaid is about forty-five, simply and tastefully dressed. She was once very pretty, but is now pinched, tense and unhappy. Daphne is eighteen, dressed for sixteen; she is cool, arrogant and sullen. Mrs. Kinkaid selects a calling card from her handbag.

MRS. KINKAID (*Giving the card, without effusiveness*): Will you say Mrs. Kinkaid, the widow of Major George Kinkaid, a friend of General Beattie! And our daughter Daphne.

MRS. McCULLUM: Mrs. Kin . . . kaid. Will you sit down, please. Mrs. Beattie is resting. I'll ask if she can see you.

MRS. KINKAID: Thank you.

MRS. McCULLUM: There are some magazines here, if you wish to look at them.

MRS. KINKAID: Thank you.

Mrs. McCullum goes out. The visitors sit very straight, scarcely turning their heads. Their eyes begin to appraise the room. When they speak, they move their lips as little as possible.

DAPHNE (*After a considerable pause, contemptuously*): Just junk.

MRS. KINKAID: The cabinet's very good.

They both gaze at it appraisingly.

When you fall, fall *that* side.

DAPHNE: We won't get fifty dollars.

MRS. KINKAID: And do that sigh—that sort of groan you did in Orlando. You've been forgetting to do that lately. Daphne! You've forgotten to take your wristwatch off. Really, you're getting awfully careless lately.

Daphne removes her wristwatch and puts it in her handbag. She rises stealthily and goes tiptoe to the back and listens. Mrs. Kinkaid has taken a piece of notepaper from her handbag, but watches Daphne's movements anxiously. As Daphne continues to listen, Mrs. Kinkaid applies herself to the notes in her hand, murmuring the words as though for memorization.

Manila, 1912 to 1913 with General Beattie and General Holabird . . . 1907 to 1911 . . . Do you remember Mrs. Holabird in West Palm Beach . . . The Presidio, 1910 . . . Oh, dear . . .

DAPHNE (*Returning to her chair, cool*): Something's going to go wrong today.

MRS. KINKAID (*Deeply alarmed*): What do you mean, Daphne?

DAPHNE: I can always tell.

MRS. KINKAID: No. No . . . How can you tell?

DAPHNE: There's going to be all hell let loose. Like that time in Sarasota.

MRS. KINKAID (*Rising, passionately*): Then let's go. Let's go at once. If it's going to be like that, I can't stand it, I really can't.

DAPHNE: Sit down! Stop making a fool of yourself.

MRS. KINKAID: This is the last time. I cannot go on with this any longer.

DAPHNE (*Harshly*): Cork it, will you!

> *Mrs. Kinkaid sits down and sobs tonelessly into her handkerchief.*

Of *course*, we've got to take risks. If we didn't take risks where'd, we be? Do you want me to go back selling *stockings?* . . . I like risks . . . and if there's going to be trouble, I *like* it. I like talking back to these old witches . . . Pull yourself together and learn your stuff. (*Pause*) Do *you* want to go back to that reception job in that hospital!?!

MRS. KINKAID (*Low, but intense*): Yes, I do, Daphne. Anything but this.

DAPHNE: Seventy a week! (*She again fixes her eyes on the cabinet*) Yes, that's not bad. It could go with the table at Mrs. O'Hallohan's. And the rugs at the Krantzes.

MRS. KINKAID: West Point, twelve. West Point, twelve.— Daphne, if you do see there may be trouble, give me the signal. You get so furious you forget to give me the signals.— Schofield Barracks. General Wilkins . . . 1909.

DAPHNE (*Eyebrows raised; she means she hears Mrs. McCullum coming*): Hickey!

> *Enter Mrs. McCullum carrying a tea tray.*

MRS. MCCULLUM: Mrs. Beattie says she'll be happy to see you. She asked me to bring you some tea while you're waiting.

MRS. KINKAID: That's *very* kind, indeed. Isn't that kind of Mrs. Beattie, Daphne?

MRS. MCCULLUM: The marmalade's from our own oranges.

MRS. KINKAID: Imagine that? —I hope Mrs. Beattie is well. Mrs. Farnsborough spoke of her as . . . as convalescent.

MRS. MCCULLUM: Thank you, Mrs. Beattie's pretty well.

> *Silence.*

Now, I think you have everything.

MRS. KINKAID: Indeed, yes. Thank you very much.

> *Mrs. McCullum goes out. Mrs. Kinkaid looks at her daughter's face anxiously.*

DAPHNE (*Looking out into space, scarcely moving her lips*): Trouble!

MRS. KINKAID (*Almost trembling; pouring the tea*): The last time!

DAPHNE: Nonsense. Just do what you have to do and get it over.

MRS. KINKAID: You're very difficult, Daphne. You're cruel.— Well, there are only six more addresses in Florida . . . and that's *all*.

DAPHNE (*Blandly*): California's as full of them as blackberries.

MRS. KINKAID: We are *not* going to California.

Daphne goes over to take her cup. She kisses her mother.

DAPHNE: Poor dear mother! (*Whispering*) You forget so easily: our house . . . our car . . . my wedding . . .

MRS. KINKAID (*Clasping her face*): Oh, I wish you were married, Daphne, and *this* were all over.

DAPHNE: Well, find me the *man*, dear. Do I ever meet any men?

MRS. KINKAID: Charles is such a nice young man.

DAPHNE (*Suddenly darkly irritated*): Are you *crazy*? Who's *he*?—Go back and study your notes. We've got to play our cards well today.

Mrs. Kinkaid's eyes have fallen on the photograph on the piano.

MRS. KINKAID: Daphne! Do you see what I see?

DAPHNE: What?

MRS. KINKAID: That photograph. Dear—

DAPHNE: What?

MRS. KINKAID: . . . The resemblance. It—it looks just like you.

DAPHNE (*A casual glance*): No, it doesn't.

MRS. KINKAID: It's amazing. (*Reopening her handbag*) I know who it is, too.

(*Reading some notes from a reference book*) "A daughter: Lydia Westerveldt, born 1912, died 1930." She's beautiful. She hasn't your eyes, dear . . . but the shape and the hair: it's amazing.

Daphne rises, stands before the photograph and gazes at it intently.

DAPHNE: Lydia . . . general's daughter . . .

"Miss Beattie, may I have the next dance?" . . .

"I'm so sorry, Lieutenant, but I've promised the next dance to Colonel Randolph."

"My daughter's away at finishing school. I don't know when she'll be back. She's staying with friends all over New England."

(*Turning to her mother, sharply*) She has a wedding ring on.

MRS. KINKAID: Do come and sit down, dear.

DAPHNE (*To the photograph*): Of course, I don't like her. She had everything she wanted. She didn't know what it was to know *nobody*, to have to spend all your time among common vulgar people, to skimp—

MRS. KINKAID: Daphne!

DAPHNE: . . . and she didn't have to see her own mother insulted (*Whirling about to face her mother*) like *you* were by Mrs. Smith.

MRS. KINKAID: Dear, I wasn't *insulted*—

DAPHNE (*Back at the photograph*): And you never knew what it was to be treated *just ghastly* by men, because you were poor; you didn't know anything. (*She spits at the picture*) There! There!

MRS. KINKAID (*Has risen; keeping her voice*): Daphne, you stop that right now, and drink your tea. Sometimes I don't know what comes over you . . .

Daphne returns, grand and somber, to her chair.

I never taught you to say things like that.

DAPHNE (*Airily*): I don't like the way she looks at me.

(*Rendered pleasurably light-headed by her outburst*) I feel better. I'm glad I talked to her. . . . Mother-mousie, we're going to be very successful today. I feel it in my bones . . . and tonight we're going to a movie, and *you know which one.* (*She hears a noise in the hall*) Hickey!

Both compose themselves for the entrance of Mrs. Beattie. Mrs. Beattie enters alone, walking with the greatest difficulty, but putting on a cordial smile.

MRS. BEATTIE: Mrs. Kinkaid, good afternoon. I am Mrs. Beattie. Don't get up, please.

MRS. KINKAID (*Rising*): Good afternoon, Mrs. Beattie. This is my daughter, Daphne.

MRS. BEATTIE (*Stopping and looking at her hard*): Good afternoon, Miss Kinkaid. Please sit down, both of you.

MRS. KINKAID: We want to thank you . . . for sending the tea. So kind.

MRS. BEATTIE (*Sitting down*): Mrs. McCullum tells me you knew my husband.

MRS. KINKAID: Mrs. Beattie . . . My husband, Major George Kinkaid, was in the Philippines at the same time as General Beattie. He was a lieutenant at that time—it was 1912 and 1913—and probably had very little opportunity to meet the General, but he knew very well a number of the members of your husband's staff—General Ferguson—then Colonel Ferguson; and Colonel Fosdick.

Mrs. Beattie nods.

I was not there at the time. I was very ill for a number of years and the doctors thought it inadvisable that I should make the trip to the Far East.

MRS. BEATTIE: Were you ever in the Far East?

MRS. KINKAID: No, I wasn't.

MRS. BEATTIE (*To Daphne*): And where were you born, Miss Kinkaid?

DAPHNE (*Slight pause*): In Philadelphia.

MRS. BEATTIE (*Turning back to Mrs. Kinkaid*): I assume that there is something that you wish to see me about?

MRS. KINKAID (*She makes a pause, and clutching her handbag begins to speak with earnest candor*): There is, Mrs. Beattie— I am faced with a problem and I have called on you in the hope that you will give me some advice. My daughter, Daphne (*Mrs. Beattie turns her eyes on Daphne*) is endowed with a most unusual singing voice. Qualified musicians have told me that she has indeed an extraordinary voice. And in addition to that voice, a deeply musical nature. Professor Boncianiani of New York, who is recognized as one of the leading teachers, has predicted a great career for her. Perhaps, if you wish—a little later—I shall ask Daphne to sing for you. My problem is this—where will I find the means to cultivate her voice? So far I have been barely able to afford a certain amount of instruction . . . naturally, in a very modest way.

She pauses.

MRS. BEATTIE: I see. You draw a pension, of course—

MRS. KINKAID: No, Mrs. Beattie, I do not. (*She takes a handkerchief from her handbag*) I do not. My husband's career in the army began most promisingly. I have here letters from his superior officers expressing the highest opinion of his work. But my husband had . . . a weakness. (*She touches the handkerchief to her nose*) I find this very hard to say . . . he was intemperate . . .

MRS. BEATTIE: I beg your pardon?

MRS. KINKAID: Somehow . . . alone in the Far East . . . he took to drinking. And on one occasion . . . under the influence of alcohol . . . he forgot himself . . . He was, I believe, impertinent to a superior officer . . .

MRS. BEATTIE: To whom?

MRS. KINKAID: To General Foley.

Pause. Mrs. Kinkaid dries her eyes.

MRS. BEATTIE: How have you made your living, Mrs. Kinkaid?

MRS. KINKAID: For a while I assisted in a small dress shop in Miami Beach. Then I was a receptionist in a hotel.

MRS. BEATTIE: And now?

MRS. KINKAID: I have not come to you with any problem about our livelihood, Mrs. Beattie. I hope to be able to sustain ourselves; it is Daphne's career—her Godgiven voice—that I feel to be my responsibility. —I would like you to hear Daphne sing. She is able to accompany herself.

She looks inquiringly at Mrs. Beattie who remains silent.

Daphne, do that French song.

Daphne has felt Mrs. Beattie's weighted glance.

DAPHNE: Mother, I don't feel like singing. I think we should thank Mrs. Beattie for the tea and go.

MRS. KINKAID: Do make an effort, Daphne. Mrs. Beattie has been so kind.

Daphne turns and looks at Mrs. Beattie who meets her gaze.

DAPHNE (*Under her breath*): Mrs. Beattie has not asked me to sing.

MRS. BEATTIE: I should very much like to hear you sing, Miss Kinkaid.

DAPHNE (*Rising*): Very well, I will.

MRS. BEATTIE (*Distinctly*): It will not be necessary to faint.

MRS. KINKAID (*Bridling*): To faint!?

MRS. BEATTIE: It will not be necessary to faint. I have understood the problem. —Sit down, Miss Kinkaid. (*Turning to Mrs. Kinkaid, with decision*) How much of what you have told me is true?

MRS. KINKAID (*Rising; with indignation*): I do not know what you mean. I have never been spoken to in such a way. Come with me, Daphne.
    (*To Mrs. Beattie*) Every word I have said is *true*.

Mrs. Beattie remains impassive, her eyes on Daphne, who has not moved from where she stopped on her way to the piano.

MRS. BEATTIE: I shall not telephone the police unless you force me to.

MRS. KINKAID (*About at the door*): The police! We have done nothing that concerns the police.

MRS. BEATTIE: They could ask you to give an account of the money you have received. —Have you an unusual voice, Miss Kinkaid?

DAPHNE (*Beginning with low contempt*): Oh, you can talk. You don't know what other people's lives are like. Our lives are just awful. You've got everything you want and you've always had everything you want. You don't know what it is for me to see my mother treated just like dirt by people she shouldn't even have to speak to.

MRS. KINKAID: Daphne! You know I've never complained—

DAPHNE: And everybody else has *cars* . . . and when they eat they eat things fit to eat. You don't know what it is to see your own mother—

Mrs. McCullum has come to the door.

MRS. McCULLUM: Mrs. Beattie, you remember what the doctor

said . . . You're not to have any excitement. I must ask these ladies to go.

MRS. BEATTIE (*Raising her hand*): I wish to hear what they have to say.

MRS. KINKAID (*Comes forward as if there had been no interruption*): Daphne has not expressed our intention correctly. Daphne is a very imaginative child and is given to exaggeration. I have never made any complaint about our lives, as far as I am concerned; but you cannot know what it is, Mrs. Beattie, to bring up a refined and sensitive girl like Daphne . . . without money and without . . . any social situation. The only girls and young men we have any opportunity to meet are coarse, and vulgar . . . often unspeakably vulgar. Daphne's place is among ladies and gentlemen. I have spent sleepless nights—many sleepless nights—trying to find some way to better our situation.

DAPHNE (*Now going to the door*): Come, Mother, she doesn't know what we're talking about. She was born ignorant . . . and her daughter went from one dance to another dance . . . and her children would have the same thing. And what right did you have to a life like that? None at all. You were born into the right cradle. That's all you did to earn it.

MRS. BEATTIE (*Firmly but not sharply to Daphne*): *Have* you a remarkable voice?

DAPHNE: No.

MRS. KINKAID: Daphne!

[*Mrs. Beattie and Daphne look at one another. Mrs. Kinkaid and Mrs. McCullum are frozen where they stand. Mrs. Beattie glances at Mrs. Kinkaid and then toward the antique cabinet on which stand the telephone and a writing kit with a pen holder and a checkbook. She moves carefully to the cabinet and pauses as if coming to an important decision.*]

MRS. BEATTIE: [Alive and together . . . that's the point.]

[*Mrs. Beattie picks up the pen and checkbook, and turns back to face Daphne and Mrs. Kinkaid, as the lights fade.*]

END OF PLAY

In Shakespeare and the Bible

(*Wrath*)

CHARACTERS

MARGET, a maid
JOHN LUBBOCK, a young attorney, twenty-seven,
Katy Buckingham's fiancé
MRS. MOWBREY, Katy Buckingham's aunt, late fifties
KATY BUCKINGHAM, twenty-one

SETTING

An oversumptuous parlor, New York, 1898.

All we need see are three chairs, a low sofa and a taboret. Two steps descend from the hall at the back into the room. A Swedish maid, Marget, introduces John Lubbock, twenty-seven, self-assured; face and bearing under absolute control.

LUBBOCK: Mrs. Mowbrey wrote me, asking me to call. My name is Lubbock.

MARGET: Yes, sir. Mrs. Mowbrey is expecting you. She will be down in a moment, sir. She says I'm to bring you some port. I'll go and get it.

> *Exit Marget.*
> *Lubbock, hands in his pockets, whistling under his breath, strolls about examining closely, one by one, the pictures hanging on the wall invisible to us.*
> *Marget returns bearing a small tray on which are two decanters and two goblets. She puts them on the taboret.*

There's port in this one, sir, and sherry in this. Mrs. Mowbrey says you're to help yourself.

LUBBOCK: Thank you. (*Still examining the pictures*) These are relatives and ancestors of Mrs. Mowbrey?

MARGET: Oh, yes. Mrs. Mowbrey comes of a very fine family.

I've heard her say that that is her father. As you can see, a clergyman.

LUBBOCK (*Casually*): She lives alone here?

MARGET: Oh, yes. She's a widow, poor lady. And very much alone. Would you believe it, if I said that no one's come to the house to call for the whole time I've been here, except her lawyer man. And, oh yes, the minister of her church.

LUBBOCK: For several months.

MARGET: Oh, I've been here about a year. But today we're going to have two callers—you, sir, and a young lady that's coming later. Yes, and I mustn't forget: when the doorbell rings for the young lady, I'm to take out the decanters before I open the door. Now I mustn't forget that. And then I'm to bring in the tea. Now, you'll help yourself, won't you?

> *Marget goes out.*
>
> *Lubbock, thoughtfully, pours himself a considerable amount of sherry and, sipping it, returns to his examination of the room and the pictures.*
>
> *Enter Mrs. Mowbrey, late fifties, handsome, florid, powdered. She wears a black satin dress covered with bugles and jet. She addresses Lubbock from the hall before descending into the room.*

MRS. MOWBREY: Mr. Lubbock, I am Mrs. Mowbrey.

LUBBOCK: Good afternoon, ma'am.

MRS. MOWBREY: You don't know who I am?

LUBBOCK: No, ma'am. I got your letter asking me to call.

MRS. MOWBREY (*Coming forward*): Won't you sit down?

> *They sit, Mrs. Mowbrey behind the taboret.*

Mr. Lubbock, I had two reasons for asking you to call today. In the first place, I wish to engage a lawyer. I thought we might take a look at one another and see if we could work together. (*She pauses. He bows his head slightly and impersonally*) I mean a lawyer to handle my affairs in general and to advise me. (*Same business*) My second reason for asking to see you is that I am your fiancée's aunt.

LUBBOCK (*Amazed*): Miss Buckingham's aunt! She never told me she had an aunt.

MRS. MOWBREY: No, Mr. Lubbock, she wouldn't. I am the

black sheep of the family. My name is not mentioned in that house.—Will you pour me some port, please. I am glad to see that you have helped yourself . . . Thank you . . . Yes, I am your future mother-in-law's sister. (*He is standing up, holding his glass—waiting*) Our lives took different directions. (*He sits down*)

But before we get into the legal matter, let's get to know one another a little better.—Tell me, I haven't seen my niece for fifteen years. Is she a pretty girl?

LUBBOCK: Yes—very.

MRS. MOWBREY: We're a good-looking family.

LUBBOCK (*Indicating the pictures on the wall*): And a distinguished one. Miss Buckingham would be very interested in seeing these family portraits.

MRS. MOWBREY: Yes. (*She sips her wine, then says dryly, without a smile*) It's not hard to find family portraits, Mr. Lubbock. There are places on Twelfth Street, simply full of them. Bishops and generals—whatever you want.

LUBBOCK (*Continuing to look at them, also without a smile*): Very fine collection, I should say.

She takes another sip of wine.

MRS. MOWBREY: Mr. Lubbock, I've made some inquiries about you. You are twenty-seven years old.

LUBBOCK: Yes, I am.

MRS. MOWBREY: You took your time finding yourself, didn't you? All that unpleasantness down in Philadelphia. What happened exactly? Well, we won't go into it. Then you gave yourself a good shaking. You pulled yourself together. Law school—very good. People are still wondering where you got all that spending money. It wasn't horse racing. It wasn't cards. No one could figure it out. Apparently it was something you were doing up in Harlem.—Certainly, your parents couldn't afford to give you anything. In fact, you were very generous to them. You bought them a house on Staten Island. You were a very good son to them and I think you'll make a very good family man.

LUBBOCK (*With a slight bow and a touch of dry irony*): You are very well informed, ma'am.

MRS. MOWBREY: Yes, I am. (*She takes another sip of wine*) On

Saturday nights you often went to 321 West Street—"The Palace," you boys called it. Nice girls, every one of them, especially Dolores.

LUBBOCK (*Mastering violence; rises*): I don't like this conversation, ma'am. I shall ask you to let me take my leave.

MRS. MOWBREY (*Raising her voice*): You and I have met before, Mr. Lubbock. You knew me under another name. I owned The Palace.

LUBBOCK: Mrs. Higgins!!

MRS. MOWBREY: My hair is no longer blond. (*She rises and crosses the room*) You may leave any moment you wish, but I never believed you were a hypocrite.

LUBBOCK (*After returning her fixed gaze wrathfully; then sitting down again*): What do you *want*?

MRS. MOWBREY: Yes, I owned The Palace and several other establishments—refined, very refined in every way. I've sold them. I've retired. I see no one—no one—whom I knew in those days. Except today I am seeing yourself. Naturally, I am never going to mention these matters again. I am going to forget them, and I hope that you will forget them, too. But it would be very valuable to me to have a lawyer who knew them and who was in a position to forget them.—I'll have a little more port, if you'll be so good.

> *Lubbock takes the glass from her hand in silence, fills it at the taboret and carries it to her. She murmurs: "Thank you." He returns and stands by the taboret, talking to her across the length of the stage.*

LUBBOCK: I don't believe you asked me here to engage me as your lawyer. There's something else on your mind. Will you say it and then let me take my leave?

MRS. MOWBREY: You were always like that, Jack.

LUBBOCK (*Loud*): I will ask you not to call me Jack.

MRS. MOWBREY (*Bowing her head slightly*): That was always your way, Mr. Lubbock. Suspicious. Quick to fight. Imagining that everybody was trying to take advantage of you.

LUBBOCK: What do you want? I don't know what you're talking about. (*He starts with fuming lowered head for the door*) Good afternoon.

MRS. MOWBREY: Mr. Lubbock, I will tell you what I want. (*He *pauses with his back to her*) I am a rich woman and I intend to get richer. And I am a lonely woman, and I don't think that that is necessary. I want to live. And when you and Katy are married, I want you to help me. (*He is "caught" and half turns*) I want company. I want to entertain. I also want to help people. I want—so to speak—to adopt some. Not *young* children, of course, but young men and women who want bringing out in some way or other. I have a gift for that kind of thing.—Even in my former work I was able to do all sorts of things for my girls.—Did you ever hear anyone say that Mrs. Higgins was mean—unkind—to the girls in her place? (*He refuses to answer; the port is going to her head. She strikes her bosom emotionally*) I'm kind to a *fault.* I love to see young people *happy.* Dozens of those girls—I helped them get married. I encouraged them to find good homes. *Against my own interest.*—Your friend, Dolores: married a policeman. Happy as a lark. (*She puts a delicate lace handkerchief to her eyes and then to her nose*)—Will you consent to be my lawyer?

LUBBOCK (*Scorn and finality*): My firm doesn't allow us to serve family connections.

MRS. MOWBREY: Oh, I don't want to have anything to do with that wretched firm: Wilbraham, Clayton, what's-its-name? All you do for me will be on your own time. I shall start giving you three thousand a year for your advice. Then—

LUBBOCK: I beg your pardon. It's entirely out of the question.

MRS. MOWBREY (*After a slight pause; in a less emotional voice*): Yes, yes. I know that you are always ready with your no! no! You haven't yet heard what I can do for you. And I don't mean in the sense of money. There is something you are greatly in need of . . . (*Pause*) . . . John Lubbock. One can see that you are a lawyer—and a very good one, I suspect.—So, you looked about you and you selected my niece?

LUBBOCK: Oh, much more than that. I'm very much in love with your niece. You should know her. Katy's an extraordinary girl.

MRS. MOWBREY: Is she? There's nothing very extraordinary about her mother. What's extraordinary about Katy?

LUBBOCK: Why, she's . . . I feel that I'm the luckiest man in the world.

MRS. MOWBREY: Come now, Mr. Lubbock. You don't have to talk like that to me.

LUBBOCK (*Earnestly*): I assure you, I mean it.

MRS. MOWBREY (*A touch of contempt*): Very clever, is she? Reads a lot of books and all that kind of thing?

LUBBOCK: *No-o.* (*With a slight laugh*) But she asks a lot of questions.

MRS. MOWBREY (*Pleased*): Does she? So do I, Mr. Lubbock, as you have noticed. (*She rises and starts toward her former seat by the decanter of port*) She asks lots of questions. I like that.—I asked her to call this afternoon.

LUBBOCK (*Startled and uneasy*): You did? Did you tell her that I would be here?

MRS. MOWBREY: No. I thought I would surprise her.

LUBBOCK: Katy doesn't like surprises. (*Preparing to leave, with hand outstretched*) I think that at your first meeting with— after so long a time—you should see her alone. Perhaps I can call on you at another time.

MRS. MOWBREY (*Still standing*): What *are* you so nervous about? It's not time for her to come yet, and besides I have this law matter to discuss with you.

LUBBOCK: Thank you.—I'll ask if I can call some other time.

MRS. MOWBREY: Anyway, perhaps she won't come. She'll have shown my letter to her mother and her mother will have forbidden her to come. Would Katy disobey her mother?

LUBBOCK: Yes.

MRS. MOWBREY (*Eyeing him*): Has Katy chosen to marry you against her mother's wishes?

LUBBOCK: Yes. Very much so.

MRS. MOWBREY: I see. Tears? Scenes? Slamming of doors?

LUBBOCK: Yes, I think so.

MRS. MOWBREY (*Leaning toward him confidentially, lifted finger*): Katy is like *me*, Mr. Lubbock. I can feel it with every word you say.

> *Still uneasy, Lubbock has been taking a few steps around the room; he looks up at the ceiling and weighs this thoughtfully.*

LUBBOCK: If you told her you were her aunt . . . Yes, I think she will come. Katy likes to know . . . where she stands; what it's all about, and that kind of thing.

MRS. MOWBREY I see. A lawyer's wife. As you suggested a few moments ago: she's inquisitive?

LUBBOCK (*With a nervous laugh*): Yes, she is.

MRS. MOWBREY: And you think I'm inquisitive, too—don't you?

LUBBOCK: Yes, I do.

MRS. MOWBREY: Well, let me tell you something, Mr. Lubbock. Everybody says we women are inquisitive. Most of us are. We have to be. I wouldn't give a cent for a woman who wasn't. And why? (*The wine has gone to her head. She emphasizes what she is about to say by tapping with jeweled rings on the taboret*) Because a good deal is asked of us for which we are not prepared. Women have to keep their wits about them to survive at all, Mr. Lubbock. (*She leans back in her chair*) When I was married I didn't hesitate to read every scrap of paper my husband left lying around the house. But (*She leans forward*) as I said, I have some business to discuss with you before Katy comes.—Do you always walk about that way?

LUBBOCK (*Surprised*): People tell me I do. I do in court. If it makes you uneasy—

MRS. MOWBREY: I would like to ask another thing. When you are married—and as a wedding present I shall give Katy a very large check, I assure you—I want you both to give me the opportunity to meet some of your friends, young people in whom I could take an interest. New York must be full of them. But most of all I want to see *you two*. I want you to feel that this house is your second home. (*Very emotional*) I will do everything for you. I have no one else in the world. I will do everything for you. (*Again she puts her handkerchief to her face*)

Now I've talked a good deal. Have you anything to say to all this?

LUBBOCK (*After rising and taking a few steps about*): Mrs. Mowbrey, I like people who talk frankly, as you do, and who go straight to the point. And I'm going to be frank with you. There's one big hitch in what you propose.

MRS. MOWBREY: Hitch?

LUBBOCK: Katy. (*He looks directly at her and repeats*) Katy. Naturally, she wouldn't have anything to say about my professional life.—And I want to thank you for the confidence you express in my ability to be of service to you. (*He looks up at the ceiling in thought*) But about those other points: I don't know. I tell you frankly, Mrs. Mowbrey, I'm in love with Katy. I'm knocked off my feet by Katy. But I feel that I don't know her. How can I put it? I'm . . . I'm even afraid of Katy.

MRS. MOWBREY (*Almost outraged*): What? A man like you, afraid of a mere girl!

LUBBOCK (*Short laugh*): Well, perhaps that's going too far; but I swear to you I still can't imagine what it will be like to be married to Katy.

(*His manner changes and he goes to her briskly as though to shake her hand*) Really, I think it's best that I say good night now. Katy will want to see you alone. So I'll thank you very much and say good-bye. And ask if I may call on you at some other time.

MRS. MOWBREY: Nonsense! What possible harm could there be—?

The doorbell rings.

There! That's the doorbell. That's Katy. It's too late to go now. Do calm down, Mr. Lubbock.

Enter Marget.

MARGET: That's the front doorbell, Mrs. Mowbrey. Shall I take out the tray?

MRS. MOWBREY: Yes, Marget. And be quick about it.

Marget scutters out with the tray.

Really, I don't understand you, Mr. Lubbock. This is not like you at all. There's nothing to get nervous about. The young girls of today are perfect geese—don't I know them! Pah!

Marget at the door.

MARGET: Miss Buckingham to see you, ma'am.

Katy, twenty-one, very pretty, stands a moment at the top step and looks all about the room.

MRS. MOWBREY (Throwing her arms wide, without rising): Ah, *there* you are, dear.

KATY (*Taking a few steps forward, her eyes on Lubbock*): Aunt Julia, I'm very glad to see you.

MRS. MOWBREY (*Apparently expecting to be kissed*): This *is* a joy!

> *Katy, approaching her, looks at her smiling, and suddenly drops her reticule which she has opened. Thus avoiding an embrace, she leans over and takes some time picking the objects up. Lubbock and Marget come to her assistance.*

KATY: Oh, how awkward of me! I'm so sorry. I'm always doing things like this. Thank you. There's my key . . . and my card case. Thank you.

MRS. MOWBREY: Marget, we're ready for tea now. I'm sure you'll want some tea, dear.

> *Exit Marget.*

KATY: Thank you, I would.—You're here, John?

LUBBOCK (*Uncomfortable*): Mrs. Mowbrey wrote me and asked me to call.

MRS. MOWBREY: Yes, dear, I've wanted a lawyer so badly. Now sit down and let me look at you.

> *Katy sits in the chair Mrs. Mowbrey has indicated.*

What a dear, beautiful girl you are!—And you're so like my father! You're like me and my father.

LUBBOCK (*Reluctantly*): Yes . . . There is something there.

MRS. MOWBREY: Oh, I've lost my looks—I know that! I've been through *great* unhappiness, but the resemblance is there, there's no doubt about it.

KATY: Did you know I was coming, John?

LUBBOCK: No, no.

KATY: Is John going to be your lawyer, Aunt Julia?

MRS. MOWBREY: I hope so, dear. I certainly hope he will be. That'll bring us all closer and closer together.

KATY: Aunt Julia . . . I scarcely remember you. Why . . . why haven't we seen you more often?

MRS. MOWBREY: Mildred, dear, your mother and I . . . let's not talk about it. I'll just say this: sometimes in families, there are people who simply can't get on together. I hope your mother's happy. I wish her every good thing in the world. If she doesn't wish to see me, that doesn't change anything. I wish her every good thing in the world. You can tell her that any time you wish, Mildred.—But Mr. Lubbock tells me you wish to be called Kate?

KATY: Yes, I do.

MRS. MOWBREY: But why?

KATY (*After looking down a moment*): That would take too long to explain, Aunt Julia.

MRS. MOWBREY: Well, you are a dear original girl, aren't you?

KATY: John, are you Aunt Julia's lawyer?

MRS. MOWBREY: He *will* be. He will be. We've just settled that. So that both my business and my pleasure—my affection, let us hope—will be close together. Oh, here's the tea.

> *Enter Marget with the tea service.*

Oh, I have such plans for you. Cream and sugar—both of you?

KATY and LUBBOCK: Thank you.

MRS. MOWBREY: You see, dear, I've lived too much alone, since my dear husband's death. That's not good. That's not right. And you are going to bring me out.—Now tell me, Katy, where are you going to live? Have you found just what you wanted?

KATY: Yes, we have.—Thank you.

MRS. MOWBREY: Splendid! Tell me, dear, don't have a moment's hesitation . . . What will it be: linen? silver?

KATY: Aunt Julia, I don't like receiving presents. I never have. I may be strange in that, but . . . I don't.

MRS. MOWBREY: Presents! But I'm your aunt—this is the family.

KATY (*Clearly*): But we don't know one another very well yet.

> *Mrs. Mowbrey is stopped short. She fumbles with her handkerchief. She begins silently to weep.*

Have you been living in New York, Aunt Julia?

MRS. MOWBREY: That was not kind, Mildred. That was not kind.

KATY (*Searching herself, softly*): I'm sorry. I'm sorry, if . . . I think I'm supposed to be a very outspoken person, Aunt Julia, but I didn't mean to be unkind.

MRS. MOWBREY (*Still drying one eye; but in a low firm tone of instruction*): That means you must have been *hurt* in life, in some way. I've seen it often.

KATY (*Another glance at John, slowly*): No, I . . . don't think I have.

LUBBOCK (*Floundering, but trying to do his part*): Katy's right, Mrs. Mowbrey. But when she does make a friend, she's a real one.

MRS. MOWBREY: *That* I believe. And so am I. And I want to prove it to you. I want you to come to feel that this is your second home. I want to be useful to you, in any way.

Do you know, Katy, that when I was a girl *I* changed my name, too? I was christened Julia; but I didn't like it. I wanted a name out of the Bible. I liked the story of Esther. I liked her courage. That's what I like—courage. Now will you tell me why you changed yours?

KATY: Well . . . I used to read Shakespeare all the time. And I liked the girls in Shakespeare. Even when I was very young . . . Every day I'd pretend I was a different one. And, you know, they . . . most of them have no fathers or mothers, or else . . . and they have to go live in foreign countries or live in a forest . . . and they even have to change their clothes and pretend they're men. They're very much thrown on their own resources. That's what they learn. There are four or five that I admired most—but I knew I wouldn't be like them. So I chose one of the lesser ones—one of the easier ones—

MRS. MOWBREY: I remember. I remember. That play. I can't remember its name—but that Kate had an awful temper. Mr. Lubbock, has our Kate got an awful temper?

Katy stiffens.

LUBBOCK: No, indeed, Mrs. Mowbrey.

KATY: No, I wish I did. I think people with a temper are lucky.

MRS. MOWBREY: Lucky! How could you wish a thing like that.

KATY: When things seem all wrong to me, I do something worse than have a temper. I turn all cold and stormy inside. It's as though something were dead in me.

MRS. MOWBREY: I understand every word of that. Katy, dear, we will be good friends.—Now surely there's some furniture I can lend you, some household appointments?

KATY (*Quietly*): Thank you very much, Aunt Julia. But, of course, we mean to live very simply. And we won't be seeing anyone for the first year or two.—Will we John?

LUBBOCK (*Floundering*): Just as you wish, Katy . . .

MRS. MOWBREY: Oh, dear! That's so unwise! My dear children, you must come and see *me*—and my friends. I have so many friends who will be delighted to meet you: artists and writers and young men in politics—so valuable for Mr. Lubbock's work. And the dear rector of my church, Mr. Jenkins.

KATY: All that's for John to decide, of course.

Katy turns inquiringly toward him, as does Mrs. Mowbrey.

LUBBOCK (*Belatedly he stammers*): Oh, we . . . won't be seeing too many people . . .

MRS. MOWBREY: There's Judge Whittaker's son for example. You'll laugh till the tears run down your cheeks. (*With confidential emphasis to Katy*) Judge Whittaker can do anything in New York—*anything* you ask him . . . Old friend of mine.

(*To Lubbock, rising*) People with influence like that—you must know them.

(*To Katy*) And then I want to take you shopping, dear. Stores where they know me. They practically *give* me the things. Great Heavens, I haven't had to pay the marked [price] for anything, for years. Friends, friends everywhere. —Now I'm going to leave you two alone together. I know you have a world of things to talk about.

Katy rises.

If you want some more tea, just ring and ask Marget for it.

KATY (*Always quietly*): Aunt Julia, I can see John perfectly well in my own home. I came to call on you.

MRS. MOWBREY (*Moving to the door*): What a sweet thing to say.—No, no. I know young people in love; don't say I don't. And beginning today I want you to think of this house as your second home. Besides, I have a present for you and I must go and get it. (*She indicates a ring on her finger*) A very pretty thing, indeed.

KATY (*Following Mrs. Mowbrey toward the door; with a touch of firmer protest*): But, Aunt Julia!—

MRS. MOWBREY: Ten minutes! I'll give you ten minutes!

She goes out. Katy turns and with lowered eyes goes slowly to her chair. She sits and covers her face with her hands.

KATY (*As though to herself*): I can't understand it . . . What a dreadful, dreadful person.

LUBBOCK (*Uncomfortable*): Come now, Katy. It's not as bad as all that . . . Of course, she's a little . . . odd; but I imagine she's been through a lot of . . . trouble of some sort.

Katy looks at him a moment and then says with great directness:

KATY: What has she done, John? (*He doesn't answer*) It must be something serious. Mother won't talk about her *one minute!*—Tell me! What is it?

LUBBOCK: Well . . . uh . . . she may have made some wrong step . . . early in life. Something like that.

KATY (*After weighing this thoughtfully*): No. My mother would have forgiven that . . . It must be something much worse.

LUBBOCK: Whatever it was it's behind her. It's in the past.

KATY (*Shakes her head; she gives a shudder*): It's there—*now.* (*Always very sincerely, this as though to herself*) I don't even know the names of things. Except what I've read about. In books. (*Brief pause*)

(*As with an effort to say such an awful thing*) Was she a . . . usurer?

LUBBOCK: What's that?—Oh, a *usurer.* (*With too loud a laugh*) NO, no—she wasn't that!

KATY: Was she a perjurer?

LUBBOCK: Katy, where do you get these old expressions? I don't know, but I guess she wasn't that.

KATY (*Gravely pursuing her thought*): *Was* she . . . that other kind of bad person. That word that's in the Bible and in Shakespeare . . . (*This takes solemn courage*) . . . that begins with "double-you" . . . with "double-you aitch"—?

This takes a minute to dawn on Lubbock. He reacts violently; with as little comic effect as possible.

LUBBOCK: Katy!! How can you say such a thing.

KATY: I don't know how to pronounce it.

LUBBOCK: Do stop this! Put this all out of your head, *please*.

KATY: But she's my own aunt. I must have some idea to go by. Mother won't say a word. She just bursts into tears and leaves the room.

LUBBOCK: Please, Katy.—For Heaven's sake, change the subject.

KATY: I don't want to know anything that it's *unsuitable* for me to know. But I don't want to live with people hiding things from me. I don't think ignorance helps anybody. I can see perfectly well that you know the answer: Was Aunt Julia that thing that beings with "double-you"?

LUBBOCK: I'm not going to answer you, Katy. This conversation *is* unsuitable. Very unsuitable.

KATY (*Who has kept her eyes on him; calmly*): Then she *was*.

LUBBOCK: No—I didn't say that. Anyway, how would I know a thing like that?—Probably, she was just connected with such things—at a distance.

KATY: How do you mean?

LUBBOCK: She wasn't in it herself . . . She just—sort of— stood by . . . I'm not going to stay here another moment. Where's that woman put my hat?

KATY: I see . . . She arranged them. That's in Shakespeare, too. She was a bawd.

LUBBOCK: Katy!

KATY: It's in the Bible, too: she was a . . . *(She pronounces the "aitch")* whoremonger.

She rises.

LUBBOCK (*Fiercely*): Stop this right now. How can you say such ugly words?

KATY: Are there any others that aren't ugly?—Anyway, now I know.

She quickly moves up toward the entrance.

LUBBOCK: Where are you going?

KATY (*From the steps*): You don't want me to stay, do you?

LUBBOCK: Think a moment, Katy. Stop and think.

KATY: Think what?

LUBBOCK: Well . . . this Bible you're quoting from . . . should have taught you to be charitable about people's mistakes. About Mary Magdalene and all that.

KATY (*Turning in deep thought*): Yes, it should, shouldn't it?— But Mary Magdalene wasn't the second thing; she was the first. (*She returns to her chair and sits, her eyes on the floor. Again as though to herself*) I don't know anything about anything. (*She suddenly looks at him and says with accusing directness*) And you're not helping me. Tell me what I should think. Are you going to be like this always? . . . When I ask questions? . . .

LUBBOCK (*Urgently*): No, Katy. I promise you. I'll answer anything you ask me!

KATY: When?

LUBBOCK: When we're married.—But not here! Not now!— Today, anyway, put all this out of your head.

KATY (*Reluctantly acquiescent, rises again*): When we're married. That's like what Mother's always saying: "When you're older; when you're older." (*Turning to him with decision*) But if she *is* those things—those things that Shakespeare said—

LUBBOCK: Don't say them!

KATY: Promise me that you'll never see her again.

LUBBOCK: Now, K-a-a-ty! She's a client. In business we can't stop to take any notice of our client's morals . . .

KATY: In business they don't? I mean: thieves and criminals? Don't men meet that kind of people all the time?

LUBBOCK (*Putting his hands over his ears*): Questions! Questions! You're going to drive me crazy.

KATY (*Looking around the room, musingly*): And all this money came from . . . that! (*Her eyes return to him*) And when she asks us to come here to dinner?

LUBBOCK: Of *course*, we don't have to come often. But she's a lonely woman who's trying to put the mistakes of her life behind her. Be kind, Katy. Be charitable!

KATY (*Weighs this, then says simply*): Have you ever seen her before?

LUBBOCK: Mrs. Mowbrey? (*Loud laugh of protest*) Of *course* not.

Katy goes to the hall. From the top step she turns and says with great quiet but final significance:

KATY: And you want me to invite her to the wedding?

Lubbock cannot answer. His jaw is caught rigid. Katy returns into the room, drawing a ring off her finger.

All I know is what I read in Shakespeare and the Bible. That's all I have to go by, John. Nobody else helps. You don't help me. I'm giving you back your ring.

She puts the ring on the taboret and goes quickly, with lowered head, out of the house. The front door is heard closing. Lubbock stands rigid. Slowly he goes to the taboret and takes up the ring. Mrs. Mowbrey appears at the hall indignant.

MRS. MOWBREY: Who went out the front door? Was that Katy?

He puts down the ring on the taboret.

LUBBOCK: Yes, Mrs. Mowbrey. She went home.

MRS. MOWBREY (*Coming in*): Without saying good-bye to me! Her own aunt! Well—there's a badly brought up girl! (*Sitting down*) What did she say?

LUBBOCK: She left no message.

MRS. MOWBREY: I'm ashamed of her, Mr. Lubbock. I never heard of such behavior. The idea!

(*Seeing the ring*) What's this? What's this ring?

LUBBOCK: She left it. It's her engagement ring.

MRS. MOWBREY: She broke her engagement?

(*Rising*) Mr. Lubbock, listen to me! You can call yourself a very lucky man. One look at her, and I could see she wasn't the right girl for you.—Left without saying one word of good-bye! I don't know what's become of the girls these days. A niece of mine—behaving like that. (*Giving him the ring and wagging her finger in his face*) Now you must put that in a safe place—and you'll find the real right girl for you. They aren't all dead *yet*. You're going to find some splendid girl and I'm going to make a second home for you here. We're going to have fun. *You only live once*, as the Good Book says.

LUBBOCK: *You* did this! Look! (*Holding the ring toward her*) She's gone.—You with your conniving and sticking your nose into other people's business. WHY the hell did you have to put your goddamned nose into my affairs?

MRS. MOWBREY: I have never allowed profanity to be used in my presence.

LUBBOCK: Well, you'll hear it now. You—with your sentimental whining about wanting friends. *You'll* never have any friends. You don't deserve to have any friends. God, have you wrecked your chances today!—While you were wrecking mine.

She has descended coolly into the room. Lubbock passes her toward the hall.

You can sit here alone for ever and ever, as far as I care. Where'd that girl put my hat?

MRS. MOWBREY: Yes, Mr. Lubbock, you go and you stay away. You have just shown yourself to be the biggest fool I ever saw. It wasn't I that lost you that girl; it was yourself. And you deserve to lose her.

LUBBOCK: How do you know what happened?

MRS. MOWBREY: I will ring and Marget will get your hat.

She pulls a bell rope. The waiting.

Katy is my niece. Every inch my niece. She put you to the test and you were . . . (*Vituperatively*) Shown up. Shown up. Oh, you men! On your high saddles.

LUBBOCK: I tried to save *you*, anyway.

MRS. MOWBREY: I never saw anyone so stupid.

Enter Marget.

MARGET: Yes, Mrs. Mowbrey.

MRS. MOWBREY: Mr. Lubbock's been looking for his hat, Marget.

MARGET: Yes, ma'am.

Marget disappears and returns with a straw hat. Lubbock takes it. Marget disappears. Lubbock lingers at the top of the stairs.

LUBBOCK: Well—out with it. What should I have done?

MRS. MOWBREY: In the first place you should have lied, of course. Strong and loud and clear. A girl like that is not ready to learn what she wants to know. And at this stage it's not your business or mine to tell her.

LUBBOCK: She said she left me because I wasn't any help to her. Is lying any help?

MRS. MOWBREY: Of course it is. I suppose you think you were trying to tell her the truth? Young man, you're not old enough to tell the truth and it doesn't look as though you ever will be. In the first place, you should have lied, firmly, cleanly. THEN, you should have shown her that you *were* her friend. Katy did just right. Katy left you standing here, because she saw that you never would be her friend—that you haven't the faintest idea what it is to be a friend. What took place here took place in my own life. It's taking place all the time. Mr. Lubbock, people don't like to be—

> *Lubbock rises, crosses the room and says aggressively and a little brutally:*

LUBBOCK: Mrs. Mowbrey, this has all been very interesting; and you've played your various cards very neatly and all that, but I want to know why you really asked me to come and see you today.

MRS. MOWBREY (*Also getting tougher*): I am coming to that. (*She pauses*) Do you prefer to stand?

LUBBOCK (*Shortly*): Yes, I do.

MRS. MOWBREY: There's one event in your life—in our lives—that I'd like you to explain to me. One night, at The Palace —it was in the spring of—you lost your head, or rather you lost control of yourself. You broke every bottle in my bar. You did like that with your arm. (*Her arm makes wide sweeping gestures, from right to left and left to right*) You terrorized everyone. You didn't strike anyone, but the flying glass could have blinded my girls. You weren't drunk. What happened? What made you do that?

LUBBOCK (*Furious, but coldly contained*): I paid for it, didn't I?

MRS. MOWBREY: Oh, Mr. Lubbock. Don't talk like a child. You and I know that there are a great many things that can't be paid for.—Was it something that Dolores said to you—or that I said to you? (*Pause*) Or did that friend of yours—what was his name? Jack Wallace or Wallop?—did he hurt your feelings? No, it couldn't be that; because you didn't strike *him*. The only thing you struck was a lot of bottles and *you weren't drunk.*

She waits in silence; finally he says in barely controlled impatience.

LUBBOCK: What of it? What of it? I lost my temper, that's all.

MRS. MOWBREY: I can understand your losing your temper at *people*, Mr. Lubbock—we all do; but I can't understand your losing your temper at *things*.

LUBBOCK: What are you trying to get at, ma'am? Out with it. Are you trying to tell me that you think I'm not fit to be the husband of your niece?

MRS. MOWBREY: No, indeed. I think you're just the right husband for her; and the more I talk to you, the more I think you're just the right lawyer for me.

Lubbock is stunned by this sudden shift in Mrs. Mowbrey's attitude.

Now, do you know what I have out in the sun porch? Do you? (*He shakes his head in confusion*) A bottle of champagne. And do you know what Lena is looking at in the kitchen? Two great big steaks.

LUBBOCK (*Slowly recovering himself*): I don't really like champagne, Mrs. Mowbrey; but would you happen to have any bourbon in the house?

MRS. MOWBREY: Bourbon! Have I bourbon? After six o'clock that's all I touch. (*Guiding him to the door*) And if you're a good boy I'll show you the list of my investments. There are one or two I'm worried about. Really worried. [(*She pauses at the top step; he beside her. She puts her hand on his arm*)] We all have disappointments in life, John—every one of us—but remember Shakespeare said—(*She smiles and taps him significantly on the chest with her jeweled forefinger*) you know—

[*She laughs and exits. He stands a moment, uncertain, then notices the straw hat still in his hand. He descends into the room, and gazes thoughtfully about. Then he places his straw hat on the taboret, turns and quickly exits in the direction Mrs. Mowbrey has taken. The Lights fade.*]

END OF PLAY

Someone from Assisi

(*Lust*)

The kitchen-garden behind the convent. A number of low benches surround the playing area. The actors' entrance at the back represents a door into the convent; it is framed by a trellis covered with vines. Opposite, the aisle through the audience represents a path to the village street.

A young girl, Pica, twelve, barefoot and wearing a simple smock, comes running out of the convent; she stares down the aisle through the audience and starts to shout in anger and grief.

PICA: No! No! Old Crazy—go home! You mustn't come here today. Go home! Go HOME!! We have someone specially important coming and you mustn't be here! Go home! You'll spoil everything!

> *Mona Lucrezia, looking much older than her forty years, comes lurching through the audience to the stage. She is crazy. Her black, gray and white hair is uncombed. She carries a large soiled shawl. She mumbles to herself as she advances.*

MONA: Don't make such a noise, child. I must think what I'm going to say when he comes. Now, *you* go away. I must think.
PICA: No, *you* go away.—Oh, this is terrible!

(*Pica turns and rushes into the convent, calling:*) Mother
Clara! Mother Clara!

MONA (*Shouting*): It's I who have someone important coming—not you. And . . . (*Worriedly*) I must be ready. It's so
hard to be ready. I must put gold on my hair . . . and perfumes, more perfumes. He'll have elephants and . . .
camels.

> *Mother Clara, thirty-one, enters and stands at the convent
> door looking thoughtfully at Mona Lucrezia. Pica passes her
> and comes toward the center of the stage.*

PICA: Mother, she mustn't be here today when *he* comes. Tell
Old Thomas to drive her away. She'll sing and make a noise
and spoil everything.—Old Crazy, *go home!* Mother Clara,
we would die of shame, if *he* heard the things she says.

CLARA (*Quietly, her gaze on Mona*): Be quiet, Pica.—Mona, do
you know me? —What is her name, Pica?

PICA: I don't know. I've forgotten.

CLARA: Go and ask Old Thomas what her name is. I don't
want you to call her Old Crazy. —Has she a home to go to?

PICA: Oh, Mother—she is very rich. But her family drives her
out of the house all day.

> *Mona has seated herself on one of the benches, her elbows on
> her knees. She is staring at the ground.*

CLARA: Go and find out what her name is.

> *Pica runs into the convent.*

Mona, do you know me? . . . Mona, do you know me? I
am Mother Clara of the Poor Sisters at Saint Damian's. Do
you know me? . . . What is your name?

MONA (*Rising; impressively*): I am who I am.—*He* is coming
today. You know I am the Queen of . . .

CLARA: What? . . . Who is coming?

MONA: The King of . . .

CLARA: Yes. What king?

MONA (*Becoming confused*): The King of Solomon. To see me.
I must be ready. He is coming . . . from France. And . . .

CLARA: From France?!!

MONA: Of course, from France. I must have presents to give him. And . . . He will have lions. And . . .

CLARA: Yes. You must be ready, Mona.

In order to induce Mona to leave the garden, Clara crosses the stage and starts walking backward through the audience.

Come. You must go to your home and make yourself ready. Look! . . . Just look! You must comb your hair beautifully. And you must *wash your face!*—Who is it you say is coming?

MONA (*Following her; angrily*): I *told* you—the King of Solomon . . . Of France. That is: French France. I didn't *love* him—*no!*; but he loved me. But now he has become a great person and he sends me all these messages.

(*Stopping at the edge of the stage, she looks at the floor in a troubled way; softly*) Did I tell you the truth? Did I love him? Did I?—Oh, he wrote such songs for me. Songs and songs.

CLARA: Come, Mona. I think you should rest, too.

MONA (*Confidentially*): If I walk slowly he will not see that I am lame. One of the boys in the street kicked me.

CLARA: Kicked . . . !! Yes, walk slowly. Like a queen. No, no, stand up straight, Mona—like a queen. You can do it. Come. What will you say when you see the king?

MONA: I shall say . . . (*Standing straight*) Oh, King of Solomon, I shall say: Change the world!

CLARA (*Astonished*): You will say that?

MONA: They throw stones at me. They kick me. Everywhere people hate people. My daughters—with brooms—they drive me away. I can't go home; I can only go home when the sun goes down. And I shall say: Oh, King, change the hearts of the world.

CLARA (*Returns to the stage; as Mona passes her on the way to the village*): That is a very good thing to say. You won't forget it?

MONA (*Loudly*): The world is *bad*.

CLARA: Yes.

MONA: Nobody is kind anymore.

CLARA: You tell your daughters that Mother Clara of Saint Damian's says that they are to let you into the house; and you will wash your face and your hair, won't you? And God bless you, dear Mona, and make you wise . . . wise and beautiful . . . for your friend.

Mona has almost disappeared. From the convent sounds of joyous cries and laughter. Pica comes running out like an arrow.

PICA (*Shrilly*): He has come, Mother Clara. Father Francis is here!

She flies back into the convent.

MONA (*Returning a few steps*): What did you say? . . . Wise?

CLARA: Yes . . . and beautiful. Good-bye, Mona. Remember. Good-bye.

MONA (*Mumbling*): Wise . . . and beautiful . . . (*She goes out*)

Francis appears at the convent door. He is forty, browned by the weather, almost blind, and with very few teeth.

Also he is very happy. Clara, joyously, and as lightly as a young girl, runs to the center of the stage and falls on her knees.

CLARA: Bless me, Father.

FRANCIS (*Kneels, facing her*): God bless you, dearest Sister, with all His love.—And now you bless me, Sister.

CLARA (*Lowered eyes, laughing protest*): Father!

FRANCIS: Say after me: God bless you, Brother Francis, and God forgive you that load of sins with which you have offended Him.

CLARA: God bless you, Brother Francis, with all His love.

FRANCIS: And . . .

CLARA (*Rippling laughter of protest*): I cannot say that, Father.

FRANCIS: I order you by your holy obedience.

CLARA: . . . And God forgive you that load of sins—Father! —with which you have offended Him.—There!

FRANCIS: Yes.

They both stay on their knees a moment, looking at one another, radiantly. Francis rises first and says with a touch of earnest injunction.

I want you to say that prayer . . . that *whole* prayer . . . for me, every day.

CLARA: I will, Father.—Now sit in the sun. The meal will be ready very soon.

FRANCIS (*Sitting*): And how is my little plant?

CLARA (*Again soft running laughter*): Your little plant is very well, Father.

FRANCIS: Let me see . . . was it ten years ago we cut off your beautiful hair and found you a bridegroom?

CLARA: Ten years ago next month.

FRANCIS: Yes . . . Never, Sister Clara, have I seen a more beautiful wedding . . .

CLARA (*Blushing with pleasure*): Father!

FRANCIS (*Softly*): . . . Except, of course, my own.

CLARA: Oh, yes—*yours.* We know all about that—to the Lady Poverty.

FRANCIS: The Lady Poverty.

CLARA: Yes.—And how are *you*, dear Father?

FRANCIS: Well . . . Well . . .

CLARA: And your eyes?

FRANCIS: Oh, Sister . . . I can see the path. I can see the brothers and sisters. I can see the Crucified on the wall.

CLARA: Oh, then, I'm so happy. I'd heard that you had some difficulty.

FRANCIS (*Emphatically*): Oh, yes, I can *see.* (*Confidentially*) Maybe I'm a little bit blind; but . . . I *hear* so well. I *hear* so much better.

CLARA: Do you?

FRANCIS: Everything talks all the time. The trees. And the water. And the *stones.*

CLARA (*Holding her breath*): What, Father?

FRANCIS: The stones. The rocks. Now, when I go up there to pray, I must say to them: "Be quiet."

CLARA: "Be quiet."

FRANCIS: "Be quiet for a while." And they are quiet.

CLARA: Yes, Father.

> *There is a moment while she digests this; then she begins again with animation.*

My sisters are so happy that you have come. Sister Agnes has made something for you. Now promise that you will eat all of it. It will break her heart if you don't.

FRANCIS: All?

CLARA (*Laughing*): Oh, it is very little. We have learned that.

FRANCIS: *All?* My stomach has grown so small . . . (*Making a ring with his thumb and forefinger*) . . . That is enough.

CLARA: We understand. But this time there is a touch—a touch of saffron.

FRANCIS: Saffron!!

CLARA: The Count sent it to us from the castle, especially for you. He remembered that you liked it . . . *before* . . .

FRANCIS: Before? Before when?

CLARA: Well . . . Father . . . before . . . Before you entered the religious life.

FRANCIS (*Agitated*): Before!!? When I was the most sinful of men! No, no, Sister Clara! Go quickly and tell Sister Agnes —no saffron! No saffron.

CLARA (*Calling sharply and clapping her hands*): Pica! Pica!

Pica enters at once.

PICA: Yes, Mother.

CLARA: Tell Sister Agnes *no* saffron in Father's dish. And do not stand by the door.

PICA: Yes, Mother.

During this interchange, Mona has returned, mumbling, through the audience.

MONA: They throw stones at me. They kick me. Hmm. But when the king comes they will learn who I am. Hmm. They will sing another song.

CLARA (*Her eyes again thoughtfully on Mona, who has seated herself on one of the benches*): She has lost her wits . . . She comes of a prosperous family, but they send her out of the house all day. I think the children torment her. She likes to come and sit here, rain or shine.—Father—she thinks she is the Queen of Sheba! And that King Solomon is coming to visit her!

FRANCIS (*Delighted*): She thinks she is . . . ! How rich she is. How happy she must be!

CLARA (*Pointing to her own forehead*): Yes—but she is touched.

FRANCIS: Touched? . . . Oh, touched.—Is she able to receive the blessed sacrament?

CLARA: No. I think not. They tell me that in church she cries out and says unsuitable things. No, she is not allowed in the church.

FRANCIS: What is her name?

CLARA: Everyone here seems to have forgotten it. They simply call her Old Crazy. We call her Mona.

FRANCIS (*Taking a few steps toward Mona*): Mona! . . . Yes, your king is coming.

MONA (*Violently*): Go away from me! I know all about your nasty filthy wicked ways!

CLARA (*Authoritatively*): Now, Mona, you must be quiet or we will send you away—with a broom, too. You know our Thomas. Our Thomas knows how to make you move.

FRANCIS (*Quiets Clara with a gesture; his eyes on Mona in reflection*): Who can measure the suffering—the waste—in the world? And every being born into the world—except One—has added to it. You and I have made it more and more.

(*He turns to Clara and adds with eager face*) Let us go to the church now and fall on our knees. Let us ask forgiveness.

CLARA: Father, we shall go to the church later. Now you have come here to take the noon meal with my dear sisters.

FRANCIS (*With a sigh, as of a pleasure postponed*): Yes . . . yes.

CLARA (*Resuming the animated tone*): You received my letter? We can't give thanks enough! More and more are coming all the time. Sometimes I'm at my wit's end to find room and food for all these girls and women who are coming to join us. Oh, but I won't trouble you with *those* things—beds and food. We always find a way.

FRANCIS: Yes. Yes. No one would believe how we always find more beds and food.

CLARA: And their happiness! From morning to night.—You will hear them sing. They have been learning some new music to sing to you.

FRANCIS (*Rising, stuttering with eagerness*): Sister C-C-Clara, let us go into the chapel and thank God.

CLARA: We will. We will. But *now*, dear Father, just for a moment, let us sit in the sun and rest ourselves.

FRANCIS (*Again resigned*): . . . Yes . . . Very well.

CLARA: Father, there is something I've long wanted to ask you. Can we talk for a moment of childish things?—Father, you *will* eat the noonday meal at our table today? You will?

FRANCIS: Sister! Sister! Can't I have it out here? *Where* I eat it is of no importance. I shall see the sisters later when I preach to them.

CLARA: Father, you hurt them.

FRANCIS: *Hurt* them?! I hurt them?

CLARA: They cannot understand it. You let Brother Avisio and Brother Juniper eat with us.

FRANCIS: Yes . . . yes . . .

CLARA: But you have never sat down with us at our table . . . Why is that? (*Lowering her voice*) My sisters are beginning to believe that you think that women are of a *lower order* in God's love.

FRANCIS: Sister Clara!!

CLARA: They have heard that you share your meal with . . . wolves and birds, but never with *them*.—Can the Father Francis whom we love—this once—sit down with us women?

FRANCIS (*Agitated slightly but compliant*): Yes . . . oh, yes . . . I will.

CLARA (*Urgently*): It is so important, Father. I work among these good women and girls. They have left everything. They have God in Heaven but they have very little on earth.

He nods repeatedly.

Thank you! Now there's another childish thing I want to ask you. Brother Avisio told me a short time ago that you were christened John. Is that true?

FRANCIS: Yes. Yes. John.

CLARA: You chose the name Francis?

FRANCIS: My friends gave it to me. But that's long ago.

MONA (*From under the hood of her shawl, as though brooding to herself*): Francis the Frenchman . . . They all called him that. That's what I called him, too.

After Francis and Clara have looked at Mona a moment:

FRANCIS: Long ago—when I was a young man. Before I found something better, I was never tired of hearing all those songs and stories that came down from France . . . about knights in armor who went about the world killing dragons and tyrants. A growing boy must have something to admire—to make his heart swell. I talked about those stories to everyone I knew. I dressed myself in foreign dress. I made songs, too—many of them. And . . . but . . .

CLARA: Why do you stop, Father?

FRANCIS: And I heard that each of these knights had a lady. (*He looks at her with pain and appeal*) I looked everywhere. I . . . I . . . looked everywhere.

CLARA: Do not talk of it, if it distresses you.

FRANCIS (*Low and urgently*): . . . May God forgive me that load of sin with which I offended him!

CLARA: Yes.

FRANCIS: I went through a troubled time . . . (*Suddenly he looks at her happily*) And then I found my lady.

CLARA (*Laughing*): Yes, we know, Father.

FRANCIS: Poverty! And I married her!

CLARA: Yes.

FRANCIS: And ever since, I go about the world singing her praises.

CLARA: Yes.

FRANCIS (*Eagerly*): Before I knew her I was a coward. Yes. I was afraid of everything: of going into the forests at night; I was afraid of hunger and of cold. I was afraid to knock at the doors of nobles and great people. But *now*—with *her* beside me—I go everywhere. I do not trouble when I go into the Pope's presence, even. I am not afraid when twenty new brothers arrive at our house: where shall I put them? How shall I feed them? *She* shows me. (*Clara nods in complete agreement*) But how can one say how beautiful she is! And . . . and (*Lowering his voice*) how severe. Sometimes I almost offend her. And then I know that her eyes are *turned away* from me! . . .

(*Suddenly raising his hands*) No saffron! No saffron!—But most of the time we live together in great happiness.

He crosses the stage, groping in his memory for an old song.

. . . That song . . . that old song I wrote for her:

> When in the darkness of the night
> I see no lantern and no star,
> My lady's eyes will bring me light.

> When in pathless woods I stray
> My feet have stumbled in despair
> My lady's eyes will show the way.

MONA: When prison chains do fetter me—

FRANCIS (*A loud cry of recognition*): Mona Lucrezia!!

MONA (*Harshly*): Shame on you! To sing that song in the ears of a holy woman! *That* is Mother Clara of Saint Damian's. Cover your ears, Mother Clara.

(*Advancing on Francis*) What do you know of Francis the Frenchman? *I* know him. He wrote that song for me.

> When prison chains do fetter me
> And it is written I must die
> My lady's eyes will set me free.

Yes, we all knew that he searched for his lady. We all knew that—the mayor's wife and Ninina Dono . . . and I . . .

FRANCIS: Mona Lucrezia.

(*Trembling, to Clara*) Leave me alone with her.

MONA: Mother Clara, they say that he goes all over the world now; that he sees the Pope and says good morning, good morning; that he's gone to Palestine to convert the Grand Turk himself—

CLARA: Do not be long, Father. The meal is almost ready.

She hurries out.

MONA (*Calling after her*): He said my body was of marble and snow—no, he said that my body was of fire and snow.

She starts leaving the stage through the audience.

He'll convert the Grand Turk. The Devil will help him. He converted the mayor's wife and me—the Devil helping him.

Francis, shaken and speechless, stands looking after her. Pica has entered stealthily from the convent. Francis appears not to hear her.

PICA: Father Francis, we did everything we could to prevent that crazy woman from coming here today. Mother Clara says that you are going to sit at table with the sisters—for the first time. You must sit quite still during the reading because

Sister John of the Nails is going to draw a picture of you that we can have on the wall. When people draw you, you have to sit very still, because when you move, they can't see what to draw—

Sounds of shouting from the street.

MONA (*Offstage*): Go away from me! Peter, put down that stone! Aiiiiiiee!
PICA: Oh, Father Francis! She's coming back again. They've been throwing stones at her.

She goes down the aisle.

Don't . . . come . . . back. We'll beat you!
FRANCIS: Come here and be quiet!

Mona lurches back, shouting toward the street. One side of her face is covered with blood. She is struck again and sinks on one knee at the edge of the stage.

MONA: Pigs—all of you. Lock your mothers up and there'll be no more of you.
FRANCIS: Come and sit down here, Mona Lucrezia.
MONA (*To Francis*): Don't strike me—*you!* Go away from me.
FRANCIS (*Authoritatively to Pica*): Get a bowl of water and a clean cloth. Put some leaves and stems of the hazel into it. And be quick.

Pica stands gaping.

Be quick! Be quick!

Pica runs off.

MONA (*Harshly to Francis*): You kicked me!
FRANCIS: No, Mona Lucrezia.
MONA: You did.
FRANCIS: Come over here and sit down. You are among friends now.
MONA (*Sitting down*): There are no friends. I don't want any friends. I had some.
    (*She stares at Francis, somberly*) Who are you? What's your name?
FRANCIS: I was christened John.

MONA: John!—Do you know who John was?

FRANCIS (*In a small voice*): Yes.

MONA: You stand there—idle as a log—and *do* nothing. If all the men in the world named John would join themselves together and be worthy of their name, the world would not be like *that*.

FRANCIS: Don't put your hand on your wound, Lucrezia. We'll wash it in a moment.

MONA (*Harshly*): Don't talk to me!

> *Silence.*

(*Then broodingly to herself*) The king will look for me. "Where is my queen?" I'll hide where he can't find me.— And I had something to tell him.

> *Clara enters swiftly with water and a cloth. She kneels before Mona.*

CLARA: Hold your face up, Mona Lucrezia.

MONA: Don't touch me! You are a holy woman. I will do it myself. Or let that log do it—that worthless John.

> *As though overcoming a powerful repulsion, Francis applies the wet cloth to Mona's forehead.*

MONA (*Striking him*): That hurts.

FRANCIS: Yes, it will hurt for a minute. Sit quiet. Sit quiet.

MONA (*With a sob, but submitting*): That hurts.

> *At a signal from Francis, Clara leaves.*

FRANCIS: There, that's better. Now your hands . . .

MONA (*With closed eyes*): They wash the dead. They washed us when we were born.

> *Silence.*

FRANCIS: Now your face again.

MONA: No! Don't touch me again. I don't like to be touched. (*She takes the cloth*)

(*Grumbling as though to herself*) On an important day like this! . . . And you one of those great good-for-nothing monks, filling your big belly with meals at other people's tables. (*Directly at him, fiercely*) God must weep!

FRANCIS: Yes.

MONA: Francis the Frenchman became a monk. I knew him. I never said to him what I should have said. It was clear in my mind, like writing on the wall; but I never said it. Whatever Francis the Frenchman wanted to do, oh, he did it. His will was like . . . ! It was that that made us break our vows. I had never deceived my husband. I told him I was afraid of God. What do you suppose he said? I told him I was afraid of losing God's love.

She stares at him.

He said: all love is one!

FRANCIS: No-o!

MONA: He said that he would make me the lady of his life and that he would do anything that I ordered him to do . . . I should have ordered him to do . . . that though that was like writing on the wall. Even then, though I was a girl, I knew that the world was a valley without rain . . . a city without food. I knew . . . I felt . . . he could . . . (*She becomes confused*)

FRANCIS (*Low*): What would you have said, Lucrezia?

MONA (*Rising*): I shall be your lady. And I command you: OWN NOTHING. No one will listen to you, if you have a roof over your head. No one will listen to you if you know where you will eat tomorrow. It is fear that has driven love out of the world and only a man without fear can bring it back.

She glares at him a moment, then sinks back on the bench.

But I never said it!

FRANCIS: Lucrezia, do you know me? I am Francis.

MONA (*Without interest*): No, you are some other Francis. I am going now.

FRANCIS (*Calling*): Pica! Pica!

MONA (*Starting to the town*): I'm tired . . . but I'm afraid of the butcher's dog . . . and the mayor's—

FRANCIS: Pica!

Pica rushes in.

I am taking Mona Lucrezia to her home. (*He indicates with his eyes*) I will need you to show me the way.

PICA: Father Francis, the sisters are ready to sit down at the table. You will break their hearts.

MONA (*Starting*): I had a stick. The boys are always taking away my stick.

Stopping.

Someone was coming to town today . . .

PICA (*Spitefully*): Yes! Father Francis himself. And you've spoiled everything!

FRANCIS (*To Pica*): Hsh!—I cannot see the path. Give me your hand.

MONA (*Turning*): Those dogs—the butcher's Rufus. Brother John, haven't you got a stick?

PICA (*Giggling*): She doesn't even know that dogs don't bite Father Francis!

MONA (*Stopping and peering at Francis*): Haven't you got a stick?

FRANCIS: No, Mona Lucrezia. I have nothing.

They go out.

END OF PLAY

Cement Hands

(*Avarice*)

CHARACTERS

EDWARD BLAKE, a lawyer, fifty
PAUL, a waiter, fifty-five
DIANA COLVIN, Blake's niece, twenty-one
ROGER OSTERMAN, Diana's fiancé, twenty-seven

SETTING

Corner in the public rooms of a distinguished New York hotel.

A screen has been placed at the back (that is, at the actors' entrance) to shut this corner off from the hotel guests. A table in the center of the stage with a large RESERVED *sign on it. Various chairs. At the end of the stage farthest from the entrance is a low bench; above it we are to assume some large windows looking onto Fifth Avenue.*

Enter Edward Blake, a lawyer, fifty. He is followed by Paul, a waiter, fifty-five.

BLAKE (*Rubbing his hands*): Paul, we have work to do.

PAUL: Yes, Mr. Blake.

BLAKE: There will be three for tea. I arranged with Mr. Gruber that this corner would be screened off for us; and I specially asked that you would wait on us. As I say, we have some work to do. (*Smilingly giving him an envelope*) There's a hundred dollars, Paul, for whatever strain you may be put to.

PAUL: Thank you, sir.—Did you say "strain," Mr. Blake?

BLAKE: I'm going to ask you to do some rather strange things. Are you a good actor, Paul?

PAUL: Well—I often tell the young waiters that our work is pretty much an actor's job.

BLAKE: I'm sure you're a very good one. Now the guests today are my niece, Diana Colvin.—You know Miss Colvin, don't you?

PAUL (*With pleasure*): Oh, yes, Mr. Blake. Everyone knows Miss Colvin.

BLAKE: And her fiancé—that's a secret still—Mr. Osterman?

PAUL: Which Mr. Osterman, sir?

BLAKE: Roger—Roger Osterman. You know him?

PAUL: Oh, yes, sir.

BLAKE: Now it's not clear which of us is host. But it's clear to *me* which of us is host. Roger Osterman has invited us to tea. He will pay the bill.

PAUL: Yes, sir.

BLAKE: There may be some difficulty about it—some distress; some squirming; some maneuvering—protesting. But he will pay the bill.

> *A slight pause while he looks hard and quizzically at Paul, who returns his gaze with knowing raised eyebrows.*

Now at about 5:20 you're going to bring Mr. Osterman a registered letter. The messenger will be waiting in the hall for Mr. Osterman's signature. Roger Osterman will ask to borrow half a dollar of me. I won't have half a dollar. He will then turn and ask to borrow half a dollar of you. And you won't hear him.

PAUL: I beg your pardon, sir?

BLAKE: He'll ask to borrow half a dollar of you, but you won't hear him. You'll be sneezing or something. Your face will be buried in your handkerchief. Have you a cold, Paul?

PAUL: No, sir. We're not allowed to serve when we have colds.

BLAKE: Well, you're growing deaf. It's too bad. But . . . you *won't* . . . *hear* him.

PAUL (*Worriedly*): Yes, sir.

BLAKE: You'll say (*Raising his voice*) "Yes, Mr. Osterman, I'll get some hot tea, at once." This appeal to you for money may happen several times.

PAUL (*Abashed*): Very well, Mr. Blake, if you wish it.

BLAKE: Now, Paul, I'm telling you why I'm doing this. You're an intelligent man and an old friend. My niece is going to marry Roger Osterman. I'm delighted that my niece is going to marry him. He's a very nice fellow—and what else is there about him, Paul?

PAUL: Why, sir—it is understood that he is very rich.

BLAKE: Exactly. But the Ostermans are not only fine people and very rich people—they have oddities about them, too, haven't they?—A certain oddity?

> *Blake slowly executes the following pantomime: he puts his hands into his trouser pockets and brings them out, open, empty and "frozen."*

PAUL (*Reluctantly*): I know what you mean, sir.

BLAKE: Have you a daughter, Paul, or a niece?

PAUL: Yes, sir. I have two daughters and three nieces.

BLAKE: Then you know: we older men have a responsibility to these girls. I have to show my niece what her fiancé is like. I have to show her this odd thing—this one little unfortunate thing about the Ostermans.

PAUL: I see, Mr. Blake.

BLAKE: I'm not only her uncle; I'm her guardian; and her lawyer. I'm all she's got. And I must show her—here she comes now—and for that I need your help.

> *Enter Diana Colvin, twenty-one, in furs. The finest girl in the world.*

DIANA: Here you are, Uncle Edward.—Good afternoon, Paul.

PAUL: Good afternoon, Miss Colvin.

BLAKE: Will you wait for tea, Diana?

DIANA (*Crossing the stage to the bench*): Yes.

> *Paul goes out.*

BLAKE: Aren't you going to kiss me?

DIANA: No!! I'm furious at you. I'm so furious I could cry. You've humiliated me. I'm so ashamed I don't know what to do. Uncle Edward, how could you do such a thing?

BLAKE (*Calmly*): What, dear?

DIANA: I've just heard that—(*She rises and strides about, groping for a handkerchief in her bag*)—you're asking the Osterman family how much allowance Roger will give me when we're married. And you're making some sort of difficulty about it. Uncle Edward! The twentieth century! And as though I were some poor little goose-girl he'd discovered in the country. Oh, I could die. I swear to you, I could die.

BLAKE (*Still calmly*): Sit down, Diana.

Silence. She walks about, dabs her eyes and finally sits down.

Diana, I'm not an idiot. I don't do things like this by whim and fancy.

DIANA: Perfectly absurd. Why, all those silly society columnists keep telling their readers every morning that I'm one of the richest girls in the country. Is it true? (*He shrugs*) I'll never need a cent of the Ostermans' money. I'll never take a cent, not a cent.

BLAKE: What?

DIANA: I won't have to.

BLAKE: What kind of marriage is that?

He rises. She looks at him a little intimidated.

Well, you'll be making an enormous mistake and it will cost you a lot of suffering.

DIANA: What do you mean?

BLAKE: Marriage is a wonderful thing, Diana. But it's relatively new. Twelve, maybe fifteen thousand years old. It brings with it some ancient precivilization elements. Hence, difficult to manage. It's still trying to understand itself.

DIANA (*Shifting in her seat, groaning*): Really, Uncle Edward!

BLAKE: It hangs on a delicate balance between things of earth and things of heaven.

DIANA: Oh, Lord, how long?

BLAKE: Until a hundred years ago a wife *had* no money of her own. All of it, if she had any, became her husband's. Think that over a minute. Billions and billions of marriages where the wife had not one cent that she didn't have to *ask* for. You see: it's important to us men, us males, us husbands that we supply material things to our wives. I'm sorry to say it but we like to think that we own you. First we dazzle you with our strength, then we hit you over the head and drag you into our cave. We buy you. We dress you. We feed you. We put jewels on you. We take you to the opera. I warn you now —most seriously—don't you start thinking that you want to be independent of your husband as a provider. You may be as rich as all hell, Diana, but you've got to give Roger the impression every day that you thank him—thank him humbly, that you aren't in the gutter.

DIANA (*Short pause; curtly*): I don't believe you.

BLAKE: Especially Roger. (*Leaning forward; emphatic whisper*) You are marrying into a very strange tribe. (*They gaze into one another's eyes*) Roger is the finest young man in the world. I'm very happy that you're going to marry him. I think that you will long be happy—but you'll only be happy if you know beforehand exactly what you're getting into.

DIANA: What *are* you talking about?

> *She rises and crosses the stage.*

I want some tea.

BLAKE: No, we don't have tea until he comes. *He* is giving us tea. Please sit down. What am I talking about? Diana, you've been out with Roger to lunch and dinner many times, haven't you? You've gotten in and out of taxis with him. You've arrived at railroad stations and had porters carry your bags, haven't you?

DIANA: Yes.

BLAKE: Have you ever noticed anything odd about his behavior in such cases?

DIANA: What do you mean?

> *He gazes levelly into her eyes. She begins to blush slightly. Silence.*

BLAKE: Then you have?

DIANA (*Uncandidly*): What do you mean?

BLAKE: Say it!

> *Pause.*

DIANA (*Suddenly*): I love him.

BLAKE: I know. But say what's on your mind.

DIANA: It's a little fault.

BLAKE: How little?

DIANA: I can gradually correct him of it.

BLAKE: That's what his mother thought when she married his father . . . After you leave a restaurant do you go back and leave a dollar or two for the waiter, when Roger's not looking? Do you hear taxi drivers shouting indecencies after him as he walks away? Have you seen him waste time and energy to avoid a very small expenditure?

DIANA (*Rising, with her handbag and gloves, as though about to leave*): I don't want to talk about this any more. It's tiresome; and more than that it's in bad taste. Who was it but *you* who taught me never to talk about money, never to mention money. And now we're talking about money in the grubbiest way of all—about *tipping*. And you've been talking to the Osterman family about an allowance for me. I feel soiled. I'm going for a walk. I'll come back in twenty minutes.

BLAKE: Good. That's the way you should feel. But there's one more thing you ought to know. Paul will help us.

He goes to the entrance at the back, apparently catches Paul's eye, and returns.

DIANA: You're not going to drag Paul into this?

BLAKE: Who better?—Now if *you* sit at ease, it will put *him* at ease.

Enter Paul.

PAUL: Were you ready to order tea, Mr. Blake?

BLAKE: No, we're waiting for Mr. Osterman. You haven't seen him, have you?

PAUL: No, I haven't.

BLAKE: Paul, I was talking with Miss Colvin about that little matter you and I were discussing. You gave me permission to ask you a few questions about the professional life in the hotel here.

PAUL: If I can be of any help, sir.

BLAKE: The whole staff of waiters is accustomed to a certain lack of . . . generosity on the part of the Osterman family. Is that true?

PAUL (*Deprecatingly*): It doesn't matter, Mr. Blake. We know that they give such large sums to the public in general . . .

BLAKE: Is this true of any other families?

PAUL: Well . . . uh . . . there's the Wilbrahams. (*Blake nods*) And the Farringtons. That is, Mr. Wentworth and Mr.

Conrad Farrington. With Mr. Ludovic Farrington it's the other way 'round.

BLAKE: Oh, so every now and then these families produce a regular spendthrift?

PAUL: Yes, sir.

BLAKE: I see. Now, have the waiters a sort of nickname for these less generous types?

PAUL (*Reluctantly*): Oh . . . the younger waiters . . . I wouldn't like to repeat it.

BLAKE: You know how serious I am about this. I wish you would, Paul.

PAUL: Well . . . they call them "cement hands."

DIANA (*Appalled*): WHAT?

BLAKE (*Clearly*): Cement hands.—What you mean is that they can give away thousands and millions but they cannot put their fingers into their pockets for . . . a quarter or a dime? And, Paul, is it true that in many cases the wives of the Ostermans and Wilbrahams and Farringtons return to the table after a dinner or supper and leave a little something—to correct the injustice?

PAUL: Yes, Mr. Blake.—Mrs. . . . but I won't mention any names . . . sometimes sends me something in an envelope the next day.

BLAKE: Yes.

PAUL: Perhaps I should tell you a detail. In these last years, the gentlemen merely *sign* the waiter's check. And they add a present for the waiters in writing.

BLAKE: *That* they can do. Well?

PAUL: Pretty well. What they cannot do—

BLAKE: —is to put their hands in their pockets. Thank you. And have you noticed that one of these hosts . . . as the moment approaches to . . . (*He puts his hands gropingly in his pockets*) . . . he becomes uncomfortable in his chair . . . his forehead gets moist? . . .

PAUL: Yes, sir.

BLAKE: He is unable to continue conversation with his friends? Some of them even start to quarrel with you?

PAUL: I'm sorry to say so.

BLAKE (*Shakes Paul's hand*): Thank you for helping me, Paul.

PAUL: Thank you, sir.

Paul goes out. Diana sits crushed, her eyes on the ground.
Then she speaks earnestly:

DIANA: Why is it, Uncle Edward? Explain it to me! How can such a wonderful and generous young man be so mean in little things?

BLAKE: Your future mother-in-law was my wife's best friend. Katherine Osterman has given her husband four children. She runs two big houses—a staff of twenty at least. Yet every expenditure she makes is on account—it goes through her husband's office—sign for everything—write checks for everything. You would not believe the extent to which she has no money of her own—in her own hand. Her husband adores her. He can't be absent from her for a day. He would give her hundreds of thousands in her hands but she *must ask for it.* He wants that picture: that everything comes from him. Why, she has to go to the most childish subterfuges to get a little cash—she buys dresses and returns them, so as to have a hundred dollars in bills. She doesn't want to do anything underhand, but she wants to do something personal—small and friendly and personal. She can give a million to blind children, but she can't give a hundred to her maid's daughter.

Diana, weeping, blows her nose.

Now you say you have your own money. Yes, but I want to be sure that you have an allowance *from Roger* that you don't have to account to him for. Money to be human with —not as housekeeper or as a beautifully dressed Osterman or as an important philanthropist—but as an imaginative human being; and I want that money to come from your husband. It will puzzle him and bewilder him and distress him. But maybe he will come to understand the principle of the thing.

DIANA (*Miserably*): How do you explain it, Uncle Edward?

BLAKE: I don't know. I want you to study it right here today. Is it a sickness?

DIANA (*Shocked*): Uncle Edward!

BLAKE: Is it a defect in character?

DIANA: Roger has no faults.

BLAKE: Whatever it is, it's deep—deep in the irrational. For Roger it's as hard to part with twenty-five cents as it is for some people to climb to the top of a skyscraper, or to eat frogs, or to be shut up with a cat. Whatever it is—it proceeds from a *fear*, and whatever it is, it represents an incorrect relation to—

DIANA: To what?

BLAKE (*Groping*): To . . .

Paul appears at the entrance.

PAUL: Mr. Osterman has just come into the hall, Mr. Blake.

BLAKE: Thank you, Paul.

Paul goes out.

DIANA: Incorrect relation to what?

BLAKE: To material things—and to circumstance, to life—to everything.

Enter Roger Osterman, twenty-seven, in a rush. The finest young fellow in the world.

ROGER: Diana! Joy and angel of my life. (*He kisses her*) Uncle Edward.—Ten minutes past five. I've got to make a phone call. To Mother. I'll be back in a minute. Mother and I are setting up a fund. I'll tell you all about it. Uncle Edward, what are you feeding us?

BLAKE: We haven't ordered yet. We were waiting for our host.

ROGER (*All this quickly*): Am I your host? Very well. You've forgotten that you invited us to tea. Didn't he, Diana?

BLAKE: You distinctly said—

ROGER: *You* distinctly said—really, Diana, we can't let him run away from his responsibilities like that. Uncle Edward, we accept with pleasure your kind invitation—

BLAKE: You called me and told me to convey your invitation to Diana. Diana, thank Roger for his kind invitation.

DIANA (*Rising, with a touch of exasperation*): Gentlemen, gentlemen! Do be quiet. The fact is *I* planned this party and you're both my guests. So do your telephoning, Roger, and hurry back.

ROGER: You're an angel, Diana. Tea with rum in it, Uncle Edward.

DIANA: Come here, you poor, poor boy. (*She looks gravely into his eyes and gives him a kiss*)

ROGER (*Laughing*): Why am I a poor, poor boy?

DIANA: Well, you are.

She gives him a light push and he goes out laughing.

BLAKE: We must act quickly now. I've arranged for some things to happen during this hour. You're going to spill some tea on your dress—no, some chocolate from a chocolate éclair.

DIANA: What?!

BLAKE: And you'll have to go to the ladies' room to clean it up. And you're going to need fifty cents. Open your purse. Give me all the change you have—under a five dollar bill.

DIANA: Why?

BLAKE: Because you'll have to borrow the fifty-cent piece from *him*.—Give me your change.

DIANA: Uncle Edward, you're a devil. (*But she opens her hand-bag and purse*)

BLAKE (*Counting under his breath*): Three quarters. Fifty-cent piece. Dimes. No dollar bills.

DIANA (*Crossing the room, in distress*): Uncle, I don't believe in putting people to tests.

BLAKE: Simply a demonstration—

DIANA: I don't need a demonstration. I suffer enough as it is.

BLAKE: But have you forgotten: we're trying to learn something. Is it a sickness or is it a—

DIANA: Don't say it!

BLAKE: And I want you to notice something else: every subject that comes up in conversation . . .

He starts laughing.

DIANA (*Suspicious and annoyed*): What?

BLAKE: To call your attention to it, I'll (*He drops his purse*) drop something. Every subject that comes up in the conversation will have some sort of connection with money.

DIANA (*Angrily drops her handbag*): But that's all you and I have been talking about—until I'm about to go crazy.

BLAKE: Yes . . . yes, it's contagious.

DIANA (*With weight*): Uncle Edward, are you trying to break up my engagement?

BLAKE (*With equal sincerity, but quietly*): No! I'm trying to ratify it . . . to *save* it.

DIANA: How?

BLAKE (*Emphatic whisper*): With . . . understanding.

Enter Paul.

Oh, there you are, Paul. Tea for three and a decanter of rum. And a chocolate éclair for Miss Colvin.

DIANA: But I hate chocolate éclairs!

Blake looks at her rebukingly.

Oh, all right.

BLAKE: And, Paul, when we've finished tea, you'll place the check beside Mr. Osterman.

Diana purposefully drops her lipstick.

PAUL (*Picking up the lipstick*): Yes, sir.

DIANA: Thank you, Paul.

Paul goes out. Diana leans toward Blake and says confidentially:

Now you must play fair. If you cheat, I'll stop the whole thing.

Enter Roger.

ROGER: All is settled. It's really very exciting. Mother and I setting up a fund where there's a particular particular need.

DIANA: What is it, Roger?

ROGER (*Laughs; then*): Guess where Mother and I are going tomorrow?

DIANA: Where?

ROGER: To the poorhouse!

Blake pushes and drops the ashtray from the table.

DIANA (*Covering her ears*): Uncle Edward, do be careful!

ROGER: In fact, we're going to three. Mother's already been to thirty—in England and France and Austria—I've been to ten. We're doing something about them. We're making them attractive. Lots of people come to the ends of their lives without pensions, without social security. We're taking the curse off destitution.

BLAKE: And you're taking the curse off superfluity.

Diana looks at Blake hard and drops her gloves.

ROGER: We're beginning in a small way. Mother's giving two million and Uncle Henry and I are each giving one. We're not building new homes yet—we're improving the conditions of those that are there. Everywhere we go we ask a thousand questions of superintendents, and of the old men and women . . . And do you know what these elderly people want most? (*He looks at them expectantly*)

DIANA (*Dropping a shoe*): Money.

ROGER (*Admiringly*): How did you know?!

Diana shrugs her shoulders.

You see, in a sense, they have everything: shelter, clothes, food, companionship. We've scarcely found one who wishes to leave the institution. But they all want the one thing for which there is no provision.

Paul enters with a tray: tea; rum; éclair; the service check, which he places on the table beside Roger; and a letter.

PAUL: A letter has come for you, Mr. Osterman, by special messenger. Will you sign for it, Mr. Osterman?

ROGER: For me? But no one else knows that I'm here.

BLAKE: By special messenger, Paul?

PAUL: Yes, Mr. Blake.

BLAKE: And is the messenger waiting?

(*Intimately*) Roger . . . the messenger's waiting in the hall . . .

ROGER: What?

BLAKE: Fifty cents . . . for the messenger.

ROGER (*A study*): But I don't think this is for me.

He looks at it.

DIANA (*Taking it from him*): "Roger Osterman, Georgian Room, etc." Yes, I think it's for you.

Roger makes some vague gestures toward his pockets.

ROGER: Uncle Edward . . . lend me a quarter, will you?

BLAKE (*Slowly searching his pockets*): A quarter . . . twenty-five cents . . . Haven't got it.

ROGER: Paul, give the boy a quarter, will you?

PAUL (*Deaf as a post*): Hot water? Yes, Mr. Osterman—

ROGER (*Loud*): No . . . a QUARTER, Paul . . . give the boy a quarter . . .

PAUL: It's right here, Mr. Osterman.

ROGER (*Has torn the letter open; to Blake*): It's from *you*. You say you'll be here. Well, if the messenger boy is from your own office, you can give him a quarter.

BLAKE (*Smiting his forehead; gives quarter to Paul*): That's right . . . Paul . . . I'll see you . . .

ROGER (*Dabbing his forehead with his handkerchief*): My, it's hot in here.

DIANA: Roger—you were saying that these old people wanted money. They have everything provided, but they still want money.

ROGER: Yes, I suppose it's to give presents to their nephews and nieces . . . to one another . . . They have everything except that . . .

   (*He starts laughing; then leans forward confidentially and says*) You know, I think one of the reasons Mother became so interested in all this was . . . (*Then he stops, laughs again, and says*) Anyway, she's interested.

DIANA: What were you going to say?

ROGER (*Reluctantly*): Well . . . she's always had the same kind of trouble. (*The other two stare at him*) Do you know that Mother once pawned a diamond ring?

BLAKE: *Your mother* went to a pawnshop?

ROGER: No. She sent her maid. Even today she doesn't know that I know.—I was at boarding school, and I'd begun a collection of autographs. More than anything in the world I wanted for my birthday a certain letter of Abraham Lincoln that had come on the market. I couldn't sleep nights I wanted it so had. But Father thought it was unsuitable that a fifteen year old should get so worked up about a thing like that.—So Mother pawned her ring.

Diana rises and crosses the room. She is flushed and serious.

DIANA: I don't think we should be talking about such things— but—let me ask one thing, Roger. Your mother has always had a great deal of money of her own?

ROGER (*Laughing*): Yes. But, of course, Father keeps it for her. More than that: he's doubled and tripled it.

BLAKE: Of course. It passes through his hands.

ROGER: Yes.

BLAKE (*Looking at Diana*): He sees all the checks. Like the old people in the poorhouse, your mother has *everything* except money?

ROGER (*Laughing*): Exactly!—The other thing the old people are interested in is food—

DIANA (*Looking down at her dress*): Oh! I've spilled some of that tea and rum on my dress. I must go to the ladies' room and have the spot taken out. Uncle Edward, lend me half a dollar for the attendant.

BLAKE (*Ransacking his pockets*): Half a dollar! Half a dollar! — I told you I hadn't a cent.

ROGER: In institutions—like prisons and poorhouses—you never have any choice—

DIANA: Roger, lend me half a dollar.

ROGER (*Taking out his purse, as he talks*): That was the awful part about prep school—all the food—(*He hands Diana a ten-dollar bill and goes on talking*)—was, so to speak, assigned to you. You never had the least voice in what it would be.

DIANA: But I don't want ten dollars. I want fifty cents.

ROGER: What for?

DIANA: To give the attendant in the ladies' room.

ROGER: Fifty cents?
  (*Rising and inspecting her dress*) I don't see any stain.
  (*To Blake*) Borrow it from Paul.

BLAKE: Paul's deaf. Roger, put your hands in your pockets and see if you haven't got fifty cents.

DIANA (*Almost hysterically*): It's all right. The stain's gone away. Forget it, please. Forgive me. I've made a lot of fuss about nothing.

ROGER (*Again touching his forehead with his handkerchief*):

Awfully warm in here. We ought to have gone to the club. These places are getting to be regular traps. Why did we come here?

DIANA: What do you mean: traps?

ROGER: You're interrupted all the time—these tiresome demands on you. I love to give, but I don't like to be held up (*Gesture of putting a revolver to someone's head*) held up every minute. (*A touch of too much excitement*) I'd like to give everything I've got. I don't care how I live; but I don't like to be forced to give anything. It's not *my* fault that I have money.

DIANA: You're right, Roger.

> *She sees Paul's service check on the table. She flicks it with her finger and it falls on the floor as near the center of the stage as possible.*

I don't think of a tip as an expression of thanks. It's just a transaction—a mechanical business convention. Take our waiter, Paul. My thanks is in my smile, so to speak. The money on the table has nothing to do with it.

ROGER: Well, whatever it is, it's a mess.

BLAKE: Once upon a time there was a very poor shepherd. It was in Romania, I think.

DIANA: Uncle!

BLAKE: Every morning this shepherd led his sheep out to a field where there was a great big oak tree.

DIANA: Really, Uncle!

BLAKE: And one day—under that oak tree—he found a large gold piece. The next day he found another. For weeks, for months, for years—every day—he found another gold piece. He bought more sheep. He bought beautiful embroidered shirts.

> *Diana is suddenly overcome with uncontrollable hysterical laughing. She crosses the room, her handkerchief to her mouth, and sits on the bench by the windows. Blake waits a moment until she has controlled herself.*

No one else in the village seemed to be finding any gold pieces.

Diana sputters a moment. Blake lowers his voice mysteriously.

The shepherd's problem was: *Where do they come from?* And *why* are they given to *him?* Are they, maybe . . . supernatural?

ROGER (*Sharply*): What?

Blake points to the ceiling.

I don't understand a word of this. Uncle Edward, do get on with it. I've never been able to understand these . . . allegories.

BLAKE: But why to *him?* Was he more intelligent—or more virtuous than the other young men?

Pause.

Now when you find a gold piece every morning, you get used to it. You get to need them. And you are constantly haunted by the fear that the gold pieces will no longer appear under the oak tree. What—oh, what—can he do to insure that those blessed gold pieces will continue to arrive every morning?

Blake voice turns slightly calculatedly superstitious; he half closes his eyes, shrewdly. His blade-like hand describes an either-or decision or bargain.

Obviously, he'd better *give.* In return, so to speak. He gave his town a fine hospital. He gave a beautiful altar to the church. (*He changes his voice to the simple and direct*) Of course, he gave. But this shepherd was a fine human being, and it was the other question that troubled him most— frightened him, I mean: Why have I been *chosen?*

DIANA (*Sober; her eyes on the floor*): I see that: he became frightened.

ROGER (*Looking at Diana, in surprise—laughing*): *You* understand what he's talking about?

DIANA: Frightened, because . . . if the gold pieces stopped coming, he'd not only be poor . . . he'd be much more than poor. He'd be exposed. He'd be the man who was formerly fortunate, formerly—what did you say?—intelligent, formerly virtuous and—

BLAKE (*Pointing to the ceiling*): Formerly favored, loved.

DIANA: Far worse than poor.

BLAKE: So he was in the terrible situation of having to GIVE all the time and of having to SAVE all the time.

DIANA: Yes . . . Yes.—Roger, I have to go.

> *She rises.*

Now, who's going to pay the bill?—Roger, you do it, just to show that you like to.

ROGER (*With charming spontaneity*): Of course, I will. Where is it?

DIANA (*Pointing*): Right there on the floor.

ROGER (*Picking it up*): I'll *sign* for it.—Where's Paul? There he is!

DIANA (*Putting on lipstick and watching him in her mirror*): Surely, it's not large enough to sign for. There's something small about signing for a three or four dollar charge.

ROGER (*Looking from one to the other*): *I* don't think so.

BLAKE: Diana's right.

ROGER (*Taking a ten-dollar bill from his purse and laying it on the bill*): Diana, some day you must explain to me slowly what Uncle Edward's been talking about.

> *Enter Paul. Roger indicates the money with his head. Paul makes change quickly.*

Paul, we're leaving.

(*To Diana*) And you must make your Uncle Edward promise not to get tied up in any long rambling stories he can't get out of.

DIANA (*To Paul*): Thank you, Paul.

BLAKE: Thank you, Paul.

ROGER: Thank you, very much, Paul.

PAUL (*As he goes out, leaving the bill and change on the table*): You're very welcome.

ROGER (*While he talks, is feverishly figuring out his change*): Because I must be very stupid . . . I can't . . . (*His hand among the coins of change, he turns and says*) Because I must say there are lots of better things to talk about than what we've been . . . (*He stops while he studies the change before him*) In fact, in our family we make it a rule never to talk about money at all . . .

Pause.

I don't think you realize, Diana, that my life is enough of a hell as it is: the only way I can cope with it is to *never* talk about it . . . what am I doing here? . . .

DIANA (*Going toward him; soothingly*): What's the matter, dear? Just leave him a quarter.

ROGER (*His face lighting up*): Would that be all right? (*She nods*) Diana, you're an angel. (*Triumphantly*) I'm going to leave him fifty cents, just to show him I love you.

DIANA: No. I'm not an angel. I'm a very *human* being. I'll need to be fed. And clothed. And—

ROGER (*Bewitched; kissing her gravely*): I'll see you have everything.

DIANA: I can look forward to everything?

ROGER: Yes.

DIANA: Like those old ladies in the poorhouse, I can look forward to—

ROGER: *My* giving you everything.

Diana hurries out ever so lightly, blowing her nose. Paul appears at the door. Blake and Roger go out. Paul, alone, picks up the tip. No expression on his face. Diana appears quickly.

DIANA: I dropped a glove.

(*She drops a dollar bill on the table*) Goodbye, Paul.

PAUL: Goodbye, Miss Colvin.

They go out.

END OF PLAY

THE SEVEN AGES OF MAN

Infancy

A COMEDY

CHARACTERS

PATROLMAN AVONZINO
MISS MILLIE WILCHICK, a nursemaid
TOMMY, a baby in her care
MRS. BOKER
MOE, her baby boy

SETTING

Central Park in New York City. The 1920s.

One or more large park benches. Some low stools at the edges of the stage indicate bushes.

Enter Patrolman Avonzino, a policeman from the Keystone comic movies with a waterfall mustache, thick black eyebrows and a large silver star. Swinging his billy club jauntily, he shades his eyes and peers down the paths for trouble. Reassured, he extracts a small memorandum book from an inner pocket of his jacket and reads:

AVONZINO: "Wednesday, April 26 . . ." Right. "Centra' Park, Patrol Section Eleven, West, Middle." Right! "Lieutenant T. T. Avonzino." Correct. Like Tomaso Tancredo Avonzino. "Eight to twelve; two to six. Special Orders: Suspect—mad dog, black with white spots. Suspect—old gentleman, silk hat, pinches nurses." (*Reflects*) Pinch babies okay; pinch nurses, nuisance. (*Puts the book away, strolls, then takes it out again for further instructions*) Probable weather: late morning, precipitation—precipitation like rain. (*Strolls*) Seven to eight-thirty, no nuisances. Millionaires on horses; horses on millionaires. Young gents running in underwear; old gents running in underwear. (*Reflects*) Running in underwear, okay; *walking* in underwear, nuisance. Eight-thirty to nine-thirty, everybody late for working, rush-rush, no time for nuisances. Nine-thirty to twelve, babies. One thousand babies with ladies. Nuisances plenty: old gents poisoning pigeons; ladies stealing baby carriages. Nuisances in bushes: young gents and young girls taking liberties. (*Hotly*) Why can't they do their nuisances at home? That's what homes are for: to do your nuisances in. (*He shields his eyes and peers toward the actors' entrance at the back of the stage; emotionally*) Here she comes! Miss'a Wilchick! *Baby!*—prize baby of Centra' Park. (*He extracts a handbook from another pocket of his jacket*) "Policeman's Guide. Lesson Six: Heart Attacks and Convulsions." No. No. "Lesson Sixteen: Frostbite." No! "Lesson Eleven: . . ." Ha! "An officer exchanges no personal remarks wid de public." Crazy! (*In dreamy ecstasy*) Oh, personal re-marks. It's personal remarks dat make-a de world go round; dat make-a de birds sing. (*Indignantly*) Nobody, *nobody* wid flesh and blood can live widout'a personal re-marks. Ha! She comes! . . . (*He steals off by the aisle through the audience*)

> *Enter from the back Miss Millie Wilchick, pushing Tommy's baby carriage. Tommy, now invisible in the carriage, is to be played by a full-grown man. Millie brings the carriage to rest by a bench. She peers up the various paths in search of Officer Avonzino. Disappointed, she prepares to make herself comfortable. From the foot of the carriage she brings out a box of chocolates, another of marshmallows, and a novel. Before sitting down she talks into the carriage.*

MILLIE: . . . lil sweet lovums. Miss Millie's lil lover, aren't you? Yes, you are. I could squeeze lil Tommy to death, yes. I could. Kiss-kiss-kiss, yes, I could. (*Again peering down the paths*) Don't know where Mr. Policerman is! Big handsome Officer Avonzino. He take care of Miss Millie and lil lover-boy Tommy . . . Hmm . . . Maybe he come by and by. (*She sits on the bench and selects a candy*) . . . Peppermint . . . strawb'ry? . . . Well, and a marshmallow. (*She opens the novel at the first page and reads with great deliberation*)

"Doris was not strictly beautiful, but when she passed, men's heads turned to gaze at her with pleasure. Doris was not strictly beautiful, but . . ." (*A squeal of joy*) Oh, they don't write like that any more!! Oh, I'm going to enjoy this book. Let's see how it ends. First, there must be one of those chawclut cream centers. (*She turns to the last page of the novel*) "He drew her to him, pressing his lips on hers. 'Forever,' he said. Doris closed her eyes. 'Forever,' she said. The end." (*Delighted cry*) They *don't* write like that any more. "For e . . . e . . . ever." Could I say "forever," if his lips . . . "e-e-v" . . . were pressed on mine? (*She closes her eyes and experiments*) . . . e . . . ver . . . for . . . e . . . Yes, I guess it could be done. (*She starts dreaming*) Oh, I *know* I could write a novel. (*She dreams*)

> *Slowly Tommy's hands can be seen gripping the side of his carriage. With great effort he pulls himself up until his head appears. He is wearing a lace-trimmed cap.*

TOMMY: Fur . . . evvah . . . Do-rus . . . nah . . . strigly boo-toody . . . (*Fretfully*) I can't say it . . . boody-fill . . . Why don't they *teach* me to say it? I want to LEARN and they won't teach me. Do-rua nah stackly . . . boody . . . Fur evvah . . . (*Near to wailing*) Time's going by. I'm getting owe-uld. And nobody is showing me *anything*. I wanta make a house. I wanta make a house. I wanta make a bay-beee. Nobody show-ow-ow-s me how-ta.

MILLIE (*Waking up*): Tommy! What are you crying about? Has 'a got a little stummyache? Has 'a got a foot caught? No. (*Leaning over him, suddenly severe*) Has Tommy wet his bed?!! No. No. Then's what's a matter?

TOMMY: Wanta make a house!

MILLIE: Wants to be petted, yes.

TOMMY (*Violently*): Wanta make a baybeee!

MILLIE: Miss Millie's lil lover wants a little attention.

TOMMY (*Fortissimo*): Chawclut. Chawclut. Wanta eat what you're eating. Wanta eat what you smell of . . . chawclut.

MILLIE: Now don't you climb up. You'll fall out. It's terrible the way you're growing.

TOMMY: Put me on the ground. I wanta learn to walk. I wanta walk. I wanta walk. I wanta find things to *eat.*

MILLIE (*Sternly*): Now Miss Millie's going to spank you. Crying for nothing. You ought to be ashamed of yourself. (*She stands joggling the baby carriage with one hand and holding the opened novel with the other*) "This little pig went to *market*." There! "This little pig . . ." Shh-shh-shh! "Doris was not strictly beautiful, but . . ." Oh, I read that. "This little pig stayed at home." (*She looks into the carriage with great relief*) God be praised in His glory, babies get tired soon . . . Asleep. (*She walks across the stage; then suddenly stops*) I don't know what I'm going to do. My life is hell. Here I am, a good-looking girl almost thirty and *nothing ever happens.* Everybody's living, except me. Everybody's happy, except ME!! (*She returns, sobbing blindly to the baby carriage*) Those silly novels—I hate them—just gab-gab-gab. Now I'm crying so I can't see which is pineapple. (*She chances to look in the direction of the aisle through the audience*) Oh, my God, there comes Officer Avonzino. (*She clasps her hands in fervent prayer*) Oh, my God, help a girl! If you ever helped a girl, help her now! (*She rapidly hides novel and candy under Tommy's blankets, and takes out another book. She arranges herself at one end of the bench and pretends to fall into a reverie*)

Enter Patrolman Avonzino through the audience. He steals behind Millie and puts his hands over her eyes. The following passage is very rapid.

AVONZINO: You've got one guessing coming to you! *Who* is in Centra' Park? Maybe who?
MILLIE: Oh, I don't know. I really don't.
AVONZINO: You've got two guessings. Maybe the mayor of Newa-York, maybe him, you think? Now you got one guessing. Maybe T. T. Avonzino—like somebody you know, somebody you seen before.
MILLIE: Oh! Officer Avonzino!!

He leaps on the bench beside her. She is kept busy removing his hands from her knees.

AVONZINO: Somebody you know. Somebody you seen before.
MILLIE: Officer, you must behave. You really must behave.

AVONZINO: Action! I believe is a action! Personal remarks and da action.

Tommy has raised himself and is staring enormous-eyed and with great disapproval at these goings-on.

TOMMY (*Loudly*): Ya! Ya! Ya! Ya! Ya!

Officer Avonzino is thunderstruck. He jumps up as though caught out of order by his superior. He stands behind the bench adjusting his tie and coat and star.

MILLIE: Why, what's the matter, Mr. Avonzino?

AVONZINO (*Low and terse*): *Him.* Looka at him. Looka at him, *looking.*

TOMMY: Ya. Ya. Ya.

MILLIE: Go to sleep, Tommy. Just nice policerman. Tommy's friend. Go to sleep.

TOMMY (*One last warning, emphatically*): Ya! (*He disappears*)

MILLIE: But, Officer, he's just a *baby.* He doesn't understand one little thing.

AVONZINO (*Blaring, but under his breath*): Oh no, oh no, oh no, oh no—he got *thoughts.* Turn-a de carriage around. I no wanta see that face.

MILLIE (*Turning the carriage*): I'm surprised at you. He's just a dear little baby. A dear little . . . animal.

AVONZINO: Miss Wilchick, I see one thousand babies a day. They got *ideas.*

MILLIE (*Laughing girlishly*): Why, Mr. Avonzino, you're like the author of this book I've been reading.—Dr. Kennick. He says babies are regular geniuses in their first fourteen months. He says: you know why babies sleep all the time? Because they're learning all the time, they get tired by learning. Geniuses, he says, imagine!

AVONZINO: *What* he say?

MILLIE: They learn more than they'll ever learn again. And faster. Like hands and feet; and to focus your eyes. And like walking and talking. He says their brains are exploding with power.

AVONZINO: What he say?

MILLIE: Well—after about a year they stop being geniuses. Dr.

Kennick says the reason why we aren't geniuses is that we weren't brought up right: we were stopped.

AVONZINO: That's a right. He gotta the right idea. Miss Wilchick, I see one thousand babies a day. And what I say is: stop 'em. That's your business, Miss Wilchick; that's my business. There's too many ingeniouses in Centra' Park right now: stop 'em. (*Tommy begins to howl. Avonzino points at him with his billy club*) What did I tell you? They all understand English. North'a Eighth Street they all understand English.

MILLIE (*Leaning over Tommy's carriage*): There, there. Nice policerman don't mean *one* word of it.

AVONZINO (*Looking at the actors' entrance; they are both shouting to be heard*): Here comes another brains. I go now.

MILLIE: Oh, that must be Mrs. Boker—I'm so sorry this happened, Mr. Avonzino.

AVONZINO: I see you later, maybe—when you get permission from the professor—permission in writing, Miss Wilchick. (*He goes out through the audience*)

> *Enter Mrs. Boker pushing Moe's carriage. Moe starts crying in sympathy with Tommy. Both women shout.*

MRS. BOKER: What's the matter with Tommy—good morning —on such a fine day?

MILLIE (*Leaning over Tommy*): What's a matter?

TOMMY: CHAWCLUT!! STRAWB'RY!! I'm hungreee.

MILLIE: Really, I don't know what ails the child.

MRS. BOKER (*Leaning over Moe's carriage; beginning loud but gradually lowering her voice as both babies cease howling*): . . . K . . . L . . . M . . . N . . . O . . . P . . . Q . . . R . . . S . . . T . . . Have you ever noticed, Miss Wilchick, that babies get quiet when you say the alphabet to them? . . . W . . . X . . . Y . . . A . . . B . . . C . . . D . . . I don't understand it. Moe is mad about the alphabet. Same way with the multiplication table. (*To Moe, who is now silent*) Three times five are fifteen. Three times six are eighteen. When my husband has to keep Moe quiet: the multiplication table! Never fails! My husband calls him Isaac Newton.—Seven times five are thirty-five. Eight times five are forty. Never fails.

MILLIE (*Intimidated*): Really?

MRS. BOKER (*Pointing to the silent carriages*): Well, look for yourself! Isn't silence grand? (*She sits on a bench and starts taking food out of Moe's carriage*) Now, dear, have some potato chips. Or pretzels. What do you like?

MILLIE: Well, you have some of my marshmallows and candy.

MRS. BOKER: Marshmallows! Oh, I know I shouldn't!—Have you noticed that being around babies makes you think of eating all the time? I don't know why that is. (*Pushing Millie in raucous enjoyment of the joke*) Like, being with babies makes us like babies. And you know what *they* think about!!

MILLIE (*Convulsed*): Oh, Mrs. Boker, what will you say next! —How is Moe, Mrs. Boker?

MRS. BOKER (*Her mouth full*): How *is* he!! Sometimes I wish he'd be sick for *one* day—just to give me a present. (*Lowering her voice*) I don't have to tell you what life with a baby is: (*Looking around circumspectly*) It's war—one long war.— Excuse me, I can't talk while he's listening. (*She rises and wheels Moe's carriage to a distance; returning, she continues in a lowered voice*) My husband believes that Moe understands every word we say.

MILLIE: Mrs. Boker!

MRS. BOKER: I don't know what to believe, but one thing I do know: that baby lies on the floor and listens to every word we say. At first my husband took to spelling out words, you know—but Albert Einstein, there—in two weeks he got them all. He would *look* at my husband, *look* at him with those big eyes! And then my husband took to talking in Yiddish —see what I mean?—but no! In two weeks Albert Einstein got Yiddish.

MILLIE: But, Mrs. Boker!! It's just a baby! He don't understand *one word*.

MRS. BOKER: *You* know that. *I* know that. But (*Pointing to the carriage*) does *he* know that? It's driving my husband crazy. "Turn it in and get a dog," he says. "I didn't ask for no prodigy," he says. "All I wanted was a baby—" (*Lowering her voice*) Of course, most of the time my husband worships Moe . . . only . . . only we don't know what to do with him, as you might say.

MILLIE: Oh, you imagine it, Mrs. Boker!

MRS. BOKER: Listen to me!—Have some of these pretzels; they'll be good after those sweets. Listen to me, Junior's at the crawling stage. He does fifty miles a day. My husband calls him Christopher Columbus.—My husband's stepped on him five times.

MILLIE: Mrs. Boker! You've got a playpen, haven't you?

MRS. BOKER: PLAYPEN!! He's broke two, hasn't he? We can't afford to buy no lion's cage, Miss Wilchick—besides, Macy's don't sell them. Now listen to me: Christopher Columbus follows us wherever we go, see? When I get supper—there he is! He could make a gefilte fish tomorrow. That child— mad about the bathroom! Know what I mean? My husband says he has a "something" mind—you know: d. i. r. t. y.

MILLIE: Mrs. Boker.

MRS. BOKER: Sometimes I wish I had a girl—only it'd be just my luck to get one of those Joans of Arcs. (*Moe starts to howl*) There he goes! Like I said: understands *every* word we say. Now watch this: (*She leans over Moe's carriage, holding a handkerchief before her mouth*) You mustn't let them smell what you've been eating, *or else*— Listen, Moe, like I was telling you: New York City is divided into five boroughs. There's the Bronx, Moe, and Brooklyn and Queens— (*Moe quiets almost at once*) See how it works?—Richmond and Manhattan.—It's crazy, I know, but what can I do about that?—Yes, Manhattan; the largest, like I told you, is Manhattan. Yes, Manhattan. (*She looks in the carriage. Silence*) Isn't it a blessing that they get tired so soon? He's exhausted by the boroughs already.

MILLIE: But he doesn't understand a word of it!!

MRS. BOKER: What has understanding got to do with it, Miss Wilchick? I don't understand the telephone, but I *telephone*.

Tommy has raised his head and is listening big-eyed.

TOMMY: N'Yak Citee divi fife burrs. Manha . . . Manha . . . Manha . . . (*He starts crying with frustration*) I can't *say* it. I can't *say* it.

MRS. BOKER: Now yours is getting excited.

TOMMY: I can't talk and nobody'll teach me. I can't talk . . .

MRS. BOKER (*Loud*): Go over and put him to sleep.

MILLIE (*Loud*): But I don't know the boroughs. Please, Mrs. Boker, just once, you show me.

MRS. BOKER: I'll try something else. Watch this! Listen, Tommy, are you listening? "I pledge legions to my flag and to the republic in which it stands." You were a girl scout, weren't you? "Something something invisible with liberty and justice for all." (*Tommy has fallen silent*) "I pledge legions to my flag . . ."

MILLIE (*Awed*): Will anything work?

MRS. BOKER (*Lowering her voice*): They don't like those lullabies and "This little pig went to market." See, they like it *serious.* There's nothing in the world so serious like a baby.— Well, now we got a little quiet again.

MILLIE: Mrs. Boker, can I ask you a question about Moe? . . . Take one of these; it's pineapple inside . . . Is Moe, like they say, housebroken?

MRS. BOKER: Moe?! Gracious sakes! Moe makes a great show of it. I guess there isn't a thing in the world that interests Moe like going to his potty. (*She laughs*) When he wants to make us a present: *off* he goes! When he's angry at us . . . oh, no! He plays it like these violinists play their violin . . . which reminds me! . . . (*Looking about her speculatively*) Do you suppose . . . I could just—slip behind these bushes a minute? . . . is that police officer around?

MILLIE: Well-ah . . . Officer Avonzino is awfully particular about nuisances, what he calls nuisances. Maybe you could go over to the avenue there—there's a branch library . . .

MRS. BOKER: Will you be an angel and watch Moe for me? If he starts to cry, give him the days of the week and the months of the year. He *loves* them.—Now where's this library?

MILLIE: Why, the Museum of National History's right over there.

MRS. BOKER (*Scream of pleasure*): Museum of Natural History!! How could I have forgotten that! Just full of animals. Of *course*! I won't be a minute, dear! . . .

> *They exchange good-byes. Mrs. Boker goes out. Millie eyes Moe's carriage apprehensively, then seats herself and resumes her novel at the last page.*

MILLIE: "Roger came into the room. His fine strong face still bore the marks of the suffering he had experienced." Oh! I imagine his wife died. Isn't that wonderful! He's *free*! "He drew her to him, pressing his lips on hers. 'Forever,' he said." Oh! "For-ever." (*In a moment, she is asleep*)

Tommy pulls himself up and stares at Moe's carriage.

TOMMY: Moe! . . . Moe!

MOE (*Surging up furiously*): Don't make noises at me! Don't look at me! Don't do anything. (*Telephone business, swiftly*) Hello, g'bye! (*He disappears*)

TOMMY: Moe! . . . Moe! . . . Talk to me something! . . . Moe, why are you thatway at me?

MOE (*Surging up again, glaring*): My daddy says I'm stupid. He says, "Stupid, come here!" He says, "All right, stupid, fall down!" I don't want to talk. I don't want to look. G'bye! (*He disappears*)

TOMMY: What does "stupid" mean?

MOE (*Invisible*): I won't tell. (*Surging up, showing his fingers; a rapid-fire jumble*) Do you know what these are? Sometimes you call them fingers; sometimes you call them piggies. One, two, six, five, four, two, ten. This little piggie stayed at home, I don't know why that is. Do you know what you do when the loud bell rings? You do this: (*Telephone business*) "Hello . . . jugga . . . jugga . . . jugga," and when you don't like it any more you say, "G'bye!" Maybe I am stupid. —But that's because MY MOUTH HURTS ALL THE TIME and they don't give me enough to eat and I'm hungry all the time and that's the end of it, that's the end of it. (*He disappears*)

TOMMY: Moe, tell me some more things.

MOE (*Surging up again*): "Stupid, come here!" "Stupid, get your goddamn tail out of here!" (*Shaking his carriage*) I hate him. I hate him. But I watch him and I learn. *You see:* I learn. And when I get to walk I'm going to do something so that he won't *be* any more. He'll be away—away where people can walk on him.—Don't you hate your father?

TOMMY: Well . . . I don't see him much. Like, once a year.

MOE: You mean: once a day.

TOMMY: Moe, what does "year" mean?

MOE: Year is when it's cold.

TOMMY (*Brightening*): Yes, I know.

MOE: Sometimes he holds out his hands and says: "How's the little fella? How's the little champ?" And I give him a look! I wasn't born yesterday. He hasn't got anything to sell to me.

TOMMY: Moe—where's your mommy? (*Silence*) Moe, she's not here. Where's your mommy? You don't hate your mommy, do you?

MOE (*Turning his face sideways, cold and proud*): I don't care about her. She's always away. She goes away for years. She laughs at me . . . with that *man*. He says: "All right, fall down, stupid," and she laughs. I try to talk to her and she goes away all the time and does, "Hello—jugga—jugga—jugga—goo-*bye*!" If she don't care about me any more, I don't care about her any more. Goo-*bye*! (*Silence*)

TOMMY: Say some more, Moe, say some more things.

MOE (*Low and intense*): Maybe I am stupid. Maybe I'll never be able to walk or make talk. Maybe they didn't give me good feet or a good mouth.—You know what I think? I think they don't want us to walk and to get good and get better. They want us to *stop*. That's what I think. (*His voice has risen to a hysterical wail*) Goddam! Hell! (*He starts throwing cloth elephants and giraffes out of the carriage*) I'm not going to try. Nobody wants to help me and lots of time is passing and I'm not getting bigger, and . . . and . . . (*Anticlimax*) I'm sleepeee . . . (*He continues to whimper*)

> Millie wakes up. She goes gingerly to Moe's carriage and joggles it.

MILLIE: Moe! What's the matter, Moe? "Rockabye, baby, in the treetop—" (*Moe wails more loudly*) Oh, goodness, gracious me. (*In desperation*) Moe! Do you know that *that* street is called Central Park West? And then there's Columbus Avenue? And then there's Amsterdam Avenue? And then there's Broadway? (*Moe has hushed*) And then there's West End Avenue. (*She can hardly believe her luck; she whispers*) And then there's Riverside Drive. (*She peers into the carriage a long time, then tiptoes to the other end of the stage; with clenched fists*) I hate babies. (*Toward Tommy*) I hate you—sticking your crazy face into my business—frightening

Officer Avonzino, the only man I've talked to in six months. I hate you—always butting in. I have a right to my own life, haven't I? *My own life!* I'm sick to death of squalling, smelling, gawking babies . . . I'd be a stenographer only I don't know anything; nobody ever taught me anything . . . "Manhattan, the Bronx"—what do I care what keeps you quiet? You can yell your heads off for all I care! I don't know why nature didn't make it so that people came into the world already grown-up—instead of a dozen and more years of screaming and diapers and falling down and breaking everything . . . and *asking questions!* "What's that?" "Why-y-y?" "Why-y-y?" . . . Officer Avonzino will never come back, that's certain! . . . Oh, what do I care? You're going to grow up to be *men*—nasty, selfish men. You're all alike. (*Drying her eyes, she picks up her novel from Tommy's carriage and strolls off the stage at the back*)

Moe's head, now solemn and resolute, rises slowly.

MOE: Tommy! . . . Tommy!

TOMMY (*Appearing*): I'm tired.

MOE: You know what I'm going to do, do you?

TOMMY: No—what, Moe?

MOE: I'm just going to lie still.

TOMMY: What do you mean, Moe?

MOE: I'll shut my eyes and do nothing. I won't eat. I'll just go away-away. Like I want Daddy to do.

TOMMY (*Alarm*): No, Moe! Don't go where people can walk on you!

MOE: Well, I *will* . . . You know what I think? I think people aren't SERIOUS about us. "Little piggie went to market, cradle will fall, Manhattan, the Bronx"—that's not serious. They don't want us to get better.

TOMMY: *Maybe* they do.

MOE: Old people are only interested in old people. Like kiss-kiss-kiss; that's all they do; that's all they think about.

TOMMY (*Eagerly*): Ye-e-es! Miss'a Millie, all the time, kiss-kiss-kiss, but she don't mean me; she means the policeman.

MOE: We're in the way, see? We're too little, that's how. I don't want to be a man—it's too hard! (*He disappears*)

TOMMY (*With increasing alarm*): Moe! . . . Moe! . . . Don't stop talking, Moe! . . . MOE!

Millie returns hastily.

MILLIE: Now what's the matter with you? I'll spank you. Always crying and making a baby of yourself.

TOMMY (*At the same time; frantic*): Moe's going away-away. He's not going to eat any more. Go look at Moe . . . *Do* something. *Do* something!

MILLIE: What is the matter with you? Why can't you be quiet like Moe? (*She goes and looks in Moe's carriage and is terrified by what she sees*) Help! . . . Hellllp! The baby's turned purple! Moe! Have you swallowed something?—(*She dashes to the audience exit*) Officer Avonzino! Officer! Hellllp!— Oh, they'll kill me. What'll I do?

Officer Avonzino rushes in from the audience.

AVONZINO: What'a matter, Miss Wilchick; you gone crazy today?

MILLIE (*Gasping*): . . . look . . . he's turned black, Officer Avonzino . . . His mother's over at the museum. Oh . . . I don't know what to do.

Officer Avonzino, efficient but unhurried, opens his tunic and takes out his handbook. He hunts for the correct page.

AVONZINO: First, don't scream, Miss Wilchick. Nobody scream. Babies die every day. Always new babies. Nothing to scream about . . . Babies turn black—so! Babies turn blue, black, purple, all the time. Hmph: "Turn baby over, lift middle . . ." (*He does these things*) "Water . . ." (*To Millie*) Go to nurses over there . . . twenty nurses . . . Bring back some ippycack.

MILLIE: Oh, Officer . . . help me. I'm fainting.

AVONZINO (*Furious*): Faintings on *Sundays*—not workdays, Miss Wilchick.

MILLIE (*Hand to head*): Oh . . . oh . . .

Officer Avonzino catches her just in time and drapes her over the bench like a puppet.

AVONZINO: "Lesson Thirty-Two: Let Mother Die. Save Baby." I get water. (*He dashes off*)

Tommy raises his head.

TOMMY: Moe! Don't be black. Don't be black. You're going to walk soon. And by and by you can go to school. And even if they don't teach you good, you can kind of teach yourself. (*Moe is sobbing*) Moe, what's that noise you're making? Make a crying like a baby, Moe.—Soon you can be big and shave. And be a policeman. And you can make kiss-kiss-kiss . . . and make babies. And, Moe—

MOE (*Appearing*): Don't talk to me. I'm tired. I'm tired.

TOMMY: And you can show your babies how to walk and talk.

MOE (*Yawning*): I'm . . . tire' . . . (*He sinks back*)

TOMMY (*Yawning*): I'm tired, tooooo. (*He sinks back*)

Officer Avonzino returns with a child's pail of water. He leans over Moe.

AVONZINO (*Astonished*): What'a matter with you!! You all red again. You not sick. Goddamn! Tricks. Babies always doing tricks. (*Shakes Millie*) Miss Wilchick! Wake up! Falsa alarm. Baby's okay.

MILLIE (*Coming to, dreamily*): Oh, Officer . . . (*Extending her arms amorously*) Oh you're so . . . handsome . . . Officer . . .

AVONZINO (*Sternly*): "Lesson Eleven: No Personal Remarks with Public." (*Shouts*) It's going to rain: better take George Washington home . . . and Dr. Einstein, too.

MILLIE: Oh! How *is* the Boker baby?

AVONZINO: Boker baby's a great actor. Dies every performance. Thousands cheer.

MILLIE (*Pushes Tommy toward exit*): Oh, I can't go until Mrs. Boker comes back. (*Peers out*)—Oh, there she comes, running. See her?

AVONZINO: You *go*. I take care of baby til a' momma comes. (*At exit Millie turns for a heartfelt farewell; he points billy stick and commands her*) Go *faint*, Miss Wilchick! (*She goes out. Avonzino addresses Moe*) I'd like to make your damn bottom red. I know you. All you babies want the whole world. Well, I tell you, you've got a long hard road before you. Pretty soon you'll find that you can cry all you want and turn every color there is—and nobody'll pay *no* attention at all. Your best days are over; you've had'm. From now on it's all up to you—George Washington, or whatever your name is.

Enter Mrs. Boker, breathless.

MRS. BOKER: Oh!!

AVONZINO: I sent Miss Wilchick home. (*Pointing toward rain*) You better start off yourself.

MRS. BOKER (*Pushing the carriage to the exit*): Has everything been all right, Officer?

AVONZINO: Just fine, lady, just fine. Like usual: babies acting like growed-ups; growed-ups acting like babies.

MRS. BOKER: *Thank* you, Officer. (*She goes out*)

Officer Avonzino, shading his eyes, peers down the aisle through the audience. Suddenly he sees something that outrages him. Like a Keystone cop he does a double take and starts running through the audience, shouting:

AVONZINO: Hey there!! You leave that baby carriage alone! Don't you know what's inside them baby carriages? . . .

END OF PLAY

Childhood

A COMEDY

CHARACTERS

CAROLINE, the oldest daughter, twelve
DODIE, her sister, ten
BILLEE, her brother, eight
MOTHER
FATHER

SETTING

A suburban house and yard.

*Some low chairs at the edges of the arena. These at first represent
some bushes in the yard of the children's home. At the back, the
door to the house; the aisle through the audience serves as a path
to the street. Enter from the house Caroline, twelve; Dodie, ten;
and, with a rush, Billee, eight.*

DODIE: Shh! Shh! Don't let Mama hear you! Car'line, Car'-
line, play the game. Let's play the game.
CAROLINE: There's no time, silly. It takes time to play the
game.
BILLEE: Play Goin' to China.
CAROLINE: Don't talk so loud; we don't want Mama to hear
us. Papa'll be here soon, and we can't play the game when
Papa's here.
DODIE: Well, let's play a little. We can play Going to a Hotel.
BILLEE (*Clamorously*): I want to be Room Service. I want to
be Room Service.
CAROLINE: You know Going to a Hotel takes *hours*. It's awful
when you have to stop for something.
DODIE (*Quickly*): Car'line, listen, I heard Mama telephoning
Papa and the car's got to be fixed and Papa's got to come

home by a bus, and maybe he'll never get here and we can play for a long time.

CAROLINE: Did she say that? Well, come behind the bushes and think.

They squat on their haunches behind the bushes.

BILLEE: Let's play Hospital and take everything out of Dodie.
CAROLINE: Let me think a minute.
MOTHER (*At the door*): Caroline! Dodie!

Silence.

Dodie, how often do I have to tell you to hang your coat up properly? Do you know what happened? It fell and got caught under the cupboard door and was dragged back and forth. I hope it's warm Sunday, because you can't wear that coat. Billee, stand out for a moment where I can see you. Are you ready for your father when he comes home? Come out of the bushes, Billee, come out.

Billee, a stoic already, comes to the center of the stage and stands for inspection. Mother shakes her head in silence; then:

I simply despair. Look at you! What are you children doing anyway? Now, Caroline, you're not playing one of those games of yours? I absolutely forbid you to play that the house is on fire. You have nightmares all night long. Or those awful games about hospitals. Really, Caroline, why can't you play Shopping or Going to School? (*Silence*) I declare. I give up. I really do. (*False exit*) Now remember, it's Friday night, the end of the week, and you give your father a good big kiss when he comes home. (*She goes out*)

Billee rejoins his sisters.

DODIE (*Dramatic whisper*): Car'line, let's play Funeral! (*Climax*) Car'line, let's play ORPHANS!

CAROLINE: We haven't time—*that* takes all day. Besides, I haven't got the black gloves.

Billee sees his father coming through the audience. Utter and final dismay.

BILLEE: Look't! Look!

DODIE: What?

ALL THREE: It's Papa! It's Papa!

> *They fly into the house like frightened pigeons. Father enters jauntily through the audience. It's warm, and he carries his coat over his shoulder. Arriving at the center of the stage, he places his coat on the ground, whistles a signal call to his wife, and swinging an imaginary golf club, executes a mighty and very successful shot.*

FATHER: Two hundred and fifty yards!

MOTHER (*Enters, kisses him and picks up the coat*): Why, you're early, after all.

FATHER: Jerry drove me to the corner. Picked up a little flask for the weekend.

MOTHER: Well, I wish you wouldn't open your little flask when the children are around.

FATHER (*Preparing a difficult shot*): Eleventh hole . . . Where *are* the children?

MOTHER: They were here a minute ago. They're out playing somewhere . . . Your coat on the ground! Really, you're as bad as Dodie.

FATHER: Well, you should teach the children—little trouble with the dandelions here—that it's their first duty . . . when their father comes home on Friday nights . . . (*Shouts*) Fore, you bastards! . . . to rush toward their father . . . to grovel . . . abject thanks to him who gave them life.

MOTHER (*Amused exasperation*): Oh, stop that nonsense!

FATHER: On Friday nights . . . after a week of toil at the office . . . a man wants to see . . . (*He swings*) his wives and children clinging to his knees, tears pouring down their cheeks. (*He stands up very straight, holding an enormous silver cup*) Gentlemen, I accept this championship cup, but I wish also to give credit to my wife and children, who drove me out of the house every Sunday morning . . . Where *are* the children? Caroline! Dodie!

MOTHER: Oh, they're hiding somewhere.

FATHER: Hiding? Hiding from their father?

MOTHER: They're playing one of those awful games of theirs.

Listen to me, Fred: those games are morbid; they're dangerous.

FATHER: How do you mean, dangerous?

MOTHER: Really! No one told me when I was a bride that children are half crazy. I only hear fragments of the games, naturally, but do you realize that they like nothing better than to imagine us—away?

FATHER: Away?

MOTHER: Yes—dead?

FATHER (*His eye on the shot*): One . . . two . . . *three!* Well, you know what *you* said.

MOTHER: What did I say?

FATHER: *Your* dream.

MOTHER: Pshaw!

FATHER (*Softly, with lowest insinuation*): Your dream that . . . you and I . . . on a Mediterranean cruise . . .

MOTHER: It was Hawaii.

FATHER: And that we were—ahem!—somehow . . . *alone.*

MOTHER: Well, I didn't imagine them *dead*! I imagined them with Mother . . . or Paul . . . or their Aunt Henrietta.

FATHER (*Piously*): I hope so.

MOTHER: You're a brute, and everybody knows it . . . It's Caroline. She's the one who starts it all. And afterwards she has those nightmares. Come in. You'll see the children at supper.

FATHER (*Looking upward*): What has the weatherman predicted for tomorrow?

MOTHER (*Starting for the house*): Floods. Torrents. You're going to stay home from the golf club and take care of the children. And I'm going to the Rocky Mountains . . . and to China.

FATHER: You'll be back by noon. What does Caroline say in her nightmares?

MOTHER: Oh! When she's awake, too. You and I are—away. Do you realize that that girl is mad about black gloves?

FATHER: Nonsense.

MOTHER: Caroline would be in constant mourning if she could manage it. Come in, come in. You'll see them at supper. (*She goes out*)

FATHER (*He strolls to the end of the stage farthest from the house and calls*): Caroline! (*Pause*) Dodie! (*Pause*) Bill-eeee!

Silence. He broods aloud, his eyes on the distance.

No instrument has yet been discovered that can read what goes on in another's mind, asleep or awake. And I hope there never will be. But once in a while, it would help a lot. Is it wrong of me to wish that . . . just once . . . I could be an invisible witness to one of my children's dreams, to one of their games? (*He calls again*) Caroline!

We are in the game which is a dream. The children enter as he calls them, but he does not see them and they do not see him. They come in and stand shoulder to shoulder as though they were about to sing a song before an audience. Caroline carries a child's suitcase and one of her mother's handbags; she is wearing black gloves. Dodie also has a suitcase and handbag, but no gloves.

CAROLINE: Dodie! Hurry before they see us.
FATHER: Dodie!
DODIE: Where's Billee gone?
FATHER (*Being bumped into by Billee as he joins his sisters*): Billee!

Father enters the house. Mother glides out of the house and takes her place at the farther end of the stage and turns and faces the children. She is wearing a black hat, deep black veil and black gloves. Her air is one of mute acquiescent grief. Caroline glances frequently at her mother as though for prompting. A slight formal pause.

CAROLINE: I guess, first, we have to say how sorry we are.
　　(*To Mother*) Shall we begin? (*Mother lowers her head slightly*) This first part is in church. Well, in a kind of church. And there's been a perfectly terrible accydent, an airplane accydent.
DODIE (*Quickly*): No, it was an automobile accydent.
CAROLINE (*Ditto*): It was an airplane.
DODIE (*Ditto*): I don't want it to be an airplane.
BILLEE (*Fiercely*): It was on a ship. It was a *big* shipwreck.

CAROLINE: Now, I'm not going to play this game unless you be quiet. It was an airplane accydent. And . . . They were on it, and they're not here any more.

BILLEE: They got *dead*.

CAROLINE (*Glaring at him*): Don't say that *word*. You promised you wouldn't say that word. (*Uncomfortable pause*) And we're very sad. And . . .

DODIE (*Brightly*): We didn't see it, though.

CAROLINE: And we'd have put on black dresses, only we haven't got any. But we want to thank Miss Wilkerson for coming today and for wearing black like she's wearing. (*Mother again lowers her head*) Miss Wilkerson is the best teacher in Benjamin Franklin School, and she's the grown-up we like best.

BILLEE (*Suddenly getting excited*): That's not Miss Wilkerson. That's—I mean—*look!*

CAROLINE: I can't hear a word you're saying, and anyway, don't talk now!

BILLEE (*Too young to enter the dream; pulling at his sisters' sleeves urgently*): That's not Miss Wilkerson. That's *Mama!*

DODIE: What's the matter with your eyes?

CAROLINE: Mama's not here any more. She went away.

BILLEE (*Staring at Mother, and beginning to doubt*): It's . . . Mrs. Fenwick!

CAROLINE (*Low but strongly*): No-o-o-o! (*Resuming the ceremony*) It wasn't so sad about Grandma, because she was more'n a hundred anyway.

DODIE: And she used to say all the time, "I won't be with you always," and things like that, and how she'd give Mama her pearl pin.

BILLEE: I guess she's glad she isn't any more.

CAROLINE (*Uncertainly*): So . . .

DODIE (*To Mother, with happy excitement*): Are we orphans now—real orphans? (*Mother, always with lowered eyes nods slightly*) And we don't have to *do things* any more?

CAROLINE (*Severely*): Dodie! Don't *say* everything. (*She consults her mother*) What do I say now?

MOTHER (*Almost inaudibly*): About your father . . .

CAROLINE: Yes. Papa was a very fine man. And . . .

DODIE (*Quickly*): He used to swear bad words.

BILLEE (*Excitedly*): All the *time*! He'd swear swearwords.

CAROLINE: Well, maybe a little.

DODIE: He *did*, I used to want to *die*.

CAROLINE: Well, nobody's perfeck. (*Slower*) He was all right, sometimes.

DODIE: He used to laugh too loud in front of people. And he didn't give Mama enough money to buy clothes. She had to go to town in rags, in terrible old rags.

BILLEE (*Always excited*): Papa'd go like this, (*Pumping his arms up and down in desperation*) "I haven't got it! I haven't got it! You can't squeeze blood out of a stone."

DODIE: Yes, he did.

BILLEE: And Mama'd say: "I'm ashamed to go out in the street." It was awful. And then he'd say, "I'll have to mortgage, that's what I'll have to do."

CAROLINE: Billee! How can you say such an awful word? Don't you ever say that again. Papa wasn't perfeck, but he would never have done a mortgage.

BILLEE: Well, that's what he said.

CAROLINE (*Emphatically*): Most times Papa did his best. Everybody makes some mistakes.

DODIE (*Demurely*): He used to drink some, too.

BILLEE (*Beside himself again*): He used to drink *oceans*. And Mama'd say, "Don't you think you've had enough?" and he'd say, "Down the hatch!"

DODIE: Yes, he did. And, "Just a hair of the dog that bit him." And Mama'd say, "Well, if you want to kill yourself before our eyes!" I used to want to die.

CAROLINE: Billee, don't get so excited; and you too, Dodie. Papa was a very fine man, and he *tried*. Only . . . only . . . (*Reluctantly*) he didn't ever say anything very inneresting.

DODIE: He was inneresting when he told about the automobile accydent he'd seen and all the blood.

BILLEE: Yes, he was. But he stopped in the middle when Mama said, "Not before the children."

DODIE: Yes, he stopped then.

CAROLINE: Anyway, we're very sad. And . . . (*She looks to her mother for prompting*)

MOTHER (*Almost inaudibly*): Your mother . . .

CAROLINE: Yes. About Mama.

BILLEE (*Hot indignation*): Mama's almost never home. She's always shopping and having her hair made. And one time she was away *years*, to see Grandma in Boston.

DODIE: It was only five days, and Grandma was very sick.

BILLEE: No, it wasn't. It was years and years.

DODIE: Well, when she was away she didn't have to say Don't —Don't—Don't all the time, all day and night, Don't— Don't—Don't.

BILLEE (*Tentatively defending her*): Sometimes she makes good things to eat.

DODIE: Beans and mash potatoes, and I just hate them. "Now, you eat every mouthful, or you don't leave the table." Ugh!

CAROLINE (*Recalling them to the ceremony*): It wasn't her fault! Only she didn't unnerstand children. I guess there's not one in a hundred hundred that unnerstands children. (*To Mother*) Is that enough, Miss Wilkerson? I can't think of anything else to say. And we've got to hurry, or Uncle Paul will come to get us, or Aunt Henrietta, or somebody even worse. So can we go now?

MOTHER (*A whisper*): I think it would be nice, you know, if you said how you loved them, and how they loved you.

CAROLINE: Yes—uh . . .

DODIE: It was awful when they got huggy and kissy. And when we got back an hour late, from Mary Louise's picnic, and Mama said, "I was frantic! I was frantic! I didn't know what had become of you."

CAROLINE (*Slowly*): She liked us best when we were sick and when I broke my arm.

DODIE: Yes. (*Exhausted pause*) Miss Wilkerson, orphans don't have to be sad *all* the time, do they?

Mother shakes her head slightly.

BILLEE: Do we get any money for being orphans?

CAROLINE: We won't need it. Papa used to keep an envelope behind the clock with money in it, for accydents and times like that. I have it here. (*She goes to Mother, like a hostess getting rid of a guest*) Thank you for coming, Miss Wilkerson. We have to go now. And thank you for wearing black.

DODIE (*Also shaking hands; conventionally*): Thank you very much.

Mother, with bowed head, glides into the house.

CAROLINE: Now be quiet, and I'll tell you what we're going to do. We've got to hurry, so don't interrupt me. We're orphans and we don't have anybody around us or near us and we're going to take a bus. (*Sensation*) All over the world. We're going to be different persons and we're going to change our names. (*Gravely she opens her suitcase. She takes out and puts on a hat and fur neckpiece of her mother's. She looks adorable*) I'm Mrs. Arizona. Miss Wilson, please get ready for the trip.

DODIE: Wha-a-t?

CAROLINE: *Miss Wilson!* Will you put your hat on, please.

DODIE: Oh! (*She puts on a hat from her suitcase*) I want to be married, too. I want to be Mrs. Wilson.

CAROLINE: You're too young. People would laugh at you. We'll be gone for years and years, and by and by, in China or somewhere, you can gradually be Mrs. Wilson.

BILLEE: I want to be somebody, too.

CAROLINE: You're only *eight*! If you don't cry all the time and say awful things, I'll give you a real name. Now we can start.

BILLEE: But aren't Papa and Mama coming? (*The girls turn and glare at him*) Oh! they're *dead*. (*More glaring*)

CAROLINE: All right. S-s-stay at home and go to s-s-school, if you want to. Papa and Mama are *happy*. Papa's playing golf and Mama's shopping. Are you ready, Miss Wilson?

DODIE: Yes, Mrs. Arizona, thank you.

CAROLINE: Don't run, but if we hurry we can each get a seat by the window.

Father enters, wearing a bus conductor's cap and big dark glasses. He casually arranges the chairs so as to indicate some of the seats of a long bus pointing toward the exit through the audience. The children form a line at the door of the bus, tickets in hand.

FATHER: Take your places in line, please. The first stop, ladies and gentlemen, will be Ashagorra-Kallapalla, where there will be twenty minutes for lunch. That's the place where you get to eat the famous heaven-fruit sandwich.

He starts punching the tickets of some imaginary passengers who precede the children.

That cat won't be happy, madam. That's our experience.

(*Severely, palping a passenger*) You haven't got mumps, have you? Well, I'd appreciate it if you sat at a distance from the other passengers.

BILLEE (*Staggered*): But that's Papa!

DODIE: Don't he silly, Papa's *away*.

BILLEE: But it looks like Papa . . . and . . . (*Losing assurance*) it looks like Dr. Summers, too.

CAROLINE: Billee, I don't know what's the matter with you. Papa wouldn't be working as a bus conductor. Papa's a man that's got more money than that.

FATHER (*To Caroline*): Your ticket, please, madam.

CAROLINE: We want to go to all the places you're going to, please.

FATHER: But you mean this to be a round-trip ticket, don't you? You're coming back, aren't you?

CAROLINE (*None too sure; her eyes avoiding his*): Well, maybe I won't.

FATHER (*Lowering his voice, confidentially*): I'll punch it on the side here. That'll mean you can use it, whenever you want, to come back here. (*Caroline takes her place on the bus.*)

> *Mother glides in and takes her place in the line behind Billee. She is now wearing a brown hat and a deep brown veil. Father punches Dodie's ticket.*

Why, I think I've seen your face before, madam. Weren't you in that terrible automobile accident—blood all over the road and everything?

DODIE (*Embarrassed; low*): No, no, I wasn't.

FATHER: Well, I'm glad to hear that. (*Dodie takes her seat behind Caroline*)

(*To Billee, punching his ticket*) And what's your name, sir, if I may ask?

BILLEE: Billee.

CAROLINE (*Officiously*): His name is Mr. Wentworth.

FATHER: Mr. Wentworth. Good morning. (*Man to man, with a touch of severity*) No smoking in the first six rows, watch that, and . . . (*Significant whisper*) there'll be no liquor drinking on this bus. I hope that's understood. (*Billee, con-*

siderably intimidated, takes his place behind Dodie. During the following he sees Mother and stares at her in amazement)

(*Father punches Mothers ticket, saying in sad condolence:*) I hope you have a good trip, ma'am. I hope you have a good trip.

MOTHER (*A whisper*): Thank you. (*She takes a place in the last row*)

CAROLINE (*Rummaging in her handbag*): Would you like a candy bar, Miss Wilson . . . and Mr. Wentworth?

DODIE: Thank you, Mrs. Arizona, I would.

BILLEE: Look! LOOK! That's Mama!

DODIE: Stop poking me. It's not. It's *not*.

FATHER: Well, now, all aboard that's going to go. (*He climbs on the bus, takes his seat, tries his gears, then rises and addresses the passengers weightily*) Before we start, there are some things I want to say about this trip. *Bus travel is not easy.* I think you'll know what I mean, Mrs. Arizona, when I say that it's like family life: we're all stuck in this vehicle together. We go through some pretty dangerous country, and I want you all to keep your heads. Like when we go through the Black Snake Indian territory, for instance. I've just heard they're getting a little—restless. And along the Kappikappi River, where all those lions and tigers are, and other things. Now, I'm a pretty good driver, but nobody's perfect and everybody can make a mistake once in a while. But I don't want any complaints afterward that you weren't warned. If anybody wants to get off this bus and go home, this is the moment to do it, and I'll give you your money back. (*Indicating Mother*) There's one passenger here I know can be counted on. She's made the trip before and she's a regular crackerjack. Excuse me praising you to your face, ma'am, but I mean every word of it. Now, how many of you have been trained in first aid—will you hold up your hands? (*Billee and Mother raise their hands promptly. Caroline and Dodie look at one another uncertainly but do not raise their hands*) Well, we may have to hold some classes later—go to school, so to speak. Accidents are always likely to happen when we get to the tops of the mountains. So! I guess we're ready to start. When we start, we often have a word of prayer if there's a minister of the gospel on board. (*To Billee*) May I ask if you're a minister of the gospel, Mr. Wentworth?

BILLEE: N-no.

FATHER: Then we'll just have to *think* it. (*Lowering his voice, to Billee*) And, may I add, I hope that there won't be any bad language used on this bus. There are ladies present—and some very fine ladies, too, if I may say so. Well, here we go! Forward march.

CAROLINE (*To Dodie, confidentially*): If it's going to be so dangerous, I think we'd better move up a little nearer *him*.

> *They slip across the aisle and slide, side by side, into the second row behind Father. Billee has gone to the back of the car and stands staring at Mother.*

BILLEE (*Indicating the veil*): Do you ever take that off?

MOTHER (*Softly, lowered eyes*): Sometimes I do.

CAROLINE: Billee! Don't disturb the lady. Come and sit by us.

MOTHER: Oh, he's not disturbing me at all.

> *Soon he takes the seat beside her, and she puts her arm around him.*

FATHER (*As he drives, talking to the girls over his shoulder*): It's hard work driving a bus, ladies. Did you ever think of that?

CAROLINE: Oh, yes. It must be hard.

FATHER: Sometimes I wonder why I do it. Mornings . . . leave my house and family and get on the bus. And it's no fun, believe me. (*Jerk*) See that? Almost ran over that soldier. And—would you believe it—I don't get much money for it.

CAROLINE (*Breathless interest*): Don't they pay you a *lot*?

FATHER: Mrs. Arizona, I'm telling you the truth: sometimes I wonder if we're going to have enough to eat.

DODIE: Why, I think that's terrible!

FATHER: And if I can get enough clothes to wear. I see that's a nice fur piece you have on, Mrs. Arizona.

CAROLINE: Oh, this is *old*.

DODIE (*Very earnestly*): But at your house you do have breakfast and lunch and supper, don't you?

FATHER: Miss Wilson, you're awfully kind to ask. So far we have. Sometimes it's just, you know, beans and things like that. Life's not easy, Mrs. Arizona. You must have noticed that.

BILLEE (*Big alarm*): Mr. Bus Conductor, look't. Look over there!

FATHER (*Galvanized; all stare toward the left*): Ladies and gentlemen, there are those goldarn Indians again! I want you to put your heads right down on the floor! Right down! (*All except Father crouch on the floor*) I don't want any of them arrows to come in the windows and hit you. (*Father fires masterfully from the hip*) They'll be sorry for this. BANG! BANG! That'll teach them. BANG! (*Billee rises and whirls, shooting splendidly in all directions*) There! The danger's over, ladies and gentlemen. You can get in your seats now. I'll report that to the Man Up There in Washington, D.C., you see if I don't. (*To Mother*) May I ask if you're all right back there?

MOTHER: Yes, thank you, Mr. Bus Conductor. I want to say that Mr. Wentworth behaved splendidly. I don't think that I'd be here except for him.

FATHER: Good! Minute I saw him I knew he had the old stuff in him! Ladies, I think you did A-number-one, too.

CAROLINE: Does that happen often, Mr. Bus Conductor?

FATHER: Well, you know what a man's life is like, Mrs. Arizona. Fight. Struggle. Survive. Struggle. Survive. Always was.

DODIE: What if—what if you *didn't* come back?

FATHER: Do you mean, if I died? We don't think of that, Miss Wilson. But when we come home Friday nights we like to see the look on the faces of our wives and children. Another week, and we're still there. And do you know what I do on my free days, Miss Wilson, after sitting cooped up behind this wheel?

DODIE (*Sudden inspiration*): Play golf.

FATHER: You're bright, Miss Wilson, bright as a penny.

CAROLINE (*Who has been glancing at Mother*): Mr. Bus Conductor, can I ask you why that lady—why she's so sad?

FATHER: You don't know?

CAROLINE: No.

FATHER (*Lowering his voice*): She just got some bad news. Her children left the house.

CAROLINE: Did they?

FATHER: Don't mention it to her, will you?

CAROLINE (*Insecurely*): Why did they do that?

FATHER: Well, children are funny. Funny. Now I come to think of it, it'd be nice if, a little later, you went back and sort of comforted her. Like Mr. Wentworth's doing.

DODIE: Wasn't she good to them?

FATHER: What's that?

DODIE: Wasn't she a *good* mother?

FATHER: Well, let me ask *you* a question: is there any such thing as a good mother or a good father? Look at me: I do the best I can for my family—things to eat, you know, and dresses and shoes. I see you've got some real pretty shoes on, ladies. But, well, *children don't understand*, and that's all you can say about it. Do you know what one of my daughters said to me last week? She said she wished she was an orphan. Hard. Very hard.

CAROLINE (*Struggling*): Lots of times parents don't understand children, either.

FATHER (*Abruptly breaking the mood*): But now, ladies and gentlemen, I have a treat for you. (*Stops the bus and points dramatically to the front right. All gaze in awe*) Isn't that a sight! The Mississippi River! Isn't that a lot of water!

MOTHER (*After a moment's gaze, with increasing concern*): But —but—Mr. Bus Conductor.

FATHER (*Looking back at her and sharing her anxiety*): Madam, I think I know what you're thinking, and it troubles me too. (*Mother has come halfway down the aisle, her eyes on the river*) Ladies and gentlemen, the river's in flood. I don't think I've ever seen it so high. The question is: would it be safe to cross it today? Look yourselves—would that bridge hold?

MOTHER (*Returning to her seat*): Mr. Bus Conductor, may I make a suggestion?

FATHER: You certainly may.

MOTHER: I suggest that you ask the passengers to raise their hands if they think it's best that we don't cross the Mississippi today.

FATHER: *Very* good idea! That'll mean we turn around and go back to where we came from. Now think it over, ladies and gentlemen. All who are ready to do that raise their hands. (*Mother and Billee raise their hands at once. Then Dodie.*

Finally, unhappily, Caroline. Father earnestly counts the twenty hands in the bus) All right! Everybody wants to go back. So, here we go. (*He starts the bus*) Now, I'm going to go pretty fast, so sit square in your seats.

(*After a pause, confidentially over his shoulder to Caroline*) I hope you really meant it when you put your hand up, Mrs. Arizona.

CAROLINE: Well . . .

FATHER: You *do* have some folks waiting for you at home, don't you?

DODIE (*Quickly*): Yes, we do.

CAROLINE (*Slowly, near to tears*): But we didn't get to China or to that river where the lions and tigers are. It's too soon to go back to where I come from, where everybody says silly things they don't mean one bit, and where nobody treats you like a real person. And we didn't get to eat the famous heaven-fruit sandwich at that place.

DODIE (*Embarrassed*): Car'line, you can do it another time.

Caroline's lowered head shows that she doesn't believe this.

FATHER (*Confidentially*): Mrs. Arizona, I'll honor that ticket *at any time*, and I'll be looking for you.

CAROLINE (*Raises her eyes to him gravely; after a minute she says, also in a low voice*): Mr. Bus Conductor—

FATHER: Yes, Mrs. Arizona.

CAROLINE: Do you get paid just the same, even if you didn't go the whole way?

FATHER: I? Oh, don't you think of that, ma'am. We can tighten our belts. There's always something.

CAROLINE (*Groping feverishly in her handbag, with a quick sob*): No! I haven't got a *lot* of money, but—here! Here's more'n two dollars, and you can buy a lot of things to eat with that.

FATHER (*Quietly and slowly, his eyes on the road*): That's real thoughtful of you, Mrs. Arizona, and I thank you. But you put that away and keep it. I feel sure that this is going to be my good year. (*After a pause*) Excuse me, may I put my hand on your hand a minute to show you know I appreciate what you did?

CAROLINE (*Shy*): Yes, you may.

He does so, very respectfully; then returns to his wheel.

DODIE: Car'line, what're you crying about?

CAROLINE: When . . . you try to *do* something for some-body . . . and . . .

FATHER (*Very cheerful and loud*): Gee whillikers! My wife will be surprised to see me back home so soon. Poor old thing, she doesn't have many pleasures. Just a little shopping now and then. (*He tosses off a snatch of song*) "The son of a, son of a, son of a gambolier . . ." I think this would be a good time to go back and say a nice word to that lady who's had a little disappointment in her home, don't you?

CAROLINE: Well, uh . . . Come, Dodie. (*Caroline goes back and sits in front of Mother, talking to her over the back of the seat; Dodie stands beside her*) The bus conductor says that everybody isn't in your house any more.

MOTHER (*Lowered eyes*): Did he? That's true.

CAROLINE: They'll come back. I know they will.

MOTHER: Oh, do you think so?

CAROLINE: Children don't like being treated as children *all the time*. And I think it isn't worthwhile being born into the world if you have to do the same things every day.

DODIE: The reason I don't like grown-ups is that they don't ever think any inneresting thoughts. I guess they're so old that they just get tired of expecting anything to be different or exciting. So they just do the same old golfing and shopping.

CAROLINE (*Suddenly seeing a landmark through the window*): Mr. Bus Conductor! Mr. Bus Conductor! Please, will you please stop at the next corner? This is where we have to get off.

(*Under her voice, commandingly*) Come, Dodie, Billee. Come quick!

They start up the aisle toward the bus exit, then turn back to Mother. Their farewells are their best party manners.

THE CHILDREN (*Shaking hands with both parents*): I'm very glad to have met you. Thank you very much. I'm very glad to have met you.

FATHER (*As Mother joins him at the bus exit*): But you'll come on my bus again? We'll see you again?

CAROLINE (*To Dodie and Billee, low*): Now, run!

> *They run into the house like rabbits. She stands at the bus door, with lowered eyes.*

Well . . . you see . . . you're just people in our game. You're not *really* alive. That's why we could talk to you. (*A quick glance at her father, then she looks down again*) Besides, we've found that it's best not to make friends with grown-ups, because . . . in the end . . . they don't act fair to you . . . But thank you; I'm very glad to have met you.

> *She goes into the house. Father takes off his cap and glasses; Mother her hat and veil. They place them on chairs. Father prepares to make a difficult golf stroke.*

FATHER: Where *are* the children?

MOTHER: Oh, they're hiding somewhere, as usual.

FATHER: Hiding! Hiding from their father!

MOTHER: Or they're playing one of those awful games of theirs. Come in, come in. You'll see them at supper. (*She goes into the house*)

FATHER (*He stands at the end of the stage farthest from the house and calls*): Caroline! Dodie! Billee-ee-ee!

> *Silence, of course. He goes into the house.*

END OF PLAY

Youth

CHARACTERS

LEMUEL GULLIVER, a shipwrecked sea captain, forty-six
MISTRESS BELINDA JENKINS, a commoner, eighteen
LADY SIBYL PONSONBY, a noble lady, twenty-four
THE DUKE OF CORNWALL, the island's governor, twenty-eight
SIMPSON, a commoner and builder, twenty
[TWO BOY GUARDS, fifteen]

SETTING

A tropical island.

At the back, an opening through a thicket leads to the principal town. Forward on the stage is a palm-thatched summer house without walls. Under its roof is a rustic table and bench; on the table some worn books. On the floor at one side of the stage is a piece of glass, fringed with moss; this represents a spring.

Gulliver, forty-six, drags himself on in the last stages of hunger and exhaustion. He sees the spring and avidly laps at it with hand and tongue. Somewhat refreshed, he lies down and closes his eyes. Then rising to a sitting position, he becomes aware of the summer house. He goes to it and opens one of the books. In great amazement he murmurs: "English! In English!"

In the distance a young woman's voice is heard lilting a kind of yodel. It ceases and is resumed several times.

Gulliver makes a shell of his hands and calls:

GULLIVER: Anyone? . . . Is anyone there?
BELINDA'S VOICE: What? . . . Wha . . . a . . . t?
GULLIVER: Is anyone there?
VOICE (*Nearer*): 'Oo are *you*?
GULLIVER (*Still calling*): I am an Englishman, madam, ship-
    wrecked on this island.
VOICE: 'Oo? . . . 'Ooh?
GULLIVER: I am Captain Gulliver, at your service, madam.

VOICE: 'Ooh?

GULLIVER: Captain Gulliver—Lemuel Gulliver of the four-master *Arcturus*, Port of London, at your service, madam.

VOICE: Oh! Lord. 'Ow old are you?

Gulliver, nonplussed, does not answer.

'Ow *old* are you?

GULLIVER: I'm forty-six years of age.

VOICE (*Just offstage*): No!! No!! *Forty*-six! 'Ow did you get here?

GULLIVER: I was shipwrecked, madam. I have been in the sea for three days, pushing a spar. I am sorely in need of food and am much dependent on your kindness.

Enter Mistress Belinda Jenkins, eighteen. She gazes at Gulliver with growing abhorrence, covers her face with her hands and turns to the entrance through which she came.

BELINDA: Oh, Lady Sibyl! 'Ow 'ideous! 'Ow unbearable!

Enter Lady Sibyl Ponsonby, twenty-four. Both are charmingly dressed as of the eighteenth century in some textile-like tapa cloth. Lady Sibyl is a great lady, however, and carries a parasol tufted with seagulls' feathers.

LADY SIBYL (*Staring at Gulliver, but with more controlled repulsion; as though to herself*): It's hall true! Then it's hall true, wot they say! (*Pronounced "si"*)

BELINDA (*To Gulliver, spitefully*): Turn your fice awigh! How can you look at Lady Sibyl?

LADY SIBYL (*With authority*): 'Old your tongue, Jenkins.

BELINDA (*Pointing*): But he's terrible! He's terrible!

LADY SIBYL (*Coldly*): Yes.—You are 'ideous to behold.

GULLIVER: I'm a plain man, madam; and in addition I have been without food and drink for three days—and with very little sleep.

LADY SIBYL (*Again as though to herself*): I have never seen an old man before. *Forty*-six, you say? It's hall true, too true.

BELINDA (*Peeking from behind Lady Sibyl*): The wrinkles, your ladyship. Nobody could count them!—Can he see? Can he hear?

LADY SIBYL (*From curiosity not kindness*): You must be suffering in every part of your body?

GULLIVER: I have suffered, madam, principally from thirst until I found this spring here; and I would be most beholden to you if *you* could also graciously give me something to eat.

LADY SIBYL: I shall never forget this moment. You are, indeed, a most pitiable spectacle.

GULLIVER (*With dignity*): I shall turn my face away if it distresses you, madam.

BELINDA: All of you is as repulsive as your face.

GULLIVER: I am as God made me and the hardships I have endured.—If you would graciously provide me with the means I could catch fish to [assuage] my hunger. I have been shipwrecked before and have sustained myself in many ways.

LADY SIBYL (*Musing*): At your age everything must be painful —exceedingly—breathing . . . and walking . . .

GULLIVER (*Loud*): Young woman, are you indeed deaf (*Pronounced "deef"*) or do you lack humanity? I am starving.

BELINDA: "Young woman!" You are talking to Lady Sibyl Ponsonby.

LADY SIBYL: Be quiet, Jenkins.—Old man, you will be given something to eat. There have been other old men on this island. They were given something to eat before they departed.

GULLIVER: I hope that will not be long.

LADY SIBYL: That will not be long.

GULLIVER: Did I understand you, madam, did I hear correctly: that you have never seen a man of forty-six before?

BELINDA: Forty-six! No one has ever seen anyone older than twenty-nine—except one that floated up from the sea, like yourself. There is no one on this island older than twenty-nine and there never will be.

GULLIVER: Merciful Heavens! What do you do with your older persons?

LADY SIBYL: I will now go and call someone to attend to your needs. You will not follow me! You will not leave this place. Today is a day of festival and it is of the highest importance that no one sees you—that is, as few as possible see you.— Jenkins, stay near him.

BELINDA: I, your ladyship!!

LADY SIBYL: Do not enter into conversation with him. (*Appraising him coldly*) I do not think he could progress far.

BELINDA (*Becoming hysterical*): Oh, your ladyship, your ladyship—do not leave me alone with him. I will become ill with the sight. (*She falls on her knees, clinging to Lady Sibyl*) I will become ill. I will become ill.

LADY SIBYL: Get up, Jenkins!—Very well, I will stay with this man. Go to the Duke of Cornwall. Draw him aside and speak to him in a low voice. Tell him that we have come upon this . . . foreigner. 'E will know what to do.

GULLIVER (*Gesturing as though bringing food to his mouth*): And tell him—

LADY SIBYL: Tell him the old man is hungry.—But, Jenkins, hold your tongue. Do not speak of it to anyone else.

BELINDA: To think that this should happen *today*—of all days! (*She sidles up toward Gulliver and examines him intently. Softly*) Think of all the years he has lived!

LADY SIBYL: Jenkins!

BELINDA (*Still scanning Gulliver; half answering*): Yes, milady.

LADY SIBYL: Jenkins! Do as I tell you!

BELINDA: Yes, milady; but I shall never see an old man again. I want to look at him . . . (*Lower*) . . . he is not as abominable as he was at first. One gets used to him, a little.—Old man, have you wives . . . and children?

LADY SIBYL: Belinda! I shall have you jailed!

BELINDA (*Turning to her, with spirit*): Your ladyship, with all due respect to your ladyship, your ladyship has been extremely severe with me for many weeks. I care not if I go to jail. As I was the first person to see this old man I ask to be permitted to have a few words with him.

LADY SIBYL: Two minutes, Belinda . . . No more.

Lady Sibyl turns her back on them and moves to the rear of the scene, striking her parasol on the floor.

GULLIVER: Yes, Mistress Jenkins, I have a wife Mary, a son John, and a daughter Betsy.

BELINDA (*Slowly, scarcely a question*): And are you very cruel to them?

GULLIVER: Madam?

BELINDA: *Old* men are cruel and nasty tempered. Everyone knows that.

Gulliver gazes deep into her eyes with a faint smile, slowly shaking his head. She continues, as if to herself.)

Your eyes are different from our eyes. Maybe some old men are a *little bit* kind.

Gulliver, as though in friendly complicity, rubs his stomach with one hand and conveys the other to his mouth.

Yes, I will hurry.—I am going, your ladyship.

LADY SIBYL: And remember, no blabbing. (*She looks toward the sun, almost directly overhead*) The games are about to begin. When you have delivered your message, take your place in silence.

BELINDA (*Curtsies*): Yes, your ladyship.

Belinda goes out. Lady Sibyl starts strolling about with great self-possession.

GULLIVER: Surely, I did not hear correctly—*no* older men?

LADY SIBYL: I have no wish to enter into conversation with you.

GULLIVER (*After a short pause, no longer able to contain himself*): By God's body, madam, you cannot be of stone! You are not a child! I have not hitherto been regarded as a contemptible being. I have been received by kings and queens and have been their guest at meat . . . I am Captain Lemuel Gulliver. I am not a dog.

LADY SIBYL: I have never seen a dog, but I think you must greatly resemble one.

GULLIVER: Madam, you have seen nothing but one small island. You are not in a position to say that you have seen anything. I am astonished that you have no questions to put to me about the world that surrounds you.

LADY SIBYL (*Lofty smile*): What questions would those be, Captain Gullibo?

GULLIVER: Madam, ignorance is a misery, but there is one still greater: a lack of any desire to increase one's knowledge.

LADY SIBYL: But I have learned much from you in this short time. You have come from that world out there (*She indi-*

cates it lightly with her parasol; her voice turns suddenly vindictive) and you have brought its poisons with you. Your visible infirmities are also marks of the country from which you came. They must be as painful for you to bear as for us to behold. However, you will not have to bear them much longer.

Gulliver gives up trying to understand her. He sinks down on the bench by the table. He is about to fall asleep.

Captain, it is not our custom for a commoner to be seated in the presence of the nobility. (*Gulliver, uncomprehending, raises his head*) I see; you are deaf (*Pronounced "deef"*). I said: it is not the custom for a commoner to be seated in the presence of the nobility.

GULLIVER (*Dragging himself to his feet; with ironic deference*): Oh . . . oh . . . your ladyship will forgive me . . . my fatigue . . . and my hunger.

Lady Sibyl puts her hand into her reticule and brings out some lozenges, which she places on the table.

LADY SIBYL: While you are waiting, here are some comfits which I have been keeping . . . for my children.
GULLIVER: For your children, Lady Sibyl?
LADY SIBYL: Our children on this island live in a village of their own. They are well tended. They are happy. That is our custom here.

In astonishment, Gulliver is about to ask a question. He corrects himself, and, bowing, says in a low voice:

GULLIVER: I thank your ladyship.

He puts two into his mouth ravenously; then takes one out for decorum's sake. A musical sound, like a rolling chord from many harps, is heard from the city. Gulliver listens in astonishment.

May I ask your ladyship the source of that music?
LADY SIBYL: You forget everything you are told. Today is a day of great festival. (*She looks at the sun*) It is beginning with the children's Morris Dance and—

GULLIVER: Oh, milady, I would greatly wish to see this festival—

LADY SIBYL (*Slight laugh, "how unthinkable"*): These will be followed by the Hoop Dance and the Dagger Dance. The Duke of Cornwall—who will be here in a moment—is the greatest victor in the Hoop Dance that has ever been known. He has won eight garlands. Moreover, he is the only man who has ever kept a kite in the air for an entire day.

GULLIVER: Ah!! He must indeed be remarkable! . . . An entire day! . . . I trust that the duke is of mature years?

LADY SIBYL (*Sharply*): I did not hear you correctly. (*Gulliver does not repeat the question*) He is naturally of mature years. He is our governor. He is twenty-eight (*Pronounced "ite"*).

GULLIVER (*Stares at her; then with dawning horror*): Great Heavens, girl! What do you do with your older persons?

LADY SIBYL: Captain Gullibo, there is no profit in pursuing a conversation on matters you are not capable of understanding.

GULLIVER (*Shouting*): You kill them. You murder them when they reach the age of twenty-nine?

LADY SIBYL: How dare you address me in that manner?—Vulgar brutish Englander! Barbarian! How could you understand customs that are based on wisdom and reason.

GULLIVER: I dread to hear them! (*Louder*) Are you able to answer me: what do you do to those who reach the age of twenty-nine?

LADY SIBYL (*Slowly; with serene assurance*): We drink the wine. We sleep. We are placed in a boat. The current carries us away.

GULLIVER: Thunder! This is hellish!

LADY SIBYL (*Putting a hand delicately on her ear*): Restrine your senile violence, Captain Gullibo.

GULLIVER: And *you*, your ladyship—are you going to drink that wine and go to sleep in that boat?

LADY SIBYL: When I am old—readily, gladly. I have four years to live. That is a very long time.

GULLIVER: And no one ever rebels? No one twenty-nine years old ever wishes to live longer?

LADY SIBYL: Captain Gullibo, you prate. You rive. You forget that you are old—very old. What I have told you is the custom of this island! Do you understand the word "custom"? . . . Would any of us *wish* to be . . .

GULLIVER (*Hand to head*): Your ladyship must permit me to sit down. (*He does*)

LADY SIBYL (*Strolling about and fanning herself*): It is understandable that the duke is occupied today. (*Severely*) Your arrival is most inopportune.

GULLIVER: The matter was beyond my control, Lady Sibyl. Little did I know that I was arriving on this happy island on the great day of the Hoop Dance. On future occasions I shall arrange it with greater propriety.

LADY SIBYL (*Looks at him and raises her eyebrows*): Future occasions, Captain Gullibo? At your age, Captain, you cannot speak with certainty of future occasions.

GULLIVER (*Returning her glance; in a low voice*): Lady Sibyl, I am thinking of your children. You will never know the joys of seeing them grow into young manhood and womanhood. You will never hold grandchildren on your knees.

LADY SIBYL: You are tedious, Captain Gullibo. I have read of those things in books.

GULLIVER: Ah, madam.—You have books, I see.

LADY SIBYL: We have one hundred and twenty-seven books, Captain.

GULLIVER (*Lowers his head in admiration; after a pause, suddenly humble and earnest*): Lady Sibyl, let me throw myself upon your mercy. You are a woman, and women in all times have tempered this rough world with mercy and compassion. I have arrived a stranger and an interloper here; I do not wish to intrude upon this happy existence. I can see that you have much influence on this island; graciously exert it on my behalf. I saw that there were boats drawn up along the shore. I am a seaman of experience. When I have been given some food to stay my hunger, be my advocate with this Duke of Cornwall—

LADY SIBYL (*Purest amazement*): Where would you go?

GULLIVER (*Pointing*): . . . That island or continent . . . those mountains . . .

LADY SIBYL (*Harshly*): I have nothing to do with such matters. Those fishing boats and their sails are fixed to the shore.

They are locked with thongs that only a few nobles can undo.—You forget that you are old—very old. Your life is over. Anyone can see that. (*She turns away*)

GULLIVER: I have a wife and children.—You said you have children?

LADY SIBYL: Naturally I have children.

GULLIVER: Look in your heart. Enable me to—

LADY SIBYL: Be silent!

GULLIVER (*Sinking onto the bench; to himself in despair*): Yes . . . yes . . . Humanity is the last thing that will be learned by man. (*He puts his head on his arms and is about to fall asleep*)

LADY SIBYL (*Walking up and down, loftily*): You may be certain that nothing will be done here that is not for the wisest and the best. We are enlightened here; and we are Christians. That strain of music you heard came from Westminster Abbey. The Archbishop of Canterbury is addressing the contestants in the games. If you were a *young* man we would be proud to show you how happy our existence is, and how perfect our institutions. This perfection is rendered possible by the fact that here we have no—

Gulliver has fallen asleep.

GULLIVER (*Mumbling*): . . . steep . . . the steep streets . . . Redriff, home! . . . Mary-Polly! . . . Polly, forgive me . . .

He falls silent. Lady Sibyl gazes at him for a moment with repugnance, then draws nearer and scans his face intently —a long gaze. When he stirs and seems about to wake, she moves away and, opening her parasol, strolls off the stage.

In deep stupor Gulliver slips off the bench and rolls under the table.

Lady Sibyl returns hurriedly; there is a suggestion of walking backward as though royalty were approaching. Enter the Duke of Cornwall, twenty-eight, very splendid in festival dress. To the early eighteenth-century costume have been added feathers and colored shells, etc. He is followed by Simpson, twenty, a commoner, carrying a tray of food. The Duke gazes fixedly at Gulliver.

LADY SIBYL: He has fallen into a swound, your grace.

DUKE: Simpson—throw some water on his face.

> *Simpson scoops some water from the mirror pool and throws it on Gulliver's face. Gulliver recovers consciousness, stirs and cumbrously extricates himself from under the table. Finally, he grasps the situation and, standing erect, confronts the Duke, eye to eye.*

Who are you?

GULLIVER: Lemuel Gulliver, your grace, captain of the fourmaster *Arcturus*, Port of London.

DUKE: How old are you?

GULLIVER: I am in my middle years; I am forty-six.

DUKE: They tell me you have been three days without food—Simpson, place the food on the table. Eat!

GULLIVER: I thank your grace. Commoners do not sit in the presence of the nobility. I shall eat when you have left to take part in the festival.

> *Pause.*

Sir, I have visited many countries and have been shipwrecked on the shores of several. In all of them, save one, I have been treated with courtesy as a citizen of England and a subject of our gracious sovereign, Queen Anne. I am indebted to you for this relief from my hunger. I trust that hereafter I may see your cities and learn of your customs. In return I shall gladly tell you of other parts of the world that I have visited; and above all of the country whose language you speak and from which your ancestors came.

DUKE (*Again a short contemptuous pause; then with a curt gesture of the hand*): You are tedious, old man.—Simpson!

SIMPSON: Yes, your grace?

DUKE: Withdraw to a distance. It is not suitable that a commoner hear this nonsense. I shall call you when it is time for you to stand watch over the captain.

> *Simpson bows and goes out. Gulliver begins to laugh to himself and, turning away, sits down.*

LADY SIBYL (*Revolted*): He is laughing!!

GULLIVER: To be young, and yet ask no questions about the country from which your ancestors came! To be young, and yet have no curiosity concerning the shore that lies upon the horizon! To be young, and yet—oh, ye immortal Gods!—to be without adventure of mind or generosity of spirit! Now it is clear to me why you so gladly bring your lives to a close at the age of twenty-nine—*gladly* was Lady Sibyl's word.

DUKE (*Bitingly*): That should not be difficult for you to understand—you, with this decay of mind and body—

GULLIVER (*Interrupting*): No! No, it is not the advance of age that frightens you on this island. (*With a sardonic smile*) A greater enemy threatens you. (*Abruptly changing the subject*) I do not wish to detain your grace from the festival and from your trophies.

DUKE: Come, Lady Sibyl.

GULLIVER: Permit me, however, one question. (*The Duke nods*) What is the name of this island and this country?

DUKE: Name? Why should it have a name?

GULLIVER: I have visited twenty countries. Each has borne a name in which it takes pride.

DUKE: Proud? All of them were proud?

GULLIVER: They were. They are.

DUKE: Among those twenty countries was there *one* that was not governed by old men—governed, misgoverned, burdened, oppressed by old men? By the pride and avarice, and the lust for power of old men? One which did not constantly war at the instigation of old men like *yourself*, to enlarge its boundaries; to enslave others; to enrich itself? We know of the War of the Roses. Or by the religious bigotry of old men—we know of the Saint Bartholomew Massacre, [the] murder of Charles, king and martyr. And when these prides of yours have obtained their lands, whose bodies are those lying upon the field of battle?—They are the bodies of men under thirty. We need no name to distinguish this country from others. Say that you are in the Country of the Young.

GULLIVER: So be it!—Since you do not wish me to encumber you longer, I request some boat with which I may rid you of my presence. (*In amazement*) How did you come here? Who brought you here?

DUKE: God!

GULLIVER: God! —Where did you acquire this distrust and hatred of the old?

DUKE: We have no boats for that purpose.

GULLIVER: The smallest would serve me.

DUKE: No boat of ours has ever made that journey and never will.

GULLIVER: Perhaps your grace will let me purchase a boat. This ring was given to me by the King of Laputa. It is of pure alchemist's gold.

DUKE: You have been here a few hours. Lady Sibyl has told me that already you have offered us insult and have spoken of our customs with contempt; and now you wish to introduce barter and trafficking, and gold!—gold, which is above all the instrument by which old men keep the younger in subjection. There is no gold and no trading here. You shall never leave this island and you shall not long envenom it. We shall make you a present for which we ask no return. We shall give you the only happiness that still lies open to you.

GULLIVER: Duke of Cornwall—Duke of Palm Trees and Sand! I wish you a happy twenty-ninth birthday. I can understand that you will gladly drink the wine and welcome the long sleep. Twenty-nine years of jumping through hoops and flying kites will have been enough. Already you are advancing toward a decay worse than age—yes, toward boredom, infinite boredom. Youth left to itself is a cork upon the waves. As we say of the young: they do not know what to do with themselves. It is only under the severity—the well-wishing severity—of your elders that you can shake from yourselves the misery of your aimless state. You elect yourselves into societies and call yourselves dukes and earls; did I hear correctly that each man on this island has several wives? You play games. What more can you ask of a thirtieth birthday than a deep slumber!

LADY SIBYL (*Ablaze*): Your grace! How can you let him speak to you so?!

DUKE: (*With a smile*): But this is what we knew; foul and embittered age! Envy and jealousy! Despising those things of which he is no longer capable. (*Whimsically to Lady Sibyl*) Perhaps we should take this man and exhibit him for all to see.

LADY SIBYL (*Covering her face*): Your grace!

GULLIVER: Yes, and for all to hear, your grace.

DUKE: And to hear.—What would you say to them?

GULLIVER: Why, I should tell them that if a man is not civilized between the ages of twelve and twenty—civilized by his elders—he will never be civilized at all.

Lady Sibyl covers her ears.

And oh, it is not an easy task. To educate young men is like rolling boulders up to the tops of mountains; the whole community is engaged in the work and with what doubtful success! For every *one* Isaac Newton or Christopher Wren there are thousands who roll to the bottom of the mountain and occupy themselves with jumping through hoops.

He sways from weakness, his hand to his head and heart.

Go to your dances and garlands. I can see that your happiness has begun to stale already. You are weary of life. Old age has marked you already.

DUKE (*With supreme complaisance*): Oh, I'm young enough! (*He calls*) Mr. Simpson! Mr. Simpson!!

The sound of music has been rising from the distance. Enter Simpson.

SIMPSON: Yes, your grace?

DUKE: Simpson, you are in charge of this man. See that he does not leave this clearing. Do not enter into conversation with him. It would suffocate you. Later I shall send someone to replace you—Lady Sibyl!

Lady Sibyl's hand has gone to her forehead; her parasol and reticule fall. She is about to faint.

LADY SIBYL: Oh, your grace . . . this sight . . . has sickened me.

DUKE (*Cold fury*): Take command of yourself!

With a gesture he orders Simpson to pick up the fallen objects. Simpson does so and holds them ready for Lady Sibyl.

LADY SIBYL (*Swaying; with closed eyes*): I must breathe a moment.

DUKE: Fool! (*He strikes her sharply on both cheeks*) Go to the city!

GULLIVER (*Taking two steps forward*): You strike her!! You *strike* her!

DUKE: We permit no weakness here—neither ours nor *yours.*

GULLIVER (*Turns and seats himself on the bench by the table*): Humanity is the last thing that will be learned by man; it will not be learned from the young.

> *Lady Sibyl has taken her parasol and reticule. She collects her dignity, but is scarcely able to leave the stage.*

DUKE: Simpson!

SIMPSON: Your grice!

DUKE: If you fail at any point in your guard over this man, you will be put to the press—and you know what press I mean. And you will be removed from your hoffice as builder and constructor. (*He looks appraisingly at Gulliver*) If he tries to leave the clearing, kick him strongly at the shinbones.

> *He goes out. Simpson takes his stand at a distance from Gulliver whom he watches intently. Gulliver returns to his meal, but seems to have lost his appetite. Again there is a sound of music from the city. Gulliver rises and listens.*

GULLIVER: Is there no way, Mr. Simpson, that I may view the games from a distance? (*Simpson shakes his head*) I am sorry. (*He eats a little*) They must be a wonderful sight . . . wonderful. Hoops and kites. (*Pause*) You strike women . . . is that often, Mr. Simpson? . . . Do you strike women frequently, Mr. Simpson? (*No reply*) . . . You are very proud of your civilization . . . when you are angry you *strike* and you *torture* . . .

> *Simpson mutters something.*

I did not hear what you said, Mr. Simpson.

SIMPSON: He is old. Strikes and tortures because 'e is old. 'E will die next year.

GULLIVER: He will be killed next year. That is not quite the same thing as merely dying. He will be killed. No wonder he is excitable, Mr. Simpson. In the normal way of life we grow of a more mild and kindly disposition with the years. (*He eats*) So you are a builder and constructor, Mr. Simpson. You are an architect. Lady Sibyl spoke of a Westminster

Abbey. I would like to see it. Did you build this Westminster Abbey, sir? (*No answer*) You have great storms in this part of the world—far greater than London has. You must build very—solidly. Have you rock here? (*Simpson points off. Gulliver rises and peers in the direction*) Coral limestone, I presume. Not easy. Arches and a vaulted roof. Ah, you should see the dome of St. Paul's. There's a sight, Mr. Simpson . . . (*He eats*) I am glad that you feel no disposition to talk, sir. I was afraid that you might ask me questions about the life led by young men like yourself in my country. (*Pause*) It would fill me with shame to describe it to you. (*He lowers his voice as though imparting a discreditable secret*) Imagine it! You would be working all the time to acquire more knowledge: from morning to night—and at night by lamplight. Think: to be a better doctor, to govern the people more wisely, *to be a better builder*, Mr. Simpson. Go down on your knees, sir, and thank your Maker that you live on this happy island where learning never penetrates, where young men are not encouraged by old men to extend their knowledge and their skill.

SIMPSON (*Loudly*): The old men drive them like slaves; the old men take the credit and the profit.

GULLIVER: The young men succeed them. They are not killed at twenty-nine. They become master builders themselves and may decide whether they will be just or unjust. However, I do not wish to talk about it. I reproach myself that I am preventing you from taking part in the games.

SIMPSON: Commoners do not take part in the games.

GULLIVER: Ah! (*He eats*)

Simpson gazes at him, brooding.

SIMPSON: I'm a builder.

GULLIVER (*Looking up at the summerhouse*): Ah!—you made this?

SIMPSON: Aye—and the new Westminster Abbey.

GULLIVER: Westminster Abbey! Then you are the chief builder.

SIMPSON: The chief builder is an earl. He has no time to build.

GULLIVER: The new Abbey is of stone—of sandstone or coral?

SIMPSON: The pillars at the corners are.

GULLIVER: And the roof? (*Simpson shakes his head. Gulliver points to the thatch*) Of thatch?—of palm boughs?

Simpson nods.

But, man, you have severe storms here. Ah! (*He looks up*) Mr. Simpson, the storm that cast me on your shores has damaged this charming . . . shelter, this pagoda. Was your Westminster Abbey able to sustain the fury of that wind and rain? (*Simpson stares straight before him*) You will not answer me, man! Your Abbey seats—what?—four hundred. Of what is your roof? Of palm fronds? (*Simpson, without moving his eyes, nods*) I see! When storm destroys your Westminster Abbey you build another. I see! I see! You don't know how to make an arch or a buttress. Oh, Mr. Simpson, do not ask me the secrets of the arch, the buttress and the dome. You are happy. Remain happy. Do not let us think of all the labor that went into those discoveries.

SIMPSON (*Taking steps toward Gulliver; in a low voice*): Sir . . . Mr. Captain . . . (*His hands describe an arch*) Do you know how to pile stone . . . so they will not fall?

GULLIVER: Believe me. Mr. Simpson, I did not arrive in this paradise in order to poison it with thoughts of progress and industry.

SIMPSON: But you *do* know?

GULLIVER: Perhaps in a hundred years some unhappy youth will be born with talent—with genius. *He* will light upon the laws of the arch. He will prove that youth stands in no need of its elders, no need of the accumulated wisdom of its ancestors. *He will make a roof* . . . Bring your ear nearer, young man: the dome of St. Paul's . . . (*His hand describes a high dome*)

SIMPSON: How high is it?

GULLIVER: How high? Sixty men standing on one another's shoulders could not touch the top of it.

SIMPSON (*Back three yards*): You are lying! All old men lie. Eat your food. Go to sleep. I ask you a question and you give me a lie. (*Simpson has raised his head*)

GULLIVER: What I said is true, but your rebuke is justified. There is no greater unkindness than to arouse ambition in a young man.—But *you* are to blame. You asked me a question. (*With assumed indignation*) A few more questions like that and you'll be proposing that we take a *boat* and cross to that shore. No I'll not go, I tell you.

SIMPSON (*Sullenly*): The boats are tied and we cannot untie them.

GULLIVER: Yes, those thongs the nobles keep . . . (*His eyes are looking off speculatively*)

SIMPSON: They're twisted and untwisted with hooks of iron.

GULLIVER: Iron?

SIMPSON: Aye, they're the only pieces of metal on the island. The nobles keep them.

GULLIVER: Very wise! Some fool might think of journeying out there . . . for knowledge and science.—Understand, young man, I'll not leave this island. Give me this day here; then bring the wine and the long sleep. Why should a man trouble his head raising domes? Fly kites, jump through hoops, beget children and sleep.

SIMPSON (*After a pause, grumbling unintelligibly*): These things you call secrets . . .

GULLIVER: I cannot understand you, sir.

SIMPSON: These things you call the secrets of the arch and the . . . batless—old men keep these secrets to themselves, that's certain.

GULLIVER (*Sternly*): Cease, Mr. Simpson, to talk of things you know nothing about.

SIMPSON: How would a young man learn them?

GULLIVER: You are asking dangerous questions, Mr. Simpson. —Let me bid you again to go down on your knees and thank your Maker that you do not live in a country where older men would urge you and struggle with you and encourage you to enrich yourself with all learning and skill.

SIMPSON: I don't believe you.

GULLIVER:—A young man would learn them by crossing that water and finding his way into a world that does not spend all its time in games and dances.

SIMPSON (*Mumbles*): I do not believe you. (*Suddenly loud*) All old men are wicked.

GULLIVER (*Simply*): I am the only old man you have ever seen.

SIMPSON (*Approaching Gulliver, the beginning of violence*): Then tell me—

GULLIVER: What?

SIMPSON: The secrets: the arch and the batless.

GULLIVER (*Backing away*): I do not know them.

SIMPSON (*Seizing Gulliver's throat*): Tell me them! Wicked old man, tell me them!

GULLIVER (*Forced to his knees*): I am not a builder. I am a doctor and a seaman.

SIMPSON (*As they struggle*): I will not let you go before you tell me—

Gulliver faints. Pause. Simpson leans over him and calls:

Old man! Old man!

Enter Belinda carrying a tray and more fruit. She starts back in consternation.

BELINDA (*Whispering*): Is he dead? . . . Have *you* killed him?

SIMPSON (*Sullenly*): No . . . he has died of his old age.

Belinda puts her ear to Gulliver's mouth.

BELINDA: I think he is still breathing. It is a swound.

Both are on their knees gazing at Gulliver.

Now I do not think he is ugly at all. I think he is a friend.

SIMPSON (*Moves away in inner turmoil*): I do not understand a word he says. He should not have come here.

BELINDA (*As before*): What a strange thing wrinkles are. (*Unconsciously she strokes her face . . . softly*) I could ask him questions all day.—Mr. Simpson, let him go back to his own people.

SIMPSON (*Harshly*): How could he do that?

Belinda slowly draws from her apron pocket a hook of iron. Simpson draws back in horror.

BELINDA (*Lowering her voice*): This is the hook that was lost last year. It was on Lady Sibyl's dressing table. I think she put it there for me to find it. I think she has hidden it to spite the Duke of Cornwall. (*She holds it out toward Simpson*) Unlock the boat and let the man go.

SIMPSON: No!

BELINDA (*Gazes at Gulliver. Pause. Low, with energy*): Go with him! . . . He is not strong enough to sail the boat alone. Go.

SIMPSON: Do not speak to me! No, I will not go . . . among other men . . . I do not know anything. *He* does not know that we commoners cannot read. Every—*over there*—would see that I am a booby.

BELINDA: Mr. Simpson! Look at him. Come close and look at him! He would be your friend . . . I think *some* old people are good.

SIMPSON: No, I will not go.

BELINDA: He is waking up. Go away and think; but take the hook.

Simpson takes the hook and goes off.

GULLIVER (*Opens his eyes. Pause. Sees Belinda*): Oh! You are here . . . Where is the young man?

BELINDA: He is nearby . . . Will you tell me your name again?

GULLIVER: Captain Gulliver.

BELINDA: Captain Gulliver. If you came to your home again what would you do first?

GULLIVER: Mistress Jenkins, I would go up the steep street—you have never seen a steep street!—I think it would be at sunset . . . I would knock at the door . . . My wife or one of my children would come to the door . . . (*Pause*) . . . Soon we would sit down at the table, and give thanks to God . . . and eat . . .

BELINDA (*Laughing, scandalized*): Captain Gulliver, you would sit down with your wife!!

GULLIVER: Do not husband and wives—

BELINDA: No—!! (*She laughs*) Sit down! No man has ever eaten with a woman—! The men eat all by themselves. The nobles in one place. The commoners in another. And the boys when they are six by themselves.

GULLIVER: And if I lived on this happy island, when would I see my daughter? (*She does not answer*) You remember your father?

BELINDA: Yes.

GULLIVER: You saw him often? You loved him?

BELINDA: But . . . men live . . . *over there* . . .

GULLIVER: The childhood of the race . . . You have slipped five—ten thousand years . . .

Simpson has returned, and half hidden, is listening.

In a thousand years, Mistress Jenkins, gradually on this island things will change. A man will have one wife and only one wife. I think when your father died at twenty-nine he was just beginning to understand (*Gulliver points to his fore-head*) what the joys of being *your* father could be—but it was too late. (*Gulliver clasps Belinda by her shoulders, sadly*) You all die here just before a new world of mind and heart is open to you.

[*The music and sounds of celebration have increased, as if approaching. Simpson breaks from his hiding place and rushes to Gulliver with the iron hook. Simpson pulls at Gulliver's arm and points toward the sea. Gulliver grasps the situation immediately, starts to go with Simpson, but looks back at Belinda. She remains motionless, staring straight ahead, and does not meet his glance. Simpson drags Gulliver off.*

Music is louder. Belinda gazes front; intense, conflicted. Pause.

Simpson reappears running. He takes both of Belinda's hands in his. They look at each other. A decision passes between them. Belinda casts one glance back over her shoulder at all she has ever known; and they run off to join Gulliver.

Music increases.

Two Boy Guards, fifteen, rush in with ropes to bind Gulliver for his ceremonial death. The Duke enters behind. They look about, see that Gulliver, Simpson and Belinda are gone. The Duke is the first to realize the implication of this absence. He stands upstage center as the Guards roughly search everywhere. Convinced that the man they were after has escaped, they turn to the Duke.

Music takes on a wild, threatening sound.

The Duke has been gazing out toward a horizon, perhaps seeing the boat moving off, perhaps contemplating his own soon wasted mortality. The Boy Guards gaze intently at him as the lights fade.]

END OF PLAY

The Rivers Under the Earth

(? Middle Age)

CHARACTERS

MRS. CARTER, mother, thirty-eight
TOM, her son, sixteen
FRANCESCA, her daughter, seventeen
MR. CARTER, their father, forty-three

SETTING

A few years ago. A point of land near a lake in southern Wisconsin.

At both sides of the stage are boxes of various sizes, but none very large—orange boxes, canned goods boxes, covered with burlap or bits of rug. These are rocks. The action of this play takes place in the dark, but I wish it to be played in bright light. Mrs. Carter, very attractive and looking less than her thirty-eight years, enters tentatively feeling her way in the dark. She is followed by her son, Tom, sixteen.

MRS. CARTER: Take my hand, Tom. I don't know where you children inherited your ability to see in the dark.

Tom passes her and starts slowly leading her forward.

TOM: It isn't dark at all. All these stars reflected in the lake.—There's a sort of path here, Mother. The rocks are at the side of it.

MRS. CARTER (*Stopping*): Fireflies. All those fireflies. (*Pause*) I don't know why it is that when I see fireflies I think of *horses*—no, of an old horse named Billy that we used to have when we were children.

TOM: Fireflies—and a horse!!

MRS. CARTER (*Still standing and smiling*): There are many associations like that one can't explain.—Why does your father

636

dislike the color green? Why do I always make a mistake when I add a six and a seven? Why have I an ever so faint tiny prejudice against people whose name begins with B— Blodgetts and Burnses and Binghams and even dear old Mrs. Becket.

Tom leads her a step forward.

TOM: I haven't got any quirks like that.

MRS. CARTER (*Stopping again*): Why have we never been able to make you eat rice?

TOM: Ugh!—I just don't like it!

MRS. CARTER: Why does your sister hate to sit in the backseat of automobiles?

TOM: Oh, Francesca's crazy, anyway.

MRS. CARTER: Oh, no she isn't. She's the most reasonable and logical of us all.

TOM: Why does Francesca hate to come here?

MRS. CARTER: What?

TOM: She hates to come out on this point of land. She told me once—but then she was sorry she told me. She told me that every now and then she dreamed that she was on this point of land, and that when she dreamed it, it was a nightmare and she woke up crying or screaming or something.

MRS. CARTER (*Thoughtful*): You mustn't tease her about it. Promise me you won't tease her about it.

TOM: All right.

MRS. CARTER: Now take my elbow and lead me to a rock that I can remember at the very tip of the point. (*As they progress*) No—all those quirks, as you call them, are like wrecks at the bottom of the sea. They mark the place where there was once a naval battle—or a storm. Why did my dear father always become angry whenever anybody mentioned . . .

—Thank you, Tom. Here it is! I used to come and sit here when I was a girl. There aren't any snakes are there?

TOM (*Competent*): One: snakes don't like this kind of pine needles; two: snakes in America don't come out at night.

MRS. CARTER: You're such a pleasure, Tom; you know everything. What I mean is: you know everything comforting.— Now you go back and do whatever it is you were doing.

Tom stands irresolute in the middle of the stage, looking up.

TOM: When do you want me to come and lead you back?

MRS. CARTER: Forget me, Tom. I can find my way back now.

Girl's voice off: "T-o-o-m! . . . Tom C-a-a-arter."

TOM (*Warningly, to his mother*): Hsh!

The voice, passing in the distance: "T-o-o-m!"

TOM: Polly Springer's always wanting something. Golly, those girls are helpless. They can't even stick a marshmallow on a fork . . . The moon will rise over *there* . . . You came to this very place?

MRS. CARTER: In those days we knew everyone in all the houses around the lake. Many times I'd come and spend the night with the Wilsons . . . or the Kimballs. (*She indicates first the right, then the left*) And I'd slip away from them, and come here; and think . . . We were told that this point had been some sort of Indian ceremonial campground . . . and a burial place, I suppose. Your father used to find arrowheads here.

TOM: What did you used to think about?

MRS. CARTER: Oh, what do young girls think about? . . . I remember once . . . I made a vow: never to marry. Yes. I was going to be a doctor. And at the same time I was going to be a singer. But I wasn't going to sing in concerts . . . for money. I was going to sing to my patients in the wards just before they turned out the lights for the night. That's the kind of thing young girls think about.

Tom has been taking this in very gravely, his eyes on the distance. He says abruptly:

TOM: But you *did* get married. And you almost never sing anymore.—I brought your guitar.

MRS. CARTER: What!?

TOM: Yes. I knew they'd ask you to sing later—around the bonfire.

MRS. CARTER: Why, Tom, you little devil. They would never have thought of it. Now don't you go putting the idea into their heads.

TOM: I didn't. I heard them talking about it. I canoed back across the lake and got your guitar . . . You don't *hate* to sing.

MRS. CARTER: Oh, I'll sing, if anybody asks me to. It's not important enough to make any discussion about.

Silence. Tom lies down in the path facing the sky, his head on his folded arms.

TOM: Right up there . . . in the Milky Way . . . There's something called a Coal Hole.

MRS. CARTER: What?

TOM: A Coal Hole. It's sort of a deep empty stocking. If Father gave me a Jaguar; and I started driving five thousand miles a minute—*starting* from up there—it'd take me hundreds of millions of years to get halfway through it.—Lake water has a completely different sound of slapping—or lapping—than water at the seashore, hasn't it? I like it best.

He shuts his eyes. Girls' voices, giggling and talking excitedly, are heard near the entrance. Tom sits up energetically and calls:

TOM: Mildred! Constance!—Is that you, Constance?

VOICE: Ye-e-s!

TOM: Get me a hamburger! Be a sweetie!

VOICE (*Sweetly*): Get it yourself, deeeer bo-oo-y.

TOM (*Lying down again; darkly*): The slaves are getting uppish at the end of the summer.

MRS. CARTER: Would these be the same trees that were here twenty years ago?

TOM: Yes. Red pines grow fast the first five years, then they settle down and grow about a foot a year. (*He turns to lie on his stomach, leaning on his elbow. He explains simply and casually*) This is really a sand dune here. Until recently there was a great big lake over all this area. When the lake shrunk, there were these dunes. Ordinarily, it takes about five thousand years for the first grasses to get their roots in and to make enough humus for small bushes to grow. Then it takes about 10,000 years for the bushes to make enough humus for the white pines. Then come the red pines. Probably it was faster here because of these rocks. They prevented the top sand from being blown away every few days. That's why the trees are so much bigger here, and over at the Cavanaughs, and around the boat club . . . Rocks.

FRANCESCA'S VOICE (*Off*): Mo-o-ther!

MRS. CARTER: Yes, dear, here I am.

Enter Francesca, seventeen, with a scarf.

FRANCESCA: Father said you'd probably be here.

TOM (*Rolling to one side*): Don't step on me, you galoot!

FRANCESCA: Oh, *you're* here.—Goodness, a regular jungle.— Father said you're to put this shawl on. He's bringing a blanket.

MRS. CARTER: I'm too warm as it is. Well, give it to me. Thank you, dear.

FRANCESCA: What are you *doing* out here?

TOM (*Bitingly*): We're talking about you. (*Imitating a teacher*) "I was just saying to Mrs. Carter: I don't know what's to become of Francesca. In all my ninety years of teaching I've never known such a problem child."

FRANCESCA (*Airily; leaving*): Tz-tz-tz.

TOM (*Urgently*): Be a sweet little flower box and get me a hamburger.

FRANCESCA: Mother, don't you let Tom have another. Everybody's laughing at him. James Wilson says he had eight.—If you want to make a howling pig of yourself, you can just get up and fetch your own. (*Leaning over him maliciously*) Of course, I don't know what Miss What's-Her-Name will think of you—gorging yourself like that.—Mother, Tom has been making a perfect fool of himself over a new girl—a cousin of the Richardsons. Anybody can see she's a perfect nothing, but there's Tom: "Violet, you didn't get any peach ice cream. Violet . . ."

TOM (*Covering her speech*): Quack-quack-quack. Honk-honk-honk.

FRANCESCA: Violet this and Violet that. (*Louder*) He even started a fight over her.

TOM (*Rising and starting off*): Quack-quack-quack! I'll be back. Honk-honk-honk.

[*Tom leaves.*]

MRS. CARTER: When you're by yourself, Francesca, you're of course much older than Tom. But when you're *with* Tom, you're younger—and *much* younger. I wish someone could explain that to me.

FRANCESCA Well, as far as I'm concerned, he's been an eight-year-old for years. And always will be.

MRS. CARTER: To get to know the best of Tom, you must learn to (*She puts her hand on her lips*) hold your tongue. It's always a pleasure to be silent with Tom. You try it someday.

FRANCESCA: Why should I hold my tongue with him?

MRS. CARTER: Have you noticed how your father holds his tongue with you?

FRANCESCA: I don't talk *all the time* when I'm with Father.

MRS. CARTER: No. But when you do, you talk so *well.*

FRANCESCA (*Softened; with wonder*): Do I? (*Kneeling before her mother*) Do I, really?

MRS. CARTER: I shouldn't have to tell you that.

FRANCESCA: Thank you.

   Enter Mr. Carter, forty-three, lawyer, with a blanket.

MR. CARTER: Mary?

MRS. CARTER: Here I am, Fred.

MR. CARTER: Try this rock. It's drier. (*He puts the blanket on a rock*) Can you see?

MRS. CARTER (*Crossing*): Yes.—What's this about a fight Tom had?

FRANCESCA: He's in a terrible mood tonight. First, that fight with the MacDougal boy—I wasn't there. Just some craziness or other.

MRS. CARTER: Do you know anything about it, Fred?

MR. CARTER: Yes. I'll tell you about it later.

FRANCESCA: But that's not really what upset him. A very funny thing happened. Before supper we were all lying around the dock and somebody said that you were going to sing tonight at the bonfire. And that boy from Milwaukee said: "Mrs. Carter sing! *She's too old!*" (*Francesca thinks this is very funny. Gales of laughter*) He'd mixed you up with Mrs. Cavanaugh!! And Paul or Herb said: "She isn't *old*. She isn't any older than . . ." their own mothers. And the boy from Milwaukee said: "Sure, she's old. She's nice and all that, but

she oughtn't to be allowed to sing." He thought Mrs. Cavanaugh was *you*!! (*More laughter*) But you should have seen
Tom's face!

MRS. CARTER: What?

FRANCESCA: Tom's face. You'd have thought he was seeing a
ghost. And the boy from Milwaukee said: "Why, she's got
all those gray hairs." (*Gales of laughter*) You remember how
at breakfast a few days ago you said you'd found some more
gray hairs?

MRS. CARTER: Yes.

FRANCESCA: And Tom was *believing* all this was about you.
Well, I thought he'd either . . . jump on the boy and kill
him, or go away and . . . maybe throw up.

MR. CARTER: What did he do?

MRS. CARTER: He canoed back across the lake to get my guitar.

MR. CARTER: Francesca, I want to talk to your mother alone a
moment.

FRANCESCA (*Touch of pique*): All right . . . but kindly don't
. . . mention . . . me.

She goes out; very queenly. Pause.

MR. CARTER: Well, what do you think about that? . . . I suppose in the code, a boy can't strike another boy for calling
his mother an old woman . . . Tom learns about old age.

MRS. CARTER: What was this other story about a fight?

MR. CARTER: Very odd. Very odd. Tom is not a bulldog type.
There's a new girl here—a cousin of the Richardsons. I don't
know her name.

MRS. CARTER: Violet.

MR. CARTER: Yes, Violet Richardson. It looks as though Tom
had taken a sudden fancy to her. She doesn't seem interesting to me—neither pretty nor individual. Anyway, he was
sitting beside her—and the MacDougal boy—the bigger
one—Ben—came up and began pulling at her arm . . . to
get her to go over where some of them were dancing. Suddenly Tom got up in an awful rage. Told him to let her
alone. She was talking to him. Not to stick his nose in where
he wasn't wanted. It all flared up in a second: two furious
roosters; two stags fighting over a doe. The MacDougal boy

backed down. I think he went home. It was all over in a second, too—but it was *real* . . . it was very real and hot.

Slight pause.

MRS. CARTER: And I thought this was going to be just one more dull picnic!

Mr. Carter lights a pipe and goes to sit on the rock where his wife had been sitting.

Fred, Tom just told me that Francesca hated to come *here*— that she had bad dreams about it? Did you ever know that?

MR. CARTER: What?—Here, this point of land!

MRS. CARTER: Can you think of any reason for it?

MR. CARTER: No!

MRS. CARTER: I'll give you a hint: a robin redbreast.

MR. CARTER: What are you getting at?

MRS. CARTER: A dead robin? . . . The children were about six and seven. We had told them there had been an Indian graveyard here. They had found a dead robin in the woods, and they set out to bury it . . . I came on: such solemn hymn singing and preaching and praying . . . That night Francesca was deathly ill—

MR. CARTER: Do I remember!! It was one of the most shattering experiences in my life!!

MRS. CARTER: Dr. Macintosh kept asking us what she had eaten, and I—stupidly, stupidly—failed to connect convulsions and hysterics with the burial of Robin Red Breast. Francesca had learned about death . . . You sat soothing her and reading aloud to her until the sun rose.

MR. CARTER: And ever since she dislikes the color red.

MRS. CARTER: And the same experience had no effect on Tom, whatever. Yet we always think of Tom as the sensitive one and Francesca as the sensible one.

MR. CARTER: I guess, growing up is one long walk among perils—among yawning abysses . . .

Silence.

Well, since you're talking about old times—I'm going to interrogate you. We've just heard that Tom had a fight. A fight over a girl named Violet. Does the name Violet bring back anything to you?

MRS. CARTER: No . . . No, why?

MR. CARTER: The color?

MRS. CARTER: No.

MR. CARTER: Think a minute.

She shakes her head.

A dress you wore?

MRS. CARTER: Fred, you wouldn't remember that! Your sister brought me back from Italy that beautiful silk. I had a dress made from it.

MR. CARTER: Go on.

MRS. CARTER: Then I bought various things to match it . . . beads . . .

MR. CARTER: I called it "your violet year" . . . perfume! . . .

MRS. CARTER: Absurd . . . just before the war . . . 1940 and '41. (*Pause*) What are you implying? Tom wouldn't have known anything about that!

MR. CARTER (*Dismissing it unhesitatingly*): Of course not. He would have been only two. (*With teasing, flirtatious intention*) It was *myself* I was thinking of. He is infatuated with a Violet, just as I was.

MRS. CARTER: Now, go away . . . to think wives wear . . . you're in the way, Fred.

MR. CARTER (*With a low laugh*): Well, I've had my troubles on that rock, too.

Tom appears at the entrance, carrying a guitar.

TOM: I could have found my way here by the smell of Father's pipe. (*He stops, closes his eyes and smells it*) Christmas is coming. You'll need some more of that tobacco. (*He gropes*) I know its name. No, don't help me . . . ah! "Bonny Prince Charlie." (*He puts the guitar on his mother's lap*)

MRS. CARTER: What's this? Oh—my guitar. Maybe they won't call for me.

MR. CARTER (*Starting off*): Are you sure you're warm enough? —Tom, do you remember coming out here with Francesca when you were six and holding a funeral over a robin redbreast?

TOM (*Lightly*): No, did I? Did I, really?—Why?

MRS. CARTER: We were just wondering, Tom.

> *Exit Mr. Carter. Tom gets down on his knees preparatory to lying down again.*

TOM: I helped the squad that was picking up the trash. I rolled the ice cream cans to the truck. I showed Polly Springer how to put a marshmallow on a fork.—I've done my duty. I can rest.

> *Silence.*

Mother, make one chord on the guitar.

> *She does a slow arpeggiated chord. Silence.*

TOM: One note of music out of doors is worth ten thousand in a building. (*He again turns over on his stomach, raises himself on his elbows*) Mother, I'm going to be the doctor that you planned to be.

MRS. CARTER: Oh!—Not an astronomer? Or a physicist?

TOM: No. That's all too far away. I'm going to be a research doctor.

MRS. CARTER (*Not hurrying*): Well, you don't have to decide now.

TOM (*Decisively*): I've decided.—Last month I thought maybe I'd be one of those new physicists. I'd find something that could stop every atomic bomb . . . I think others'll get there before me . . . Besides, that's not hard enough. Any Joe will be able to find that one of these days. I want something harder . . . something nearer. For instance—

> *Voice offstage: "MRS. CAAAR-TER." Nearer: "MRS. CAAAR-TER!"*

MRS. CARTER (*Raising her voice*): Ye-es. Here I am.

VOICE: The bonfire's starting. They want you to come and sing.

MRS. CARTER: Is that you, Gladys? Tell them to start singing. I'll come soon.

VOICE: All-riiight.

MRS. CARTER: You were saying you wanted to do something harder.

TOM: Harder and *nearer*. (*Beating the ground*) There's no reason people have got to grow old so fast. I guess everybody's got to grow old some day. But I'll bet you we can discover lots of things that will put it off. I'll bet you that three hundred years from now people will think that we were just stupid about, well, about growing old so soon . . . I haven't any crazy idea about people living forever; but . . . it's funny: I don't mind getting old, but I don't like it to happen to other people. Anyway, that's decided. (*He puts his head in his arms and closes his eyes as though going to sleep*) It's great to have something decided. (*Pause*) Mother, what was the name of that nurse I had when I was real young, the southern one?

MRS. CARTER: Miss . . . Miss Forbes.

TOM: What was her first name?

MRS. CARTER: Let me think a minute . . . Maude? No. (*Trouvé*) Madeleine!

TOM: Do you remember any teacher I had back then that was named . . . Violet?

MRS. CARTER: . . . N-n-n-o.

TOM (*Dreamily*): There must have been somebody . . . I remember . . . it was like floating . . . and the smell of violets. Golly, I go crazy when I smell them. I'll tell you why I was so polite to old Mrs. Morris—you remember? She had perfume of violets on her. Why don't you ever wear that, Mother? Don't you like it?

MRS. CARTER (*caught*): Why, it . . . never occurred to me.

TOM: That's an idea for a Christmas present, maybe.

Voices: "MRS. CAAAR-TER!"

MRS. CARTER: Here they come.

Enter Mr. Carter.

MR. CARTER: Do you feel like singing or not? They're making a fuss about you down there.

MRS. CARTER: Why not?

Enter Francesca, running.

FRANCESCA: Mother, they're stamping their feet and—

MRS. CARTER: I'm coming.—I . . . (*She starts tuning the guitar. Going out*) What'll I do, Tom? I'll do . . .

[*They are*] *out. Silence.*

FRANCESCA: The fireflies . . . the moon.

> *Mr. Carter takes the blanket from the rock, carries it across the stage and wraps it around the rock he formerly sat on; then, sitting on the floor, leans his back against it.*

Your pipe smells so wonderful in the open air. (*She starts quietly laughing*) Papa, I'll tell you a secret. *Years* ago— when I went away to summer camp—do you know what I did? I went into your study, and I stole some of that tobacco. I put it in an envelope. And in the tent after lights out, I'd take it out and smell it . . . Why do they call it "Bonny Prince Charlie"? (*Pause; dreamily*) I like the name of Charlie . . . I've never known a stupid boy named Charles. Isn't that funny? They all have something about them that's interesting. (*She starts laughing again*) But I'll tell you something else: all Freds are terrible. Really terrible. You're the only Fred (*Laughing and scarcely audible*) that I can *stand*.

MR. CARTER: Look at the moonlight just hitting the top of the boat club. (*She turns on her knees and draws in her breath, rapt. Mr. Carter drawing his fingers over the ground*) When I was a boy I found all sorts of things here. I made a collection and got a prize for it. Arrowheads and ax heads . . . I used to come out here and think—on this very rock.

FRANCESCA (*Glowing*): Did you?—What did you think *about*?

MR. CARTER: That someday maybe I'd have a family. That someday maybe I'd go into politics.

FRANCESCA: And now you're senator!

MR. CARTER: Tom's not interested in this place as a *human* place. He's always talking about it as a place before there were any human beings here. But even as boy, I used to think all that must have gone on here.—Initiations—

FRANCESCA: What?

MR. CARTER: Initiations into the tribe. And councils about those awful whiteskins. And buryings. (*Pause*) On this very rock I decided to become a lawyer.

FRANCESCA (*Moving a few feet toward him on her knees*): Papa, why was I so mean to Mother?

MR. CARTER: Mean?

FRANCESCA (*Bent head, slowly*): Yes, I was. When I was telling that story about the boy from Milwaukee . . . mistaking Mother for an old woman, like Mrs. Cavanaugh. I knew I was mean while I was doing it. (*She sobs*) And why am I mean about Tom? I *am*. I *am*. (*Sinking lower on her heels*) I'm terrible. I'm unforgivable.—But *why?*

MR. CARTER: Are you mean about yourself? (*She stares at him*) Yes, now you're being mean toward yourself!—Could you imagine building a house on this point?

FRANCESCA: No . . .

MR. CARTER: Because you'd have to cut down so many trees?

FRANCESCA (*Slight pause*): No . . . I could do it without cutting down the best trees.

MR. CARTER: Why couldn't you imagine building here?

FRANCESCA (*Lightly*): I wouldn't.

MR. CARTER: No *reason?*

FRANCESCA (*Affectionately*): Why do you keep asking me when you can *see* that I don't want to answer.

MR. CARTER: Oh, I beg your pardon.

FRANCESCA (*In a loud whisper*): I don't like this point. I've never liked it.

MR. CARTER (*Walking back and forth, right to left*): Well, isn't that funny—people feeling so differently about things.

[*Mr. Carter holds out his hand and Francesca moves closer and takes his hand. They both look into the distance, lost in their thoughts and feelings, as the lights fade.*]

END OF PLAY

WRITINGS ON THEATER

Foreword to
'The Angel That Troubled the Waters and Other Plays'

I<small>T IS</small> a discouraging business to be an author at sixteen years of age. Such an author is all aspiration and no fulfillment. He is drunk on an imaginary kinship with the writers he most admires, and yet his poor overblotted notebooks show nothing to prove to others, or to himself, that the claim is justified. The shortest walk in the country is sufficient to start in his mind the theme, the plan and the title, especially the title, of a long book; and the shortest hour when he has returned to his desk is sufficient to deflate his ambition. Such fragments as he is finally able to commit to paper are a mass of echoes, awkward relative clauses and conflicting styles. In life and in literature mere sincerity is not sufficient, and in both realms the greater the capacity the longer the awkward age. Yet strange lights cross that confusion, authoritative moments that all the practice of later maturity cannot explain and cannot recapture. He is visited by great depressions and wild exhilarations, but whether his depressions proceed from his limitations in the art of living or his limitations in the art of writing he cannot tell. An artist is one who knows how life should be lived at its best and is always aware of how badly he is doing it. An artist is one who knows he is failing in living and feeds his remorse by making something fair, and a layman is one who suspects he is failing in living but is consoled by his successes in golf, or in love, or in business.

Authors of fifteen and sixteen years of age spend their time drawing up title-pages and adjusting the tables of contents of works they have neither the perseverance nor the ability to execute. They compass easily all the parts of a book that are inessential. They compose dignified prefaces, discover happy quotations from the Latin and the French, and turn graceful dedications. This book is what is left of one of these projects.

The title was to have been *Three-Minute Plays for Three Persons.* I have lately found one of my early tables of contents for it, written in the flyleaves of a First Year Algebra. Quadratics in those days could be supported only with the help of a rich marginal commentary. Usually these aids to education took the shape of a carefully planned repertory for two theaters, a large and a small. Here my longer plays were to alternate with *The Wild Duck* and *Measure for Measure* and were cast with such a roll of great names as neither money nor loyalty could assemble. The chapter on Combinations and Permutations ended short by several inches, and left me sufficient space to draw up a catalogue of all the compositions I had heard of that were the work of Charles Martin Loeffler. This list of *Three-Minute Plays* was drawn up in Berkeley, California, in the spring of 1915. It contains several that have since been rejected, two that are in the present volume, "Brother Fire" and "Proserpina and the Devil", and the names of many that were unwritten then and that still, through the charm of their titles, ask to be written.

Since then I have composed some forty of these plays, for I had discovered a literary form that satisfied my passion for compression. Since the time when I began to read I had become aware of the needless repetition, the complacency in most writing. Who does not know the empty opening paragraphs, the deft but uninstructive transitions, and the closing paragraphs that summarize a work and which are unnecessary to an alert reader? Moreover, their brevity flatters my inability to sustain a long flight, and the inertia that barely permits me to write at all. And finally, when I became a teacher, here was the length that could be compassed after the lights of the House were out and the sheaf of absurd French exercises corrected and indignantly marked with red crayon. In time the three minutes and the three persons became a habit, and no idea was too grandiose—as the reader will see—for me to try and invest it in this strange discipline.

There were other plans for this book. There was to have been a series of Footnotes to Biographies, suggested by Herbert Eulenberg's *Schattenbilder*, represented here by the Mozart, the Ibsen, and the St. Francis plays. There were hopes of a still more difficult series. Dürer's two sets of woodcuts illustrating the Passion were to serve as model for a series of plays that would be meditations on the last days of Our Lord. Two of them are in this book. There was to have been a series illustrating the history of the stage, and again, two of them are in this book. How different the practice of writing would be if one did not permit oneself to be pretentious. Some hands have no choice: they would rather fail with an oratorio than succeed with a ballad.

During the years that these plays were being written I was reading widely, and these pages are full of allusions to it. The art of literature springs from two curiosities, a curiosity about human beings pushed to such an extreme that it resembles love, and a love of a few masterpieces of literature so absorbing that it has all the richest elements of curiosity. I use the word *curiosity* in the French sense of a tireless awareness of things. (It is too late to arrest the deterioration of our greatest English words. We live in an age where *pity* and *charity* have taken on the color of condescensions; where *humility* seems to mean an acknowledgment of failure; where *simplicity* is foolishness and *curiosity* is interference. To-day *hope*, and *faith* itself, imply a deliberate self-deception.) The training for literature must be acquired by the artist alone, through the passionate assimilation of a few masterpieces written from a spirit somewhat like his own, and of a few masterpieces written from a spirit not at all like his own. I read all Newman, and then I read all Swift. The technical processes of literature should be acquired almost unconsciously on the tide of a great enthusiasm, even syntax, even sentence-structure; I should like to hope, even spelling. I am thinking of some words of Renan commenting in the *Souvenirs d' Enfance et de Jeunesse* upon his education: *"Pour moi, (je) crois qua la meilleure manière de former des jeunes gens de talent est de ne jamais leur parler de talent ni de style, mais de las instruire et d'exciter fortement leur esprit sur les questions philosophiques, religieuses, politiques, sociales, scientifiques, historiques; en un mot, de procéder par l'enseignement du fond des choses, et non par l'enseignement d'une creuse rhétorique."*

The last four plays here have been written within a year and a half. Almost all the plays in this book are religious, but religious in that dilute fashion that is a believer's concession to a contemporary standard of good manners. But these four plant their flag as boldly as they may. It is the kind of work that I would most like to do well, in spite of the fact that there has seldom been an age in literature when such a vein was less welcome and less understood. I hope, through many mistakes, to discover the spirit that is not unequal to the elevation of the great religious themes, yet which does not fall into a repellent didacticism. Didacticism is an attempt at the coercion of another's free mind, even though one knows that in these matters beyond logic, beauty is the only persuasion. Here the schoolmaster enters again. He sees all that is fairest in the Christian tradition made repugnant to the new generations by reason of the diction in which it is expressed. The intermittent sincerity of generations of clergymen and teachers have rendered embarrassing and even ridiculous all the terms of the spiritual life. Nothing succeeds in dampening the aspirations of the young to-day—who dares use the word "aspiration" without enclosing it, knowingly, in quotation-marks?—like the names they hear given to them. The revival of religion is almost a matter of rhetoric. The work is difficult, perhaps impossible (perhaps all religions die out with the exhaustion of the language), but it at least reminds us that Our Lord asked us in His work to be not only as gentle as doves, but as wise as serpents.

THE DAVIS HOUSE
LAWRENCEVILLE, N.J.
June, 1928.

'The Long Christmas Dinner':
Notes for the Producer

NINETY YEARS are traversed in this play which represents in accelerated motion ninety Christmas dinners in the Bayard household. Although the speech, the manner and business of the actors is colloquial and realistic, the production should stimulate the imagination and be implied and suggestive. Accordingly gray curtains with set pieces are recommended for the walls of the room rather than conventional scenery. In the center of the table is a bowl of Christmas greens and at the left end a wine decanter and glasses. Except for these all properties in the play are imaginary. Throughout the play the characters continue eating invisible food with imaginary knives and forks. The actors are dressed in inconspicuous clothes and must indicate their gradual increase in years through their acting.

The ladies may have shawls concealed which they gradually draw up about their shoulders as they grow older.

At the rise of the curtain the stage should be dark, gradually a bright light dims on and covers the table. Floods of light also are directed on the stage from the two portals. The flood from stage Right should be a "cool" color, and the one from stage Left "warm." If possible all lights should be kept off the walls of the room. (It may be possible, when this play is given by itself, to dispense with the curtain, so that the audience arriving will see the stage set and the table laid, though in indistinct darkness.)

Experience has shown that many companies have fallen into the practice of playing this play in a weird, lugubrious manner. Care should be taken that the conversation is normal and that after the "deaths" the play should pick up its tempo at once.

'The Happy Journey':
Notes for the Producer

Aｌｔｈｏｕｇｈ the speech, manner and business of the actors is colloquial and realistic, the production should stimulate the imagination and be implied and suggestive. All properties, except two, are imaginary, but their use is to be carried with detailed pantomime. One of these two is the automobile, which is made up of four chairs on a low platform. In some productions, because of the sight lines of the auditorium, it has been found necessary to raise slightly the two rear chairs of the automobile. The second is an ordinary cot or couch.

The Stage Manager not only moves forward and withdraws these two properties, but he reads from a typescript the lines of all the minor (invisible) characters. He reads them clearly, but with little attempt at characterization, even when he responds in the person of a child or a woman. He may smoke, read a newspaper and eat an apple throughout the course of the play. He should never be obtrusive nor distract the attention of the audience from the central action.

It should constantly be borne in mind that the purpose of this play is the portrayal of the character of Ma Kirby, the author at one time having even considered entitling the play "The Portrait of a Lady." Accordingly, the director should constantly keep in mind that Ma Kirby's humor, strength and humanity constitute the unifying element throughout. This aspect should always rise above the merely humorous characteristic details of the play.

Many productions have fallen into two regrettable extremes. On the one hand actors have exaggerated the humorous characters and situations in the direction of farce; and on the other hand, have treated Ma Kirby's sentiment and religion with sentimentality and preachy solemnity. The atmosphere, comedy, and characterization of this play are most effective when they are handled with great simplicity and evenness.

A Preface for
'Our Town'

For a while in Rome I lived among archeologists, and ever since I find myself occasionally looking at the things about me as an archeologist will look at them a thousand years hence. Rockefeller Center will be reconstructed in imagination from the ruins of its foundations. How high was it? A thesis will be written on the bronze plates found in New York's detritus heaps—"Tradesmen's Entrance," "Night Bell."

In Rome I was led through a study of the plumbing on the Palatine Hill. A friend of mine could ascribe a date, "within ten years," to every fragment of cement made in the Roman Republic and early Empire.

An archeologist's eyes combine the view of the telescope with the view of the microscope. He reconstructs the very distant with the help of the very small.

It was something of this method that I brought to a New Hampshire village. I spent parts of six summers tutoring at Lake Sunapee and six at the MacDowell Colony at Peterborough. I took long walks through scores of upland villages.

And the archeologist's and the social historian's points of view began to mingle with another unremitting preoccupation which is the central theme of the play: What is the relation between the countless "unimportant" details of our daily life, on the one hand, and the great perspectives of time, social history, and current religious ideas, on the other?

What is trivial and what is significant about any one person's making a breakfast, engaging in a domestic quarrel, in a "love scene," in dying? To record one's feelings about this question is necessarily to exhibit the realistic detail of life, and one is at once up against the problem of realism in literature.

William James used to warn his students against being impressed by the "abject truth." Most works in realism tell a succession of such abject truths; they are deeply in earnest, every detail is true, and yet the whole finally tumbles to the ground —true but without significance.

How did Jane Austen save her novels from that danger?

They appear to be compact of abject truth. Their events are excruciatingly unimportant; and yet, with *Robinson Crusoe*, they will probably outlast all Fielding, Scott, George Eliot, Thackeray, and Dickens. The art is so consummate that the secret is hidden; peer at them as hard as one may; shake them; take them apart; one cannot see how it is done.

I wished to record a village's life on the stage, with realism and with generality.

The stage has a deceptive advantage over the novel—in that lighted room at the end of the darkened auditorium things seem to be half caught up into generality already. The stage cries aloud its mission to represent the Act in Eternity. So powerful is the focus that it brings to bear on any presented occasion that every lapse of the author from his collaborative intensity is doubly conspicuous: the truth tumbles down into a heap of abject truths and the result is doubly trivial.

So I tried to restore significance to the small details of life by removing scenery. The spectator through lending his imagination to the action restages it inside his own head.

In its healthiest ages the theater has always exhibited the least scenery. Aristophanes's *The Clouds*—423 B.C. Two houses are represented on the stage, *inside* of one of them we see two beds. Strepsiades is talking in his sleep about his racehorses. A few minutes later he crosses the stage to Socrates's house, the Idea Factory, the "Thinkery." In the Spanish theater Lope de Vega put a rug in the middle of the scene—it was a raft in mid-ocean bearing a castaway. The Elizabethans, the Chinese used similar devices.

The theater longs to represent the symbols of things, not the things themselves. All the lies it tells—the lie that that young lady is Caesar's wife; the lie that people can go through life talking in blank verse; the lie that that man just *killed* that man—all those lies enhance the one truth that is there—the truth that dictated the story, the myth. The theater asks for as many conventions as possible. A convention is an agreed-upon falsehood, an accepted untruth. When the theater pretends to give the real thing in canvas and wood and metal it loses something of the realer thing which is its true business. Ibsen and Chekhov carried realism as far as it could go, and it took all their genius to do it. Now the camera is carrying it on and is in great "theoretical peril" of falling short of literature. (In a world of actual peril that "theoretical peril" looks very far-fetched, but ex-college professors must be indulged.)

But the writing of the play was not accompanied by any such conscious argumentation as this. It sprang from a deep admiration for those little white towns in the hills and from a deep devotion to the theater. These are but the belated gropings to reconstruct what may have taken place when the play first presented itself—the life of a village against the life of the stars.

In an earlier draft of the play there were some other lines that led up to those which now serve as its motto. The Stage Manager has been talking about the material that is being placed in the cornerstone of the new bank at Grover's Corners, material that has been chemically treated so that it will last a thousand or two thousand years. He suggests that this play has been placed there so that future ages will know more about the life of the average person; more than just the Treaty of Versailles and the Lindbergh Flight—see what I mean?

Well, people a thousand years from now, in the provinces North of New York at the beginning of the Twentieth Century, people ate three times a day—soon after dawn, at noon, and at sunset.

Every seventh day, by law and by religion, there was a day of rest and all work came to a stop.

The religion at that time was Christianity; but I guess you have other records about Christianity.

The domestic set-up was marriage, a binding relation between a male and one female that lasted for life.

. . . Anything else? Oh, yes, when people died they were buried in the ground just as they were.

Well, people a thousand years from now, this is the way we were—in our growing-up, in our marrying, in our doctoring, in our living, and in our dying.

Now let's get back to our day in Grover's Corners. . . .

'Our Town':
Story of the Play

IN the first act the author genially outlines the history of the town, which is Grover's Corners, N.H., and something of the character of its citizens. Then he carries you into the houses of the Gibbs and Webb families, substantial homes containing substantial folks. You arrive at breakfast time and are carried through one entire day in the lives of these good people.

The second act concerns the love affair between young George Gibbs and little Emily Webb, and thus culminates in a moving wedding scene, which contains all those elements of poignant sorrow and abundant happiness that make for solemnity and impressiveness.

In the third act we are led to the cemetery on the hill, where many of the townspeople we have come to know so well are patiently and smilingly awaiting not "judgment" but greater understanding. Into their midst is led the bride, a little timid at first, a little wishful to go back to life, to live again with her memories. But she is shown how impossible, how futile it is to return. The past cannot be re-lived. Living people, humans, occupied with their petty occupations and small thoughts, know little of true joy or happiness. Truth is to be found only in the future.

'Our Town':
Some Suggestions for the Director

I T is important to maintain a continual *dryness* of tone,—the New England understatement of sentiment, of surprise, of tragedy. A shyness about emotion. These significances are conveyed by the eyes and a sharpening and distinctness of the voice. (So in the Stage-Manager on the Civil War veterans: "All they knew was the name, friends,—the United States of America. The United States of America." And in all the dealings of the mothers with their children where a matter-of-factness overlays the concern.)

———

It has already been proven that absence of scenery does not constitute a difficulty and that the cooperative imagination of the audience is stimulated by that absence. There remain, however, two ways of producing the play. One, with a constant subtle adjustment of lights and sound effects; and one through a still bolder acknowledgment of artifice and make-believe: the rooster's crow, the train and factory whistles and school bells frankly man-made and in the spirit of "play." I am inclined to think that this latter approach, though apparently "amateurish" and rough at first, will prove the more stimulating in the end, and will prepare for the large claim on attention and imagination in the last act. The scorn of verisimilitude throws all the greater emphasis on the ideas which the play hopes to offer.

———

It seems advisable that at the opening of the play where the audience is first introduced to pantomime and imaginary props, that Mrs. Gibbs and Mrs. Webb in the preparation of breakfast perform much of their business with their backs to the audience, and do not distract and provoke its attention with too distinct and perhaps puzzling a picture of the many operations of coffee-grinding, porridge-stirring, etc.

———

At the beginning of the wedding scene there is an abrupt change of approach. The audience is hearing the thoughts of the characters and is seeing a symbolical statement of attitudes which never were consciously expressed by the characters in their daily life. This change is greatly aided by the entrance of the bride and groom through the aisles of the auditorium; and by the fact that it is accompanied by the very soft singing of the hymns by the congregation. It would be well that George on arriving on the stage draws back well toward the proscenium, indicating that this scene does not literally take place in the church or before the church. After Mrs. Gibbs's line: "George! If anyone should hear you! Now stop! Why, I'm ashamed of you!" George passes his hand over his forehead, as though emerging from a dream, and with a complete change of manner, returning to realism, explains: "What? Where's Emily?" Mrs. Gibbs and George do not touch each other during the scene until she straightens his tie, and the strong emotion is indicated by tension, not by weeping. In the following scene between Emily and her father, however, Emily is in tears and flings herself into her father's arms.

—

The Stage-Manager-Clergyman's speech: "I've married two hundred couples in my day," etc., is not delivered to the village congregation before him, but across their heads, an almost dreamy meditation, during which the tableau on the stage "freezes."

In the last act it is important to remove from the picture of the seated dead any suggestion of the morbid or lugubrious. They sit easily; there is nothing of the fixed and unwinking about their eyes. The impression is of patient composed waiting.

Emily's revisiting her home and her farewell to the world is under strong emotion, but the emotion is that of wonder rather than of sadness. Even the "I love you all, everything!" is realization and discovery as much as it is poignancy.

T.W.

'Our Town'—
From Stage to Screen

A correspondence between
Thornton Wilder and Sol Lesser

THIS lively and friendly correspondence between Thornton Wilder, author of *Our Town*, and Sol Lesser, who made the screen version of the play, will provide an illuminating insight both personal and technical into the translation of an excellent play into an excellent motion picture. It may, moreover, serve as a pleasant antidote for the large literature that already exists on the unpleasant relationship between a dramatist and a motion picture producer who adapts his play to the screen. It is obviously only a part of the exchange of letters which dealt with all the phases and details of production.

—Editors' Note

October 5, 1939

Dear Thornton:

Ever since my last letter to you, Frank Craven and I have been working on the script (First Rough Draft), and we found ourselves contradicting some of our first impressions, so we are sending to you herewith the revised yellow pages to substitute for the pages of the same numbers in the script you have on hand. I would recommend that you insert these revised pages before reading the script through from beginning to end. . . .

Sincerely,
Sol Lesser

New York, Oct. 7, 1939

Dear Mr. Lesser:

Forgive my delay in answering these letters and reporting on this material. After our five lively days in New York, I went to Woollcott's island, and took up work on the essays I've long planned to write and, as always in such cases, I shut the whole world off in order to concentrate.

663

Considering the screenplay pp. 1–79 (the second installment is waiting for me in New Haven, and I shall find it there this afternoon):—

I feel that now the point has come in the work, as I foresaw, when my feelings must often give way before those of people who understand motion-picture narrative better than I do. It's not a matter of fidelity to my text—since I doubt whether there has ever been a movie as faithful to its original text as this seems to be—it's just a matter of opinion, and my opinion should often give way before that of those who know moving-pictures thoroughly.

I. For instance, in the opening. Mr. Morgan appearing at the door of his drugstore, and saying: 'Well, folks, we're in Grover's Corners, New Hampshire . . .' seems to me far less persuasive and useful than the opening over the jig-saw puzzle. The puzzle opening has the advantages:

(1) Of setting the background against the whole United States, that constant allusion to larger dimensions of time and place, which is one of the principal elements of the play; and

(2) Of giving the actor and audience that transitional moment between talking-one's-thoughts and addressing-a-theatre-audience from the screen, that Sacha Guitry found necessary, too. It would seem to me that each occasion that Mr. Morgan addresses the audience directly should have some such preparation: from monologue to address.

II. In the episodes during the evening it would seem to me that (pp. 38ff) there should be constantly maintained by the camera the view of the whole town—our feeling that *there* is choir rehearsal; *there* are the children at work; *there* is Dr. Gibbs reading. These episodes are very slight to be received in succession; but all gain when they are given with an air of being simultaneous. At present the camera directions don't pick up the whole town until page 49.

III. I forget whether it's in the book or not, but I like the addition of one line to Mr. Morgan's speech on p. 69—I think the meaning is clarified and enlarged as follows:

MR. MORGAN. Well, before we get on with this wedding, I think we should know how it all began—*this plan to spend a lifetime together; I'm awfully interested in how big things like that begin.* You know . . . you're twenty or twenty-two, etc.

IV. Re your telegram.

I can see how you may feel that it is best not to give Emily's birthday in the opening scene. I shall send you from New Haven my suggested lines.

V. As to the date.

1919–1923 would be all right with me. It closes out those horse-and-buggy pre-automobile days which may have been a part of the much-discussed 'nostalgia' which people found in the play. I can't for the life of me think of any events that could substitute for Treaty of Versailles and the Lindbergh Flight. Death of Grover Cleveland?

Anyway I shall be writing you on Monday from New Haven, with the rest of the screenplay in hand.

In the meantime, all my cordial regards to you and your family and to Frank.

Sincerely ever,
Thornton

CULVER CITY, OCTOBER 11, 1939

Telegram to Thornton Wilder

YOU PERSUADE ME TO RESTORE JIGSAW PUZZLE OPENING. AM TRYING TO FIND DEVICE TO MAINTAIN FEELING OF WHOLE TOWN AT NIGHT. AGREE THAT MORGAN'S SPEECH PAGE 69 SHOULD BE ENLARGED TO INCLUDE THE ADDITIONAL LINES.

SOL LESSER

Oct. 9, 1939
New Haven, Conn.

Dear Sol:

Returning to New Haven I found the yellow pages of corrections and now have everything before me.

The cuts in Mrs. Gibb–Mrs. Webb shelling beans are all right with me; also the transferred speeches from the Stage Manager to Mrs. Gibbs in the last act. Also the omission of the Birthday Scene from the opening sequence.

My only worry is that—realistically done—your wedding

scene won't be interesting enough, and that it will reduce many of the surrounding scenes to ordinary-ness.

Did you ever see a wedding scene on stage or screen that followed through normally?

Either it was interrupted (*Smiling Through* and *Jane Eyre* and *It Happened One Night*), or it showed the bride hating the groom (*The Bride the Sun Shines On*), or some other irregularity.

On the stage with *Our Town* the novelty was supplied by

(1) economy of effect in the scenery.

(2) the minister was played by the Stage Manager.

(3) the thinking-aloud passages.

(4) the oddity of hearing Mrs. Soames' gabble during the ceremony.

(5) the young people's moments of alarm.

You have none of these—by a close-up of Mrs. Soames even her gabble will lose its oddity and shock. Here is a village wedding and the inevitable let-down when it all runs through *as expected*.

Now, Sol, it's just you I'm thinking about; will you have as *interesting* a picture as you hoped?

This treatment seems to me to be in danger of dwindling to the conventional. And for a story that is so generalized that's a great danger.

The play interested because every few minutes there was a new bold effect in presentation-methods.

For the movie it may be an audience-risk to be bold (thinking of the 40 millions) but I think with this story it's a still greater risk to be conventional. This movie is bold enough in the last sequence, but apart from the three characters who talk straight into the audience's face, there's less and less of that novelty and freedom and diversion during the first forty minutes.

I know you'll realize that I don't mean boldness or oddity for their own sakes, but merely as the almost indispensable reinforcement and refreshment of a play that was never intended to be interesting for its story alone, or even for its background. . . .

All my best to all, as ever,

Thornton

October 19, 1939

Dear Thornton:

Tomorrow I am sending you a revised first draft script, in which you will note that we have re-captured those elements omitted from the first rough draft, and in which we have incorporated the further suggestions made in your letters to me. You will also find several new ideas which I hope, will please you. . . .

It was a great satisfaction to me today when we rewrote the wedding scene and used the technique of exposing the characters' thoughts. I see now, more clearly, the purpose of the wedding as you originally intended. I ask you also to edit these lines with fullest sense of their import. The more I consider this scene, the more value I see in its original form.

I urge you to point out to me wherein you think the picture lapses into conventionality. While this is only our Revised First Draft, I feel we can, without danger, add boldness and novelty, even though our thoughts up to date have not produced anything further than the script shows. . . .

Frank Craven has just done a picture for Paramount in which he played the part of a druggist. Whether this would identify him as the same druggist in our picture I can't say, but I've decided to play safe; so instead of establishing Mr. Morgan as a druggist we have played him as the proprietor of the general merchandise store. I give you this explanation now so you do not fall over backwards when you read the establishing scene of Mr. Morgan in the script.

I know you will not hesitate to speak your mind freely, and I await your further comments, criticisms and suggestions with great eagerness.

Gratefully,
Sol Lesser

New Haven, Connecticut
October 29, 1939

Dear Sol:

The 'Revised First Draft' is before me. Before I speak of it in general I shall take up the few notes I have made. . . .

Page 106. I hate to seem like 'Vain Author thinks every Word Sacred', but it does seem to me that the cuts in the

Death-and-Immortality speech do something to it—in its present shape it reads like a sweetness-and-light Aimee Mac-Pherson spiel. I don't feel violently about this, but suggest omitting 'lot of thoughts . . . but there's no post office', and restoring after: '. . . There's something way down deep that's eternal about every human being.' Some of the original lines there, and placing 'Yes, all these important things . . . grow kinda pale around here' to its position after the 'Something eternal' paragraph—and then omitting the 'And what's left? What's left when memory's gone . . . and your identity, Mrs. Smith?' In other words: The idea of the Relinquishing Earth-Associations follows the Something Eternal-Passage.

However, as I say, I don't feel very strongly about this, and I leave it to your judgment. . . .

The Wedding Scene is Better. I still think it's not fresh enough. I don't think that realistic boys in a realistic village would hoot and guy a friend on his way to his wedding. That's Dead-End-Kids city life. And it's pretty sententious of Mr. Morgan to say out loud to a friend: 'There are a lot of things to be said about a wedding. And there are a lot of thoughts that go on during a wedding.' . . .

The papers say that this script has been sent me for my approval. My approval it certainly has. My demurring is just between you and me, Sol, not as to whether it's a good treatment and a faithful transcription—that it already is—but whether for your joy as well as mine, it is a movie that beats other movies—and which the public and the critics will receive as a deep movie experience. For that I feel that there is still some more work to be done.

All my best to you all, as ever,

Thornton

November 2, 1939

Dear Thornton:

I have your letter of October 29th, and let me say that I find the greatest stimulation in your suggestions and counsel. You actually put steel in my backbone in my determination to carry this script through to its finality in as faithful a translation of its original as it is possible in our medium.

In speaking to trained motion picture technicians, both

writers and directors, I have had to face several challenges, but I have always discarded those minds who do not see eye to eye with me in the matter of technique and the fulfilment of the poetic intent of your original writing. Many observations from these sources, however, have made (for the time being at least) some impression on me, and while I am still analyzing them in my own mind I feel that I need your deductions as to their value.

I do hope you will not permit yourself to feel, to use your own words, 'any inexperience in movie values'. While agreeing that the medium of the screen is entirely different from the stage, still I hold that if we properly translate the situations from stage to screen, audience emotions will be the same looking at the picture as looking at the stage play. I might use this as an example of a difference: A person might attend a Hollywood Bowl Concert and hear *Aïda* played for fifteen minutes by a full symphony orchestra, and thoroughly enjoy it. That same person attending a motion picture theatre and hearing *Aïda* played by the identical orchestra in identical fashion might be thoroughly bored before it is half finished. There is an important difference. One will grow tired of looking at the orchestra on the screen. Something must accompany it which would entertain through the eye as well as the ear. . . .

I now come to a question which needs your guiding answer. It has been suggested for movie purposes a means be found to attach the third act to circumstances already within the play. I suppose by this it is meant that perhaps there should be a problem affecting the married life of Emily and George growing out of the differences in their mentalities. I cite the following only as an example:—

Emily is brighter than George; in her youth she has the best memory in her class—she recites like 'silk off a spool'—she helps George in his mathematics—she is articulate—George is not—she is 'going to make speeches all the rest of her life'. . . .

Query: Could it be Emily's subtlety in the soda-fountain scene that causes George to make the decision not to go to Agricultural School? The audience gets this, but George feels it is his own voluntary thought. He makes the decision not to go.

Could Emily, after death, re-visit her fifth wedding anniversary . . . and now see her mistake?

Emily in life is likely to have been over-ambitious for George, wanting him to accomplish all of the things he would have known had he gone to Agricultural School, but which he has had to learn mainly by experience. In a single scene we could establish that George did not develop the farm as efficiently and as rapidly as Emily thought he should have. She continued to get ideas out of newspapers and books as she did out of her school books, and had tried to explain them to George, but he was slow in grasping them. She had been impatient very often. Someone else's farm may have been progressing faster than George's and she may not have liked that. . . .

Now she sees this. She remembers she was responsible for his not going to Agricultural School. She has overlooked many of George's virtues—she took them all for granted. All this was her mistake. . . .

Could there be a great desire to live, to profit by what she has just seen, rather than go back to the grave—should she long to live—would the audience, witnessing this picture, pull for her to live—and she does?

Others tell me that this, or something like it, would give the picture more appeal for the forty millions, and that it would only change the expression of your philosophy, not the philosophy itself, which would be retained.

Now tell me frankly, Thornton, what you think. Would it help or hurt the structure? Does it give rise to something that you think might be done within the scope of your original purpose? . . .

There is one other thing that you were right about—we do need some kind of an introduction for Simon Stimson; and there are many other points which we must discuss personally.

I hope that the advancing of the First Rough Draft to its multigraphed stage has not made you feel other than that the play is in process of being made ready for the screen—a screen-play writer is the next in order.

Sincerely,
Sol Lesser

Sunday, Nov. 12, 1939
New York

Dear Sol:

My letters seem only to make you unhappy about the work and God knows I don't mean that.

The important thing is that I do think it's a very good script as it is now, and when I do express some reservation about some portion or aspect of it, I don't seem to be able to offer anything concrete to propose in its stead.

However, I feel pretty concrete about trying to dissuade you against showing Emily returning to her fifth wedding anniversary and regretting that she had been an unwise wife.

(1) It throws out of the window the return to the 12th birthday which you feel is sufficiently tied up with the earlier part of the picture, but which is certain of its effect.

(2) It introduces a lot of plot preparation in the earlier part of the picture that would certainly be worse than what's there now. Scene of George running the farm incompetently. Scene of Emily upbraiding him.

(3) It makes Emily into a school-marm 'improving' superior person. The traits that you point out *are* in her character, her 'good in classes', her desire 'to make speeches all her life'—but I put them in there to prevent her being pure-village-girl-sweet-ingenue. But push them a few inches further and she becomes priggish.

(4) The balance of the play reposing between vast stretches of time and suggestions of generalized multitudes of people requires that the fathers and mothers, and especially the hero and heroine, be pretty near the norm of everybody, every boy and every girl.

If this is made into ineffectual-but-good-hearted-husband and superior-interfering-wife, the balance is broken.

It's not so much new 'plotting' that is needed, as it is refreshing detail-play over the simple but sufficient plot that's there.

As to the new approach—the use of a model town—that you mentioned over the phone:

I'm very glad for one thing, that it brings back Mr. Morgan speaking from 1940. The more I think of it the more I see that that will be a great gain.

If the picture can avoid Giant Man looking over Toy Village—like Grover Whalen showing a model World's Fair to visitors in his office—then everything's fine. . . .

Cordially ever,
Thornton

HOLLYWOOD, DEC. 4, 1939

Telegram to Isabel Wilder
WHAT MAKE OF CAR WOULD THORNTON LIKE FOR CHRISTMAS

SOL LESSER

NEW YORK, NY, DEC. 5, 1939

Telegram to Sol Lesser
THORNTON DOESN'T DRIVE ANY MORE BUT HAS ALWAYS SAID IF HE HAD CAR WANTED A CHRYSLER CONVERTIBLE WITH RUMBLE SEAT

ISABEL WILDER

December 26, 1939—10:34 P.M. E.S.T.

Dear Sol:

Just to show you that I'm not stuck up because I own the most beautiful car in town (even the Cartwrights turn their heads when I go by now) I'm writing on my old paper. All my sisters were back for Christmas and you never heard such squeals. Everybody had to be taught all the gadgets. When they found there were little red lights that went on when your oil and gas were low—that slew 'em; and the two speeds on the windshield—oh, and the defroster; and a top that goes up and down without anybody losing their temper. Well, well—first I was so astonished I didn't know what to do, but ever since I've been getting more proud and pleased every hour. A thousand thanks, Sol! I wish you were here to see what a big success it is. . . .

Thornton

January 5, 1940

Dear Thornton:

Your two letters, December 26 and New Year's Eve, arrived at the same time, and I feel confident that from them we have achieved the desired result; so the changes have been incorporated into our script, which now takes the form of a Final Screenplay. A copy of this will go forward to you within the next two or three days.

We decided to change the opening of the picture order in to eliminate all mechanical feeling. Our minds out here have all agreed that this final choice is smoother and better. I fought right along to retain the jig-saw puzzle opening to get the illusion of many small towns that make up the United States, but unquestionably this will assert itself in the picture proper. Our conclusion was that this sort of thing has been done too many times to make it worth while, even though it would serve a purpose.

The picture itself will be treated in an unconventional manner with regard to camera set-ups, following our original idea of introducing properties intended to accentuate the moods and to visualize something deeper than just the mere dialogue.

For instance, in the Simon Stimson episodes, with the scenes played in moonlight, the photography will accentuate the black and white shadows. The little white New England houses, which look so lovely in other shots, will look naked and almost ghostly in relation to Simon Stimson, to whom they did not offer nice lovely homes but a cold world which ruined him.

As a further example: When we come to Mrs. Gibbs on the morning of the wedding, we will see her through the kitchen window grinding the coffee, but in the foreground the flowerpots will be dripping in the rain to accentuate the general mood, so that Mrs. Gibbs is almost a secondary element in this scene.

And just as another example: When Rebecca is crying in her room the morning of the wedding, we see her little pig bank tied by a ribbon to a corner of the bed, which will remind the audience of what Rebecca likes most in the world. I think this little effect will give as much to an audience as if we had a whole scene about her.

I mention these little points merely so you will have them in mind when you read the script. . . .

Sol Lesser

January 9, 1940

Dear Thornton:

Under separate cover I am sending you a final shooting script of *Our Town*. Even though it says 'final' we are still working, not only for new bold effects but also for simplification, and I will appreciate very much any further word from you in criticism or suggestion.

I have a feeling that it might be helpful to you in visualizing this script to meet Harry Horner who could show you a number of the sketches that he has prepared and which in a great many cases have acted as a stimulant to our art designer here. I can't commence to tell you my enthusiasm for the sketches that have so far been prepared. They are indeed artistic, and I think we will get a very unusual result.

Most of the conversational scenes will be played in very close shots, eliminating scenic proportions, in order to capture the original purpose of the play—the non-use of scenery—but at the same time we will have a beautifully scenic production in the places where scenery will serve its purpose. . . .

With all good wishes, I am

Cordially,
Sol Lesser

January 9, 1940

Dear Thornton:

Does it occur to you that we should expose as a premise early in the picture 'that human beings do fairly move about in self-preoccupied matter-of-factness—admitting that human beings are inadequate to experience'—all as demonstrated in the last act? If this could be accomplished subtly, yet thoroughly understandably to the forty million, perhaps the third act will take on a still added value.

As an example, Craven says: 'And there comes Howie Newsome and Bessie delivering the milk'—adding—'Howie, you know, does one of those services that we just naturally take for granted.'

While I realize that this premise 'cannot be taken as a motto for this picture', do you feel, as I do, that it is an important collateral—which when exposed should have everyone in the audience right where we want him?

Think this through for me, and let me hear.

Cordially,
Sol Lesser

Jan. 13, 1940

Dear Sol:

. . . . Re planting unobtrusively the notion of everybody's inevitable self-preoccupation.

I should suggest that the idea is not so much suggested by the service a Milkman renders—the American Mind assumes that what you get money for cannot be classed as benevolence—but by some picture of a person's not noticing another's need or claim or call. (Chekhov's plays are always exhibiting this: Nobody hears what anybody else says. Everybody walks in a self-centred dream.) Children perpetually feel it as a rebuff:

'Mama, mama, look what I found—isn't it *wonderful?*'

'Yes, dear, now go and wash your hands.'

It is certainly one of the principal points that the Return to the Birthday makes; when I read the script today I'll be thinking over a way to incorporate some advance indications of it in the earlier part of the picture.

All my best,
Thornton

Monday Morning
Jan. 15, 9:45 A.M.

Dear Sol:

I hope you're as completely pleased and reconciled as I am to the simplifications in the last act—

I append a few notes, but they're not important and not meant to wrinkle your brow now when you have so many other things to think about.

(1) *Shot 314.* Cat arches its back at presence of dead Emily.

I should think it would trouble the scene and distract the audience's mind to introduce here the notion of ghosts and of animals being aware of ghosts. The cat's arched back would suddenly set off a train of spooky associations—haunted houses and animosity against, and dread of, the dead. . . .

Re the Opening. You have thought it over a thousand times

and I defer to your judgment, but this opening lacks the largeness that might be there. On the stage, though the whole U.S.A. was not mentioned, the largeness of design was conveyed by the bareness of the stage and the surprise of the direct address to the audience. It may be that during the work of production you will feel the other opening recurring to you. . . .

So shooting will begin any day now. All my best to all the forces. How splendid Fay Bainter and Beulah Bondi will be; and Tommy Mitchell. . . .

All regards,

Ever,
Thornton

January 17, 1940

Dear Thornton:

I have your letter of January 15th, which arrived in the midst of our happy excitement incidental to the starting of the picture.

The cast is now practically complete:

DR. GIBBS	Thomas Mitchell
MRS. GIBBS	Fay Bainter
MR. WEBB	Guy Kibbee
MRS. WEBB	Beulah Bondi
NARRATOR	Frank Craven
EMILY WEBB	Martha Scott
GEORGE GIBBS	William Holden
HOWIE NEWSOME	Stuart Erwin
MRS. SOAMES	Doro Merande
REBECCA GIBBS	Ruth Toby

I have taken careful note of your comment, and accordingly the cat will not arch its back in the presence of dead Emily. We have deleted the remarks before the wedding; and have reduced the uncle-ishness of Frank Craven, editing his remarks in accordance with your suggestions, and we are now energetically employing what remains of our faculties to devise a new opening. We are all of one opinion here now—that the Narrator should not be too much attached to the story as the druggist. He doesn't have the freedom of the original manager, and I am certain we will come up with what will be the right idea before many nights have passed.

We have been searching, but haven't found the emotional reason for Craven starting the story back in 1901, nor have we exactly identified the location where we pick him up. Everyone seems to feel that the opening should have a feeling of air, broadness and scope, rather than being confined in a set or in front of a store, but we can't put our finger on it.

And so the remaining major problems are: the opening, and the situation about which I still expect to hear from you, which will lay down early in the picture some advance indication of the premise exposed by Emily's summing up in the last act.

It is difficult for me to convey to you the extent of my obligation to you for the support that you have given me and the value of your corrections. . . . We should not consider the script settled until the picture is finished shooting, and there is no difficulty about changing any scenes. There will be a practised orderliness, even while the picture is being photographed, which will permit us to improve where the opportunity affords. . . .

Sincerely,
Sol Lesser

January 17, 1940

Dear Thornton:

. . . You are going to get a real thrill, Thornton, when you see on the screen the production of the graveyard sequence as designed by Mr. Menzies. There is great inspiration from the time the mourners under their umbrellas come into the graveyard. We never show the ground—every shot is just above the ground—never a coffin nor an open grave—it is all done by attitudes, poses and movements—and in long shots. The utter dejection of Dr. Gibbs—we have his clothes weighted down with lead weights so they sag—the composition of Dr. Gibbs at the tombstone is most artistic—and as Dr. Gibbs leaves the cemetery the cloud in the sky gradually lifts, revealing stars against the horizon—and as the cemetery itself darkens a reflection from the stars strikes a corner of the tombstone which is still wet from the recent rain, and the reflection (hilation) seems to give a star-like quality—and the scene gradually goes to complete darkness. We get a vast expanse of what seems to be sky and stars. When this dissolves to the dead people this same reflection of hilation appears to touch the brows of the dead. It is lovely—something quite bold! Well, if it comes out on the screen as we hope, we will get that feeling of joy.

> Cordially,
> *Sol Lesser*

Monday, Jan. 22, 1940, 4:10 P.M.

Dear Sol:

First: Re suggestions for Additional Business. You notice I've noted 14 O.K.'s; 3 O.K., but finicky; and 6 reservations.

'O.K., but finicky' means the kind of detail-business which might get a laugh, or a moment's pleasant 'recognition' chuckle, but which might break the curve of a scene or (still more serious) establish the wrong tone for the picture. A few more stealing-doughnuts; dish-towel-errors; four-spoonfuls-of-sugar; drinking-coffee-out-of-saucers; mothers-looking-behind-sons'-ears—and the audience would be justified in believing they're in one of those pictures Quaint Hayseed Family Life. (I saw a striking example of this establishing the wrong tone last week on the New York stage. Barry Fitzgerald and Sarah Allgood played the first act of *Juno and the Paycock* in the tone Drunken Irishmen and Tyrannical Wives are very very funny. But Sean O'Casey meant that drinking and shift-lessness are the ruin of Ireland—so when Sean O'Casey got around to showing the ruin in the rest of the play, the audience felt that he'd switched his message, and resented it.) . . .

> *Thornton*

Wed. afternoon

Dear Sol:

The new opening's fine.

I shudder at the way you spare no expense. Fences, bridges, nut-trees, distant villages, scarecrows—!

It's fine.

I'm sorry I came home too late yesterday to get my answer off to your telegram about the beginning of work. I wish I could see all those fine actors and fine people gathered together.

And a look at you up in your office when every minute you want to be down in the middle of it.

Sol, I thought I'd found a place to insert that nobody-pays-any-attention-to-anybody motif.

EMILY. Mama, I made a speech in class today and I was very good.

MRS. WEBB (*Abstractedly*). Hm. I mustn't forget that bread in the oven. . . . What, dear?

EMILY. Oh, Mama! You never listen to what we're telling you. I said I made a very fine speech in class today.

MRS. WEBB. What was it about? Etc. Etc.

But now I'm afraid of it. Because it puts the burden of self-centredness on Mrs. Webb again, who bears the burden in the last act. (A woman from California!! wrote me, asking me whether the meaning of the play was that New England mothers were so severe that they had no responsive love for their children!!)

I wish I could attach some such brief hitch in the dialogue to somebody else than Mrs. Webb. Mrs. Gibbs could 'take it' but I can't find the place (George's spending-money—Rebecca's 'Mama, do you know what I love most in the world, do you?') without its unnecessarily blocking the forward movement.

Well, I carry the problem around with me wherever I go and will report to you if I see something.

All my best to 1041 and allied departments.

Thornton

February 21, 1940

Dear Thornton:

. . . We are finishing up this week with those of the cast who did not finish last week. They are dropping off like flies. Another twelve days should see the picture completed.

Everyone—not only the 'Yes Men'—yes, everyone is most enthusiastic, and I think we have something quite different in novelty, both from the photographic and story-telling stand-point. Now if the motion picture public wants this kind of a story—all is well. I think we have considerable insurance in the well-known players, Mitchell, Bainter, Bondi, Kibbee,

Erwin and Holden, and Craven for metropolitan New York prestige. . . .

Cordially,
Sol Lesser

March 21, 1940

Dear Thornton:

Well, Thornton, I've managed to work myself into a jam. Or at least I think it's a jam, which is just about as bad, I suppose. Maybe you can help to extricate me. It's a sort of puzzle, and it all comes about with respect to the ending of the story.

The first serious thing to decide is whether we should let Emily live or die. There are two schools of thought here, as naturally there would be. But I find myself bouncing from one side to the other, and I just hate myself because I can't make up my own mind. It is true that we can rely upon a preview, showing both endings alternately, but it is in the event that we choose the happy ending where the problem really lies.

Doug Churchill, who wrote the review for *Red Book*, has counselled me to use the happy ending. He has given us a very flattering review, which he concludes by saying (as nearly as I can remember his words):

'The picture differs from the original play in only one respect: the ending—Emily lives. Those who are purists and who loved the play will be outraged, but to those countless others, like myself, who have during the running of the picture come to love Emily as well as the other characters, it is a most satisfactory and logical conclusion. And since, indeed, this ending has been arranged with the permission of the author, who is there amongst us to criticise? It is a beautiful, inspiring picture' . . . .

Cordially,
Sol Lesser

New Haven, Conn.
Easter Night

Dear Sol:

Sure, I see what you mean.

In the first place, I think Emily should live. I've always thought so. In a movie you see the people so *close to* that a different relation is established. In the theatre they are halfway abstractions in an allegory; in the movie they are very concrete. So, insofar as the play is a generalized allegory, she dies—we die—they die; insofar as it's a concrete happening it's not important that she die; it's even disproportionately cruel that she die.

Let her live—the idea will have been imparted anyway.

Cordially ever,
Thornton Wilder

MAY 9, 1940

Telegram to Thornton Wilder

I AM SENDING THIS WIRE TO YOU AFTER WHAT I CONSIDER A MOST UNUSUAL AND SUCCESSFUL PRESS PREVIEW. THE VERDICT WAS ONE HUNDRED PER CENT UNANIMOUS VERY FAVORABLE FROM BOTH PRESS AND LAY AUDIENCE. . . . DID YOU EVER SEE A DREAM WALKING? THAT'S ME AS I DICTATE THIS WIRE. . . . I FEEL IT IS SAFE TO SAY THAT PICTURE WILL NOT DISAPPOINT ANYONE. AFFECTIONATE REGARDS

SOL LESSER

Preface to Three Plays:
'Our Town,' 'The Skin of Our Teeth,' 'The Matchmaker'

Toward the end of the 'twenties I began to lose pleasure in going to the theater. I ceased to believe in the stories I saw presented there. When I did go it was to admire some secondary aspect of the play, the work of a great actor or director or designer. Yet at the same time the conviction was growing in me that the theater was the greatest of all the arts. I felt that something had gone wrong with it in my time and that it was fulfilling only a small part of its potentialities. I was filled with admiration for presentations of classical works by Max Reinhardt and Louis Jouvet and the Old Vic, as I was by the best plays of my own time, like *Desire Under the Elms* and *The Front Page*; but at heart I didn't believe a word of them. I was like a schoolmaster grading a paper; to each of these offerings I gave an A plus, but the condition of mind of one grading a paper is not that of one being overwhelmed by an artistic creation. The response we make when we "believe" a work of the imagination is that of saying: "This is the way things are. I have always known it without being fully aware that I knew it. Now in the presence of this play or novel or poem (or picture or piece of music) I know that I know it." It is this form of knowledge which Plato called "recollection." We have all murdered, in thought; and been murdered. We have all seen the ridiculous in estimable persons and in ourselves. We have all known terror as well as enchantment. Imaginative literature has nothing to say to those who do not recognize—who cannot be *reminded*—of such conditions. Of all the arts the theater is best endowed to awaken this recollection within us—to believe is to say "yes"; but in the theaters of my time I did not feel myself prompted to any such grateful and self-forgetting acquiescence.

This dissatisfaction worried me. I was not ready to condemn myself as blasé and overfastidious, for I knew that I was still capable of belief. I believed every word of *Ulysses* and of Proust and of *The Magic Mountain*, as I did of hundreds of plays when I read them. It was on the stage that imaginative narration became false. Finally, my dissatisfaction passed into resentment. I began to feel that the theater was not only inadequate, it was evasive; it did not wish to draw upon its deeper potentialities. I found the word for it: it aimed to be *soothing*. The tragic had no heat; the comic had no bite; the social criticism failed to indict us with responsibility. I began to search for the point where the theater had run off the track, where it had chosen—and been permitted—to become a minor art and an inconsequential diversion.

The trouble began in the nineteenth century and was connected with the rise of the middle classes—they wanted their theater soothing. There's nothing wrong with the middle classes in themselves. We know that now. The United States and Scandinavia and Germany are middle-class countries, so completely so that they have lost the very memory of their once despised and ludicrous inferiority (they had been inferior not only to the aristocracy but, in human dignity, to the peasantry). When a middle class is new, however, there is much that is wrong with it. When it is emerging from under the shadow of an aristocracy, from the myth and prestige of those well-born Higher-ups, it is alternately insecure and aggressively complacent. It must find its justification and reassurance in making money and displaying it. To this day, members of the middle classes in England, France, and Italy feel themselves to be a little ridiculous and humiliated. The prestige of aristocracies is based upon a dreary untruth, that moral superiority and the qualifications for leadership are transmittable through the chromosomes, and the secondary lie, that the environment afforded by privilege and leisure tends to nurture the flowers of the spirit. An aristocracy, defending and fostering its lie, extracts from the arts only such elements as can further its interests, the aroma and not the sap, the grace and not the trenchancy. Equally harmful to culture is the newly arrived middle class. In the English-speaking world the middle classes came into power early in the nineteenth century and gained control over the theater. They were pious, law-abiding, and industrious. They were assured of eternal life in the next world and, in this, they were squarely seated on Property and the privileges that accompany it. They were attended by devoted servants who knew their place. They were benevolent within certain limits, but chose to ignore wide tracts of injustice and stupidity in the world about them; and they shrank from contemplating those elements within themselves that were ridiculous, shallow, and harmful. They distrusted the passions and tried to deny them. Their questions about the nature of life seemed to be sufficiently answered by the demonstration of financial status and by conformity to some clearly established rules of decorum. These were precarious positions; abysses yawned on either side. The air was loud with questions that must not be asked. These audiences fashioned a theater which could not disturb them. They thronged to melodrama (which deals with tragic possibilities in such a way that you know from the beginning that all will end happily) and to sentimental drama (which accords a total license to the supposition that the wish is father to the thought) and to comedies in which the characters were so represented that they always resembled someone else and not oneself. Between the plays that Sheridan wrote in his twenties and the first works of Wilde and Shaw there was no play of even moderate interest written in the English language. (Unless you happen to admire and except Shelley's *The Cenci*.) These audiences, however, also thronged to Shakespeare. How did they shield themselves against his probing? How did they smother the theater—and with such effect that it smothers us still? The box set was already there, the curtain, the proscenium, but not taken "seriously"—it was a convenience in view of the weather in northern countries. They took it seriously and emphasized and enhanced everything that thus removed, cut off, and boxed the action; they increasingly shut the play up into a museum showcase.

Let us examine why the box-set stage stifles the life in drama and why and how it militates against belief.

Every action which has ever taken place—every thought, every emotion—has taken place only once, at one moment in time and place. "I love you," "I rejoice," "I suffer," have been said and felt many billions of times, and never twice the same. Every person who has ever lived has lived an unbroken succession of unique occasions. Yet the more one is aware of this individuality in experience (innumerable! innumerable!) the more one becomes attentive to what these disparate moments have in common, to repetitive patterns. As an artist (or listener or beholder) which "truth" do you prefer—that of the isolated occasion, or that which includes and resumes the innumerable? Which truth is more worth telling? Every age differs in this. Is the Venus de Milo "one woman"? Is the play *Macbeth* the story of "one destiny"? The theater is admirably fitted to tell both truths. It has one foot planted firmly in the particular, since each actor before us (even when he wears a mask!) is indubitably a living, breathing "one"; yet it tends and strains to exhibit a general truth since its relation to a specific "realistic" truth is confused and undermined by the fact that it is an accumulation of untruths, pretenses, and fiction. The novel is preeminently the vehicle of the unique occasion, the theater of the generalized one. It is through the theater's power to raise the exhibited individual action into the realm of idea and type and universal that it is able to evoke our belief. But power is precisely what those nineteenth-century audiences did not—dared not—confront. They tamed it and drew its teeth; squeezed it into that removed showcase. They loaded the stage with specific objects, because every concrete object on the stage fixes and narrows the action to one moment in time and place. (Have you ever noticed that in the plays of Shakespeare no one—except occasionally a ruler—ever sits down? There were not even chairs on the English or Spanish stages in the time of Elizabeth I.) So it was by a jugglery with time that the middle classes devitalized the theater. When you emphasize *place* in the theater, you drag down and limit and harness time to it. You thrust the action back into past time, whereas it is precisely the glory of the stage that it is always "now" there. Under such production methods the characters are all dead before the action starts. You don't have to pay deeply from your heart's participation. No great age in the theater ever attempted to capture the audience's belief through this kind of specification and localization. I became dissatisfied with the theater because I was unable to lend credence to such childish attempts to be "real."

I began writing one-act plays that tried to capture not verisimilitude but reality. In *The Happy Journey to Trenton and*

Camden four kitchen chairs represent an automobile and a family travels seventy miles in twenty minutes. Ninety years go by in *The Long Christmas Dinner*. In *Pullman Car Hiawatha* some more plain chairs serve as berths and we hear the very vital statistics of the towns and fields that passengers are traversing; we hear their thoughts; we even hear the planets over their heads. In Chinese drama a character, by straddling a stick, conveys to us that he is on horseback. In almost every No play of the Japanese an actor makes a tour of the stage and we know that he is making a long journey. Think of the ubiquity that Shakespeare's stage afforded for the battle scenes at the close of *Julius Caesar* and *Antony and Cleopatra*. As we see them today what a cutting and hacking of the text takes place —what condescension, what contempt for his dramaturgy.

Our Town is not offered as a picture of life in a New Hampshire village; or as a speculation about the conditions of life after death (that element I merely took from Dante's *Purgatory*). It is an attempt to find a value above all price for the smallest events in our daily life. I have made the claim as preposterous as possible, for I have set the village against the largest dimensions of time and place. The recurrent words in this play (few have noticed it) are "hundreds," "thousands," and "millions." Emily's joys and griefs, her algebra lessons and her birthday presents—what are they when we consider all the billions of girls who have lived, who are living, and who will live? Each individual's assertion to an absolute reality can only be inner, very inner. And here the method of staging finds its justification—in the first two acts there are at least a few chairs and tables; but when Emily revisits the earth and the kitchen to which she descended on her twelfth birthday, the very chairs and table are gone. Our claim, our hope, our despair are in the mind—not in things, not in "scenery." Molière said that for the theater all he needed was a platform and a passion or two. The climax of this play needs only five square feet of boarding and the passion to know what life means to us.

The Matchmaker is an only slightly modified version of *The Merchant of Yonkers*, which I wrote in the year after I had written *Our Town*. One way to shake off the nonsense of the nineteenth-century staging is to make fun of it. This play par-

odies the stock-company plays that I used to see at Ye Liberty
Theatre, Oakland, California, when I was a boy. I have already
read small theses in German comparing it with the great Austrian original on which it is based. The scholars are very bewildered. There is most of the plot (except that our friend Dolly
Levi is not in Nestroy's play); there are some of the tags; but
it's all "about" quite different matters. My play is about the aspirations of the young (and not only of the young) for a fuller,
freer participation in life. Imagine an Austrian pharmacist
going to the shelf to draw from a bottle which he knows to
contain a stinging corrosive liquid, guaranteed to remove
warts and wens; and imagine his surprise when he discovers
that it has been filled overnight with very American birch-bark
beer.

The Skin of Our Teeth begins, also, by making fun of old-
fashioned playwriting; but the audience soon perceives that it
is seeing "two times at once." The Antrobus family is living
both in prehistoric times and in a New Jersey commuters' sub-
urb today. Again, the events of our homely daily life—this time
the family life—are depicted against the vast dimensions of
time and place. It was written on the eve of our entrance into
the war and under strong emotion and I think it mostly comes
alive under conditions of crisis. It has been often charged with
being a bookish fantasia about history, full of rather bloodless
schoolmasterish jokes. But to have seen it in Germany soon
after the war, in the shattered churches and beerhalls that were
serving as theaters, with audiences whose price of admission
meant the loss of a meal and for whom it was of absorbing interest that there was a "recipe for grass soup that did not cause
the diarrhea," was an experience that was not so cool. I am very
proud that this year it has received a first and overwhelming
reception in Warsaw. The play is deeply indebted to James
Joyce's *Finnegans Wake*. I should be very happy if, in the
future, some author should feel similarly indebted to any work
of mine. Literature has always more resembled a torch race
than a furious dispute among heirs.

The theater has lagged behind the other arts in finding the
"new ways" to express how men and women think and feel in
our time. I am not one of the new dramatists we are looking

for. I wish I were. I hope I have played a part in preparing the way for them. I am not an innovator but a rediscoverer of forgotten goods and I hope a remover of obtrusive bric-a-brac. And as I view the work of my contemporaries I seem to feel that I am exceptional in one thing—I give (don't I?) the impression of having enormously enjoyed it.

Notes On 'The Alcestiad'

ALCESTIS chose to die for her husband. We are often told that soldiers die for their country, that reformers and men of science lay down their lives for us. Who commands them? Whence, and how do they receive the command?

The story of Alcestis has been retold many times. When her husband, Admetus, King of Thessaly, was mortally ill, a message came from Apollo saying that he would live if someone volunteered to die in his stead. Alcestis assumes the sacrifice and dies. The mighty Hercules happened to arrive at the palace during the funeral; he descended into the underworld, strove with Death, and brought her back to life. The second act of my play retells this story. There is, however, another legend involving King Admetus. Zeus, the father of gods and men, commanded Apollo to descend to earth and to live for one year as a man among men. Apollo chose to live as a herdsman in the fields of King Admetus. This story serves as the basis of my first act. My third act makes free use of the tradition that Admetus and Alcestis in their old age were supplanted by a tyrant and lived on as slaves in the palace where they had once been rulers.

On one level, my play recounts the life of a woman—of many women—from bewildered bride to sorely tested wife to overburdened old age. On another level it is a wildly romantic story of gods and men, of death and hell and resurrection, of great loves and great trials, of usurpation and revenge. On another level, however, it is a comedy about a very serious matter.

These old legends seem at first glance to be clear enough. One would say that they had been retold for our edification; they are exemplary. Yet on closer view many of them—the stories of Oedipus, of the sacrifice of Isaac, of Cassandra—give the impression of having been retained down the ages because they are ambiguous and puzzling. We are told that Apollo loved Admetus and Alcestis. If so, how strangely he exhibited it. It must make for considerable discomfort to have the god of the sun, of healing and song, housed among one's farm workers. And why should divine love impose on a devoted couple the decision as to which should die for the other? And why (though the question has been asked so many millions of times) should the omnipotent friend permit some noble human beings to end their days in humiliation and suffering?

Following some meditations of Søren Kierkegaard, I have written a comedy about the extreme difficulty of any dialogue between heaven and earth, about the misunderstandings that result from the "incommensurability of things human and divine." Kierkegaard described God under the image of "the unhappy lover." If He revealed Himself to us in His glory, we would fall down in abasement, but abasement is not love. If He divested Himself of the divine attributes in order to come nearer to us, that would be an act of condescension. This is a play about how Apollo searched for a language in which he could converse with Admetus and Alcestis and with their innumerable descendants; and about how Alcestis, through many a blunder, learned how to listen and interpret the things that Apollo was so urgently trying to say to her.

Yet I am aware of other levels, and perhaps deeper ones that will only become apparent to me later.

Noting the Nature of Farce

S URELY highly civilized societies can never enjoy farce, farce which depends on extreme improbability and on the laughter aroused by the spectacle of someone's mental and physical anguish.

These long-lost twins that arrive in the same town; these girls dressed as boys that are not recognized by their closest friends; these deceived husbands under torment; these guardians beaten by mistake; these respectable and distraught ladies with men hidden all over their rooms.

Farce would seem to be intended for childlike minds still touched with grossness; but the history of the theater shows us that the opposite is true. Farce has always flourished in ages of refinement and great cultural activity.

And the reason lies where one would least expect it: farce is based on logic and objectivity.

The author of a farce may ask his audience to concede him two or three wild improbabilities, but thereafter he must proceed with an all the more rigorous consequence. The laughter is an explosion of almost grudging concession: "Yes, granted that premise, these things would inevitably follow."

The School for Scandal simmers along among a thousand mild improbabilities; it is a comedy; but *The Importance of Being Earnest* shows us what would be bound to happen if a man invented an invalid brother who needed his attendance whenever he wished to shirk a tedious engagement, and what would happen if his friend decided to impersonate this brother.

The pleasures of farce, like those of the detective story, are those of development, pattern, and logic.

A "pure" farce would be all pattern and would admit no mixture. Comedy, which is the clarification of unsocial human traits through exaggeration, may benefit by a dash of farce, especially toward the close of the evening; but farce dare not lean too far toward the exposition of character.

She Stoops to Conquer is not primarily about a man who mistakes a private house for an inn, which would be farce; but about a man so shy that he cannot converse at ease with a

691

"lady of quality," which is comedy. *Twelfth Night* is not about a girl who dresses as a man in order to make her way out of destitution; but about a girl who is clear-eyed in a world of misguided "humorous" beings.

Since farce is an intellectual exercise, the only ornament it welcomes is the additional intellectual pleasure of lines of social comment and generalization. It is significant that "the fires of the French Revolution were lighted" during a soliloquy in Beaumarchais's *The Marriage of Figaro*; and the early farces of Molière cast a host of proverbial expressions into the French language.

And the cruelty of farce?

Theorists since Aristotle—whose lecture-notes on this matter were unfortunately lost—have tried to analyze the springs of laughter. In this century two distinguished hands have written books on the subject, Bergson and Freud.

Bergson says that we laugh when we see man—man who prides himself on living by choice, reason, and free will—reduced to being a victim of the same forces that govern things. Pretentious man reduced to an automaton is funny; a scrubwoman who slips on a banana peel is less funny than a bank president in a silk hat.

Freud says our laughter is a release of a grudge against a universe which has since infancy crossed our ambitions and defeated our egocentric wishes. Civilization, however, has educated us; we do not wish, even in our own eyes, to be transparent in the revelation of our wounded pride. We cannot give vent to our animus until incongruity or the verbal ingenuity of wit gives us the pretext and the permission.

A lady who had forgotten that Whistler hated Turner said to him: "Oh, Mr. Whistler, my husband has discovered in a secondhand shop what he thinks are two real Turners. Will you come and tell us whether they are real Turners or imitation Turners?" "Well, ma'am," replied Whistler, adjusting his monocle, "that is a fine distinction."

Wit is the permitted suspension of decorum and the retaliation of the underdog.

There has never been a "pure" farce. Terence's *Andria* is

crossed with melancholy; Goldoni's *The Liar* is perfect in ingenuity and design, but is forever straying off into psychological
finesse; Nestroy's *The Talisman* delays in Dutch genre-
painting of three social strata. Perhaps—as with the "pure" detective story—it would not be so desirable after all. Perhaps a
wavering among other elements makes it bearable: toward humor, its natural enemy, for humor is the acknowledgment of
one's kinship with frailty; toward character-drawing; toward
picturesqueness, a static quality; even toward pathos—perhaps
all these are necessary to keep it from the ultimately empty triumph of its two fundamental drives: logic and objectivity.

Some Thoughts on Playwriting

Four fundamental conditions of the drama separate it from the other arts. Each of these conditions has its advantages and disadvantages, each requires a particular aptitude from the dramatist, and from each there are a number of instructive consequences to be derived. These conditions are:

I. The theater is an art which reposes upon the work of many collaborators;
II. It is addressed to the group-mind;
III. It is based upon a pretense and its very nature calls out a multiplication of pretenses;
IV. Its action takes place in a perpetual present time.

I

THE THEATER IS AN ART WHICH REPOSES
UPON THE WORK OF MANY COLLABORATORS.

We have been accustomed to think that a work of art is by definition the product of one governing selecting will. A landscape by Cézanne consists of thousands of brushstrokes each commanded by one mind. *Paradise Lost* and *Pride and Prejudice*, even in cheap frayed copies, bear the immediate and exclusive message of one intelligence. It is true that in musical performance we meet with intervening executants, but the element of intervention is slight compared to that which takes place in drama. Illustrations:

1. One of the finest productions of *The Merchant of Venice* in our time showed Sir Henry Irving as Shylock, a noble, wronged, and indignant being, of such stature that the merchants of Venice dwindled before him into irresponsible schoolboys. He was confronted in court by a gracious, even queenly Portia, Miss Ellen Terry. At the Odéon in Paris, however, Gémier played Shylock as a vengeful and hysterical buffoon, confronted in court by a Portia who was a *gamine* from the Paris streets with a lawyer's quill three feet long over her ear; at the close of the trial scene Shylock was driven screaming about the auditorium, behind the spectators' backs and onto

the stage again, in a wild Elizabethan revel. Yet for all their divergences both were admirable productions of the play.

2. If there was ever a play in which fidelity to the author's requirements was essential in the representation of the principal rôle, it would seem to be Ibsen's *Hedda Gabler*, for the play is primarily an exposition of her character. Ibsen's directions read:

Enter from the left Hedda Gabler. She is a woman of twenty-nine. Her face and figure show great refinement and distinction. Her complexion is pale and opaque. Her steel-gray eyes express an unruffled calm. Her hair is of an attractive medium brown, but is not particularly abundant; and she is dressed in a flowing loose-fitting morning gown.

I once saw Eleonora Duse in this rôle. She was a woman of sixty and made no effort to conceal it. Her complexion was pale and transparent. Her hair was white, and she was dressed in a gown that suggested some medieval empress in mourning. And the performance was very fine.

One may well ask: Why write for the theater at all? Why not work in the novel, where such deviations from one's intentions cannot take place?

There are two answers:

1. The theater presents certain vitalities of its own so inviting and stimulating that the writer is willing to receive them in compensation for this inevitable variation from an exact image.

2. The dramatist through working in the theater gradually learns not merely to take account of the presence of the collaborators, but to derive advantage from them; and he learns, above all, to organize the play in such a way that its strength lies not in appearances beyond his control, but in the succession of events and in the unfolding of an idea, in narration.

The gathered audience sits in a darkened room, one end of which is lighted. The nature of the transaction at which it is gazing is a succession of events illustrating a general idea—the stirring of the idea; the gradual feeding out of information; the shock and counter-shock of circumstances; the flow of action; the interruption of action; the moments of allusion to earlier events; the preparation of surprise, dread, or delight—all that is the author's and his alone.

For reasons to be discussed later—the expectancy of the group-mind, the problem of time on the stage, the absence of the narrator, the element of pretense—the theater carries the art of narration to a higher power than the novel or the epic poem. The theater is unfolding action and in the disposition of events the authors may exercise a governance so complete that the distortions effected by the physical appearance of actors, by the fancies of scene-painters, and the misunderstandings of directors, fall into relative insignificance. It is just because the theater is an art of many collaborators, with the constant danger of grave misinterpretation, that the dramatist learns to turn his attention to the laws of narration, its logic, and its deep necessity of presenting a unifying idea stronger than its mere collection of happenings. The dramatist must be by instinct a storyteller.

There is something mysterious about the endowment of the storyteller. Some very great writers possessed very little of it, and some others, lightly esteemed, possessed it in so large a measure that their books survive down the ages, to the confusion of severer critics. Alexandre Dumas had it to an extraordinary degree; while Melville, for all his splendid quality, had it barely sufficiently to raise his work from the realm of nonfiction. It springs, not, as some have said, from an aversion to general ideas, but from an instinctive coupling of idea and illustration; the idea, for a born storyteller, can only be expressed imbedded in its circumstantial illustration. The myth, the parable, the fable are the fountainhead of all fiction and in them is seen most clearly the didactic, moralizing employment of a story. Modern taste shrinks from emphasizing the central idea that hides behind the fiction, but it exists there nevertheless, supplying the unity to fantasizing, and offering a justification to what otherwise we would repudiate as mere arbitrary contrivance, pretentious lying, or individualistic emotional association-spinning. For all their magnificent intellectual endowment, George Meredith and George Eliot were not born storytellers; they chose fiction as the vehicle for their reflections, and the passing of time is revealing their error in that choice. Jane Austen was pure storyteller and her works are outlasting those of apparently more formidable rivals. The theater is more exacting than the novel in regard to this faculty and its presence constitutes a force which compensates the dramatist for the deviations which are introduced into his work by the presence of his collaborators.

The chief of these collaborators are the actors.

The actor's gift is a combination of three separate faculties or endowments. Their presence to a high degree in any one person is extremely rare, although the ambition to possess them is common. Those who rise to the height of the profession represent a selection and a struggle for survival in one of the most difficult and cruel of the artistic activities. The three endowments that compose the gift are observation, imagination, and physical coordination.

1. An observant and analyzing eye for all modes of behavior about us, for dress and manner, and for the signs of thought and emotion in oneself and in others.

2. The strength of imagination and memory whereby the actor may, at the indication in the author's text, explore his store of observations and represent the details of appearance and the intensity of the emotions—joy, fear, surprise, grief, love, and hatred—and through imagination extend them to intenser degrees and to differing characterizations.

3. A physical coordination whereby the force of these inner realizations may be communicated to voice, face, and body.

An actor must *know* the appearances and the mental states; he must *apply* his knowledge to the rôle; and he must physically *express* his knowledge. Moreover, his concentration must be so great that he can effect this representation under conditions of peculiar difficulty—in abrupt transition from the non-imaginative conditions behind the stage; and in the presence of fellow actors who may be momentarily destroying the reality of the action.

A dramatist prepares the characterization of his personages in such a way that it will take advantage of the actor's gift.

Characterization in a novel is presented by the author's dogmatic assertion that the personage was such, and by an analysis of the personage with generally an account of his or her past. Since in the drama this is replaced by the actual presence of the personage before us and since there is no occasion for the intervening all-knowing author to instruct us as to his or her inner nature, a far greater share is given in a play to (1) highly

characteristic utterances and (2) concrete occasions in which
the character defines itself under action and (3) a conscious
preparation of the text whereby the actor may build upon the
suggestions in the rôle according to his own abilities.

Characterization in a play is like a blank check which the
dramatist accords to the actor for him to fill in—not entirely
blank, for a number of indications of individuality are already
there, but to a far less definite and absolute degree than in the
novel.

The dramatist's principal interest being the movement of
the story, he is willing to resign the more detailed aspects of
characterization to the actor and is often rewarded beyond his
expectation.

The sleepwalking scene from *Macbeth* is a highly com-
pressed selection of words whereby despair and remorse rise to
the surface of indirect confession. It is to be assumed that had
Shakespeare lived to see what the genius of Sarah Siddons
could pour into the scene from that combination of observation, self-knowledge, imagination, and representational skill,
even he might have exclaimed, "I never knew I wrote so well!"

II

THE THEATER IS AN ART ADDRESSED
TO A GROUP-MIND.

Painting, sculpture, and the literature of the book are certainly
solitary experiences; and it is likely that most people would
agree that the audience seated shoulder to shoulder in a concert hall is not an essential element in musical enjoyment.

But a play presupposes a crowd. The reasons for this go
deeper than (1) the economic necessity for the support of the
play and (2) the fact that the temperament of actors is prover-
bially dependent on group attention.

It rests on the fact that (1) the pretense, the fiction, on the
stage would fall to pieces and absurdity without the support
accorded to it by the crowd, and (2) the excitement induced
by pretending a fragment of life is such that it partakes of ritual
and festival, and requires a throng.

Similarly, the fiction that royal personages are of a mysteriously different nature from other people requires audiences,

levées, and processions for its maintenance. Since the beginnings of society, satirists have occupied themselves with the descriptions of kings and queens in their intimacy and delighted in showing how the prerogatives of royalty become absurd when the crowd is not present to extend to them the enhancement of an imaginative awe.

The theater partakes of the nature of festival. Life imitated is life raised to a higher power. In the case of comedy, the vitality of these pretended surprises, deceptions, and *contretemps* becomes so lively that before a spectator, solitary or regarding himself as solitary, the structure of so much event would inevitably expose the artificiality of the attempt and ring hollow and unjustified; and in the case of tragedy, the accumulation of woe and apprehension would soon fall short of conviction. All actors know the disturbing sensation of playing before a handful of spectators at a dress rehearsal or performance where only their interest in pure craftsmanship can barely sustain them. During the last rehearsals the phrase is often heard: "This play is hungry for an audience."

Since the theater is directed to a group-mind, a number of consequences follow:

1. A group-mind presupposes, if not a lowering of standards, a broadening of the fields of interest. The other arts may presuppose an audience of connoisseurs trained in leisure and capable of being interested in certain rarefied aspects of life. The dramatist may be prevented from exhibiting, for example, detailed representations of certain moments in history that require specialized knowledge in the audience, or psychological states in the personages which are of insufficient general interest to evoke self-identification in the majority. In the Second Part of Goethe's *Faust* there are long passages dealing with the theory of paper money. The exposition of the nature of misanthropy (so much more drastic than Molière's) in Shakespeare's *Timon of Athens* has never been a success. The dramatist accepts this limitation in subject matter and realizes that the group-mind imposes upon him the necessity of treating material understandable by the larger number.

2. It is the presence of the group-mind that brings another requirement to the theater—forward movement.

Maeterlinck said that there was more drama in the spectacle

of an old man seated by a table than in the majority of plays offered to the public. He was juggling with the various meanings
in the word "drama." In the sense whereby drama means the
intensified concentration of life's diversity and significance he
may well have been right; if he meant drama as a theatrical
representation before an audience, he was wrong. Drama on
the stage is inseparable from forward movement, from action.

Many attempts have been made to present Plato's dialogues,
Gobineau's fine series of dialogues, *La Renaissance*, and the
Imaginary Conversations of Landor, but without success.
Through some ingredient in the group-mind, and through the
sheer weight of anticipation involved in the dressing-up and
the assumption of fictional rôles, an action is required, and an
action that is more than a mere progress in argumentation and
debate.

III

THE THEATER IS A WORLD OF PRETENSE.

It lives by conventions: a convention is an agreed-upon falsehood, a permitted lie.

Illustrations: Consider at the first performance of the *Medea*,
the passage where Medea meditates the murder of her children. An anecdote from antiquity tells us that the audience
was so moved by this passage that considerable disturbance
took place.

The following conventions were involved:

1. Medea was played by a man.

2. He wore a large mask on his face. In the lip of the mask
was an acoustical device for projecting the voice. On his feet he
wore shoes with soles and heels half a foot high.

3. His costume was so designed that it conveyed to the audience, by convention: woman of royal birth and Oriental
origin.

4. The passage was in metric speech. All poetry is an
"agreed-upon falsehood" in regard to speech.

5. The lines were sung in a kind of recitative. All opera involves this "permitted lie" in regard to speech.

Modern taste would say that the passage would convey
much greater pathos if a woman "like Medea" had delivered

it—with an uncovered face that exhibited all the emotions she was undergoing. For the Greeks, however, there was no pretense that Medea was on the stage. The mask, the costume, the mode of declamation were a series of signs which the spectator interpreted and reassembled in his own mind. Medea was being re-created within the imagination of each of the spectators.

The history of the theater shows us that in its greatest ages the stage employed the greatest number of conventions. The stage is fundamental pretense and it thrives on the acceptance of that fact and in the multiplication of additional pretenses. When it tries to assert that the personages in the action "really are," really inhabit such-and-such rooms, really suffer such-and-such emotions, it loses rather than gains credibility. The modern world is inclined to laugh condescendingly at the fact that in the plays of Racine and Corneille the gods and heroes of antiquity were dressed like the courtiers under Louis XIV; that in the Elizabethan Age scenery was replaced by placards notifying the audience of the location; and that a whip in the hand and a jogging motion of the body indicated that a man was on horseback in the Chinese theater; these devices did not spring from naïveté, however, but from the vitality of the public imagination in those days and from an instinctive feeling as to where the essential and where the inessential lay in drama.

The convention has two functions:

1. It provokes the collaborative activity of the spectator's imagination; and

2. It raises the action from the specific to the general.

This second aspect is of even greater importance than the first.

If Juliet is represented as a girl "very like Juliet"—it was not merely a deference to contemporary prejudices that assigned this rôle to a boy in the Elizabethan Age—moving about in a "real" house with marble staircases, rugs, lamps, and furniture, the impression is irresistibly conveyed that these events happened to this one girl, in one place, at one moment in time. When the play is staged as Shakespeare intended it, the bareness of the stage releases the events from the particular and the experience of Juliet partakes of that of all girls in love, in every time, place, and language.

The stage continually strains to tell this generalized truth and it is the element of pretense that reinforces it. Out of the lie, the pretense, of the theater proceeds a truth more compelling than the novel can attain, for the novel by its own laws is constrained to tell of an action that "once happened"— "once upon a time."

IV

THE ACTION ON THE STAGE TAKES PLACE
IN A PERPETUAL PRESENT TIME.

Novels are written in the past tense. The characters in them, it is true, are represented as living moment by moment their present time, but the constant running commentary of the novelist ("Tess slowly descended into the valley"; "Anna Karenina laughed") inevitably conveys to the reader the fact that these events are long since past and over.

The novel is a past reported in the present. On the stage it is always now. This confers upon the action an increased vitality which the novelist longs in vain to incorporate into his work.

This condition in the theater brings with it another important element:

In the theater we are not aware of the intervening storyteller. The speeches arise from the characters in an apparently pure spontaneity.

A play is what takes place.

A novel is what one person tells us took place.

A play visibly represents pure existing. A novel is what one mind, claiming to omniscience, asserts to have existed.

Many dramatists have regretted this absence of the narrator from the stage, with his point of view, his powers of analyzing the behavior of the characters, his ability to interfere and supply further facts about the past, about simultaneous actions not visible on the stage, and, above *all*, his function of pointing the moral and emphasizing the significance of the action. In some periods of the theater he has been present as chorus, or prologue and epilogue, or as *raisonneur*. But surely this absence constitutes an additional force to the form, as well as an additional tax upon the writer's skill. It is the task of the dramatist so to coordinate his play, through the selection of episodes and speeches, that, though he is himself not visible,

his point of view and his governing intention will impose themselves on the spectator's attention, not as dogmatic assertion or
motto, but as self-evident truth and inevitable deduction.

Imaginative narration—the invention of souls and destinies
—is to a philosopher an all but indefensible activity.

Its justification lies in the fact that the communication of
ideas from one mind to another inevitably reaches the point
where exposition passes into illustration, into parable, met-
aphor, allegory, and myth.

It is no accident that when Plato arrived at the height of his
argument and attempted to convey a theory of knowledge and
a theory of the structure of man's nature, he passed over into
storytelling, into the myths of the Cave and the Charioteer;
and that the great religious teachers have constantly had re-
course to the parable as a means of imparting their deepest
intuitions.

The theater offers to imaginative narration its highest possibilities. It has many pitfalls and its very vitality betrays it into
service as mere diversion and the enhancement of insignificant
matter; but it is well to remember that it was the theater that
rose to the highest place during those epochs that aftertime
has chosen to call "great ages" and that the Athens of Pericles
and the reigns of Elizabeth I, Philip II, and Louis XIV were
also the ages that gave to the world the greatest dramas it has
known.

Richard Beer-Hofmann's
'Jaakobs Traum'

R ICHARD BEER-HOFMANN in *Jaakobs Traum* retells the story of the deception which Rebecca and Jacob played upon Isaac and interprets the vision which came to Jacob at Bethel. In the unfinished trilogy to which this play serves as prologue he recounts the life of King David.

The retelling of the great myths forms a large part of the literature of all countries; the last fifty years have shown a surprising increase in this form of literature. In the light of Beer-Hofmann's distinguished achievement it is of interest to consider the problems which accompany the treatment of such themes and, in particular, his solution of them.

A number of origins may be ascribed to the myth, and any definition of the myth should reflect the variety of such origins and the possibility of any given myth being at one or other of the phases through which all myths pass.

A myth at the moment when it is employed as the basis of a work of literature, however, may be defined a story:

1. Whose historical authenticity is so far irrelevant as to permit to the narrator an assumption of omniscience in regard to what took place;

2. Whose antiquity and popular diffusion confer upon it an authority which limits the degree of variation that may be employed in its retelling; and

3. Whose subject matter is felt to have a significance which renders each retelling a contribution to the received ideas of the entire community to which, in a very real sense, it belongs.

Such a definition, however, still includes the animal fables of worldly wisdom and the fairy tales of childhood.

A fourth clause in the definition must be sought further.

The most persistent myths are stumbling blocks; they are not reassuring but disturbing. The writer who sets out to retell them discovers that a mere filling-in of the story with visual and psychological details is not sufficient. The survival of these stories seems to be due to their being questions and not answers in regard to the human situation.

Their tenacity is endlessly surprising. They are among the few things of which it may be said with assurance that they have a long future. Speculations as to their origin do not sufficiently explain this persistence. Anthropologists assure us that they may have come to us from any of three sources or from any combination of the three. They may have been put forward to explain natural phenomena. Helen and Siegfried, the golden-haired, were each originally the sun, hidden by the clouds, captured by the Trojans and by the Nibelungen. Myths may be the reports of historical events and persons, exaggerated in the course of innumerable retellings, assimilated to natural phenomena and reinforced by emotional fantasies, religious, patriotic, or instinctual. They may testify to the relations of tribes and races and the syncretism which took place among their religions. Under this interpretation Europa and the Bull-God should be understood to read Europa the Cow-Goddess and Zeus the Man-God; Leda, and not her lover, was the swan. Psychologists are saying that many myths have their origin in the unavowed fantasies of the subconscious and that an Oedipus is slain in every family and that a Moses is sanctified by his murderers in many a religion.

These elements may play a large part in the formation and persistence of many myths. In those, however, which are most frequently retold another element is more constantly recognizable and is more frequently seized upon by the poets who in successive ages have chosen to retell them.

They are questions and not answers in regard to the human situation. In the majority of cases the questions seem to have to do with the mind disengaging itself from the passions or finding its true position in the presence of the established authorities, human or divine. They are concretizations of man's besetting preoccupation with the mind and the mind's struggle to know itself; and each retelling requires that some answer be furnished to the question that infuses every part of the story.

These stories, then, are not reassuring, but disturbing. Soothing stories have been plentiful in all ages—and to the

philosophical sense few stories are as soothing as adventure
stories—but each of these circulates for a time and is forgotten. To survive, a story must arouse wonder, wonder in both
the senses in which we now employ the word: astonishment
at the extent of man's capability for good and evil, and speculation as to the sources of that capability. Not least troubling
have been those which seem to have been raised by dogma to
the realm of the unquestionable. Nor have all the resources of
the greatest writers engaged upon their acknowledged masterpieces been able to bring to definite solution the problems set
by these old stories. Certain of them seem to grow even more
urgent with the passing of time. Those, for instance, concerning Prometheus, Satan, Adam, Faust, Phaëthon, and Icarus
converge upon a number of related questions: Can intellectual
advance be made without disobedience? Must intellectual inquiry and mastery over nature be paid for by self-destruction?
At each retelling, such stories as those of Job, Oedipus, Orestes
(Orestes-Hamlet), Cassandra, and Tristram break through the
established interpretations and re-insist upon questions which
appeared to have been settled. Sometimes a figure of myth
seems—like Ulysses of the *Odyssey*—to have achieved a state of
rest, to be merely exemplary; but the great writers of the successive ages do not permit a characterization of such vitality to
remain unquestioned. Sophocles and Euripides dealt harshly
with him; Dante showed him under eternal torture in Hell;
Shakespeare mocked him as the mouthpiece of a glib worldly
wisdom; through him Tennyson voiced the all-but-despairing
aspiration of his time; James Joyce in a vast parody made him
an image of modern man, abashed and rootless, but "long-
enduring" and "of many devices."

The story of the command which Abraham received to sacrifice Isaac is so appalling that only a mind which is cruel to itself can gaze at it fixedly. In the last century, however, Søren
Kierkegaard wrung from it a reading of such power that, like a
strong wind, it is blowing through the thought of the foremost religious philosophers of the Greek Orthodox, the Roman Catholic, and the Protestant faiths.

Jaakobs Traum retells two disturbing myths. Behind the
story of Rebecca's fraudulent substitution of Jacob as leader of

his people one hears Kierkegaard's urgent question: "Is there a teleological suspension of the ethical?" Beer-Hofmann does not hesitate in his answer, either in this play or in *Der Junge David*: there is a line of succession in the leadership of men that is indicated by spiritual insight and which is justified in overriding the customs and received opinions of any localized community.

The second myth retold is that of God's message to Jacob at Bethel, the famous promise to the Jewish people:

. . . and in thee and in thy seed shall all the families of the earth be blessed. And behold I am with thee and will keep thee whithersoever thou goest, and will bring thee back into this land; for I will not leave thee, until I have done that which I have spoken to thee of.

Beer-Hofmann's interpretation of these words avoids none of the difficulty of understanding them in the light of the thousands of years of persecution; with prophetic power he describes the new trials which were to be visited on the Jewish people during the years following the writing of the play. There are few more impressive passages in modern literature than those in this work wherein it is developed that suffering can be experienced as a "distinction." It is a doctrine which is not easy to express in words; those in comfort do not wish to hear it and those under trial are wary of receiving facile consolations. Beer-Hofmann's statement irresistibly recalls three other passages on the subject: Milton's two sonnets on his blindness and the invocation to Light in *Paradise Lost*; Pascal's prayer on his illness; and the Baron von Hügel's letters on "the uses of pain," written to a friend dying of an incurable disease.

There are three pitfalls in the way of writers who undertake to retell a myth: they may seek to transpose it into rationalistic and realistic terms; they may seek to make it the vehicle of autobiographic identification; and they may rely solely upon its antiquity and accumulated authority for force, without convincing us that they have wrestled with the basic ideas inherent in the story and found their authority within their own creative vision. It is instructive to see the way in which Beer-Hofmann has avoided each of these dangers.

A myth, passing from oral tradition into literature, moves most congenially into poetry and particularly into the poetic drama. Even the most rationalistic reader consents to receive as *given* the elements of the supernatural and the incredible that are involved in these ancient stories. Their validity rests on the general ideas they contain. The novel carries with it the inevitable requirement of presenting the realistic atmosphere of the daily life, which in the case of such ancient stories means the accompaniment of varying amounts of archeological and anthropological learning. The characters whom we have endowed with the life of significant ideas must be endowed with a different kind of life—that of the recognizable quotidian. The noble narratives which Thomas Mann has based upon the story of Joseph occasionally exhibit the constraint imposed by this transposition. So great, however, is the gulf between the two kinds of reality that it can be said that it has seldom been bridged in either direction, save by parody, a method peculiarly suitable to this literary problem. By this method Cervantes achieved the force of myth against the background of the Spanish roads and taverns of his time. A result in the opposite direction, from sublimity to the naturalistic, frequently skirts the ludicrous, a danger that even the suave tact of Renan did not escape in his *Vie de Jésus.*

Among the most interesting aspects of *Jaakobs Traum* is the art with which Beer-Hofmann gradually moves from the relatively realistic presentation of Isaac's ranch at the opening and by gradual infusion of other-worldly elements prepares us for the vast perspectives of the close.

Der Junge David is not based on mythical material. The chapters of the Books of Samuel which it retells are historical narrative. But the great prologue which is *Jaakobs Traum* has established the framework and tenor of the world of myth, which is universal application and basic issues, and it may be assumed that the conclusion of the trilogy would have carried the retelling of David's life back into the thought-world presented to us at the close of the prologue.

Myths do not easily lend themselves to being retold as the vehicle of an individual author's self-identification. They come to us molded by the pressure of innumerable storytellers and listeners; their heroes and heroines are legion. The writers who announce themselves as Cassandra, as Cain, as Dedalus arouse in us a feeling of embarrassment. The gulf between the mythical type and the isolated individual is too great for any writer to cross; assertion passes into rant and pathos into bathos. The myth is everyman's and no man's. It is not impossible that the lack of organic directness in Shelley's *Prometheus Unbound* is a result of the poet's inability to decide as to the extent to which he will project himself as the great revolutionary of Greek tradition.

Beer-Hofmann has a profoundly urgent message to convey. Nothing indicates the elevation of his thought more clearly than the way by which this message comes to us divested of personal assertion yet of undiminished intensity. It is unnecessary to enlarge upon the third of the three pitfalls I have indicated above: he does not rely on the solemn authority of the Biblical story to project his work; all has been thought through and made his own. He has accomplished the ultimate requirement of this type of literature: to preserve the universality of a story which is the property of the whole world without robbing it of its immediacy to each individual who addresses himself to it.

Those already familiar with the original text will discover with pleasure that the present translation is both faithful and musical. The fact that Beer-Hofmann worked closely with the translator, weighing over the exact shade of his intention, has furnished us a number of readings which are particularly precious, constituting as they do a sort of gloss or amplification of the original.

It is to be hoped that *Der Junge David* will also soon be presented to English readers.

The loss which the world of letters sustained with the death of Beer-Hofmann will be felt for a long time. It is a consolation, however, to know that an ever widening circle of readers will come to know the beauty and power of his work.

Sophocles's 'Oedipus Rex'

O NE of the remarkable aspects of the survival of literary
masterpieces down through the centuries is the diversity
of reasons which the successive ages have found for admiring
them. They are like great, slowly revolving lamps which turn a
different face to each new generation that confronts them.
Many of them have outlasted the spoken life of the language in
which they were written and the social and religious ideas that
played a large part in their inspiration, but such is their depth
and variety that ever new aspects emerge to replace those
which have lost their immediacy. The *Aeneid* was intended to
be an inspiring appeal to patriotic emotion; then for centuries
it was held to be a prophetical allegory of the Christian dispen-
sation; for a time it was looked upon as a book of magic, and
fortunes were told through the blindfold singling out of a line
from its pages; now it is most often praised for its passages of
melancholy and pathos. For centuries *The Divine Comedy*
served as a poem of piety and instruction; now even the foremost Italian critic regards it as a conglomerate of poetry and
non-poetry and advises the reader to cull from its vast doctri-
nal scaffolding the intermittent moments of poetic and dramatic force. We have much anecdotic evidence that *Don
Quixote* was originally received as boisterous comedy; now it is
the peculiar treasure of the reflective. Similarly, the *Oedipus
Rex*, though it contains much that has commanded uniform
admiration in every age, presents a number of aspects which
were more impressive to the Greeks than they are to us, and
others, indifferent or imperceptible to the contemporaries of
Sophocles, which particularly engage the modern mind. It is
the task of the attentive reader first of all to reconstruct, as far
as he is able, the values which were most apparent to the original audience. In the *Oedipus Rex* there was one that exceeded
even its technical ingenuity, its psychological truth, and its eloquence, and that was its religious force. Apollo does not appear upon the scene, but the terror of his presence and his will
is the true subject of the play. There has been little religious
drama in Europe since the Greeks, and the theater has lost one

of its most powerful effects—the shudder and awe induced by the presence of the numinous, by the *tremendum* of religious experience; and in order to do justice to this play we, over twenty centuries later, must attempt to recover something of this emotion.

When at the first performance Oedipus appeared at the doors of his palace and spoke the opening lines of the play, the Greek audience gazed at him not only with full knowledge of his past involuntary crimes and of his future misfortunes, but with an additional apprehension which may be underestimated by the modern spectator. They saw in him a man under the shadow of the hereditary curse which pursued all the descendants of Labdacus, a shadow recently enhanced by a second curse laid on his father by Pelops—the same Pelops who was himself accursed and whose malediction is wrought out in the lives of his own descendants, Agamemnon, Orestes, Electra, and Iphigeneia. In the eyes of the original audience the actions and motives of such a man would be understood to express the constant pressure of a force for destruction beyond his own control. In the same way, in the play about his daughter Antigone, the modern reader may forget that for the Greeks the heroine's courageous action and lofty sentiments were enhanced by the fact that she was not only the daughter of a great house, but a child of incest and enmeshed in the doom that weighed upon her family from the curses that had been pronounced upon it.

It is not difficult to see how the idea of the hereditary curse could develop in primitive society. It satisfied the longing for a balance of justice whereby a powerful, wicked man could be rendered uneasy in the belief that because of his enemy's curse his descendants would suffer in his stead, and whereby a wronged man with no power of direct retaliation could be comforted through the assurance that his curse had struck terror into his enemy's mind. Yet it is difficult to see how the Greeks throughout that century of unparalleled swift growth in philosophic thought could cling so tenaciously to this vestige of rudimentary ethics. It is doubly interesting, therefore, to watch the way in which the tragic poets sought to elevate the hereditary curse—an unavoidable *datum* in the legendary material they were transferring to the stage—and to raise it from the realm of superstition to religious insight. In the *Oedipus Rex*, the *Antigone*, and the *Oedipus at Colonus*, Sophocles has muted the allusions to the curse and has placed the action of a pursuing vengeance in the hands of Apollo under his attribute of presiding deity over the purity of the home. The Athenian audience knew that the pestilence with which the play opens had been sent by him; within one hundred lines of the opening Creon arrives from the god's temple at Delphi, followed presently by his priest Teiresias. The theatrical excitement inherent in this opening scene can best be illustrated by reference to another Greek play, the *Choephoroi* or *Libation-bearers* of Aeschylus. There the tomb of the still unavenged Agamemnon is in view of the audience. The Furies are imagined to be hovering near it, clamoring for the death of the murderers, Clytemnestra and Aegisthus. Electra turns about it, brooding on her revenge. Orestes, in disguise, returns from his long exile and makes his vows before it. The Queen has been visited by terrifying dreams and brings her offerings to appease it. The air is charged; to borrow an expression from children's games, the stage is "warm" and it grows to a white heat during the progress of the play. Similarly, the *Oedipus Rex* opens at the moment that the "other world" has chosen to intervene in human affairs, to set in motion the train of events that will bring to light the enormities in Oedipus's past. The action of *Macbeth* and *Hamlet* is likewise instituted by supernatural agencies, but the witches and the ghost of Hamlet's father are easily understood as externalizations of the promptings within the protagonists' minds. In the Greek plays, however, the gods are objective forces and the audience received the anguish of Oedipus and the suicide of Iocasta as being required by a power greater and "other" than subjective fancy, and under a necessity more significant than the hereditary curse which Sophocles has elevated to a larger fatality, the cleansing will of Apollo.

It is this concentration of the punishment in the hands of Apollo which gives to the play its character of cruelty; for Apollo is punishing a patricide and an incest which had long since been predicted by his oracles and which depended for their fulfillment on slight and easily preventable coincidences. Oedipus's cry:

Apollo, friends, Apollo was he that brought these my woes to pass,
these my sore, sore woes . . .

seems to be as true of their having taken place originally as of
their being punished now. When a modern dramatist under-
took to retell the same story, he called his play *The Infernal
Machine*, and the impression that both plays make upon us is
that of an innocent man's being driven into a trap of vindictive
ingenuity and of then being punished for it with equal malice.
The *Oedipus Rex* seems to say: Destiny is engaged in the conscious preparations of man's humiliation. During the play, all
absorbed in the mounting tension, Sophocles does not stop to
consider the problem of Oedipus's responsibility for his involuntary crimes; but this is not the poet's last word on the life-
story of his hero. In the *Oedipus at Colonus*, which tradition
tells us was written some forty years later, he shows us Apollo
making amends and repentant of the part he had played. In
the later tragedy word comes from the oracle at Delphi that in-
estimable benefits will accrue to whatever country affords hospitality and sepulture to the aged outcast, and at the close of
the play Oedipus dies accompanied by many signs of divine
favor. It is as though Sophocles, like his hero, had been troubled
during the intervening years by all the philosophical questions
that inevitably arise from the earlier play, and as though he too
had seen that it was indeed those "pure and awful gods"
whom Oedipus had invoked who were ultimately responsible
for his misfortunes. Had the *Oedipus at Colonus* disappeared
with the reported eighty or ninety other plays of Sophocles,
the *Oedipus Rex* would have remained no less a masterpiece of
tragic art, but it would have been one degree further removed
from us by reason of this extreme picture it presents of the
helplessness of man. The catastrophes in the plays of Euripides, as in those of Shakespeare, proceed from flaws in the protagonists' characters rather than from the implacable workings
of circumstance. The sufferings that men endure as a result of
their weaknesses are no less "tragic," but they do not imply a
universe in which the human struggle for felicity is doomed in
advance to frustration. When people in general conversation
today refer to the "starkness of Greek tragedy" it is this play that
has primarily established the idea; but it is well to remember

that the two most notable contributions to the form, Aeschylus's trilogy dealing with Agamemnon and his children, and the two plays of Sophocles dealing with Oedipus, both conclude in a spirit of reconciliation and hope.

The consideration of Oedipus's guilt brings us to another element in the play, an idea in regard to human behavior so deeply imbedded in the Greek mind that its understanding requires of us a particular exercise of the historical imagination. Any exceptional endowment, they believed, or any responsible position which a man might hold constituted a moral danger and rendered him liable to a state of pride, of excessive self-confidence, of *hubris.* Under *hubris* a man lost his spiritual discernment. All exceptional achievement was a provocation to arrogance, and the Greeks watched the kings and heroes of their epic poems and tragedies with a particular excitement for signs of this moral blindness. It was in the light of this law that they saw Achilles withdraw from the battle, Agamemnon sacrifice his daughter and later accept the treacherous flattery of his wife, Creon condemn Antigone, and Oedipus at the opening of this play insult Creon and the priest of Apollo, Teiresias. The Greek distrust of the exceptional did not apply only to the possession of notable advantages, however; it constituted a rule for behavior in the daily life of the average individual as well. Of the two inscriptions on the temple doors at Delphi, "Know thyself" has become the more famous, but the other, "Nothing too much," was more characteristically Greek. The idea recurs with particular frequency in the work of Sophocles. When he came to treat the subject of Electra, the whole play became a study in perilous excess and rings with such admonitions as "Weep not too much," "Rejoice not too much," and "Love not too much." In the *Oedipus Rex* the first sign that the King is in danger of succumbing to this excessive self-confidence arrives with his acceptance of the words spoken by the priest of Zeus:

> It is not as deeming thee ranked with the gods . . . but . . .

The sentence implies the possibility of such a comparison which no mere rhetorical negative could save, and the Greek audience knew that his failure to repudiate the implication was a sign that his downfall was imminent. Oedipus's responsibility for the crimes in the past does not present itself to Sophocles as a problem until he writes the *Oedipus at Colonus*; he is absorbed by the sins into which Oedipus falls during the action of the play—those he finds reprehensible enough, as the third choral ode shows.

The reason for Sophocles's indifference at this stage of his life to the ethical problems behind his story may lie in a trait of his character on which the few surviving fragments of his biography throw some light. We are told that his attitude to the religious ideas of his time was that of unquestioning piety. In one play, now lost, he had occasion to present the utterances of a blasphemer, and an Alexandrian critic tells us that the speeches were singularly ineffective. Whereas both Aeschylus and Euripides were engaged throughout their lives in purifying the mythical heritage and pouring into it a wealth of didactic innovations, Sophocles was generally content to retell the old stories without examination of their often savage principles. Even with the example before him of Aeschylus's treatment of the Orestes story as an argumentation against the tribal requirement of eye-for-an-eye revenge, Sophocles shows us an Orestes obediently accepting the duty of murdering his mother and closes the play with such satisfaction at the achievement that one critic has described it as "a mixture of matricide and high spirits." It may be that it is Sophocles's readiness to reproduce the traditional legend and his serene acceptance of Apollo's dictates that lend to the *Oedipus Rex* its character of cruelty, and it therefore becomes all the more interesting to know that later, in the *Oedipus at Colonus*, he changed his views upon its meaning.

If these religious elements in the play were nearer to the minds of the ancients, there remains another which has attracted attention in modern times: the psychological interest in the old myth which has rendered Oedipus's name a label for certain recurrent patterns in behavior. Modern psychology holds that myth-making is one of the means whereby the generalized truths of human knowledge find expression and particularly the disavowed impulses of the mind escape the "censor" of acquired social control and find their way into indirect confession. Myths constitute the dreaming subconscious soul of the race telling its story. Greek mythology is peculiarly rich in these formulations of generalized truth. Prometheus, the benefactor, is perpetually the rebel against authority. Cassandra stands forever as the wisdom that is unable to warn the crowd. The heel of Achilles and the choice of Hercules have passed into proverbial expression. The newer psychologists claim to have discovered that in the infantile life every child feels himself to be the rival to the father for the mother's love and harbors and finally suppresses the death-wish against the father. In the majority of cases the phase is outgrown but remains in the subconscious in the form of a sense of guilt. Whatever truth this theory contains would help to explain the haunting power which this play has continuously exercised and the strange fact that the critics from antiquity to the present day constantly refer to the "universality" of the figure of Oedipus, who would seem on the contrary to be a man struggling in highly exceptional circumstances. This attribute of universality is further enhanced by the secondary myth which represents him as the man who was able to answer the riddle of the Sphinx:

> What is it that goes first on four feet, then on two, and finally on three?

The answer itself is mankind, and the myth seems to say that Oedipus represents man setting out on the journey of self-knowledge and inquiry. If it is true that readers and audiences have followed this tragedy with a profound unconscious self-identification with the accurst and guilty hero, then the message of the *Oedipus at Colonus* declaring that the gods absolve mankind of the crimes in which it had no choice becomes an affirmation comparable to that contained in the Book of Job.

At the festival where it was first produced the *Oedipus Rex* obtained the second prize. The winning play has long since been forgotten, and the *Oedipus Rex* has probably been revived more frequently than any other play of antiquity. At the close of the last century, in the great performance of Mounet-Sully, it was one of the most popular productions of the Comédie Française. Max Reinhardt's productions of it attracted vast audiences throughout the German-speaking world and England. Sir John Martin-Harvey toured with it for many years in England and America. The plays by Voltaire and

Dryden modeled closely upon it enjoyed great success in their day. The second prize remains in the record, however, for our instruction. It would seem that no play could make a more immediate effect. It is a triumph of construction, an intricate "detective story," wherein two avenues of inquiry after a long, mounting progress of increasing tension finally meet in a passage of compact force forty lines long. It is a demonstration of psychological skill. The figure of the Queen is drawn with great precision, shielding her husband from the knowledge she foresees approaching, alternately condemning and upholding the authority of the oracles as best suits the direction of the argument at the moment, and finally giving up the struggle.

The characterization of Oedipus displays the same combination of large-scale draftsmanship and specific detail: the mind caught in the whirlpool of dread, long unable to credit the evidence before him (Voltaire, the embodiment of French reasonableness, refused to see the psychological truth of this blindness, and exclaimed: "He who was able to read the riddle of the Sphinx was unable to see what would be apparent to a child of ten!") and betraying his inner turmoil by lapses of the tongue and by abrupt and all but incoherent transitions in his questionings.

Perhaps the second prize which the Athenian judges conferred upon the play should remind us primarily that masterpieces are difficult. Their survival and the diversity in their appeal are evidence that they come to us from a removed thought-world not easy to penetrate. Sometimes their difficulty proceeds from an inner necessity on their authors' part continually to innovate in form and subject matter. This was the case with Euripides, each of whose works was a new scandal to his contemporaries and who never received a first prize in the dramatic contests throughout his long career. Sometimes the difficulty proceeds, as in the case of the second part of Goethe's *Faust* and of the last quartets of Beethoven, from the extreme condensation and symbolic formulation that the artists' long meditations have converted into an almost "private language." During the years following the appearance of such works the public has the opportunity of adjusting itself to them; other works are composed under their influence by less original hands, and finally a body of critical commentary collects about them to facilitate their understanding. But the difficulty is eternally there, and as it is not essentially a difficulty of style or manner but of a relation to life, it is our duty to insist on rediscovering it and wrestling with it. The aids to masterpieces are often nothing but means to avoid their fundamental power and reduce to matters of "taste" and "interest" what should be a perpetually renewed conflict.

One may venture to suggest that the difficulty of the *Oedipus Rex* lies in two realms. In the first place, it is not easy to accord one's adherence, moment by moment, to a mind that treats so painful a subject with such composure. We are accustomed to seeing a greater conformity between style and matter: the imaginative tumult in Michelangelo's composition for the Judgment Day; the impassioned extensions of language and syntax in Aeschylus's treatment of the crimes of the *Oresteia*. Sophocles nowhere betrays this human participation in the overwrought emotions of his characters, and many distinguished scholars and critics have found something "chilling" in the measured beauty of the language and the impeccable intellectual ordering of the action. Sophocles's name is often linked with those of Raphael and Mozart, artists who chose to efface from their work all evidence of the emotional stress they underwent in contemplating the tragic background of life. It is not easy to follow such natures, but this deep equanimity before the spectacle of evil is one of the exacting values of the play. A still greater difficulty, however, resides in the fact that we rise to a prolonged act of concentration. There are no other examples in literature of so single-minded a discipline. The Elizabethan tragedies, by the use of sub-plots and the frequent change of scene, invited an intermittent relaxation; the *Antigone* even has moments of humor; the *Oresteia* has lyrical digressions and episodes in varying mood. Time after time in the *Oedipus Rex* our minds fall back, unwilling to carry the weight of realization and forever ready to follow the action on easier levels, as ingenious narrative or as absorbing characterization. Having chosen a subject in the realm of the incommensurable, the will of the gods, and having, through reasons in his own temperament, refused to endow it with the mitigating element of a sympathetically emotional treatment, Sophocles trans-

ferred it with an inflexible purity to the realm of the mind.
This evocation of pity, terror, and religious awe under the control of an elevated objectivity estranged his contemporaries. In
the intervening years the world has corrected the error, but it
remains as drastic an experience as on the occasion of its first
performance, and its rewards are in proportion to its difficulty.

Foreword to
'Three Comedies
by Johann Nestroy'

D URING the forties and fifties of the last century a famous
actor-dramatist of Vienna was observed on a number of
occasions, sitting alone in a café in the late afternoon. His
manner became increasingly agitated. The hour of seven was
approaching when the curtain must rise on his performance.
He was trying in vain to call a waiter's attention, but shrank
from rendering himself conspicuous. Finally a fellow guest
would raise his voice and call out: "*Herr Ober*, can't you see
that Herr von Nestroy wishes to pay his bill?" Yet an hour later
this same shy actor, released from his torment at the café-table,
would advance toward the audience with an introductory
monologue and song, expressing in his carriage and in the
glances of his large brilliant eyes an unbounded insolence. The
words he uttered and the pantomime that accompanied them
attacked his public's most cherished illusions. Later, when he
rose to be manager of his company he never directed the productions himself. He lacked the courage to "correct" his fellow actors' performances. He arrived promptly at rehearsals,
letter-perfect in his rôle. When scene-shifters bumped into
him, it was Nestroy who tendered a deferential apology. There
have been other examples of writers famous for aggressive and
arrogant wit who have been mild and self-effacing in private
conduct. Dr. Sigmund Freud, who delighted in Nestroy's
work, has described wit as "the retaliation of the underdog."

Satire is aggressive. Cynicism is a devaluation of prevailing
standards. What and whom was Nestroy attacking? Why did his
audiences submit to—and even welcome—the large element in
his writing and performance that was so obviously intended to
render them uncomfortable?

Nestroy played in "second class" theaters—in the so-called
Vorstadt, the suburbs that had recently been included in the
new metropolis. The Viennese aristocracy and the "nicely"

cultivated public attended the Burgtheater which offered long
verse tragedies generally dealing with antiquity or the Middle
Ages (occasionally these were by great hands; in *Der Talisman*
Nestroy alludes to Grillparzer's *Ottokars Glück und Ende*).
Nestroy's plays were felt to be "low." Though the majority of
them picture the emerging newly wealthy middle classes, the
parts he wrote for himself embody figures from a lower level
of society—servants, apprentices, adventurers, and proletariat
ne'er-do-wells.

Satire flourishes when society is passing through a state of
transition, and transition contains elements of social and cultural revolt. The upward movement of a hitherto depressed
stratum is accompanied by pretension, insecurity, and gau-
cherie. Two centuries earlier Molière was ridiculing these manifestations in *La bourgeois gentilhomme*, *Les femmes savantes*,
and other plays. Goldoni was constantly occupied with them
and often at his best, as in *La casa nuova*. Beaumarchais laughed
and shook his fist. It is not necessary to be a card-carrying
Communist to observe that a large part of European literature
during the last two centuries—tragic and comic—has been
concerned with "class warfare." Numberless are the works,
headed by the Don Juan and Faust legends, that derive a large
part of their force from the seduction of a peasant girl by a
man of privileged background. (Nestroy affords a powerful
treatment of this situation in *Der Unbedeutende*.) Vienna was
in social and political ferment. When finally the short-lived
"March Revolution" of 1848 broke out in Austria, Nestroy himself manned the ramparts and wrote two comedies to celebrate
the victory—disconcerting plays, however, for his satire was
directed at both the oppressors and the liberators. For cynics
there are no Utopias and little hope of meliorism. Satirists, like
Swift, Voltaire, and Gogol, may declare their intention of
bettering mankind, but one is left with an impression of their
resigned acceptance of the doctrine of man's imperfectibility.
We are often told that the object of comedy is to expose stupidity, restrain excess, unmask hypocrisy, and to chastise vice.
Each of the masters returned repeatedly to certain targets:
Aristophanes flayed his contemporaries' passion for political
bungling (of little interest to Nestroy); Molière attacked medical quackery and religious hypocrisy (Nestroy has little to say

about doctors and *never* alludes to religion). Most satirists, in so far as they are permitted—particularly those working in the late Middle Ages and early Renaissance—have exploited the scatological and the pornographic. Accounts of Nestroy's performances as an actor give the impression of having been accompanied by a constant play of obscene implications, yet scarcely a word of such matter can be read in the printed texts that have come down to us. This daring material appeared in Nestroy's rôle only and was conveyed by him in extempore improvisation and in glance, pause, and gesture. The censor threatened, critics voiced their outrage, a portion of the audience protested; but Nestroy could not restrain himself; his daemon drove him on. Two plays in this volume show very clearly where such material could have been inserted: Titus in *Der Talisman*, climbing up the social ladder, is the object of infatuation of a succession of women he despised and insulted; and the scurrilous Nebel in *Liebesgeschichten* (Moon in *Love Affairs and Wedding Bells*), pretending to make love to a rich and foolish spinster. In other words, Nestroy is not merely undermining the sentimental attitude to love, but the very instinctive drive itself. He depicts a sort of faun for whom one female is as acceptable as another.

The inner target of Nestroy's satire was the very ethos of Vienna's newly stabilized bourgeoisie: the pleasure-loving geniality, the famous *Gemütlichkeit*. In a play *Unverhofft*, written in the year following *Der Zerrissene* (*A Man Full of Nothing*), the character played by Nestroy himself says: "Only an unintelligent man can fail to see the omnipresent havoc underlying the apparently innocuous *Gemütlichkeit*." What revolted Nestroy in his native city was not only the narrowness and coldness of heart that characterize all such milieux, but its predominant and stultifying characteristic of sentimental complacency—the smugness of small-town citizens living in a newly conscious metropolis. In the center of every play we find this Nestroy-figure, this disillusioned but clear-sighted outsider —often amoral, but never self-deluding—exposing the pretension of his audience, ridiculing their defenses, denouncing their sloth and the damage inflicted by their mindless subservience to outworn conventions.

Why did his public find enjoyment in this drastic devaluation of its self-image? Members of a parvenu social stratum are like adolescents, absorbedly self-conscious. They love to hear themselves discussed. They peer into mirrors. Even to hear themselves ridiculed becomes a "school of manners." But they soon tire of mere abuse; the darts must be accurate. The *vis comica* is always painful, but it is compelling in proportion to its truth. And Nestroy, aided by employing *their own dialect*, was unerringly actual. His wit cut to the quick. He walked a perilous tightrope and often suffered for his insolence. Enormously successful plays alternated with abject failures. (A number of those failures are now among the most admired of his works.) Finally, with the years his temper became milder. The rôles he wrote for himself in *Der Unbedeutende*, *Kampl*, and *Mein Freund* are still sharp-eyed and harsh spoken, but at heart they reveal themselves as merely kindly curmudgeons.

Of Nestroy's fifty major plays scholars have found only two which were not adaptations of novels or plays by others—the majority of them from the French. It is astonishing to observe with what fidelity he followed the plot structure of his foreign source. The invention of narrative patterns—"plotting"—did not interest him. Far more astonishing is the alteration he effected through the imposition of his own dialogue and characterization. Consider *Der Talisman*, for example: the young hero of *Bonaventure*, a vaudeville-comedy by Duperty and F. de Courcy, is the conventional young opportunist of French farce who reacts with banal surprise to the succession of wigs that circumstance offers him. In *Der Talisman*, Titus is the social pariah—victim of the prevailing prejudice against red hair—who avidly seizes each opportunity to advance himself. In Nestroy's hands the prejudice against red hair becomes a symbol of all the senseless ideas on which a *gemütlich* public nourishes itself. Titus is *aware* of it and, remaining in close rapport with the audience by means of asides, monologues, and songs, invokes their complicity in his heartless and even cruel advancement. (That is: in the dryness of heart that underlies the *Gemütlichkeit* and that snatches at any occasion for pleasure or wealth, no matter whom one tramples upon.)

Principally, however, Nestroy was forgiven his cynicism

because of his extraordinary mastery of language. It is this that has lead to the proverbial assumption in Vienna that "Nestroy is untranslatable," by which is also meant untranslatable even into German (an exaggeration that can be laid to local pride; the distortion imposed by the dialect is less exotic than that found in Hauptmann's Prussian and Silesian plays). Similarly it is said of the great actor-dramatist of Naples today, Eduardo de Filippo, that he is untranslatable even into Italian. Nestroy avails himself of the German language's tendency to compound nouns, forcing adjectival forms from polysyllabic (and polyglot) substantives, wrenching startling associations of ideas from puns, and illuminating philosophical concepts by the use of droll mixed metaphors. Most jokes lose their savor in translation and perish under dissection. The greater part of this verbal acrobacy is entrusted to the Nestroy-figure and hence derives a special fascination in the mouth of a character at the bottom of society. Under a light screen of dialect *he* speaks a highly sophisticated German; his is the only superior intelligence in the play. The same pungency and force are found in the utterances of Shakespeare's clowns—half beggars, the lowest of the servants, parasites at rich men's tables. Through *independence* of *mind* the despised outsider elevates himself to the rank of a penetrating judge of society and its mores. Diogenes, the Cynic, is reported to have lived in a tub.

It has been a pleasure to learn that Mr. Max Knight and Mr. Joseph Fabry, who know their Vienna well, have faced the challenge of introducing Nestroy to English readers. It is, as far as I have been able to discover, the first time that this attempt has been made. I hope that this volume will find many readers and that the authors will be encouraged to translate other plays of the great Austrian and that in time his work will be presented in our theaters.

George Bernard Shaw

SOMEWHERE Shaw writes:

> I am more responsible than anyone outside of Scandinavia for the
> improved position of women in the modern world, and women
> in the mines of South America and in the mills of Bombay are in-
> debted to me, even though they do not know my name.

It is an impressive boast. One wonders why he does not add to
the number of his beneficiaries some hundreds of thousands of
wives who, having discovered that their amiable bridegrooms
are brutes, are better able to protect themselves and their children. One might also expect to find him pointing with pride at
the innumerable enemies he has made, including those property owners who have been made more publicly responsible
for what takes place throughout those holdings which had
seemed to lie at such a vast distance from them.

We are indeed aware that society owes a large debt to Shaw;
but it is important that we attempt to estimate the extent of
the debt and in what ways and through what channels he was
effective. This brings us to a consideration of the rôle performed by the Man of Letters as Reformer, and thinking of
Shaw we are to keep in mind the work of Voltaire and Diderot
and Ibsen and Dickens, to say nothing of those even greater
writers whom the hurried and impatient reformers never think
of including among the builders of our social institutions.

During the last quarter of the last century Irishmen were reminding each other with increasing intensity that their country
had endured seven centuries of oppression. Their brains were
continually suffused with fantasies of the death-wish against
the invader and they never ceased from intoning the names of
the martyrs who fell in those ever renewed and ever repressed
rebellions. What are the results of seven centuries of hatred
and frustration? One of the manifestations among Irish men of
letters was the withdrawal into esoteric mystical constructions
infinitely remote from the agitations of the market-place; another was the cultivation of a histrionic bellicosity—histrionic,
not because it was unreal but because so much of it required
that the Irishman continually seek out or invent ever new ob-

jects for his aggression. We see the same thing frequently in men and women who have spent their childhood (or who retrospectively imagine that they have spent their childhood) under a senseless and immitigable tyranny.

The result for Bernard Shaw was that he did not know what he knew, he was not visited by any ideas, save in contradiction to some already established error. He was incapable of thinking in pure gratuity; he could only think by ricochet. Hence, his thought was always contentious; its energy was sustained by exaggeration and it glittered with those illuminations derived from striking a half-truth which are inseparable from wit. Further, he was unable to express a thought without being aware of its repercussion in Audience. He was Audience-ridden, Audience-fettered, and that is a very sorry thing to be.

I was once invited to lunch by the Shaws in their apartment in Whitehall Court. I observed immediately that Shaw had the handshake of a shy man, the rapid tender and withdrawal. He seized the conversation one beat too soon—and not from vanity but from dismay. He stood with his back to the hearth and harangued the guests on the virtues of vegetarianism. "I shall outlive you all," he cried, beating his chest. "In a few minutes you will go into the next room and my dear wife will offer you the decaying carcasses of animals. . . ." That is what it is to be dependent on reaction. Even in the anecdotes of his gaiety— and he was not gay on that day—the pressure upon him was like an anguish. And no wonder he was shy, for to live by one's effect on others—even if it includes insulting those whom one feels to be worthy of contempt—is a dependence very close to servility.

The social effectiveness of Shaw's writings had by its very nature to be indirect. It was not his books and plays in themselves which began to crack and melt the great icebergs of British inertia. His particular kind of wit and exaggeration were precisely the kind which hardens the sinner in his sin. British society was so deeply imbedded in its institutions, so self-evident seemed the continuation of its inequities (it has never been difficult to ascribe the world's inequities to God's will, "as the dear Bishop so reassuringly explained to us last Sunday at St. Cuthbert's") that the sharpest attacks against it rang in their ears as frivolity and flattery. At its worst we see this operation in the librettos of W. S. Gilbert: they pretended to be corrosive; in fact, they were little short of soothing.

Shaw's social effectiveness was rendered possible by vulgarization. He was digested and rephrased by bright young men (and now that this twentieth century advances we can say for the first time in history that such work is also being carried on by bright young women, and we are partially indebted to Shaw that we can say it). The thousands of wives who saw *A Doll's House* within the first half-century of its appearance themselves went home revolving long thoughts; Dickens's debtors' prisons, his Dotheboys School and his Circumlocution Office aroused an immediate uneasiness in every self-respecting reader. Vulgarizers those writers had also, but the works themselves were masterpieces and masterpieces energize with or without mediation. Shaw was a bright young man who vulgarized Ibsen and Ellen Key and Nietzsche, but he produced no masterpieces and the radiance of his brightness was obscured by his frenetic need of Audience's immediate praise and blame.

So now, partly as a result of Shaw's vigorous writing, millions of women in industry receive larger wages and work shorter hours and millions of wives know that if their husbands turn unamiable they are in a better position to take their children and walk out of the front door. These are great and merciful advances. It would be rash, nevertheless, to affirm that the totality of society is further advanced in its right to the pursuit of happiness than it was fifty years ago. Nor would one, on the other hand, compare these reformers to men who lift a yoke from one pair of shoulders only to discover that it has fallen on another, or to surgeon apprentices who are able to lance a patient's boil but who cannot purify a patient's blood. Misery and inhumanity never sleep, nor are they so easily abolished; they merely displace themselves. The trouble with the immediate and topical reformer is that he has an incomplete conception of the human need. Shaw attacked the institution of marriage without having any instinctive sympathetic understanding of the nature of woman; and he attacked the abuses of property without having any clear picture of the relation of property to the life in a home—especially the life of the workingman

who would presumably benefit in a society under socialism.
Like all Audience-fettered writers, he found it very difficult to
be attentive to how freedom operates in other people. He has
testified to his lifelong indebtedness to Charles Dickens. From
Dickens he borrowed the outer contours of characterization;
his cockney *raisonneurs*, for example, have some of the impudence and self-assurance of Dickens's originals; but he could
not borrow Dickens's joy in the spontaneous separateness of
everyone who has ever lived. It is to this that people refer
when they say of certain writers: "All the characters talk like
the author."

This trait furnishes another reason why Shaw's work depended on its vulgarization by bright young people and it
throws light on a certain obtuseness whereby he could allocate
so much credit to himself for a worldwide reformation. It is
perhaps fortunate that such reformers enjoy so largely the
sense of initiating a cause and of carrying it on singlehandedly,
as Shaw did relative to the improved situation of women. At
most we must see him as an accelerator. As far back as 1860
Queen Victoria had been trembling with indignation at the
advancing tide. She hoped to curb "this mad, wicked folly of
Women's Rights, with all its attendant horrors, on which her
poor mad sex is bent."

Shaw affected to be in dialogue with Shakespeare all his life.
He invented the fiction that everyone had always misunderstood Shakespeare and attributed to him many great qualities
which he did not possess and remained blind to other qualities
which he (Shaw) would now indicate. Shaw's quarrel with
Shakespeare lay deeper, however. In one of the prefaces he
draws a parallel between Shakespeare and John Bunyan. (I am
writing these lines while convalescent in a hospital and furnish
only a paraphrase of the text.)

Five pages of Bunyan are worth a hundred by these myriad-minded
opalescent-men who refrain from advancing to the ramparts of the
struggle for human betterment and planting their banners there.

But it was Shakespeare who did so much toward preparing
the improved situation of women. It is a poor writer who cannot arrest the attention of his readers with the presentation of

an erratic young woman or with, at best, the picture of an admirable young woman, like Gretchen or Tess or Anna Karenina, caught up in situations that result in havoc and destruction. Shakespeare was one of the few writers in all literature who could present a young woman as both virtuous and interesting. He fashioned nine of them and they continue to affect the spiritual weather of the world. A number of them he places in situations of utter destitution (several are not even permitted to acknowledge that they are women), but they are unafraid, resourceful, observant, and thoughtful, and they are singularly exempt from the notion that they ceased to have any significance save in relation to some man. All of them are finally married, but we have the sense that they would have remained no less the objects of our admiration had we known them many years later as spinsters. There is food for thought in observing how few sisters they have (Nausicaä joins hands with Natasha Rostov) in world literature and how many notable writers attempted the task and failed. The vulgarization of Shakespeare was not carried on by bright young men writing editorials but by millions of persons in many lands gazing with emotion and delight at the way in which, to borrow a phrase of our grandfathers, Shakespeare "bore witness" for womankind.

The theater appears to be the most Audience-subservient of the arts. Like a magnet, it attracts all sorts of Audience-infatuate natures. It has another face, however; at its best it is the purest of the modes for presenting the human situation. Its masters have passed through all the solicitations of self-assertion and have come out on the farther side. To them the audience in the theater is neither student nor flatterer nor fool —Molière to the contrary—nor even judge. It is mere humanity, shoulder to shoulder—the dramatist in their midst—agaze at this mirror held up to nature. Shaw achieved no complete play at this elevation. Occasionally we are aware of it in a first act—those of *John Bull's Other Island* and *The Doctor's Dilemma*, for instance. He announced that he had written *Heartbreak House* "in the manner of Chekhov" and, again, for one act the example of the great Russian has lifted him above himself, the women particularly seeming to be alive in their

separateness and their freedom; but soon thereafter the solicitations of self-assertion win the field. Millions have taken delight in these plays and will continue to do so for some time; it
is only in juxtaposition to masterpieces that we are able to per-
ceive that there is a difference.

SHADOW OF A DOUBT

A Screenplay

Part One

The New Jersey marshes near Jersey City. Soot and waste heaps.
Then some streets at the edges of the towns in early evening.
Working men's rooming houses.
An abandoned station on a siding with the sign: "Passaic, New
Jersey."
More rooming houses.
In the room of one of these houses considerable light comes in the
windows from the street lights outside.
Uncle Charlie is bulky; about forty-seven; well, but a bit ostenta-
tiously, dressed; red carnation in his buttonhole. His fleshy,
slightly florid face is set in fatigue and bitterness. His movements
alternate between tense stillness and rapid nervous precision.
He empties his pockets on the top of the bureau, papers, purse, ci-
gars, glasses. Some of the objects fall on the floor.
Without taking off his hat or shoes he lies down on the bed, hands
clasped behind his head, and stares up at the ceiling.
Knock on the door. He makes no response. Second knock.
The landlady, Mrs. Martin, puts her head in, and hems apolo-
getically.

MRS. MARTIN: Two men were here and asked for you while you
was out, Mr. Spencer. Young man and a kinda older man. I
think they was sorry you wasn't in. (*Pause.*) I guess they'll be
back, though, I saw them up at the corner about an hour ago
when I went to the A and P for a minute. I just wanted to
change your towels, Mr. Spencer, I hope I'm not disturbing
you. (*She goes to the washstand.*) You look kinda tired to me
and that's a fact. Have you got a headache or something? I
think maybe you need a real rest, that's what I think.—Why,
Mr. Spencer! You oughtn't to leave all that money lying
around that way. Always makes me nervous to see money
lying around. Everybody in the world ain't honest, you
know.—Though I must say I haven't had much trouble that
way. Some people say New Jersey has a bad reputation for
things like that, but I haven't had much trouble, I'll say that.
(*She goes to the door.*) Well, wouldn't you want I should turn

733

out the light and you can get a good rest? You'd better lock
the door when I'm gone. (*He nods slightly.*) I think those
two men'll be back. Looked to me like they were really sorry
you was out.

UNCLE CHARLIE (*without change of expression*): Well, if they
come back, Mrs. Martin, you show them right up this time.

MRS. MARTIN: I'll do that, Mr. Spencer, I'll do that.

UNCLE CHARLIE: Up to now I've always been out when they
came. Yes sir, they've never found me in yet. (*Pause.*) Funny
thing,—they've never seen my face once. No, Mrs. Martin,
your friends have never clapped eyes on me in all their born
days. But I'm in this time. Everything's got to end some
time or other. You can show them right up when they come.

MRS. MARTIN (*bewildered; softly*): Yes, Mr. Spencer.

> *She turns out the light and shuts the door. In the streaked
> shadows we see his eyes staring at the ceiling. Suddenly he
> turns over with a choking noise and we see the bulk of his
> back and his fists pounding into the pillow in impotent rage.
> He springs from the bed and gulps down two glasses of water
> at the washstand. He turns on the light, then stands motion-
> less, staring at the floor. Crosses to window; sees two men in
> the street. Breathing heavily he can be heard whispering:*

UNCLE CHARLIE: What do they know? They're bluffing. They
don't know anything. They've nothing on me. (*Sudden fever
of activity. Crams money, papers, etc., into his pockets and goes
out. Foot of the stairs. He calls "Mrs. Martin." She appears.
Same concentrated pause, eyes on the ground.*) I'm going away
on a business trip. Just collect the things I've left upstairs
and put them aside somewhere. 'be back some day. (*He
gives her a ten-dollar bill.*)

MRS. MARTIN: Why, Mr. Spencer, you don't owe me a penny.
No, no, Mr. Spencer, I couldn't take it, I really couldn't.

UNCLE CHARLIE (*eyes on the distance*): Why . . . find something to do with it. Find something or other. It's only
money,—that's all it is. Throw it away. (*He goes out the front
door. On the top step he takes a deep breath and straightens his
shoulders.*)

> *In the street, not far from the house, two men are waiting*

under the trees; one on each side of the sidewalk, though sev-
eral yards apart. He walks straight down the walk between
them. They make no move until he's passed. One turns to fol-
low him; the other quickly crosses the street. In another de-
serted street Uncle Charlie suddenly turns into an alleyway.
By the time the two men arrive there is no sign of him. He
has given them the slip.
A telephone booth.
Uncle Charlie holds the receiver to his ear. In his other hand
is a heap of silver change.
The two men are helplessly searching.

UNCLE CHARLIE: Yes, it's under fifty words. How much money
  do I have to have ready? All right, I have it. . . . Wait a
  minute. What town am I in now? . . . All right I'm ready.
  It's going to Mrs. Joseph Newton, Santa Rosa, California.
  . . . "Dear Emma, am going to pay you a visit at last, arriving about next Thursday. Will wire train." (*Same dead*
  pause.) "Give my love to everybody, especially our little Charlie." No, cross out that last,—from . . . "especially our
  little Charlie . . ." euh . . . "Much anticipation. Your affectionate brother, Mouser" . . . M . . . O . . . U . . . .
  No, say "Your affectionate brother, Charles." There's no return address. No, don't read it to me. Here's the money. A
  quarter, a quarter, a quarter. . . .

Sound of ball registering the coins. Dissolve to long view of the
valley in which Santa Rosa lies. Sound of distant church bells
repeats sound of coins. Shots closer into village. The Newton
House. The window of Young Charlie's room. Enter room.
Young Charlie is lying on her bed, staring at the ceiling.
Both the disposition of her room and her mood are reminis-
cent of Uncle Charlie's in the earlier sequence. Young Char-
lie is 18. Very pretty. Capable of high spirits, but with a
strong sense of responsibility. Her present mood is without
self-pity or tearful exaggeration. The sound of the telephone
ringing downstairs is heard. She turns her head slightly,
then returns to her fixed gaze at the ceiling. Cut to sitting
room of the Newton home, downstairs.
Ann Newton, 10, bespectacled, competent and solemn, is ly-
ing on her stomach on the floor of the sitting room, reading.

*Book in hand, her eyes glued to the page, she goes to the wall
telephone, kicking before her a footstool that will enable her
to reach the height of the mouthpiece. During the following
she continues reading.*

ANN: Hello, this is Ann Newton, Mrs. Henderson. No, my
Mama isn't home yet. Yes, Mrs. Henderson, I'll tell her to
telephone you at the telegraph office . . . before nine
o'clock. Thank you very much, Mrs. Henderson. (*Not taking
her eyes from the page she returns to her former place on the
rug. Her father appears in the dining room behind her. Mr.
Newton is 45, lanky, absentminded. A wing of pepper-and-
salt hair falling over one eye. He carries two cheap magazines
with lurid covers, of the pulp mystery story type. Puts them in
table drawer.*)

MR. NEWTON (*over his spectacles*): Where's your mother?

ANN (*without raising her eyes from the page*): Mama's not home
yet and Roger's not home and Mrs. Henderson says there's
a telegram for Mama at the telegraph office and Charlie's in
her room.

MR. NEWTON: Telegram, eh? Who could'a died? Your aunt
Sarah? Cousin Walter? Automobile accident, I expect, or
cleaning one of his guns. (*He makes a clucking noise.*) Always
was a careless fellow. . . . Well Ann, aren't you going to
kiss your poor old father when he comes home from work?
—All tired out at the bank, answering foolish questions?
(*Ann, still without taking her eyes off the book for more than a
second, goes to him and throws her arms around his neck. She
catches a word or two behind his head even during the kiss.*)
Now don't go hurting your eyes reading.

ANN: No, Papa.

MR. NEWTON: Charlie's in her room, eh? (*He starts upstairs.*)

*Cut to Young Charlie, lying on her bed. Knock at the door.
No response from her. Another knock. . . .*

YOUNG CHARLIE: Come in, Papa, come in.

MR. NEWTON (*pushes the door ajar, but does not come far into
the room*): Now, now, now, now, what's the matter, my girl?
Keck!! Minute I came into the house I could feel you were

low in your mind about something. Something preying on your mind, Charlie? What is it, something I've done? (*Silence. He searches his memory.*) No, no. What is it, eh? Keck.

YOUNG CHARLIE (*without moving her eyes*): Papa, I'm at the end of my tether. It seems to me right now that I give up. I'm very sorry, but I give up. (*Her father whistles sympathetically.*) Papa, I think a family's the most wonderful thing in the world, but our family's just gone to pieces with laziness and wickedness and there's nothing to be done about it and I give up.

MR. NEWTON: Charlie! Things aren't as bad as that. I got a raise at the bank only last month, you know.

YOUNG CHARLIE: Money has nothing to do with it. It's a hundred years since anybody in this house said anything nice to anybody else. We're all to blame. We're not a family. We're just a run-down boarding house. Mama's run-down boarding house. Papa, you forgot today was your wedding anniversary.

MR. NEWTON: Gee whillipers! How could I come to do that! Keck!—anyway, Charlie, at our age your mother and I don't take much stock in such things.

YOUNG CHARLIE: Well, it's no pleasure to me to talk to people who don't take much stock in such things, so you can go out and close the door behind you when you go.

MR. NEWTON (*reproachfully*): Charlie!

YOUNG CHARLIE: Papa, at table you eat like a tramp. You sit down before you're called. You grab at things before Mama has even put them on the table. So naturally you don't notice that Roger is growing up even worse than you are. And all you read are those trashy mystery magazines so that you can talk them over afterwards with . . . *Mr. Hawkins.* Aren't you ashamed when your own daughter, 10 years old, is reading *Ivanhoe?* What books can she talk to you about, when all you read is rubbish?

MR. NEWTON: Now, Charlie, everybody needs relaxation in their own way.

YOUNG CHARLIE: But it's especially Mama I'm thinking about. (*At last, some animation.*) She's the best mother in the world; but, Papa, we have to do something about it. She doesn't take care of her looks anymore. Sometimes, just from nerves, she gets that kind of cooking-stove craziness. Papa, we must save Mama.

MR. NEWTON: You're right, Charlie. You're absolutely right.— But now you watch me. I'll reform. I'll reform so fast—

YOUNG CHARLIE (*resuming her former mood*): I don't believe in good intentions anymore. All I'm waiting for is a miracle. So you can go out and shut the door behind you.

MR. NEWTON: Charlie!

> *Mrs. Newton pushes the door wider open, but does not come in. Mrs. Newton is 40; untended good looks; neither anxious nor complaining, but just meeting day-to-day demands without hope or discouragement.*

MRS. NEWTON: What's the matter, Charlie? Joe, what's the matter?

MR. NEWTON (*evasive*): Well, seems like . . . uh . . .

YOUNG CHARLIE (*rises*): Father forgot it was your wedding anniversary; I've become a nagging old maid, and you went downtown in that awful old hat you promised me you'd throw away.

MRS. NEWTON: Goodness! What on earth does it matter what hat I put on?

YOUNG CHARLIE (*interrupting her, putting her arms around her, with mysterious authority, as though she had a secret*): Mama, I'm going downtown to send a telegram.

MRS. NEWTON: Why Charlie, who do you know to send a telegram to? (*Young Charlie starts downstairs bringing the others down with her, including Roger, age 8, who has appeared in the hall.*)

YOUNG CHARLIE: I know just the person to come and save us, a wonderful person who'll come and shake us all up, so we'll be good and dignified and intelligent again.

MRS. NEWTON: Charlie, have you gone crazy? What do you mean "save us"?

YOUNG CHARLIE: Come on downtown with me—dinner doesn't matter. Nothing matters as much as this. It's really quite simple, Mother: it's as though we were all on a raft sinking. The years go by and we get worse and worse. It's as though we were all sinking in a marsh of some kind.

ANN (*from the floor*): Mama, Mrs. Henderson says to call her up at the Telegraph office about a telegram.

YOUNG CHARLIE: And all the time there's been the one real, right person to save us. Mama, what's Uncle Charlie's address?

MR. NEWTON: Charlie!! You're not going to ask Uncle Charlie for money!!

YOUNG CHARLIE (*in the door onto the porch*): No! No! That wouldn't help us—what's his address?

MR. NEWTON: Emma, Mrs. Henderson says you're to call her up about a telegram. I expect Cousin William has killed himself at last.

MRS. NEWTON (*not hearing him*): The last address we had— now, Charlie, if you've forgotten it I'm not going to tell you.

YOUNG CHARLIE: I remember,——Philadelphia.

ANN: Mama, you don't hear me. Mrs. Henderson says there's a telegram for you.

MRS. NEWTON: Anyway, think of asking a busy man like that to come all this way for nothing— Now don't go, Charlie. I have to phone a minute. (*She goes to the telephone.*)

YOUNG CHARLIE: He'd come for me. I'm named after him. With each present he sends me a special message. Besides, we're the only relatives he has in the world. (*She leaves the house.*)

MRS. NEWTON: Telegraph office! One-eight-one, isn't it?— Besides, stop and think! None of us have seen him for ten years. One-eight-one, please— Who'd be sending me a telegram?

MR. NEWTON: If it isn't Cousin William's killed himself, it's my sister Sarah's been walking in her sleep again and has fallen off the roof-pole.

MRS. NEWTON: Hello? Yes, this is Mrs. Newton, Mrs. Henderson.

ANN: She's not deaf, Mama.

MRS. NEWTON: Yes. . . . Thursday. Did you say Thursday, Mrs. Henderson?

MR. NEWTON: Funeral Thursday? Long ways off!

MRS. NEWTON: Thank you, Mrs. Henderson, very much. (*She sits down.*) I declare I've got to sit down. It's downright uncanny! Nobody's dead, Joe. Uncle Charlie's coming. He's in Passaic, New Jersey, and he'll be here Thursday. Charlie can sleep in Ann's room and tomorrow morning, Joe, you go downtown and buy that blue serge suit you've been putting off so long.

ANN and ROGER: Uncle Charlie's coming *here?*

MRS. NEWTON: Go and catch Charlie and tell her. (*She rushes to the porch and calls:*) Charlie! Charlie! (*She goes down the porch and calls:*) Charlie! (*Roger helps her. Finally she gives up.*)

MRS. NEWTON (*continuing*): Well, she's out of reach. Mrs. Henderson will tell her in time and stop her sending her telegram.

Local Telegraph office. Young Charlie is at one of the desks about to tear up her fourth attempt at phrasing a telegram. She is chewing her pencil and frowning. Over her shoulder, we see:

"Mr. Charles Oakley,
   Bellevue-Stratford Hotel,
    Philadelphia, Penna.
Dear Uncle Charlie in making your plans for the next half year do what you can to come and see us."

Some customers finish their business and withdraw and Mrs. Henderson sees Young Charlie.

MRS. HENDERSON: What! Are you there, Charlie? We just telephoned a telegram up to your house.

YOUNG CHARLIE (*half hearing*): I know.

MRS. HENDERSON: I was just going to send it by Bill Forest. Can you take it when you go home?

YOUNG CHARLIE: Yes.

MRS. HENDERSON (*extending it*): It's from your uncle that your mother told me about—(*She turns away abruptly to answer the phone.*)

Young Charlie rises, takes it, and puts it down on the desk where she has been writing. She slowly tears up her sketches, murmuring under her breath.

YOUNG CHARLIE: He's coming. . . . He heard me. (*She holds it a moment, then tears it open and reads it. We see her*

moving rapidly along the crowded street, saying to herself:)
Thursday . . . time, hurry up. . . . Time, go fast. . . .
Time, hurry up! (*The rhythm of her words and her feet change
during the dissolve to the sound of railroad wheels.*)

*Pullman car, sunset. One berth is still made up. The baize
curtains very conspicuous in the middle of the car. In the
seat beyond, a foursome is playing bridge. Porter parts the
curtains.*

PORTER: Mr. Otis! Mr. Otis!

UNCLE CHARLIE'S VOICE: Yes, porter?

PORTER: We're getting right near Santa Rosa, Mr. Otis. You
want to be ready when we get to Santa Rosa.

UNCLE CHARLIE: Thank you, porter. I'm all dressed. I'm ready.
You'll help me, won't you?

PORTER: Yes, sir. Your baggage is all out and ready. How you
feelin', Mr. Otis?

UNCLE CHARLIE: I'm pretty well. I'm pretty well, porter.

DOCTOR'S WIFE: Fred, tell the porter you're a doctor. Ask him
if there's anything you can do.

DOCTOR: Bella, I'm on vacation. Don't I ever get any vacation?

DOCTOR'S WIFE: Nonsense. It's only human. Porter, come
here.—Porter, my husband's a doctor, and if there's anything he can do. . . . What seems to be the matter?

PORTER: Oh, mam, he's an awful sick man. When he got on
the train he was all right . . . but oh, mam, he got awful
sick since.

DOCTOR: We're waiting for your bid, Bella.

*The station platform, sunset. Young Charlie stands waiting
with her arm through her father's. Ann holds her other
hand. Roger, awed, stands beside his father. Mr. Slocum
passes pushing a baggage cart.*

MR. SLOCUM: Hear it? That's the whistle for Mill River bridge.
Won't be three minutes now. A mile a minute,—that's the
way you reckon it. (*He passes out of sight.*)

ANN: When you've got to wait for something, Charlie, the best
thing to do is close your eyes and count up to a hundred:
one, two, three, four.—

MR. NEWTON: The watched pot never boils, that's what they say.

YOUNG CHARLIE: Don't count, Ann, just wait.—Papa, I have a funny feeling that now that it's really coming, maybe this isn't what I wanted after all.

MR. NEWTON: Your Uncle Charlie's coming can't do much more good than it's done already. Anybody'd think your mother was a different person; goes around the house singing hymns all day. Lost ten years off her age.

YOUNG CHARLIE: Maybe it's wicked to hope too much.

ROGER: I hear it, I hear it.

YOUNG CHARLIE: Papa, you watch that end, and I'll watch up here. (*Roar of the train.*)

> *Young Charlie, holding her hat, turning uncertainly right and left. Uncle Charlie descends feebly, supported by the two porters and the doctor. The doctor's wife solicitously looking down from the car's platform.*

UNCLE CHARLIE (*feebly*): Gently, gently.—I can't thank you enough. You've all been very good. (*He presses money into the porter's hands.*)

PORTER: Thank you. Thank you, Mr. Otis.

UNCLE CHARLIE: God bless you all.

> *Train whistle. View of stationmaster, warning, train starts. Uncle Charlie straightens himself, takes a deep breath, and changes his expression. Young Charlie has been peering at him.*

YOUNG CHARLIE: Are you—? Are you—?

UNCLE CHARLIE: Who's that? Is that my niece? Is that Charlie? (*She flings herself into his arms.*)

YOUNG CHARLIE: You've come at last!—Uncle Charlie! At first I thought you were sick!!! Pa—pa; here he is.—Uncle Charlie, you're not sick! Why. That was the *funniest* thing!

UNCLE CHARLIE: Sick? I?—Well, Joe, how are you? Haven't changed a bit.

MR. NEWTON: How are you, Charles?

UNCLE CHARLIE (*squats down on his haunches and puts out his hand*): And this is Ann. Well, well, well.

ANN (*retreating against Young Charlie*): Thank you very much.

ROGER: I saw the bed on the train. I saw the bed on the train.

YOUNG CHARLIE (*kneeling by a suitcase and reading the labels*):

Mexico City, Buenos Aires, Quebec, London, Naples, Uncle Charlie!!

MR. NEWTON: Well, now, we must get this baggage into the car. Emma's cooking dinner. She couldn't come to the station. (*They move off to their car. Mr. Slocum peers at them over his spectacles.*)

> *Front of the house. The car drives up. Mrs. Newton, flushed and self-conscious, appears on the porch, standing at the head of the stairs. Voices from the car:*

UNCLE CHARLIE: Now, Charlie, those handbags are too heavy for you.

YOUNG CHARLIE: I can carry anything.

UNCLE CHARLIE (*suitcase in hand, starts up the walk, drops the suitcase, and cries*): Emma Spencer Oakley, as I live! Don't move! Emmy Oakley of 46 Burnham Street, St. Paul, Minnesota, the prettiest girl on Burnham Street, and still is.

MRS. NEWTON: Charles! The same old Charles! (*She puts out her hand, self-consciously. Ann and Roger fling themselves against her skirts.*)

ANN: Mama, nobody got off the train, only him.

ROGER: Mama, I could see one of the beds on the train where people go to sleep.

MRS. NEWTON: Children, be quiet. Well, Charles, I'm very happy you could arrange it.

UNCLE CHARLIE (*embraces her boisterously, but does not kiss her*): Little sister Emmy.—Now, now, don't cry.

MRS. NEWTON (*smiling*): How did you remember that?—46 Burnham Street. I hadn't thought of that for twenty years.

UNCLE CHARLIE: Funny thing, Emmy.—I keep remembering the old days. There's nothing like those old days. The whole world since,—!! (*He makes a face and gesture of dismissal and distaste. The others come up the stairs with the baggage.*)

MR. NEWTON: How does he look to you, Emmy? Same old Charles, eh?

MRS. NEWTON (*holding the door open for him*): Charles, I hope you didn't eat your dinner on the train?

UNCLE CHARLIE: Haven't eaten for days, Emmy. Saving up for your cooking. (*Looking about at the sitting-room.*) Well, well, well.

MRS. NEWTON: Now, Joe, you show him upstairs to his room.

In the sitting-room. Mr. Newton's and Roger's backs can be seen trudging upstairs with the bags. Uncle Charlie turns at the foot of the stairs and puts his hand on Young Charlie's shoulders, turning her so that the light falls on her face.

UNCLE CHARLIE: Let me get a good look at our young Charlie. (*He scans her face genially.*) Makes your life complicated when you're as pretty as that, eh, Charlie?

YOUNG CHARLIE: Oh, there are lots of girls prettier than I am, Uncle Charlie; doesn't cause me any trouble.

UNCLE CHARLIE: Lots of beaus hanging around the house, Emmy?

MRS. NEWTON: She hasn't fallen in love yet, Charles, as far as I know. I don't know, she's wrapped up in this home. Sometimes I think she's more like my sister than my daughter. I expect the right man'll come along one of these days; but it'd be more than I could bear to lose her. I'll say that.

UNCLE CHARLIE: And what do you say, Charlie?

YOUNG CHARLIE (*passionately, but smiling*): I love what I have right here. Papa and Mama and the children. I don't want it to change except to get better and better, and that's why I'm so glad that you've come, Uncle Charles.

UNCLE CHARLIE: Why, what can I do?

YOUNG CHARLIE: Why, you can keep us all at our best,—that's all.

UNCLE CHARLIE (*turning*): We'll see. We'll see. (*He starts up the stairs. Mr. Newton reaches down from above and takes his suitcase.*)

MR. NEWTON: You have Charlie's room, right here at the head of the stairs.

Uncle Charlie alone in his room. With no expression on his face he slowly looks about him.
1. On the table beside his bed: a bible and a copy of a cheap edition; collection of American humor.
2. On the wall, Whistler's Mother.
3. On the bureau: a bouquet of flowers, and a graduation of Young Charlie; white dress; mortar-board hat; diploma in hand.

Kitchen: Mrs. Newton peering in the oven. Door opens like a whirlwind. Roger puts his head in.

ROGER: Don't burn anything, whatever you do. (*Whirlwind disappearance. Ann enters.*)

MRS. NEWTON: Now everybody keep out of this kitchen and leave me alone. Where's Charlie?

ANN: Why's everybody so excited? (*She goes out. Enter Young Charlie.*)

YOUNG CHARLIE: Is there anything we've forgotten?

MRS. NEWTON (*rubbing her hands on her apron and looking about*): No . . . no . . . seems to me. . . . (*Young Charlie goes to her and puts her arms around her, in silence.*) Charlie! How funny you're acting!

YOUNG CHARLIE: Oh, Mama . . . everything'll be all right, everything'll be all right. How wonderfully things work out in the world, Mama!

MRS. NEWTON (*patting her arm*): I'm glad you're happy, dear; but goodness, Charlie! don't start setting your heart on miracles. Like I always say: life's life. Be glad of everything good that comes,—but medium pleasure and medium grief, that's all I count on.

YOUNG CHARLIE: Oh, Mama! I'll take the big joys even if I have to get the big troubles, too. (*She goes out. Suddenly Uncle Charlie framed in doorway.*) OH!

The dinner table—the duck has been eaten. Uncle Charlie has been holding forth.

UNCLE CHARLIE: It wasn't one of these big expensive yachts, Joe, but it was well appointed; you know what I mean,— everything nicely put together. (*He suddenly pauses; looks deflated; coughs.*) However, what am I talking about? All that's another story. Let's talk about you. Charlie, that's the prettiest dress I ever saw.

YOUNG CHARLIE: I think so, too.

MRS. NEWTON: Charles!—don't you remember?

UNCLE CHARLIE: Remember? Remember what?

MRS. NEWTON: You're joking.

YOUNG CHARLIE: Why, Uncle Charlie, you gave it to me.

UNCLE CHARLIE: I did?!

YOUNG CHARLIE: Don't you remember? Of course, I've grown. I just had to make a few changes.

UNCLE CHARLIE: Great Scott, I've been forgetting something all this time. Ann! Roger! Shut your eyes. (*He fumbles under his chair and brings out two packages which he places on the children's plates. They contain a water pistol with holster and a woolly elephant.*) Get ready, get set, open 'em! (*The children start opening their packages with cries. Uncle Charlie places another before Mr. Newton.*) Joe, a little thing I picked up in Philadelphia. Thought it might come in useful.

MR. NEWTON: What's this? Presents? Now, Charlie, nobody ought'a get presents at my age. (*He starts unwrapping a fine wrist-watch.*)

UNCLE CHARLIE: Emmy, two mementos for you. Mother gets two, it's only right.

MRS. NEWTON: Charles! You shouldn't have! (*It's a fur neck-piece.*) Charles! What would I look like in a thing like that!

YOUNG CHARLIE: Yes, Mama, it's wonderful. It's just right. I've always wanted you to have one of those. (*Uncle Charlie now extends toward her a leather case which opens, and shows restored daguerreotypes of their father and mother.*)

MRS. NEWTON: Charles!! Where did you find these?

UNCLE CHARLIE: Am I right? You didn't have them?

MRS. NEWTON: No . . . no . . . I've never had them. (*Young Charlie comes up behind her and looks at them with deep emotion.*)

YOUNG CHARLIE: Is that . . . grandpa and grandma?

MRS. NEWTON: Yes.

UNCLE CHARLIE: Oh, the old times were best. Everything that's happened since can't compare with 'em. The world's gone down hill, hasn't it, Emmy?

YOUNG CHARLIE (*goes to Uncle Charlie and flings her arms around his neck*): Uncle Charlie, I don't have to live any more. I've lived enough. Anybody who's been as happy as I am doesn't have to grow old.—Just look at us. Just look at us: we're happy. For once we're happy.

UNCLE CHARLIE: Don't you want to see your present?

YOUNG CHARLIE (*backing to the kitchen door*): No, Uncle Charles, I don't want a present. I have everything. I don't want another thing. (*She goes into the kitchen.*)

MR. NEWTON: We've got a high-strung daughter. Yes, sir. But she's never been as high-strung as this. Smartest girl in class at school. Won the debate against East Richmond High School single-handed. High-strung; but she's got more brains in her little finger than all the girls in California put together.

Uncle Charlie rises, a little box in his hand.

UNCLE CHARLIE: I'll give her this in the kitchen.

The kitchen. Young Charlie, her back against the electric icebox, looks at him smiling as he enters.

YOUNG CHARLIE: I ask you as a favor; don't give me anything.
UNCLE CHARLIE: Nothing?
YOUNG CHARLIE: You're you, Uncle Charlie. That's enough. —Besides, what can we give you that makes up in the least way for all that you've done for us.
UNCLE CHARLIE: What have I done?
YOUNG CHARLIE: But you have only to look at us. Look at Mama. I never hoped to see such a change. Besides, there's another reason why I don't want you to give me a present.
UNCLE CHARLIE: And what's that?
YOUNG CHARLIE (*with a mysterious smile, moving to one side*): Maybe it'd spoil things if I told you.
UNCLE CHARLIE: No. Tell me.
YOUNG CHARLIE: Uncle Charlie, you and I aren't just any uncle and niece. Mother's always said that you and I are alike. And I know we are. She said she can't describe what it is. One day she said that nobody could ever be sure what we were thinking. And another day she said that you and I were alike because whenever we had any trouble on our mind we never let other people see it. I guess what she means is that we're proud. Anyway, whatever it is, I know it's true. We're kind of . . . twins. And I'm sure twins don't give each other presents.
UNCLE CHARLIE (*taken aback*): Twins? That's a mighty fine thing to be.
YOUNG CHARLIE: It's a very serious thing to be, too. Because we can read one another's thoughts.
UNCLE CHARLIE: You can read my thoughts?

YOUNG CHARLIE: You'll see. You wait and see. We're no ordinary uncle and niece.

UNCLE CHARLIE: Well, let me be ordinary just for one minute and give you my present. Put out your hand. (*She puts out her hand. He slips a ring on her finger. It contains a large flat emerald. She withdraws and looks at it. Then says sincerely but lightly:*)

YOUNG CHARLIE: Thank you, Uncle Charlie.

UNCLE CHARLIE: But you haven't looked at it.

YOUNG CHARLIE: I don't have to look at it. If you gave me a penny postcard or the San Francisco Bay, it'd still be the same thing. I'd say: thank you!

UNCLE CHARLIE: Let me show it to you. A good emerald, a really good one, I mean, is one of the most beautiful things in the world. (*She looks at it calmly and suddenly becomes more excited.*)

YOUNG CHARLIE: But you've written something in it; that's different!

UNCLE CHARLIE: No, I haven't. But I'll do it; I'll have it done next week.

YOUNG CHARLIE: Why, yes, you have, Uncle Charlie. It's very faint. It's way down deep under the stone. (*Closeup of the emerald. Gradually one sees the words: "T. S. from B. M. Atlantic City, 1912." Finally they fill the whole screen.*) Why . . . who are they?

UNCLE CHARLIE (*his face dead and expressionless, in a low voice*): The jeweller rooked me. The jeweller rooked me.

YOUNG CHARLIE: It doesn't matter.

UNCLE CHARLIE: The jeweller rooked me. (*Trembling with rage, his fists clenched.*) There's a sample for you. The whole world's crooked. From top to bottom, the whole world's crooked.

YOUNG CHARLIE: Uncle Charlie, it doesn't matter. I like to think that someone else was happy with this ring, too. It's been in and out of other people's lives. I like it even more than before.

UNCLE CHARLIE: There's a sample for you. (*Crossing the room, trembling.*) Oh, Charlie, I hope you never get to know what a hell this world is.

YOUNG CHARLIE (*going to the icebox, kneeling and taking out*

six frozen desserts): Not where you and I . . . and Mama
. . . and the rest of us . . . are.

UNCLE CHARLIE: Give it back to me. I'll have it fixed.

YOUNG CHARLIE: No. It's perfect as it is. And see how it fits
me. (*Taking up a tray of desserts.*) Now, Uncle Charlie, if you
bring the coffee-pot off the stove, we'll surprise them with
what good service we can give them. (*As she moves toward
the dining room door, she starts singing to the syllable "la" the
first eleven notes of the "Merry Widow" Waltz.*)

> *Cut to the family seated at table.*
> *During the following conversation, the Merry Widow Waltz
> can be faintly heard from the sound-track.*

MRS. NEWTON: Charles, why don't you settle down out here in
the West?

UNCLE CHARLIE: That's what I'm thinking of doing. In fact,
I've decided. Pretty soon I'll go and look San Francisco over.
. . . Yes, looks to me like I'm going to open up a whole
new chapter in my life—"turn over a new leaf," as they say.

YOUNG CHARLIE (*hums a short phrase of the Merry Widow
Waltz*): La-la-la-la.

ANN: You shouldn't sing at table.

UNCLE CHARLIE: Among other things, Joe, I'm going to
transfer some of my money from the East. Why not deposit
it in your bank until I can find something to invest it in? Do
you accept deposits in your bank?

MR. NEWTON: Yes, sir, that's one thing we do.

UNCLE CHARLIE: How about calling on you tomorrow
morning—open an account? Say thirty-forty thousand, just
to start things off?

MR. NEWTON (*gaping*): Do you mean it?

UNCLE CHARLIE: Why not? You're sound, I hope?

MR. NEWTON (*swallowing*): Oh, yes. Oh, yes.

MRS. NEWTON: Goodness, Charles! Is that the way men do
things like that? I give more thought than that to buying a
spool of thread.

YOUNG CHARLIE (*during the last speech has again hummed the
first eleven notes of the Merry Widow Waltz*): Excuse me
singing, Ann; but there's that tune going around in my head

and I can't stop it. If I could only remember its name, I guess it'll stop. (*She sings the first eight notes.*)

MRS. NEWTON (*chin in hand, groping*): Seems to me I know that.

YOUNG CHARLIE: I think when a tune teases you like that, it means that someone else has got it going on in their heads, too. Do you know what I mean? It jumps from head to head. (*Shot of Uncle Charlie eating—no reaction.*) Sometimes I've been going down the street and some tune has been tormenting me, and suddenly I hear somebody whistling it in the next block.—What is it, Uncle Charlie? (*She sings the first eight notes.*)

UNCLE CHARLIE (*dead pan*): I don't know.

MRS. NEWTON: It's on the tip of my tongue. It's got a name that everybody thought shocking when I was a girl. My mother wouldn't allow me to say it in the house.

UNCLE CHARLIE: No—it's the Blue Danube Waltz.

YOUNG CHARLIE: Of course. That's it. (*Short pause. Rising.*) No! I know what it is. It's the Merry— (*Closeup of Uncle Charlie's hand deliberately upsetting his drinking glass. Confusion. He rises in loud apology.*)

UNCLE CHARLIE: I beg your pardon. Forgive me, Ann. Did it go in your ice-cream?

MRS. NEWTON: That's all right, Charles. Don't think about it a minute. We do it every day.—Joe, there's Herbie Hawkins, scratching at the window to get in. (*Herbie can be seen through the windowpane, abashed, cap in hand.*) Come in, Mr. Hawkins. Come in. Mr. Hawkins is a friend of Joe's, Charles. They talk over books and magazines together. (*Enter Herbie. He carries three copies of detective story magazines with lurid covers.*) Can we give you some supper, Mr. Hawkins?

HERBIE: No thanks. I've had mine.

MR. NEWTON: Herbie, I'd like you to meet my brother-in-law. Charles, this is Mr. Hawkins.

UNCLE CHARLIE: Glad to know you, Mr. Hawkins. Glad to know you.

MRS. NEWTON: Now while we do the dishes, Charles, you stretch out on the sofa and read the evening paper. Mr. Newton can read it when you're finished.

UNCLE CHARLIE: Emma, you remember I'm pretty good at the dish-cloth myself.

MRS. NEWTON: Well, your first few days we're going to pet and spoil you.

YOUNG CHARLIE (*ensconcing her uncle on the sofa*): Here's another pillow. May I have that pillow, Mr. Hawkins? And here's the paper, Uncle Charlie. Pass it, will you, please?

> *The front porch. Mr. Newton and Herbie have drifted outdoors. Mr. Newton from the hall table-drawer has extracted two detective-story magazines.*
> *They talk to one another with suppressed excitement and long, judicious pauses.*

MR. NEWTON: Wife's brother come on a visit . . . New York man . . . good for the children, you know what I mean?

HERBIE: In business?

MR. NEWTON: Takes himself very serious. How's everything?

HERBIE (*indicating a magazine with his thumb*): Seen this week's?

MR. NEWTON (*reveals an identical copy*): Hngh.

HERBIE (*awed whisper*): Somethin'! Believe me, somethin'!

MR. NEWTON: You don't say!

HERBIE: Microbes on a lipstick. One of these here chorus-girls.

MR. NEWTON: Don't tell me, don't tell me!—Microbes on a lipstick, eh? H'mmm! I finished that other number.

HERBIE (*eagerly*): Death-ray in a fountain-pen number?

MR. NEWTON: No . . . no. . . . Soprano in a church choir, kick—could it be done, do you think? Everybody kneeling in prayer that way?

HERBIE: Why not, Joe? Have all their heads bowed, wouldn't they?

MR. NEWTON (*as they drift off under the trees; in the tone of an expert*): A fella'd have to be pretty, pretty smart to get by with that.

> *Cut to sitting room.*
> *Uncle Charlie opens the paper. His eye darts rapidly from item to item. On Page 3, something arrests his attention.*

Slight reaction. He reads the news item further. Strong reaction; he crushes the paper down against his knees. He glances about the room. No fireplace, no hiding place. He stops to think. His eyes fall on Ann. He rises and becomes playful.

UNCLE CHARLIE: Ann, Ann.

ANN: What?

UNCLE CHARLIE: Come here, Ann.—Did you ever make a house out of newspapers? See what I mean? First, you stretch 'em all out on the ground. Then you take a chair; and another chair. See? And then you . . . look . . . you cut out a door. Now if you can crawl in there. . . . Don't you want to? (*He rips the item from the paper. Ann is not amused. He folds the torn fragment and puts it in his pocket.*)

ANN: It's Papa's paper. (*Roger dashes into the room and stands thunderstruck at the door.*)

UNCLE CHARLIE: Hey, Roger—there you are! Look what we have here. An esquimeaux's igloo. Get the idea?

ROGER: But . . . it's Papa's paper.

UNCLE CHARLIE: You're right. You're dead right. I should have thought of that. Well, in a minute we'll fold it right up and your father won't know the difference. (*He is obviously worried by the conspicuous tear. He extracts the whole double page and folds it into smaller and smaller squares and puts it in his pocket. Roger and Ann draw nearer, tempted.*)

ANN: Can you make hats out of it?

UNCLE CHARLIE: Hats? Let me see. Hats. You show me how, Ann.

ROGER: I can make darts. I've made lots of them.

Enter Young Charlie.

YOUNG CHARLIE: Why, Ann! Roger! What are you doing? You know you can't do that until Papa's finished.

UNCLE CHARLIE: Don't scold them, Charlie. It's all my fault. I began it. We felt like playing games here.

YOUNG CHARLIE (*on hands and knees*): Anyway, no harm's done. Page 5 . . . page 1 . . . page 22. Seems to me the paper gets bigger every day. . . . Part 2 . . . where's page 3-and-4 and 11-and-12? That's funny. Ann, help me look. It must be around here somewhere. Roger, help me look.

Page 3-and-4. Why, that's the funniest thing I ever heard. Did you go out on the porch with it somewhere?

UNCLE CHARLIE (*looking behind the sofa*): Certainly is curious.

YOUNG CHARLIE: Well, maybe Papa won't notice it, if we fold it very neatly . . . see . . . very evenly. (*Closeup of his hand pushing down larger pages in his pocket.*)

> *Lapse of a few hours. The family's going to bed.*
> *Dissolve: fade in on Uncle Charlie lying in bed in shirt-sleeves. Coat hanging on bedpost—pages of folded newspaper visible.*

UNCLE CHARLIE: Come in.

YOUNG CHARLIE: I brought you some water.

UNCLE CHARLIE: Thank you, Charlie. Good night. Sweet dreams. (*At the door, Young Charlie turns and says conspiratorially, teasing:*)

YOUNG CHARLIE: Uncle Charlie, I know something. I know a secret that you think I *don't* know.

UNCLE CHARLIE: A secret? What?

YOUNG CHARLIE: There was something in the evening paper about you.

UNCLE CHARLIE: About me?

YOUNG CHARLIE: Tell me what it was. Show it to me. I won't tell anyone. (*She comes nearer to him.*)

UNCLE CHARLIE: What? The evening paper?

YOUNG CHARLIE: Yes. *That's* why you played that game with Ann and Roger. Uncle Charlie, tell me what the newspaper said. Anything that interests you interests me.

UNCLE CHARLIE: Now, now. . . . Just something about some people I know. (*Young Charlie picks the page out of his pocket; runs and stands with her back to the door. As she holds the paper, the full double-page unfurls, showing the hole made by the torn fragment.*)

YOUNG CHARLIE: There! (*Uncle Charlie goes to her and seizes her wrist.*)

UNCLE CHARLIE: Charlie! It's none of your business!!

YOUNG CHARLIE: Uncle Charlie! You're hurting me! (*She gazes fascinated at his hand. We see his hand relaxing.*)

UNCLE CHARLIE (*lighter tone*): Forgive me. I keep forgetting how strong I am. . . . That news-item, it's just a bit of foolish gossip about someone I knew once. Forget all about it. It's just a lot of nonsense.

YOUNG CHARLIE (*can't take her eyes off his hand, now down at his side*): But it must be *something*. (*She goes blindly out of the room. He goes to the door and calls genially after her:*)

UNCLE CHARLIE: Good night. Get a good rest.

YOUNG CHARLIE (*composing her face, and for the first time "acting" a friendly manner*): Good night, Uncle Charlie. Same to you.

> *Transition to sequence showing the various members of the family in their bedrooms.*
> *Bedroom of Mr. and Mrs. Newton. Mr. Newton is sitting up in bed reading a mystery story magazine. Mrs. Newton, dressed in a wrapper, is sitting before a table rubbing cold cream into her face. On the table is a basin of water and a propped-up mirror.*

MR. NEWTON (*looking at her over his glasses*): I never thought I'd live to see the day when you'd be putting goose-grease on your face in the middle of the night. Like one of these here chorus-girls.

MRS. NEWTON: I know. I feel as foolish as I look. But I promised Charlie I'd do it, and I am. Now that Charles is here, we've all got to smarten up a bit. You, too. I hope he doesn't find out that a grown man like you wastes his time reading carloads of those trashy mystery stories, filling your head full of blood and gore. (*She starts rapidly passing an ice-cube over her forehead and cheeks. Mr. Newton peers at her in alarm.*)

MR. NEWTON: What are you doing now? *Freezing your face?*

MRS. NEWTON: Joe, you tend to your business and I'll tend to mine. If I'd begun doing this long ago I wouldn't have lost the secretaryship of the East End Woman's Club.

MR. NEWTON (*grunts*): I haven't seen any signs that you girls elect one another to office on grounds of beauty.

MRS. NEWTON: Joe, if Charles does deposit all that money in your bank, won't it bring you a lot of credit? (*She turns and looks at him speculatively.*) I wouldn't be surprised if Mr. Greene promoted you to the Loans department.

MR. NEWTON (*not raising his eyes from the page*): Don't count your chickens before they're hatched. (*Mrs. Newton returns*

to her treatments and plucks a hair out of her eyebrows):
Ouch!—Well, I can't see any end to the good effects that
Charles' visit's going to have on this family of yours. Charlie's
in such a happy state that I'm almost beginning to worry
about her.

MR. NEWTON: Charlie's a high-strung girl.

MRS. NEWTON: Yes, she is. But she's solid as a rock, too. Joe,
did you ever stop to think that Charlie never cries? I don't
think I've seen Charlie in tears more than three or four
times in her whole life.

MR. NEWTON: She takes after me.

MRS. NEWTON: Nonsense! She's an Oakley through and
through. She's as like Uncle Charlie as two peas in a pod.
Now that he's here I can see it every minute. Ann and Charlie are Oakleys; it's Roger that takes after you, always trying
to scare yourself—

> *Cut to Roger. He is kneeling on his bed in his pajamas. He is
> wearing the belt and holster and is aiming the toy revolver
> at an enemy. This was Uncle Charlie's present.*

ROGER (*softly*): I give you three to come out of that door and
give yourself up, Fred Bergin. All right, then. I'm sorry to
have to do it. (*He carefully empties the water from the water-
pistol into a flower-vase beside the bed.*

> *Cut to Ann's room. Two beds. Ann is looking up at Charlie
> who in night-dress is standing over her with a candle.*

ANN (*sleepily*): How long is Uncle Charlie going to stay in our
house?

YOUNG CHARLIE: Sh . . . sh . . . go to sleep, Ann. I hope
he stays a long time.

ANN: Hasn't he got a house of his own to stay in?

YOUNG CHARLIE (*kissing her*): Turn over and go to sleep, now.
Good night.

ANN: Good night.

> *Charlie gets into her own bed. Blows out the candle. In the
> moonlight we see her sitting up, gazing happily before her.
> She starts to hum the Merry Widow Waltz.*
>
> *Cut to Uncle Charlie's room. He is sitting up on the bed,*

fully dressed, except for his coat. He is smoking a cigar with great satisfaction. Distant whistle and bell of train.

Cut to railway station platform. A train is pulling out. From the far end of the platform two men are coming towards us. They are Jack Graham and Fred Saunders. They are carrying suitcases and Saunders has the photographic paraphernalia on his back. They get nearer and grow to ominous size on the screen.

Part Two

Shot: outside of the house.
Cheerful music.
Uncle Charlie's breakfast in bed. The tray is spread out on his knees. Mrs. Newton is talking to him vivaciously.

UNCLE CHARLIE: Ah, you're spoiling me, Emma, you're spoiling me. Breakfast in bed!

MRS. NEWTON: It won't hurt to be coddled your first day. Though I must say, Charles, you're the first person in this town that ever had breakfast at ten-thirty in the morning. And while you've been sleeping the whole town's been talking about you.

UNCLE CHARLIE: About me?

MRS. NEWTON: Yes, indeed. The phone's been ringing at ten-minute intervals. The newspaper wants to interview you. The Woman's Club I belong to—in fact, I used to be secretary of it, Charles, when I was younger—they want you to speak to them.

UNCLE CHARLIE: Do I have to make speeches?

MRS. NEWTON: Not unless you want to. We'll talk it over later.

UNCLE CHARLIE: Where's Charlie?

MRS. NEWTON: Oh, she's cleaning the house. She'll be here in a minute, I expect. But Charles, you're not the only person that's in the limelight this morning. The Newton family's going to be dragged out into public attention, too.

UNCLE CHARLIE: How do you mean?

MRS. NEWTON: Well, a very nice-spoken young man called on me this morning. He said his name was Graham. And he said he wants to interview everybody in the house.

UNCLE CHARLIE: What for?

MRS. NEWTON: Seems he's been sent around the country by a committee or institute or something to pick out representative American families and ask them questions. It's a kind of poll. It's called the . . . the . . . National Public Opinion Survey . . . or something like that.

UNCLE CHARLIE: Oh!—How did he happen to pick you out?

MRS. NEWTON: Well, he said something about typical United States families. I told him right off that we're not a typical family at all. When he starts asking questions, Charles, he'll be able to see that he's made a big mistake. My three children —each in their own way—are many times superior to certain other families I might name. Between you and me, he'll find he's just wasting his time.

UNCLE CHARLIE: But you still haven't explained how he happened to pick you out.

MRS. NEWTON: That's what I asked him, first thing.

UNCLE CHARLIE: What did he say?

MRS. NEWTON: I can't remember, exactly . . . he said he'd looked around . . . and that's what he'd decided.

UNCLE CHARLIE: So he's going to ask you a lot of questions. Well, you can leave me out of it.

MRS. NEWTON: Not only questions. He's going to take photographs, too.

UNCLE CHARLIE: Oh.

MRS. NEWTON: Yes, there are two of them and one takes photographs.

UNCLE CHARLIE: There are two of them, are there?

MRS. NEWTON: He said not to dress up specially, but to move around just as though it were an ordinary day.

UNCLE CHARLIE (*pushing his tray aside; making it impressive*): Emma, I think you've done a foolish thing. A downright foolish thing. Why do you want to expose your family to a pack of snoopers? *I* thought you had more sense than that.

MRS. NEWTON: But Charles— (*Enter Young Charlie.*)

YOUNG CHARLIE: Good morning, Uncle Charlie.

UNCLE CHARLIE: Good morning. What do you know about this?

MRS. NEWTON: Charlie wasn't here. But, Charles, the way he put it, it was a useful thing to do . . . it was like a . . . our duty as citizens. It's something the government wants.

UNCLE CHARLIE: Oh, the government's in it, is it?

MRS. NEWTON: Maybe not exactly . . . I don't know; but it's for the public good. And Charles, of course I told him you were here, and he seemed very interested.

UNCLE CHARLIE: I won't have anything to do with it. I'm just a visitor here. And my advice to you is to slam the door in his face.

MRS. NEWTON: You don't have to meet him, if you don't wish to, Charles. I know he'll be disappointed.

YOUNG CHARLIE: *I* wish you'd consent, if only for the reason that we could have a photograph of you. He'd give us one free.

UNCLE CHARLIE: No, ma'am. No, thank you. I've never been photographed in my life, and I won't be photographed now.

MRS. NEWTON: Why, Charles, I have a photograph of you.

UNCLE CHARLIE (*astonished*): I tell you, there are none!

MRS. NEWTON (*taking a small snapshot out of an envelope*): I guess you've forgotten all about it. (*Young Charlie moves around by her uncle's shoulder to look at it. It is the photograph of a boy of 9; high forehead; singularly idealistic expression.*)

UNCLE CHARLIE (*taken aback*): 39 Burnham Street.

YOUNG CHARLIE (*in awe*): Uncle, how beautiful!

UNCLE CHARLIE (*after looking at it a moment, under his breath*): Oh, Emmy, if we could only turn back the clock. (*Pause.*) The whole world's gone down hill.

The photograph fills the screen. Over it we hear Mrs. Newton's voice:

MRS. NEWTON: I can remember the day it was taken just as though it were yesterday. You'd thrown a snowball and hit the policeman—what was his name?

UNCLE CHARLIE (*sharply*): No!

MRS. NEWTON: You certainly did. And Mama wouldn't speak to you the whole rest of the day, except when we had that appointment at the photographer's. Don't you remember— Mama cried all the way home.

Camera returns to take in the room. Uncle Charlie pushes the photograph back at her almost roughly.

UNCLE CHARLIE: Doesn't do to look backward or forward.— That's my philosophy. Keep your eyes on the present moment—that's all we can manage. Now you girls run away. I've got to dress and go downtown to the bank. Charlie's going to have lunch with me downtown, special treat.

MRS. NEWTON: Well, Charlie! Don't be late for the question-naire-man. He's coming at four o'clock.

> *The streets of the town.*
> *Passing crowds. Traffic policeman's whistle, etc. Young Charlie and Uncle Charlie on their way to the bank. They enter the bank.*

YOUNG CHARLIE: There's Papa over at that window. (*They go up to the window.*)

UNCLE CHARLIE: Hello, Joe. Can you stop embezzling for a minute and give me a little attention? (*Mr. Newton, horrified, looks to right and left. He leans forward and says in a frightened whisper:*)

MR. NEWTON: Charles . . . uh . . . we don't joke about such things in here.

UNCLE CHARLIE (*louder still*): What if there is a little shortage in the books at the end of the month? I wouldn't think much of a bank clerk who couldn't cover up a little shortage. (*He laughs loudly.*) Isn't that right, Charlie? (*Mr. Newton laughs feebly.*)

YOUNG CHARLIE: Uncle Charlie! Everybody can hear you!

UNCLE CHARLIE: Good thing if they can. Banks are always trying to put on a solemn show. Doesn't fool me. Everybody knows what they are. (*He makes the gesture of rubbing his thumb against his forefinger and winks.*) Well, Joe, let's see your president.

MR. NEWTON: You still thinking about opening an account, Charles?

UNCLE CHARLIE: Yes, sir.

MR. NEWTON: Then you wait right here and I'll speak to Mr. Greene.—But Charles, Mr. Greene doesn't understand jokes, like I do.

UNCLE CHARLIE: Well, he understands forty thousand dollars, don't he? Listen, Joe, the whole world's a joke, and everybody knows it. You can't change me at my time of life.

MR. NEWTON: I'll be back in a minute. (*He can be seen passing behind the backs of the other tellers and entering the president's office.*)

YOUNG CHARLIE: Uncle! You shouldn't tease Papa that way.

UNCLE CHARLIE: I'm not teasing anybody. I hate this stuffy

awe about banks. What are they so righteous about? They're strong-boxes and money-lenders, and that's all I want from them.

YOUNG CHARLIE: Look, he's making us the sign to come in.

The president's office.
Mr. Greene is a very solemn man. Mr. Newton is whispering in his ear.

MR. GREENE: You don't say, Joe. Well, ask him to come right in. Thirty thousand dollars?

MR. NEWTON: Thirty or forty, Mr. Greene.

MR. GREENE: Ask him right in. And Joe—

MR. NEWTON: Yes, Mr. Greene?

MR. GREENE: We won't forget this—you know what I mean?

MR. NEWTON: I'll . . . I'll . . . I'll call him. (*Mr. Newton beckons to Uncle Charlie and Young Charlie, who come into the office. The other tellers crane their necks and whisper among themselves while the introductions are made and cigars lighted.*)

UNCLE CHARLIE (*big-city man*): Yes, Mr. Greene, I'm thinking of settling down in the West. Great country. Great country. No doubt about it.

MR. GREENE: We think so, don't we, Charlie?—What's been your occupation, Mr. Oakley?

UNCLE CHARLIE: Well, looking at it from all sides—I guess you could call me a promoter. I've done a little of everything. Real estate . . . shipping business. . . . It's not hard to make money, Mr. Greene. The only difficult thing is keeping interested in it.

MR. GREENE (*stung*): I beg your pardon?

UNCLE CHARLIE: Well, you know as well as I do that there's more money lying around for the first person that comes along to pick up than you can shake a stick at. Yes, sir. The only trouble with making money is that it's boring.—Well, let's get down to our business. (*He reaches in his pocket and takes out a bulging purse.*) As I was saying—since I've decided to settle down in the West, I said to myself: why not deposit some of my loose cash in my brother-in-law's bank.

MR. GREENE: Loose cash, Mr. Oakley?

UNCLE CHARLIE: Yes.—You see, I'm funny that way, Mr. Greene. I like to know where my money is.

MR. GREENE (*his eyes popping at the bills*): You make it a custom to carry large sums in bills?

UNCLE CHARLIE (*counting them out*): Yes, sir. All my life. Until money's invested . . . twenty . . . twenty-five . . .

MR. GREENE: It's a risk, Mr. Oakley. On trains. In hotels.

UNCLE CHARLIE: Never lost a cent in my life, Mr. Greene. Dogs don't bite you unless you're afraid of them. Thirty . . . thirty-five . . . forty. Let's say forty. We'll start with that.

MR. GREENE (*a little coldly*): Now if you'll write the deposit slip, Mr. Oakley.

UNCLE CHARLIE: Yes, sir.

MR. GREENE: I must say that this has never happened to me in all my experience. Sometimes some farmers back in the hills bring in a few hundreds they've been keeping in a sock. But larger transactions have always been carried on by check.

> *Young Charlie is standing by him as he fills out the blank. She says, playfully:*

YOUNG CHARLIE: Why do you do things different from other people, Uncle Charlie?

UNCLE CHARLIE (*raising his head; sharply*): I've pulled myself up in the world from a side-street in St. Paul, Minnesota. I wouldn't be where I am if I'd consented to do things as other people do.

YOUNG CHARLIE (*taken aback; puts her arm lightly around his shoulder*): Uncle Charlie, I wasn't criticizing you. I was only joking.

UNCLE CHARLIE: There you are, Mr. Greene. Now, Charlie, you can show me the town and then we'll get some lunch. Good morning, Mr. Greene.

MR. GREENE: Good morning, sir. Happy to serve you. Joe, you can see Mr. Oakley to the door.

UNCLE CHARLIE: See you tonight, Joe. (*At the door, Uncle Charlie is very amused by something. He says confidentially to Mr. Newton:*) Keep your eyes open, Joe. You'll have his job in two years. Watch everything. (*He leaves Mr. Newton open-mouthed.*)

Two men waiting in a car. A bus approaches. They go up the steps when they see Young Charlie and Uncle Charlie are on the bus.

Uncle Charlie and Young Charlie are returning to the house, laden with parcels. On the front porch Jack Graham and Saunders are standing, about to ring the bell. Saunders carries three cameras and much apparatus.

YOUNG CHARLIE: Why, there are those questionnaire men. They're a whole hour early.

UNCLE CHARLIE: —I'm not going to have anything to do with them.

YOUNG CHARLIE: Uncle Charlie, I'll see that you aren't disturbed at all. You don't have to speak to them if you don't want to.

UNCLE CHARLIE: They turned your mother's head. I thought better of her than that. (*Young Charlie runs up to the porch where the men have been waiting.*)

YOUNG CHARLIE: Good afternoon. I suppose you're the men who arranged with my mother to interview us. I'll call her.

JACK: My name's Graham, Miss Newton. This is Fred Saunders.

YOUNG CHARLIE: Won't you come in? (*They step aside and wait for Uncle Charlie, who walks past with a slight nod—and starts up the stairs to his room.*) I'll call my mother—Mother! Mother! Here are the men from the government. (*Uncle Charlie, on the stairs, receives this with a slight turn of his head. Mrs. Newton enters from the kitchen.*) Mother, this is Mr. Graham and Mr. Saunders.

JACK: I know we're early, Mrs. Newton. I hope you'll forgive us. We have a crowded schedule.

MRS. NEWTON: Why . . . ugh . . . one time's as good as another, I guess,—though my husband won't be back from the bank until after five and the children are away at school. Won't you both sit down? (*She sits and folds her hands, self-consciously. Jack takes out a notebook and turns the pages judicially.*)

JACK: Hm. There's a good deal of this I'll get later . . . names; ages; car; electric icebox;—Mr. Newton owns this house, Mrs. Newton?

MRS. NEWTON: Yes, oh yes. We bought the house fifteen, sixteen years ago.

JACK: May Mr. Saunders take some photographs, Mrs. Newton?

MRS. NEWTON: Yes, if you wish to. (*Saunders starts setting up his apparatus.*)

JACK (*turning pleasantly to Young Charlie*): There are six persons living here in the home?

YOUNG CHARLIE: Five.

JACK: Five? You mean you're not counting the gentleman who just came in the door with us?

YOUNG CHARLIE: My uncle's just visiting us for a few days.

MRS. NEWTON (*interrupting, effusively*): You see, he's from the East. He's on a kind of vacation and I think we'd better not disturb him. We'd better leave him out of the whole thing.

JACK: I hope not, Mrs. Newton; for my purposes I should collect the opinions of everyone in a home.

YOUNG CHARLIE: I'm sorry, but—we've promised him that he won't be disturbed.

JACK (*still pleasantly. With pencil poised over his note-book; his eyes resting on Young Charlie appraisingly*): Since you've been kind enough to let us visit your home, Miss Newton, I hope you aren't going to make any exceptions now.

YOUNG CHARLIE (*rising*): We must, Mr. Graham. I'm sorry.

JACK: This project we're on—

YOUNG CHARLIE (*firmly*): I'm sorry, Mr. Graham, if that's the case, I think you'd better choose some other family.

Now Jack's looking at her hard. However, he decides to give way.

JACK: I wouldn't like to do that, Miss Newton. We agree to anything you say. (*Turning to Mrs. Newton.*) Do you and Mr. Newton belong to any clubs, Mrs. Newton—

Cut to Uncle Charlie on the upper landing listening down the stairs. He turns to his room and paces up and down. Dissolve to the kitchen. Mrs. Newton is being photographed as she is making a cake. She is talking vivaciously to Jack. Young Charlie is listening, uneasily.

MRS. NEWTON: . . . no one could have been kinder. Twice a year he's sent presents to the children, simply beautiful presents. And when you think that he's such a busy man,—always travelling. Once they came from Mexico, even. And once, from Newport, Rhode Island. But, of course, we're all his relatives in the world. We're all he's got.

Saunders' flashbulb goes off.

JACK: If you'll raise your hand a little higher, Mrs. Newton, please—what's your brother's occupation, Mrs. Newton?

MRS. NEWTON: Well, I don't know exactly. I suppose it's just those things men do. . . . What they call "big business."

YOUNG CHARLIE: But, mother, these gentlemen want to know about a lot of other things besides Uncle Charlie.

JACK: Yes, indeed. Now I wonder if you'd let us take a few notes about the house upstairs, Mrs. Newton. (*To Young Charlie:*) Perhaps you'd be kind enough to show us around?

MRS. NEWTON: Yes, Charlie. You go up and— (*Young Charlie starts up the stairs—halfway up she turns and says:*)

YOUNG CHARLIE: What is it you especially want to see upstairs? (*She reaches the landing and starts to turn left. Jack immediately behind her points to Uncle Charlie's closed door.*)

JACK: What room is this?

YOUNG CHARLIE: That's my room, but we've given it to my uncle during his visit.

JACK: We want to get an idea of all the rooms. Let's begin here.

YOUNG CHARLIE: But . . . I don't want to disturb him. Maybe he's taking a nap.

JACK: Is there a back stairs from this floor?

YOUNG CHARLIE: Yes, the stairs down to the kitchen are at the end of the hall.

JACK (*playing with a coin in his hand, smiling*): I bet you half a dollar, Miss Newton, that your uncle isn't here.

YOUNG CHARLIE (*smiling back*): I don't bet, Mr. Graham. But I think he *is* here.

JACK: All right: let me knock. (*He raises his hand to knock.*)

YOUNG CHARLIE (*a little troubled, but much taken with Jack*): Well,—you'd better let me do the knocking. (*She knocks lightly.*) Uncle Charlie! (*She knocks again.*) Uncle Charlie, can we come in? (*The young people grin at one another. Suddenly Jack opens the door and shows that the room is empty.*)

JACK: See?

YOUNG CHARLIE: Now how could *you* be sure of that?

JACK: Can Fred take a picture or two?

YOUNG CHARLIE: Yes,—but I can't imagine it being interesting to anybody. (*Saunders goes in.*)

JACK: Oh, a young woman's room is part of it all. (*Jack closes the door and stands with his back to it.*)

YOUNG CHARLIE: Mr. Graham, why did you choose our family?

JACK: I don't know. We just looked around. Why *not* choose your family. (*Pleasantly:*) You've nothing to hide, have you?

YOUNG CHARLIE: No.—Sometimes I wish we had.—You know, your asking all those questions downstairs, and your taking these photographs gives me a funny feeling.

JACK: How do you mean?

YOUNG CHARLIE: The feeling that maybe, after all, we are the average family. Are we?

JACK: No, indeed. I've visited a great many families. You're a very exceptional one.

YOUNG CHARLIE: In what way?

JACK: Well, in a number of ways. But to begin with, you're much nicer than the average family. I love your mother.

YOUNG CHARLIE (*gives him a grateful smile and becomes more confidential*): If you'd come here a week ago I don't think you'd have felt that way about us.

JACK: Why not?

YOUNG CHARLIE: We've improved. My uncle's visit has waked us up. It's not only that he's such a fine man himself, but there's something about him that puts everybody at their best.

JACK (*lowers his eyes a moment*): But you say you haven't seen him for ten years. And, after all, he only arrived last night. Maybe you're . . .

YOUNG CHARLIE: Why is it that—downstairs and up here— you keep bringing the conversation back to Uncle Charlie? And now it seems as though you were warning me not to admire him too much. (*Suddenly we see a shadow cross her face. She touches her wrist reflectively. Her glance turns toward the room, remembering where Uncle Charlie touched her wrist.*) Your friend's taking a long time in my room. I hope he isn't disturbing anything. My uncle's very neat and particular.

JACK: Oh, Saunders is always very careful.—Miss Newton, I have to collect some information about the town, too. I was going to ask your mother if you might show me about the town this evening. I've rented a car for the purpose.

YOUNG CHARLIE (*laughing*): I'll give mother permission to let me go. I'll show you the firehouses and the reservoir—

Uncle Charlie's head appears coming up the back stairs. Jack knocks three times with his fist on the door behind him. Uncle Charlie comes down the hall.

JACK (*raising his voice*): Is this your uncle you were telling me about?

YOUNG CHARLIE: They're just photographing the room, Uncle Charlie. They'll be out in a minute.

The door opens. Saunders appears with a camera, shoulder-high. A flashbulb goes off.

UNCLE CHARLIE (*smiling*): No, sir. I'm sorry. I don't like to be photographed. I'll have to ask you to give me that reel.

YOUNG CHARLIE: But, Uncle Charlie, we're all having our pictures taken.

UNCLE CHARLIE (*lightly—hand extended*): Give it to me,—or I'm afraid I'll have to break the camera.

YOUNG CHARLIE: You're joking, Uncle Charlie!

UNCLE CHARLIE (*ignoring her*): I'm sorry. Give it to me.

JACK (*with lowered eyes*): Give it to him, Fred. (*Uncle Charlie grasps it, and is about to go in his room.*)

YOUNG CHARLIE: But, Uncle!—Mother's on that reel, too. (*Uncle Charlie is suddenly trembling with rage.*)

UNCLE CHARLIE: It's a free country, Miss Newton. Everyone has a right to decide whether they wish to be photographed or not. Good afternoon. (*He closes the door sharply behind him.*)

YOUNG CHARLIE: Oh, dear—why should he be angry about an ordinary thing like that!

Mrs. Newton's anxious face appears at the bottom of the stairs.

MRS. NEWTON: What's the matter? What's the matter, Charlie?

Young Charlie and the men start coming downstairs.

YOUNG CHARLIE: I'm afraid we've made Uncle Charlie angry.

MRS. NEWTON: Now, how could you do that? Mr. Graham, you understood that my brother wasn't to have any part in this.

YOUNG CHARLIE: But, Mama, he *is* unreasonable.

JACK (*putting his notebook away*): Mrs. Newton, there's always one part of my work I don't like. Naturally, families don't like to be disturbed. When the reports are published, though, I think you'll be able to see that any inconvenience like this has been justified.

MRS. NEWTON: Of course, I'm glad if we can be of any service . . . but it's too bad that— (*She looks up the stairs.*)

JACK: That's all we have to do in the house, but there's one more favor I'd like to ask of you. There's some material I have to get about the town itself. I wonder if you'd let Miss Newton come to dinner with me and show me about afterwards.

MRS. NEWTON: That's up to Charlie. . . . I . . .

YOUNG CHARLIE: I'd like to, Mother. (*They've moved out to the porch.*)

JACK: That's very good of you. If I could call for you, Miss Newton—about half-past six?

YOUNG CHARLIE: Thank you. I'll be ready.

The men tip their hats and go off. Mrs. Newton and Young Charlie stand on the porch looking after them.

MRS. NEWTON: Really, Charlie, I can't make up my mind whether he's a nice young man or not.

YOUNG CHARLIE: Oh, yes, he is, Mother. I think he's a little different, because . . . because he's serious about what he's doing.

MRS. NEWTON: Well,—

YOUNG CHARLIE: I'd begun to think that young men were never really serious about anything.

And yet a puzzled look crosses her face. Dissolve to a look-out point on a hill above the town. Night— Young Charlie and Jack are standing by a low stone wall. The car is beside them, its lights turned off.

YOUNG CHARLIE (*happy animation*): I'll never forget the look on that man's face.

JACK: What man?

YOUNG CHARLIE: Why, the man who owns the shooting gallery. It was bad enough when you made a hundred per cent on his hardest targets—but when you did it standing on your head!—Where on earth did you learn to do a thing like that?

JACK: Oh, just picked it up. (*He turns away.*)

YOUNG CHARLIE: However, I keep forgetting that I'm here to be instructive. Where was I—oh, yes. (*She turns back to the view—pointing.*) I should say that in all those parts of town, most of the people own their own houses, just as we do. (*Jack has been softly whistling the Merry Widow Waltz.*) You're not listening to me. In fact, I don't think you're interested at all. When I began you took everything down in your notebook; now you don't take anything down and you whistle. Do I tell all these things badly?

JACK: No, no. You're a very well-informed citizen, Miss Newton. The more I hear you discuss Santa Rosa, the more I admire you.

YOUNG CHARLIE: I can't get it out of my head that it's all rather mysterious. And yet you're certainly interested in *something*. You come into our house and ask all those questions and take all those photographs—as though you were a spy or a detective or something. (*She says this casually; but he suddenly turns his head in alarm. She sees this; stares at him, takes a few steps backward, and says in a low voice:*) You're from the police! You're a policeman!

JACK: Hm. I guess I'm a pretty bad one.

YOUNG CHARLIE (*with a cry*): But we have nothing to hide!

Jack takes both her hands at the wrist, urgently.

JACK: Listen! Sit down! I'm trying to help you, you and your mother. I'm trying to save you both from any unnecessary suffering.

YOUNG CHARLIE: My mother? My mother?

JACK: Sit down a moment.—Do you realize how little you know about your uncle?

YOUNG CHARLIE: Everything I know is good.

JACK: Maybe it is. I hope so. Maybe we're mistaken—but you say you haven't seen him for ten years. He only arrived in town yesterday. You've never even known his address.

YOUNG CHARLIE: What . . . do you think he's done? Why are you suspicious about him?

JACK: All over the country they're hunting for a man with some very serious charges against him. We know very little about this man we're hunting for. One little thing, however, *does* connect him with your uncle.

YOUNG CHARLIE: It can't be. It's all a mistake.

JACK: Yes, we think the real man is in the East somewhere—up in Massachusetts and Maine. But we have to learn all we can about your uncle. He may be the man we're after.

YOUNG CHARLIE: What is it that you suspect?

JACK (*a slight pause*): It's not right to tell you . . . until we're sure.

YOUNG CHARLIE: It would kill my mother!—What should I do? What can I do?

JACK: You can tell us anything that would help us—anything you've noticed. The more we know, the easier it will be to take him away with as little publicity as possible.

YOUNG CHARLIE: Arrest him? Here?

JACK: No one need know,—with your help in the house—

YOUNG CHARLIE: Don't talk to me. Don't talk to me for a minute. I've got to get used to this— (*She walks away from him and stands looking down at the town. Jack starts whistling softly the Merry Widow Waltz, Young Charlie lifts her head; she calls from a distance:*) Why are you whistling that tune . . . the *Merry Widow Waltz*?

JACK: Was I? . . . Hm, that's strange. There's a sort of connection between that tune and the things this man is suspected of.

YOUNG CHARLIE (*wide-eyed, taking a step forward*): —What connection could there be?

JACK: I'm sorry. I didn't mean to say that. It's nothing.

YOUNG CHARLIE (*returning to him*): Tell me. What can I do?

JACK: I leave that to you. Is there anything you have to tell me now?

YOUNG CHARLIE: No, of course not.

Pause—Jack turns and looks over the town.

JACK: Now you see what I meant when I said that there's one part of my work that I don't like. But just the same—

YOUNG CHARLIE (*softly*): You're from the police!

JACK: Look at all the lights of the towns. Most of those people live and die without being disturbed by anything like this. (*He looks in her face.*) That takes a lot of watching.—You're one of the few,—the one in every thousand—who has to come up against it. This is your chance to help. I'm going to count on you to help. That's all.

Young Charlie goes to her seat in the car.

YOUNG CHARLIE: I'll try.

In silence Jack climbs into the driver's seat and starts the motor.

JACK: If we learn anything I'll let you know. And in the same way, you let us know. We're at Brown's Tourist Camp. If we do find something it'll be your business to persuade your uncle to leave town. You tell us when he goes and how, and we'll arrest him in some other town. (*He starts driving.*)

YOUNG CHARLIE: Does Uncle Charlie know that you're from the police?

JACK (*throwing up his head; with a short laugh*): Oh, yes.

YOUNG CHARLIE: What can anybody do?

JACK (*driving—out of the corner of his mouth*): You're intelligent. You're grown up. Keep up your nerve and be brave. . . . That's all you have to do.

Cut to street in front of the Newton home. Young Charlie is getting out of the car.

JACK: We're in this together. I'll do anything I can for you. And remember, as I said: maybe he's not the man.

YOUNG CHARLIE: I can't believe he's done anything really

bad. I'm going to prove to you that he's not the man you're looking for.

JACK: That's right. That's what we're here to prove. Can I say,—goodnight, *Charlie?*

YOUNG CHARLIE: Yes . . . goodnight, Jack.

She hurries toward the house. She stands in the dark looking in at the brightly lighted windows. In the sitting room Uncle Charlie's back is to her, but she sees her mother leaning forward in her chair and listening to him with admiring affection. From among the trees Mr. Newton and Herbie come walking with long thoughtful pauses. Herbie follows a few yards behind with dog-like admiration.

HERBIE: Do you think they could'a caught her, Joe?—right in the middle of a circus going on? and she standing on top of a horse?

MR. NEWTON (*turning and frowning at him*): Nothing's ever been done without leaving some evidence around, Herbie. Don't forget that. Why, *you* can't even go downtown and buy a cigar, Herbie, without leaving a dozen clues for the right man to pick up.

HERBIE: You don't say so, Joe?

MR. NEWTON (*seeing Young Charlie*): Who's that? Is that you, Charlie?

YOUNG CHARLIE: Yes, Papa. I was just getting some air before going to bed.

MR. NEWTON: Well, don't catch your death of cold. Go in and talk to your Uncle Charlie. He's been asking about you.

YOUNG CHARLIE: No, I think in a minute I'll just go up the back way to bed. I'm tired.

MR. NEWTON: Suit yourself.

YOUNG CHARLIE (*kissing him and clinging to him a moment*): Goodnight, Papa. Take care of yourself.

MR. NEWTON: Eh, you're choking me. Goodnight. (*Mr. Newton and Herbie move on. Before they disappear we hear the last murmurs of their conversation.*) You see, Herbie, all a body's got to do is to develop his powers of observation. . . .

Young Charlie goes up the back stairs. She listens on the landing. Uncle Charlie's voice floats up the stairs.

UNCLE CHARLIE: The chief thing in the education of children, Emma, is to see that they understand what the world's really like. Now you and I were brought up to a lot of nonsense—

Young Charlie is about to go in her own room when her eye falls on the shut door of Uncle Charlie's room. She opens it, turns on the light and looks around. She doesn't know what to do first. She opens a bureau drawer or two. She opens the drawer of the bedside table.

Her eye falls on the wastepaper basket. The double sheet of the newspaper has been torn into many pieces. She gathers them together and carries them into her own room. Ann is sleeping in one of the beds. She lights a candle and starts putting the pieces together on the counterpane of her bed.

Cut to the pieces all put together. The pattern of the torn-out fragment emerges.

Ann wakes and sits up, blinking and shielding her eyes.

ANN: What game is that you're playing, Charlie?

YOUNG CHARLIE: Sh. . . . Go to sleep, Ann. It's just a recipe I was looking for in the paper. And it's been torn out. Too bad.

ANN (*lying down*): They have all the papers in the library. The new ones and the old ones.

YOUNG CHARLIE (*glances at clock*): It closes at nine. Oh, well, it doesn't matter; perhaps I'll go tomorrow. (*Crushes together the pieces of paper.*) Now go to sleep, Ann. Goodnight.

ANN: Goodnight.

YOUNG CHARLIE (*blows out the candle. Then starts running down the back stairs, whispering*): It can't be anything bad . . . it's nothing at all. I can prove that it's nothing at all. (*She runs through the streets of the town, her hair flying behind her. She starts across the curb against the policeman's signal.*)

MR. MORTON: Just a moment, Charlie. What do you think I'm here for?

YOUNG CHARLIE: I'm sorry, Mr. Morton.

MR. MORTON (*blows whistle*): All right now.

She catches a glimpse of a clock: four minutes of nine.
She arrives at the steps of the library. The reading-room lights go out as she reaches the steps. There is a faint light in

the front hall. She tries the door. It is locked. She knocks and finally beats on the door. The spinster librarian appears behind the glass; she shakes her head reprovingly; she is saying something. She points at some wall-clock.
Closeup through glass of Young Charlie, her lips moving in urgent request. At last the Librarian opens the door:

LIBRARIAN: Really, Charlie! You know as well as I do that this library closes at nine o'clock. I can't make any exceptions for individual cases—

Young Charlie brushes past her.

YOUNG CHARLIE: Please forgive me, Miss Corcoran. There's something in a newspaper that I have to see—
LIBRARIAN: I must say I'm very much surprised!
YOUNG CHARLIE: I won't be a minute, Miss Corcoran. (*Young Charlie has stumbled into the darkened reading-room and made for the farther corner. The Librarian, still injured, turns on the reading-room lights and continues grumbling.*)
LIBRARIAN: The library hours give plenty of time for everyone to make use of the privileges. I shall give you three minutes, Charlie—

She withdraws into her office. Young Charlie stands before the racks where the day's newspapers are hanging. She tries them and rejects them. On the shelves nearby she finds the recent issues ranged in piles. She picks up the paper she's looking for and at last isolates the pages. She draws with her finger the design of the last torn fragment. Suddenly she sees:

POLICE CLOSE IN ON HUNTED CRIMINAL
Boston, Mass., Feb. 8. In their search for the so-called "Merry Widow" murderer, the police have thrown a cordon around the North Eastern States and the announcement of his arrest is expected daily. (*The Merry Widow Waltz is heard faintly from the sound-track.*) A peculiarity of the case lies in the fact that no photograph of the suspected man has ever been obtained and all the names he has used are thought to be aliases.

When found he will be charged with the murder of three, and perhaps four, wealthy women. His victims have uniformly been widows of large means living in resort hotels and this fact has led to his being given the name of the "Merry Widow" murderer.

His latest victim, on January twelfth, in Gloucester, Mass., was Mrs. Bruce Matthewson, the former musical comedy star, known to audiences at the beginning of this century as "the beautiful Teresa Schenley."

The "T. S. from B. M." inscribed below the emerald becomes isolated from the newsprint and fills the screen. The Merry Widow Waltz issues from the sound-track, fortissimo. View of Young Charlie, dragging herself from the room. Voice of the Librarian:

LIBRARIAN: I really must close the library now, Charlie. I hope you've found what you wanted. As you know, the library will be open tomorrow at nine o'clock. . . .

Stunned, Young Charlie walks home.

Part Three

The Waltz still faintly heard.
Long view of house.
Cut to Mrs. Newton before stove.
Uncle Charlie strolls to kitchen window.

UNCLE CHARLIE: Emma.

MRS. NEWTON: Yes, Charles?

UNCLE CHARLIE: Where's Charlie? Here it is four o'clock and I have not seen her all day?

MRS. NEWTON: Shh. She's asleep and I don't want to wake her. (*Lap dissolve. Outside Young Charlie's door. Mrs. Newton knocks lightly.*) Are you awake, dear? Uncle Charlie's been asking for you all day. (*Listens and retires.*)

Lap dissolve to sitting-room.

MRS. NEWTON: I'm glad she's had a good rest. She's been looking tired lately. She says she'll be down to dinner.

Closeup reaction of Uncle Charlie. Slight expression of concern.
Lap dissolve to Young Charlie coming out of her room. Her face shows anxiety and watchfulness. As the sound of Uncle Charlie's voice floats up the stairs, her expression changes to repulsion. She goes toward the back stairs.

UNCLE CHARLIE'S VOICE (*amid roars of his own laughter*): See, Joe? Thought he was in the National Bank and it turned out to be one of these burial vaults; so I said to him— (*The voice fades out.*)

Mrs. Newton is kneeling before the oven, peering in at the roast. She is humming the Merry Widow Waltz. She is so occupied that she does not see or hear Young Charlie enter by the back stairs. Young Charlie can be seen changing her expression: she assumes an air of cheerful but firm generalship and says to her mother:

YOUNG CHARLIE: Now, Mother, from now on I'm going to

take charge of the dinner. You go in and talk to Uncle
Charlie.

MRS. NEWTON: How are you feeling now, Charlie?

YOUNG CHARLIE: I feel fine. I must have been more tired than
I thought. I took a nap and I slept like a log all afternoon.

MRS. NEWTON: Uncle Charlie's been asking for you again. And
that nice young man came twice and asked after you. I looked
in and saw you were asleep and I wouldn't disturb you.

YOUNG CHARLIE: Well, I'm ready for anything. I'm going to
serve the whole dinner. (*She kneels and looks into the oven.*)
Have you skimmed the gravy yet?

MRS. NEWTON (*taking off her apron and fluffing her hair, hums
a bar of the Waltz*): Yes, I have.

YOUNG CHARLIE: Whatever you do, Mama, don't hum that
tune any more. I've almost got it out of my head and I don't
want it to get started again. Please remember that: don't hum
that tune, and, Mama, don't you get up from the table. You
just sit there and be a lady without a single care on your mind.

MRS. NEWTON: If you say so, but at least I'll carry in the soup.
(*She opens the door to the dining-room with tureen in her
hands.*) Roger, dinner's almost ready. Have you washed your
hands? Charles!—Joe!—you can sit down at the table, if you
like. (*Ann enters the kitchen.*)

UNCLE CHARLIE'S VOICE: Where's our Charlie? Where's our
Charlie, I've missed her all day.

MRS. NEWTON: She'll be in in a minute, Charles. (*Ann has been
pulling her skirt, trying to whisper something. Mrs. Newton
lets the kitchen door fall closed.*)

ANN: Mama.

MRS. NEWTON: What is it?

ANN: Mama, I want to ask you something.

MRS. NEWTON: What is it you want? I can't hear you. Don't
whisper. What is it you want?

ANN: I want to sit by you.

MRS. NEWTON: What? Don't you like sitting by your Uncle
Charles?

ANN: I want to sit by you.

YOUNG CHARLIE: Let her change with Roger, if she wants to.

MRS. NEWTON: Certainly not. Uncle Charles might think that
. . . certainly not.

YOUNG CHARLIE: Oh, mother,—let her change if she wants to.

MRS. NEWTON: All right; but I don't like it.

YOUNG CHARLIE: Go on in. Go on in. (*She practically pushes them through the door. Then she stands listening at it, her face concentrated in loathing.*)

The dinner-table. Mrs. Newton seats herself at head and serves soup.

Joe Newton   Young Charlie

Mrs. Newton [ ] *Uncle Charlie*

Ann   Roger

Mr. Newton is catching a quick view of the first page of the newspaper. Uncle Charlie becomes aware of the change of seating at his left.

UNCLE CHARLIE: Hel-lo! What's this? Have I lost my little girl?

MRS. NEWTON (*hastily*): I want them both to have a chance to sit by you, Charles.

UNCLE CHARLIE (*but with his eyes on Ann*): Roger: wait till you see your new present; sent for it yesterday. You'll open your eyes.

MRS. NEWTON: Now, Charles, promise me,—not another thing.

MR. NEWTON (*handing Uncle Charlie the paper*): Nothing special in the paper as far as I can see. Want a look, Charles?

The kitchen. Young Charlie prepares herself to enter the dining-room—she faces the door—almost nose to it—and takes a deep breath. Suddenly she turns, goes back to the other end of the kitchen, gropes in her handbag, and takes out a lipstick. She goes to a cracked hanging mirror and applies the stick with a concentrated look on her face.

The dining-room. Uncle Charlie has been glancing through the inner side of the newspaper with increasing satisfaction.

UNCLE CHARLIE: As you say, Joe: nothing special tonight. Nothing special. (*But he continues to glance through the back pages. Young Charlie enters. During the following speeches she moves about, taking up the empty soup plates. On her entrance she receives an ovation.*) There you are! Here's Charlie at last, folks.

ROGER: Hey!!

MR. NEWTON: Yes, here's our girl.

YOUNG CHARLIE (*drily, deprecating the welcome*): I live here.

MR. NEWTON: Where you been, Charlie?

MRS. NEWTON: She was asleep. She slept like a log all afternoon.

UNCLE CHARLIE (*with a wink*): Are you sure?

YOUNG CHARLIE: I've been dreaming about you, Uncle Charlie. Perfect nightmares— Mama, as I'm going to be in and out all the time, you come up here and sit in my place by Uncle Charlie.

MRS. NEWTON: Charlie!

YOUNG CHARLIE: We may not have him with us forever, so you get a good visit with him now. (*She stands holding out her chair for her mother. Mrs. Newton rises and comes to it.*)

MRS. NEWTON (*shocked*): Why, Charlie, what a thing to say! I hope he stays with us a good long time.

YOUNG CHARLIE (*smiling brightly at Uncle Charlie*): Well, we have to face the fact that we'll lose him some day or other, don't we?

UNCLE CHARLIE (*over his newspaper, gets this and has been watching her musingly*): Yes, that's what I like,—people that look facts in the face.

MRS. NEWTON (*patting his hand, though he's still holding the newspaper*): Charlie didn't mean a thing by that,—not a thing.

Ann is standing beside him, about to take his soup plate from under the folds of his paper.

UNCLE CHARLIE: Want to see the funnies, Ann? They're right here.

ANN (*removing his plate; lowered eyes*): I don't read at table.

UNCLE CHARLIE: Ann, you're right. I'm forgetting all my manners. Thank you for the lesson, little lady. Roger, will you go and look at the back of the icebox and bring me a big red bottle you see there? (*Roger goes out.*)

YOUNG CHARLIE: Anyway, now that Father's finished with the

paper, you can do anything you like with it. We throw them away,—or we just line bureau drawers with them. (*She goes out into the kitchen. Now Uncle Charlie is uneasy.*)

MRS. NEWTON: Ann, go out and help Charlie bring in the vegetables.

UNCLE CHARLIE: How late was Charlie out last night,— gallivanting about with that young journalist, or whatever you call him?

MRS. NEWTON: She got back quite early. I was surprised. I went to take a look at Ann and there was Charlie already asleep by quarter of ten. She must have gone up the back way.

UNCLE CHARLIE: Did she see him today?

MRS. NEWTON: No. He called twice, but I wouldn't disturb her.

UNCLE CHARLIE: What do you think of him, Emma?

MRS. NEWTON: I? . . . Why—uh . . . he seems to be a very nice young man. (*Uncle Charlie raises his eyes significantly and clutches his napkin in his fist. Roger returns with a bottle of Burgundy—he places it beside Uncle Charlie.*) Goodness! What's that, Charles? Wine?!!

UNCLE CHARLIE: St. Paul said: Take a little wine for thy stomach's sake.

MRS. NEWTON: But, Charles, we *never, never,*—in fact, we've all taken the pledge. Ann took it just last week.

UNCLE CHARLIE: This is what's called Sparkling Red Burgundy, Emma. In hospitals they give it to invalids.

MR. NEWTON: That's a fact, Emma,—it's a tonic for anybody that's run down.

MRS. NEWTON: You can do what you think best, but I won't touch it.

UNCLE CHARLIE: Roger! (*He whispers a direction to him. Roger returns in a moment with four glasses. Young Charlie enters with the roast, which she places before her father. She sits down in her place with lowered eyes.*)

MRS. NEWTON: Charles, the bank president's wife, Mrs. Greene, is president of our women's club. She called up this afternoon again. She wants to know the title of the speech you're going to make for us. She has to give it to the newspapers.

UNCLE CHARLIE: It's got to have a title, does it? Let's see. Shall we give 'em current events, or a travel talk?

MRS. NEWTON: Oh, travel, Charles! We get current events every week.

MR. NEWTON (*serving*): Fact is, Charles, Rotary and Kiwanis are fighting over you now. Mr. Greene's Rotary, and he wants you for them; and I'm Kiwanis, and it looks like I've got to produce you for them.

MRS. NEWTON: Do you make many speeches, Charles?

UNCLE CHARLIE: Oh, it's one of those things you can't get out of when you're in public life. Easier to do 'em than refuse 'em.

MRS. NEWTON: Mrs. Greene says I'll have to introduce you at the lecture. I know I'll die of fright before I ever get on the platform.

UNCLE CHARLIE: Now, Emma, listen to what I'm saying to you—when you've got some kind of test or ordeal ahead of you,—see?

MRS. NEWTON: Yes, Charles. (*Uncle Charlie starts unwinding the wire from the neck of the bottle.*)

UNCLE CHARLIE: First, prepare your speech or make your plan,—whatever it is—thoroughly. Then don't think about it again. Nothing in the world is difficult if you just fix your will on it. Do it!!—but don't let your imagination fool with it beforehand, or afterwards. (*He now is rubbing the neck of the bottle with a rotary motion and pulling at cork.*) No, just take it for what it's worth. Realize that it'll all be over in a few moments. Don't keep turning it over in your mind. Soon it'll be in the past—and you'll be thinking of other things. There! Like that! (*He pulls the cork. Young Charlie has been watching his hands with fascinated horror. She shuts her eyes, but recovers herself.*)

MRS. NEWTON: Oh, Charles, you always did do things easily.

UNCLE CHARLIE (*pouring out the glasses*): What kind of audience will it be?

MRS. NEWTON: Oh, we're middle-aged women, mostly. Pretty busy with our homes, most of us.

UNCLE CHARLIE: That's right. You're doing something. (*Young Charlie abruptly drains half her glass. Uncle Charlie falls into brooding thought for a moment, then continues from some deep resentment.*) In the cities it's a different matter. Thousands of middle-aged women . . . their husbands spent forty and fifty years building up a fortune . . . work, work, work. They die and leave their money to their wives. And what do *they* do? You can see them in the hotels, by the thousands, . . . eating great meals . . . playing bridge all afternoon and all night . . . diamonds sparkling all over their big chests. Vapid, useless lives. Thousands of them. . . .

YOUNG CHARLIE (*a cry wrung from her*): But they're human beings!!

UNCLE CHARLIE (*as though awakened*): Are they? Barely . . . and there are some other things best not talked about. Gigolos and what not. I'm not a man to set himself as better than the next man; but, by God, there are certain things I can't stand. (*Calming down.*) But there! Forget it. Charlie, you're not eating your dinner. (*Young Charlie hastily picks up her fork.*)

   Herbie Hawkins appears at window, as before.

MRS. NEWTON: Joe, I see Mr. Hawkins coming around the house to see you again. I'll bet he has some more of those trashy magazines. . . . I declare, he always seems to come while we're eating dinner. (*She calls:*) Come in, Mr. Hawkins. Come in. (*Herbie, cap in hand, abashed, enters, and mumbles "Good evening, M's Newton. . . . Good evening, Mr. Oakley."*) Won't you sit down and have some dinner with us, Mr. Hawkins?

HERBIE: No thanks, 'had mine. (*He sits stiffly on a chair in the corner of the room. He exposes one magazine on his lap and tries to catch Joe Newton's eye, by indicating it with his thumb, as much as to say: "Have you seen this one?" Mr. Newton rises nonchalantly.*)

MRS. NEWTON: Now, Joe. You aren't going to leave the table until you've eaten your dinner?

MR. NEWTON: Just going to say how-do-you-do to Herbie. (*He approaches Herbie. Herbie in suppressed excitement gouges out the magazine with his thumb.*)

HERBIE: Seen this one?

MR. NEWTON (*looking at him through narrowed eyes, significantly; master mind*): Yes— What did I tell you? She killed him in the bath-tub. Held him under.

HERBIE: Pretty strong for a woman.

YOUNG CHARLIE (*half-rising; with a touch of hysteria*): Honestly, Papa, do you have to talk about such things all the time? Papa, I don't want to hurt your feelings, but I wish you'd find something different to talk to Mr. Hawkins about. All I hear is this whispering about crimes and horrible things.

MRS. NEWTON: Why, Charlie, it's Papa's relaxation.

YOUNG CHARLIE: Isn't there anything else to read? Is that the only thing you can talk about? I don't want to hurt your feelings, Papa, but sometimes I think I'll go crazy.

MR. NEWTON (*dignified*): Mark my words, young lady,—it takes a good head to ferret out these things.

YOUNG CHARLIE: Can't we hold on to the little peace and quiet we've got without dragging in crimes and murders all the time?

MRS. NEWTON (*as Mr. Newton returns to his chair*): Joe, Charlie must get a vacation at the seaside. Charlie dear, you're tired. I've been noticing it for some time now.

YOUNG CHARLIE (*mastering herself, and trying to smile*): Perhaps I am. . . . I'm sorry . . . excuse me, everybody. (*She leans over and kisses her father.*) Especially Papa. Maybe I'm just hungry. (*She pretends to attack her food again.*)

UNCLE CHARLIE: I think anybody'd be tired who'd had to show Santa Rosa to that busy-body young man who's been haunting the house these days.

MR. NEWTON: Which reminds me: he stopped in at the bank and asked me some questions today.

UNCLE CHARLIE (*smiting the table*): Why do you stand for it? Emma, I can't for the life of me see why you let him put foot in the house? What business has he got?

MRS. NEWTON: Why, it's an excellent thing he's doing—

UNCLE CHARLIE: Do you *really* know what he came for? To find out whether you had an electric icebox and a furnace? In my opinion, he's made a fool of you. I'm not even sure he's what he pretends to be.

MRS. NEWTON: What do you mean, Charles? Do you mean he's from an insurance company, or something?

YOUNG CHARLIE: No, Mother. Of course, he's conducting a poll.

UNCLE CHARLIE (*relaxing*): Well, you ought to know. You've spent a lot of time with him.

YOUNG CHARLIE: Yes, we went up to Prospect Point and looked down on the lights of the town. (*She pauses in thought.*)

UNCLE CHARLIE: What did you two talk about up there? Electric iceboxes? (*He starts to laugh uncontrollably.*) That's it . . . electric iceboxes.

YOUNG CHARLIE (*calmly, lowered eyes*): Yes, and the school-system . . . and the city bond issues, and—(*she raises her eyes and looks at him*)—you.

UNCLE CHARLIE: Me? What's there to say about me?

MRS. NEWTON: Charlie, you haven't eaten a thing.

YOUNG CHARLIE: Well, naturally he couldn't see why you should be so upset about a mere photograph.

MR. NEWTON: What photograph?

YOUNG CHARLIE: He thought you must be a difficult person to live with. But I told him—

MRS. NEWTON: Charlie, what are you talking about?

Young Charlie rises and goes toward her uncle.

YOUNG CHARLIE: I told him about how wonderful you were to us all. And how your visit was making new persons out of us. And of how I want to remember you as you were on the first night you came here,—when you gave Mother those photographs of your father and mother.

UNCLE CHARLIE (*rising*): Charlie,—

YOUNG CHARLIE: And I told him how we'd miss you if you went away. (*She is now very near him—closeup of her eyes, as she says:*) Don't go. Don't go. Just think of us. We're the only relatives you have in the world. Think of us sometimes. (*She turns and says almost lightly to her mother:*) Mama, I'm going to take a walk. I'll be back soon. (*She goes out of the house.*)

The whole family has risen in surprise.

MRS. NEWTON: I don't know what's come over Charlie. That's the most foolish talk I've ever heard in my life. Roger, run after her and ask her to come back.

UNCLE CHARLIE: No. I'll go—Where do you suppose—?

MRS. NEWTON: She often goes for walks. . . . Surely she doesn't know that young man well enough to call on him—

UNCLE CHARLIE: You sit down and finish your dinners. I'll catch up with her. (*He hurries out.*)

MRS. NEWTON: Joe, there's something very strange going on. Haven't you any ideas? You think you're so clever at ferreting things out. Why can't you do something? (*Dissolve on Mr. Newton's helpless face.*)

> *This flight through the streets differs from that which Young Charlie made on the previous evening in that we see her over the shoulders of Uncle Charlie who is following her a few yards behind.*
>
> *At first he calls "Charlie" several times, then realizes that she hears him, but does not wish to stop.*
>
> *At one corner she runs by accident into the arms of the town policeman.*

YOUNG CHARLIE: Excuse me, Mr. Morton.

MR. MORTON: Well! Well! You're always running along the street at night. Where were you going in such a hurry last night?

YOUNG CHARLIE (*manages to laugh*): Just doing an errand, Mr. Morton.

> *Uncle Charlie catches up with them.*

UNCLE CHARLIE: Let me walk along with you, Charlie.

MR. MORTON: Is this gentleman your uncle I've heard about, Charlie?

YOUNG CHARLIE: Uncle Charlie, this is Mr. Morton.

MR. MORTON: Glad to meet you. What's the name?

UNCLE CHARLIE: Oakley. Charles Oakley. Glad to meet you, Mr. Morton.

MR. MORTON: Keep an eye on your niece, Mr. Oakley. I'll have to give her a ticket for speeding one of these nights. City ordinance about running on these sidewalks.

UNCLE CHARLIE: Hear that, Charlie?—I'll watch her, officer. Good night. (*They walk on a few steps. He grasps her arm and says:*) What's on your mind? What's troubling you, Charlie?

She releases herself and gains several yards on him. In a long shot we see her crossing a street. Mrs. Greene stops her and engages her in effusive conversation. Again Uncle Charlie catches up and is introduced to Mrs. Greene. They excuse themselves from her.

Finally Uncle Charlie catches up with Young Charlie as she is passing the Have-One Bar. He grasps her arm even more firmly.

UNCLE CHARLIE: I've got to talk to you. Where can we go.— In here.

YOUNG CHARLIE: You're hurting my arm again.

UNCLE CHARLIE: Then come in—

YOUNG CHARLIE: I've never been in a place like this. I can't go in.

UNCLE CHARLIE: Yes, you can. There are some things I've got to ask you. (*He has opened the door and practically pushed her in. Neon lights, juke-box—garish orchestra-stand with no orchestra. Booths along one side of the wall. The juke-box is playing so loudly that they can scarcely hear one another speak.*)

YOUNG CHARLIE: You shouldn't make me come in here. It's an *awful* place.

UNCLE CHARLIE: What does it matter where we are?

Louise, the waitress, comes toward them,—weak-minded type; vacant, melancholy.

LOUISE: Hello, Charlie. (*To Uncle Charlie:*) Hello.

YOUNG CHARLIE: Hello, Louise. Uncle Charlie, this is Louise Finch; she was in my class at school. This is my uncle, Louise.

LOUISE: Glad to meet you. (*To Charlie, who keeps her head down:*) I never seen you here before. I only been here two weeks anyway. I used to see you at Kern's Drug Store. I was fired from there. There were too many things to remember. Oh, I been in half the restaurants in town, there are too many things to remember.

UNCLE CHARLIE: What'll you have, Charlie.

YOUNG CHARLIE (*her head still down*): I'll have a chocolate ice-cream soda.

LOUISE: Oh, we don't have that. We don't have anything like that.

UNCLE CHARLIE: Bring Charlie a ginger-ale. I'll have a double brandy.

LOUISE: I think we have brandy. I'll see. (*She wanders off, vaguely.*)

UNCLE CHARLIE (*hard*): What did that young fellow tell you? What did he say to you about me?

YOUNG CHARLIE (*with sudden spirit*): He doesn't know anything. It doesn't matter what he knows.

> *The juke-box suddenly stops. In the silence, Uncle Charlie clears his throat, pulls himself together and changes his manner; kindly.*

UNCLE CHARLIE: Now, why can't we talk this over quietly, like old friends? We're old friends. We're more than old friends. You said so yourself. Tell me, Charlie,—has something that I've done or said upset you? (*He puts out his hand to touch her elbow confidentially—she suddenly glares at him.*)

YOUNG CHARLIE: Don't you touch me, Uncle Charlie!!

UNCLE CHARLIE (*the wind knocked out of him; then tense again*): What did he tell you? What did that boy tell you?

YOUNG CHARLIE: He has nothing to do with it. I hope he *never* knows.

UNCLE CHARLIE: Well, now, Charlie, there's something I've been meaning to tell you ever since I came to town. You're the head of the family—anybody can see that—I've thought there's something you ought to know. Charlie, my life hasn't exactly been what I'd like it to have been. I've been careless, that's a fact. I've made some foolish mistakes, I confess it. Nothing serious, you know,—just foolish mistakes. What's the matter?

> *Young Charlie hasn't been listening to him. Her eyes have been fixed on his hands. He becomes aware of her fascinated gaze, and slowly withdraws his hands from the table and hides them.*

UNCLE CHARLIE (*shaken*): Now don't start imagining things, Charlie. Imagining things don't get anybody anywhere.

YOUNG CHARLIE (*her eyes fixed on where his hands were; very much "imagining things"*): How . . . could . . . you . . . do . . . things like that? My mother's own brother . . .

you . . . who came here, so we thought, you were the best person in the world. . . . However long I live I don't think I'll ever be happy again.

UNCLE CHARLIE (*with a touch of anguish*): Tell me, tell me— tell me what is it you know?

> *Young Charlie fumbles in her handbag—brings out the ring and puts it on the table between them, and looks Uncle Charlie for the first time in the eyes, forcefully.*

YOUNG CHARLIE: I know everything.

> *At this moment, Louise comes to the table, carrying a tray.*

LOUISE: I'm sorry I was so long. It's always a long time here.

> *Uncle Charlie seizes the double brandy and drinks it in one draft.*

UNCLE CHARLIE: I'll have another double brandy, please.

LOUISE: Yes, sir—Charlie, before you go out—I mean before you go home, maybe you want to buy a chance.

YOUNG CHARLIE: A what, Louise?

LOUISE: A chance in a raffle. My God, haven't you heard about it? It's for the new gymnasium at St. Aloysius' Church. Mr. and Mrs. Lombardino—my God, give a diamond clip, and everybody's buying chances for the raffles. I bought one— they cost a quarter, but I won't win. It's not costume jewelry, it's real. I guess if I won it I'd die of the shock. (*She has been holding some soiled tickets in her hand.*)

UNCLE CHARLIE: Here's a dollar. Give Charlie four chances.

LOUISE: Four!!! Oh, Charlie, you'll— (*As she counts out the tickets on the table, she sees the emerald ring.*) Oh—oh! Whose is that? Ain't that beautiful? Can I pick it up? Is it—? (*She's about to say "real" but rejects the thought.*) Anyway, it's just as beautiful as if it were. (*She puts it down reverently. She moves away in almost dreamy dizziness, murmuring:*) I'm funny that way—I just love jewelry. (*Louise has replaced the ring on Young Charlie's side of the table. Young Charlie now puts out her hand and pushes it away.*)

YOUNG CHARLIE: Why don't you go away? Why don't you leave us alone? Go. Go tomorrow. You have nothing to do with us. (*She looks at the ring and shudders. She puts her hands up to her face.*) How could you do such horrible things? How could you be that kind of person? (*She rises, about to leave in sheer revulsion.*)

UNCLE CHARLIE (*no longer uneasy*): Sit down. *Sit down.* You're in a public place. (*She sits down but faces sideways.*) I don't know how you came to find out—whatever it is you think you know. But there's something much more important that you don't know. (*He puts the ring in his pocket.*) What do you know?—all of you who live in places like this? Nothing. What are you all?—sleepwalkers—blind. You might as well learn once and for all, that the whole world's crooked. It's one big foul sty. Rip down the fronts of houses and in every room you'll find liars and swine and cheats. Get it into your head; the central fact about the world is that it's Hell. It always was and it always will be. Whatever I've done may not be very pretty. But it's of no importance. It's nothing. It's nothing compared to what's going on every day. Wake up. Learn something. You people in Santa Rosa are in no position to judge anybody's actions.

Sick to her stomach, Young Charlie rises and goes toward the door.

LOUISE (*from the bar*): Are you going, Charlie? (*She brings the second brandy to Uncle Charlie who drinks it down and gives her two dollars. He rejoins Young Charlie at the door.*)

YOUNG CHARLIE: All I ask is that you go,—before you're found out, and before everybody knows about it and it breaks my mother's heart.

UNCLE CHARLIE: Who's going to find me out—your friend Graham?

YOUNG CHARLIE: I don't know. (*Looking him in the face.*) Even if I don't tell him what I know, he may find out any minute.

Uncle Charlie thinks a moment, then says with contemptuous dismissal:

UNCLE CHARLIE: And he may not— Anyway, I can't leave now. They'd think— I can't leave until they've gone.

Young Charlie, as though from despair, continues out of the door into the street. They walk home in silence.

*As they reach the sidewalk before the Newton home, he stops,
is about to put his hands on her shoulders to emphasize his
point; but restrains himself.*

UNCLE CHARLIE: Listen, Charlie, you've got to help me.

YOUNG CHARLIE: Help you?

UNCLE CHARLIE: We're related, aren't we? I'm your own flesh
and blood. (*He lowers his voice.*) Listen, Charlie—a week ago
I was at the end of my tether. I'd been keeping out of reach
of them for years. But there's an end to the amount of running a man can do. I was ready to give up and let them take
me. (*Pause.*) Then I got the idea of coming out here for one
last chance. Give me this chance. Those two men—your
friend, Graham—they're *not* sure I'm the man they're after.
There's another man in the East who used to go around with
me; they're trying to catch him. Give me this one chance,
Charlie.

YOUNG CHARLIE: Yes, yes. Take your chance, but go.

UNCLE CHARLIE: I'll go; but give me a few days. And help me
cover up . . . help me get away. Charlie, you've got to. I'm
your mother's brother.—Mislead them. Let me escape.

YOUNG CHARLIE (*drawing back and standing up straighter*):
Uncle Charlie, I won't do anything to hurt you; but I won't
do anything to help you. Whatever you do you've got to do
it by yourself.

UNCLE CHARLIE: Haven't you any feelings? Haven't you any
feeling for me? (*She lowers her head with distaste.*) Do you realize where they'd send me? They'd send me to the—

YOUNG CHARLIE: Don't say it!

UNCLE CHARLIE: The electric chair.

YOUNG CHARLIE (*indicating the house*): You go in first. . . .
I'll come in . . . in a few minutes.

UNCLE CHARLIE (*starting up the walk*): I count on you, Charlie
—don't forget; you said it yourself. We're not any ordinary
uncle and niece. Whatever I've done . . . we're twins. (*He
enters the house. The sitting room. Mr. Newton smoking; Mrs.
Newton knitting. Uncle Charlie puts on a jovial manner.*)
East, West; home's best.

MRS. NEWTON: Where's Charlie?

UNCLE CHARLIE: She's all right. She's calmed down. We had a

good talk. She just stopped to talk to a friend. She'll be here in a minute.

MR. NEWTON: She acted very strangely at dinner, Charles. I didn't like it at all.

UNCLE CHARLIE: She's a fine girl, a fine girl. But—as you said —high-strung. With a brainy girl like that you've got to expect it—it's part of the brains.

MRS. NEWTON (*not entirely reassured*): Just the same we'll send her to the seashore—to your sister Sarah, Joe.

MR. NEWTON: Sarah walks in her sleep. Not fit company for anybody.

MRS. NEWTON: I kept something hot on the stove for you, Charles.

UNCLE CHARLIE: Don't need it. We had something downtown. I think I'll turn in. Big day tomorrow.

MRS. NEWTON (*hopefully*): You mean you're coming to church with us?

UNCLE CHARLIE: Fine idea! Maybe I will. (*Going past her, he taps his sister's shoulder.*) Yes, Emma, you ought to be mighty proud of a girl like that.

MRS. NEWTON (*smiling*): I am, Charles, and I'm glad you think so. I always thought you two'd get on fine together. Good night.

UNCLE CHARLIE: Good night. (*He goes upstairs.*)

> *Young Charlie from the porch looks in the window at the peaceful picture of her father and mother. Ann appears at the foot of the stairs in her nightgown, and is saying something. Her parents laugh. Mr. Newton gets up, picks Ann up in his arms and carries her upstairs to bed.*
> *Young Charlie leans against the porch post, sobbing.*
> *Pull back: long view of the house.*
> *Dissolve to view of church-door, seen from across the street between the backs of Jack and Saunders who stand waiting by their car. The congregation is emerging from the doors. Church bells are ringing. The Newton family comes out— minus Uncle Charlie—and Ann runs out into the middle of the street.*

SAUNDERS: There's the young one. Call her over.

JACK: Hsst. Ann!

ANN: Hello. (*She comes over.*)

JACK: Can you ask your sister to come over here a minute,—ask her quietly, if you can. Tell her we'll meet her just around the corner. (*Pointing.*)

ANN: Yes, I'll get her. (*She is seen nudging Young Charlie, who is seen telling her parents that she and Ann will walk home.*)

Cut: around the corner the men are strolling slowly. Ann and Young Charlie, hand in hand, catch up with them.

YOUNG CHARLIE: Do you want to speak to me?

JACK: Saunders has something important to say to you.—Ann, you come and walk with me.

Close shots of Young Charlie and Saunders.

YOUNG CHARLIE: Is there something new you know?

SAUNDERS: No, it's not new. It's that photograph we took.

YOUNG CHARLIE: Why—you gave the film to my uncle.

SAUNDERS: We gave him the wrong film. We have the photograph all right. If your uncle is the man we're hunting for, that photograph can lead to his arrest in a very short time.

YOUNG CHARLIE: How—?

SAUNDERS: No photograph is known of the man we're looking for. All we have to do is to send this one to our San Francisco headquarters; it will telegraph to New York where it will be shown to some witnesses. Within a few hours we would be told to arrest your uncle; or he would be cleared and we'd be called off the job.

YOUNG CHARLIE: You've sent the photograph?

SAUNDERS: No. Out of consideration for you and your family, we've held it up. Graham told me you were trying to urge your uncle to leave town.

YOUNG CHARLIE: I've tried. I'm doing what I can.

SAUNDERS: You realize what would happen here? Every newspaper in the country would carry the story. There'd be a couple of hundred reporters camping out on your front lawn. If there's going to be an arrest, we'd rather do it in another town.

YOUNG CHARLIE: I know. I know. Oh, Mr. Saunders,—it would kill my mother. How much time will you give me?

SAUNDERS: An associate of ours is passing through town at

four o'clock, on his way to San Francisco. We'll have to give it to him.

YOUNG CHARLIE: I'll speak to my uncle after dinner. Thank you, Mr. Saunders, for what you've done for us. Thank you.

SAUNDERS: Miss Newton, we're surprised about one thing: you seem to take it for granted that your uncle's the man we're hunting for.

YOUNG CHARLIE (*covering up quickly*): Do you think he's the man?

SAUNDERS: It's not important what I think. I merely have to collect all the information I can. You don't seem to want to know what the charges are.

YOUNG CHARLIE: Oh, I told Jack I don't want to hear them. I don't want to hear them.

Jack joins them.

SAUNDERS: Well, in return for what we've done—and it was quite an exception to our usual way of doing things, Miss Newton—we hope we can count on you to tell us anything that you know and that would help us. And especially when your uncle's leaving town and how.

YOUNG CHARLIE: Yes, yes, I will.

SAUNDERS: And anything else. If he's a guilty man—you're too intelligent, and I hope too public-spirited—to try to help him in any way.

YOUNG CHARLIE: I won't do anything to help him, but— (*Turning to Jack.*) He's my own uncle. You can't ask me to spy on him, you can't ask me. . . . I'm not the police.

JACK (*taking her arm; earnestly*): Think, Charlie, think: there are no family ties when it comes to crime! Try to realize what crime is. Every citizen is a member of the police, when it comes to *that*. (*He looks into her eyes, and smiles.*) Since you like serious things, that's serious.

YOUNG CHARLIE: Yes, yes. (*To Saunders:*) I'll see that he leaves town this afternoon, and I'll let you know.

SAUNDERS (*smiling encouragingly*): And after all,—the photograph may show that he had nothing to do with the case we're on.—Ann,— (*Ann comes up and puts her hand in Saunders'.*)

ANN: Yes, Mr. Saunders?

YOUNG CHARLIE: You two know one another?

SAUNDERS: Oh, we're old friends. Ann answer questions very, very well. We play questions and answers. And Ann plays very very well.

YOUNG CHARLIE: Come along, Ann. We have to help with Sunday dinner.

> *Cut to Young Charlie and Ann going up the walk to the front door of the Newton home.*
> *Uncle Charlie is standing, expansively, on the top step. On the bottom steps, Mr. Newton and Herbie Hawkins are sitting with space enough for Young Charlie to go up the steps between them.*
> *Uncle Charlie waves from the porch.*
> *Young Charlie waves back.*

YOUNG CHARLIE: Don't you want to pick some flowers for the dinner table, Ann?

ANN: Yes. (*She goes off. This leaves Young Charlie strolling and lingering at the foot of the stairs.*)

MR. NEWTON (*to Herbie*): Was there anything special on the noon radio, Herbie?

HERBIE: No. Not that I can think of.

UNCLE CHARLIE: How was church, Charlie? Did you have a full house? Turn anybody away?

YOUNG CHARLIE: No . . . everybody got a seat.

UNCLE CHARLIE: Glad to hear it. Show's had such a long run I thought maybe attendance was falling off a bit.

HERBIE: Oh, yes—there was one thing on the radio—

YOUNG CHARLIE: We prayed for you, Uncle Charlie, very earnestly.

> *Uncle Charlie's shoulders start shaking with laughter.*

HERBIE (*looking around—guardedly*): —they said—they caught that fella. That fella they call the Merry Widow murderer.

> *Tense reactions on the part of Young Charlie and Uncle Charlie.*

MR. NEWTON: They caught him—where?

HERBIE: In the state of Maine—Portland, Maine. Didn't catch him, exactly. He was running away from the police at the airport, but police was just about to nab him when he ran plunk into the propeller of an airplane.

MR. NEWTON: You don't say—hew-ie!

HERBIE: I guess that closes that pretty final.

MR. NEWTON (*whistles in awe*): You don't say.

> *Slowly Uncle Charlie straightens himself, adjusts his tie, blandly.*

UNCLE CHARLIE: Well, I'll go upstairs and get ready for dinner. Feel maybe I can eat a good dinner today. See you at dinner, Charlie. (*He turns and goes into the house. Young Charlie goes up the stairs and into the house. At the foot of the stairs up to the second floor she looks up, hears her uncle whistling the Merry Widow Waltz, then lowers her eyes and stands, lost in thought.*)

> *On the upper landing shot of Uncle Charlie. He looks down the stairs and sees the figure of Young Charlie.*
> *His eyes narrow; the whistling dies away on his lips.*

Part Four

Uncle Charlie's room. He is pacing up and down, then goes to the window, looking down into the street in front of the Newton home. Again Young Charlie is in his line of vision.
She is standing at the curb waiting impatiently for Jack.
Jack's car drives up. He is alone. He gets out and comes toward Young Charlie.
Uncle Charlie pushes his window open wider to hear what they say.

JACK: Well, Charlie, I have some good news for you. (*A passing automobile drowns out his explanation and her reply.*) —so there's nothing to worry about!—Why aren't you happier about it?

YOUNG CHARLIE: Of course, I'm happy.

JACK (*looking about*): Where can we go to talk things over. We can't go riding—I'll tell you why in a minute. But let's get away from here.—You still look as though you have something on your mind.

> *Shot of Uncle Charlie—expression of increasing concern.*
> *Cut to Jack and Young Charlie who have strolled around the house and are approaching the garage.*

YOUNG CHARLIE: No, really.—Look!

JACK: I can't get over the fact that you're not more relieved and everything. We don't have to send the photograph. We've been called off the job.

YOUNG CHARLIE: I am relieved.

JACK: I imagined you'd been working yourself into a fever trying to get your uncle out of town.

YOUNG CHARLIE: Jack, I'm so relieved that I don't want to think about it any more. I want to pretend the whole awful thing's over.

JACK (*turning and taking her hands*): *Pretend* it's over? It *is* over. I'm glad you never knew what we suspected him of.— But Charlie, I have something else to tell you.

YOUNG CHARLIE: What?

JACK (*again looking about*): Where on earth can we go? There! Let's go in the garage. (*One of the garage doors is open. The car is out.*)

YOUNG CHARLIE: You'll like it. Look!—Here's a sort of workbench for carpentering. That's Father and Roger. Here are stacks of Papa's old magazines. These marks against the wall are our heights as we grew bigger. There I am—aged seven —What else did you have to tell me?

JACK: This case has cleared up and—

YOUNG CHARLIE: —you must go.

JACK: Yes.

YOUNG CHARLIE (*slowly sinking down on the work-bench*): Of course. You have to go. I don't know what's the matter with me—I hadn't thought of that. I must be crazy. (*She bends her head and starts to cry.*)

JACK (*going quickly toward her*): But I'll be back very soon.

YOUNG CHARLIE (*looking up quickly*): I'll be alone again.

JACK: A very short time. There's nothing you're afraid of, is there? As far as we're concerned, your uncle's— There's nothing you're afraid of, is there?

YOUNG CHARLIE: No. No.—Jack,— (*She looks into his face. Her lip trembles. She is about to tell him everything. Then in her hesitation she turns her head and her eyes fall on her mother's gloves.*) Look! There are my mother's Sunday gloves that she thought she'd lost. (*She rises and slowly goes to get them.*) She's always losing something. (*During the following scene she holds the gloves and smoothes out the fingers.*) Are you really going to come back?

JACK (*tenderly*): Charlie, you don't understand. I'm not just coming back to see you. I'm coming back to marry you, if you'll let me. I love you. I've never been in love before, in my life. I'd heard about it. I suppose I didn't really believe it. But for two days now I've felt like the first person in the world who ever fell in love. Can't everybody see that I'm different? I breathe differently. I walk differently. I think differently. And the chief thing I think is that you're the most wonderful girl a man ever fell in love with. (*He takes her hands.*)

YOUNG CHARLIE (*laughing softly and turning her head*): I love you, but I thought I'd never, never tell you. I thought I'd keep it a secret.

He kisses her.

JACK: Dearest Charlie! You've been through a very hard time. (*He kisses her again.*) But it's all over— You haven't said yet whether you'll marry me.

YOUNG CHARLIE: Yes, I will—(*she rises, with a mixture of abandon and uneasiness*)—and as soon as you want. Is that something a girl shouldn't say?

JACK (*happily*): No. No. It's just the thing—but Charlie, before I ask you again, there's something I want to say. And while I say it I think I ought to get as far away from you as I can in here. It's something we've got to be very sensible about. (*He walks backward to the further corner of the garage and is about to speak, when the open leaf of the garage door swings halfway to and then swings open again, squeaking shrilly on its hinges.*)

YOUNG CHARLIE: What is it, Jack?

JACK: I love you most in the world and next to you I love my work. You wouldn't want me to give that up, would you? When I first went into it, Charlie, I thought it was interesting and adventurous; but since then it's become a lot more than that. I believe in it more and more. While I'm away, Charlie, drive up to that place on the mountain and look down on the town and remember what I said. There are a lot of ugly evil things in the world that all those families shouldn't have to know about it. Let them do their work and bring up their children. But I'm one of the persons who has to know about such things so as to be able to fight against them. Would you be willing to be the wife of a man like that?

YOUNG CHARLIE (*going to him with outstretched arms*): Yes, yes. (*While she is in his arms, the garage door swings to with a violent noise. They are in the half-dark.*)

JACK: Oh, let it stay.—Charlie, I have to say goodbye now. It's four o'clock and we're all going. (*He gives her an envelope.*) Here are my addresses for every day of the week. Write me every day. I'm your husband,—do you realize that? And the first thing I require of you is to write me every day. And I'll write you. Goodbye. (*He tries to open the door. It sticks. At last with a great effort he gets it open.*)

Emerging into the sunlight, they come upon Uncle Charlie strolling nearby.

UNCLE CHARLIE: Well, well. What have you two been locking yourself in the garage for?

JACK: Hello, Mr. Oakley. I was just saying goodbye to Charlie and the old door got stuck. How are you? I've got to say goodbye. (*He shakes his hand.*)

UNCLE CHARLIE: Oh, so your work's over?

JACK: Yes, but I'll be back, I guess.

UNCLE CHARLIE: Oh, you're coming back?

JACK: Yes, I want to come back and see Charlie again.

UNCLE CHARLIE: Is that so? Well, she's a fine girl. She's the thing I love most in the world and that's a fact. You can travel up and down the whole country and you won't find a girl like Charlie. Have a good trip, Mr. Graham, and don't take any photographs without permission. It's a free country, you know.

JACK: Well, let's have a talk about freedom some day, Mr. Oakley. (*He nods and turn to Young Charlie.*) I'll go in and say goodbye to your mother. Let me give her the gloves.

YOUNG CHARLIE: I'll come with you.

Uncle Charlie follows them with his eyes.
Cut to sitting room. Mrs. Newton is talking.

MRS. NEWTON: He has a real sense of humor, too. Practical jokes and . . . he gets into scrapes. (*She waves her hand, smiling at her memories.*) There was even one time—I've never told the children about this—when he actually changed his name! (*Lowering her voice—confidentially.*) I expect some designing woman was annoying him and he just wanted to be rid of her. For half a year we had to write him under the name of Chapman O'Higgins. Think of it—Chapman O'Higgins.

JACK (*pleasantly*): Is that so.—Chapman O'Higgins.

MRS. NEWTON: Hurry up, Charlie, have you those cookies ready for Mr. Graham to take on his trip?

Enter Young Charlie with a cake-box.

YOUNG CHARLIE: There.

JACK: Many thanks. Goodbye, Mrs. Newton, and say goodbye to the rest of the family for me.

MRS. NEWTON: Goodbye, and come back soon.

> *Young Charlie and Jack go down to the car, passing Uncle Charlie on the porch, with a wave of the hand.*
> *Mrs. Newton joins her brother on the porch.*

JACK (*from car*): You have all the addresses. Remember,—don't forget to write.

YOUNG CHARLIE: No.—Goodbye.

JACK (*indicating Young Charlie*): Take good care of her.

UNCLE CHARLIE: I will. I certainly will.

> *Young Charlie takes step forward with raised hand and calls:*

YOUNG CHARLIE: Jack! (*But is not heard. Behind her falls the shadow of Uncle Charlie going into the house.*)

> *Dissolve to upper hall. Young Charlie is calling down the stairs, reading from a shopping list in her hand.*

YOUNG CHARLIE: Butter . . . brown sugar . . . green thread . . . library book . . . is there anything else?

MRS. NEWTON'S VOICE: I think that's all. Aren't you coming this way?

YOUNG CHARLIE: I'm in a hurry. I'm cutting through the back lots. I'll be home about five.

> *The back stairs. Young Charlie starts down them; loses her foothold, swings and catches herself on the banister just in time. She screams.*

MRS. NEWTON: Charlie, what's the matter?

YOUNG CHARLIE: I almost . . . let me stop and get my breath.

MRS. NEWTON: I've told you a hundred times about those stairs. They're too steep and rickety to tear up and down them as you do. Are you hurt, dear?

YOUNG CHARLIE: No. (*She comes down slowly.*)

MRS. NEWTON: Charlie! You might have broken your neck! (*Young Charlie looks up.*)

> *Cut to Uncle Charlie's room. He is lying on the bed smoking a cigar, and looking up at the ceiling with half-closed eyes. Dissolve to a telephone booth. Young Charlie with address book in her hand—speaking.*

YOUNG CHARLIE: You're positive Mr. Graham's not there? . . . But I just called Los Angeles. If he does come in will you tell him to call Miss Newton? No, that's all, he'll understand.

> *Dissolve to the sitting room: Roger and Uncle Charlie are playing slap-jack. The sequence is punctuated by the slow bangs of their game. Mrs. Newton is sewing; Ann reading; Mr. Newton and Herbie can be seen talking at the dining room table, their heads close together.*

ROGER: Slap-jack!!—My hand got there first, Uncle Charlie.

MRS. NEWTON: Do you have to be so noisy, Roger? Charles, you mustn't make a wild Indian of him.

ROGER: Your turn.

> *Closeup: Young Charlie at the top of the stairs. She comes down the stairs, holding three letters.*

YOUNG CHARLIE: Ann!—Mama!—do you want to take a walk with me downtown to the post-office?

> *Mrs. Newton rises and goes to her, anxiously.*

MRS. NEWTON: How do you feel, dear?

UNCLE CHARLIE (*slam bang*): Slap-jack!! (*Rising.*) I'll go with you, Charlie.

ROGER: I couldn't see it,—everybody was talking so. Mama, don't talk when people are playing games.

MRS. NEWTON (*continuing to Young Charlie*): Really, I can't get over it. Joe,—Mr. Hawkins,—why don't you boys go upstairs and fix those steps right now? You're so good at carpentry work.

MR. NEWTON: We will. (*He goes on talking to Herbie.*)

MRS. NEWTON: This house is getting old, that's all there is about it. We've had it sixteen years ourselves,—Joe! How long had the Stevensons lived in this house before we bought it?

MR. NEWTON: Long time. They raised their children here.

MRS. NEWTON: Now, Charlie, you just lie down and get a good rest. Roger will take your letters to the post-office when he's finished his game.

UNCLE CHARLIE: I'll be with you in a minute, Charlie. Emma, you're right. The house is falling to pieces. I'll give you a new one.

MRS. NEWTON (*scandalized*): Charles! Why!! I couldn't think of such a thing. Now, Charles, don't you say another word. The idea!

UNCLE CHARLIE: Why, you're my own sister, aren't you? Charlie, your mother is trying to disown me.

YOUNG CHARLIE: I like this house as it is.

Here Uncle Charlie makes a false slap-jack.

UNCLE CHARLIE: Slap-jack.—No!

ROGER: You've gotta forfeit. You've gotta forfeit. That's not a jack.

UNCLE CHARLIE (*giving him the three cards*): Emma, tomorrow morning, Charlie's going to drive us around those new residence developments. If we can't find what we want, we'll build one.

MRS. NEWTON: Joe, don't you listen to what Charles is saying. We don't need a house.

Mr. Newton has come strolling to the partition between the two rooms.

UNCLE CHARLIE (*his eyes on Young Charlie*): I'm not only going to give you a house; but the kitchen's going to have every labor-saving device that money can buy. You're too pretty a woman, Emma, to spend six hours a day struggling with a stove out of the Dark Ages.

MRS. NEWTON: Joe, don't you answer him.

UNCLE CHARLIE: What do you think, Charlie? Can't a brother do that for the only kin-folk he's got in the world?

YOUNG CHARLIE: That's a matter for you to decide between you. I like this house as it is.

UNCLE CHARLIE: There's another thing I'm thinking of doing,

Emma. I want you to help me. Something for the town. In memory of our father and mother. We'll give it together—you and I. Children's playroom at the hospital—something like that. Think it over.

ROGER: Slap-jack!! Now you've only got four cards, Uncle Charlie—You've only got four cards. (*Jumping up and shouting:*) I'm beating you all hollow. When the game's over you'll wish you were dead.

YOUNG CHARLIE: Roger! Where on earth did you pick up manners like that?

MRS. NEWTON: Really, I don't know what's happening to him.

UNCLE CHARLIE (*rising*): I resign the game, Roger. You can have it!

MRS. NEWTON: Roger, Ann,—run around to the garage and get the hammer and some nails. We'll fix the back-stairs right now. This house will last a good twenty years yet, Charles. (*Roger and Ann go out.*) And Joe, I want to show you and Mr. Hawkins some other things you can fix while you're about it. Start along both of you. (*Mr. Newton and Herbie go resignedly into the kitchen. Mrs. Newton turns to Uncle Charlie and puts her hands on the lapels of his coat.*) But, Charles, I don't want to seem ungrateful. Even the *thought* that you want to do such things for us is kindness enough. We who love you have to save you from your own goodness and generosity. (*She kisses him.*) But if you want to do something in the name of Papa and Mama, that's different. They loved children; and they loved you. I won't say anything against your doing a thing like that, if you want to. (*Much moved, she goes into the kitchen.*)

UNCLE CHARLIE: Charlie! I want to see you for a minute. Haven't had a chance to say a word to you for quite a while. . . . Well, Charlie, that whole matter's blown over. It needn't have taken place at all. Let's try and forget all about it.

YOUNG CHARLIE: When are you going?

UNCLE CHARLIE: Come, come, there's no need for hurry. We're all happy here. You heard what your mother just said.

YOUNG CHARLIE: When are you going?

UNCLE CHARLIE: I wasn't joking about that house. I'll give it to you. I'm not going—not yet. If I settle down and go into business, I've got to have a place where I'm known, where I'm a respected citizen—where I've a bank and a family,— where people *know* me. A man can't operate without having a bank. Now this whole trouble's blown over. Even your young what's-his-name doesn't suspect a thing. I don't leave this town until everybody feels about me as though I'd lived here for ten years.

YOUNG CHARLIE (*menacingly*): I see.

UNCLE CHARLIE: The best thing for you to do is to accept the fact that we're as big friends as we ever were. We've been through an anxious business together. I daren't think what would have happened, if your mother'd gotten wind of what was going on.

YOUNG CHARLIE (*taking a step forward*): I hate lies. I hate keeping secrets from people. Sometimes I wish I'd told my mother the whole thing from the first moment I knew it.

UNCLE CHARLIE: I thought you'd come to an idea like that. *How do you think she'd have taken it?*

YOUNG CHARLIE: Now it's not important how she'd take it.

UNCLE CHARLIE: Well, what have you got to tell? Who'd believe you? A waltz tune ran in your head. You didn't like some initials in a ring. You connected it all up with a news-paper clipping.

YOUNG CHARLIE: Go away. Go away, or I'll kill you myself,— that's what happens to a person who has to live near you. (*She stares at him a moment, then plunges out of the room. Uncle Charlie smiles coolly, then has his belated reaction of rage.*)

> *Long view of house. Windows lit.*
> *Dissolve to the front of the garage. Evening. Uncle Charlie in dinner coat, red carnation in button hole, emerges from garage doors, smoking a cigarette. Satisfied, he brushes off his hands and strolls around the back of the house. Cut to Young Charlie, in her best evening dress, at the telephone.*

YOUNG CHARLIE: Is that you, Mrs. MacCurdy? My mother's been trying to reach you for two days. . . . Did you find her well? Isn't that fine. . . . Well, Mrs. Blodgett tells Mother that you and Dr. MacCurdy are going to my uncle's lecture tonight . . . and we wondered if you couldn't come in afterwards and meet him . . . just a few friends, the

Greenes and the Phillipses. . . . That's fine, we'll look forward to seeing you. And Mrs. MacCurdy, tell Dr. MacCurdy we all thought it was a splendid sermon last Sunday. . . . Oh, didn't you hear? There are so many people coming to the lecture that they've moved it to the High School Auditorium . . . then we'll see you tonight. Goodbye.

Crane to Uncle Charlie emerging on the landing upstairs, overhearing the end of this conversation. He adjusts his tie casually. Mr. and Mrs. Newton come out of their room behind him. Mr. Newton has begun to put on his dress-suit. He is in stocking feet.

MRS. NEWTON: Well, the children can sit on our laps. Charles can sit up in front with Charlie.

MR. NEWTON: Tight squeeze for everybody. Wouldn't be surprised if I bust my coat.

MRS. NEWTON: Joe, if you'd only learned how to drive the car yourself!

MR. NEWTON: We'll do it this way. Charles will sit—

YOUNG CHARLIE (*from the foot of the stairs*): Mama, Uncle Charles can sit in back with Papa, and Roger and Ann can fit in perfectly well beside them—

UNCLE CHARLIE: Now, now! This is very easily settled. I have it all worked out. I'm sending for a taxi for you. Charlie and I can go on in the car alone. (*Reaction from Young Charlie.*)

YOUNG CHARLIE: No,—Uncle Charlie, you go in the taxi. You'll be much more comfortable.

ROGER: I want to go in a taxi; I want to go in a taxi.

UNCLE CHARLIE: Of course you do—so that's settled. Emma, start phoning for the taxi now,—and Charlie?

YOUNG CHARLIE: Yes?

UNCLE CHARLIE: Why don't you go and get the car out of the garage?

YOUNG CHARLIE (*ignoring Uncle Charlie*): Mama, Father can go with Uncle Charlie in the taxi. I'll drive all of you.

UNCLE CHARLIE: No, I wanted you to hear me go over my speech.

Mrs. Newton starts downstairs—Young Charlie meets her at the foot of the stairs.

MRS. NEWTON: Ann, you telephone Mr. Abercrombie for a taxi.

YOUNG CHARLIE (*in a whisper*): Mama, I want you to come with us. Papa can go with Uncle Charlie. I insist on it.

Shot of Mrs. Newton's face, bewildered.

MRS. NEWTON: I don't understand what all the fuss is about. (*She goes out through the front door. Uncle Charlie, after a last glance down, is seen going along the upper hallway toward the back stairs.*)

Mrs. Newton comes into the sitting-room, still in his stocking feet.

MR. NEWTON: Emma, where are my shoes? Can't find a thing.

MRS. NEWTON: I polished them myself and put them on a newspaper in the kitchen.—Roger, run upstairs and get your father's collar and tie.

Mr. Newton goes into the kitchen to get his shoes.

ANN: Mama, you'd better recite your speech to me just once more.

MRS. NEWTON: I'd better take another look at those sandwiches—Where's Charlie?—Oh, yes, she's out getting the car. (*Roger brings the collar and tie.*) Now hold still, Joe.

As she starts tying her husband's tie—cut to the garage—night. Young Charlie comes across the lawn and turns on the garage light from the outside. After some difficulty with the doors she enters. The car's engine is running. She runs to driver's seat and is assailed by the fumes. She reels with faintness and covers her nose with her scarf. She gropes to find the car key and can't find it. Mutters, "Where's the key?" Shot of the garage door slowly and firmly closing. Young Charlie starts coughing. She goes to the door to open it, and struggles with the door.
Cut to sitting room. Mrs. Newton is tying her husband's white tie.

MR. NEWTON: I'll be the only man there that's been fool enough to dress up.

MRS. NEWTON: Joe, we've been over that before. Nothing to

be ashamed of in dressing correctly. Charles! Charles! I hope
you're almost ready. Now, Joe, you can go upstairs and get
your coat on. You look very nice.

*Mr. Newton goes upstairs, meeting Uncle Charlie coming
down.*

UNCLE CHARLIE: It's getting late, but the lecture can't begin
without me— By the way, what's the news? (*He turns on the
radio.*) Air's getting kind of cool, don't you think? (*He closes
a window.*)

VOICE FROM RADIO: —Mothers, do you realize what a musical
education means to your children? Start Junior on the violin
now. Get little Betty a child's size cello. Hartman's has vio-
lins ranging from twelve dollars; cellos from twenty dollars.
Make your home a place of musical happiness—

MRS. NEWTON: Charles, I know I'll forget my speech of introduction. At first I thought of telling a joke about you.

UNCLE CHARLIE: A joke about me—

MRS. NEWTON (*confidentially; whispering*): Yes, about that time
you changed your name to O'Higgins.

UNCLE CHARLIE: I did! You're mistaken.

MRS. NEWTON: Don't tell me you've forgotten it. It was about
twelve years ago. The time you borrowed a hundred dollars
from Joe, and you wanted the cheque addressed to you as
Chapman O'Higgins.

UNCLE CHARLIE (*petrified—after a pause*): I'd forgotten it.
Emma, be a good girl and never mention it to a soul. Not
to a soul. I was a young fella. I was foolish. I could get in
trouble about that. Emma,—cashing a cheque under an assumed name. You wouldn't want to get me in trouble,
would you, Emma?

MRS. NEWTON: Of course not, Charles.

UNCLE CHARLIE: Then promise me you'll keep that under
your hat. Just forget it.

MRS. NEWTON (*patting his hand*): Of course I will, Charles.

*Uncle Charlie goes to switch the radio dial. A symphonic
broadcast comes through, very loud.*

MRS. NEWTON (*shouting*): Does it have to be so loud, Charles?

UNCLE CHARLIE (*with pantomime*): . . . hear all the instruments . . .

ROGER: I like it loud.

Mr. Newton and the children are coming downstairs.

MR. NEWTON: Well, let's get started.

Herbie's terrified face appears at one of the windows. He is trying to shout something, but no one hears him.

MRS. NEWTON: I don't know why Charlie's so long.

Herbie's face has appeared at another window. Finally he rushes in on them through the front door.

HERBIE: Help everybody. Charlie's caught in the garage. She's suffocatin'. Something's the matter with her.

MRS. NEWTON: Oh!—Joe! Charles—hurry!

Uncle Charlie becomes a model of resourcefulness.

UNCLE CHARLIE: Have you a flashlight, Emma. (*It is produced from a table drawer.*)

MRS. NEWTON: Here it is! What can have happened. Joe!

They run out the front door and around the house. Uncle Charlie finally gets the garage doors open. He steps over the unconscious girl, and we see him inserting the key in the car and turning the engine off. He has tied the handkerchief about his face.

UNCLE CHARLIE: Keep back, everybody. Which one of you could have left the engine running? Keep back, Joe. (*He lifts Young Charlie tenderly from the floor and carries her out on the lawn. He takes a magazine from Herbie's hands and starts fanning her.*) Joe, there's a flask of whiskey in the top drawer of my bureau—get it and hurry. (*He starts slapping her face.*) Charlie! Charlie! Our dear Charlie! Wake up.

MRS. NEWTON: God help us. God help us. God help us.

UNCLE CHARLIE: Emma, start rubbing her feet. Roger, run in and get the evening paper,—something better to fan her with. (*Mrs. Newton kneels on the grass and starts rubbing Young Charlie's feet. Young Charlie opens her eyes and closes them again.*) That's right. —Charlie! Charlie!

Young Charlie opens her eyes and gazes at Uncle Charlie a moment. She murmurs something.

MRS. NEWTON: Here's Mama, dear.

Ann suddenly bursts into tears and flings herself on Young Charlie and is about to stifle her.
Uncle Charlie pushes Ann away and leans over Young Charlie.

UNCLE CHARLIE: What are you trying to say, Charlie?

YOUNG CHARLIE (*faintly, but with unmistakable hatred*): Go away. Go away.

UNCLE CHARLIE: She wants you, Emma. Come and hold her. (*She revives quickly. Mr. Newton rushes up with the whiskey.*)

MRS. NEWTON: Here, dear, take this. Uncle Charlie says it's good for you. It's whiskey.

YOUNG CHARLIE (*sitting up*): I don't want it. I won't take it. (*She shuts her eyes and takes some deep breaths.*)

MRS. NEWTON: Joe, call Dr. Phillips.

YOUNG CHARLIE: No, I'm all right. I'll be all right in a minute. Papa, put your elbow down. I want to get up.

UNCLE CHARLIE: Well, it's been a wonderful escape. Someone must have left the engine running. They say it happens thousands of times every year.

MRS. NEWTON (*in tears; flinging herself on Uncle Charlie*): She might have died. We owe everything to you. You knew just what to do.

We'll put off the lecture. There isn't going to be any lecture.

YOUNG CHARLIE: No. You're all going to the lecture. There's the taxi now. I'm all right. Go on—all of you.

MRS. NEWTON: Charlie, I wouldn't leave you for the world.

YOUNG CHARLIE (*almost totally recovered—moving her mother to the taxi*): I'll sit on the porch a while and get a lot of air. I want to be alone.

MRS. NEWTON (*struggling*): I wouldn't think of it.

YOUNG CHARLIE: Get in, Ann.—You see I'm perfectly well. I could go to the lecture myself; but I'll stay home and get things ready for the party.

MRS. NEWTON: But, Charlie!—

YOUNG CHARLIE: Who found me in the garage? The last thing I remember—

MR. NEWTON: Herbie Hawkins heard you beating on the door. (*All look at Herbie. He is proud, but embarrassed. He keeps one eye on Mr. Newton.*)

HERBIE: I heard this gasping and beating on the door . . . and I figgered twan't no car behaving that way . . . must be a human being. That's what I figgered.

MR. NEWTON (*lofty approval*): Quick thinking, Herbie.

YOUNG CHARLIE: Thank you, Mr. Hawkins. Goodbye.

MRS. NEWTON: Charlie, I *want* to stay with you.

YOUNG CHARLIE: Mr. Hawkins, will you take Roger?

ROGER: I wanted to go in the taxi. (*Roger is taken toward Herbie's car.*)

UNCLE CHARLIE: I don't feel like giving a lecture. When I think what might have happened to the best little girl in California.

The cab door slams. Mrs. Newton puts her head out of the window.

MRS. NEWTON: Are you sure you'll be all right, Charlie,—first, the stairs— (*Cab starts. Two passers-by obscure the last departures. The taxi drives off. Young Charlie waves. She hurries into the house.*)

Lap dissolve: the telephone.

YOUNG CHARLIE: . . . can you tell me where he is? I've already called up the Hotel California in Fresno. He's not there and he hasn't been there. (*Turns, a moment of indecision then dashes upstairs. In Uncle Charlie's room she rips open drawers. Finds ring in envelope in suitcase, after scattering objects around. Fade out on her emerging from room, looking at ring—face filled with decision.*)

Outside of house. Cars pulling up.
Then to Young Charlie's room. Young Charlie is sitting in bed. From below the sounds of cars arriving; laughter. Reflections of headlights circle about the room. She rises. Her face is pale and resolute.
Cut to front hall.

Mrs. Newton and Uncle Charlie go upstairs.

UNCLE CHARLIE (*calling*): Charlie! Charlie!

MRS. NEWTON: I'll see how she is. (*Goes to Young Charlie's room.*)

Uncle Charlie pauses, goes into his room, and is astonished at the disorder. Abrupt cut to Young Charlie's room. Enter Mrs. Newton.

MRS. NEWTON: How are you now, dear? I could scarcely bear it, sitting there. How do you feel?

YOUNG CHARLIE: I'm all right, Mama. How was the lecture?

MR. NEWTON (*off*): Charles! Charles! Everybody's waiting for you.

MRS. NEWTON: Charlie, it was *wonderful.* Everybody's been heaping me with compliments. Really it was *wonderful.* And Uncle Charlie was so *funny*—we laughed and laughed.— I've got to go down and put the coffee on.

YOUNG CHARLIE: I'll be down in a minute.

Shot follows Mrs. Newton going downstairs in the distance. The sitting room. The party is in progress, the Greenes, Dr. and Mrs. Phillips, Rev. and Mrs. MacCurdy. Uncle Charlie has just joined the party. Pop of him opening champagne. He fills their punch glasses.

REV. MACCURDY: Of course, I have deep convictions about the evils of strong drink. But when I think that our great government uses champagne for the christening of battleships—well, I think that makes an exception of it. Mrs. MacCurdy and I will not partake of it ourselves; but we're glad to see you enjoying yourselves.

UNCLE CHARLIE: Emma, I want to propose a toast to—(*he looks up the stairs*)—did Charlie say she was coming down?

MRS. NEWTON (*passing sandwiches*): Yes, she said she'd be down in a minute.—Mrs. Greene, do you like anchovy? And those are eggs.

MR. GREENE: May I propose a toast: to our esteemed visitor,— to the man who's made the best speech heard in this town since William Jennings Bryan, and to a very good fellow— Mr. Charles Oakley!

UNCLE CHARLIE: That's very kind of you, Mr. Greene. (*Pleased hubbub. Uncle Charlie keeps looking anxiously toward the stairs.*)

> *Cut to Young Charlie's room. She is feverishly applying lipstick and staring at herself in the mirror.*
> *She dashes to the door. Then turns and goes back to apply one more dab of lipstick.*
> *Cut to sitting-room.*

UNCLE CHARLIE: Save something in your glasses, friends, for one more toast . . . a person who's very dear and precious to us all. We're hoping she'll join us in a moment.

> *Shots from group to group.*

DR. PHILLIPS: Carbon monoxide poisoning is a very sad affair, a very sad affair. I had a case of it in Petaluma just last year . . .

MRS. NEWTON: To think, Dr. Phillips, that my brother knew just what to do! Really, it was a miracle he was there.

UNCLE CHARLIE (*to Mr. Newton*): It's an old car, that's what's the matter. What are you doing with a car like that? Joe, I'm getting you a new one tomorrow. (*He catches sight of Young Charlie coming slowly downstairs; louder:*) Emma, what you need's a new car. I saw the very thing downtown this morning. Here she is. (*He now sees Young Charlie's face. Her eyes are fixed on him with significant determination. Camera dollies in until the ring on her finger is seen. He pauses a moment, alarmed; then raises his glass in her direction.*) Charlie, you're just in time for a farewell toast,—I am sorry to say—my farewell toast.—(*The group turns back toward Uncle Charlie.*) My dear family and my good friends, tomorrow morning I must leave Santa Rosa,—not for long, I hope. Let us lift our glasses to this beautiful town.

MRS. NEWTON: Charles! —Did I hear you say—?

UNCLE CHARLIE: Yes, my friends. I've been called away and must leave on the early morning train; but like every other visitor I shall never cease to feel myself drawn back to the city of hospitality, kindness and homes.

> *Hope and relief on Young Charlie's face. She takes off ring*

and puts it in her vanity case. Herbie passes her a glass. Mrs. Newton has been so overcome that first she sits down, then rises:

MRS. NEWTON: But, I don't understand, Charles. You talk as though you were going away for a long time. And you've changed your mind so suddenly. We've made all our plans for tomorrow. We were going to see the ocean . . . and the redwoods. (*She rises.*) And, Charles, you've only just come. We're just beginning to know you.

UNCLE CHARLIE: Oh, I'll be back before long, Emma. I've been arranging with Dr. Phillips about our little memorial at the hospital—

MRS. NEWTON: But we haven't begun to thank you,—(*cut to Young Charlie's face as she sits with lowered eyes, holding her glass*)—for so many things, and for the biggest thing of all, for saving Charlie's life. . . . Oh, yes, you did! We owe that to you. We'll never, never forget it.

Dissolve to railroad station, the next morning. From between the shoulders of Jack and Saunders we see the farewells taking place at the other end of the station platform. The Newton family is surrounding Uncle Charlie. The Mac-Curdys and the Greenes are getting out of their cars and going up to shake hands with him.

SAUNDERS: All right. The minute the train crosses the town line . . . a mile and a half down.

JACK: Thanks, Fred.

SAUNDERS: There he is all right,—the great Chapman O'Higgins.

The train coming into the station sweeps by them.
The farewells. Mrs. Newton is crying. Mr. Newton is embarrassed. Ann and Roger are uncomfortable. Young Charlie is relieved and high-spirited.

UNCLE CHARLIE (*to the Greenes and the MacCurdys*): Oh, yes, I'll be back. Can't say exactly when. You know what business is like.

MR. GREENE: We'll be looking for you, Mr. Oakley. We feel like you're one of us,—don't we, Margaret?

MRS. GREENE: Our club will never forget the evening you gave us.

REV. MacCURDY: The gift you've made to our hospital—our dear suffering children will bless you for years and years to come.

Uncle Charlie turns to his sister and takes both her hands in his. They talk in low voices. She looks up at him adoringly.

REV. MacCURDY (*to Mr. Greene*): Very touching. . . . The ties of family life and the home . . . deep.

A porter has descended from the train and carried his bag into the car. A conductor is standing, watch in hand.

MR. NEWTON: Better get on, Charles. We'll watch you.

UNCLE CHARLIE: Ann, Roger, come and see the train. Have we a minute, conductor?

CONDUCTOR (*his thumb on his watch, weightily*): Yes, yes—a minute or two. (*He strolls down to the next car platform.*)

ROGER: Mama, there's time. I want to see the rooms. Mama, I want to see the rooms.

UNCLE CHARLIE: Charlie, bring them in. You can see that they get off all right.

The children hurl themselves onto the car steps.

YOUNG CHARLIE: Well, just a minute.

Uncle Charlie from the steps waves for the last time.

MRS. NEWTON: Be sure and write to us, Charles.

UNCLE CHARLIE: I certainly will. I'll send you my address and you write me.

MR. NEWTON: Yes, don't forget to write.

UNCLE CHARLIE: Yes, write you often. And you write me. Joe. Goodbye.

EVERYBODY: Goodbye. Goodbye.

The compartment. The children dash in and out examining things. At the door Uncle Charlie is talking to the porter.

UNCLE CHARLIE: Porter . . . a large black briefcase . . . very important to me . . . I swear I thought I saw it being carried into that next car. Go and look for it.

PORTER: Yes, sir. (*He hurries off. The train whistle sounds.*)

ANN: Charlie, the train's starting. We gotta go.

ROGER: The train's starting.

UNCLE CHARLIE: Plenty of time. Run along; we'll follow you. (*The children dash along the corridor and off. Uncle Charlie at the door detains Young Charlie.*) Just a minute, Charlie. Plenty of time. Just a word or two I'd like to say. You won't regret this.

YOUNG CHARLIE: There isn't time. I have to run.

UNCLE CHARLIE: I'll come out to the platform with you. (*Comes down corridor, holding her arm.*) You did a fine thing for your mother. You were right not to let her know. After all, she's not very strong.

YOUNG CHARLIE: We're leaving the station. (*They reach the platform. The door has been closed. He opens it quickly. She stands on the steps shrinking from the jump. Uncle Charlie grasps her upper arm in a grip of iron. He murmurs soothingly.*)

UNCLE CHARLIE: Wait . . . just a little faster. Just a little faster.

> *Young Charlie turns blazingly on him.*

YOUNG CHARLIE: You won't! You won't! (*They start to struggle.*)

> *Cut to Jack and Saunders passing without hurry along the compartments of a car.*

JACK: Still in the town.

> *Cut to Uncle Charlie and Young Charlie in a furious struggle. Young Charlie, with a powerful hold on the iron rail, twists her body and by crouching, pulls herself up to the platform. As Jack appears on the platform he is in time to see Young Charlie give her uncle a tremendous push, levering herself just as the oncoming train is about to pass the open door. Uncle Charlie's hold is broken and he falls.*
> *Dissolve in a crash of noise and lights.*
> *Dissolve to an impressive funeral procession passing through the square of the town. The hearse, a score of automobiles. Solemnized crowds line the streets.*

*Quick glimpses into the automobiles carrying the mourn-
ers—in the first limousine Mr. Newton mutely presses his
wife's hand, as she weeps into a black-edged handkerchief.
Beyond her, Young Charlie looks resolutely out of the window. The two children are sitting sideways on the adjustable
seats, darting their heads out of the window to count the automobiles in the procession.*

ANN: Twelve.

ROGER: Eleven.

ANN: There's twelve.

ROGER: That last one don't belong to us. It's just somebody
driving for fun.

ANN: Yes, it does too belong to us. It's Herbie Hawkins, and
he *likes* funerals.

MR. NEWTON: Children, if you can't sit quiet you can go home.

Glimpse of Jack with the Greenes.

MR. GREENE: No, we don't grow much alfalfa around here.
That's grown farther south.

MRS. GREENE (*fumbling a black-edged handkerchief*): Oh, my
father grew miles of alfalfa.

JACK: You don't say.

*Cut to the last car. Herbie driving his own. With a sedate
lift of an eyebrow he acknowledges the greetings of an ac-
quaintance on the sidewalk.*

*The church door. People going in. Mr. and Mrs. Newton
with Ann and Roger close behind them. Young Charlie
pauses with one foot on the stair. Jack catches up with her.
Without exchange of signals she turns from the door and
starts toward the street at the side of the church.*

*The sidewalk under the church windows. Both sides of the
street are lined with cars. Organ music is coming from the
church.*

*Young Charlie and Jack are moving very slowly. They come
to a stop.*

YOUNG CHARLIE: I did know more than I could tell you. . . .
Will you ever forgive me?

JACK: Yes, oh, yes. (*He kicks some gravel in the path, thoughtfully. The minister's voice comes through the window.*)

REV. MacCURDY: Santa Rosa has gained and lost a son,—a son that she can be proud of. Brave, generous— (*His voice fades out.*)

YOUNG CHARLIE: Jack, *he* said that the whole world was just one big heap of lies and evil, and that people like us—(*a movement of the hand indicates the congregation in the church*)—have no idea what the world's really like. You'd know. Is it as bad as that?

JACK (*turning and looking in her face*): No, of course not. (*Taking her hand.*) It's not necessary that they know about whatever bad there is. But it takes a lot of watching.

They move on slowly, hands clasped. The organ in the church swells.

CHRONOLOGY

NOTE ON THE TEXTS

NOTES

Chronology

1897   Thornton Niven Wilder born April 17 in Madison, Wisconsin, second child of Amos Parker Wilder and Isabella Thornton Niven. (He is named after grandfather Thornton McNess Niven, Jr. [1836–1908], a Presbyterian minister who served as chaplain under General Thomas "Stonewall" Jackson during the Civil War, and great-grandfather Thornton McNess Niven [1806–1895], a Hudson Valley engineer and builder. Father, born 1862 in Calais, Maine, the grandson of a Revolutionary War veteran, graduated from Yale in 1884 and received a Ph.D. in political economy; he became a renowned public speaker, and edited and eventually owned the *Wisconsin State Journal*. Mother, born 1873 in Dobbs Ferry, New York, was the great-granddaughter of Arthur Tappan [1786–1865], co-founder of the American Antislavery Society; she did not attend college but acquired an excellent education in literature, languages, music, and art, wrote poetry, and translated from Italian and French. Parents married on December 3, 1894; their first child, Amos Niven, was born in 1895. Thornton's twin brother died at birth).

1898   Sister Charlotte Elizabeth born.

1900   Sister Isabel born.

1905–07   Through his Yale friend William Howard Taft, then Secretary of War, Amos Wilder is appointed consul general in Hong Kong. Family arrives in China on May 7, 1906. Thornton briefly attends local German school. Returns to the United States in October 1906 with mother and sisters, living in Berkeley, California. Studies violin and piano, and sings in Episcopal church choir. Attends McKinley and Emerson public schools. Conducts home theatricals. Watches rehearsals and has walk-on parts in productions at the University of California's Greek Theater.

1909   Father is posted to Shanghai and has home leave to visit family in California.

1910   Sister Janet Frances born. Thornton travels to China with his mother and sisters Isabel and Charlotte in December.

1911–13   After a brief stay at a German school in Shanghai, attends
           British-run China Inland Mission School 450 miles away
           in Chefoo (Yantai), where Henry Luce is a fellow student.
           Early in 1911, because of her health and political instabil-
           ity in China, mother takes two youngest children to Italy,
           where they remain for two years. In 1912, Thornton re-
           turns to America and joins brother Amos at the Thacher
           School in Ojai, California, where he co-writes and directs
           his first play, *The Russian Princess*, playing the role of the
           villain, the Grand Duke Alexis. Father refuses to allow
           him to play Lady Bracknell in school production of *The
           Importance of Being Earnest*. Mother returns to Berkeley
           in spring 1913, reuniting the Wilder children under one
           roof; Thornton transfers to Berkeley High School, where
           he is active in the dramatic and vaudeville clubs and be-
           gins writing a series of three-minute plays. Is an indif-
           ferent student but a voracious reader: reads Shakespeare,
           Dickens, Henry James, Scott, and German classics. Sees
           Sarah Bernhardt, Sidney Howard, and Sir Johnston Forbes-
           Robertson perform. In summer 1913, goes to San Luis
           Obispo, where he spends first of several summers doing
           farm work.

1914–15   Father resigns from the Consular Service for medical rea-
           sons and relocates to New Haven, Connecticut, to assume
           post of General Secretary of the Yale-in-China program.
           Thornton graduates from Berkeley High School in June
           1915. At father's insistence, enrolls in the fall at Oberlin
           College. Writes to a former teacher: "I have [my father's]
           promise in writing for one year only. Then Yale, and I
           hope Prof. [George Pierce] Baker's class for post-
           graduate at Harvard."

1916–17   Stays two years at Oberlin, where he befriends fellow stu-
           dent Robert Maynard Hutchins, studies the organ, con-
           tinues writing plays, and publishes in the *Oberlin Literary
           Magazine*; finds a mentor in English professor Charles H.
           Wager. During the summers, works on farms in Kentucky,
           Vermont, and Massachusetts. In September 1917, enrolls
           at Yale (repeating sophomore year), where his contempo-
           raries include Hutchins, Luce, Stephen Vincent Benét,
           Reginald Marsh, John Farrar, and Philip Barry. Important
           teachers are William Lyon Phelps and Chauncey Brewster
           Tinker.

1918–19   Wilder continues busily seeing plays, writing mostly
           drama, including several full-length plays, among them

The Trumpet Shall Sound. In 1918, wins the John Hubbard Curtis Prize for his short story *Spiritus Valet*. Spends summer 1918 working as clerk in the War Industries Board in Washington, D.C. In September 1918, joins the Army's First Coast Artillery Corps stationed at Fort Adams, on Narragansett Bay outside Newport, Rhode Island; is discharged as a corporal and returns to Yale shortly after war's end. Reviews plays for the *Boston Evening Transcript*, and is critical of conventional melodrama and frothy comedies; is active in Yale's Elizabethan Club. First three acts of four-act play *The Trumpet Shall Sound* are published in the *Yale Literary Magazine*.

1920   *The Trumpet Shall Sound* receives Yale's Bradford Brinton Award after its final act is published in the *Yale Literary Magazine*. Wilder graduates from Yale in June, and works on Connecticut farm during the summer. In the fall, begins an eight-month residency at the American Academy in Rome, informally studying archeology. (He later wrote: "For a while in Rome I lived among archeologists, and ever since I find myself occasionally looking at the things about me as an archeologist will look at them a thousand years hence.")

1921   Writes to his mother in April 1921: "I have found an Italian playwright whose plays I adore, the Sicilian Luigi Pirandello. Philosophical farces, actually,—strange contorted domestic situations illustrating some metaphysical proposition. . . ." Attends the first performance in Rome of Pirandello's *Six Characters in Search of an Author*. Is introduced to modern German expressionist drama. Meets Ezra Pound. Concludes his postgraduate year abroad with a six-week stay in Paris, where he begins writing "Memoirs of a Roman Student," which becomes his first novel, *The Cabala*. Reads Proust, Flaubert, and Madame de Sévigné. In June accepts offer, arranged by his father, to teach French at the Lawrenceville School, a preparatory school for boys near Princeton, New Jersey. Meets Stark Young on the return voyage.

1922–24 Establishes himself as a successful teacher and assistant dormitory master at Lawrenceville and as a speaker in local literary circles; reads extensively in seventeenth- and eighteenth-century French literature in the Princeton library; works on drama and *The Cabala* and attends theater whenever possible in New York, Trenton, and Philadelphia, where, in 1923, he meets producer and director

Max Reinhardt. Publishes pieces in the magazine *S4N*, and brief excerpts from *The Cabala* in *The Double Dealer*, a New Orleans literary journal. Continually writes plays. In 1924, makes the first of many stays at the MacDowell Colony in Peterborough, New Hampshire, where he meets Edwin Arlington Robinson and other authors, painters, and composers. Requests and is granted a two-year leave from Lawrenceville.

1925 Studies for a master's degree in French literature at Princeton and works to complete *The Cabala*, which is accepted for publication by Albert and Charles Boni in November. Covers Broadway for *Theatre Arts*.

1926 Writes to a friend in January: "I am full of plays that can't get written. I can't sleep. I am hateful." *The Cabala* is published to critical acclaim in England and America; in April *The New York Times* hails "the debut of a new American stylist" and calls it a "magnificent literary event." Starts work on *The Bridge of San Luis Rey* at the MacDowell Colony during the summer. In the fall, chaperones a young man around Europe; is introduced to Ernest Hemingway by Sylvia Beach in Paris. Is unable to attend December premiere of his revised version of *The Trumpet Shall Sound*, directed by Richard Boleslavsky, at the American Laboratory Theatre in New York, a production that is reviewed unfavorably.

1927 After living in Connecticut while working on *The Bridge of San Luis Rey*, returns to Lawrenceville in July as master of Davis House. In November, *The Bridge of San Luis Rey* is published by Albert and Charles Boni to immediate acclaim on both sides of the Atlantic. (To a friend, he later wrote: "It seems to me that my books are about: what is the worst thing that the world can do to you, and what are the last resources one has to oppose it. In other words: when a human being is made to bear more than human beings can bear—what then? . . . *The Bridge* asked the question whether the intention that lies behind love was sufficient to justify the desperation of living.") During Christmas holiday in Miami, meets boxer Gene Tunney and producer Jed Harris.

1928 Meets F. Scott Fitzgerald and Edmund Wilson at Fitzgerald's house in Delaware. Writes to Fitzgerald that he enjoys teaching at Lawrenceville and will probably remain there "for ages"; "a daily routine is necessary to me: I have no writing habits, am terribly lazy and write seldom." In May, delivers the Daniel S. Lamont Memorial Lecture at Yale, his first major public lecture, on "English Letters and Letter Writers." Rents a house for his mother and sisters Isabel and Janet for an extended stay in and around London. Travels to Europe, and studies the work and techniques of European dramatists and theater companies by attending performances in Germany, Austria, and Hungary. Is awarded the Pulitzer Prize for *The Bridge of San Luis Rey*. Hikes the Alps and motors through the south of France with Tunney; begins work on novel *The Woman of Andros*. In November, *The Angel That Troubled the Water and Other Plays* is published; some of the plays are published in periodicals. Wilder accepts a commission to translate novel *Paulina 1880* by Pierre-Jean Jouve for Longmans, Green (the translation, never published, may not have been completed; the manuscript is almost certainly lost).

1929   Returns from Europe in January and, under lecturing contract with the Lee Keedick Agency, sets out on a two-month cross-country lecture tour. His royalties and related professional fees are now the main support of his parents and two youngest sisters, and in March he buys property on Deepwood Drive in Hamden, Connecticut, to build a house for the family, referring to it later as "The House *The Bridge* Built." Sister Isabel and lawyer J. Dwight Dana increasingly assume duties of caring for his business and domestic arrangements. Wilder travels to Europe with mother; sees Tunney and Hemingway. Film (mostly silent, with a segment in sound at the end) of *The Bridge of San Luis Rey*, directed by Charles Brabin, is released.

1930–31 Accepts invitation from his close friend Robert Maynard Hutchins, now president of the University of Chicago, to serve as a part-time visiting lecturer in classics and writing at the university for spring quarter of 1930; the appointment, during which he teaches no more than two quarters each year, extends through 1936. *The Woman of Andros* is published in February 1930 and becomes a best seller; in *The New Republic,* Marxist critic Michael Gold attacks it and Wilder's previous work for ignoring social issues. Develops close, lifelong friendships with Ruth Gordon, Alexander Woollcott, and Sibyl Colefax. *The Long Christmas Dinner and Other Plays in One Act* is published in January 1931.

1932–33 Wilder is asked to translate from German and adapt *The*

Bride of Torozko, a play about anti-Semitism in a small Hungarian town by Hungarian playwright Otto Indig, but project stumbles (play is eventually staged on Broadway in 1934, and Wilder is not credited). In summer 1932, begins to work intensively on novel *Heaven's My Destination*. Wilder's translation of André Obey's play *Le Viol de Lucrèce* opens late in 1932 in New York as *Lucrèce*, starring Katharine Cornell and Brian Aherne and directed by Guthrie McClintic; it runs for 31 performances. *Lucrèce* is published by Houghton Mifflin in 1933. Reads the European comedies of Nestroy, Raimund, Goldoni, and Lessing, "just to make sure," he writes later to Ruth Gordon, "that I've expunged every lurking vestige of what Sam Behrman and George Kaufman think comedy is."

1934 Wilder goes to Hollywood to work on a film treatment of *Joan of Arc* for RKO studios, to star Katharine Hepburn and to be directed by George Cukor; film is never made. Also does writing jobs for Sam Goldwyn, including work on *We Live Again* (film based on Tolstoy's novel *Resurrection*) and *Dark Angel*. Turns down other major film assignments (as he will later do). Back at the University of Chicago, meets Gertrude Stein, who comes to lecture in November.

1935 *Heaven's My Destination* is brought out by his new publisher, Harper & Brothers, in January. Stein's *Narration: Four Lectures* is published with an introduction by Wilder. During a leave of absence from University of Chicago in 1935, he spends six months in Europe in the summer and fall, seeing Stein, Alice B. Toklas, Franz Werfel, Max Reinhardt, Pablo Picasso, and Sigmund Freud. Upon returning to America tells reporters that he intends to "abandon" the novel in favor of writing only plays, viewing the novel's omniscient voice as "out of gear with twentieth-century life" and drama "the new vehicle to succeed the narrative form." His journal notes include ideas for ten plays, among them "M Marries N" (an early working title for *Our Town)* and *The Merchant of Yonkers*.

1936 Father dies on July 2. Wilder resigns from University of Chicago. Begins work on *Our Town*. Stein's *Geographical History of America*, with an introduction by Wilder, is published.

1937 Completes his Lee Keedick public-lecture contract, writing his brother: "The new life's begun. Taught my last class. Delivered my last lecture. The living is wonderful, and alarming; but I've plunged jubilantly into work and play no. #1 is almost done; plays no. #2 (on the Arabian Nights) and #3 ('Our Town' . . .) all planned out, as are several more." As a favor, works on a new "acting version" of Ibsen's *A Doll's House* for Jed Harris and Ruth Gordon. Works on plays at the MacDowell Colony in June. In July, travels to Paris as the first American delegate to the Institut de Coopération Intellectuel of the League of Nations, and delivers a lecture in French; sees E. M. Forster, Orson Welles, and Coco Chanel. Visits Stein and Toklas at their home in Bilignin, and attends Salzburg Festival. Retires for the fall to seclusion in Ruschlikon, near Zurich, to complete *Our Town*. Writes Sibyl Colefax in October: "Lord! What I got myself in for. A theologico-metaphisico transcription for the *Purgatorio* with panels of American rural genre-stuff." In December, after a successful tour, his version of *A Doll's House* opens on Broadway.

1938   After one performance in Princeton and a week's run in Boston, *Our Town* opens on Broadway on February 4 to mostly favorable reviews. Later that spring, Wilder is awarded his second Pulitzer Prize. Moves to a hotel in Tucson, Arizona, to complete *The Merchant of Yonkers*. Works on *The Alcestiad*. In September, takes over the role of the Stage Manager in *Our Town* for two weeks. *The Merchant of Yonkers* opens on Broadway on December 28, to a disappointing reception.

1939   Travels in Mexico and Texas, then goes to Europe in May and stays through the end of June; sees Jean Cocteau, Ruth Draper, Gertrude Stein, and Sibyl Colefax. Returns home and plays the Stage Manager in summer-stock productions of *Our Town* in Pennsylvania and Massachusetts. Describes his enthusiasm for James Joyce's *Finnegans Wake* as his "constant new companion." Devotes fall to nonfiction, except for an adaptation for Broadway of *The Beaux' Stratagem* for producer Cheryl Crawford, which he does not finish. Completes statement on the nature of theater ("Some Thoughts on Playwriting," published in 1941) and an introduction for an edition of *Oedipus Rex* (not published until 1955). Producer Sol Lesser appeals for his help in adapting *Our Town* for the screen, a task that involves meetings and continuous collaboration via letters and telegrams over several months.

1940   Stirred by news of events in Europe and inspired by ideas in Joyce, Wilder begins working on a play called *The Ends of the Worlds* that will become *The Skin of Our Teeth*. Attends May 22 premiere in Boston of film version of *Our Town*, directed by Sam Wood and starring William Holden and Martha Scott. Acts in summer-stock productions of *Our Town*. Goes to Quebec City for several weeks to work on *The Skin of Our Teeth*.

1941   Puts aside work on play to travel in late winter and spring to Colombia, Ecuador, and Peru at behest of the State Department's Bureau of Educational and Cultural Affairs, for which he studies Spanish intensively. Reads the letters of Simón Bolívar. To amass funds for his family in case of military service, teaches a double load during the summer term at the University of Chicago. Travels to England with John Dos Passos as American representatives to the International Committee of PEN; meets with H. G. Wells, Edith Evans, E. M. Forster, and Cecil Beaton. Resumes work on *The Skin of Our Teeth* late in the year.

1942   Completes *The Skin of Our Teeth*. In May 1942, is accepted into the Army Air Intelligence and declares he would take "the khaki veil with an explosive cry of relief." Before reporting for duty, goes to Hollywood to write the screenplay for Alfred Hitchcock's *Shadow of a Doubt*, based on a scenario by Gordon McDonnell. On June 26, begins six weeks of basic training in Miami. Transfers to Harrisburg, Pennsylvania, for Intelligence School, and is then assigned as a captain to the headquarters of the 328th Fighter Group at Hamilton Field, California, and later to Washington, D.C. After previews in New Haven, Baltimore, and Philadelphia, *The Skin of Our Teeth* opens on Broadway on November 18. The next month, in *The Saturday Review of Literature*, Joseph Campbell and Henry Morton Robinson attack the play as stolen "in conception and detail" from James Joyce's *Finnegans Wake*, a charge Wilder chooses not to answer publicly, although he writes that "the ant-like industry of pedants, collecting isolated fragments, has mistaken the nature of literary influence since the first critics arose to regard books as a branch of merchandise instead of an expression of energy."

1943   In spring, Wilder is awarded his third Pulitzer Prize. Receives promotion to major on April 15, and is shipped overseas to the intelligence section of the Twelfth Air Force in Constantine, Algeria, and later to Algiers, where he is involved in planning operations. Is promoted to lieutenant colonel on August 27, 1944, and is posted to Caserta, Italy.

1944   Spends three days in Rome, his first visit since his American Academy residency. Directs all-military production of *Our Town* in Caserta. Second film adaptation of *The Bridge of San Luis Rey*, directed by Rowland V. Lee and starring Lynn Bari, Francis Lederer, and Alla Nazimova, is released. *The Skin of Our Teeth* and *Our Town* are produced in Switizerland; the latter, again directed by Jed Harris, has its first major New York revival.

1945   Wilder goes to Belgrade in February for performance of Serbo-Croatian version of *Our Town* staged by Tito's Partisans. During the Italian campaign, continues to prepare intelligence material and interrogate prisoners. Is awarded Bronze Star. Returns to America in May and is discharged from the Air Force in September. Because of poor health, cannot accept the post of cultural attaché at U.S. embassy in Paris. Resumes work on *The Alcestiad* but puts it aside in November to start the novel *The Ides of March*. Reads Kierkegaard and avidly follows periodical literature on the new vogue of existentialism.

1946   In January at Yale, meets Jean-Paul Sartre, who asks him to translate his play *Morts sans sépulture*. Travels from the Gulf Coast to the Yucatan Pennisula to Washington, D.C. Works on *The Ides of March*. Mother dies on June 29. Wilder writes short play in honor of the Century Club's centenary and records radio broadcast of *Our Town* for Theatre Guild on September 29. Receives Order of the British Empire (O.B.E.) for wartime service.

1947   Spends a month in Mexico and moves on to Florida, working on *The Ides of March*. Writes in April to his agent: "I hate being alone. And I hate writing. But I can only write when I'm alone. So these working spells combine both my antipathies." Is awarded honorary doctorate by Yale in June. Completes introduction to Gertrude Stein's *Four in America* in July, and finishes *The Ides of March* in the fall.

1948   Travels to London in January to consult about Laurence Olivier's production of *The Skin of Our Teeth*. Meets T. S. Eliot, V. S. Pritchett, Kenneth Tynan, and Peter Ustinov. Sees Sartre in Paris in February. *The Ides of March* is published in March. In an interview, he says: "Modern man has taken such pride in the exploration of his mind that he has forgotten there must be some laws governing that exploration. Whether it comes under religion or ethics or mere judgment, such laws must be found and respected. Otherwise the mind leads him straight to self-destruction. So my book is Caesar's groping in the open seas of his unlimited power for the first principles which should guide him." Plays Mr. Antrobus in summer-stock productions of *The Skin of Our Teeth* in Massachusetts, Connecticut, and Pennsylvania. By this time, has embarked on his voluminous scholarship on the career of Spanish dramatist Lope de Vega (1562–1635), a passion comparable to his long devotion to *Finnegans Wake*. In November, lectures for two weeks at the University of Frankfurt on "The American Character as Mirrored in Literature," and later at universities of Heidelberg and Marburg; spends two days in Berlin meeting students during the Berlin Airlift. Continues on to Switzerland, Italy, and Spain. His translation of Sartre's *Mort sans sépulture* is produced Off Broadway as *The Victors* in December to mixed reviews.

1949   Wilder returns to Hamden. Works on a new play, *The Emporium*. Visits Ezra Pound at St. Elizabeths Hospital. Is awarded honorary degrees by New York University and Kenyon College. Delivers lecture "World Literature and the Modern Mind" on the occasion of the Goethe Bicentennial at the Aspen Festival in June, where he also extemporaneously translates addresses by Albert Schweitzer and José Ortega y Gasset.

1950   Travels in Europe in spring; sees Max Beerbohm, Sacheverell Sitwell, and Noel Coward. Returns to the United States to accept honorary degree and perform in *Our Town* at the College of Wooster. Plays Stage Manager in *Our Town* at the Wellesley Summer Theatre, "the twelfth company I've played it with," he writes to Laurence Olivier and Vivien Leigh, adding "I advise every playwright to get somehow somewhere *that* side of the footlights." Accepts appointment as Harvard's 1950–51 Charles Eliot Norton Professor of Poetry, a position requiring six public lectures to be published by Harvard University Press. Moves into Dunster House in September; in addition to lecturing, agrees to teach large American literature class, and accepts scores of invitations to talk and meet with students and groups in Boston area. Lectures on Thoreau, Poe, Melville, Dickinson, and Whitman in a series titled "The American Characteristics in Classic American Literature."

1951   Collapses from exhaustion March 9 and is hospitalized for several weeks. Resumes lighter schedule. Gives the 1951 Harvard Alumni Association's Commencement Address on June 21. Calls the Harvard experience the hardest year of his life. Receives honorary degrees from Harvard and from Northwestern University in June. That fall, travels to Europe to revise his Norton lectures for publication, a project that is ultimately never completed.

1952   Throughout the year, works on various projects: the Norton lectures, *The Emporium*, *The Alcestiad*, a possible screenplay for Vittorio De Sica, and a Christmas pageant play called *The Sandusky, Ohio, Mystery Play*. In May, is awarded the Gold Medal for Fiction by the American Academy of Arts and Letters. In June, receives honorary degree from Oberlin. Spends summer at MacDowell Colony. In September, heads the American delegation to a UNESCO congress in Venice. Travels to Paris to meet with Ruth Gordon and Tyrone Guthrie, who have asked him to consider revising *The Merchant of Yonkers*. Versions of three of his Harvard lectures are published in the *Atlantic Monthly*.

1953   Returns to America and resumes work on old projects. Is featured on cover of *Time*, June 12. Returns to MacDowell Colony late summer. Continues to work on *The Emporium*; finishes revisions of *The Merchant of Yonkers*.

1954   *The Merchant of Yonkers* opens successfully as *The Matchmaker* at the Edinburgh Festival in June, directed by Tyrone Guthrie and starring Ruth Gordon. "If I do finish *The Emporium* by July I'll be a very blithe fellow, indeed, and a public nuisance in Edinburgh. Of course, if I could finish the four-year-late Harvard lectures, too, all Europe would rock," he writes to Gordon. After a well-received tour, *The Matchmaker* opens a successful run in London. Wilder goes to the Berlin Festival in September, and travels on to Hamburg, Paris, and southern France to work on *The Alcestiad*, which he describes as "a humdinger— the true extension of the *Our Town–Skin* line."

1955–56   On August 22, 1955, *The Alcestiad*, retitled *A Life in the Sun*, opens at the Edinburgh Festival, directed by Guthrie and starring Irene Worth, to generally negative reviews. Wilder begins collaboration with composer Louise Talma on an opera based on *The Alcestiad*. In November *The Matchmaker* moves on to the United States where Wilder is initially involved in production details, but he is in

Europe when the play opens on December 5, 1955, on Broadway, where it runs for 486 performances, Wilder's Broadway record. Works and travels in Europe; returns to the U.S. in March 1956. In June, drives to Mexico and back; as has been his lifelong habit, travels to different cities, different continents to work and "regenerate": "What do all of these long stays abroad mean, but my eternal effort to find a time and a place when I can follow an idea through," he writes in May.

1957   Along with *The Happy Journey to Trenton and Camden*, two new one-act plays, *Bernice* (starring Ethel Waters) and *The Wreck on the Five-Twenty-Five*, are performed at Congress Hall in West Berlin in September 1957, with Wilder in the cast. Is inducted into the prestigious German society Orden Pour le Mérite für Wissenschaften und Künste. In October, is awarded the German Book Sellers Peace Prize in Frankfurt, the first American to receive this prize, delivering an address, "Culture in a Democracy," in German to audience of two thousand guests. Is awarded honorary degree by the Goethe University (Frankfurt) and receives Austria's Medal of Honor for Science and Fine Arts.

1958   In Washington in February, receives a medal from the Peruvian government. Works on two cycles of one-act plays, "The Seven Ages of Man" and "The Seven Deadly Sins," intended to be performed on an arena stage. Works with Norman Bel Geddes on "epic film" called *The Melting Pot*, but project ends when Bel Geddes dies in May. Contributes preface to *Three Plays by Thornton Wilder: Our Town, The Skin of Our Teeth, The Matchmaker.* In August Paramount Pictures releases a film version of *The Matchmaker*, directed by Joseph Anthony and starring Shirley Booth, Anthony Perkins, and Shirley MacLaine.

1959   Travels in Europe. "It's not quite clear to me what I'm doing in Europe," he writes. "I seem to remember that I came here to work, and work went fine on the boat and then I got joined to various human communities. . . . But, boy do I work! The lives—the life-stories that I've entered." Back in the U.S., he deals with business matters, works to finish his "Seven Deadly Sins" plays, and in August acts as the Stage Manager in *Our Town* at Williamstown, Massachusetts, his final appearance as an actor.

1960–61   Continues work on "Seven Deadly Sins" and "Seven Ages of Man" play cycles. Offers to help Katharine Hepburn and Spencer Tracy fashion a movie from *The Skin of Our Teeth*, but nothing comes of the project. Helps Jerome Kilty adapt *The Ides of March* for the stage. Adapts *The Long Christmas Dinner* for use as a one-act opera libretto set by composer Paul Hindemith; in German translation, the opera premieres in Mannheim, West Germany, on December 26, 1961.

1962–64   *Plays for Bleecker Street* (comprising three one-act plays: *Someone from Assisi, Infancy,* and *Childhood*) opens Off Broadway January 11, 1962, and enjoys a successful run. In German translation, the Wilder-Talma opera based on *The Alcestiad* opens in Frankfurt on March 1, 1962, to 20-minute ovation. Wilder presents "An Evening with Thornton Wilder" to President Kennedy's cabinet in Washington, D.C., on April 11. On May 20, 1962, departs for a long retreat in the Arizona desert; by late May is in Douglas, Arizona. Here he stays 20 months, initially in a hotel, and by the fall of 1962 in an efficiency apartment. By the end of the year has put aside work on his "Seven Deadly Sins" and "Seven Ages of Man" plays and begins working on a novel that becomes *The Eighth Day.* In March 1963, reveals this work for the first time to his family, describing his story as "*Little Women* being mulled over by Dostoevsky." Theatrical adaptation of *The Ides of March*, starring John Gielgud and Irene Worth, opens in London in June 1963 but soon closes. Wilder leaves Douglas in late November 1963 to accept the Presidential Medal of Freedom in the White House on December 1, announced the previous July by President Kennedy but conferred by President Johnson after Kennedy's assassination. *Hello, Dolly!*, a musical adaptation of *The Matchmaker*, opens on Broadway, on January 16, 1964; royalties provide Wilder financial security for the rest of his life.

1965–67   Wilder resumes extensive foreign and domestic travel, working almost exclusively on *The Eighth Day.* On May 4, 1965, Lady Bird Johnson awards him the National Book Committee's first Medal for Literature at the White House. He completes *The Eighth Day* and reads proofs in Innsbruck, Austria, in November 1966. *The Eighth Day* is published on March 29, 1967; it is a critical and financial success, and receives the National Book Award for Fiction. In September 1967, Wilder buys second home at Katama Point on Martha's Vineyard with his sister Isabel.

1968–75 Travels often, with stops in Paris, Munich, Milan, Venice, Zurich, Cannes, Florida, New York, and Martha's Vineyard. Begins to suffer from circulatory problems; eye problems and hearing worsen. Toys with many writing ideas, but settles into writing a series of semi-autobiographical chapters. One of them, drawing on many affectionate visits to Newport, Rhode Island, grows into his novel *Theophilus North*, written between April 1972 and April 1973 and published in October 1973; critically praised, it becomes a best seller. Wilder continues to travel but is more and more confined to Hamden home. Begins work on sequel to *Theophilus North*. Spends summer of 1975 on Martha's Vineyard; is operated on in September for a cancerous prostate. Dies of an apparent heart attack at home in Hamden on December 7, 1975.

Note on the Texts

This volume collects all the plays that Thornton Wilder published in book form in his lifetime (except for the translation of *Lucrèce*), as well as a number of unpublished, more or less unfinished plays written in his later years. It does not include several plays written during his school years, some of which were published in periodicals such as the *Oberlin Literary Magazine*, the *Yale Literary Magazine*, and *S4N*. This volume also contains 14 essays and short pieces by Wilder about the theater, as well as the screenplay he wrote in 1942 for Alfred Hitchcock's film *Shadow of a Doubt*.

The Angel That Troubled the Waters and Other Plays (New York: Coward-McCann, 1928) collects sixteen "three minute plays for three persons," some composed as early as 1915. Written more for reading than for production, these plays were not reprinted in Wilder's lifetime. The Coward-McCann edition contains the text printed here.

The Long Christmas Dinner and Other Plays in One Act (New York: Coward-McCann; New Haven: Yale University Press, 1931) collects the plays "The Long Christmas Dinner," "Queens of France," "Pullman Car Hiawatha," "Love and How to Cure It," "Such Things Only Happen in Books," and "The Happy Journey to Trenton and Camden." Wilder had withdrawn "Such Things Happen Only in Books" from production by 1946, and omitted the play when the volume was reprinted by Harper & Row in 1963. It was restored in *The Collected Short Plays of Thornton Wilder, Volume I*, edited by Donald Gallup and A. Tappan Wilder (New York: Theatre Communications Group, 1997). Some changes, having mainly to do with the sequence of lines and with some details of stage business, were made to the texts of "The Long Christmas Dinner" and "The Happy Journey" in the acting editions published by Samuel French in 1934. The changes in "The Long Christmas Dinner" were made, according to Gallup and A. Tappan Wilder, "by Alexander Dean, the director, and were apparently sanctioned by the author," and are incorporated in their edition. However, the 1963 Harper & Row edition does not incorporate these changes, which seem designed chiefly to make certain points of the play's action more explicit and conventional. For these reasons, and because the source of the changes in the acting editions is not well established, the text printed here is taken from the 1931 edition of *The Long Christmas Dinner and Other Plays in One Act*, published by Coward-McCann and Yale University Press.

Our Town was published by Coward-McCann in 1938, the same year the play opened on Broadway. An acting version was published by Coward-McCann in cooperation with Samuel French in 1939. When *Our Town* was included in *Three Plays* (1957), Wilder incorporated significant revisions; it is not known when these revisions were made, or whether they had accrued gradually during the period from 1938 to 1957. Cass Canfield of Harper wrote to Wilder's sister Isabel (acting as his representative) in November 1956 that he was "delighted" to learn that Wilder "will have ready the definitive text of *Our Town* between December 1st and 15th." Around the same time, Isabel Wilder wrote to Beulah Hagen of Harper that "work on the 'definitive' *Our Town* text is about to get underway." The text in the present volume is therefore taken from the 1957 Harper & Row edition of *Three Plays*.

The Skin of Our Teeth was published by Harper in 1942, the same year it opened on Broadway. The text of this edition was regarded by Wilder as final, and is the source of the text printed here.

The Matchmaker is a revised version of Wilder's play *The Merchant of Yonkers*, which was published by Harper in 1939, the same year that it opened on Broadway. Although *The Matchmaker* was published as a separate volume in London by Longmans in 1957, in the United States its first book publication was in *Three Plays* (1957), for which Wilder provided a revised typescript of the play. Richard H. Goldstone and Gary Anderson note in *Thornton Wilder: An Annotated Bibliography of Works By and About Thornton Wilder* (New York: AMS Press, 1982): "The final speech of *The Matchmaker*, through a typist's error, is corrupt in the published version. R. H. Goldstone's biography, *Thornton Wilder: An Intimate Portrait* (New York: Saturday Review Press/Dutton, 1975), contains Wilder's corrected version, p. 234." The text printed here is from the 1957 Harper & Row edition of *Three Plays*, with correction of the error noted above.

The Alcestiad, which Wilder had begun writing in the late 1930s, was first produced by Tyrone Guthrie in 1955 in Edinburgh. Wilder was dissatisfied with the play and revised it, adding the accompanying "satyr play" *The Drunken Sisters*; the revised version was translated into German and produced in Zurich in 1957. *The Alcestiad* and *The Drunken Sisters* first appeared in book form from Harper & Row in 1977, in a version "drawn," according to Donald Gallup, "from both the earlier English acting version and a German version published in 1960." The 1977 Harper & Row edition contains the text printed here.

"The Marriage We Deplore" was written in June 1917 when

Wilder was a sophomore at Yale. Prepared by Donald Gallup, it was first published in *The Collected Short Plays of Thornton Wilder, Volume II*, ed. A. Tappan Wilder (New York: Theatre Communications Group, 1998), which contains the text printed in this volume.

"The Unerring Instinct: A Play in One Act" was written in 1947 for the National Conference of Christians and Jews, as a contribution to their "NCCJ Scripts for Brotherhood" program, which distributed the script to schools and dramatic clubs. The play was first published in book form in *The Collected Short Plays of Thornton Wilder, Volume II*, from which the text in this volume is taken.

Thornton Wilder began *The Emporium* in 1948, and continued to work on the play on and off for many years, but never completed it to his satisfaction. In 1948 he described the play to a journalist as "a typical American success story and a spine-chilling melodrama . . . a combination of Horatio Alger and Kafka . . . and there'll be a little bit of me in it, too." A draft of the first two scenes of the play was published as an appendix to *The Journals of Thornton Wilder: 1939–1961*, ed. Donald Gallup (New Haven, CT: Yale University Press, 1985) and was subsequently included in *The Collected Short Plays of Thornton Wilder, Volume II*. Two additional scenes, neither of which have previously been published, are included here. The texts of all four scenes from *The Emporium* included here are taken from Wilder's holograph manuscript in the Thornton Wilder Archive of the Yale Collection of American Literature, Beinecke Rare Book and Manuscript Library.

The plays presented here as "Plays for Bleecker Street" (the title was devised by Donald Gallup, based on Wilder's use of that title for a smaller grouping of the plays included here) were to form part of two cycles of seven plays each, "The Seven Deadly Sins" and "The Seven Ages of Man." Begun in 1956, the cycles were not completed by Wilder. He completed six of the projected plays—"Childhood," "Infancy," "Someone from Assisi," "The Drunken Sisters" (later paired with *The Alcestiad*), "Bernice," and "The Wreck on the Five-Twenty-Five." Of the remaining plays included, "A Ringing of Doorbells," "In Shakespeare and the Bible," "The Rivers Under the Earth," and "Youth" were left in a nearly completed state and are presented here in texts prepared by F. J. O'Neil; "Cement Hands" is taken from a text prepared by Donald Gallup. "Bernice" was first published in German translation in *Die Neue Rundschau 71*, no. 4 (1960) and in English in the *Yale Review 85*, no. 2 (April 1997). "The Wreck on the Five-Twenty-Five" was originally published in the *Yale Review 82*, no. 4 (October 1994) and included in *The Best American Short Plays 1994–1995* (New York: Applause Theatre Book Publishers) and in *EST Marathon '95: The Complete One-Act Plays* (Lyme, NH:

Smith & Kraus, 1995). "A Ringing of Doorbells," "In Shakespeare and the Bible," and "Cement Hands" were first published in *The Collected Short Plays of Thornton Wilder, Volume I*, in texts based on manuscripts in the Thornton Wilder Archive. "Someone from Assisi" was first distributed in an acting edition by Samuel French in 1964. "Infancy" was first published in an acting edition by Samuel French in 1970. "Childhood" was first published in the *Atlantic Monthly*, November 1960, and later in an acting edition published by Samuel French in 1970. "Youth" was first published in *The Collected Short Plays of Thornton Wilder, Volume I*. "The Rivers Under the Earth" was first published in *American Theatre 14*, no. 3 (March 1997). The present volume takes the texts of these plays from *The Collected Short Plays of Thornton Wilder, Volume I*. It retains in brackets the stage directions and, in one instance, a single line of dialogue added by F. J. O'Neil (based on, he writes, conversations with Wilder) to provide endings for the plays he edited, and which are in brackets in *The Collected Short Plays*; editorial explanations by O'Neil are included in the Notes.

Under the rubric "Writings on Theater," this volume collects most of Wilder's writings about his plays and those of other playwrights.

The text of "Forward to *The Angel That Troubled the Waters and Other Plays*" is taken from the first edition of the book, published by Coward-McCann in 1928.

"Notes for the Producer: *The Long Christmas Dinner*" and "Notes for the Producer: *The Happy Journey*" were first published in the Samuel French acting editions of those plays, published in 1933 and 1934 respectively. The texts printed here are taken from these editions.

"A Preface for *Our Town*" was published in *The New York Times*, February 13, 1938, and later collected in *American Characteristics and Other Essays*, ed. Donald Gallup (New York: Harper & Row, 1979), which contains the text printed here.

"*Our Town*: Story of the Play" and "*Our Town*: Some Suggestions for the Director" are taken from the Samuel French acting edition of *Our Town*, published in 1939.

"*Our Town*—From Stage to Screen," is taken from *Theatre Arts*, where it was published in November 1940.

"Preface to *Three Plays: Our Town, The Skin of Our Teeth, The Matchmaker*" was first published in that volume (New York: Harper & Brothers, 1957). (An abridged version was published in *Harper's*, October 1957, under the title "A Platform and a Passion for Two.") The preface was included in *American Characteristics and Other Essays*, which is the source of the text printed here.

"Notes on *The Alcestiad*" was published as a program note for the Tyrone Guthrie production of the play at Edinburgh in 1955, and first appeared in book form in *The Collected Short Plays of Thornton Wilder, Volume II*, which is the source of the text printed here.

"Noting the Nature of Farce" was first published in *The New York Times*, January 8, 1939, and was collected in *American Characteristics and Other Essays*, which is the source of the text in this volume.

"Some Thoughts on Playwriting" was first published in *The Intent of the Artist*, edited by Augusto Centeno (Princeton: Princeton University Press, 1941). It was collected in *American Characteristics and Other Essays*, which is the source of the text printed here.

"Richard Beer-Hofmann's *Jaakobs Traum*" was the introduction for an English translation of the play by Ida Bension Wynn (New York: Johannespresse, 1946). It was collected in *American Characteristics and Other Essays*, which is the source of the text printed here.

Written in 1939, "Sophocles's *Oedipus Rex*" was the introduction for an edition of the play, translated by Francis Storr, published by the Heritage Press (New York, 1955) under the title *Oedipus the King*. It was collected in *American Characteristics and Other Essays*, which is the source of the text in this volume.

"Foreword to *Three Comedies by Johann Nestroy*" introduced the book of that title, translated by Max Knight and Joseph Fabry, which was published by Frederick Ungar (New York, 1967). The text of the Ungar edition is used here.

Written in 1968, "George Bernard Shaw" was first published in *American Characteristics and Other Essays*, the source of the text printed here.

Wilder was approached in May 1942 by Alfred Hitchcock to adapt "Uncle Charlie," an unpublished scenario by Gordon McDonell, for the screen. The screenplay, entitled *Shadow of a Doubt*, was written over a six-week period just prior to the start of Wilder's military service. He worked in close collaboration with Hitchcock and his wife, Alma, writing the script by hand and revising on the basis of daily discussions. After Wilder completed his version, further changes were made by Alma Hitchcock, and the writer Sally Benson was brought in to write some additional dialogue. The film opened in 1943. Although Wilder was unhappy with some of the additional dialogue, the finished film adheres quite closely in structure and pacing to his original draft. The text used here is taken from the final typescript containing handwritten changes by Wilder from the Beinecke Library, emended in some cases by consulting Wilder's holograph (from the Alfred Hitchcock papers in the Margaret Herrick Library at Fairbanks Center for Motion Picture Study) as well as a later typescript incorporating subsequent revisions.

The texts of the original printings chosen for inclusion here are presented without change, except for the correction of typographical errors. Spelling, punctuation, and capitalization are often expressive features and are not altered, even when inconsistent or irregular. The following errors have been corrected: 25.27, *After*; 31.15, Mediterannean; 31.23, it to; 31.28, Mediterannean; 34.6, could sleep; 35.1, me we where; 45.7, CONSTANZA; 67.2, mother; 67.8, RODERICK; 101.24, heads; 107.13, *The*; 122.36, Gabrielle the; 138.8, Arthur and; 138.23, Laurenceville; 156.35, MRS; 175.9, *kitchen*; 186.25, Y'know.; 197.19, mother'n; 244.36, NEGROES *file*; 251.32, *place*; 263.23, *into*; 324.23, *cupbroad*; 336.3, this a; 360.14, *exit*; 367.3–5, adventure. So [sentence dropped]; 395.4, die from; 452.25, *into*; 460.14, What did; 510.19, instance?"; 526.21, DAPHNE:; 537.38, mother?; 605.4, perfeck; 614.12, Dodie; 653.24, sentence-struction; 653.31, *l'enseinement*; 659.21, et; 676.28, Dere; 678.17, dish towel-errors; 694.1, *Playwrighting*.

Notes

In the notes below, the reference numbers denote page and line of this volume (the line count includes headings). No note is made for material included in standard desk-reference books. Biblical quotations are keyed to the King James Version. For more biographical information than is contained in the Chronology, see Gilbert Harrison, *The Enthusiast* (New Haven, CT: Ticknor & Fields, 1983) and Linda Simon, *Thornton Wilder: His World* (Garden City, NY: Doubleday, 1979). Grateful acknowledgment is made to Jackson R. Bryer, Penelope Niven, Robin Gibbs Wilder, and Tappan Wilder for their assistance with the Chronology.

THE ANGEL THAT TROUBLED THE WATERS AND OTHER PLAYS

5.1   *Nascuntur Poetæ*]   From the Latin adage "Nascuntur poetae, fiunt oratores" ("Poets are born, orators are made").

5.3   *Piero di Cosimo*]   Italian painter (c. 1462–1521).

5.8   *chlamys*]   A short mantle, fastened at the shoulder, worn usually by men in ancient Greece.

8.18   Melusina]   A figure in French and German folklore. Because she offended her father in defense of her mother, Melusina was transformed every Saturday into a serpent from the waist down. When she married Raymond, Count of Lusignan, she made him vow never to visit her on Saturday, but he hid and viewed her metamorphosis. Melusina left her husband and wandered the earth until doomsday.

8.31   JEPHTHA'S daughter]   See Judges 11.

11.3   *the Siddons . . . O'Neill*]   Sarah Siddons (1755–1831), Anna Oldfield (1683–1730), and Anne Bracegirdle (c. 1674–1748) were famous English actresses; Eliza O'Neill (1791–1872) was a celebrated Irish actress.

21.21   joss]   A Chinese idol. The word is a corruption of the Portuguese *deos*, from Latin *deus*, "god."

22.22–23   the Portagee's]   Slang for the Portuguese's.

25.13   *Carolus . . . magister*]   Charles of Benicet, master in gold and silver.

25.32   *fidelitas carior vita*]   Faithfulness dearer than life.

27.1   *Childe . . . Came*]   The title of an 1855 poem by Robert Browning, which draws on an old Scottish ballad cited in *King Lear* (III.iv). Wilder conflates the ballad with the story of Charlemagne's knight Roland or Orlando, slain at Roncevaux in his emperor's defense, who was the hero of the twelfth-century *Song of Roland*.

34.5   *Ave Maris Stella!*]   Hail, Star of the Sea!

34.36   *Flos undarum!*]   Flower of the waves!

40.1   *Now . . . Malchus*]   The title is taken from John 18:10: "Then Simon Peter having a sword drew it, and smote the high priest's servant, and cut off his right ear. Now the servant's name was Malchus. Then said Jesus unto Peter, Put up thy sword into the sheath: the cup which my Father hath given me, shall I not drink it? Then the band and the captain and the officers of the Jews took Jesus, and bound him."

43.7   Salieri's]   Antonio Salieri, Italian composer (1750–1825), court composer and later Kapellmeister in Vienna.

43.29   *servus*]   Latin for "servant," used as a greeting in Austria (as in the formal "your servant").

44.17–19   Excellency . . . lady]   Count Franz Georg von Walsegg-Stuppach (1763–1827), first mentioned by name at 45.17–18, sent an anonymous messenger to Mozart in 1791 to commission a requiem mass in memory of his young wife, Anna. As stated in the play, he claimed to have written works he had commissioned from others.

46.33   *miserere nobis*]   Have mercy upon us: from the *Agnus Dei* sung before communion during Mass ("Lamb of God, who takes away the sins of the world, have mercy on us").

48.1   *Hast . . . Job?*]   The title is drawn from Job 7:12. The temptation of Christ by Satan is recounted in Matthew 4:1–11, Mark 1:12–13, and Luke 4:1–13.

51.3   *Dime Museums*]   From the mid-nineteenth century until the early twentieth century, dime museums, named for the price of admission, were popular collections of exotic man-made and natural curiosities. Their success made millionaires of entrepreneurs such as P. T. Barnum.

THE LONG CHRISTMAS DINNER AND OTHER PLAYS IN ONE ACT

62.38–39   "Take a little wine for thy stomach's sake."]   Cf. I Timothy 5:23: "Drink no longer water, but use a little wine for thy stomach's sake and thine often infirmities."

81.3   the true heir to the French throne]   Louis Charles (1785–1795?), the second son of Louis XVI and Marie Antoinette, came to be known as "the lost dauphin." He became the dauphin in 1789, on the death of his older brother. Imprisoned with the royal family in 1792, he was proclaimed Louis XVII by royalists after his father's execution in 1793. He died in prison, though tales about him swirled, including rumors that he escaped and another boy was substituted for him in his cell.

83.16   Le Petit Salon] New Orleans social club for ladies.

88.30   *La loi—c'est moi.*] "I am the Law," a play on Louis XIV's "L'Etat, c'est moi" ("I am the State").

100.1–4   "There's so much . . . Stevenson] Not said by Robert Louis Stevenson; usually attributed to Kansas governor Edward Wallis Hoch (1849–1925).

100.13   *The Vision of Sir Launfal*] A long verse romance (1848) by James Russell Lowell (1819–1891) based on an Arthurian legend. The quotation is from the Prologue to Part First.

100.13   William Cullen—] American poet William Cullen Bryant (1794–1878).

100.20–22   "On the road . . . bay."] From "Mandalay" by Rudyard Kipling (1865–1936), published in his *Ballads and Barrack Room Ballads* (1892).

100.22–23   Frank W. Service] The Tramp is undoubtedly thinking of the poet Robert W. Service (1874–1958).

100.32–33   "Throw . . . today-ay] From the 1888 hymn by Edwin Smith Ufford (1851–1929).

101.1–8   Ich . . . hervorgebracht] "I am the workman who lost his life here. While blasting for this bridge which at this very moment you are crossing . . . I was struck by a falling boulder. I speak now as a ghost in this play. 'Fourscore and seven years ago our forefathers brought forth on this continent a new nation . . .'"

101.24–25   "If you can . . . you] The opening lines of Kipling's poem "If—" (1910).

102.10–11   *Elihu Vedder's Pleiades*] Allegorical figures in "The Pleiades," painting (1885) by American artist Elihu Vedder (1836–1923).

102.16–20   "Are you not . . . realities] A paraphrase of doctrines found both in Plato's *Phaedrus* and in his *The Republic* (book 7).

102.23–26   "What else . . . creature] Cf. the *Discourses* (1, 16, 19–21) by the Stoic philosopher Epictetus (c. 55–c. 135).

102.32   "And we began to say] From Augustine, *Confessions*, book 9.

106.13–14   "I do not ask . . . me."] From Cardinal John Henry Newman's 1833 hymn "Lead, Kindly Light."

107.17–19   "I was . . . years."] Cf. the second verse of "Lead, Kindly Light": "I was not ever thus, nor pray'd that Thou /Shouldst lead me on; /

I loved to choose and see my path; but now / Lead Thou me on! / I loved the garish day, and, spite of fears, / Pride ruled my will: Remember not past years!"

113.36   panto] Slang for "pantomime," a traditional Christmastide entertainment in Britain.

118.7   Nell Gwynne] English actress (1651–1687) and mistress of King Charles II.

123.30   Enoch Arden] Eponymous hero of Alfred Tennyson's 1864 poem.

143.25–28   "There were . . . gold] The opening lines of "The Ninety and Nine" (1868) by Scottish poet Elizabeth C. Clephane (1830–1869), which became widely known when set as a hymn by Ira D. Stankey (1840–1908) in 1874.

OUR TOWN

145.1   OUR TOWN] *Our Town* was first performed at the McCarter Theatre, Princeton, New Jersey, on January 22, 1938. Three days later, it began a weeklong run at Boston's Wilbur Theater, and opened in New York at Henry Miller's Theatre on February 4, 1938. The play was produced and directed by Jed Harris. Costumes were designed by Helene Pons; technical direction was by Raymond Sovey; the music was arranged and the organ played by Bernice Richmond. The cast was as follows:

Stage Manager	Frank Craven
Dr. Gibbs	Jay Fassett
Joe Crowell	Raymond Roe
Howie Newsome	Tom Fadden
Mrs. Gibbs	Evelyn Varden
Mrs. Webb	Helen Carew
George Gibbs	John Craven
Rebecca Gibbs	Marilyn Erskine
Wally Webb	Charles Wiley, Jr.
Emily Webb	Martha Scott
Professor Willard	Arthur Allen
Mr. Webb	Thomas W. Ross
Woman in the Balcony	Carrie Weller
Man in the Auditorium	Walter O. Hill
Lady in the Box	Aline McDermott
Simon Stimson	Philip Coolidge
Mrs. Soames	Doro Merande
Constable Warren	E. Irving Locke
Si Crowell	Billy Redfield
Baseball Players	Alfred Ryder, William Roehrick, Thomas Coley

Sam Craig . . . . Francis G. Cleveland
Joe Stoddard . . . . William Wadsworth
People of the Town: Carrie Weller, Alice Donaldson, Walter O. Hill, Arthur Allen, Charles Mellody, Katharine Raht, Mary Elizabeth Forbes, Dorothy Nolan, Jean Platt, Barbara Brown, Alda Stanley, Barbara Burton, Lyn Swann, Dorothy Ryan, Shirley Osborn, Emily Boileau, Ann Weston, Leon Rose, John Irving Finn, Van Shem, Charles Walters, William Short, Frank Howell, Max Beck, James Malaidy.

150.2   Canuck] Slang for Canadian, specifically for French-Canadians.

150.11   Bryan] William Jennings Bryan (1860–1925), known as "the silver-tongued orator," ran for president three times.

160.10   MacPherson's gauge] An authority on population figures, Logan Grant McPherson (1863–1925) was employed by American railroads as a statistician, and his computations were used by government and commercial agencies.

166.24   *"Blessed . . . Binds."*] The popular hymn "Blest Be the Tie That Binds," with words taken from the poem "Brotherly Love" (1782) by English clergyman John Fawcett (1740–1817).

167.32   "Art . . . Languid?"] The words of this hymn were written by the eighth-century Judean monk known as Stephen of Mar Saba; it was translated from the Greek in 1862 by John Mason Neale (1818–1866) and set to music in 1868 by Henry W. Baker (1818–1877).

175.19–21   Middle West poets . . . love life] Cf. the closing lines of "Lucinda Masters," from *Spoon River Anthology* (1915) by Edgar Lee Masters (1869–1950): "What is this I hear of sorrow and weariness, / Anger, discontent and drooping hopes? / Degenerate sons and daughters, / Life is too strong for you— / It takes life to love Life."

181.27–28   book . . . chickens] E. W. Philo, *The Philo System of Progressive Poultry-Keeping* (1911).

190.35–36   *"Love Divine, All Love Excelling"*] A hymn written in 1747 by Charles Wesley (1707–1788); it has been given several musical settings.

196.4   Woodlawn] The 400-acre Woodlawn Cemetery, established in 1863, is in the Bronx, and is a prominent burial ground for the New York City community.

196.13–14   Daughters of the American Revolution] A women's professional service organization founded in 1890. Membership is restricted to lineal descendants of patriots of the American Revolution.

211.1   THE SKIN OF OUR TEETH] See Job 19:20: "My bone cleaveth to my skin and to my flesh, and I am escaped with the skin of my teeth."

The Skin of Our Teeth opened at the Schubert Theatre in New Haven, Connecticut, on October 15, 1942, and traveled to Baltimore, Philadelphia, and Washington, D.C. It opened in New York at the Plymouth Theatre on November 18, 1942. The play was produced by Michael Myerberg, and directed by Elia Kazan. The sets were by Albert Johnson, costumes by Mary Percy Schenck. The cast was as follows:

Announcer	Morton DaCosta
Sabina	Tallulah Bankhead
Mr. Fitzpatrick	E. G. Marshall
Mrs. Antrobus	Florence Eldridge
Dinosaur	Remo Buffano
Mammoth	Andrew Ratousheff
Telegraph Boy	Dickie Van Patten
Gladys	Frances Heflin
Henry	Montgomery Clift
Mr. Antrobus	Frederic March
Doctor	Arthur Griffin
Professor	Ralph Kellard
Judge	Joseph Smiley
Homer	Ralph Cullinan
Miss E. Muse	Edith Faversham
Miss T. Muse	Emily Lorraine
Miss M. Muse	Eva Mudge Nelson
Usher	Stanley Prager
Usher	Harry Clark
Drum Majorettes	Elizabeth Scott, Patricia Riordan
Fortune Teller	Florence Reed
Chair Pusher	Earl Snydor
Chair Pusher	Carroll Clark
Conveener	Stanley Weede
Conveener	Seamus Flynn
Conveener	Aubrey Fassett
Conveener	Stanley Prager
Conveener	Harry Clark
Conveener	Stephan Cole
Broadcast Official	Morton DaCosta
Defeated Candidate	Joseph Smiley
Mr. Tremayne	Ralph Kellard
Hester	Eulabelle Moore
Ivy	Viola Dean
Fred Bailey	Stanley Prager

213.22 Genesis 11:18] "And the LORD God said, It is not good that the man should be alone; I will make him an help meet for him."

215.22 midst . . . death] "In the midst of life we are in death: of whom may we seek for succour, but of thee, O Lord, who for our sins art justly displeased?" From the Burial of the Dead service in *The Book of Common Prayer*.

217.24–25   *Peg . . . Bat*]   Popular Broadway shows in their time: *Peg o' My Heart* (1912), by John Hartley Manners (1870–1928); *Smilin' Through* (1919), by Allan Langdon Martin (pseudonym for Jane Murfin and Jane Cowl); and *The Bat* (1920), by Avery Hopwood (1882–1928) and Mary Roberts Rinehart (1876–1958).

217.30–31   I who've played *Rain . . . Lady*]   Tallulah Bankhead was in the cast of *Rain* (1935), adapted for the stage by John Colton and Clemence Randolph from Somerset Maugham's 1921 story "Miss Thompson," but did not appear in *The Barretts of Wimpole Street* (1931) by Rudolf Besier (1878–1942), or *First Lady* (1935) by Katherine Dayton and George S. Kaufman (1889–1961).

219.32   raped . . . Sabine hills]   According to legend, Roman soldiers abducted women of the Sabines, a tribe in ancient Italy, to help populate Rome. The subject has often been depicted by artists, including Giambologna, Poussin, and David.

225.18–19   *Tableau by Raphael . . . triangle*]   Raphael frequently used a triangular composition in his paintings; see, for example, his "Canigiani Holy Family" (1507) and "Sistine Madonna" (c. 1513).

234.9   HOMER:]   The opening lines of Homer's *Iliad*: "Sing, Goddess, of Achilles' vengeful wrath, / The son of Peleus who caused the Achaeans so many woes, / so many brave souls sent to Hell. . . ."

234.17   MOSES:]   The opening lines of Genesis: "In the beginning God created the heaven and the earth. And the earth was without form, and void; and darkness was upon the face of the deep. And the spirit of God moved upon the face of the waters."

238.5   "THE STAR" . . . LONGFELLOW]   Most likely either Longfellow's poem "The Evening Star" or "The Light of Stars."

255.14   Equity]   Actors' Equity Association, founded in 1913, is the labor union representing American actors and stage managers.

265.1   *"la fille du regiment"*]   The regiment's daughter.

268.18–20   "After experience . . . futile—"]   Cf. Baruch Spinoza (1632–1677), opening of "On the Improvement of the Intellect" (written around 1662, published posthumously in 1677).

268.28–29   "Then tell . . . not—"]   Wilder acknowledged that he made up this quotation as if it had been a question posed in Plato's *Critias*.

268.34–38   "This good estate . . . wonderful."]   An excerpt from Aristotle's *Metaphysics*, reworked from item 39 in the anthology edited by Robert

Seymour Bridges, *The Spirit of Man: An Anthology in English & French from the Philosophers & Poets* (London and New York, 1916).

285.1 THE MATCHMAKER] *The Matchmaker* is a revision of an earlier Wilder play, *The Merchant of Yonkers*, that was first published in 1939 and first performed at the Colonial Theatre, Boston, on December 12, 1938. It opened in New York at the Guild Theatre on December 28, 1938. It was presented by Herman Shumlin, directed by Max Reinhardt; the designer was Boris Aronson, and music was composed by Alexander Hass. The cast was as follows:

Horace Vandergelder	Percy Waram
Ambrose Kemper	Bartlett Robinson
Joe Scanlon	Philip Coolidge
Gertrude	Carrie Weller
Cornelius Hackl	Tom Ewall
Ermengarde	Frances Harison
Melchior Stack	Joseph Sweeney
Mrs. Levy	Jane Cowl
Barnaby Tucker	John Call
Mrs. Molloy	June Walker
Minnie Fay	Nydia Westman
A Cabman	Edward F. Nannery
Rudolph	Max Willenz
August	Peter Struwel
A Cook	Maida Reade
Miss Van Huysen	Minna Phillips

An English production of *The Merchant of Yonkers* opened at the Embassy Theatre in London on December 27, 1951, directed by Andre Van Gyseghem and starring Raymond Lovell as Horace Vandergelder and Sophie Stewart as Dolly Levi. The published edition of *The Merchant of Yonkers* includes this dedication: "To MAX REINHARDT with deep admiration and indebtedness."

In 1953, Wilder revised *The Merchant of Yonkers* and retitled it *The Matchmaker*. This version, written for the Edinburgh Festival and first tried out in Newcastle, opened at the Royal Lyceum Theatre, Edinburgh, on August 23, 1954. It was directed by Tyrone Guthrie, and designed by Tanya Moiseiwitsch. The cast was as follows:

Horace Vandergelder	Sam Levene
Cornelius Hackl	Arthur Hill
Barnaby Tucker	Alec McCowan
Malachi Stack	Patrick McAlinney
Ambrose Kemper	Jerry Stovin
Joe Scanlon	Peter Sallis
Rudolf	Timothy Findley
August	John Milligan
Cabman	Peter Bayliss
Dolly Levi	Ruth Gordon

Irene Molloy	Eileen Herlie
Minnie Fay	Rosamund Greenwood
Ermengarde	Prunella Scales
Gertrude	Henzie Raeburn
Flora Van Huysen	Esmé Church
Cook	Daphne Newton

After ten weeks on the road, it opened at the Theatre Royal, Haymarket, in London, on November 4, 1954. The part of Ambrose Kemper was played by Lee Montague, and A Musician by Peter Sallis. The next year it came to America, produced by the Theatre Guild and David Merrick, opening first at the Locust Street Theatre, Philadelphia, on October 27, 1955, where the part of Horace Vandergelder was taken by Eddie Mayehoff; next at the Colonial Theatre in Boston, on November 14, 1955, with Loring Smith as Horace Vandergelder; and finally at the Royale Theatre in New York, on December 5, 1955. In the Broadway production Loring Smith played Horace Vandergelder, Robert Morse played Barnaby Tucker, Alexander Davion played Ambrose Kemper, Charity Grace played Gertrude, William Lanteau played Rudolf, Philip Leeds played Joe Scanlon and A Musician, and Christine Thomas played Cook.

In the 1957 edition of *Three Plays*, Wilder included the following note: "This play is a rewritten version of *The Merchant of Yonkers*, which was directed in 1938 by Max Reinhardt and is again dedicated to MAX REINHARDT with deep admiration and indebtedness."

286.24–27   This play . . . Oxenford] First staged in Vienna in 1842, *Einen Jux will er sich Machen* (*He Just Wants to Have Fun*) is a play by popular and influential Austrian playwright and actor Johann Nepomuk Nestroy (1801–1862), a master of burlesque comedies laced with social satire. John Oxenford (1812–1877) was a playwright, critic, and translator, notably from the German. His play *A Well Spent Day* was first performed in 1835.

301.30   Her duck! Her steak!] "The following passage—adapted from a scene in Molière's *L'Avare*—has been cut in recent performances" (note in *Three Plays*, 1957). The passage extends from Mrs. Levi's "Her duck! Her steak" to her "No exaggeration" (301.40). Cf. Molière, *The Miser*, II.v.

302.17–18   Lochinvars] Lochinvar is a romantic hero in the long narrative poem *Marmion* (1808), Canto V, by Sir Walter Scott (1771–1832).

302.22   I hope . . . hm] "Following passage—also based on Molière—has generally been cut in performance" (note in *Three Plays*). The passage extends from Vandergelder's line here to Mrs. Levi's "Yes, sir, that's money." Cf. Molière, *The Miser*, II.v.

323.23   Raritan Canal] Canal built in the 1830s in central New Jersey to connect the Delaware River and the Raritan River, to help transport freight by barge between Philadelphia (and the coal mines of eastern Pennsylvania) to New York City.

328.34   *"Tenting tonight*]   With words and music written in 1863 by Walter Kittredge (1834–1905), this was one of the most popular and haunting of
all songs during the Civil War.

338.35   *"Les Patineurs" waltz*]   *Les Patineurs Valse* ("Skaters' Waltz"), an
1882 salon favorite composed by Emile Waldteufel (1837–1915).

345.23   *"The Sidewalks of New York"*]   Song (1894) with words by Charles
B. Lawlor (1852–1925) and music by James W. Blake (1862–1935); its chorus begins with the well-known lines, "East Side, West Side, / All around the town."

363.29   Trinity Church]   Church at Broadway and Wall Street in Lower
Manhattan, founded in 1697. The present building on the site was built in
1846, and includes a neo-Gothic spire.

THE ALCESTIAD

369.1   *The Alcestiad*, retitled *A Life in the Sun*, was performed at the 1955
Edinburgh Festival. It opened on August 22 at The Church of Scotland As-
sembly Hall, The Mound, produced by the Edinburgh Festival Society and
Tennant Productions Limited, directed by Tyrone Guthrie, and designed by
Tanya Moiseiwitsch. The cast was as follows:

Apollo	Michael David
Death	John Kidd
First Watchman	Laurence Hardy
Alcestis	Irene Worth
Aglaia	Madeleine Christie
Teiresias	Geoffrey Dunn
Boy	David Gloag
Admetus	Robert Hardy
First Herdsman	Philip Guard
Second Herdsman	John Scolan
Third Herdsman	Peter Fox
Fourth Herdsman	Peter Duguid
Hercules	Rupert Davies
Second Watchman	Peter Baylis
Epimenes	Alexander Davion
Cheriander	Michael Bates
Agis	Robert Speaight
First Guard	Timothy Findley
Third Guard	John Greig
Fourth Guard	David Saxby
Servants	Jennifer Wright, Mary Wylie

People of Thessaly: William Robertson, John Macdonald, William Lyon
Brown, Joyce Allan, Betty Thorburn, Joyce C. Kerr, Ann Tirard, Helena
Gloag, Ann Gibson, Peter Smallwood, Pat Magee

Unfavorable criticism of the production led Wilder to withdraw the acting rights. He next revised the play, added the satyr play, *The Drunken Sisters*, and in a German translation by Herberth E. Herlitschka (*Die Alkestiade: Schauspiel in drei Akten mit einem Satyrspiel Die Beschwipsten Schwestern*), it was successfully produced at the Schauspielhaus in Zurich, opening on June 27, 1957. It was directed by Leopold Lindtberg, with sets by Teo Otto, costumes by Elisaveth Schmid, and music by Rolf Langnese. The cast was as follows:

Apollo	Erich Schellow
Der Tod	Peter Oehme
Ein alter Nachtwächter	Erwin Parker
Alkestis	Maria Becker
Aglaja	Traute Carlsen
Teiresias	Herman Wlach
Ein Knabe	Ronald Brunner
Admetus, König von Thessalien	Peter Lühr
Ein Hirt	Wolfgang Stendar
Ein junger Nachtwächter	Claus A. Landsittel
Epimenes	Alfons Höckmann
Cheriander	Peter Brogle
Agis, König von Thrakien	Heinz Woester
1. Leibgardist	Hans Jedlitschka
2. Leibgardist	Kurt Brunner
3. Leibgardist	Friedrich Braun
Rhodope, eine Dienerin	Edith Golay
Klotho	Elisabeth Wenger
Latchesis . . . Parzen	Josy Holsten
Athropos	Angelica Arndts

This German text was published by S. Fischer Verlag in April 1960. The original English acting edition and the later German version were used to make the final English version, edited by Donald Gallup, and published in November 1977, two years after Wilder's death. An acting edition, with a foreword by Wilder's sister Isabel, was published in 1980. The first American professional production, under the title *Alcestis and Apollo*, was mounted by the Great Lakes Shakespeare Festival in Cleveland, Ohio, on August 25, 1978. An operatic version of *The Alcestiad*, with a libretto by Wilder and music by Louise Talma (1906–1996) was published in 1978 by Carl Fisher as *The Alcestiad: An Opera in Three Acts*. In a German translation by Herberth E. Herlitschke, it had its world premiere at Frankfurt's Alte Oper on March 2, 1962, directed by Harry Buckwitz, with Inge Borkh in the title role.

371.16   Pherai]   An important town in Thessaly. According to myth, Admetus was its founder and first king.

375.5   Pelias, King of Iolcos]   Ruler of a town in Thessaly; he sent Jason and his Argonauts in search of the Golden Fleece.

398.33–34   the Nemean lion . . . the stables of King Augeas] Two of the twelve labors imposed on Hercules by King Eurystheus, whom Apollo had ordered Hercules to serve in atonement for the murder his own wife and children in a fit of madness. The people of Nemea had been threatened by a ferocious lion, which Hercules killed by grasping it in his arms and squeezing it to death. Afterward he wore the lion's skin. Augeus, king of Elis, kept a huge herd of oxen in a stable he never cleaned; Hercules diverted a river through the stable to cleanse it.

407.2   the Hydra] Another of the labors of Hercules was to kill the Hydra, a many-headed water snake. When he at first struck off one of the monster's heads, two others grew in its place. With the help of his charioteer, who applied a brand to each new wound, Hercules eventually killed the Hydra.

UNCOLLECTED PLAYS

447.1   *The Marriage We Deplore*] Not published during Wilder's lifetime, this play was written when Wilder was a sophomore at Yale, and is dated "June 10, [19]17."

449.20–21   Forbes-Robertson] Sir Johnston Forbes-Robertson (1853–1937), renowned English actor who was considered the greatest Hamlet of his day.

450.27–28   *Billie Burke's*] Stage and movie actress Mary William Burke (1884–1970), wife of Broadway producer Florenz Ziegfeld.

453.1   *The Unerring Instinct*] This play was written in late 1947 at the request of the National Conference of Christians and Jews, whose "Scripts for Brotherhood" program distributed it free to schools and dramatic clubs throughout the country until at least the mid-1960s. Accompanying publicity material described it as the "story of a woman whose fears and sweeping judgments of people are swept away when she is shown how susceptible she is to nonsensical talk. For high school and adult groups."

456.34–35   Al Smith . . . States?] Alfred Emanuel Smith (1873–1944), four times elected governor of New York between 1918 and 1926, was the Democratic candidate for president in 1928, and lost to Herbert Hoover.

461.6   Kate Smith] Kathryn Elizabeth Smith (1907–1986), a popular singer best known for her rendition of Irving Berlin's "God Bless America."

461.6   Mary Pickford, born Smith] Mary Pickford (1892–1979), born Gladys Smith, actress and glamorous star of the silent-movie era.

462.1–2   SCENES . . . *Emporium*] In 1948, steeped in his readings in existentialism, Wilder began work on a new play, *The Emporium*, which he intended, in the words of his literary executor Donald Gallup, to be "influenced by both Kierkegaard and Gertrude Stein, combining the atmosphere of Kafka's *The Castle* with a Horatio-Alger theme." By the next year he had drafted several scenes, which he read to friends, but he grew uncertain of their order and direction, and abandoned them. Between 1952 and 1954 he resumed work on the play, and commented on its progress to the press. For instance, in 1953 he told a German reporter: "The mysterious divine plan is not accessible to us. Eternity will balance the ledger; we are only agents and sufferers. I am attempting to shape these thoughts in a parareligious form in my new drama 'The Emporium.' I have been working on it for three years now, but I am in no hurry. I follow the inner law of maturation without pressure."

Two scenes from the play—the first two in this volume—were printed as an appendix in Donald Gallup's 1985 edition of Wilder's journals. Two more scenes, seemingly complete in themselves, have been added here. Excerpts from Gallup's edition of the journals show Wilder's thoughts on the play while he was working on it:

HMS "Mauretania," Eve of arriving at Cobh, September 21, 1948. My new play.
In May an elderly woman whom I did not know wrote me from Washington. She said that Dr. [Les] Glenn in church had recounted my "Empress of Newfoundland" story and thanked me for it. It did not then occur to me that it would serve as a project. I rejected it as I did most of the others as being sentimental. During my last week at home, however, I reread Kafka's *The Castle* with mounting excitement and, resolving to do a play of Kafka's atmosphere, the Newfoundland story suddenly slid into place as furnishing a possible framework for such a project. Dining alone with Mrs. [X] one night, I outlined such a play, combining it with the Horatio-Alger idea.

Now on board ship it has given me two nights of almost total insomnia and is in a fair way to determine itself as the next work I shall offer.

At present its state is as follows:

(1) An opening scene in an orphanage. A boy, aged about ten, has run away. Alarm over the countryside. Boy brought back. Superintendent and wife plead with him. His mutism. His whispered declaration that he wants to "belong." Dream atmosphere—they are and are not his parents.

(2) Scene Two. Tom [his name is later changed to Daniel, and finally to John] has been placed on a farm. Scene opens with wife holding lamp and calling to Tom hiding behind barn. Pleading that he will apologize to the farmer in order to escape daily beating; the real resentment of farmer is that Tom will not call him father. (Night scene, but in this scenery-less play, lights are not lowered to represent darkness. The upheld lamp is not even lit, but understood as lit. Tom, mute and distrustful, stands in theatre aisle, advancing and retreating.) Farmer returns; whips Tom offstage. Tom attacks him; reenters. Seizes locket about the neck of farmer's wife. Her treasure: a medal for faithful service long ago at the Emporium in the City. The beauty, wonder, and mystery of the Emporium.

(3) Perhaps Tom's first interview as applicant to work in the Emporium. Or boarding-house in New York: his efforts to get near the Emporium.

Here disturbance at back of theatre auditorium: a patron has heard that this play has a prologue: it has been omitted this evening; he insists on

seeing the whole play. It is explained to him that it is not certain that the prologue is by the author; [that] it was found one morning under Mr. [Arthur]
Hopkins's door; that it gives the play a different meaning, etc. Patron insists.

Prologue. A nephew of either Mr. Fitch or Mr. Westman of the Emporium
seems likely to inherit a high office in the store. The draught or potion.

So far is becoming firm.

Difficulties are: how to make Part Two—the effort to convey the Kafka-
Castle character of the Emporium, Tom's agonized desire to belong to it,
etc.—how to convey it as drama, and to do it without leaning too closely on
The Castle. And how to prevent Scene Two of Part One from too closely re-
sembling a scene from Faulkner's *Light in August*—Joe Christmas's flight
from his foster-parents.

It may be that Part Two will take an entirely different turn: the story of a
girl also burningly fixated on the Emporium. Alger theme of marrying the
boss's daughter.

*The Gresham Hotel, Dublin. Wednesday, September 23 [22], 1948. Of "The Em-
porium" (New Working-title of the Play, già "Pluck and Luck").*

Another night of insomnia, begoaded by the play straining to be born.
This time I am well along in Part Two. Another: "old idea": that of the person emerging from a long prison term, has coalesced with my theme. . . .

It is not impossible that most of the material that I've been thinking up
during these feverish nights may turn out to be bad, but that is the way it's
done. One becomes aware of the central idea of the play tearing around in
one's head trying to find the clothes in which it must be dressed, or, rather,
the concrete elements on which it must feed, picking up old motifs and re-
jecting them, or suddenly discovering that they will serve, modifying them to
its purposes and then, with a rush, expanding them and exploring their unexpected possibilities.

Hotel Russell, [Dublin,] September 25, 1948. Of "The Emporium."

A bad day yesterday. I attacked the Prologue, got quite a ways with it, and
then recognized that it was all wrong. I still have no idea how I shall be able
to manage, but after today's work I feel confident that it is there, waiting
somehow, and can be done.

Today, in spite of a bothersome change of hotel just after lunch, I wrote
Scene Four (The Employment Office) as far as Tom's "false exit." I finished
writing the passage under strong emotion; it can hardly be as good as that, but
I feel that it hits the tone and gets the stride better than any of the sections
written so far. Vaguely during the morning I had said to myself that I would
try that "employment interview" next; but I shrink from doing it. It presented
itself then as a not very vital interrogation of Tom, based upon a few easily
foreseen motifs and climaxed by his presentation of Mrs. Graham's medal. As
I lay down to take a much-needed nap, I asked myself how I could start the
scene, *i.e.,* establish the atmosphere of the employment agency. I . . .
thought of the Employment Office addressing a few words to a waiting

queue offstage (last night [his sister] Isabel and I stood so long in queue for Charlie Chaplin's [film] "Monsieur Verdoux" that we finally gave it up); then suddenly the idea came of having the queue in the audience, in fact the audience itself. There was no sleeping after that and I got up and wrote the Scene.

Now the play takes shape and a new concern enters my mind. The play as it now projects itself will be all right, but it will have for me the drawback of being about one thing: the baffling search for the Right Way. I am disappointed in plays that turn endlessly on one subject (*Othello* has always seemed to be for this reason less rich than the other tragedies). I would like to run some counter-motif into this one. . . .

[Hotel Russell, Dublin,] the Next Morning.

Before I fell asleep last night I made myself face the fact that not only have I not got an ending to this play, I haven't even got a middle body to it. That note I made about wishing to enrich the texture with other interests was a projection of my uneasiness that by Scene Six, I should have exhausted even the primary interest.

What I dimly see is that Tom must go through the *noche oscura del alma* [dark night of the soul], the abysmal despair about the Emporium's concern for him, followed by his frenzied repudiation of all that the Emporium once meant to him: which leaves it to Laurencia to show that she "lives always in the Emporium" and to be unshaken by the fact that in any relation to the Emporium, human beings are always in the wrong.

Steffani Hotel, St. Moritz, December 27, 1948. "The Emporium."

. . . I see that I don't yet know how to write this play. I haven't thought deeply enough. If this is all I've got I'd better throw it away. It has been wildly shallow in me to think that the ticket-buyer in Row Q could ever understand that the Laurencia I have so far devised could represent the Knight of Perfect Resignation, or She Who Is Always in Abraham's Bosom— those to whom Faith is both self-evident and also hourly re-won; that Tom (henceforward, perhaps, called Daniel) could similarly be understood for several scenes as exhibiting the *Angst* before the Good. My concern is of course not with the spectator in Row Q, but with myself in Row Q, and as always any stupidity comes from the fact that I have not found the common-common way of stating these things—*i.e.*, of feeling them validly in myself; for if they are not common-common they are not good enough for me. I have found them in books (in Kierkegaard), but if they are not in me (or potentially, with passion potentially in me) they have no business messing up my play. . . . Oh, the difficulty of establishing the Emporium as the Excellent, as Gertrude [Stein]'s Human Mind [as set forth in her 1936 *The Geographical History of America, or The Relation of Human Nature to the Human Mind*, for which Wilder wrote an introduction], and at the same time making it somehow fleetingly represent what centuries have called God—as the Other. Here I must clearly depart from Kafka's overstrained frustration, while still clinging to Kierkegaard. . . .

[Claridge Hotel, Atlantic City, N. J.,] May 7, 1949. "The Emporium."

At least during the sketches these next few days to try another attack: that all-out allegorical of which I have been afraid hitherto.

That it is a *Pilgrim's Progress*.

That it is the Decision of Hercules.

To balance continuously the Three Categories, the Bad, the Good, and the Other.

Here the difficulty will be to find and to plant three mouthpieces, the *raisonneurs*, or the "explanations."

I hate allegory, and here I am deep in allegory. . . . The Orphanage, then, is Childhood; it is the Family; it is the World into which the Child is dropped as an "orphan": it is neither Good nor Bad, but both. Its alternations between Good and Bad disorganize the Child, prepare the Anxiety, and hence prepare him for the claims of the Other.

The Farmhouse of Act [i.e, Scene] Two is the Bad—the Bad all the worse for representing in Mrs. Graham a relapse from the Other. Mr. Graham [the farmer] is the Bad—*i.e.*, the Self exploiting itself under the guise of the Good. The difficulty will be to get this into the dialogue.

The difficulty of Scenes Three and Four will be to show how Daniel's thirst for the Other turns into hatred and dread of the Other—and most difficult to make it clear (*i.e.*, explain it) to the audience.

Sunday [August 9, 1953].

I have reached the point where Mr. Craigie offers John the store and his daughter's hand. If this is to be the first scene of the play I am in a world of difficulties. The audience which receives this at 8:45 [p.m.] is in the presence of mere story-telling. Its only interest can be in what-will-happen-next. My dimensions are not wide and poignant enough to generate in this audience a passion to know, also, what happened before. This, then, is either not the first scene, or it is not correctly written. The play should begin with a vast reversal or a coming-to-himself.

Peterborough, [N.H.,] Tuesday, August 18, 1953.

Vacillation. Insecurity in progress. But what it comes down to is that I cannot make any decision about form or anecdote until I discover the next characteristic of the Store—the next image or merely fact or symbol—to feed the curiosity of the audience which is the true life of the play. And the difficulty lies in the fact that I must present the characteristic under the form of a department store's operation. And what I am looking for is something dealing with the fact that the Absolute "sells" primarily to the individual and is only individually perceived. And this I must do by presenting the contrast of this method to the method employed over at Craigie's. The classic way of presenting this is, I suppose, Hans Christian Andersen's story of the King who has no clothes. Each person sees the Emporium and its goods differently; while Craigie and all its objects are of equal valuation to all its customers . . .

September 7, 1953.
Twisting and turning. Rewriting scene after scene. Forever trying to focus and define the two great problems behind this play: what is the Emporium?; and how to bring into highlight the qualities it has in common with a department store while attenuating and veiling the qualities it *hasn't* in common. . . .

February 16, 1954.
But what my play above all lacks is passion—which, in all the forms that passion could take, is here the *movement* of the passion of people seeking the "Right Way." I feel that it is present in the first scenes, but it slips away, somehow, between the scenes. The figure of John must be a hot-winging arrow that carries the whole play with it. And it seems to me that the reason I've lost it is that I haven't been clear in my head as to what obstacle it is that prevents his being invited to enter the Emporium. I shy away from facing this problem because every side-glance at it seems to lead toward moralizing *platement* [French: dully]: he lacks humility; he refuses to renounce worldly success, etc.

But we decided—didn't we?—that the qualification of the Emporium-worker was that he could "do a thing alone"—nay, that nothing worthwhile was done save unaided (whereby G[ertrude]. S[tein]. enters the play). There too all the pitfalls of eupeptic moralizing lurk, but less flagrantly; this introduces, rather, the pitfalls of the sentimental and pathetic. So that John can be represented as desiring the G. and S. and yet incapable of seeing that success, etc. are forms of dependency. Now it would seem that for this we need a *raisonneur* or *raisonneuse*, probably several.

Let me return to the text and see what I can do.

Walked downtown.

Now it seems to me that we can follow this line: Scene One: Orphanage; Scene Two: The Graham Farm; Scene Three: First Floor of the Emporium; Scene Four: The Employment Office; Scene Five: First Floor of the Emporium (terminating with John's dream). . . .

February 23, 1954.
. . . What the play needs is a larger deeper happier immersion on my part in what it's all about. Today the emphasis is on *happier*, for the sign that all is going well in this portentous and often painful subject matter will be that it will be permeated with the comic.

Oh, the form isn't bold and splendid and revolutionary enough. That's why I'm so inhibited and tentative and scratchily groping.

Now let me put down some of the fancies that have been crossing my mind in this matter of form,—not because they are the *eureka*, but because they give me imaginative practice in bold form-shattering invention.

(Before I put them down I want to add another thing: when I find the right form—the right statement for this cosmological comedy—wouldn't it be wonderful if I could do it without those names of celebrated orphans—those names of the painters and music-makers of the Emporium? To other people—but not to me—they bring in the smell of professor and historian. Not to me, because "culture" is in me a second nature. Hitherto it has always seemed to me that the "comic" aspect of their introduction into the play—the anachronistic game, for instance,—saved them from the academic stink—but *even* I, as I have expressed it several times in the Journal, am aware that in those names, through those names, is felt the hated didactic formal-symbolic strain. After all, Kafka did it without names.) . . .

June 17, 1954.

. . . It's the Hero I haven't got right—the Hero and the Girl. Since the play, by very reason of its mode of staging, to say nothing of the vast impli-cations of the theme, the wrestling with the Absolute, is about the type Hero, let's do the eternal Hero myth. I have been too much drawn into the Kafka hero, the frustrated pre-condemned struggler. That's not my bent; I'm not the stuff of which nihilists are made; I'm not even sympathetic toward the broken-winged; all that derived from a mimetic sympathetic admiration for the Kafka vision, perhaps merely for the Kafka art, the virtuosity with which he could present his maimed soul. I want to liberate myself from the Kafka hero—and can we call Hero the man who dies "*wie ein Hund*" [like a dog; from final line of Kafka's *The Trial*]?—while at the same time retaining that element in Kafka which is real to me, the seduction and the ambiguity and the terror of the Absolute?

So back to the Hero.

Let us bear in mind the eternal myth-patterns of the Hero—viewed not only as the Exceptional Man but as the potential in every man. His birth is surrounded with mystery. At first all he knows is the beatific, timeless, effort-less floating in the womb. Then he is separated from that nirvana—the ego emerges as he becomes aware of an Outside which is not the self. He has two mothers: the benignant goddess of all living and the baleful enemy-mother who wishes to retain him in nirvana, to draw him back to the chaos of in-stinctual life. He has two fathers: the warrior-worker-creator to emulate; and the jealous old man who wishes to restrain and maim and kill him. He sets out on the quest for a treasure: the treasure is a virgin. He must win her through trials and perils.

At once I see that I have wasted time over the choice between Emporium and Craigie. (Yes, there is a play there, a theme there, but it is secondary to the more basic theme of the Hero's journey—and it has led me all this time into a resort to the tiresome moralizing side of my "formation.")

Let us say that our Hero does get into the Emporium at once, but at the ground floor: he is a package-wrapper in the basement.

The Girl is the daughter not of Craigie's but of the Emporium. She is guarded against young heroes, because even Excellence becomes tyrannical and conservative-petrified. The Emporium is old-fashioned and airless; the

Hero wins the daughter of the Emporium and the power to refresh and renew it.

Now I can play with this business of the Older Actress playing the successive Good and Bad Mothers; and the Older Actor playing the Good and Bad Fathers. The Orphanage-Mother is Good, but against John's being sent away. The Orphanage-Father is Stern-Justice. The Farmer's Wife is in one scene both Good and Bad. (Can that be done?)

There is in the first Emporium Scene (this is just groping now) no Laurencia? John comes up at closing time from the bowels of the Emporium and inveighs against its airlessness, etc., and hears, again, about the Virgin-Princess.

It also sounds (1) excruciatingly schematized and (2) oriented toward a sunburst of a happy-ending; but let's see what can be done with it. . . .

466.29   Gustav Froebel Foster] Friedrich Wilhelm August Froebel (1782–1852), German educator, established the first kindergarten in 1837.

467.21   Joseph Severn Foster] Joseph Severn (1793–1873), English painter and friend of John Keats.

496.1   PLAYS FOR BLEEKER STREET] While staying in Saratoga Springs, New York, during the summer of 1956, Wilder began a series of "Four-Minute Plays for Four Persons," reminiscent of his much earlier series, "Three-Minute Plays for Three Persons," the best of which were gathered in *The Angel That Troubled the Waters and Other Plays.* Almost at once, the plays began to exceed the limitations he had imposed, and he began specifically to envision them for an arena stage, or theater in the round. In 1957, he published *The Drunken Sisters* in the *Atlantic Monthly,* and used it as the satyr play to conclude *The Alcestiad.* That same year, he agreed to let the American National Theater and Academy stage *Bernice* and *The Wreck on the Five-Twenty-Five* as part of a program of short American plays (others were by Eugene O'Neill, Tennessee Williams, and William Saroyan) to dedicate the new Congress Hall in West Berlin. Wilder withdrew the plays, but in 1958 he began working again on what he came to see as a series based on the Seven Deadly Sins, the order of which was established by spring 1959: *The Drunken Sisters* (Gluttony), *Bernice* (Pride), *The Wreck on the Five-Twenty-Five* (Sloth), *A Ringing of Doorbells* (Envy), *In Shakespeare and the Bible* (Wrath), *Someone from Assisi* (Lust), and *Cement Hands* (Avarice). In May 1959 he agreed that the Circle in the Square Theatre, with its arena stage ("the beauty and power of the arena stage," he wrote, "is that it diminishes all that is not in the high sense poetic"), could produce the series when he had completed it. A year later, it was still unfinished, and Wilder had begun work on a new series of plays based on the Seven Ages of Man. With fourteen plays in mind, he decided to let the Circle in the Square, located on Bleeker Street in New York City, mount three of them as an evening called *Plays for Bleeker Street,* which opened on January 11, 1962. The plays were *Infancy, Childhood,* and *Someone from Assisi.* The theater planned to add the remaining plays to the repertory as they were ready, over a period of six years. But none of the other plays were staged in his lifetime, and he did not complete the Seven Ages of Man series.

496.3 *Bernice*] First produced in English at the Congress Hall in West Berlin, in September 1957. In the cast were Ethel Waters and the author, along with Hiram Sherman and John Becher; the director was Lamont Johnson. The play was published in a German translation by Herberth E. Herlitschka as *Berenike, oder Der Stolz* in *Die Neue Rundschau 71*, no. 4 (1960), and first published in English in *The Yale Review 85*, no. 2 (April 1997). The American stage premiere took place as part of "The Thornton Wilder Play Festival" at the Hill School in Pottstown, Pennsylvania, on February 18, 1997. In his journal for December 2, 1956, Wilder writes: "'Bernice' is salvaged from the scenario I sent to Vittorio De Sica when he asked me to work with him on a movie ['Rain in Chicago,' based on Ben Hecht's 1943 novel *Miracle in the Rain*, a project eventually abandoned]. It does not use the principal idea behind that scenario (then called 'Jones')—the experimental assumption of roles in life in order to discover one's essential function; but the returned convict and the Negress as advisor are from the original."

507.1 *The Wreck on the Five-Twenty-Five*] First staged at the Congress Hall in West Berlin in September 1957 (in English). In the cast were Lillian Gish and Hiram Sherman, along with John Becher and Cynthia Baxter; the director was Lamont Johnson. First published in *The Yale Review 82*, no. 4 (October 1994). The American stage premiere took place in May 1995, as part of "Marathon '95," a series produced by the Ensemble Studio Theatre in New York. In his journal for November 24, 1958, Wilder writes: "'The Wreck on the Five-Twenty-Five' will require the addition of a few words to show that the type of despair into which the hero falls is, precisely, in Dante's sense, an unwillingness to accept the gifts of life: 'Sullen we were in the bright air.' [Cf. *Inferno*, Canto 7, lines 121–24]"

513.35 Rotary] Rotary International, a worldwide network of service clubs, was formed in Chicago in 1905. Its name derives from the early practice of rotating club meetings among members' offices. Its motto is "Service Above Self."

514.25 "*Valencia*"] Spanish composer José Padilla (1889–1960) wrote many zarzuelas, operettas, and popular songs. His international celebrity is largely based on "Valencia," a *pasodoble* from his 1924 zarzuela *La bien amada*.

515.20–21 breathes . . . dead] "Breathes there a man with soul so dead, / Who never to himself hath said, / 'This is my own, my native land!'": the opening lines of Canto Sixth of *The Lay of the Last Minstrel* by Sir Walter Scott (1771–1832).

520.1 *A Ringing of Doorbells*] First published in *The Collected Short Plays of Thornton Wilder, Vol. I*, ed. Donald Gallup and A. Tappan Wilder (New York: Theatre Communications Group, 1997). The bracketed material at the end of the play is based on research in the Thornton Wilder Collection at Yale's Beinecke Library by F. J. O'Neil. His note about the end of "A Ringing of Doorbells" is included in *The Collected Short Plays* as an afterword to the play:

In June 1957, Thornton Wilder wrote in his journal that *In Shakespeare and the Bible* and *A Ringing of Doorbells* were plays he could "terminate any day, but which will never be finished" [*Journals*, June 14, 1957].

The author's manuscript of *A Ringing of Doorbells* ended abruptly with this exchange:

MRS. BEATTIE (*Firmly but not sharply to Daphne*): Have you a remarkable voice?

DAPHNE: No.

MRS. KINKAID: Daphne!

MRS. BEATTIE:

Just how "terminated" is the play? The answer would appear to be: all but Mrs. Beattie's last line. After dinner one evening at his home in Hamden, Connecticut, Thornton Wilder read aloud to me a nearly complete draft of this play and spoke of his plan to bring the story to a logical, but unconventional, conclusion. Mrs. Beattie, as envious of the Kinkaids as they are of her, wants to help them in spite of their attempt to trick her. A fair solution then to the missing last line seemed to be a reprise of Mrs. Beattie's earlier line: "Alive and together . . . that's the point," as her summing up at the point of decision. The stage directions that I added are consistent with what appears to be Wilder's intention. Combining the antique cabinet and the telephone, both already established in the text, with a writing kit and checkbook, allows a moment of suspense as Mrs. Beattie moves toward the desk, and the a final tableau as she turns back to face the Kinkaids, checkbook in hand.

524.24   (*She is out*)]   Added in *Collected Short Plays, Vol. I*.

532.27–36   (*Mrs. Beattie . . . fade.*)]   Added in *Collected Short Plays, Vol. I*. (see note 520.1).

533.1   *In Shakespeare and the Bible*]   First published in *The Collected Short Plays of Thornton Wilder, Vol. I*.

543.31   Kate]   Heroine of Shakespeare's *The Taming of the Shrew*.

551.26–27   (*She . . . arm*)]   This stage direction, as well as the two parenthetical stage directions that follow (at 551.28–29 and 551.31–35), were added in *Collected Short Plays, Vol. I*. The passages are based on research in the Thornton Wilder Collection at Yale's Beinecke Library by F. J. O'Neil. His note is included in *The Collected Short Plays* as an afterword to the play:

The author's manuscript of *In Shakespeare and the Bible* existed in three nearly completed drafts, the latest of which had a number of rewrites, additions and corrections toward a fourth draft. Pages and sections of the earlier drafts, which were lined-through or crossed-out, have been examined but have not played a significant part in assembling this version of the play. Wilder's habit of throwing out what he emphatically rejected ("The writer's best friend is his wastebasket," is a motto he often articulated), but keeping around what he might refer to again and *use* again provided a richly marked road map to the play printed here.

Wilder leaves us wondering whether John will succumb to the strong impulse to grab success at any cost. For this reason I added stage directions (in brackets) at the end to give John a moment to collect his thoughts, wonder what the right path is, and then, at least for the moment, to cave in.

552.1   *Someone from Assisi*]   First produced in New York as one of the three "Plays for Bleecker Street" at the Circle in the Square Theater, *Someone from Assisi* premiered on January 10, 1962, directed by José Quintero. It starred Sandra MacDonald, Betty Miller, Dolores Dorn, and Lee Richardson. The script, reproduced from a typed copy, was distributed by Samuel French in 1964. Its first commercial publication was in *The Collected Short Plays of Thornton Wilder, Vol. I*, ed., Donald Gallup and A. Tappan Wilder (1997). While musing in his journal (November 24, 1958) on his group of plays about the Seven Deadly Sins, Wilder wrote: "As I groped in the extremely difficult problem of 'exemplifying' *Luxuria*, there came back to my mind that notion I had long had of doing a St. Francis before the conversion: that saints are monsters of nature that have hesitated, been good and evil at their extremes. This promises to be a most extraordinary play, indeed, and full of matter not often said." And on December 7, while in Salzburg, he added: "The difficulty of 'Someone from Assisi' is to carry the burden of two tremendous elements as subordinate to elements that must overweigh them—*i.e.*, brief summarized sketches of the characteristics of a St. Francis and a St. Clara as merely contributive to the idea of the Erotic as Destroyer and the Erotic as Creative."

559.25–26   you were christened John]   St. Francis of Assisi (1182–1226) was born Giovanni di Bernadone. His mother (whose name was Pica) was of French origin and when she died his father gave him the pet name of Francesco ("Little Frenchman").

566.1   *Cement Hands*]   The first public reading of this play took place on April 15, 1997, at the University Club in New York as part of "A Wilder Evening," the MacDowell Colony's celebration of the Thornton Wilder Centennial. The reading was directed by Elizabeth Diamond, and starred Kevin Kline, William Meisle, Sarah Knowlton, and Thomas McCarthy. Originally entitled "The Cabots," *Cement Hands* was first published in *The Collected Short Plays of Thornton Wilder, Vol. I*. In a journal entry dated July 2, 1960, Wilder wrote: "I wrote my little play 'Cement Hands' about avarice among the generous and philanthropic millionaires. It is a failure, and I shall probably have to tear it up; but it exhibits the beginnings of some good analysis. And, as so often, it started me thinking after the work was written."

584.1   *Infancy*]   First produced in New York as one of the three "Plays for Bleecker Street" at the Circle in the Square Theater, it premiered on January 10, 1962, directed by José Quintero. It starred Jack Dodson, Mary Doyle, Macintyre Dixon, Charlotte Jones, and Richard Libertini. An acting edition was published by Samuel French in 1961. It was included in *The Collected Short Plays of Thornton Wilder, Vol. I.*

591.24   Richmond]   Staten Island.

599.1   *Childhood*]   Published in 1960 in the *Atlantic Monthly* (November) and in an acting edition by Samuel French. First produced in New York as one of the three "Plays for Bleecker Street" at the Circle in the Square Theater, it premiered on January 10, 1962, directed by José Quintero. It starred Debbie Scott, Susan Towers, Philip Visco, Betty Miller, and Dana Elcar. In his journal for March 24, 1960, Wilder wrote: "In *Childhood*, I use something I none too clearly remember from *The Interpretation of Dreams* (and by the light of that book, observed in my own dreaming): that an important person in one's dream, whom one's censor does not wish to identify and acknowledge, appears veiled or masked, or seen from the back only. So my children's father and mother."

614.8–9   "The son . . . gambolier]   "The Son of a Gambolier" is a traditional English, or possibly Scottish, folk song. *Gambolier*: a worthless fellow, given to drink and carousing.

616.1   *Youth*]   First published in *The Collected Short Plays of Thornton Wilder, Vol. I.* , in which F. J. O'Neil, whose research and editing helped establish the text, writes:

> The author's manuscript existed in a partial typescript, which contained Wilder's handwritten corrections interleaved with several handwritten pages of clearly indicated revised material. The author's manuscript ended with Gulliver's speech to Belinda, spoken while Simpson listens hidden from their view. To conclude the play for production, I felt it would be helpful to take into account Wilder's most plausible intention: that Swift's Gulliver, only borrowed for this adventure, be returned safely to London and his place in English literature.
>
> What then of Simpson and Belinda? Belinda had earlier insisted to Simpson that Gulliver was not strong enough to make the trip alone. Her plea that Simpson accompany Gulliver in the escape strongly suggests that Wilder intended Simpson and Gulliver to leave the island together. Simpson had been sent off with the tool that unlocks the boats. Further, there is the duke's threat that Simpson will be put to the press if he fails in his guard duties. Will Belinda stay behind to face the wrath of the duke? Gulliver has developed a strong paternal feeling for her and, in addition, she

and Simpson are commoners, both of age, both bright and interested and curious by nature: a matched set to be saved on Gulliver's "ark."

And the duke? Wilder often placed characters in a position where, experiencing an epiphany, they catch a glimpse of what lies ahead. *Youth* seems constructed for just such a moment. The twenty-eight-year-old duke, himself within a year of his enforced demise, returns as he must, accompanied by his callow bullyish guards. Might Wilder perhaps have wanted us to wonder what the duke feels about the defeat of his will and authority in the light of what he will not be able to avoid in a year's time? Those questions hang in the added final tableau [in brackets here at 635.10–36].

616.8   TWO . . . fifteen]   Added in *Collected Short Plays, Vol. I*.

618.14   assuage]   Inserted in *Collected Short Plays, Vol. I*.

626.30   Saint Bartholomew massacre]   French Catholic violence against Huguenots that began on St. Bartholomew's Day (August 24) in 1572.

626.30–31   the murder . . . martyr]   Charles I (1600–1649), deposed when England's monarchy was overthrown, was put on trial for treason and beheaded. "The" was added in *Collected Short Plays, Vol. I*.

627.8   Laputa]   In Part III of *Gulliver's Travels*, Gulliver visits the floating island of Laputa, whose inhabitants are preoccupied with theoretical scientific speculations.

635.10–36   *The music . . . fade.*]   See note 616.1.

636.1   *The Rivers . . . Earth*]   Published in *American Theatre 14*, no. 3 (March 1997), and included in *The Collected Short Plays of Thornton Wilder, Vol. I.*, in which F. J. O'Neil, whose research and editing helped establish the text, writes:

> The place of *The Rivers Under the Earth* in Wilder's schema of short plays is ambiguous. In its first draft it was entitled *Children*. That title was dropped in later drafts. Students of Wilder have speculated that he finally meant the play to represent middle age, since *Childhood* was the title given to one of the three "Plays for Bleecker Street," produced in 1962 at Circle in the Square in New York City.
>
> Wilder had written in his journal [for June 14, 1957]: "I planned [*Rivers*] to arrive at a culmination illustrating—so recurrent in me—the relations between a daughter and a father." I added the final stage direction (in brackets) to illustrate this idea in a concluding tableau [in brackets here at 648.27–29]. The author's manuscript had ended with the line:

> MR. CARTER (*Walking back and forth, right to left*): Well, isn't that funny—people feeling so differently about things.

640.38   *Tom leaves*]   Added in *Collected Short Plays, Vol. I*.

644.31–32   "Bonny Prince Charlie"]   Known as "The Young Pretender" or as "Bonnie Prince Charlie," Charles Stuart (1720–1788), grandson of the deposed King James II of England and Ireland, led an insurgent Jacobite rebellion and was defeated at the Battle of Culloden in 1746.

646.17   *Trouvé*] Found.

647.3   *They are*] Added in *Collected Short Plays, Vol. I.*

648.27–29   *Mr. Carter . . . fade.*] See note 636.1.

WRITINGS ON THEATER

651.1   *Foreword . . . Plays*] Written for the first edition (Coward-McCann, 1928).

652.9   Charles Martin Loeffler] German-born American composer (1861–1935).

652.26–27   a sheaf . . . corrected] At the time he was writing some of these plays, Wilder was working as a French instructor at the Lawrenceville School.

652.32–33   Herbert Eulenberg's *Schattenbilder*] In 1911, Herbert Eulenberg (1876–1949), German writer and poet, published *Schattenbilder* (*Silhouettes*), a collection of brief portraits of such historical figures as Mozart, Goethe, Shakespeare, Michelangelo, Napoleon, and Byron.

653.20   I read . . . Swift.] I.e., the writings of Cardinal John Henry Newman (1801–1890) and Jonathan Swift (1667–1745).

653.24   Renan] French philosopher and writer Ernest Renan (1823–1892) published his *Memories of Childhood and Youth* in 1884. In English, the passage quoted from it reads: "Myself, I believe that the best way to shape young people of talent is never to speak to them of talent or style, but to instruct and strongly excite their minds with philosophical, religious, political, social, scientific, and historical questions; in a word, to proceed by teaching the essence of things, and not by teaching a hollow rhetoric."

654.16–17   Our Lord . . . serpents] See Matthew 10:16.

655.1   '*The Long . . . Produce*'] A preface to the acting edition of *The Long Christmas Dinner*, published by Samuel French in 1933.

656.1   '*The Happy . . . Producer*'] A preface to the acting edition of *The Happy Journey to Trenton and Camden*, published by Samuel French in 1934. When Wilder chose this play to be included in *This Is My Best*, ed. Whit Burnett (New York: The Dial Press, 1942), he prefaced it with the following note, dated April 13, 1942:

The form in which this play is cast is not an innovation but a revival. The healthiest ages of the theatre have been marked by the fact that there was least literally representative scenery. The sympathetic participation of the audience was most engaged when their collaborative imagination was called upon to supply a large part of the background.

It is perhaps a sad commentary on the kind of people who go in for amateur stage production to say that in many productions of the play I have seen "Ma" has been permitted, or directed, to play her role sentimentally, and the closing moments have been drenched in tears, ostentatious piety and a kind of heroic self-pity. The play is a testimonial of homage to the average American mother who brings up her children as instinctively as a bird builds its nest and whose strength lies in the fact that whatever stress arrives from the circumstance of life, she strives to maintain an atmosphere of forward-looking industry and readiness.

657.1–2   *A Preface for 'Our Town'*]   Published in *The New York Times*, February 13, 1938, nine days after the play first opened on Broadway.

660.1–2   *'Our Town . . . Play*]   First published in the acting edition of the play (Samuel French, 1939), as was "*'Our Town': Some Suggestions for the Director*" (661–62).

663.1–2   *'Our Town' . . . Screen*]   The 1940 film of *Our Town* was adapted from the play by Wilder, Frank Craven, and Harry Chandlee. It was directed by Sam Wood, with music by Aaron Copland. The film starred William Holden, Martha Scott, Frank Craven, Beulah Bondi, Fay Bainter, Thomas Mitchell, and Guy Kibbee. It earned Academy Award nominations for Best Picture, Best Actress (Scott), and Best Score. Sol Lesser (1890–1980), a Hollywood producer best known for his series of *Tarzan* movies, served as the film's producer. This selection of their correspondence concerning the project was published *Theatre Arts 24* (November 1940), 815–24.

663.31   Woollcott's island]   Alexander Woollcott (1887–1943), critic and member of the Algonquin Round Table of wits. The island he purchased is Neshobe, in Lake Bomoseen, Vermont.

664.22   Sacha Guitry]   Alexandre-Pierre Georges Guitry (1885–1957), Russian-born French playwright, actor, innovative film director, and screenwriter.

666.5–7   *Smiling Through . . . On*]   The films *Smiling Through* (1932), *Jane Eyre* (1934), and *It Happened One Night* (1934); Will Cotton's Broadway play *The Bride the Sun Shines On* (1931).

668.2–3   Aimee MacPherson spiel]   Aimee Semple McPherson (1890–1944) was a flamboyant evangelist, founder of the Foursquare Church, and a popular radio personality in the 1920s.

668.18   Dead-End-Kids city life]   Five young actors from Sidney Kingsley's 1935 Broadway play *Dead End* were recruited for a series of films of the late 1930s and the 1940s—the most famous of them was *Angels with Dirty Faces* (1938)—and the phrase "Dead End Kids" became a byword for trouble-making youths. The actors were Billy Halop, Bobby Jordan, Huntz Hall, Leo Gorcey, Bernard Punsly, and Gabriel Dell.

672.2   Grover Whalen] Whalen (1886–1962), nicknamed "Mr. New York," was appointed by Mayor Fiorella La Guardia as New York City's official greeter, and in 1935 became president of the New York World Fair Corporation.

674.9   Harry Horner] Austrian-born designer Harry Horner (1910–1994), a production designer for *Our Town*.

677.27   Mr. Menzies] William Cameron Menzies (1896–1957), Academy Award–winning art director, designed the production of the *Our Town* film.

678.22–23   New York stage . . . *Paycock*] Arthur Shields's 1940 revival of *Juno and the Paycock*, the 1924 play by Sean O'Casey (1880–1964), starred Barry Fitzgerald (1888–1961) as The Orator and Sara Allgood (1879–1950) as "Juno" Boyle. Both actors had played these roles in Alfred Hitchcock's 1930 film adaptation of the play.

682.1–3   *Preface . . . Matchmaker'*] First published in *Three Plays* (1957).

682.12–15   classical works . . . *Page*] Innovative Austrian-American director and author Max Reinhardt (1873–1943) directed Wilder's *The Merchant of Yonkers* (1938) on Broadway. Louis Jouvet (1887–1951) was a renowned French actor and producer. The Old Vic is one of the oldest and most famous of London theaters. *Desire Under the Elms* by Eugene O'Neill (1888–1953) was first performed in 1924. *The Front Page*, by Ben Hecht (1894–1964) and Charles MacArthur (1895–1956), opened on Broadway in 1928.

684.22–23   Shelley's *The Cenci*] *The Cenci: A Tragedy in Five Acts* (1819).

689.1   *Notes . . . Alcestiad'*] Written as a program note for the original Edinburgh Festival production of the play in 1955.

691.1   *Noting . . . Farce*] First published in *The New York Times*, January 8, 1939, 12 days after *The Merchant of Yonkers* opened on Broadway.

691.22   *The School for Scandal*] Play (1777) by Richard Brinsley Sheridan.

691.23–24   *The Importance . . . Earnest*] Play (1895) by Oscar Wilde.

691.35   *She Stoops to Conquer*] Play (1773) by Oliver Goldsmith.

692.16   books . . . Bergson and Freud] *Le Rire* (*Laughter*, 1901), by French philosopher Henri Bergson; *Der Witz und seine Beziehung zum Unbewussten* (*The Joke and Its Relation to the Unconscious*, 1905) by Sigmund Freud.

694.1   *Some . . . Playwriting*] First published in *The Intent of the Artist*, ed. Augusto Centeno (Princeton: Princeton University Press, 1941).

694.26–31   Irving . . . Gémier]   Henry Irving (1838–1905), whose original name was John Brodribb, was one of the great actors of his time, and the first ever to be knighted. Ellen Terry (1847–1928), English actress, played Portia in Irving's 1879 production of *The Merchant of Venice*. Firmin Gémier (1869–1933) was a French actor and director.

698.17   Sarah Siddons]   English actress (1755–1831) whose most celebrated role was her portrayal of Lady Macbeth.

699.40   Maeterlinck said]   In the essay "The Tragical in Daily Life" (1896), by Belgian playwright, poet, and essayist Maurice Maeterlinck (1862–1949).

700.9–10   Gobineau's . . . Landor]   *La Renaissance* (1877), by French essayist Arthur de Gobineau (1816–1882); *Imaginary Conversations*, by the English poet and writer Walter Savage Landor (1775–1864), was published in several editions, the final in 1846.

704.1–2   *Richard . . . Traum'*]   Wilder's introduction to Ida Benison Wynn's translation of *Jacob's Dream* (New York: Johannespresse, 1946), a play by the Austrian dramatist and poet Richard Beer-Hofmann (1866–1945).

704.6   unfinished trilogy]   The projected trilogy *Die Historie von König David* (*The Story of King David*), which included *Der junge David* (*The Young David*, 1933).

706.34   Kierkegaard wrung from it]   In *Fear and Trembling* (1843), a book-length study of Abraham's near-sacrifice of Isaac.

707.1   Kierkegaard's urgent question]   See *Fear and Trembling*, Problema I.

707.10–13   and in thee . . . thee of]   Genesis 28:14–15.

707.25–26   Milton's two sonnets . . . *Lost*]   "When I consider how my light is spent"; "Methought I saw my late espousèd saint"; and *Paradise Lost*, Book III, 1–55.

707.26–27   Pascal . . . illness]   Blaise Pascal, *Prière pour demander à Dieu le bon usage des maladies* (*A Prayer Asking God to Make Good Use of Sickness*, 1659).

707.27   the Baron von Hügel]   Baron Friedrich von Hügel (1852–1925), Austrian-English religious writer.

708.11–12   the noble . . . Joseph]   Mann's trilogy of novels, *Joseph and His Brothers*, written between 1933 and 1942.

708.21   *Vie de Jésus*]   *Life of Jesus* (1863) by Ernest Renan (see note 653.24).

710.1   *Sophocles's . . . Rex'*]   The introduction to Francis Storr's translation was written in fall 1939, and first published by The Heritage Press in 1955.

710.18–19   the foremost Italian critic] Benedetto Croce (1866–1952).

713.4–6   a modern dramatist . . . *Machine*] Jean Cocteau (1889–1963), French poet, designer, filmmaker, and playwright, author of *La machine infernale* (1934).

716.34–35   Mounet-Sully] Jean Mounet-Sully (1841–1916), French actor noted for his portrayal of Oedipus in Jules Lecroix's 1888 translation, *L'Oedipe roi*.

716.38   Sir John Martin-Harvey] John Martin Harvey (1863–1944), English actor.

716.39–717.1   The plays by Voltaire and Dryden] Voltaire's *Oedipe* (1718) and Dryden and Nathaniel Lee's *Oedipus* (1678).

720.1–2   *Foreword . . . Nestroy*] From *Three Comedies*, "translated and fondly tampered with by Max Knight and Joseph Fabry" (New York: Frederick Ungar, 1967). The three comedies were *A Man Full of Nothing* (*Der Zerrissene*, 1844), *The Talisman* (*Der Talisman*, 1840), and *Love Affairs and Wedding Bells* (*Liebesgeschichten und Heiratssachen*, 1843).

721.4   Grillparzer's . . . *Ende*] *King Ottakar's Rise and Fall* (1823), historical tragedy by Austrian poet and playwright Franz Grillparzer (1791–1872).

721.16   Goldoni] Carlo Goldoni (1707–1793), Italian playwright whose comedy *The New House* premiered in 1760.

721.25   *Der Unbedeutende*] *The Man of No Importance* (1846).

722.25   *Unverhofft*] *Unforeseen* (1845).

723.14–15   *Kampl,* and *Mein Freund*] *Kampl oder Das Mädchen mit Millionen und die Nähterin* (*Kampl, or the Millionairess and the Seamstress*) and *Mein Freund* (*My Friend*) premiered, respectively, in 1852 and 1851.

724.5–6   dialect . . . plays] German dramatist and novelist Gerhart Hauptmann (1862–1946) made use of dialect in plays such as *Before Sunrise* (1889) and *The Weavers* (1893).

724.7–8   Eduardo de Filippo] Italian playwright and screenwriter (1900–1984).

725.1   *George Bernard Shaw*] Written in 1968 (while Wilder was in the hospital recovering from minor surgery), this essay was published posthumously, in *American Characteristics and Other Essays*, ed. Donald Gallup (New York: Harper and Row, 1979).

727.11–12   Dickens's . . . Office] See *Nicholas Nickleby* (1839) and *Little Dorrit* (1857).

727.17   Ellen Key] Swedish suffragist and writer (1849–1926).

729.16   Nausicaä]   Pretty young girl whom Odysseus encounters during his wanderings in *The Odyssey*.

729.17   Natasha Rostov]   Heroine of Tolstoy's *War and Peace*.

731.1   *Shadow of a Doubt*]   Alfred Hitchcock sent a telegram to Wilder in the spring of 1942, asking him to write the screenplay for his next film, his sixth to be made in America. Wilder wrote to Alexander Woollcott on May 12: "Mr. Hitchcock of the thriller movies wants me to come out to California for six weeks and write the screen treatment of a movie. He recounts the plot. It's about American small-town life and big-city murderer. I'm a consultant on small-town life to the tune of fifteen thousand dollars and murder has no secrets from him. The plot he recounts is corny. I very much doubt whether I can supply one convincing small-town speech. And I haven't got six weeks. [Wilder was scheduled to report for army training in Miami on June 26.] But I'm going to compromise with time, art and money. And go for five weeks for ten thousand dollars." The plot Hitchcock had in mind originated in a newspaper story about a man from New York, visiting his family in California, who was discovered to have strangled several women back east. Writer Gordon McDonnell read the story, researched it in some depth, and started writing a play based on the material. Unable to finish it, he met with Hitchcock, who was interested in the story and purchased McDonnell's seven-page scenario, then titled "Uncle Charlie." Wilder and Hitchcock would meet in the morning to discuss the screenplay, and Wilder would work on it during the afternoon and evening. Hitchcock recalled: "We weren't quite sure how to start the picture and Thornton said, 'Well there's this short story by Hemingway where a man is lying in bed in the dark, waiting to be killed.' I, who fear being influenced by anyone in my work, was astonished that a great writer should not be afraid of another writer's influence." When it was time for Wilder to leave California, Hitchcock rode with him on the luxurious Super Chief, "The Train of the Stars," departing Los Angeles for Chicago on June 22, 1942, so that they could continue to work on rewrites. Later, Sally Benson was brought in to re-do some dialogue, and Hitchcock's wife, Alma, worked on continuity. Although Wilder remarked that he had enjoyed his collaboration with Hitchcock immensely, he was not pleased with the anglicizing changes made to his dialogue, later writing to his friend Ruth Gordon: "Months after I wrote *Shadow of a Doubt* I slipped into a neighborhood movie house and saw it. But I was robbed of any experience such as you had,—because Mrs. Alfred Hitchcock in order to get a credit—had intervened and rewritten the American-rural dialogue into Strand-Magazine Golders Green."

Years later, in an interview with Peter Bogdanovich, Hitchcock said that "from the point of view of suspense and character," *Shadow of a Doubt* was his best film. "For once there was time to get the characters into it. It was the blending of character and thriller at the same time. That's very hard to do."

737.33   *Ivanhoe*]   Novel (1819) by Sir Walter Scott (1771–1832).

749.9   *the "Merry Widow" Waltz*]   The celebrated melody from the 1905 operetta, *Die lustige Witwe*, by Franz Lehár (1870–1948).

750.17   the Blue Danube Waltz]   The famous waltz, *An der schönen blauen Donau* ("On the Beautiful Blue Danube"), was originally written in 1867 for male chorus by Johann Strauss, Jr. (1825–1899).

Library of Congress Cataloging-in-Publication Data

Wilder, Thornton, 1897–1975.
  Thornton Wilder : collected plays & writings on theater /
    J. D. McClatchy, editor.
      p. cm. — (The Library of America ; 172)
  Includes bibliographical references (p.).
  ISBN-13: 978–1–59853–003–2 (alk. paper)
  ISBN-10: 1–59853–003–8 (alk. paper)
      I. McClatchy, J. D., 1945– II. Title: III. Title: Thornton
Wilder, collected plays and writings on theater. IV. Title: Collected
plays and writings on theater.

PS3545.I345A6   2007
12'.52—dc28   2006048620

THE LIBRARY OF AMERICA SERIES

The Library of America fosters appreciation and pride in America's literary heritage by publishing, and keeping permanently in print, authoritative editions of America's best and most significant writing. An independent nonprofit organization, it was founded in 1979 with seed money from the National Endowment for the Humanities and the Ford Foundation.

*This book is set in 10 point Linotron Galliard,
a face designed for photocomposition by Matthew Carter
and based on the sixteenth-century face Granjon. The paper
is acid-free lightweight opaque and meets the requirements
for permanence of the American National Standards Institute. The
binding material is Brillianta, a woven rayon cloth made by
Van Heek-Scholco Textielfabrieken, Holland. Composition by Dedicated Business Services. Printing by
Malloy Incorporated. Binding by Dekker Book-
binding. Designed by Bruce Campbell.*

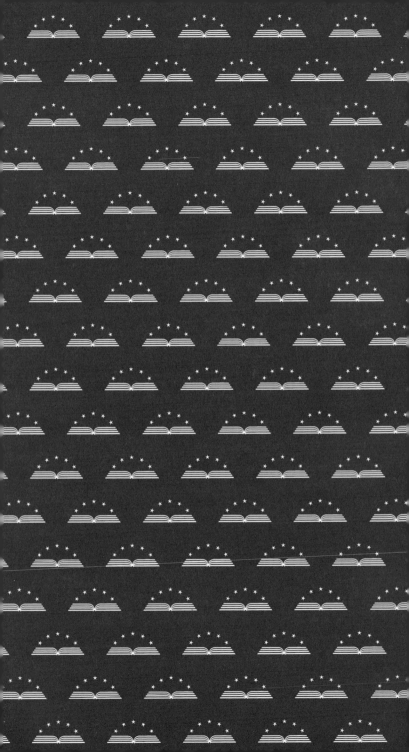